Argentine Riptide

Other Books by Tina Assanti Books:

By Tina Assanti
Italian Bones of Contentions
Italian Bodies of Change
The Kingdom of God and Playboys

Pioneer Women Series E-Books
Letters of a Woman Homesteader
Letters from an Elk Hunt by a Woman Homesteader

By Liesje Wagner
Corrie and the Rose Accordion
Bully Swan Gone
Argentine Riptide

ARGENTINE RIPTIDE

A Phyl Redington Adventure:

MILITARY COUPS, NAZI INTRIGUES, EVA PERON

A Novel Inspired by True Events

LIESJE WAGNER

TINA ASSANTI
Stories of the Human Spirit

TINA ASSANTI BOOKS

Copyright © 2024 by Tina Assanti Books

Paperback ISBN: 978-1-7381778-0-6
Ebook ISBN: 978-1-7771774-9-2

All rights reserved. No part of this publication, either writing or images, may be reproduced, distributed, or transmitted in any form or by any means, including photocopying, recording, or other electronic or mechanical methods, without the prior written permission of the publisher, except in the case of brief quotations embodied in critical reviews and certain other noncommercial uses permitted by copyright law.

All attempts have been made to verify the information contained in this book: Argentine Riptide, but the author and publisher do not bear any responsibility for errors or omissions. Any perceived negative connotation of any individual, group, or company is purely unintentional. Furthermore, this book is intended for entertainment only, and as such, any and all responsibility for actions taken by reading this book lies with the reader alone and not with the author or publisher. This book is not intended as medical, legal, or business advice, and the reader alone holds sole responsibility for any consequences of any actions taken after reading this book. Additionally, it is the reader's responsibility alone and not the author's or publishers to ensure that all applicable laws and regulations for the business practice are adhered to.

Published by Tina Assanti Books © 2024

Cover designed by Rade Rokvic and book printed at Willow Publishing

www.tinaassantibooks.com

8 Wendy's Lane, Brighton, Ontario K0K 1H0

I thank my family and friends for their patience as
I share my passion. My dear friend, Clay,
for feeling he should definitely listen to every detail,
and the community of Brighton and the surrounding beauty.
A special thank you to my editor, Vic Schukov.

Liesje Wagner

This book has to be dedicated to Beverley Phillips.
Dear friend and inspiration.
And, of course, to her Auntie Phyl.

PREFACE

In the waiting instant I opened the box, the room spun inward, pulling me into its vortex. This is a true story. The only kind that matters. And it blew my mind.

While visiting my dear friend Bev Philips, in Kitchener, I was led into a corner of her bedroom inflicted with paper and boxes. She stopped at a collapsible table and pointed out a small box. She told me it contained letters belonging to her deceased Auntie Phyl. She said her aunt was "one of those characters who deserved to be written about."

I hear that an awful lot from friends and acquaintances.

Bev insisted Auntie Phyl was different. She was a real-life Auntie Mame, a Rosalind Russel, complete with cigarette holders, servants, and all. She lived a beautiful if not incredible life with the love of her life, her American husband, Stuart Redington.

There were photos and postcards scattered everywhere across the table. Judging by the postmarks, it looked like Phyllis and Stuart lived a high life in exotic places. I browsed through the letters stuffed in the box and noticed they started in 1935 and ended in 1961. Being a student of history, I intuitively knew I would enjoy reading them if nothing else. I told Bev the same.

Intrigued, I took the box home and put it aside for several months as I completed another project. Still, the unread contents haunted me, waiting for me to release them like genies in a lamp. I could not help but set off on Phyl's marked trail as soon as possible.

After reading only four letters, and corroborating details through a bit of research, I felt moved to build a more complete picture in my mind, to understand Phyl and the context in which she wrote. Then I called Bev. There were pertinent details she had not told me. I was curious as to why, and when I shared them with her, she said it was all news to her, too. I asked if she had read the letters. No, but she knew they had to be good from what she remembered of her aunt's magnetic nature.

Oh, I said. The letters are good, alright. I was hooked. Phyl was speaking to me from beyond.

I researched every letter. I digested every line. Every nuance. Every innocent implication and referral. Every word appeared to be thrown into a conversation as if it was nothing. Phyl admitted several times in her letters she couldn't write about certain things she wished she could. Mesmerized, I had to dive into what she *wasn't* writing. What she *wasn't* saying. Like the veiled lady in black standing apart from a funeral service.

I was to discover that Phyl and Stuart were thrown onto a mounting wave of history and adventure in beautiful Buenos Aires at a time when this magnificent city was still the Babylonic Paris of the West. As foreigners, they were not necessarily welcomed. But trade had reopened with the United States, and Stuart was sent down to Buenos Aires as a salesman for a British Commonwealth office of Remington Rand Typewriters. It didn't hurt that Phyl was Canadian, a British Commonwealth citizen. Britain was Argentina's largest trading partner at the time.

Unsettling, wicked things stirred in the world. Hitler, a manipulating, self-minted Chancellor, hypnotized his Germany, herding his black dogs into the fold. And, although neutral, Argentina strongly leaned toward Nazism, a disturbing trepidation to the Americas in the western hemisphere. Fascism also took hold, as did Communism. The Americans felt they had very little control.

Enter Stuart, the American, who, it turns out, wasn't just a lowly British Commonwealth salesman. Upon graduation from Princeton University in the early 1930s, he was conscripted into J. Edgar Hoover's new G-Man program - the Government Men - the forerunner of the FBI. When trade finally resumed between the United States and Argentina, he was sent as a squeaky-clean, unofficial ambassador, married to a citizen of the British Commonwealth, with "instructions" to be part of a group of informants, all in the name of peace.

The story of Phyl and Stuart begins at the tail end of the Depression when Buenos Aires was still a wealthy center of the West. It takes us through the Nazi intrigues before and during World War 2, numerous violent elections and military coups; it includes Phyl crossing paths with Eva Perón on a movie set when the latter was still Eva Duarte, an angry, struggling teenage actor. Phyl and Stuart rubbed shoulders with the wealthy Argentine elite. They befriended ambassadors and their wives, dined with politicians and royalty, and entertained foreign servants.

Priceless.

The more I read the letters, the more evident it was that Canadian Phyllis May Redington did not live as most people did. Her's was a life of intrigue, mystery, luxury and adventure. Phyl saw history in the making. In her own way, she *made* history. And practically everything she experienced was humbly interwoven between the lines of these seemingly simple letters in a box.

This book is the story Phyl could not tell.

Liesje Wagner

"There's a lot I can't talk about here but this place is killing me."

*"It's starting to feel like I'm caught in an Argentine riptide
and I won't know how to get out of it if
we don't call this quits. People die in riptides."*

—*Phyllis May Redington*

Chapter One
1934, Toronto, Ontario, Canada
Dreams, a Young Man, and a Door Opens

"People die in riptides, right Phyl?"

El clutched at Phyl as they rode the crest of a wave of retreating movie goers pushing through the lobby of the Palace Theatre.

"Yes. Of exhaustion, usually."

"Why was this movie called Riptide then? I didn't see an ocean. No one drowned. I don't get it."

"Silly, it was about Norma Shearer, or the woman she played, being pushed and pulled, practically drowning in the passion and romance of it all." Phyl gently pushed back against someone leaning into her. "That's why the second title of Opposing Forces in Woman. She was continuously torn."

El pondered as she watched where she was stepping on the popcorn-strewn carpet.

"And you wanna know something?" Phyl continued, in her excitement, slowly pushing along.

"What?"

"I feel I'll have a life just like that." She struggled to take off a glove to scratch her palm. "I feel it in my bones."

"What do you mean? Like opposing forces in yourself?"

Phyl laughed. "No. Like I'm going to be in the moving pictures, too." She pulled her glove back on. "And something about those wonderful tuxedoes, evening gowns, and fancy cigarette holders." Phyl gave her best friend a coy look as she pretended to hold up a cigarette holder. "Like it's natural to me."

"Oh, Phyl. As if." El giggled.

The young women finally burst through the cinema's front doors as the crowd erupted into the damp, drizzly Toronto night. Phyl spied a newspaper stand under a canvas covering between two potted bushes along the cement curb and squeezed passed others to get to it to grab a paper from under the cloth. She handed two copper pennies to a shivering, wet paper boy sitting on the edge of one of the planters. She folded the paper and stopped, then squinted through the light drizzle at the marquee above their heads.

"Do you think I look like her, El?" She looked back at her friend. "Like Norma Shearer?" She grinned and posed, her blue eyes sparkling under the marquee lights. She wore the same trench coat as El, an old, red beret tilted back on her brunette head.

El's eyes watered from the sting of the cool air. She comically studied Phyl's pose this way and that. "Turn around," she demanded.

Phyl twirled on the spot, then hiked her coat and dress, and did a high kick. "Look at me. I'm a Ziegfeld Folly girl. I want to dance, dance, dance."

A passing elderly lady said, "Young woman, how can you do such a thing in public? Honestly." She was led by an older man sporting a silver-topped cane. Both looked like they had stepped out of Victorian England and were indignant about navigating through an unruly crowd.

"Oops!" winced Phyl, looking around, embarrassed.

El laughed so hard she leaned against Phyl, looking back at the elderly couple with wide eyes.

Phyl smiled. She waved the couple away. "Never mind. I consider every 25 cents I spend going to these films as a serious investment in how to better myself. I learn how to dance, walk, talk," she said with a British accent, "Eat, drink, dress and smoke like a lady."

"Well, it's working, Phyl." El took Phyl's arm as they marched in unison to the crossing at the corner of Pape and Danforth. They stepped back as a horse clomped by pulling an old heavy wagon. The nag's hoofs exploded through a deep puddle, splashing the cracked sidewalk in front of them.

Phyl glanced up the Danforth and pointed at an oncoming streetcar. They hurried across to the south side, dodging two Ford Model A's and a Packard. They clambered onto the streetcar with other movie theatre folks, including a young boy with a cap, who tried to race past the driver without paying. The driver grabbed him by the ear and forced him to pay.

"Two transfers, please," Phyl requested. She threw seven cents into the meter and took the chits from the conductor. El did the same. Slowly, they made their way to the very back as the streetcar screeched and hobbled along. They plopped into cracked, horse-hair seats and looked back at the massive Palace sign in front of the theatre adjacent to a line-up of new stores. The once large theatre had just had shops built into the facade. The stores were rented out to generate income to support the theatre. Everybody did what they could to survive this Great Depression.

Phyl sat up to face El. "I mean it. I just know that there's something special I have to do in my life, and it isn't living in Toronto taking dictation and pounding a Remington Rand typewriter all day. That's why I took this business course. I wanted to better myself. I don't wanna just get married and have babies, and then, well, that's it for the rest of my life." She shuddered.

"What's wrong with getting married and having babies?"

"Yeah, what's wrong with getting married and making babies?" interrupted the young boy with the cap as he slid onto the bench behind them. He made an obscene expression and wiggled his eyebrows like Groucho Marx.

El and Phyl gasped as they turned to look at him. "Do you mind?" demanded Phyl. "We're having a private conversation here."

The boy sunk into the shadows of his seat, grinning.

Phyl sighed and looked at her best friend. They had worked together at the grocers, but Phyl took that correspondence course and got a job at the Remington Offices downtown. While El sorted fruit and vegetables closer to home, Phyl was now a downtown girl, a typist, and took dictation from the president of the Toronto Division office, Mr. Schuler. "Nothing," she answered, in a lower voice but loud enough to be heard over the streetcar's screeching and a nosy brat. "But it doesn't feel like me." She looked down at her hands. "I didn't mean to imply it's bad for everyone. For some girls, I guess it must be a dream."

El pensively studied Phyl rocking with the motion of the streetcar. She had started dating Phyl's brother, Claude Jr., six months prior, and had her own dreams. "Phyl, I know it was hard for you when your mother died …"

"I don't know what you mean. I don't think I even remember," Phyl lied. She remembered the sounds of desperate gasps, a slow torturous end. A memory of her mother suffocating to death, drowning in her own lung fluids.

"I know you blame yourself. But your whole school was infected. They say 50 million people died from the flu in the entire world. How could a six-year-old be responsible for something like that?"

"If they had only closed the schools a month before, El. Then my mother wouldn't have died and become one of the 50 million." Phyl lifted her chin and took a deep breath. "I've come to terms with it, though. That's fourteen years ago. But the fact is, it *was* me: *I* brought the Spanish Flu to the house, and one by one, we all got sick. First me, then Claude and Dad and Mom. We pulled through, but Mom…"

"Hey," yelled the young boy behind them. "Do you know where the term 'hanky-panky' comes from? It's from people kissing through their handkerchiefs during the flu. Get it? Doing the panky through a hanky." The young intruder laughed suggestively.

El reached out and swatted the young man. "Sit somewhere else, you snot nosed kid!" The boy scrambled out of the seat and stumbled as he reached for overhead handlebars to move away. They watched him with piercing eyes until he settled halfway down the streetcar, squeezing in between people.

"For crying out loud. What is he? Ten?" asked El.

"Notice how little kids always have runny noses? They're always fighting some germ or another." Phyl looked out the window. "They're walking pestilences. Like I was."

"Oh, come now, Phyl. You sound as if you hate children." El leaned in. "I know you better than that. I think you would make a wonderful mother." She swallowed. "I would love to have our children grow up together. In fact, I would want you as their godmother."

Deep down, Phyl understood El had hopes and plans with her brother, Claude Jr. That she and Phyl would be happy housewives with children of the same ages playing together. But it wasn't who *Phyl* was and she suddenly sensed there would be days in the future when she would let her best friend down. The thought saddened her and she softened. She smiled gently at El and, as a way of changing the subject, she pointedly shook the newspaper flat and fingered the pages. She forced herself not to think of their own future, instead, searched and finally found what she was looking – an article about the exhibition and Toronto's future. A welcome distraction. She straightened the paper out, folded it once, and held it up in the slow strobes of the passing streetlights.

"Oh, here we are about the CNE Ex show." She squinted as she focused on the words. "*There will be revolutionary changes in urban life,*" she read aloud. "*Due to largely improved means of transportation and industrial production and the extraordinary improvement of the chief western rail and motor traffic highways, by a hundred years from now, it will have continued to be duplicated along the eastern waterfront far past Scarboro' Cliffs.*" Phyl looked wide-eyed at El. "Wow, isn't that something?"

"No kidding," replied Eleanor.

Phyl went back to reading. "*Nor must the aeroplane be overlooked in laying out transportation plans for the Toronto of 2034.*"

"Gosh, I'd love to go on an aeroplane one day."

"*Civic services may not change to such a degree as transportation facilities. And Toronto, in 2034, will be as full of television sets as it is today for telephones. Every house will have movies on tap.*"

"Who would have walls big enough!" exclaimed El. "Just imagine Hollywood whenever I want! Oh, my gosh, I would be in Seventh Heaven. Rudy Valentino all day."

"Jean Harlow!"

"Cary Grant." El grinned, pretending to swoon.

"Wouldn't that be something?" Phyl folded the paper, and placed it on her lap. She looked down and caught sight of a headline at her fingertips as her body jostled in tandem with the streetcar. She held up the paper and squinted, trying to keep it from shaking. *"Argentina Holds Election: Democrats Win.* They had a newsreel about that just before the movie."

"What's that?"

"This headline on Argentina. Remember the newsreel after the Mickey Mouse cartoon? Most of the political speech went over my head, but I got the message it was a military coup, didn't you? I loved seeing the palm trees, the broad, wide avenues and monuments, and the elegant people going up and down the boulevards." She sighed and placed the paper back on her lap. She thought of warmer and exotic lands. Faraway places, you can only get to by fancy ships. Like in films. Like that Argentina.

"Uh-oh. I know that look." El looked at her askance. "She's dreaming again."

Phyl looked sideways and wiped at the grimy window and watched the street lights go by, the bare trees, the old churches. Such a contrast to the newsreel on Argentina. Everything looked so grey. So sad and poor, ill-kept. The Depression was still in full force but, by now, most people had adapted to a stringent life of want and need. She was tired of being poor. This made Phyl, all the more, have big wishes to fulfill. She was tired of seeing houses peeling their paint, the coal-stained buildings and garbage-strewn parks and abandoned yards. Cardboard and material tents dotted every space where a cop hadn't frightened the homeless away. She smiled as El touched her shoulder and waxed on about how Norma Shearer looked so glamorous in *Riptide*, in all her different costumes, make-up, hair, and dazzling smile. Almost in response, Phyl gave El her own dazzling smile and pointed at herself for emphasis.

"Almost as beautiful," El jested. "And the men in white jackets and tuxedos, and tails. How glamorous."

"Indeed. How very glamorous. Won't find those in good ol' T.O. Which reminds me. Tell me, again, why you're interested in my brother? He's far from glamorous. He hunts and fishes, and he stinks all the time. He frightens the ducks away when he passes wind, for crying out loud."

El laughed. "Oh, he cleans up pretty nice when he's off to go to work. K starches his collar pretty nice, I must say."

"I don't know, El. I love my brother, but you deserve better."

El shook her head. "Phyl, it's not just that. If things go in a certain way, we'd be family, you and I. And I simply love K."

Phyl was taken aback.

"Now wouldn't that be a hoot?" El's eyes danced. "Didn't think of that, huh?"

Phyl didn't have the heart to shoot down such extraordinary innocence. Of course, she knew that's what El wanted. But the passion with which El spoke of such mundane things frightened her. Her friend wanted so little out of life. That, in itself, was a mystery. "You're right," she answered as a good friend. "And you're right about K. My Dad lucked out there. What a saint."

Phyl shared a three-quarter bed with K in the dining room of a tiny two-bedroom home on Pickering Street. One of the two bedrooms belonged to her Dad, Claude Sr. The other small bedroom was used by her brother, Claude Jr. Phyl's father was still not divorced from her stepmother. In 1934, this was close to scandalous. It was a long story, and not a very nice one. The neighbors talked about how her father's housekeeper lived full-time in the house, wink-wink, nudge-nudge. There was no choice but to share a bed together; she and K. They certainly ensured the neighbors knew they did!

Two transfers later, El and Phyl stepped off the streetcar into a thick mist at the corner of Pickering Street and Gerard. They looked back at the young boy grotesquely squishing his face against the window. They watched him for a moment as the streetcar rambled away. "Good night, Phyl. See you maybe tomorrow night?" El shivered in the cold.

"*Maybe*? Come on. You wouldn't miss the Jack Benny Show for the world. And it's an excuse for you to spend time with Claude Jr."

El looked sheepishly at Phyl and held a daintily gloved fingertip to her lips, feigning innocence. Phyl jostled her arm and turned. "See you tomorrow night!"

"Good night, Rochester!"

Phyl laughed. "Good night, Jack!"

Phyl opened the storm door and entered her enclosed front porch. In the gloom, she grabbed the brass doorknob of the peeling, front door, and jiggled the knob to free it from the brass latch plate. She stepped onto a wooden floor scarred by generations of tolerance. Tony, her crazy mutt, barreled into the narrow hallway from a small kitchen in the back. His long tail flung like a loose rudder, banging on all sides of the hallway. The walls suffered unwashable brown streaks along the whole length, a testament to an eternity of gleeful welcomes. As usual, he had been waiting for her under the small, enamel kitchen table by the back door. The kitchen was always a little warmer than the rest of the modest house.

"Tony! Did you miss me? Come here, you." She scrunched up the happy dog's face and smooched his nose. Satisfied, he romped two steps ahead of her and danced on the braided brown rug before disappearing into the living room. He being dark-haired, it was hard to keep her eyes on him as he bolted in and out of the shadows and the Spartan pool of light under the hallway's overhead bulb. He bounced around the corner into the living room once again. Phyl smiled and straightened the braided rug with her foot and bent to unlace her wet shoes, only to be attacked anew. He jumped at her face. She laughed in response, and he accidentally licked her tongue then rushed off.

Phyl sputtered, wiping her mouth and tongue with her sleeve. "Ah, geeeeee."

K emerged in the hallway, holding a faded teatowel. Her hourglass figure stressed her frayed shift, patterned with tiny violet blossoms. Her hair, salt-and-peppered prematurely from chronic worry, was swept and pinned on the top. Tendrils of hair betrayed her session over a hot washbasin. Colorful cheeks endowed her with an innocent look, her hazel eyes as enduringly kind.

"So, was it nice?" She smiled, absently wiping her hands on the teatowel.

Phyl flipped her hair out of her eyes, and wiped her mouth one last time. "Ring a ding, ding!" She straightened up. "You should come with us next Saturday, K. I could put up the bread for your ticket."

K waved at her. "Oh, I'm too old to sit so long. And that Palace Theatre is too rich for my blood."

Phyl took off her gloves. "K, you deserve some pleasure. You can't go taking care of everyone else, cleaning people's homes, and caring for your mother without doing some little thing for yourself."

"Oh, don't you worry about me none."

Phyl inhaled a familiar smell. Home smell. And she could tell by the pall of smoke hovering under the bare light bulb above her that her father had been smoking a storm with his stogies by the coal fire. "Hey, Pops," she called out.

"Father, to you." Claude Jr. stepped out of the living room and leaned against the chipped trim of the entranceway into the living room. Tall, moon-faced and fresh, he grinned the same dazzling smile his sister sported. He wore a worn woollen vest and tie, his best clothes for work at the mattress factory office. His detachable collar spread out from both sides of his neck mimicking a swan's wings.

"You know our father forbids slang in the house. 'Ringa ding, ding?'" he said, as he fingered the faux paint on the door trim made to look like oak grain by the finesse of a goose feather; Phyl had done that. It looked pretty classy. "How's El?" he asked.

Phyl hung her trench coat on a twisted wire hook in the closet under the stairway leading up. She tried not to notice the tired Victorian wallpaper glued onto crumbling plaster. She wished she could hang her coat elsewhere, where spiders didn't lodge in her sleeves overnight. She always shook her coat before going out. "Oh, El's the cat's pajamas. She's coming over for the Jack Benny Show tomorrow night."

"Well, I may not be home."

She jumped at Claude Jr. and slapped his shoulder with her gloves. "Don't you dare do that to El. You know she's only coming just to sit in the same room as you."

"It's my musky scent. The girls go crazy over it."

"Moose stink more like"

"Or fish guts," laughed K.

Claude Jr. grinned proudly at the two women and shrugged.

"It's a mystery, for sure," Phyl said. She stepped past K and her brother to see Claude Sr., in his usual faded ruby-red armchair with mahogany trim, chipped by who knows what. It was like that when they found it at Kensington Market. They had a friend cart it across town with his horse and buggy in exchange for a couple of good Sunday meals and a front seat at the radio.

Phyl's father frowned over a book sprouting dog-eared pages resting on his bald corduroy pants. His was a tough, rugged look, a face cracked by the elements. He raised a strong forearm to adjust his stogie, his muscles stringy and bulbous from wrestling wayward beasts and shovelling mountains of steaming dung for more than two decades at the Riverdale Zoo. Behind Claude Sr. hung several rifles and shotguns. At his feet, were day old papers. Framed prints of pheasants and hunting dogs graced the mantle over the coal stove. The cracked ceiling had a solar system of yellow stains from years of smoke. Beside him, behind the scattered newspapers, stood his frayed clarinet and saxophone cases. He still played the odd weekend or evening. It's how he met K. She had been taken by him in his fancy uniform when he played with the band at the local gazebo five summers before. He was quite the lady's man at the time.

In the background, a lazy tick-tick of an old brass clock of a hunter and his dog. It sat on a marble-topped, corner table. Next to his chair, a heavy brass cigarette stand, with a black glass ashtray which was continuously emptied by K, into a corrugated ashcan at the back door. By extension, K almost smelled as bad as Phyl's Dad.

Phyl handed the paper to him. His eyebrows shot up, and he leaned over and took it from her. "Kinda late in the day to get a Globe & Mail."

"It's still the news, Dad." She watched him unfold the paper. In their family, you couldn't get enough of the news. "Are you feeding the animals in the morning, Dad?"

He widened the newspaper to its full width, his stogie clamped between fore and middle finger, crooked pinky raised elegantly. "Someone's gotta feed and clean the crap out of those stalls," he growled.

Phyl studied his handsome, creased face. He hadn't had a lot of sleep lately with extra hours at the zoo. "How're the elephants doing? Did Maizie give birth yet?"

He looked up puzzled. "Maizie? Oh, Maizie. No, though we're a little concerned that it hasn't happened yet. But then, we really don't know what to expect. It's the first time we're having a live birth of an elephant. Quite a special occasion. Reporters are standing by."

Claude Jr. flopped onto a nearby horsehair settee and held out his hand. "Dad's gonna be a celebrity in the papers."

Sr. looked up. "Not necessarily." He glanced at Jr.'s extended hand. "What do you want, son?"

"Can I have the Funnies?"

Sr. shifted, flipped through sections, and tossed the Funnies onto the settee next to his Jr. "Son, you should read what intelligent people read."

"Dad, this relaxes my brain. All the better to think with tomorrow. Oh, wait. Tomorrow is a day of rest. I guess I don't need to use my brain for a couple of days then." He laughed.

"Like you ever use it," teased Phyl. "I really don't know what El sees in you." She looked at the clock. Almost 10:00 p.m. She called out to K who had retreated back to the kitchen. "K? I'm going to get ready for bed." She turned to her father. "Good night, Dad."

"Good night, Phyllis." Claude Sr. didn't look up as he continued to read. Jr. did the same, except with the Funnies.

Phyl slid open a wooden door separating the dining room from the living room. She slid the door shut behind her and quietly undressed, after carefully pulling the paper shades down on the two dining room windows. She sat at the dressing table and pulled out her brush. Almost in meditation, she separated her short, bobbed hair into individual fronds, twisting a couple into pin curls with bobby pins. She stopped to light an Export "A" cigarette and contemplatively banished the smoke to the ceiling.

She thought of the new employee who was starting on Monday. She had been part of dictating, sending and receiving mail concerning him. He had an exciting background, but something was off. She absentmindedly flicked ash into a chipped, brown glass ashtray and wondered. Why did a bright, rich, American kid go from the prestigious St. Andrew's private school north of Toronto to New Jersey, and graduate Princeton in '28, to work for Remington Rand in big, exciting New York City, only to be transferred to dull Toronto as a simple salesman of typewriters? Phyl was very bright also, and to her it didn't make sense. She wondered secretly if he was a dud.

She took another drag, squinted against the smoke, and carefully balanced the cigarette on the ashtray, then continued to twist her hair into tiny spindles. That mystery, she thought, was best kept for Monday. The far-reaching, much greater and convoluted mystery that was her future was still far from making its entrance. Looking back, she might say, careful what you wish for in an adventurous life – You might just get what you want.

* * *

Monday morning, Phyl masterfully slammed and clicked and flicked the sturdy round keys and carriage return lever of a heavy Remington typewriter. Remington-Rand, originally E. Remington and Sons, was founded in 1816 in North Carolina by an American gun maker, Eliphalet Remington. It was said that after finishing second in a shooting contest, his self-made flintlock so impressed everyone he immediately acquired enough orders to start a business. By late 1874, his sons had the engineering wherewithal to help create the first typewriter, causing a revolution in industry and communication. Quite a jump from the banality of firearms to benign, helpful machines that eased social communication. Phyl, hungry for knowledge, was proud to know this. She truly wanted to understand how success came about in business.

She looked over at the moving shadows of two men reflected on the frosted window of Mr. Schuler's office. A meeting had been underway when she arrived at 8:30. The voices were steady, but she couldn't make out what they were saying. There was outburst of laughter, which wasn't normal for her boss. Earlier, she had hung her trench coat next to a dark camel hair coat and noticed a brown felt Trilby hat with a black Petersham band on a hook above the coat. The combo smelled of something bigger than little ol' Toronto. She blinked at the stark difference between the quality of her coat and that of the stranger's. She felt rather provincial and was surprised at her feeling of insecurity. "Why, for crying out loud?" she thought, as she straightened out her dress, patted her hair, and busied herself at her desk.

Fifteen minutes later, Mr. Schuler threw his door open and ushered out a young man in a grey wool suit, white shirt, and a heavily-starched collar. His wool tie was black, blue, and white diagonal stripes. Phosporous green eyes hid laughter in their corners. He had a small toothbrush mustache – carefully trimmed – set over the softest smile she'd ever seen on a man. As he stepped out of the office, his eyes sparkled, swept over her and two employees behind her. He faced Mr. Schuler, smiling broadly.

Phyl didn't know where to look. She dropped her hands, tucked them under her desk, and desperately searched for papers that did not exist. What should she do? Pretend she didn't notice him? His presence was spell-binding.

"How are John and Bessy doing? The hotel doing fine?" asked Mr. Schuler of the young man.

"Apart from some of the rheumatism and his lungs, father still bangs the floors with his cane when he's upset, and my mother has been doing much of the work since the Crash. In fact, she reupholstered over 100 chairs all by herself last year. However, they did rehire two employees. But money's uncomfortably tight."

Staring at him unabashedly, Phyl noticed a slight change in his face. His forehead creased ever so slightly. He cared very much for his parents, she could see. She guessed the rich kid had problems, too.

"Miss May."

Phyl jumped. She tore her eyes from the young man, looked at Mr. Schuler, and blinked.

"Miss May, this is Mr. Redington. Stuart, I would like to introduce you to Miss May, my secretary. She'll make sure you have all the supplies you need. Miss May?"

Phyl jumped out of her chair, accidentally knocking the chair over. "Oh," she gasped, looking down at her accident scene. "What a nincompoop!"

Stuart lunged quicker than what he was required to, and righted the bulky chair for her. He lightly wiped down the seat with a strong-looking hand, a move that was more for gentlemanly show than necessity.

A twinge of uninvited warmth rose from Phyl's neck to her cheeks. She was in unfamiliar territory. Open range to the inexperienced. She gathered her wits together in random bits and straightened up all too awkwardly for her own comfort. Salvaging her womanly dignity, chin up, she smiled politely. The performance only made her seem that much sweeter to the young man.

"Right this way, Mr. Redington. We have your desk and office ready for you."

A slight shiver went down her spine.

* * *

Two months passed. Well into better weather, it was a beautiful Friday in May, so it wasn't a risk for her to rush the four blocks to lunch outside of the office for a change. Woolworth's grilled cheese day was Phyl's all-time favorite – cheap and satisfying, sitting at a counter. Music and chatter all around always lifted her spirits, and helped prepare her for a promising and fun weekend. But it had to be a quick trip, and she tried to leave a few minutes before noon to beat the rush and not have to wait too long to be served. Having almost run the entire distance, she hurried panting into the popular store. She spied a red leather stool near the end of the long faux-marble dining counter.

She squeezed through shoppers and diners to grab it. With a "harrumph," she made it and plopped down. The stool turned slightly under her weight, and she grabbed the Art Deco counter for balance. Over the tinny intercom, she caught the fun lyrics to "Ain't We Got Fun?"

Every morning, every evening
Ain't we got fun?
Not much money, oh, but honey
Ain't we got fun…?

Phyl picked up a menu, though she only wanted the grilled cheese. She liked to pretend she had enough money to choose anything. It was a fun game.

"Well, hello there, Miss May."

Phyl looked next to her into Stuart Redington's green, laughing eyes. She blushed. She put down the menu and started to take her gloves off, still trying to recover from her girlish stumbles.

"Well, hello, Mr. Redington. I didn't know you were sitting there."

He held out his hand. "I think you might call me Stu by now, out of the office?"

Phyl politely shook his hand, which felt strangely intimate. She blushed even more and withdrew her hand. "Stu," she nodded slowly as if to measure if having done so was too suggestive.

The waitress suddenly appeared, uninvited due to the ripe circumstance of two people wanting to get to know each other, and looked at them, a Statue of Liberty poised with pad and pencil.

"Well, what would you like to order?" he smiled at Phyl, and motioned to the waitress.

Phyl looked at the menu for no reason, and smiled. "Grilled cheese and a coffee, please."

"Make that two," Stu said, with the appropriate number of fingers raised, for the hard of counting. He twisted to face her as the waitress left for the order counter behind her.

"Two Jacks!" the waitress yelled at the short order cook. "I'll get your Belly Warmers in a sec," she hurriedly informed Stu and Phyl as she rushed to make fresh coffee.

"So, Miss May." He paused, hoping she'd suggest using her first name.

She pointedly didn't and looked at the counter.

He grinned and persevered. "May I know more about you?"

She looked up. "Like what?" Stifling self consciousness, she wondered if she had answered correctly.

"Well, like, do you have brothers and sisters? Are your parents still living? Are you planning to overthrow company management?"

Phyl laughed, at once put at ease by this charming man with green eyes. She leaned a little closer, but far from striking distance, so that he could hear her better over the din. "I have one brother. His name is Claude Jr., and we live with our Dad. My mother died when I was young –"

"Oh, so very sorry."

"It was a long time ago. But I couldn't stay with my Dad, so he kept my brother, and I stayed with my aunt and uncle. But I moved back during high school after Dad got a housemaid. Her name is K, or at least that's what I call her. Short for Katherine. She's nice. She takes care of the house and feeds us."

"Your Belly Warmers," the waitress announced as she plunked down two green jadeite mugs full of steaming coffee, and a little plate with two spoons. She banged down tin containers of sugar and cream from further up the counter. "Your Jacks are comin' up."

"Thank you," smiled Stu. He turned attentively to Phyl as he handed her the cream and sugar.

Phyl poured the cream into her coffee. "My Dad works at Riverdale Zoo."

Stu leaned closer and smiled. "No kidding. That must be interesting work."

Phyl brightened up even more. "It is. He loves it. He does have a peculiar smell when he comes home." She laughed. "Right now, we've been celebrating. We had the first baby elephant born on Canadian soil a couple of months ago. Isn't that grand? Dad hopes to be superintendent one day, as he wouldn't mind not having to worry about cleaning out of the stalls in particular. It's kind of heavy work."

"Dangerous, too?"

"Well, it can be if you step into the wrong cage at the wrong time." She laughed again.

"Wouldn't want to act out Daniel in the Lion's Den?" he joined in with his own laughter.

"No." She stirred her coffee as the "Jacks" were served. She eyeballed the lovely, grilled cheese before seeking the ketchup. Stu reached on his side for a bottle and handed it to her.

"Did you know that ketchup was used as medicine a hundred years ago?"

She chuckled. "No." She poured a dollop on the edge of her plate, grabbed half of her sandwich, and held it up. "Bon appetite."

He picked up his, and they 'toasted' their halves.

"I was thinking. I'm new to Toronto, although I attended school north of here. I'd love to know the city better. How about you showing me a few things? The weather's getting pretty nice now. If you'd rather your brother tag along as chaperone, I don't mind."

Phyl was delighted. She thought of El and Claude Jr. and how marvelous and proper it was to go out as two couples. "Yes, I think that could be arranged. I wouldn't mind doing that at all. He has a girlfriend, my best friend, El. Could she also tag along?"

"Absolutely. The more the merrier."

"Wonderful! There are so many things to do here. In fact, the flowers are out in bloom on Toronto Island. And it's a beautiful view of the city from there. You'd be impressed at how tall the Royal York Hotel is. It's the tallest structure in Toronto."

He laughed. "I worked in the Big Apple, remember? Concrete jungle and skyscrapers?"

Phyl nodded, smiled and chewed. She jiggled her head at her own silliness. "You're right. This ain't New York, that's for sure. How about this weekend? Where do you live?"

"I rent a flat in one of the larger homes in Rosedale."

"Oh, how posh," she jested. "Do you know how to get to Union Station from there?"

"I do, indeed, Ma'am."

"Then I'll arrange it with my brother and El, to join us. We'll meet you at Union Station and go from there. We'll show you Toronto Island, Centre Island, and Hanlon's Point Amusement Park, and we'll check out the Royal Canadian Yacht Club. Their clubhouse is beautiful. There's a beach, though it's too cold to swim, I should think." She took another bite. "Do you mind if I take my dog, Tony?"

Stu laughed. "No, I love dogs. Great to have Tony around." He looked up at the wall clock as he chewed. "We must make tracks in about five minutes. Do we want to be back on time?" he asked mischievously.

"You might get away with not being on time, but not me. Mr. Schuler counts the seconds when I'm late. So, yes, Mr. Redington, we do have to make tracks soon."

"I guess we better chow down, then."

Phyl enjoyed the rest of her grilled cheese almost as much the handsome company, while they listened to the chatter of happy people and the tinny lyrics to "Life is a Song."

> *Life is a song. Let's sing it together.*
> *Let's take our hearts and dip them in rhyme,*
> *Let's learn the words. Let's learn the music together.*
> *Hoping the song lasts for a long, long time.*

Phyl felt it in her bones - it was going to be a great Spring and Summer.

* * *

El took along her Brownie to take photos of the group sitting on the large rocks along the Island's waterfront, at the top of the bridge in Centre Island,

and on the cool sands of the Beach. Claude Jr. and Stuart spent most of their time discussing soup kitchens, Hooverville in New York, President Roosevelt, fishing, and their futures. Phyl posed for Eleanor, sitting on a blanket in the grass or hamming it up in front of trees.

"Wow, they're gettin' on like a house on fire," said El, watching Claude Jr. laugh and gesture at Stuart. "Stu sure is nice, Phyl."

Phyl agreed, not as if it was a sudden revelation. They were giddy and lagging behind the two gentlemen. Phyl walked Tony on his broad leash. They strolled along the sidewalks toward the Ferry, through flower gardens bursting with color and swarmed by buzzing bees. Tiny sparrows flitted in and out of the blossoming cherry trees all about, and pecked at the dirt between purple and pink petunias and yellow begonias. Tony perked up whenever a bird flew close to his head. He snapped at cherry blossom petals floating in the air, and sniffed at every weed growing out of cracks in sidewalks.

Occasionally, Phyl had to gently tug at Tony's leash to keep him moving along. She didn't really mind. She felt a nice little buzz and enjoyed the sun's warmth on her face. She wore a white short-sleeved blouse and black skirt, and her arms and ankles already showed some color. The fuzziness around the brain was because Stuart had just treated them to a new fancy drink called the "Martini" at the Manitou Hotel on the main drag of Centre Island. She was happy, felt classy and carefree. A Martini! So posh! Oh, it was a perfect day. So perfect, she almost forgot about the Depression.

Earlier, while they were sipping their cocktails, she and Claude Jr. invited Stuart and El back to their house for dinner. She didn't want such a lovely day to end, and had already given K a call on a pay phone to tell her there'd be two extra mouths to feed. K didn't mind at all.

El looked at her shoes well-dusted from the day's activities. "Seeing all that old furniture piled together in front of that apartment building this morning was so sad. So many people are being evicted. Where do they all go?"

Phyl was not unaware that her own shoes and gloves also showed wear and tear from the day. She wished she had other daytime shoes and taken along a clean pair of gloves.

"Let's not think about that, El." Phyl suspected El was a sad drunk. Phyl certainly wasn't. She happily threw her arms out at the sky and almost hit a lady strolling by. She quickly apologized, then turned to El. "Let's pretend all is well and this ugly Depression is finally cleaned up and behind us."

"But it's not. We didn't make the last mortgage payment on our house." El's bottom lip threatened to quiver, Phyl could see.

"Oh, no." Phyl stopped walking and faced her. "You were able to so far."

El briefly looked away as people walked around them. "With Mother not well, the doctor had to come to the house four times last month." She took out a handkerchief from inside her skirt pocket. She briefly held it to her eyes, sniffed, then folded it again. "I don't know how we'll catch up."

"El, don't worry. Between Claude Jr. and I, we can help. It's just one month you missed, right?"

El dropped her hands in angst. "Yes, but I can't let you do that!"

"Dad's got a good job, El. And K still has a few clients for cleaning houses. They don't rely on Claude Jr. and me as much as your mother and father rely on you. Let us do it, okay?" Phyl dropped her chin and looked up from under her lids at El, challenging her to give her a smile.

"Do you think this will ever end?" El asked quietly.

Phyl took her arm, and they continued, quickening their step. She sighed, taking in the lovely breeze off Lake Ontario. Carousel music from the park helped keep her spirits up. "Not everyone's having it so bad. People like my boss, Mr. Schuler, seems to be doing well enough. He just bought a boat."

El nodded toward Stuart. "He seems to be okay, too."

"Oh, Stu? He may come from money, but, apparently, his parents are on the verge of bankruptcy. If it isn't the economy killing their hotel business, it's flooding from the nearby river, and the whole downtown is underwater. The town, Wilkes-Barre, can't maintain the shoreline anymore. No money in the town coffers. The roads are bad. Everything's working against them right now. Who can afford to stay at a hotel, right? But now that Prohibition is over, their bar seems able to carry itself. Barely."

"We know where the money goes, right? Hooch and the flicks," El looked at Phyl sadly.

"Yeah, well. People need outlets." Phyl squeezed El's arm. "Fortunately, we have ours and today, it's a gorgeous day. El, mark my words. The way I feel now, I think there's only good stuff waiting for the both of us." She raised her hand, holding the leash straight up in the air, almost choking Tony. "And for the whole world!" Tony felt the happiness and joined in with a bark.

El looked at the dog and laughed. "I hope you're right."

"You can bet I am!" Phyl saw Stuart turn to look back at her. He waved and smiled. He wore a white jacket, white shirt, and a fun striped tie, along with white slacks and white shoes. A very well-dressed young man on an early summer day. She waved excitedly and grinned.

"Come on, you're lagging behind, step it up!" yelled Claude Jr. in dark jacket and slacks. "We'll miss the ferry, and I'm hungry!" Like Clark Gable, he had his fedora slanted back on his head and was working on growing a pencil mustache.

The two ladies, uplifted by such acceptable testosterone specimens in their company, locked arms and quickened their steps.

The lovely aroma of roasted chicken and potatoes, onions, and carrots wafted through the little house on Pickering Street. There was also a little hint of cinnamon in the air, guaranteeing K's famous buns for dessert. Phyl and El helped peel the vegetables and returned to entertain the gentlemen, leaving the radio on low for a bit of Bill Boyd's Cowboy Ramblers fiddle music in the background. Claude Sr. sat smoking in his chair, talked out about his work at the zoo, the successful birth of the baby elephant, and the newspapermen who came to see it. He spoke of his music, and his hunting and fishing days. Now he was eyeing Stuart standing at the front of the living room with his hands in his pockets, bending over to study photographs on a marble side table.

Stuart picked up a tarnished, silver-framed photo of Claude Jr. and Phyl. Taken in 1920, Phyl was only 8, and Jr. was 10 standing stiffly with his hands at his sides. He wore a white shirt, black slacks and his tie was askew. Little Phyllis sat sadly on what looked like a white metal, patio chair, wearing a white frock, white socks on her crossed ankles, and a massive white bow on top of her long, dark pipe curls.

"A sweet patootie!" teased Stuart. He looked back and grinned boyishly.

Claude Jr. cleared his throat loudly, in apparent correction. He hovered at the mantel, giving up the settee to El and Phyl. "Just to let you know, Father doesn't like slang." Claude Jr. motioned to his father with his head.

Stuart looked over at Sr., who frowned at him, piercing blue eyes enhanced by generous, blue light from the windows. Stuart observed Sr.'s fingers on his left hand slightly keeping beat with the fiddle music on the radio, so he hoped Claude Sr. wasn't too upset. Stuart, a naturally capable observer, knew he was being sized up.

"Er, sorry, Mr. May. No disrespect meant, sir. I was teasing your daughter, actually." He motioned to Phyl on the settee. "I guess we had such a fun day today. I'm still in that frame of mind." Stuart respectfully returned the framed photo onto the table and looked back at Phyl, who grinned at him.

She stood up. "Well, I'll help K set the table. We're going to squeeze around the kitchen table, Stu, I hope you don't mind. The more, the merrier, right? Claude Jr., could you get the chair out of the dining room?" Phyl paused at the doorway to the hallway, looking back at her brother who was about to step away from the mantle when Stuart suddenly held him back.

"No, let me. Where's the chair?"

Phyl pointed at the dining room door. "In there. Thank you, Stu."

Stuart opened the wooden sliding doors and stopped. He looked around. He had expected a dining room. Not what looked like a bedroom. Phyl appeared next to him.

"K and I sleep here. It's comfortable. Dad and Claude Jr. are in the bedrooms upstairs."

Stuart looked around the room, back into the living room, and then at Phyl. He nodded, looked back in the room again, and spotted the chair at the make-up table. Stuart walked over and saw two brushes, two housecoats on nails on the wall, and a little bed for two people. He pulled his eyes away and smiled at Phyl as he carried the chair past her to the kitchen. Phyl carefully slid the wooden doors shut.

She wondered how this remarkable young man's mind discerned.

She would learn soon enough.

* * *

Days later. Stuart sat on the corner of Phyl's desk. She looked up from her Dictaphone and then around the office. No one was there, and Mr. Schuler's door was closed. She visibly relaxed.

"Yeeees? Can I help you, Mr. Redington?"

"I was thinkin'."

"Yeeees?"

"You know how we went through your enclosed porch to get into the house?"

She chuckled. "Yeeeees?"

"Well, you have an excellent back door for people to go in and out of. If I winterize that front porch, that could be a swell little bedroom for you. And K could have the dining room all to herself."

Phyl sat back. "You've been pondering this all this time? I knew it bothered you that K and I shared a bed."

"Lots of people share beds. Especially now, but if there's a better way, why not?"

Phyl straightened up. "Oh, I don't know if K would like everyone always traipsing in and out while she stands at the stove cooking."

Stuart blinked. "Well, I think I recall a window off to the side in the kitchen, and the doorway is over by the sink, icebox, and stove. Why not move the door to the window so people bypass where K works? And that way, she has a window to look out of instead of a solid door."

Phyl blinked. She brushed her hair back behind her ears. "Okay. But we only have one bed."

Stuart stood up and put his hands together in supplication. "Do not be offended," he said. "But if your father would let me, I will get you a bed, nightstand, and dressing table that would fit into the porch." He pointed at his chest. "I will arrange for the winterizing and the door changing."

"But your parents rely on the money you send back."

Stuart paused to present a proper proposal. "Listen, I have two brothers and a sister. And half-brothers and sisters. They're also helping. Let me do this. You helped El and her parents. What goes around comes around."

Phyl felt her breath fail her momentarily. A strange sensation. She wasn't a crier, far from it. But she believed her tears were building up to a storm level. She blinked them back. She turned to the Dictaphone and typewriter and put the headphones back on. She looked at Stuart sideways. "I will stay out of it. My father may not know how to respond to your suggestion of buying me a bed and everything else that goes into a bedroom," she said softly so as not to cry.

To save her from herself, Stuart looked away at the linoleum floor. "I hadn't thought of that. I guess it *would* sound a little forward."

Phyl typed, then stopped. "I've always wanted a black and white checkered linoleum floor."

Stuart looked up in surprise.

"A heavy hint," she said, giving him a look and then continued typing.

Stuart smiled, nodded to himself, and called Phyl's father that night to ask permission to change his daughter's sleeping arrangements.

* * *

"If Claude Jr. and I ever have our own home, I would like to have a black and white checkered linoleum floor in my hallway and kitchen just like this. It's so fresh and rich-looking." El was sitting on Phyl's new bed. Her foot reached out to straighten the new little rug by the bed. Sleeping on a folded blanket against the wall nearby, Tony groaned and shifted his weight, stretching his dangly legs for a moment before curling them underneath again. He continued to snore slightly.

Phyl had chosen a pink tufted bed cover, shams, and a matching pink rug by the bed. She felt spoiled. And she felt terrific. She looked at the polished wood furniture glowing warmly in the setting sun, which peeped through the lace curtains at new latticed windows of the enclosed porch. She had sturdy blinds she could pull down, an overhead light, and two bedside lamps. She had a floor lamp in the corner by the old armchair which used to be in the room she shared with K. When Stuart bought a new armchair for her - mahogany armrests and upholstered in cream, tufted material - she passed it on to K. She felt guilty having so much new beauty around her while K simply inherited a larger space, albeit her own bed and complete privacy. She needed an excuse to see K's eyes widen happily at seeing a new piece of furniture sitting in the corner of her own bedroom.

K was elated. So much so, she had utterly rearranged the dining room and retrieved an heirloom quilt and announced she deserved to use such a good cover. Better than leaving it in a cedar chest with mothballs for the next generation.

Everyone desperately needed uplifting away from the pall of poverty hovering over them. The news was never good, it seemed. The only good news was occasional updates on the French-Canadian Dion quintuplets born in May. On the negative side, everyone was carefully watching this Adolph Hitler and his Brown Shirts over in Germany. Mr. Hitler had made himself ultimate ruler of the country. She learned words she'd never heard before like Fuhrer, Reich Chancellor, National Socialists. The American authorities had also finally caught and shot Bonnie and Clyde back in April. Even in death, making a big splash in the news. The police finished John Dillinger in July. There was so much violence all over the world, it seemed. It was high time to make home feel more comforting and secure.

El held up her engagement ring to let the sun play on the little ruby set in gold. Two tiny little diamonds sat in chiseled gold grooves on each side of the red gem. "I wish mother would let us set the date now."

"Is there a hurry?"

"Yes, I ache to have my own little kitchen. My own little family. And I don't like to let things hang like this. Neither does Jr. But Mother needs to arrange someone else to move in to care for her." She paused. "And she will miss what little I make with my wages, for sure."

"But you got the ring on the finger. That's what you were aching for just months ago. Progress, El, progress." Phyl picked up a Maclean magazine from the old armchair and flopped into it. She tossed the magazine onto the bed. Someone knocked on her new bedroom door. She looked up. "Yes?"

Jr. opened the door and poked his head in. He looked at El on the bed. He gave her a Cheshire cat grin.

"Ooo, creepy," quipped Phyl.

"Hey, do you think Stuart would like to come with Dad and me to Lake Scugog for some fishing in a couple of weeks?"

"Wow, did Dad suggest that?"

"No, I did. But I know Stu likes to fish. 'N Dad's impressed with what he did for you and K."

"Well, no can do. I know for a fact Stuart's on some mysterious business trip to Washington, D.C. I arranged it all for him. He's going down by train and taking a few days to check in on his parents in Pennsylvania while there."

"Boy, Sis, you have control over his whole life – his work life, and you're his private life. You have him wrapped around that little finger of yours."

Phyl stiffened. "I certainly do not! He's his own man!"

"Oh, Phyl, don't let your brother get to you. He's teasing you." El got up off the bed and stepped to Jr. "Claude, you know that kind of teasing means you're implying she's using him. You know she takes that kind of talk as an insult."

"I certainly am NOT using him." Phyl sat back, her chin lifted defiantly. She crossed her arms over her summer top.

Jr. dared to step further into the bedroom, seeing El was still hanging onto his arm and it was like permission to enter. "Well," he tipped an imaginary hat. "I apologize. I did not mean to imply any such thing." He turned to El. "So, are you ready for an early movie?" He looked at Phyl. "Sis? Wanna come?"

"No, there's lots of daylight left. I think I'll take Tony for a walk."

At the sound of his name and "walk," Tony suddenly awoke and jumped up, tail wagging, tongue hanging. He looked up at El and Claude Jr., then back at Phyl who grinned and leaned forward. She clapped her hands and patted her lap. Tony took a run and jumped. He was a little big for a slim little lady. Phyl grunted under the weight. She patted Tony on his side. "Good boy."

The phone rang in the hallway. Three times. Their code. Claude Jr. looked back and let go of El, and disappeared. The girls and dog heard him answer the phone. He chatted and came back.

"Phyl, it's Stu."

Phyl threw Tony off her lap and jumped up. El and an excited Tony followed her out of the bedroom. Jr. went to get his money-clip while El hung around to see what the call was about. Tony sniffed at Phyl's feet, then went to where his leash hung off the closet doorknob. He dropped onto his side and waited.

"Hi, Stu. How are you?" Phyl had to yell on the phone so he'd hear her. She looked at El and pointed at the wooden phone. She gave a thumb's up. "Tomorrow? Oh? How nice! Just one moment!" Phyl let the earpiece hang loose against the plaster wall and it swung back and forth on its thick wire, retracing a series of crescent moon marks already on the plaster. Phyl scurried to the kitchen. She stopped for a second and turned to El. "You two have plans for tomorrow, right?"

"Yes, my parents invited Claude Jr. over for the afternoon and to stay for supper." El looked at her expectantly. "Why do you ask?"

Phyl put up a finger. "K!" Phyl continued into the kitchen. She came out. "K must be outside with Dad." She hurried back into the kitchen and opened the new kitchen door leading onto the new little porch overlooking the still old backyard. Claude Sr. was smoking his stogie on a wooden folding chair while K was hanging the wash. "K?"

K turned and looked over her shoulder as she held a sheet against the clothesline. "Yes, Phyl?"

"How would you and Dad like to come with Stu and me to Guelph for a picnic tomorrow? Stu's old school buddy just bought a car, and we can use it."

Phyl's Dad looked up from his newspaper. "What kind of car?"

K laughed from the wash line. "Does it matter?" She squinted at him in the sun.

"It sure does." Claude Sr. took out his stogie and flicked the ash into the grass. "How much did his friend pay for it?"

"Twenty-five big ones."

"Piece of junk. I won't trust it."

"Dad," Phyl protested, slanting her head in disapproval.

He waved her away. "It makes a difference." He turned slightly toward K who stood watching him. "Guelph is over fifty miles away. We don't want the car to break down. The roads between here and there are rudimentary at best." He turned to Phyl. "Why Guelph?"

Phyl raised her hands and dropped them. She exchanged a confused look with K. "I don't know. It's what he suggested." She rested her hands on her hips. "I'd love to go. The Speed River runs through it, and they have a beautiful church in the middle of the city."

"Papists."

"So, it's a beautiful cathedral. The park is gorgeous. And they have lovely cafés there."

K waved at her. "He's just trying to give you a hard time, Phyl. We'd love to go. Ask Stu what he wants in the picnic basket. We can rustle something together now or first thing in the morning."

Phyl hurried back through the kitchen and grabbed the earpiece away from Tony, who was licking it. "Hello?" she yelled. She listened and then laughed. "Oh, that was Tony licking it. Hahahaha. Yeah, I guess it would sound like a swamp monster. It's a go, Stu. What time?"

El stood standing in the hallway but turned as Claude Jr. appeared next to her. She looked at Phyl again. Her eyes sparkled, and a smile slowly appeared on her face.

"What 'you smiling about?" Claude Jr. asked as he put his money clip in his back pocket.

"Just a feeling." She smiled at Phyl, who was listening to Stuart talking at the other end.

Phyl waved back and watched Claude Jr. and El leave through the kitchen. "Uh-huh, uh- huh. Okay. Will do. You wanna talk to Dad? Okay. See ya tomorrow then. I'll let Dad say bye. I'll go walk Tony. Just one moment." Phyl dropped the earpiece again and quickly grabbed the leash off the doorknob. "Come, Tony. Let's enjoy this beautiful evening before the mosquitoes come out to devour us!" She guided Tony out the back door as she called, "Dad! Stuart wants to talk to you!"

* * *

9:00 a.m. the next morning. While the sun warmed the dew and coal dusted weeds, the silence was desecrated by an old Ford, its engine rattling on old rubber tires looking suspect and wobbly. The flat top rounded the corner and chocked onto a dirt driveway. Stuart in whites, got out, and put the blocks to the tires. Claude Sr., overdressed in a heavy suit, tie, and summer hat, came out from the back of the house, holding an Ontario 1934-35 Official Government Road Map. He took one look at the car and shook his head like a priest giving a patient his last rights.

"You think that jallopy'll get us to Guelph and back," he inquired. "Today?"

Phyl hurried from the back of the house. K followed with Tony on a leash and was slightly bent from the strain of a big picnic basket. Stuart dashed up the driveway to take it from her.

Phyl addressed the car doctor. "Dad. Stuart knows what he's doing. Don't you, Stu?"

"Good morning, K," Stuart smiled over at K. "And good morning, young damsel."

Phyl looked up at Stuart with a pleased expression. "Good morning, Mr. Redington." She wore a white cloche hat, her standby short-sleeved white blouse, and a black skirt. Not unlike a new woman, she was also sporting new white shoes and gloves and a brooch pinned at the V-neck.

"You look very summery, I must say," he said, pleased.

"Good morning, Stuart. Thank you for arranging this today," said K.

"My pleasure indeed!" He motioned to the basket. "And thank you for going to all this trouble."

"No trouble at all," smiled K, patting her hair with her free, gloved hand.

"You're not taking my family in that dilapidated wreck, are you?" yelled Claude Jr. hanging out from the upstairs bedroom window.

"Shhh. Neighbors might still be sleeping." Phyl looked around at the neighboring homes.

"After that entrance with this piece of junk? I'd be surprised they're still sleeping two blocks over," joked Jr., but this time in a loud whisper.

Claude Sr. gave K a look, then at Phyl. "Stuart, I should ask, you do have a license?"

"Yes, sir. And I pride myself in being somewhat of an expert in the management of cars."

Phyl peered at her father as she reached the car. "Oh, come on, Dad. We'll be fine."

Sr. looked at Stuart who glanced back at him as he put the basket on the running board, lashing it with a hemp rope. Sr. motioned to the basket. "How do we open the doors with that thing lashed there?"

"You just climb in from the other side. Just slide over." Stuart kept working on the rope, straightening and leveling the basket, and looking for places to feed the rope through.

"You think that hemp rope'll keep that on? You know what conditions those roads are?"

"Dad." Phyl looked sad. Her mouth drooped. K came over and patted her on the shoulder.

"Claude, I can slide into the back there, fine. No problem at all," said K. She was dressed quite crisply; a tiny hat with veil, cream gloves, shoes, and a white summer dress with a dropped waist.

Stuart put another knot into the rope and straightened out. "Yes, sir, I do think we'll be fine. I've been to Guelph a few times. It's a journey but worth it on a nice day." He pointed at the map in Claude Sr.'s hand. "And you won't need that. It's a simple route. We go from here to Highway 5, till we hit Highway 6, and then straight North to Guelph."

"Well, you never know if there are detours, young man. Detours, construction, road mishaps. You get off the beaten track, and you're doomed."

Stuart hustled to the other side of the dusty black car and opened the back and front doors, motioning for everyone to climb in. K slid into the back, and Phyl joined her with Tony, who squeezed in and sat on the car floor between K and Phyl.

Claude Sr. looked at Stuart pointedly before climbing into the front and sliding over to his seat. "How am I supposed to get out if something happens?" he complained as he grunted in place on the front bench. He sat up straight and sighed heavily. He looked back to ensure the women were fine.

Stuart waved up at Claude Jr., who returned the wave and cupped his mouth and whispered loudly, "I'd like to see how you start it without waking the rest of Kingdom Come at this hour."

Stuart waved him away and went to the front of the car. He grabbed the handle of the crank and turned it over. Nothing. Tried again. This time the engine exploded into harsh coughs. A flock of sparrows bolted from a neighboring apple tree and cats scooted from under bushes. The car jiggled and argued while standing in place. Stuart quickly took away the blocks and climbed in behind the wheel. Everyone waved at Claude Jr. as the car backed out and sputtered North to Gerard Street, neighbor's eyes peering through curtains watching it until it disappeared around the corner.

It was scorching and sticky inside the car. Most of the way, they had to keep the windows almost closed to a crack to prevent road dust from billowing in. Roads changed from graded dirt to gravel, and stone. At one point, a distance was of seashells and sand clay. Where the seashells came from, nobody could say. The Ford averaged about 20 miles to the gallon and didn't need new water in the radiator. Unfortunately, Tony's dog breath filled the car, and K had to sprinkle Eau de Cologne on her handkerchief and hold it to her nose several times just to give herself a break from the intense mustiness in the car.

They hiccoughed to a stop once to let Tony out for a break in the tall grass along the deserted highway. The next time, they stopped because Claude Sr. needed a break. He pointed out the window to a cluster of trees. "There," he motioned to Stuart. "Stop around here."

Stuart slowed down onto the dirt shoulder and turned off the Ford. He clambered out, put the blocks behind the wheels, and helped Claude Sr. slide over and climb out.

Two cars rumbled by. One honked horn in acknowledgment of a fellow car; the second slowed down to see if their group had car trouble. Stuart waved, shook his head, and motioned them to go on.

Phyl opened her door, and the two ladies and a very hot dog exited for blessed, fresh air. Phyl waved her handkerchief at her face, then yanked Tony's leash a little tighter to herself as she walked toward the edge of the shoulder. The dog was anxious to bolt and explore the tall grass. "My goodness, it's getting warm. How much longer, Stu?" asked Phyl.

K held out her hand for the leash and took Tony, leading him to the other side of the car.

Stuart hadn't counted on the fact that the dog and older man would need stops. He looked at his watch and peered further up Highway 5. "At this rate, I'd say another hour and a half."

"An hour and a half!" K exclaimed. "Why, if we wait a little longer, we might as well have our picnic lunch here along the highway." She gazed beyond the surrounding fields, and distant farm houses, barns, cows and horses. "It's quite pretty here."

Relieved by a positive statement, Phyl relaxed a little. She checked for dust on the hot black surface of the car before cautiously resting her arm against it. She was about to take a cigarette out of her little purse but thought better of it as she looked over and saw her father disappearing into the trees.

"Say, I should tell you something, Phyl." Stuart leaned back against the car, next to her.

She pointed at the dust and brushed off his shirt sleeve.

"Oh, that's okay. I suppose you heard Remington Rand has been trying to get into the South American market?"

"I've seen the letters, yes."

"Well, Argentina has signed a treaty with Britain to open up trade for three years. Argentina's still not open to trading with the United States, but there's a chance we can do business through the Toronto office as British subjects."

"Oh?" She squinted at him, curiously.

"Yes, and, well, because I'm an American working for a British firm, head office in New York thought I would be the perfect candidate. They would like to gain the trust of the Argentines. They're hoping they can eventually establish a solid American base there."

Phyl stood ram rod straight. She dropped one hand and tucked the other under her underarm. She looked at Stuart, appalled. She blinked several times as her brain scrambled to think of something to say.

"All right, let's hit the road!" yelled Claude Sr., retracing his path through the tall grass to the shoulder of the highway. He looked up at the sun. "We might just make it by noon."

They had their picnic at a lovely spot beside the fast-flowing Speed River before moving on to see the Gothic Revival-style church, Basilica of Our Lady Immaculate. Phyl felt like she had travelled to Europe as she stood staring up at the fancy, tall spires. Inside, it was welcomingly cool and dark and breathtaking. The sunlight flowed through a myriad of stained-glass windows, creating a feast for the eyes. All the gold and silver within the church came to life in a shower of brilliant color. Claude Sr. didn't come in, choosing to smoke outside and stayed with Tony as the others went in to marvel at the architectural splendor.

Later, Phyl sadly stood at the bottom of the grand, stone steps leading up to the limestone Ontario Agricultural Building. She felt heartbroken at the thought of Stuart going to Argentina. She had many questions but didn't have an opportunity to be alone with him long enough to ask.

"I especially found the samples of deformed baby animals in jars very fascinating. I've never seen such a thing, have you, Phyl, dear?" asked K.

Phyl sadly shook her head. "No, never. I may have some nightmares about them actually." As Stuart approached her, she braved a smile for him but her lip quivered, and that darn feeling pestered her.

Stuart turned to Claude Sr. and K. "Would you mind if I walk a bit with Phyl alone?"

K looked over at Claude Sr., who was lighting his stogie. "I think a walk would be fine," K said. She looked over the vast, trimmed lawn and pointed at a bench under a spreading maple tree, its leaves almost lime green. "I wouldn't mind resting my poor feet."

Sr. nodded. "It's time for my smoke. You kids go ahead. I didn't like the sound of that muffler, so after my smoke, I'll mosey on over to the car and check the muffler and motor mount."

Stuart smiled. "Oh, right. Okay. Thank you, sir. We won't be long." Stuart gently held Phyl's upper arm. He led her in the opposite direction toward one of the other limestone buildings on the campus. As they fell into step, he put her arm through hers. They sauntered into a shaded alley between two buildings. From there, they heard a gramophone playing Bing Crosby singing "Brother Can You Spare a Dime?"

They used to tell me I was building a dream
With peace and glory ahead
Why should I be standing in line
Just waiting for bread?
Once I built a railroad, I made it run
Made it race against time
Once I built a railroad, now it's done
Brother, can you spare a dime?

Stuart led her past from the music. Then he stopped, dipped his hand into his pocket, and kept it there. "Phyl, I know you are very upset. But I want you to know that if this Argentina thing happens, it won't be for another year."

"Oh," she said hopefully.

"But, I do not want to be away from you. I can't see any other option than this." He bent his knee and pulled out a little red, velvet jewelry box. He opened it to reveal a small gold ring with a beautiful aquamarine stone.

Phyl's heart leapt. It was the last thing she expected. She looked wide-eyed, into Stuart's hopeful eyes. The wrinkles next to them crinkled slightly.

"Please, Phyl, will you marry me?"

Phyl surprised herself when she burst into tears. Stuart took out his handkerchief and handed it to her as if already prepared to do so.

She wiped her eyes and nose, and nodded wordlessly. "Yes, oh, yes." She laughed, half crying.

Stuart stood, took the ring out of the box, then took her left hand. He slipped it on. It was a little large. They laughed. "I can have that made smaller."

Phyl nodded. "I know. It's beautiful. I've never seen such a beautiful ring."

"It's aquamarine. It matches your bright and delightful disposition." He grinned and blinked, thinking for a moment. "And your very beautiful blue eyes. Phyl, I'm so very happy."

Phyl looked around. "Oh, my goodness. My father."

"That's okay. I spoke to your father about it first. He knows."

"When on earth did you do that?"

"Last night, remember I asked to talk to him on the phone? I asked him out for a coffee at the corner. He was home before you got back from your walk."

"Is that why he's in such a bad mood?" she laughed.

"He doesn't want to see you go. Especially if it means you are going as far away as Argentina. In his opinion, you might as well fall off the face of the earth. And I think he secretly hates Americans." He squeezed her hand lovingly. "But I promised to have you back after two years."

They stood looking at each other. The breeze gently tossed their hair. She admired his long, boyish face and gentle look. She stood on tiptoes and kissed him. "I don't know what to say."

"Well, you've already said enough to make me happy for the rest of my life." He smiled softly. "I've also told my parents, and they want to meet you. So, we came up with a plan. I spoke to Claude Jr."

"What? Am I the only one who didn't know?"

"Jr. is going to chaperone us when we go by train to see my folks. I spoke to Mr. Schuler."

"Mr. Schuler!?"

"He says it'll be okay to take you in October before things get hectic for Christmas. We're staying in my folks' hotel. They would want the wedding in Wilkes-Barre because I have a bigger family who would want to attend, plus they would like to see us married at the same church I was baptized in. And the reception will be in the ballroom of the hotel."

"Oh, Stu, down in Wilkes-Barre? I don't know if my Dad could... If we could afford..."

"As the father of the bride, he'll cover the cost of your wedding dress, the preacher, Maid of –"

"Yes, El!"

"He will cover the cost of her dress and both your flowers. My folks will cover the rest, plus train tickets for your Dad, K, Claude, and El. What ya think?"

"And when do you think we should marry?"

"Well, a year is respectable. Yes? A little less, perhaps. Early next Spring? And we can stay in my flat for the few months after we're married before we board a ship for Argentina."

Phyl laughed. "Argentina! By ship! What a honeymoon!"

"Well, no. Our honeymoon will be a week in New York after the wedding."

Phyl's mouth dropped. "Can we afford all that?"

"We have relatives in Manhattan who'll be in Europe for a few months. So, it only costs us a train ticket from Wilkes-Barre, Pennsylvania, and then a ticket home to Toronto through Montreal after that."

Phyl felt faint. It was all so sudden and so much. Even a good shock is still a shock to the system, and she thought she might throw up just for good measure. She grabbed her stomach. "Oh, Stu."

Stuart held her tightly for a moment, then let go. He fluttered his hand at her face for oxygen and laughed. "Too much, huh?"

"If this indicates how exciting our lives will be together, I'll just have to get used to it, I guess."

Stuart paused, as if harvesting a profound message whispered to him from a place only angels know. She felt suddenly an inexplicable stop in the Earth's rotation. It even seemed like a complete stoppage in time. When whatever message from beyond was relayed, Stuart spoke thoughtfully.

"Phyl." He followed the path of a passing cloud. "I promise we'll always have an exciting life. You'll never get bored with me."

She squeezed his arm and, in her excitement, almost fell sideways. "Oh, Stu, can we go somewhere and have a Martini to celebrate? I'm just dying for one."

"Can't, my dear. It's Sunday. We're in Ontario, remember?"

"Oooooh, darn."

"But there's hooch in the boot. Why don't we make a toast before heading back home?"

"Sounds like the cat's meow! And I can't wait to tell El!" Phyl suddenly stopped him from leading her back out into the sun. "Oh, wait. Unless El already knows, too."

Stuart shook his head. He grinned. "Nope, that's for you to tell."

"Oh, my God. She's going to go berserk!" Phyl jumped up and straddled Stuart, laughing. Someone wolf-whistled from overhead and Stuart and Phyl looked to see two young men leaning out of a window. Phyl got down and held up her hand. "Look! We're engaged!"

One of the two young men disappeared briefly, reappeared, and emptied a metal waste basket of paper, which fluttered down over Stuart and Phyl's heads. Phyl screamed as Stuart grabbed her hand and they ran off to rejoin the others.

Chapter Two
October 1934, Train to Pennsylvania

"The more I know of Argentina, the more I wonder why the company is crazy enough to send us there."

Phyllis looked at her brother seated across from her, then at Stuart next to her. "All I read about are military coups. Guns and generals and destruction. I'm tired of all that stuff. I can remember the Great War and all those broken, young men coming home, and we're still in this godforsaken Depression."

Stuart looked down his nose at her from where they sat on a leather bench in a packed train compartment. It was dark outside. They had watched the sunset over Buffalo an hour before and he could tell the day had been hard on Phyllis. She was getting mighty tired. He shifted to make room for her in the middle of their bench. "Phyl, here, lie down. I'll roll up my coat, and you can rest your head on my lap."

Phyl remained sitting, staring out the window, rocking to the train's rhythm. She didn't answer.

"Sis, you okay?" asked Claude Jr. He leaned forward, his elbows resting on the table between them, careful to slightly shift the train-ware ashtray out of harm's way. He frowned and blinked at her, seeing her downtrodden expression, her staring out into the darkness at nothing. He looked at Stuart, who slightly shrugged. "Sis, are you having second thoughts about hitching with Stu? You can be honest. No one would blame you." He chuckled as he shot another glance at Stuart, who glowered at him.

Stuart tore his eyes away from Jr. "I should've pushed for a sleeper." He looked glumly at the tabletop and started fidgeting with a cigarette package.

Phyl turned to Stuart. "No, Stu, your parents are already helping us with this trip. I'm fine without a bed." Her bloodshot eyes looked at the other passengers. Women, men, and a few children. Everyone sitting with various bags and rolled-up coats. Not quite time to sleep, but some had already succumbed to the rocking motion of the train. She sighed deeply and looked at her hands. She clasped and unclasped her fingers. She took off a glove and slightly adjusted her engagement ring to center on her finger.

"Look, I know I should've been more forthcoming about the what's and why's." Stuart touched her hand, covering her engagement ring with a warm and comforting hand.

Jr. frowned at his brother-in-law-to-be. "What do you mean, more forthcoming? What don't we know? Now, if you've been hiding something…"

"No. I just didn't think it was that important, really."

Phyl looked at Stuart as if in confessional.

Stuart spread his hands on the little table. "Okay. You know I went to Princeton."

Phyl nodded silently. She frowned and shifted her body impatiently.

"I also went to Military College before that."

"Oh?"

"And my degree in Princeton was in English."

Phyl raised her chin. "Yeeees?"

"I also studied economics."

"Okay?"

"Up until the Justo administration in Argentina…"

"The Military Coup guy," she emphasized, sitting up.

Stuart held up a finger. "Okay, so, the basic premise of a healthy economy for any country is trade."

Phyl looked confused. "Wait, wait, wait," she said, holding up her hands. "What does Military College, what you studied at Princeton and military coups in Argentina have to do with trade?"

"Um. Well. First of all, it makes me an all-round capable guy."

"All-round capable guy," Phyl quietly repeated. "How's that?"

"Okay. Just hear me out and let me start again. Roosevelt keeps a Good Neighbor Policy, right?"

"Meaning?"

"Meaning the U.S. no longer desires to manipulate economies through political tampering. We, as in the United States, but I'm sure it applies to you guys in the British Commonwealth, need to focus on issues at home to get through this Depression. So, we've basically become isolationists."

"Iso-whats?" asked Claude Jr.

"Countries cut back on exports and imports and concentrate their money and attention on crumbling infrastructure, food shortages, and homelessness."

"We're not doing a very good job," said Phyl. She wondered what this had to do with a wedding.

"I agree. It isn't working. So, now we are told that the secret to climbing out of this Depression is to look to trade again. However, under pressure by the Brits, the United States had to agree to cut down on imports of Argentine beef and, instead, buy beef and lamb from you guys to help keep *you* afloat. Argentina didn't like being dropped by the U.S. and is not enamored with us at present. So, it's been an uphill battle generating trade with them again."

Phyl shook her head in frustration. She looked at Claude Jr.

Jr. shrugged and shook his head in turn. "He's lost me, Sis. It's already over my head."

Phyl turned to Stuart. "Stu, this doesn't mean anything to me." She motioned to Claude. "To us. I'm frightened of military coups. Beef or no ridiculous beef, I don't care to go. And what does beef have to do with Remington Rand typewriters, anyhow?"

"It's the building up of relations that counts in the end. We're trying to get more Americans into Argentina but Argentines frown on any kind of interference by us, and any perceived gain by us will be suspect. Besides, it would be wise for North America to rely on its closest source of meats. In good or difficult times." He paused and looked at the brother and sister team. "Don't you agree?"

"But what about us? The British Commonwealth? Shouldn't we be upset with you, the Americans, by withholding important trade?"

Stuart took a deep breath and shrugged. "It's all political."

"Hey, hold on there, buddy. Are you sayin' what I think you're sayin'?"

Stuart looked at him impatiently. "What am I 'sayin', Claude Jr.?"

"Are you marryin' my sister 'cause she's a British subject, so you can go to Argentina on some United States booboo business?"

"Stuart!" Phyl's eyes widened, and her mouth dropped.

"OH, COME NOW!"

"Stuart, keep your voice down," shot Phyl.

Stuart fumed and pursed his lips. Quietly, he spoke but with intent. "The Brits have an advantage. Two years ago, lucky *they* signed an agreement with Argentina called the Roca – Runciman Treaty, which guaranteed Argentina a beef export quota but only equivalent to 1932 – three years ago. However, in exchange, Argentina reduced tariffs on British goods, but to 1930 rates. It's all about compromise."

"Good for us Brits, but what has that got to do with you guys?" he asked Stuart.

"You mean me, as in American?"

Claude nodded.

"Okay. We've created a loop hole: Remington Rand Toronto is under the British umbrella even though Head Office is in New York. It's a stretch, but these agreements comprise tons of small print in endless pages, and by slipping in a paragraph or two pertaining to piggybacking on the Brits, we can get away with…." Stuart lowered his voice and leaned in over the table toward

Claude Jr. "We can get away with establishing an office base in Buenos Aires as a British enterprise."

Phyllis crossed her arms and looked at the moving black scenery outside the window. A glow in the sky signaled they were approaching a town. "This is a touch more than I can handle. I still want to know: What does a military regime have to do with typewriters?" she muttered, over her shoulder.

Jr. sat back and raised and dropped his hands. "Sis, everyone needs to type memos and letters. You know, you being a typist, far better than me."

Phyllis tipped her head to the side and shrugged. "I guess."

"So, are your parents as upset as Dad is about us going to the 'ends of the earth,' as he put it?" Phyls' sad eyes looked into his inquisitively.

Stuart's eyebrows raised, and he shook his head. "Nope."

Phyl sat back and blinked. "Nope? Not one iota? They're not afraid for you?"

Stuart made a quizzical face. "Why should they be? It's all part of what one does to get ahead and make it big in this world. Believe it or not, there is a world outside of Toronto the Good!"

"Stuart!" Phyl frowned.

Jr. grinned. "I like that. Make it big. That's what I want to do."

"Yeah, you would." Phyl turned to her brother and shook her newly-cropped bob.

"Phyl, we discussed our goals with this opportunity in Argentina. We want to have financial stability, right? It's not impossible. Working as a salesman is fine, but it's hand-to-mouth. Making this special contract has bonuses tied to it. And it leads to other opportunities. I could forever say goodbye to a little salesman's job in a Toronto office. Remember? We want to work hard for a couple of years and then come back and put a down payment on our own home. Phyl. Our own *home*."

"Well, maybe I'm being difficult here, but I still don't understand how one lives under a military regime with guns on every corner. I have nightmares of people walking around with guns in their belts."

"It's not the Wild West, Phyl. You'll see."

Phyl's eyes saddened more, yet she felt a twinge of hope. And perhaps excitement.

Stuart took her hand.

"Hey there, hold your horses." Claude Jr. grinned and looked at Stuart's hands pointedly.

"You're taking your role as chaperone too seriously, Jr." Stuart continued holding Phyl's hand. Comforting, he spoke. "Let's you meet my folks first, Phyl. We'll take one step at a time. Together."

Phyl smiled. "Sounds good."

"Great." Stuart slapped the table. "Now, where's that dining car? Let's go have a nightcap."

"I'm all for that," announced Jr. as he scrambled from behind the table and straightened his jacket. He picked up his fedora. "Let's go. I'm hooked on those Martinis. Stu, you're a bad influence."

Stuart grinned. He helped Phyl off the bench, and put on his hat. "I certainly try my best."

Phyl followed them down the aisle while something tugged at the back of her mind. Something foreboding. Something yet to come. She glanced at the other passengers while her ears tuned into the locomotive's repetitive rhythm. It sounded fine. Nothing amiss. For now. She shivered and decided a Martini or two was just what the doctor ordered.

* * *

"We have 200 rooms, but we only use 50. We're lucky if half of them are ever occupied at one time."

Stuart's mother, Bessy, trailed a hand along the top edge of a brocade chair she had reupholstered. With her other hand, she pushed a rogue lock of grey hair back into her bun at the nape of her neck. Grey eyes, accustomed to detail and years of customers' faces and expressions, seemed worried and distracted. Her thin lips frozen in a benign smile, she nervously straightened her lavender sweater over her mid-shin, navy-blue dress. Comfortable shoes and thick stockings betrayed her conservative personality.

"We were doing quite fine before the Crash. We were able to send Stuart and Robert to university. Unfortunately, my younger son, Ed, has to wait." Bessy turned to Phyl, who stood at the hotel room window looking down six floors to Pennsylvania Avenue. "Which I hope won't be too long." She clasped her hands. "You do know, that Stuart promised to help put his brother through university once he is established." She cleared her throat. "Once *you* are established." Bessy wrung her hands and waited.

Phyl turned and smiled. "Oh, yes. I do know, Mrs. Redington. And I totally agree. I know from the paperwork that Stuart isn't going to make us rich quick, and it's going to be a lot of hard work in Argentina. I mean, we don't even speak Spanish. But perhaps after a year or so, we should be able to do something for him." She nodded. "I'm okay with that. That's what family does."

Bessy softened her smile. She sighed and looked at a faded green carpet. "I certainly don't have the right to complain. Some don't have a roof over their heads. John and I have a choice of two hundred beds outside of our penthouse." Bessy adjusted her spectacles as she chuckled nervously, dryly. "But no matter what standing one may have, one still has bills to pay, and if the money isn't flowing, well..."

"Certainly."

Bessy motioned to her. "Shall we? I'm so anxious to show you the dining room downstairs. It would be a wonderful place for the wedding reception. It can seat 200 at a time."

"Yes, that would be very nice." Phyl took another look around the room. A gold-trimmed mirror over a dark-oak nightstand, a table, a brass floor lamp with satin shade and dangling pearls, seemed grand enough. If she looked closely, however, she would see wear and tear. Nevertheless, it sure beat her Dad's two-bedroom house and her bedroom porch in Toronto.

"You'll be staying in a room a little smaller than this on the first floor. Your brother is next to you, and Stuart sleeps in his room in the Penthouse." She looked at her thin gold watch, "Marita should be home soon. She works as a clerk at the Town Office. She is so looking forward to meeting you."

"Well, I am certainly looking forward to meeting my future sister-in-law. Thank you."

Bessy waited for Phyl to leave before she took a last look around the room and shut the door.

"I love Freddy Martin and his Orchestra, don't you?" Marita asked Phyllis, speaking over the tinny, scratchy music.

> *I saw stars, I heard a birdie sing, so sweet, so sweet,*
> *The moment I fell for you. I saw stars,*
> *I heard an angel say, 'Wake up, wake up*
> *Your wonderful dreams come true.'*

Like her brother, Marita had laughing green eyes, and her hair, cropped into a short bob similar to Phyl's, was the same dirty blonde. Marita wore red lipstick and little ruby stones in her ear lobes. She wore her dark brown jacket and skirt from work. She and Phyl were nursing gin and tonics, standing by the upright piano as they listened to the gramophone perched on a side table by a velvet settee.

"Marita, Darling, please put the music down. We can't think here," called Bessie.

Phyl looked to where Bessie and John, Stuart's mother and father, were sitting chatting with him.

Marita moved the louver over the horn to minimize the volume of the music.

Phyl looked closer at Marita's earrings as she bent over. "You have pierced ears?"

Marita straightened up and put her finger to her lips. "Shhh, no one actually noticed save you. I felt quite rebellious." She shook her hair so that the bottom edge of her bob covered her ear lobes. Then she pushed her hair back behind one ear to model an earring again for Phyl. She grinned and, with a wink, she shook her hair loose again. She giggled. "Do you ever feel rebellious?"

Phyl was taken aback. "Well, I think I'm adventurous, but I don't know about rebellious."

Marita laughed. "You have to be, to be with my brother. He has big ideas. He's like a comet streaking across the sky, and you have to grab onto his tail for dear life."

Claude Jr., standing nearby at a window also listening to Freddy Martin and his Orchestra, suddenly turned. He took a sip from his scotch on ice and wandered over, shaking the glass to hear its luxurious sound in a glass. "I have really big ideas, too." He smiled at Marita.

Short and petite, Marita looked up at Claude Jr. as if he were Hercules. "You do?" She straightened up, pushed back her little shoulders, and deftly pulled at the bottom of her jacket.

"Sure," Jr. said, putting his hand in his trouser pocket. He rocked on his feet. "I have dreams."

"I find your Canadian accent so amusing," she said.

"I didn't know Canadians had an accent," laughed Claude Jr.

Phyl moved a little closer to her brother. She could tell there was chemistry between her brother and her future sister-in-law. "And what are your dreams, Claude Jr.?"

"They're for me to know, Sis," he joked.

"And El to find out?" She looked at Jr. knowingly.

Marita, eyes aglow, looked up at Phyl. She smiled. "And who is this "L"?"

"El, short for Eleanor. She's my best friend."

"Oh, how lovely." Marita reached up and touched one of her earrings.

"And she happens to be Claude Jr.'s fiancée." Phyl grinned at her brother's pointed look at her.

"Oh. I'm sorry." Marita turned politely to Claude Jr. "You have a fiancée?" Boldly, she looked him up and down. "Too bad."

Jr., his moon face glowing, raised his eyebrows at Phyl. "Well, I don't know what to say to that." He looked pleasingly down at Marita, who coyly swayed side to side as she looked at him sideways and smiled. "But I think I will take that as a compliment." He bowed his head slightly to Marita. "Thank you."

Marita's eyes glistened. "You're welcome."

Phyl's heart skipped a beat. She didn't quite know how to steer the conversation away from budding, unwanted relationships. She had to protect El, somehow. "Um," she started as she looked around the Redington's living room. In reality, there were so many things she could easily ask. The room was full of artifacts from exciting places around the world. Some things were a complete mystery to her. But artifacts apart, the room itself was fascinating.

The Redingtons lived on the upper level of the Hotel Redington, where their windows looked out in four directions seven floors up. On the one side, she saw the dark swath of the Susquehanna River four blocks away, lights twinkling along its shoreline in the October night. She could see past lit houses onto a black expanse on the North and East Sides. These were still very green fields surrounded by trees in brilliant Fall colors of red, yellow and orange. The railroad and lit station were quite evident.

On the South Side, the city sprawled a little further past a market square, ending in darker neighborhoods of humble homes, though she noted earlier they were much larger than hers in Toronto. Here and there, outside of the downtown area, dirt roads. Very few cars were in evidence in town, but she had seen private little barns for horses and wagons before the night set fully.

"You know," she finally said, "I think Wilkes-Barre is a strange combination of a small city and quaint little neighborhoods. And you're right on the edge of farmland."

"That's where a lot of the goods come from for market. From there, and by train, of course. But when you look the other way, across the Susquehanna River, you can almost see our house in Kingston."

Phyl looked out the window across the black swath of river. "Is it on the water?" she asked.

"No, but it has a nice view of the water and has a bit of land. It's rented out now. Fortunately, the tenants pay their rent on time. It's kind of why we're keeping our head above water. I miss living there."

"Can I see it sometime?" asked Phyl, intrigued.

"Sure, maybe we can take a drive out there." Marita chewed at a nail. "By the way, have you talked about where you'll settle eventually, you being Canadian and Stu American?" Marita looked at Phyl with a quizzical look. "Hmmm?"

Phyl thought for a moment. She couldn't stand the idea of not coming back to Toronto after their adventure in Buenos Aires. It hadn't even occurred to her that Stuart may want to live in Pennsylvania.

"No, we haven't."

"Stuart's always wanted to build a house in Kingston. Did you know that?"

"No. Stuart never mentioned it," said Phyl, frowning.

"Oh well, maybe he didn't get around to sharing that with you." Marita approached a carpet-covered table and reached for a pink quartz box. She opened the gold-trimmed lid to expose unfiltered cigarettes. "In Spring, we can smell the pig and cow manure spread over the fields. It's quite pungent." She took a cigarette and offered it to Phyl, who took it gladly. "But you get used to it."

"Sis, put the cigarette back. Claude Jr. whispered, motioning back to Bessy and John.

Phyl looked at her future in-laws on the large settee opposite Stuart. She shrugged. "Marita is having one. And these cigarettes are obviously meant for anyone to enjoy. I'm not a child, Claude."

He sighed, looked back at Stuart and his parents, then turned and took a cigarette. He tapped it on his hand before patting his vest for his lighter.

"Here, we have matches coming out of our ears." Marita handed him a book of matches, allowed him to light her cigarette, then waited while he lit Phyl's.

"What kind are these?" asked Phyl, exhaling. "They're stronger than I'm used to."

"What do you smoke in Canada?"

"Export 'A's."

"'Never heard of them." Marita watched Phyl remove a loose piece of tobacco from the tip of her pink tongue. "These are Camels."

Jr. closed the book of matches and looked at it. "'Hotel Redington, 200 rooms of solid comfort. Modern, Fireproof, European. Wilkes-Barre. John A. Redington, Jr., Manager.'" He looked at Marita. "Your Dad's a Junior, too?"

"Yeah, my grandfather started the hotel in better days. Who knows how long we'll still be here. We could be kicked out any day by the bank." Marita looked wistfully around the room. "Oh, well. Everyone's having a hard time. We're just lucky we have our own bar downstairs. Lots of drinky-poos." She grinned, holding up her gin and tonic. Marita turned to her parents. "Mother, when do we go down for dinner?"

"We're not, Marita. They're bringing it up. We're just waiting for your brothers. They want to sit in on the discussion as to how this wedding will be organized."

Marita turned to Phyl. "My brothers are always late. By the way, I'm sure your best friend will be your Maid of Honor? Have you told her yet?"

Phyl finished her drink. "It's the first thing I did after she screamed and left me deaf. But that was before I realized we were getting married in Pennsylvania. She won't be able to come down and join us."

Marita's smile vanished, and she looked down at the floor. "Oh. I'm so sorry. We're a ghastly family. We're probably railroading you to have the wedding down here." She paused. "Is it because of the distance? Or she can't take the time? I know it takes a while, going down and back by train. Maybe a full week by the time she's done with the wedding."

Phyl fingered her empty glass. Claude Jr. took it wordlessly and slipped away to refresh it for her. She watched Jr.'s back distractedly. "El's mother isn't well," she whispered to Marita. "And they really can't miss the lost wages. The distance might have something to do with it, certainly." She smiled sadly. "We didn't imagine this when we used to dream about our weddings. I'm afraid she's very hurt."

"I'm sorry."

Phyl looked around for a chair. Her feet were killing her. She chose an elaborate armchair closest to the piano. Marita followed suit and sat in a matching chair. "My feet are killing me."

"It's amazing how many steps you take just going around this hotel. That's why we're all so slim," Marita laughed. "What about your father? He'll be coming, surely?"

Phyl grimaced. "That's another challenge. Dad's not too pleased." She leaned back in her chair. "I'll be honest with you. Like everyone else, we have no money. Dad can't take the time off, not that much. He only gets two weeks in the summer, and fishes, and, well, it's complicated."

"Complicated?"

"We're embarrassed to say. He's separated. It's ugly. And there's more."

"Oh dear."

"He doesn't like me to be gone for two years in Argentina."

"It's only two years. Surely, he can't see that as a big deal."

"He thinks any number of things could happen. The ship might sink. I may get kidnapped."

Marita laughed then made a face. "Well, that's no fun for you. I'm sure. It's hard dealing with parents who expect other things from you." She looked over at her own parents. "I know. It seems that whatever I would love to do just doesn't fit into *their* plans."

Phyl sadly looked and wondered what to say.

Marita waved at her. "Old hat. Not worth talking about. Maybe another day."

Phyl watched as Stuart explained something to his parents. They were so obviously focused on their son. "Well, maybe there's still time to figure this out on my end," she said. "And because your parents are covering almost all the cost, I really don't have any right to complain. I'm humbled and so moved that – especially now – Stuart and I could have such a lovely wedding and reception. So, though it upsets things at home, getting married here, in the end, is a blessing."

"You could always have another wedding reception at home for those who can't make it."

Phyl's eyebrows shot up. "Oh, wow. That's a good idea, Marita. Thank you. That just might work." And though she knew it would be far too much to expect, she immediately knew where she would want it. "The Old Mill," she whispered. "I've always wanted to see the Old Mill."

"That sounds quaint."

"Oh, I've only seen it from the outside. It's very posh."

"Posh is nice."

A brass engraved rotary phone next to the large settee rang shrilly. Bessie turned her attention from Stuart and answered the phone. She said a few words, then hung up.

"There's a telegram for you at the front desk, Stuart, dear."

"Oh." He stood up.

"No need." Bessie put up her hand as she settled back into the settee. "Sam's bringing it up."

Phyl, hearing the exchange, tapped the ash off her cigarette into a tall floor ashtray and stood up. "Were you expecting a telegram from anyone, Stu?" she asked, as she walked toward him.

"Nope." Stuart shook his head and leaned back into his armchair. He yawned. He had been reading during the night to acquaint himself with the Roca – Runciman Trade Treaty.

The stylus slipped off the end of the track on the phonograph record, and Marita lifted the needle.

"Marita, could we have some Stravinsky for a change, please?" said Bessie.

Marita looked back at her mother just as a knock came on the door. "That was fast," she said. She saw her father, John Redington, holding up his hand.

"I'll get that. I've been sitting on this couch far too long." With a grunt, John struggled off the couch and grabbed his wooden cane. He found his balance and walked toward the door. Bessie took a moment to reach up and tug at his rumpled smoking jacket as he passed. He quickly slicked a few hairs over his bald head and opened the door to find Sam, the only bellhop they had on hire. "Hello, Sam, and thank you." John took a telegram from Sam, who smiled and nodded.

"Your dinner should be comin' up soon, Mr. Redington, sir."

"Thank you, Sam. Much appreciated." John closed the door absentmindedly looking down at the envelope. "Who on earth would be sending you a telegram, Son?"

Stuart stood up and took the telegram. He looked at both sides of the envelope, took a fancy letter opener in the shape of a sword held out by his mother, and sliced the end open.

Phyl moved closer, curious as well. She watched Stuart read the telegram. It was short and concise. He folded it up, put it back into its envelope, and tucked it into his jacket pocket. He looked up to see everyone looking at him expectantly. "Uhm, I have to go to Washington first thing tomorrow."

"Tomorrow? For how long?" asked Bessie. "We still have so much to plan."

"Just for the day."

"What on earth for?" asked Phyl, confused. "And can you do that in a day?"

"Oh, yes. Hop on the train, go for the day, hop on the train, come home," offered Marita. She placed another record on the gramophone. She wound the handle, and the subtle, rising notes of Stravinsky's "The Firebird" gently filled the living room.

The door banged open suddenly, and Stuart's two brothers, Bob and Ed, came laughing through the entrance. Bob threw his fedora on a small chair next to the door and stepped to his mother, kissing her on the cheek. "Sorry, we're late, Ma. Got held up."

"We bumped into William," continued Ed, taking off his British-style woolen cap and throwing a magazine at Stuart, who caught it in mid-air. "He asked me to give this back to you."

Stuart looked at the magazine.

"Who is William?" asked Phyl.

"He's my best friend. We went to school together. William Goeckel. He'll be my Best Man."

Phyl jiggled her head, slightly perturbed. "Oh, lovely. Something else I didn't know about our wedding. I hope I get to meet him on this trip, then?"

"Yes, you are, Phyl," said Bessie. "The night before you return to Toronto, we'll have all the details sorted, and everyone involved in the wedding party, save for your relatives who are not here with us, will have dinner in the dining room downstairs." Bessie folded her hands and smiled.

"Hi, Phyl," Bob smiled. "Did you keep busy today?"

Phyl looked up at her future brother-in-law, who hovered over her. Taller than Stuart. "Your Mother has kept me busy," she smiled. "My feet are killing me. I think I saw every crevice in the Hotel."

Bob laughed and Ed, next to him, smiled and nodded his head. "That would be like Mother." Ed turned and pointed at the magazine in Stuart's hand. "William said he found that most interesting, by the way. Wished he could be part of some of the new programs coming up."

"Well, he can't. I don't have the heart to tell him. One has to go through rigorous examinations, but not having a degree disadvantages him." Stuart placed the magazine on the table by his parents.

Phyl stepped over to look at it. "May I?" she asked Stuart, reaching toward the magazine.

"Oh, yes. You might find the articles quite interesting yourself." Stuart scratched at his cheek as he studied her. Then he looked at his sister. Marita made a face and rolled her eyes.

Phyl read the front page. "American Foreign Service Journal. Looks interesting."

"For future G-men," offered Marita, taking a deep drag on her cigarette.

The notes of Stravinsky built to a crescendo mirroring Phyl's confusion and sudden obscure, panic. Something didn't make sense. "Future G-men?" She frowned at Stuart. She saw ash drop off her own cigarette from the corner of her eye. She gasped. "Oh, I'm so sorry!" She looked down at the carpet.

Bessie got up and picked up a little fancy brass dustpan and horsehair brush. "That's all right. I have something for just this kind of accident. It happens all the time when John recharges his pipes."

Phyl mutely watched Bessie kneel and brush the offending ash onto the little pan.

"There. No problem whatsoever."

Phyl blinked. "What's a G-man?"

"Government man. J. Edgar Hoover's idea." Marita subdued the volume on Stravinsky. Everyone felt the tension.

Phyl looked at Bob and Ed, then Stuart. "Who is J. Edgar Hoover?"

Ed laughed. "Don't you know anything up there in the North with the Eskimos?"

"I don't live with Eskimos. I live in a city called Toronto, in Upper Canada." She was testy. "Canadians don't always know what's going on down here. Do you know what's going on up there? What's the capital city of Canada? I bet you think it's Chicago or Detroit. Do you know we drink milk, eat bread, and are struggling just as much with this Depression that you Americans probably started?"

"Oops," said Marita. She downed her drink.

Stuart put up his hands. "Okay. A bit of tension here. I should speak to Phyl alone." He looked at Phyl. "Ed didn't mean anything by that. But you have a point, Phyl. It's silly to expect you to know everything here. Let's take a walk down the hall. Dinner's almost here, and we'll talk before it arrives."

Phyl kept her grasp on the magazine and allowed herself to be gently maneuvered through the door into the hallway. She stood by frowning as Stuart quietly closed the door against his family and Stravinsky. He walked her a few steps away from the door.

Phyl walked slowly, embarrassed and confused, watching her feet on the hallway runner. She didn't know what to say or even what to ask. Her heart was pounding against her ribs. She had no idea how what she had said could've tumbled out of her mouth as it did. She hoped she didn't upset her future in-laws. Everything seemed to be running ahead of her, and she'd lost sight of what they had come down for in the first place – meeting her future in-laws and planning a simple wedding. Her father was upset she was marrying an American, upset that she would be gone to a foreign country on the other side of the world for two years, and upset that the wedding was in Pennsylvania. It might as well be on the other side of the moon, for all he could do about that.

She felt sick to her stomach, and tears welled up in her eyes. She wiped at a tear cascading down her burning cheek. She dug into her skirt pocket for a handkerchief with her free hand but gave up. Then she looked at the magazine again and opened it to the first page. There was a full-page ad about the New Yorker Hotel. It announced, "25% reduction to diplomatic and consular service…applies only on rooms $4 a day or more…" She stopped walking. She turned to Stuart and held the open magazine up to him.

Stuart wordlessly took it. He closed it and rolled it up in his hands. He tapped his left palm with it. He sighed and measured his words. "Phyl, when I graduated from Princeton, I automatically got a subscription to this magazine." He held up the rolled-up magazine. "The government tries to entice graduates into working for a special program for peace. It's very interesting, especially if you like to know what's going on behind the scenes. Wait." He opened the magazine and flipped through the pages. "Here's an example. I just love this. This is an interview with the Secretary of State and he was asked: *Mr. Secretary, in looking back over the two years you have been in office, what would you say were the major accomplishments?* And Secretary Hull said, *The maintenance and promotion of peace, both political and economical, throughout the world, has been the primary purpose of American Foreign policy. Virtually everything accomplished or hoped for falls under one of these two headings. In seeking to consolidate and promote political peace, this Government has dedicated itself unequivocally to the policy of the good neighbor as enunciated by President Roosevelt. We have consistently endeavored to cooperate with other nations of the world in strengthening the machinery of peace and devising new ways of -* "

Phyl felt she'd pushed him in a direction she hadn't anticipated. "What has this to do with us?"

Stuart held up his hand for her patience. "Wait. …*in devising new ways of preventing the possibility of war.*" He looked at her pointedly, eyebrows raised, looking earnest. The gloom in the hallway softened his features. He was a little boy trying to reason with his parent about buying a new toy. He continued reading. "*At the Montevideo conference, five important and hitherto dormant peace pacts were signed, and a new era of Pan-American cooperation and understanding was ushered in.*"

"Pan-American?" asked Phyl. She tilted her head and looked at him sideways. "Okay."

He continued. "*Plans for the construction of an inter-American highway which, when complete, should further strengthen the friendly ties now existing between North and South America.*" He looked at Phyl. "They're also looking to control the manufacturing and traffic of arms with Europe. Phyl, there's Hitler spewing fear-based threats. And Argentina is a massive country with ties to Germany, a desperate and devasted country suffering greatly because of the demands of the last Great War."

Phyl frowned. "No, don't say that. The last Great War. That's implying more war. No one wants that again." She did a cutting motion with her hands, palms down. "Absolutely no one."

"There are things you and most people don't know. Argentina is housing German immigrants. They're forming clubs and have all the earmarks of becoming a concern if something should erupt in Europe. Argentina is a wealthy country led by unstable military coups. Leaders hunger to strengthen alliances with anyone who would make them rich, or at least pull them out of their own Depression. At the same time, they're blind to what's brewing under their noses. They hate and fear *us*. And yet…"

Phyl shook her head. "I still don't know what this has to do with us."

"Economic peace is part of this control, Phyl. Opening trade with Argentina, a country that can explode in ways we cannot comprehend and desperate to strengthen themselves through unhealthy alliances, could pose a deadly threat to the rest of the world. The Secretary of State believes that a program of trade agreements is most important." He continued to read, "*Trade agreements, together with the maintenance of the open-door policy, synonymous with commercial fair play, leads to the restoration of world trade and, to a measurable extent, of world peace.*" Stuart slapped the page and pointed to it. "I want to have a hand in this. Prevent a world in which any son of mine traipses off to another war."

Phyl breathed heavily. She suddenly felt weak. As if gravity was far too much for her petite body. "Stu," she whispered, "why are you so worried about things that seem so far away?"

"Because Phyl, I have been taught this one thing: Each one of us, as an individual, can make a difference. Big or small. And I want to make a difference."

"And how does going to Buenos Aires selling typewriters have anything to do with preventing a future war our children may have to deal with?"

"Think about it. Even though I am a salesman, I would also become somewhat of a diplomat. An ambassador of small stature. I prove to Argentines, who are suspicious of all Americans, that I am a man of integrity. I represent the United States through my own positive traits and beliefs. It may sound grandiose, a little salesman trying to sell typewriters in a country whose language we have yet to learn while wanting to do his bit for world peace. And what kind of man would do that, right? Someone with higher ideals. Someone who doesn't just make a living selling the latest Remington Rand typewriter to some government official. Someone who also creates a bond of trust." He paused for effect. "*With* an Argentine government official who climbs up the proverbial political ladder. An official who may have the power to sway the currents within the political realm. Who may even become president one day."

Phyl's mind quickened. She thought of how Remington used to make weapons. They would have the capability to do so again, yes? Their factories and machinery could easily be converted to manufacturing arms and amunition. So, was this the true motive for Remington Rand? "Is this to *prevent* war, for sure? Not to generate business for creating and supplying weapons, in *case* of war?" She tilted her chin. "You remember that that's what Remington was before, right? A manufacturer of guns?"

Stuart looked at her, and his mouth dropped in awe. "Woman, you are astute in ways I was unaware of." He held up his hands. "And I don't mean that as an insult." He dropped his hands and looked closely at her. "No, I have never heard anything of that kind of thinking."

Phyl leaned back against the wall and rested her hands on the wainscoting on both sides of her. She crossed her legs at the ankles. "So, this meeting in Washington?"

"I'm sure it's to fill me in on what they require of me. And us. But it also gives me a chance to let them know what I am willing to do and what I'm not willing to do."

"You, or us?"

"Well, I'm sure they don't keep you in mind but, of course, I would only accept parameters you are comfortable with, Phyl. And we would be married. An advantage for them although it limits my security clearance."

Phyl snorted. "Security clearance," she repeated. "Why didn't you say anything before?"

"I wanted to wait to get all the facts, first. I thought you'd appreciate that more than conjecture. I didn't want you to start fearing things which were not valid."

Phyl pointed at him and herself. "And this marriage. Are they okay with this? I mean, it sounds like they consider everything. I haven't gone through examinations. I'm not a woman who could be – what did Marita call it? A G-man?"

Stuart swallowed hard.

"Is there something I should know?"

"Okay. It helps that I'm being sent down by a British Commonwealth office, Remington-Rand Canada. It helps I'm marrying a citizen of the British Commonwealth. Yes, it helps we do not have children."

"Of course, we don't have children! We're not even married yet, Stuart," she almost spit.

"I mean, I had already said we were not planning to have children immediately."

Phyl's mouth dropped. The elevator down the hall dinged. They looked in the direction of the polished brass doors. Knocks and squeaks announced a heavy elevator reaching their floor. Phyl turned to Stuart. "You told them this without even discussing it with me first?"

"*Do* you want children right away?"

"No, you know that. We discussed that. But it seems odd spreading that around with strangers. How long do we have to wait for children?"

Stuart looked over at the elevator as the doors slowly slid open. "Just the two years." He kept looking as a large food tray on wheels appeared. It was manhandled over the space between the floor and the elevator itself. Hidden from view, Sam swore under his breath as he carefully lifted his hidden end of the cart, then appeared with everything balanced carefully on top.

Phyl lowered her voice. "And how I didn't know you wanted to live in Kingston one day? I never even heard of Kingston until Marita mentioned it!"

Stuart made a face. "That Marita!" He looked over just as Sam looked up from where he stood in front of the closing elevator. His brown eyes widened in embarrassment. He grinned his big bright smile.

"Sorry, Master Stuart. Miss May. I didn't know you were there. You must have heard me cussing. I just didn't want anything to spill from the cart."

Stuart jumped forward and took a large tureen off the top of piled dinner plates. "Not to worry, Sam. You should hear me when I'm frustrated."

"Ha!" offered Phyl. "You should get *me* hot under the collar, Sam, and you'd be seeing blue for a week!" Phyl stepped over, took a covered casserole off the bottom rack, and eyed Stuart pointedly before turning and leading them back to the penthouse. "If you had waited another minute, you would have witnessed something quite grand."

Stuart watched Phyl's back, her hips swaying as she stomped into the penthouse. He sighed deeply. The worst of it was over.

So, he thought.

Chapter Three

1935 Summer, Lake Ontario, Letting El Down and Jorge

Phyl's short hair rose slightly with a sudden gust off Lake Ontario. She sat in her whites and the newest style of shorts on the most enormous rock she could climb along the shore off Scarborough Bluffs. White sneakers with laces, ankle socks, shorts, and a crew neck top with short sleeves made her look older. She wore oversized, black sunglasses and red lip color. She raised her hand and studied her engagement ring and simple gold wedding band. She looked at Stuart, also in his whites, with a schoolboy tie of blue, green, and white stripes. He sat reading on a small boulder, his bare feet burrowed in the sand. He was hunched over a leather pocket book, his elbows resting on his knees.

Phyl inhaled deeply. The air wasn't cold, hot, dry, or too wet. It was perfect. A good-sized fish jumped about a hundred feet away, and she quickly looked to see, too late. With her Dad and Claude Jr. fishing at Lake Scugog every chance they had, she was curious to see what jumped so that she could tell them she saw a pickerel or a bass. Perhaps they wouldn't have to pine to fish so far away. But then she realized it wasn't just the act of fishing that was paramount for the men. Of course. They also like to sleep fully clothed on primitive bunk beds, fry eggs and bacon over an open fire, and generally slum it for days at a time. Fishing off Scarborough Bluffs would still mean having to shave. Lake Scugog was a paradise if one preferred to live like a Sasquatch. Phyl pondered this side of her father and brother.

She sighed at the thought of her father.

Claude Sr. had finally come around. He didn't come to the wedding. The ceremony was in a Catholic Church – dirty Papists to him. He would never have been able to walk her down the aisle, either. It just wouldn't do. The shame attached to his being separated was difficult for people to accept. Plus, they didn't know how to explain K's relation to everyone else. It was easier to let the Redingtons organize everything in Pennsylvania and wait for the special Toronto reception after the wedding.

After they visited Stuart's folks in October, Stuart was able to explain a few more points to Claude Sr., which helped warm her father to Buenos Aires a bit more. Stuart had returned from Washington with news that he was to be on a foreign mission while in Argentina. There wasn't much the government could promise this early in the game money-wise, but by going down as an unofficial agent of the American Foreign Service, he and Phyl did not have to fade into the woodwork and find themselves entirely alone if times were to get tough. There were connections to be made that would help ensure their safety and the assurance of supplemented rent and support for emergencies. After Stuart explained all this, Claude Sr. chose to see it as the whole United States government was watching out for his daughter. He finally said, "Well, you couldn't get any better than that."

Stuart was just as happy to know that when he shook someone's hand in Argentina, his primary goal was to be the good American, which was just as important as the amount of money he was to earn. He felt confident he would find enough allies in the government to help ensure that Remington-Rand would eventually offer him excellent terms for a beginning salesman dispatched to a foreign country.

The fact that Sr. settled down somewhat helped Phyl relax into marriage, Stuart noticed. Of course, El wasn't happy. She didn't get to be Phyl's Maid of Honor. He sensed there was still a bit of tension between her and Phyl. He also suspected El had discovered Jr.'s indiscretions with his sister, Marita, during and after the wedding ceremony. Jr. and Marita were like two peas in a pod, and they added up to trouble. Stuart was terribly disappointed in his sister.

As if reading his thoughts, Phyl suddenly spoke.

"I still can't get over Claude Jr. taking Marita away from the reception. He shouldn't have come. I knew there would be trouble the moment he laid eyes on her that first trip."

"Well, he and El are still together. Their wedding's still on." Stuart closed his book and looked at the cover, thoughtfully tracing the embossed leather with the ball of his thumb.

"And that newspaper article about our wedding got names wrong." Phyl turned her head and looked over her shoulder at him. She reached out a hand. "Do you still have the clipping?"

Stuart opened the book and pulled out a paper clipping. He got up off the rock and took it to her. His bare feet sunk into the sand between stones, seagull feathers and snail shells. She sat up straighter, lowered the sunglasses onto the tip of her sun-touched nose, and peered at the clipping with bright eyes.

"*Redington – May. The marriage of Miss Mildred May…*" She grimaced. "Who the hell is this, Mildred? How can they mix that up with Phyllis? My one time in the newspaper, and they get it wrong."

"Local rags always get things wrong." Stuart climbed onto the rock beside her, but not until he brushed aside bits of pebble and looked around for seagull droppings on the warm, granite surface.

"I know, but my name? The bride?" She continued to read. "*Daughter of Claude May of Toronto, and Stuart G. Redington, son of Mr. and Mrs. J. A. Redington of Kingston, took place this afternoon in St. Theresa's Church in Beaverton. Rev. J.J. O'Leary officiated. Miss Marita Redington and William Goeckel of this city were the attendants. The bride, who was given in marriage by her brother, Claude May, wore an eggshell canton crepe gown trimmed in brown fur. She wore a matching hat and a shoulder wrap.*" She flattened the clipping on her knee against the lake breeze and ironed it with both hands. "I loved that wedding dress."

"Your father almost had a heart attack when he heard how much it cost."

"I know. I can't help it if I have expensive taste, but I figured I am, after all, his only daughter. Besides, El likes it. She's taking it to a tailor to refit it and Dad's paying. So that's also going to be Dad's and K's wedding gift to her and Claude Jr." Phyl pushed back her sunglasses, handed the clipping to Stuart, and tilted her face to the sun. "Is Buenos Aires on the water like this?" she asked, eyes closed.

Stuart shooed a fly from his face. "Yes. It's on the Samborombon Bay, part of the Atlantic Ocean. Across from Uruguay and not quite across from Montevideo."

"Oh, goody," she smiled, keeping her face up to the sun and eyes closed. She inhaled deeply again and sighed. "I can just imagine palm trees around us right now."

"Have you ever seen a palm tree?"

Phyl opened her eyes and looked at him, smiling. "No. All the more, I'll love them." She kept smiling at him. He could see her eyes slightly closed behind the dark lenses. She kept a steady gaze on him.

He felt his loins stir. He leaned over and gently kissed her. She kissed back and placed a hand on his neck. He pulled back. "Happy?"

She nodded. "Uh-huh."

He lifted her hand and kissed it. He leaned in again and whispered. "Where is your dog?"

Phyl gasped and pulled back, looking along the shore and up at the Scarborough Bluffs behind her. She jumped up. "That dog. Probably rolling on a rotting fish. Here, Tony!" She whistled harshly.

Legs pounding and deep breathing from behind bushes announced her large, black dog, wet and covered in sand. Tony attempted to climb their rock. Phyl lifted up her hands. "No! Stay, Tony!"

Tony sat on his haunches and looked expectantly from Stuart to Phyl. He licked his lips while his behind rocked side to side from the force of his whipping tail, creating a deep well in the sand. Little, exposed insects scrambled in panic.

"Ugh. What shall we do with you, huh? You need a bath." She scratched behind the dog's ear. "I wish I could take you with me." They could not take Tony on any ship. "You have to stay with Boppa!"

"Who is Boppa?" asked Stuart.

"Dad, of course. Haven't you heard me say, Boppa, before?"

He laughed. "No."

"Well, it's just for a couple of years." She pulled Tony closer for a roughing of his head with her other hand. "Right, Tony? Just two years." She held up two fingers to the dog. Tony licked them.

Stuart looked at his watch. "We should head back to your Dad's. Supper will be ready in an hour. But first, we swing by the flat. I'm expecting a telegram telling us the departure date."

"I didn't know that. That's kind of important, don't you think?" She frowned at him. "You have a habit of not telling me everything, Stu."

"Oh, don't I?" He squinted at her like a little boy. She was steadily cataloging his nuances.

Phyl climbed down from the rock and brushed her bare legs of debris. "No, you don't. Could you please improve on that?"

"I'll try," he grinned.

"Now I'm nervous. We can't miss El and Claude Jr.'s wedding on Christmas Day. Crossing my fingers that we leave just after."

"Well, cross away. We'll find out soon enough."

Phyl looked at her legs. "Should I change? I really shouldn't go around wearing these shorts. I already got a dirty look from someone when I got out of the car up on the road."

Stuart took off his summer sweater and wrapped the sleeves around her middle, tied them, then pulled and yanked down on the sweater. It covered her entire midriff down to her knees. "There, you're a little more decent now."

"It's a good thing you're a knight in shining armor," she laughed.

Stuart looked her up and down, appreciatively. "Well, my job is to help beautiful damsels in distress. If the shoe fits…"

"Hmm," Phyl whispered, wiggling her eyebrows. "And the shoe fits so very nicely," she teased.

He grinned and slapped her behind.

She looked around. Seeing no one, she pulled his face down and kissed him on the lips.

"All righty, that's enough of that." Stuart pushed her away. "We'll miss dinner, at this rate."

"Who cares about stupid food?"

"You should know, you married a man with a hefty appetite," he laughed.

"As do I. But it ain't for food!"

Stuart's jaw dropped. "Well, well, well. Cheeky. I think I've created a little monster."

Phyl grinned coyly before jumping to the rock to retrieve her bag. "Come on, Tony! Let's race Stuart back to the car!"

Mesmerized, Stuart watched Phyl's behind as she scrambled after Tony up the steep drive toward the car park. He sighed contentedly. He looked once more over the lake and spied a distant sail. He quietly watched it for a few seconds. So peaceful. He thought of the new world and peace. He thought of the developments in Germany. And felt there was a disconnect there somewhere.

Phyl whistled shrilly from the top of the hill, dislodging his reverie.

He smiled, scooped up his sneakers and socks, and trudged up along the grassy edge of the drive.

* * *

Jr. dug into his roast beef, carefully keeping gravy over the morsel. "You know when you're goin' yet?"

Phyl's heart skipped a beat. She quietly watched her brother while she cut into her Yorkshire Pudding. She looked at Stuart, then past K at El. It'd been a while since they all had Sunday dinner together. El was sadly looking down at her plate as she slowly chewed. Phyl could tell El was still hurting very much. Marita. She gritted her teeth at the thought of how stupid her brother was. She wondered if El would ever get over it. Her friend's glow had been gone since Spring. Now Phyl was going to make it worse. Phyl felt absolutely sick about having to let El down yet again.

Stuart put his knife and fork down and wiped his mouth with his napkin. He squinted against the sun pouring in through the living room windows, which cast spears of laser light through the sliding doors into the dining room. K now slept in Phyl's porch bedroom, so the dining room was finally used for dinners. K got up and slid the dining room doors against the light. "Thank you, K," said Stuart.

"So?" said Claude Sr. Everyone stopped eating.

Stuart cleared his throat. "I received the telegram this afternoon."

"What did it say?" asked Jr.

Phyl watched El cross her slender fingers in front of her dinner plate and bite her lip.

"We're leaving Toronto on the first or second of November by train." Stuart moved his plate forward slightly, more out of nervousness. "First, we stay with the folks. We need a week or so to straighten out what we're taking along with us on the ship, arrange for passports, visas, get our shots. One has to wait a certain period of time after one gets them. Then I have one more meeting in Washington. I still haven't sorted out the details of my work contract with the company, but it should be carved in stone by then. Then, as part of an extended honeymoon," he pointedly looked at Phyl, who smiled nervously back, "we stay for a few days in Manhattan. I'll be close to head office for any last-minute details, and we'll catch a few shows."

He tried to make light of the plans, but didn't score any points

"But what is your final departure date," asked K.

"November 19 with an arrival date of December 17 in Buenos Aires."

The clatter of a fork dragged everyone's attention to El, who dragged her eyes over to Phyl.

"El, I'm so sorry." Phyl stared at El's pained expression. She felt intense remorse.

Shaking, El pushed her chair back. "Excuse me." Her voice quivered. She placed her napkin on the table, opened the heavy sliding door and left the dining room. Everyone listened to the steps creaking up the staircase. They heard her enter the water closet and slam the clasp down on the door.

No one spoke for a few moments.

"I'm so sorry, Claude," said Phyl.

Claude Jr. sighed and blinked at her. Then at Stuart.

"Just don't get mugged while you two are gallivanting about in New York," growled Claude Sr. His brown hair, threaded with grey, was thick and generally unruly but kept very short on the sides. Stragglers stubbornly stuck out on top. As if reading everyone's mind, K reached and patted them down.

"Poor El. Nothing's going the way she planned," mumbled K.

Phyl looked at Stuart.

Stuart scratched a cheek and shook his head. "Yes, well, this is all generally because of me. I can't control this big machine set in motion. It's complicated. It's not a simple transfer."

"I agree. It's all quite abnormal." Claude Sr. didn't look up. "You meet, you marry far away we can't come, a party too posh for my taste, and Phyl's not working after all that money invested in her."

"It's not lost, Dad. The business course gave me a couple of more skills."

"Like I said, money wasted."

"Dad," Phyl feebly replied.

Claude Jr. reached over the table to touch his sister's hand. "Dad quit it. It's all part of moving forward. It's not wasted. She caught this big fish with it, didn't she?" He tried to laugh.

Phyl looked at Stuart with widened eyes.

"Sir, I'm sorry my presence has caused such an upset in everybody's lives here. I don't know what to say. It's all very unfortunate," said Stuart.

"Just promise to take care of my daughter."

"Yes, sir. I promise you this will all be worth it."

"Worth missing our wedding?" Jr. asked.

"Claude, you know what he means. Come down and visit us. There is an opportunity here for you and El. For Dad and K. Look at the big picture."

"And who can afford the time and money?" asked Jr. dryly.

"Why are you so closed-minded?"

"Why are you so selfish?"

"Me? And what of you and Marita? Was that not selfishness on your part?" snapped Phyl. She threw her napkin onto her plate. "Excuse me." Phyl got up and ran out of the dining room, up the stairs and to the water closet door. She stood listening for a moment. She could hear El sniffling. Then she heard the water run. She knocked gently on the door. "El? Are you alright?"

"I'll be right out."

Phyl waited, head down, until El undid the clasp of the door. She opened it but kept looking down as she stepped out and past Phyl into the narrow hallway. Phyl reached out and held onto the bottom of El's light summer blouse sleeve. "El, I'm so sorry things seem out of step with all your plans."

El shook her head. "I understand. You're not in charge. It's Stuart's work."

"If we were in charge, we would choose a date after your wedding. But Stu couldn't sway Head Office. I think it all comes down to the authorities in Buenos Aires. Or in Washington. They're the ones organizing the tickets for the ship, customs, passports, visas, a place to stay once we get there…" She let go of El's sleeve and covered her eyes. "Oh, I feel so awful. So very bad. And so, so sad." She dropped her hands and looked at El pleadingly. "You can't move the date up?"

El shook her head. "No, it's what Mother wants. A Christmas Wedding. And it gives her sister time to sort out her own life so that she could come and live with her once I move out. The flat we're renting won't be available until the first of January. I'd hate to impose on K by staying here very long, and I certainly wouldn't want to be at Mother's after we're married. I wouldn't rest a moment because I'd be worried that Claude wouldn't be happy." El covered her face. She shook her head.

Phyl stroked El's hair. It was hot and muggy in the hallway, and her palms were sweaty, but she stroked anyhow. "El, I'm going to make up for all of this. I don't know how, but I promise I will."

El gently took Phyl's hand, keeping it between her palms. "It's alright."

"And I'm sorry about Stuart's sister."

El looked straight into Phyl's eyes. She blinked back tears. "That's what is eating away at my heart, Phyl. Not so much that I couldn't be at your wedding. We had a nice reception at the Old Mill, and I got to do a few things for you there. It ended up being very nice."

Phyl felt more hopeful. "Yes, it was lovely at the Old Mill."

"Very posh," they said in unison.

"I wish you could've been my Matron of Honor, Phyl, but I wouldn't force you to trade those palm trees in Argentina for an afternoon at my wedding and all the headaches that go with it. I'd rather do what you're doing. Start a new life."

Phyl looked into her eyes with a slight smile. "You're going to be okay?"

They heard the men and K talking in low tones downstairs. El nodded. "I could've broken off the engagement, Phyl, but chose not to. There are reasons why Jr. fell for Stuart's sister. He's been pushy with me, but I insisted on waiting and it's a long engagement. So, I guess, in a way, it's my fault."

"Absolutely not! Don't even think that way."

"Well, an engagement of two years is unreasonable. But it was what Mother wanted."

Phyl took El's hands. "Let's hope Mother doesn't control everything once you're married."

"Oh, our Claude Jr. will see to that. He's not too fond of her," smiled El.

Phyl laughed through her tears. She felt more at peace. "You can bet on that."

* * *

"Oh, my gosh, it's cold. Don't they put the heat on in these trains?"

Phyl shivered under a steamer rug. She'd put on layers of clothing she had packed in her smaller suitcase, but it was still insufficient. So, Stuart talked the porter into finding what heavy rugs or blankets he could find that were available for her to use.

Stuart looked around the compartment. Frost formed inside the windows, but most passengers appeared to be far more comfortable than Phyl. They dressed for winter as normal folk did. As *he* did.

"Phyl, I told you to dress down and warm. There's no one to impress."

"I wanted to look nice for your parents. Besides, I didn't pack many heavy things because we're going to Argentina. Why would I need to? It's hot down there."

Stuart chuckled and shook his head.

"What?" Phyl didn't look amused.

"It may be damn hot down there, but they have winters, too, Phyl."

"Snow?"

"Well, not that I know of."

"Well, then."

Stuart sat back and shuffled closer to her to share his warmth. "Okay, then."

"Stu, do you think Dad and K will come and see us off in New York?"

Stuart put the bulk of a rug around her. "Let's hope. You'll be gone for two years, after all."

"Yes, but they saw us off at Union Station at 1:00 a.m. this morning. Perhaps in another four weeks, they may not see the value in coming all the way to New York. All that money and time."

She dug under the rug, pulled out a light pink envelope, and took out a round card. It was shaped like a life ring with a Scotty dog looking through, its little pink tongue hanging out. "Bon Voyage!" was across the top. The card opened to a sketch of a rope leading to the words, "If I owned a Big Bark, I'd follow you! Claude, Dad, K." Phyl held it up for Stuart to read. He nodded his head and chuckled again.

"I'm going to miss Tony. 'Hope he'll be okay."

Stuart patted her on the shoulder. "He'll be fine." They sat quietly rocking with the train, its rhythm lulling them into passivity. Stuart noticed Phyl was quite pale. "Are you alright?"

Phyl shrugged. "I suppose." She brushed away an imaginary hair from her nose. "Is this a woolen rug? I'm allergic to pure wool."

"And we're going to Argentina, where alpaca wool is in everything?"

Phyl scratched her nose and forehead. She shook her head. "I can't wait to see the palm trees."

"You keep saying that."

"Oh, Stu. We're so lucky." She cuddled up to him.

He put his feet on the bench under the table. "It's a good thing we have a sleeper car. I'd hate to be dead tired getting to the folks and stay tired as we scramble around getting things done. That ship will depart without us if we're not careful. We'll be so dead tired when we're finished in New York that we'll sleep in and not get to the docks on time."

"That sounds like a nightmare," Phyl said as she snuggled even more. She gazed at Stuarts's handsome profile. "Stu?"

"Hmm?"

Her blue eyes sparkled. "Can we go to the sleeper car now?"

Stu's grin slowly spread across his face. "Well, it wouldn't hurt to get some beauty sleep. Right?"

"Uh-huh."

* * *

"Oh, my God, Stu, we'll miss the boat! What's wrong with that stupid Remington-Rand!"

Phyl sat on the bed, about to pull her hair out. They were on the 19th floor of the Commodore Hotel in New York at the generosity of the company. The ship was to depart at 5:00 p.m., and it was 1:00 p.m. Stuart was held up because their contract had been amended without any warning, and Stuart had to go to Head Office to discuss the changes. He had just called to tell her what the amendments were.

They had, in good faith, left all behind in Toronto four weeks prior. In the meantime, they spent a couple of weeks arranging visas, shots and saying goodbye to Stuart's parents. He also had another meeting in Washington, and they spent the last week in Manhattan doing last-minute details and enjoying the city bedecked with Christmas lights and ornaments. Snow piled along the city streets, in the way of mounds of garbage. People milled, holding up traffic, and horns blared day and night. Even from their height, the din kept Phyl up at night, but she was still thrilled to be there.

They had done everything Stuart had promised for their second trip to Manhattan. She had seen the Empire State Building and Statue of Liberty and did some window shopping at all the grand stores. Best of all, they saw "The Children's Hour" at the Maxine Elliott's Theatre.

She told Stuart that everything was ready downstairs at the Bell Hop's and that his parents, his brothers and sister, and his Aunt Ruth and Uncle Roz from Brooklyn were standing by at a deli, waiting for confirmation that the departure indeed was at 5:00 p.m. on the HMS Southern Prince. They were all hoping to share a fancy meal somewhere before they piled into taxis for the grand send-off at the Piers.

"That's why I called. I really can't approve these amendments without talking to you first, Phyl."

"But Stu, what on earth could they have changed that is so potentially deal-breaking? I don't understand. Can't we sort it out later?" She eyed the passports at the edge of the bed. What wasn't already downstairs waiting to go was ready at the door. She had her gloves, coat, and rubber overshoes ready. She was anxious they should leave soon to have a leisurely goodbye meal with everyone.

"They changed my wages from American dollars to *pesos*, and, Phyl, here's the zinger that I think you'll be disturbed by, especially seeing your father didn't like you being away for two years."

"Yes?"

"The contract is for three years."

Phyl was stunned. "I don't understand how they can do that. You signed the papers already."

"That's what I think but we don't have a choice. Right now, the exchange rate for the dollar and *peso* seems to be equal. They argue that everything is much cheaper anyway, so we still stand to gain."

"But the three years, Stu."

"I'll see if they'll pay for you to visit Toronto during those three years. Why don't I do that?"

Phyl nodded to herself. "That's the least they could do, those –"

"Careful what you say. They'll be our livelihood."

"Well, you know what I mean."

"Rest assured. I certainly do. We'll work it to our benefit somehow, Phyl."

* * *

Pandemonium ruled the frozen Piers. Despite a small passenger list of 30 on the HMS Southern Prince – it held refrigerated cargo – another ship was departing that evening, and a wall of well-wishers filled the brightly-lit, snow-lined dock area. Copious amounts of steam escaped huge funnels, and horns blew at intervals. Spotlights lit up the sides of the ships. Bells rang. People laughed, cried, whistled, called, and waved handkerchiefs at family and friends lined along decks. Breaths hung ghostlike in the crisp air before blown away. Snowflakes made people blink, and a sharp breeze kicked up from the choppy Hudson River. Lingering tugboats created a deep wash blending with river white caps which smashed against the wharves and sprayed the crowd. Icicles hung from thick dock lines. Workers, layered against the weather, puttered as best they could, readying for departure. The main gangplank was hauled in.

Phyl huddled against Stuart's chest. She held her scarf against her face and waved her handkerchief. Each time, icy wind blew up her sleeves forcing her to lower her hands to warm her wrists. She could see Stuart's parents were tired of the cold, too. Marita clung to her mother. Stuart's brothers grinned and chatted with their aunt and uncle as they shuffled to stay warm. She bent closer over the icy railing, cupped her face, and yelled at her in-laws. "You don't have to stay. Go inside!"

"They can't hear you," yelled Stuart into her ear, his breath warming her ear lobe.

"I know. But they're freezing."

"That's okay. Look, we're moving."

Phyl peeked over the railing and saw the gap between the ice-covered hull and wharf widen. "Oh, Stu. We're off! Oh my gosh, we're going!" She clung to him and he squeezed her. They waved joyously. "I'm trying to memorize their faces, but I can't see them clearly anymore." She jumped, waved with both hands, ignored the freezing cold on her exposed wrists, and yelled, "Bye! Bye!" The passengers near them joined in with their own renewed enthusiasm in waving and yelling goodbye.

Likewise, everyone on shore vigorously waved and called.

Slowly, the ship was maneuvered by three black and maroon tugboats. Ear-shattering horns blew. The distance from the wharf grew, and Stuart motioned they should go. "Let's watch from inside."

"Will they still see us through the windows?"

"I doubt it, but if it makes you feel better, just keep waving your handkerchief at the window." Stuart led Phyl in through the closest doorway, and they stepped to the side. Condensation flowed down the icy steel bulkheads. The wind blasted through the open doorway, but they were still protected from the worst. Phyl moved to the closest porthole and waved her handkerchief against the thick glass misted over with their breath. Soon, the lengthening distance made it difficult to see where everyone stood. Stuart held her shoulders and led her deeper into the ship.

"How do we find our cabin?" she asked.

Stuart pulled out paperwork and peered at it under a storm lamp. He looked and saw a purser and waved at him. Together, the three found their cabin – a simple room with one large porthole and bunk beds. It had a sink, but they shared the main washrooms and showers further up the corridor with other passengers, males and females separated.

Phyl hit her ankle on the high metal threshold of their heavy doorway and winced. "Ouch, why are the thresholds so high?"

"In case of flooding, Ma'am," said the purser, as Stuart handed him a tip.

"Flooding?" Phyl dumbly asked.

"For when we take on water," the purser innocently replied.

Phyl looked as if she was going to faint. Stuart hugged her and thanked the purser. The purser stepped high over the threshold and slammed the heavy metal door shut. Phyl eyed the door with its massive hinges, then looked over at the bunk beds. She looked at Stuart.

Stuart made a comical face.

Phyl looked at their luggage piled under and around the sink, and felt the deep rumble and shaking of everything around her. She threw her arms up as if to grab something. "Oh my gosh!"

"We're now under full power. No more tugboats." He looked out the porthole eagerly and eyed the Statue of Liberty lit in the dark. "Oh, Phyl. You should see this."

Phyl listed to the porthole and squeezed her face close to Stuart's. Their breath frosted the glass. Stuart wiped the glass. Phyl sighed as she looked at the Statue of the gallant lady. "Oh, Stu."

"I know."

"I hope I get used to this noise." Phyl's nostrils twitched. "And the smell!" She stood back. "How do we sleep? And what if I get seasick? That would be so embarrassing."

"There are buckets galore, Phyl. But you're tough. You'll be fine. You've got weeks to get used to this." He stepped away from the porthole and undid his coat, checking out their little cabin.

"I sure hope so." She brightened up. "Let's get a drink and celebrate. I'm dying for a smoke."

"Grand idea, so am I." Stuart helped with Phyl's coat and took off his hat. Phyl sat on the lower bunk and took off her rubber overshoes. They scurried out of the cabin and looked up and down a well-lit corridor. "Which way to the bar?" Stuart asked a passing purser leading yet another passenger. The purser gave them instructions, and Phyl studied the passenger. A dark-skinned, elegant-looking man looked directly back at her, and smiled. She smiled back. There was no reason to do otherwise.

Stuart led her to another level of the ship. Many passengers had beaten them to the bar, chatting with fellow voyagers, comparing stories and backgrounds. Phyl noticed the same gentleman from the corridor entering the bar. She watched him approach the bar. He caught her watching and came to them directly. Phyl sidled closer to Stuart, who nodded at the stranger. The gentleman held out his hand.

"Good evening, I am Jorge Piñiero," he said in very cultured English. "We are neighbors, I see."

"Oh?" asked Stuart, shaking Jorge's hand.

"Yes, he was the passenger with the purser who gave us directions," Phyl said.

Jorge's eyes lit up as if he was impressed by her observational skill. She thought, maybe.

She put her cigarette onto an ashtray and held out her hand. Jorge bowed, brushed his lips over her gloved hand, and let it go.

"Oh," she couldn't help but say. She blinked and smiled.

"Oh, yes. I'm Stuart Redington, and this is my lovely wife, Phyl."

"Enchanted," smiled Jorge.

Phyl had never seen a gentleman such as Jorge. Dark, almost black, brown eyes, dark skin, thick black eyebrows, black hair slicked back. It shone like highly polished wax under the lights. His suit was of lighter color and fabric, and his collarless shirt was white. His neck was adorned with a bright purple satin cravat. Beautiful gold cufflinks peeked from his cuffs and a gold ring with a large diamond adorned his left ring finger. She had never seen such a large ring on a man before. He wore very strong cologne.

"Are you from Argentina?" she asked.

He bowed his head. "Yes. I have an *estancia* with my brother there. We also have a vineyard and cattle ranch. I have a home in Buenos Aires and an apartment in New York. If you would excuse my boldness, but I believe you are the young couple sent down by Remington-Rand?"

Stuart straightened up. He looked at Phyl pointedly before replying to Jorge. "Yes, we are."

Jorge turned to the bartender and ordered a drink and another round for Stuart and Phyl, instructing him to take the order to a table. He motioned to Stuart and Phyl to follow him to one of the round dining tables bolted into the ship's floor. "Shall we get comfortable?" he asked.

As they settled, Jorge sat back and straightened his jacket.

"You look like you know your way around the ship," said Stuart.

"The Southern Prince and I are old friends. I come to New York quite often on business." The drinks arrived with fancy coasters and an ashtray. Jorge took his glass and held it up in the air toward them. "Cheers, as you say in America."

They clinked glasses and took a sip. Jorge put his glass down precisely in the middle of the coaster and took out a gold cigarette case and lighter. Phyl saw he had manicured fingernails. She had never seen a manicure on a man before. She wondered what else was extraordinary about the stranger. She watched as he opened the case and offered Stuart and her a cigarette. They each took one, and Jorge lit them as he continued talking.

"I am assigned to help orientate you to our end of the globe on business. You see, I am one of those Argentines interested in increasing and maintaining good trading relations with the rest of the Americas, especially our largest and wealthiest neighbor."

"I don't know about the wealthy part. We're struggling with the same Depression as you are," Stuart said, exhaling smoke. He coughed into his fist. "Although I know we're keen on strengthening trade with your country, specifically."

"Does that mean you won't mind if I ask you questions?" Phyl asked. "I'm inquisitive about many things. Not just trade. I wonder about stoves and ice boxes and shopping." Phyl put her glass down and sat back in an elegant armchair, cigarette in the air like she'd seen in the movies. Slowly, she started taking off one glove. Like she'd seen in the movies. Then she put the cigarette between her lips as she pulled the other glove off. She placed both gloves on the table's edge and took the cigarette out of her mouth. Every move was watched closely by their host.

"As you would say, fire away. I am to put myself out to no end to help you two adjust. And, as you can imagine, we have lots of time on this journey. By the time you arrive in Buenos Aires, you should have all your questions answered." He smiled and nodded.

Stuart jumped in. "If you don't mind me asking, Jorge, your accent. It's not particularly Spanish."

Jorge laughed. "No, you are right. We actually speak French at home."

"French?" asked Phyl. "Are you French?"

Jorge laughed again. "Oh, no. I'm very much an Argentine through and through. Actually, this is a perfect starting point in our conversation about Argentina. You see, in Argentina, many of us are fluent in French. We like to proliferate French ideas and literature. We are quite knowledgeable about French works of science, philosophy, art, music, and mathematics."

He sat slightly to the side and crossed his legs, careful to straighten out the crease in his trousers. "It's scarce for a member of the Argentine gentry not to be very French. We spend a good amount of time in France. Many of us send our children there for school. In fact, we have more French newspapers, books and magazines in Argentina than we do English or other foreign languages. Our women are the most modern because our fashion certainly is influenced by France." Phyl looked again at Jorge's bright cravat and his gold ring. "As a result, we have some of the world's most beautiful and elegant women. Though," Jorge motioned his head to Phyl, "None as beautiful and elegant as your wife, and I say this sincerely."

Phyl felt the wind knocked out of her. She blinked and wondered if she heard correctly. Both men looked at her. Stuart looked quite bemused. She felt herself blush, and she fidgeted. "Oh, my. Well, I don't know about that." She didn't know where to look. They hadn't shown her that in the movies.

Jorge smiled. "In Argentina, women accept compliments with grace and confidence. You deserve to do so in both cases." He continued. "As I was saying, you will see when you arrive in Buenos Aires, the layout and architecture are quite French. We have grand parks and monuments, and the city is fashioned after the 19th-century French beautification systems of diagonal avenues and botanical gardens, including an excellent train system to ease traveling through the city, though, interestingly, the system is quite British. However, even our sidewalks look very French," he laughed.

"Is that why there is such a large French presence in Mexico, Panama, and certain sections of Central and South America?" asked Stuart.

Jorge looked at Stuart appreciatively. "Yes. You see, it's the Latin base of the language and culture. We are all Latin countries. In fact, Buenos Aires is the largest Latin city after Paris. It rivals the most beautiful cities of Europe." He flicked the ash off his cigarette carefully over the ashtray. He leaned back. "That does mean we do not have an internationally mixed populace. We have many immigrants – French, Italian, Spanish, and Basque. Also, German. And, of course, we have a tremendous number of British. In fact, most of the money invested in Buenos Aires is British, concerning public transportation and shipments by train. All in all, there is quite an interesting mix of countries represented in my homeland. There is a famous saying in an old travel book about Argentina. I forget who the author was, but said he was surprised that the cook of the house he stayed in was from Spain; the chauffeur from Paris; the valet from Germany; the cook's assistant was Galician; the First Butler – or as we say in Argentina, *Majordomo* - was English; the Second Spanish Basque. The host's father was German, his mother Argentine, and he was married to a French-Basque girl. His one son was at Cambridge University, the other at Heidelberg, and his daughter was engaged to a young North American."

"Oh my, that's a lot of different languages at once," offered Phyl.

"It sure is. When you speak so many languages, I can see why one would have a cultured accent such as yours, which could be difficult to trace to any one language," laughed Stuart.

"Precisely. Unfortunately, there have been changes in the wind." Jorge's eyes seemed to stare at the far side of the dining room. "Some of the more beautiful buildings once owned by the gentry have been confiscated and converted into government buildings and military palaces." He waved in the air. "But then, that is another story." He suddenly stood up. He bowed slightly. "I must apologize. If you would excuse me, I promised to send a telegram to my wife that we have departed from New York."

Phyl reached out and touched his sleeve. "When will we talk again? I have so many questions about the military coups. They worry me."

Jorge looked at the other passengers, then looked deeply into Phyl's face. His own softened. "Tomorrow. But fear not. We are prisoners on this ship for the next several weeks. And, quite honestly, I couldn't think of being imprisoned with more gracious a couple as the both of you."

Stuart stood to shake hands. "Thank you, Jorge. It's truly a pleasure."

"My dear Stuart Redington. The pleasure is all mine." The ship lurched, and Jorge deftly did a two-step to keep his balance. Stuart fell back into his chair. "We've left the harbor and are in the open ocean. The swells are particularly large this time of year. You may want to watch the lights along the shore or see the glow over Atlantic City. It will help keep seasickness at bay. I will see you at breakfast."

Phyl grabbed hold of a chair and looked around. Glasses tinkled behind the bar, and their drinks, coasters and ashtray slowly edged from one side of the table to the other. Phyl's eyes widened in surprise. "Stu, let's go back to the cabin. Just in case."

"Just in case what?" asked Stuart.

Phyl swallowed. "Just in case of you-know-what."

"Well, you can have the can. I'm going to glue myself to the porthole to watch the lights go by to keep my stomach at bay." He held up a fist to his face and belched quietly. "I think we better hurry."

* * *

By the time HMS Southern Prince checked in at Trinidad-Tobago for customs, two weeks later, Phyl and Stuart knew every one of the passengers and crew by last names, if not by first. Some disembarked in Trinidad-Tobago, and a few got on board for the remaining two weeks down the east coast of South America. Phyl and Stuart made it a point to, at least, have one conversation with them all.

One of the first things Phyl noticed, after acquiring her sea legs and spending more time on deck, was the color of the Gulf Stream. She couldn't find the words to describe it properly. A blue of many layers - blue vermillion, plus navy, with a certain transparency in its depth of color. She found it hard to define. Equally impressive, there were so many pin-prick stars amongst familiar constellations, it seemed there was hardly any black in the void of space. And something magnificent appeared on the first night she wandered along the deck. Fairy-like light shone eerily in the crests of the bow waves and in the ship's wake, like a cold fire lit with the glow of tiny plankton. Jorge explained it to her later while standing at the rail, watching the magic show both above and beneath the waves.

"They call it the Burning of the Sea."

"That's a strange way of describing it. Fire under the sea." The rumble beneath the deck was ever present. Phyl had surrenderred to the ship's rhythms long ago. She was one with the beauty around her.

"Christopher Columbus once said that it was like the light of a wax candle moving up and down. But the Greeks attributed the effect to their god Poseidon and his nymphs."

They were waiting for Stuart to join them. He had gone to the cabin to get more cigarettes, and they were to participate in a game of cards in the lounge. It was unusual to be left alone with Phyl, but Jorge made sure she didn't feel threatened. He kept a respectful distance at the railing, though attentive.

A full moon was crisp, as if cut out of the sky with a knife. The sky and the sea seemed to be synchronous. In addition to the phosphorescence of the plankton, one could tell the moon's magnetism on the ocean waters made Phyl feel quite heady. Jorge watched, mesmerized by her innocent passion. Suddenly, something broke through the surface of the moonlit waves and she looked just in time to see the shadows of two dolphins splash back into the dark ocean continuum.

"Oh, look. Dolphins again!" screamed Phyl, pointing over the rail. Throughout the trip, dolphins raced along with the ship, and she had seen jellyfish for the first time. Off the coast of Florida, a passenger had called out at the sight of a giant swordfish breaking the surface. And she could swear she sometimes saw shark fins slicing alongside, but Stuart always insisted they were dolphins.

She turned to Jorge. "Are there sharks off the beaches in Buenos Aires?"

"Certainly, but they rarely attack. Why do you ask? Are you a swimmer?"

"Oh, yes." She turned back to the moon and the ocean. The breeze blew delightfully through her hair. She licked the ocean salt off her lips. She inhaled deeply and felt like she was bathed in the freshest and healthiest of air. "Growing up, Dad would pick me up with my brother. I was living with my aunt and uncle after my mother died. But Dad made sure that I came along whenever he went fishing or camping. Lake Scugog, usually. Sometimes, Lake Simcoe. I would go swimming at the drop of a hat. I also learned how to shoot a gun, by the way. Sometimes I'd go shooting for pheasants."

"We have much hunting in Argentina. You know we hunt ostrich?" Jorge turned and leaned on the railing with his back. He hung his elbows over the edge.

Phyl stared at him. "No. Really?"

"You and Stuart will come up and hunt. We have good fishing holes, too."

"Oh, we would love that!" Phyl saw Stuart come out onto the deck. "Stu, guess what? We're going hunting for ostrich!"

"Oh, we are, are we?" he said, amused. "We'll have a lifelong supply of feather dusters."

Phyl slapped him on the arm.

Stuart held out his arm. "Shall we? We have a card game to join. I believe they're waiting for us."

Phyl happily took Stuart's arm. She turned to Jorge, who followed in their wake. "Oh, Jorge, you must talk to me tomorrow about the military coups. You've purposely put off my questions about them."

Jorge raised a finger. "It isn't that I don't want to discuss them. It's just, well, let's say, a very sensitive subject, and one has to be careful as to who may overhear. I do have enemies."

Phyl and Stuart stopped in mid stride. She looked at Jorge, frowning. "Enemies? You? You are so charming and delightful and generous."

Stuart frowned. "You're one of the good guys, Jorge. Who are these other guys to watch out for?"

"With the rise of mass politics, a person like me is considered a tyrant. I am, they claim, to be an exploiter of the worker. They say that people like my brother and me lack any useful social function."

"Jorge, you provide meat, wine, and fruit for the market." Stuart shrugged and shook his head. "I can't think why anyone should consider that not 'useful.'"

Jorge smiled slightly and raised his shoulders. "It's complicated. And it's a discussion for another day. But it would have to be in your cabin or mine. Too many ears everywhere else."

Stuart put his hand on Jorge's shoulder. "That's a deal. But it's a must. We have to have this discussion. I think we should know these things."

"Indeed, it would be helpful." Jorge politely nodded for them to go on.

Stuart turned and led a perplexed Phyl into the ship's interior. Suddenly the moonlight wasn't so pure and all-consuming. The new world they were about to enter began to cast a shadow over her joy. What ever were these two men alluding to?

* * *

They dined every night with Jorge, sometimes at the captain's table. Phyl's dream of the high life in gowns and men wearing tails had come true. Jewelry sparkled and everyone looked as if they stepped off a Hollywood soundstage. One evening, an elegantly-dressed Phyl sat between the captain and a young, handsome Cuban. Stuart and Jorge smoked across from her. A new band had come onboard at Trinidad and Tobago and brought a distinct Latin zest to the festivities. There was a piano player, two accordionists, two guitar players, a violinist and bongo drummers. They played the new tango.

"Oh, my gosh, Stu," exclaimed Phyl. "Is that the tango?" she faced Jorge, excitedly. They had just finished an appetizer of salmon, ham and beef in white wine.

"Indeed," chuckled Jorge. He dabbed his linen napkin at the corners of his soft, full lips. "It certainly is a tango."

"Please dance with me, Stuart."

Stuart grimaced. "I'm not a dancer, Phyl. I wouldn't know where to start."

"Would you like to learn how to dance the tango?" asked the beautiful young man. They had been introduced, but Phyl had forgotten his name. The young Cuban stood and bowed to Stuart. "Sir, would you allow me to instruct your beautiful wife as to how to dance the tango? It would be my distinct pleasure." He had a very strong Spanish accent, very cultured. He sported a vibrant purple and green tie and a tight outfit with a high waistband, the only gentleman without tails in the dining room.

Stuart fidgeted and felt some shame he was supplanted by a younger, more resolute man.

"Oh, Stu, you won't mind, would you?" Phyl pleaded. "I would love to learn!"

Stuart folded when he saw her eagerness. He nodded to the Cuban. "If my beautiful wife would like to, fine with me."

Stuart stood and pulled Phyl's chair back for her. Eyes aglow, she looked at the Cuban keenly, not wanting to break the spell. She walked around the decked table and offered her hand. She carefully lifted the hem of her long gown with her free hand. As they walked onto the small dance floor, Jorge leaned over to Stuart.

"If I may say, my friend, your wife may have a problem adjusting to our society." The bongo drums and accordions were loud enough that he had to raise his voice.

Stuart stopped watching Phyl and the young Cuban and turned to Jorge, concerned. "How so?"

"In our country, or any of the Latin American countries, including Cuba," Jorge nodded towards Phyl and the young man, "Phyllis will be continually propositioned. She will attract no end of attention. Someone may even attempt to kidnap her."

Stuart laughed. Then the color drained from his face. "Excuse me?"

"I'm quite serious. She can never leave the house alone. She can with you, a friend, or a maid. But never alone. She would only invite trouble." Jorge leaned back as a waiter took away his plate.

"But that would be impossible. Phyl is a free spirit."

Jorge shook his head. "Married women stay at home, have children, on average about one child every two years. And men, we work, but we also play."

Stuart leaned on his elbow. He reached over and nervously rubbed his cigarette case with his thumb. "You're saying men go out and leave their wives alone at home?"

"Every Argentine man has a good wife who bears him children. But outside the home, he plays."

"You mean with other women?" Stuart's eyebrows shot up. "We call that adultery."

Jorge shrugged. "We call that playing. It's the custom. Each country is different."

"But Argentina is a religious country, yes?" asked Stuart.

"Indeed. But we also know how to enjoy life. It works very well."

"But don't women feel misused? What of your wedding vows?" Stuart wanted another drink. He looked for an available waiter and raised his hand when he saw one.

"Women know when they marry that that their husbands will have one or two mistresses on the side," Jorge continued. He watched Phyl being led through suggestive poses by the young Cuban. Stuart followed his gaze. His face reddened and he dropped his hand.

"One or two?" Stuart's voice broke.

"I have two. And one in New York for while I go there for business," Jorge said matter of factly.

Stuart stared at the tablecloth. It seemed to him, a new world was unrolling in front of him. A world he did not anticipate.

The music changed to a rhumba. Phyl squealed with joy as the Cuban showed her how to stand and shift her weight from one foot to the other, short steps, hips swaying suggestively.

Stuart scratched the side of his neck nervously. "I will keep this under advisement. I'll have a talk with her, though she won't be too happy."

"Perhaps it would be better coming from me while the three of us are together. I will certainly make a point of how much respect she will demand as your wife. She will lose who she is, however, as she will only be known as *Señora de Stuart Redington,* but she will gain in power over the running of the household. You will have a maid. And service people, even the unruliest of men, will respect her. But only if she remains in her place."

Jorge leaned back as the waiter placed a Prussian Salad of cold beets and hard-boiled eggs with dressing in front of him. He watched as one was put in front of Stuart and Phyl's place.

Stuart grabbed the waiter's arm. "I'd like a whiskey on the rocks, please." The waiter nodded and as he left to go to the bar, Stuart raised a finger. "Make that a double!"

Jorge continued. "I hope our Argentine ways do not diminish her brilliant light."

Stuart looked down at his hands, clasped in confrontation on the table's edge. Suddenly, he lost his appetite. He sadly looked at Phyl, laughing as she tried to keep step with the Cuban. "Brilliant light," he repeated. His eyes hardened. He pushed his salad away.

"Not to worry, Stuart. My wife, Angelica, and I, will certainly include her in as many activities as she will allow while you are consumed with your work. We will even take her to the *estancia*."

"You'll keep her busy hunting ostrich?" asked Stuart. "While I work?"

Jorge laughed. "If that is what it takes for her to be happily occupied, my friend."

"Wait a minute, wait a minute." Stuart threw his napkin over the Prussian Salad. He stood up, pushed his chair as far back as he could and turned to Jorge. "Jorge, I do not appreciate how you talk about my wife."

Jorge looked confused. "My friend, I tell you this." He put his right hand over his heart. "I will always respect your wife and your marriage. I am very open about how beautiful and charming Phyl is, but I will never take advantage of our friendship. I am much too fond of the both of you."

Stuart pointed at Jorge. "Is this how you help others acclimatize? Become so very friendly?"

Jorge looked at Phyl and the Cuban on the dance floor. Phyl had gotten into the short steps and undulations of the rhumba and she looked ravishing. He pointed to her. "She's a very good dancer. She could become professional." He looked back at Stuart, who was impatiently eyeing him. Now Jorge pointed at him, at Phyl and at himself. "But this," he said, "is sincere. I have never invited anyone to my *estancia* or home and I consider you family. I know my wife and children will become very fond of you. Please," he said, as he held out his hand.

Stuart refused to take it.

Jorge pulled back his hand. He shrugged. "Tomorrow, we talk about politics. My cabin. Right after breakfast. Does that suit you?"

"No, it doesn't suit me. I don't want you in the same room as my wife."

The rhumba stopped and another tango started, but Phyl motioned to the Cuban she wanted to stop. She returned elated, sweaty and a new woman. Stuart stood by as she was helped to her seat by the Cuban. She picked up her napkin and fanned her cleavage. "Wow, I'm hot." She looked down at the Prussian Salad. "Good Lord, more food!"

Jorge laughed so hard, he coughed.

"What?" smiled Phyl.

Jorge shook his head and waved her away. "*Wow, Good Lord.* You have such an endearing way of speaking English. Are all Canadians like you?"

Phyl grinned, her eyes sparkled, sweat shone on her forehead and chest. "I guess," she laughed.

"Well, I must say, Canadians are very charming." Jorge pointed at her salad. "Now, just be a good girl and eat, *Señora de Redington*! You need to renew your energy."

"That's it," announced Stuart. He grabbed Phyl's upper arm and bodily lifted her from her chair.

"STU!" Phyl looked up at him, appalled.

"Don't ask," muttered Stuart.

"Stuart, we have some very important things to discuss. We arrive in Buenos Aires day after tomorrow. While we are on the ship the three of us have more privacy."

Stuart fumed at Jorge. He pointed at him as he secured his grasp on a confused Phyl. His voice broke with emotion. "Why is it that everything you say, Jorge, sounds disgustingly suggestive to me?"

The band politely continued to play, but the dancers and diners were all watching Stuart, Phyl and Jorge. Stuart glared at everyone, then back at Jorge. He looked at the captain and shook his head. "I apologize, Captain. Forgive me, but..." He pointed wordlessly at Jorge, as if he would say more, but gave up. He put an arm protectively around Phyl's shoulder and marched her out of the dining room.

Jorge raised his hands and dropped them and said to the captain, "*C'est l'amour!*"

The captain said, "Ah, yes." Others within earshot nodded, laughed and chuckled, and simply continued on with their eating.

Jorge picked up his fork and happened to look up at the Cuban. The Cuban shook his head and said, "*Americanos.*"

Chapter Four
Crash Course on Argentine Politics and Babylon Buenos Aires 1935

Phyl and Stuart stood arm in arm in the hot, tropical breeze, gazing at the distant rocky shoreline. They held onto the ship's railing as they swayed side to side on the higher observation foredeck, as close to the bow of HMS Southern Prince as they could get. Below them was out of bounds except to crew. Grey and white lifeboats were tightly lashed in topsy-turvy style, looking like upside-down miniature whales. This was where the crew dropped and retracted massive anchors and carefully coiled thick anchor rode. Today, the workers, their sea legs engaged, swayed and lurched as they focused on elegantly arranging the heavy dock lines, lugging, stretching, and folding them back and forth along the wet deck. The organized rope started to look like a giant sleeping anaconda, coiled and stretched between a dozen newly-painted air-scoop towers, all gleaming brilliantly white in the tropical afternoon sun and sounding like giant, moaning, empty beer bottles.

Their high perch above the bow offered Phyl and Stuart an excellent view, though they were still too far out in the Argentina Basin and Atlantic Ocean to see the entrance to the Buenos Aires docks. Still, distant tendrils of smoke marked where other ships were docked. They curiously looked at the low-lying yellow and brown streak hanging over the old city. Phyl jumped as the ship's bone-rattling horn bellowed behind them. She grabbed her chest and felt it resonate with the nautical moan from the deepest of hell, and she laughed into the wind. She reached up and removed hair from her watering eyes and the corner of her mouth. She grinned like a silly Cheshire Cat.

A black and maroon pilot boat, acrid-looking smoke spewing from its large funnel, rocked and rolled toward them at great speed from the direction of the city. Phyl could see men on the bow, swaying and ducking from the spray while looking toward their ship.

Beneath her feet, the ship trembled and complained loudly as it fought to maintain its course against the deep Atlantic swells. It fought a wind on its nose and opposing currents from the mouth of Samborombon Bay – *Bahia de Samborombón* with Uruguay to the North on the starboard side. Phyl and Stuart looked at the rugged Uruguayan cliffs reaching like giant castles.

Phyl saw tiny, gleaming-white structures. "Oh, Stu, look!" she called excitedly. "I bet those are fancy hotels all lined up along a beach! That must be Montevideo! Oh my gosh, that's where the Pan-American meeting was we heard about in the news! It's so close to Buenos Aires!"

Stuart looked at the pilot boat. "That boat's going quite a clip. It's running with the current."

"What did you say?" yelled Phyl over the overwhelming noise around them.

Stuart leaned toward her and pointed at the oncoming pilot boat. "They're coming at quite a clip. And we're fighting against the current to stay in one place."

Phyl nodded. "Fascinating." She inhaled deeply and squeezed Stuart closer to herself. "There's no awful sewage smell at last," she yelled.

"That's because the wind is on the nose, blowing back the stink."

"I won't miss *that* smell," she laughed. Phyl sniffed the air again. "There's something else in the wind." There was a hint of floral, a touch of dust, along with smells similar to the ship's sewage. "Flowers. Almost like perfume but something rotting underneath."

Stuart studied the pollution over the city. "I'd say it's Buenos Aires itself that we're smelling."

She leaned her head against his chest and frowned. She had expected, of all the places they had stopped south of New York, that Buenos Aires would be the most exceptional. Sacred. She expected to smell fresh ocean air, warm sandy beaches, and exotic flowers found only in Paradise. She sighed. She looked up into the bright sky. The deepening blue turned into an almost black hue towards the heavens. Large sea birds with massive wing spans hovered overhead, floating on the wind. Two pelicans flew by at a slant, toward Uruguay. Suddenly, a healthy-looking seagull landed with a flutter on the railing near them. It dropped a slither of white feces.

"Good omen," laughed Stuart.

The bird looked at them this way and that, its feathers ruffled by the strong wind. It shook its wings straight, poked at them with its beak, then looked skyward at the larger birds. Other seagulls, swooping and hovering over the upper decks, called and screeched. The winged visitor replied and flew away with a clatter of stiff feathers to join them.

"They sure look fatter than those at Lake Ontario," Stuart yelled. Something caught the corner of his eye, and he looked to see Jorge, hatless and in sunglasses, climbing over the top of the nearby ship's ladder that led from the lower decks. He stiffened, and faced forward again. Phyl sensed his change of mood and peeked back.

"Oh, it's Jorge, Stu."

"I know." Stuart's face went rigid.

Phyl stepped away from Stuart as Jorge came closer but kept a hand on the rail for support. Jorge nodded at Phyl as he slicked back wayward hairs, and stood with his feet apart for balance, smiling sweetly. "I'm sure it's hard to believe it's almost December with this heat." He looked at her fondly and took a deep breath to bellow again. "A little topsy turvy season-wise for you Northerners, yes?"

Phyl looked at Stuart, who rocked with the ship and stared forward. She looked back at Jorge, shrugged, and smiled politely. "Yes, very much so." She kept her voice loud. "It's nice to have a tan in late November. Just like Paradise should be." She smiled, eyebrows raised.

"Are you packed and ready?" He stepped closer and held the rail behind her, eyeing the work left behind by the seagull. "You have hours before we disembark. We are held up by a Nazi rally in the Port."

Phyl looked at Stuart. "We heard something was amiss. I didn't realize it was a rally."

"They're forever pushing Nazi ideology and trying to widen their membership base. They're like mosquitos. Buzzing everywhere, ready to prick you with their Super Aryan Race Theory. They're not making any friends in a country made up mostly of darker-skinned people."

"Odd," offered Phyl.

"Yes. Just remember, we'll be tying up at the dock by 11:00 tonight, and one last dinner is served in about an hour." Jorge took off his sunglasses, looked at his gold watch, and tapped it. He folded his sunglasses and slipped them over the top button of his Panama shirt, then grabbed the rail again. He studied Stuart's unwelcoming profile and pondered as he sucked at his lower teeth. Phyl looked at him wide-eyed, then at Stuart. Jorge continued, "Stuart, we had a terrible misunderstanding."

Stuart spread his hands along the railing and looked further down the Argentine coast.

"Stuart, it is essential I brief you on the government and how it runs," yelled Jorge, looking around to ensure no one else was nearby. "It is not only my duty to do so, but it will also benefit your mission on behalf of your company. You should know new government departments have yet to be organized. I don't think you are aware of that." Jorge moved closer to Stuart, stepping almost in front of Phyl, and he lowered his voice. "Offices are not all established. Prime time for a bright, young salesman to get acquainted with those in charge of such infrastructures, yes?" He winked at Phyl, who smiled back.

Stuart nodded to himself. He turned and faced Jorge. "I apologize. Indeed, it behooves me to know whatever is useful for my company." He sounded perturbed.

Phyl spoke up. "And, also, for the Foreign…"

"Yes, Phyl. Also, for, er, that," Stuart added, glancing around for eavesdroppers. He peeked down at the workers. They couldn't possibly overhear. Still, it was nerve-rattling thinking secrecy was of utmost importance. Did it really matter, he wondered?

"I think we can talk here. And perhaps, if Phyl would like, she can get ready for dinner at her leisure?" He looked kindly at Phyl.

Phyl looked surprised but understood. She pushed her hair back behind her ear. "Oh, okay. Unless Stu wants me to stay and listen?" She looked at Stuart questioningly.

Stuart shook his head. "No, Phyl. I'd rather you go. Jorge and I will talk here. We're okay."

Phyl got on her tiptoes and gave Stuart a peck on his suntanned cheek, then she smiled at Jorge and quickly left to go aft and down to their cabin. "I'll see you in the cabin?" She stopped and turned, her hands out for balance.

"No, I'll meet you in the dining room. Have a drink if I'm not there right away."

Phyl nodded, looked at the two men with concern, then turned and left them to their privacy.

Jorge leaned against the railing, took his gold cigarette case out of his pant pocket, and offered Stuart a cigarette. He took one as well, cupping his hands against the wind around the lighter. It took a while, but he finally lit both cigarettes. They turned back to face the bow of the ship. "We should stand very close, Stuart. I do not want my voice to carry."

Stuart turned to him. "Alright."

Jorge turned sideways to face Stuart.

Stuart felt uncomfortable but knew he had to do this. He moved a touch closer. "Shoot."

Jorge chuckled. "*Shoot*. Such an American expression."

"I *am* an American."

"I did not mean anything by that." Jorge looked at Stuart sideways. "Let me begin. I do not know how much you know about what has transpired in Argentina since the beginning of the Depression. The Crash, as you say." He took a drag while waiting for Stuart to respond.

Stuart tilted his head a little. "I know the basics, but it is confusing."

"I'll give you a broad overview but hope not to bog you down with too many details because our politics can be mercurial and challenging to keep track of." Jorge cleared his throat. "General Justo, our *presidente*, took over four years ago, November 1931. The military demanded fair and open elections, but they banned opposing candidates and organized a system that was basically fraudulent and ensured that Justo won hands down, anyway. He was supported by the conservative party known as the *Concordancia*."

"I hadn't heard of the *Concordancia*."

"Good. The *Concordancia* is an alliance between the National Democratic Party, the Radical Civic Union – who helped depose former president, Yrigoyen – and the Independent Socialist Party. Like other countries, Justo thought the best way for Argentina to survive the Depression was to reduce public expenditure. So, he restricted currency circulation, thinking it would strengthen the public coffers. Of course, just like every other country, he saw it wasn't the magic cure, and instead, like your Roosevelt, he emphasized public infrastructure works. To support this, he created the National Office of Public Highways, which is expanding the road network – something quite overdue. This helps to bring foods to market and for people to traverse easier for business. He also created the National Grain Board and the National Meat Board and, just this past year, he created the Central Bank of the Argentina Republic."

"A lot of forced growth." Stuart indeed saw sales opportunities everywhere.

"Yes, this is where you come in, and when I say you, I mean the United States *through* our longstanding financial relations with the British Empire."

"Okay."

Jorge jiggled his head. "The Brits are more tolerated than Americans, and they have done much for my country." Jorge looked back. He saw Phyl's face peeking out over the ladder. Her eyes widened, her mouth dropped open, and her head popped out of sight. He grinned and turned to Stuart.

Phyl sat down and balanced herself on one of the treads of the ship's ladder going down to the lower deck. She was afraid of a fistfight, and hung back to check. But what she saw were two men conversing seriously and closely. She agonized over the fact that Jorge saw her doing such an asinine thing as spying on them. She took a deep breath. It was what it was.

She checked her watch, a slim decoration. She hadn't changed the time since leaving New York, as the voyage was in the same time zone. However, Argentina had daylight savings time, and she forgot whether she had to set the clock forward or back. She gave up, stood up carefully, and walked along the well-scrubbed deck, a hand on the rail. She headed toward the entrance into the ship closest to her cabin. She passed wooden deck chairs with folded woolen blankets. She eyed her reflection in all the portholes. She was going to miss this ship. The music, the dancing, the food, the view, the ocean…But reality was about to set in, and she had misgivings. The fun of the trip was what it was. But it wasn't their mission.

She smiled at passengers who recognized her. "Hello," she said to a woman sitting with a little girl on her lap in a deck chair. She continued on. She put her hand in her wide, white pants pocket and felt for her cabin key. She wore a short sleeve black top with a crew neck, a white necktie, and white earrings. To add a a bit of sport, she wore white running shoes, in womanly liberation. It was delightful to be so warm, beautiful, and tanned at the end of November. She wished El could see her now. She wished El could be there with her. Of course, she wished the world for El.

She pondered her and Stuart missing the wedding. So caught up in preparation for the trip, she hadn't even planned a gift for El and Claude Jr. Another embarrassing letdown for El from her presumable best friend. She agonized over her failings. She thought, even if she sent a gift in the coming week, it wouldn't arrive for months, primarily if it was held up at Customs. Perhaps she could write K and ask her what was missing from El's Hope Chest. Maybe K wouldn't mind buying it. She would figure out how to reimburse K. It was all so very complicated now. She thought, adventure is not simple.

She was beginning to realize she had a very selfish streak. After all, she made the time to buy things she needed for the trip. She could've taken a moment and bought a special gift in New York and mailed it to Toronto from there. She shook her head at her own shortcomings.

She absentmindedly looked over the rail at the pilot boat below which had arrived alongside the ship and was haphazardly keeping lines tied between it and the heaving, sleek hulk. She watched the pilot time his jump perfectly, leaping from the rocking boat and disappearing into the ship's belly. She continued walking, wondering if other people were as short-sighted and selfish as she was. She decided she would make up for it somehow. She didn't know how. But she was determined to figure that one out.

Sad and disappointed in herself, Phyl speedwalked to an entrance of the ship. She yanked at a heavy, watertight door, deftly stepped over the threshold, and disappeared.

Jorge, his heart warmed at the concern Phyl had shown, didn't let on to Stuart that Phyl had been spying and, instead, continued to brief Stuart. "Justo needed to restore international trade, and he managed to restore meat exports to Britain but at 1932 levels."

"I know. Through the Roca-Runciman Treaty," said Stuart. "I read up on that before we left."

"Precisely. Now, Justo is trying to ensure we sign another treaty of a further three years when the present one expires next year." Jorge whisked ash off his chest.

"I see," said Stuart, watching Jorge's movements. He held his own cigarette as far to the side as possible and flicked the ash away to the back of them.

"He wants to rejoin the League of Nations."

Stuart turned and looked straight into Jorge's face. "Wow. Is this public knowledge or is it…?"

Jorge shook his head and smiled at him. "No, Stuart. This is not public knowledge."

Stuart's eyes widened. He newly appreciated his association with Jorge. "Alright." He realized all this intel under the guise of typewriter sales was going to be a familiar and dangerous companion.

"We stand to gain some foothold with this present treaty and its extension, but we have some nationalistic sectors who complain that Britain will gain the most and are not too happy with our *Presidente Justo*." Jorge adjusted the turned cuffs of his short sleeves blown loose by the wind and looked around for a deck ashtray. Giving up, he bent over and dropped the cigarette onto the deck. He caught it rolling away with his foot and ground it with his toe. He made sure all the embers were dead. "After the coup of '31, Justo imprisoned former President Alvear, Ricard Rojas, Pueyrredon…"

"I recognize President Alvear but not the other two."

Jorge waved at him. "No matter." He slid his palms along the sides of his greased head to ensure his hair was still in place. He rubbed his palms together, awkwardly took out a handkerchief, and wiped his hands before putting the cloth back into his pocket and grabbing the rail again. "There were many uprisings and attempted revolts. Some violence, people killed, but not like days of old. Justo kept our other former president, Yrigoyen, under house arrest until he died. He was a very ill man."

"I understand he had diabetes?"

Jorge dismissed the sky with a free hand. "He was eighty. It was his time. But he was a brilliant diplomat and tactician. A true waste of a bright human being. In the meantime, Justo allowed Alvear to return from exile. Alvear groomed Justo for this. Did you know?"

Stuart shook his head.

"Alvear was disappointed at Justo's manipulation of the election. He demands fair elections. Alvear vowed there would be no violence as long as Justo stopped fraudulent elections forever more."

"Goodness, big promises. Hard to keep in a military regime, I would imagine."

"Indeed. He is actually a doctor. Dr. Alvear. Did you know, he is the first and only president to have quarreled with the Pope?"

"No kidding."

"Hmm. He fell in love with and married a Portuguese opera singer, Regina Pacini. We don't marry for love here; taking on an artist as a spouse while in office is a major taboo. It was a national scandal." He rubbed his cheek. "I must shave before dinner." He played at the ash streak on the deck with the toe of his shoe. "I understand you studied under Professor Fran Fetter at Princeton."

Stuart looked at Jorge, surprised. "Yes, economics."

Jorge nodded. "A good friend of mine."

Stuart's appreciation of this man grew. "Small world," he said quietly. He sensed the wind had slightly lessened in strength. He relaxed a little and let go of the rail and turned to lean against it. He crossed his arms. He realized he had never asked Jorge how he was affected, both by the Depression and the military coups. "And how does this affect you and your brother?" he asked.

"It was challenging. It still is. There was much fighting between us and the meat packers. We had to destroy much of our cattle. Very unfortunate." Jorge secured the sunglasses hanging onto a shirt button. "There were no international markets until the trade was renewed through the Roca-Runciman Treaty. But by then, the *peso* took a plunge and, as I said, we are trading at three years ago prices. But because of the devalued *peso*, they're not really at '32 prices. It's been tough maintaining our cash flow. Fortunately, I have investments in France and New York which, though also threatened by the Depression, are much stronger than our entire investment in our own country."

Jorge, shorter than his newest partner in espionage and secrecy, looked up into Stuart's face. "And the masses – well, they are not too fond of us old patron families. Our wealth and power threaten them." He paused. "There is much poverty, and the rift between the classes is great. But our wealth is misunderstood. We keep the country and economy together. We know exactly what the land can take regarding grazing or farming. We have generations of experience. Unfortunately, the uneducated, who vote and are heady with this new power, cannot see that. You give them land, and they farm it until it is no longer fertile. Stripped for years and useless. They don't have eyes to see. They only see what they *don't* have themselves and want what we have at all costs, but they are without the experience, education, and deep roots in our history to maintain quality production and management."

The setting sun glowed between two large funnels on the ship and struck Jorge's face. "Most of us, *estancieros*, are conservative, but there is a new business middle class and they, surprisingly along with some of the newer *estancieros*, are radical and tend to lean for the masses. Well-meaning but entirely misdirected. Unless carefully managed, they are potentially dangerous for our country." His eyes became crystals in the sun. "And many are emotionally driven. It's frightening."

Stuart noticed light brown and black speckles in Jorge's brown eyes. And his enhanced face showed quiet depths. He saw a touch of fear there, too. Looking at a deep crease between Jorge's brows, he realized he saw much suffering. He was looking unfettered into Jorge's soul. He remembered that Jorge thought as a Frenchman and that recognizing the crazy, unleashed mania through which the masses were motivated during the French Revolution was reflected in his own people. He knew that it must subconsciously play a role in Jorge's thinking. Cultural differences or not, Stuart realized he was in the presence of a very influential, and quietly powerful man. He saw the wisdom with which the Powers-That-Be used in directing Jorge to assist him and Phyl. He suddenly felt so fortunate. And humbled.

Jorge reach into his vest pocket and removed a slip of paper for Stuart. "Once you settle, I will contact you."

Jorge took a long look at the deck below, then behind them. "You will come to our home in the city as soon as possible, and Angelica will help Phyl run a household. You and I will continue to talk, my friend. In the eyes of the world, we have established a friendship, and that is what it will continue to appear to be. We have the freedom to exchange information whenever we meet. As well, I have many powerful friends. You will meet them. Many of them will pass on information that will help our country remain strong. We are most concerned, in particular, about the Nazi influence on our military, the church and our schools. We have quite a large Germanic population, you may know. I believe it is most important to have the United States as an ally, for us who still have some economic clout, in the face of such challenges and political unrest. We are ears and eyes on the ground for you lot."

He pointed to the slip of paper. "First: some practical business. Your company has arranged a pension in one of the suburbs, but it will not suit you. Call this number and tell them you are my friend. This person will help you find lodging more to your liking until your permanent home is ready."

"How do I get a hold of you?"

"I will contact you. You will not be lost to me."

Stuart looked down at the paper. "Thank you," he said. He looked around, overwhelmed with emotion, and noted that the pilot must have boarded because the feel of the movement under his feet, he surmised, meant he was at the helm and heading for the distant docks. The ship's speed increased, so did the strength of the wind. Spray violently assaulted the bow once again and the ship's nose raised and lowered, crashing into oncoming steep waves. Jorge and Stuart were sprinkled lightly by the ocean shower, even at their height.

"Jorge, listen. I must apologize. I was very unreasonable at dinner the other night. I treated you like a brute. I'm sorry." He held out his hand. "Friends?" He squinted against another spray and waited.

Jorge looked at Stuart's outstretched hand, smiled, and took it. He nodded wordlessly. He patted Stuart on the upper arm as a more substantial gush of spray reached their deck. "I hope we can help each other, not just me for you. But as I said the other night, we are more than friends. Family. You are at a disadvantage, Stuart. I knew more about you before I met you than you know of me through all our conversations on board. As I've said, I've grown quite fond of the two of you."

Stuart hadn't realized so much planning, time, and energy were invested in them by people they didn't even know, hidden behind the scenes. Stuart had gained a true friend from this group. He was at a loss for words. He could only think to at least express his gratitude. Jorge had turned to start heading to the ladder leading below.

With a cracked voice, Stuart said, "Thank you, Jorge." He stepped forward and grabbed a surprised Jorge. He hugged him. "I hope we deserve all that you have done for us."

"My friend," Jorge said, patting Stuart on the back and leading him to the ladder. "We have only just begun. But I must remind you of one very important point."

"Yes?"

Jorge's face softened. "You cannot tell all to Phyl. But you can share just enough to allow her to understand the nature of what it is you are actually doing here. It would help your marriage greatly."

Stuart clenched his jaw. "She's pretty bright and inquisitive. I've learned to be more discreet. Even deflective."

Jorge smiled. "You'll get the hang of it."

"Oh, boy," Stuart laughed nervously.

* * *

"Good Lord, these Argentines take so long to do anything."

Phyl stood tired and weary. It was 2:00 in the morning, and a customs agent was slowly going through her baggage. Every once in a while, the agent stopped to take a sip of coffee from a cup beside him. A hot plate and kettle near his station and peers, kept the coffee flowing. His hooded eyes constantly looked up at her and Stuart, like they were going anywhere, then over the crowd crammed into the large crumbling stone warehouse, then over to his tired co-workers, then to her and her things. So tedious. He took another sip and lingered over her underwear. Phyl groaned and leaned on Stuart, in front of his own exposed suitcase contents.

"Is it my imagination, or is he purposely taking his time going through my smalls?" she said.

Stuart glanced disapprovingly at the agent and her suitcase. "I don't know what they're looking for. We went through Customs in Trinidad-Tobago. Maybe they're looking for guns?"

A male passenger in a rumpled linen suit and sweating profusely leaned in. "They don't care about guns. Instead of a silver spoon, they're born with a pistol in their mouths here."

Phyl's eyes, strained by the ugly fluorescent lighting hanging from the rafters, widened and looked up at Stuart. Just past him, she noticed men waving frantically from a dirty-looking plate glass window at the end of a long hall. Her attention interrupted by something fluttering against her cheek. She waved it off, then squealed when she saw it was an alien-looking bug.

Stuart frightened the bug away and slapped another one on his neck.

"Ugh," she shivered, then pointed up. "Look there, Stu. Is it my imagination, or are those men trying to get our attention?"

Stuart looked to see if they were waving at others near them. He looked again and pointed at himself questioningly. The men all nodded. "Oh. That must be Mr. Minor, Remington-Rand's General Manager for Argentina. I think I recognize him from his company photo."

Mr. Minor and two other men wore Panama hats. Mr. Minor wore a black kerchief tied at his neck and a rumpled linen suit. The other two wore loose, light-colored pants and Panama shirts. They motioned they would wait at the main doors, and Stuart nodded he understood.

"Oh, Stu," lamented Phyl, smelling diesel and sewage. "We're finally here, it's more foreign than I expected. So different from what we're used to."

"You're not alone, there."

Their first impression of Buenos Aires was a train wreck. Earlier, as HMS Southern Prince maneuvered into position dockside by tugboats, a heavy mist had drifted in and covered everything. Feeble lights along the wharf glowed eerily in the pitch black, and everything was wet and dripping. Horns blew everywhere, unseen traffic roared, cars honked, and people shouted. It almost felt like a revolt. Music reached their ears, but they knew not where from. Bells rang, and towering cranes squeaked and banged overhead as they finally tied dockside.

Just before, Phyl shivered in the strangely cool and humid heat. She looked from the lit cranes overheard down to the wharf of shadows where dock workers slowly secured dock lines. They still had time before disembarking, so they lingered on deck, hoping to catch the flavor of this new and exotic city. But so far, it was not at all what they had expected.

Phyl peered into the black depths of the roiling waters as she waited by the rail. She saw a bloated dead dog. She cried to Stuart, who came over and looked. The body tossed by swells circumnavigated garbage, driftwood, and giant floating clumps of slimy sewage. She tore her eyes away. She found a deck chair to sit on to recuperate. The smell of the docks was atrocious – a combination of oil, rot, urine, and something else dank and disgusting. "What is that smell?" she whined.

Stuart called her back to the rail and pointed out the low tide. "There's a two-and-a-half-foot tide here. See the walls of the wharf?" He directed her gaze. "See how high the wall of barnacles has grown? That's all underwater at high tide, but when exposed, it can smell pretty bad."

Phyl looked closely at the shells and writhing barnacles. Dark-moving bugs crawled over everything. "Oh my god, are those giant cockroaches?" she asked, appalled, her eyes riveted at large, leathery entities milling about the barnacle shells, in and out of the shadows created by the ship's lights and those of the wharf.

"Don't worry, unless you fall in, you won't have to get close to them," Stuart joked.

An hour later, Phyl stood in the warehouse waiting, looking everywhere on the ground for wayward cockroaches and was being glared at by an uncouth agent browsing her intimates.

Thirty minutes later, they were finally outside. Phyl and Stuart eyed flyers scattered on the wet pavement. A filthy, torn material of red, black and some white lay in a gutter. Minor kicked at it.

"Swastika flag. Crazy krouts."

"That was the rally earlier?" asked Stuart.

"Yeah." Minor looked at his watch. "Thanks to them, we're now finally getting you to your beds in the unseemly hour of ..." He was cut off when a black and yellow Ford rumbled up. Minor and his two cohorts whisked Stuart and Phyl into the taxi. They were also desperate to get home and just as drenched with sweat. They all squeezed into the cramped car which smelled of cheap perfume. Minor explained that everyone, including the men, wore perfume in the city. Phyl asked for the window to remain open so that she could breathe while they raced in and out of the busy night traffic to a pension out in a suburb called, Belgrano.

Pensions were glorified boarding houses, at one time old grand houses. This particular place looked all right on the outside. It had high stone walls and tall palm trees, very Spanish with tiled steps and clay pots along the walkway. However, it was depressing and unwelcoming inside. The carpet was bare, the tile floor cracked. Old, faded brocades, statues of the Virgin Mary in corners, on tables, and on shelves throughout a dark hallway. It was ancient and smelled terribly musty. Other guests, surprisingly still awake and chatting or reading, were sitting smoking in the front lounge. Some looked at them with suspicion once they heard them speak English, and Phyl immediately sensed they assumed the two of them were American. She was so tempted to say "Canadian" but was too tired to communicate in a language she knew nothing about.

By the time they settled into their room on the third floor, it was well after 2:30 in the morning, and, combined with a sudden wave of homesickness, they miserably sat huddled together, listening to the city's noises outside their window. Phyl cried from stress and disappointment, and Stuart was terribly frustrated. Like a couple of babies, they were utterly overwhelmed by their alien surroundings.

At one point, Phyl said, "Why are we going through this? Remind me?"

Stuart took her hand. "Phyl, it's going to be worth it." He motioned to the dark, dank room and the moisture-covered, plaster walls. "Your Dad, El, the challenges with Remington-Rand, Washington. I know we're wrestling with the angels, Phyl. But we're going to push and we're going to make enough money to put a nice, big fat down payment on our own house back home."

"Which home? Toronto? Kingston?"

"It doesn't matter at this point, Phyl. We'll know in a few years. We may be changed by then and want something completely different."

"Oh, no, Stu, I have to get back to Dad and Claude Jr. and El. We're going to be godparents to their children. We have to go back."

Stuart sighed. "Like I said, we'll see. We'll figure it out. But in the meantime, we're fast tracking our future. Plus," he raised his eyebrows, his watery eyes holding her gaze, "I wanted to feel I was working on behalf of something big. I hope that I can say I've made a little bit of a difference."

Phyl sniffed and nodded, and together they lay back onto the worn, tufted dusty pink bed cover, their fingers interlocking, their legs hung over the edge of the bed.

The next day, after a sleepless night fully clothed, Phyl and Stuart grabbed their bags and got out of there. Minor was upset when he came to call and saw them checking out, but Stuart and Phyl were determined to find a nearby hotel instead. Minor helped get them to the City Hotel, where they found a room that was much more comfortable and welcoming.

Minor suggested Stuart take a week to settle in before starting work at the office. The next day, following a peaceful night's rest, Stuart decided to follow up on Jorge's contact.

On their third morning in the city, they landed a small furnished apartment while they waited for a long-term home. They packed their things into a taxi once again, said goodbye to the friendly doorman at the City Hotel, signed the papers with the landlord, and immediately moved in. After dropping their bags, they immediately went out to explore.

Phyl admired blossoms of all kinds and colors which flourished along the edges of sidewalks, in parks, and at the bases of fountains and monuments. Latin music came from all directions. Palm fronds swayed above them as they strolled, making the sun waltz electrically across the shaded sidewalks. It finally started to feel like Paradise. Phyl was so pleased, she couldn't help but grin. She listened to the staccato Spanish spoken around her, and the odd moment she recognized a word in German, Italian, French, and what she thought must be Portuguese. At one point, tiny squealing noises broke through the surrounding din. She walked over to a bush to discover a thin, sad-looking dog with three puppies.

"Stu. Puppies!" Stuart wordlessly took her arm, gently pulled her away from the bush and made her continue her stroll. "But the poor puppies. We should do something." But Stuart ignored her pleas.

After crossing wide boulevards and side streets, they had quite the appetite and chose the first restaurant that looked reasonably clean to stop in. Inside, there were only Spanish speaking people, all talking exceptionally loud and fast, at a ricochet clip. Phyl and Stuart sat at their table and nearly went crazy trying to read the menu.

No one in the restaurant could translate for them and, even with Stuart's rudimentary Spanish, the menu items had such fancy names, there was no way to know what they described. Even though the British had invested in the city's infrastructure with magnificent sums of money, and even though the menus were translated from Spanish into three other languages – French, German, and Italian – there was not a single English word. At least, not in this neighborhood.

They had no choice but to order by pointing at what people were eating next to them. However, they did not realize how many servings were included. First, came the appetizer: a plate of salami, ham, beef, and another form of meat they did not recognize, all done in a white wine sauce. Then came roast chicken with prunes, caramelized onions, and cold beets, followed by the same

Prussian salad they were acquainted with onboard ship, served with hard-boiled eggs and dressing. Phyl had enough after the salad, and Stuart was close to ordering dessert, when a bowl of soup was set before them with a glass of wine.

While they struggled through the soup, they were served a chicken liver omelette and an inch-thick steak with potatoes and more wine. Finally, they were served ice cream topped with fresh pineapple and strawberries, which came with a tall flute glass of champagne. Then elegant cups and saucers were placed before them, and thick black coffee was poured, accompanied by short glasses of port.

Phyl thought she was going to be sick. She wiped her mouth with her napkin for the umpteenth time and looked at Stuart with tortured eyes. "Oh, Stu. I don't feel so good."

"Well, no one forced you to eat it all." Stuart pondered whether he could finish a strawberry.

Phyl looked at the other diners, who all had no problem eating massive amounts of food in one sitting. "How come they're not all five hundred pounds?"

Eyes bloodshot, Stuart scanned the noisy room. Even though Jorge had alluded to the most beautiful and elegant women in the world being in Buenos Aires, he saw couples all on the rotund side. The women were hefty, thick legged with thick midriffs. He surmised they were married couples, not men with mistresses. Then again, a man wouldn't take a mistress to a restaurant. Jorge had spoken of nightclubs and secret cafés with partitioned rooms, live bands, performers, and live dance shows. He looked at Phyl's green face. "This is going to cost us an arm and a leg."

As if reading his mind, the waiter jabbered in Spanish and slapped the bill onto the table and ran off with his white cloth over his arm. Like every Argentine man they met, including Jorge, the waiter's hair was slicked back, shining like a round mirror, depositing a cloud of perfume in his wake. Stuart picked up the bill and squinted. "What?" he almost yelled.

"What?" asked Phyl, frowning. "A lot?"

"Oh," said Stuart. "Sorry, I thought it said 2,000 *pesos*. It's 20. I think this meal costs us two dollars US."

Phyl's mouth dropped open. "Are you serious?"

"And that includes the tip," Stuart read further.

Phyl gazed at their remaining dirty plates and glasses on the table. "Well, I guess we're not going to starve to death, even if we don't make a go of it. Our savings and your advance will at least guarantee that. Too bad you're paid in *pesos* on par. It still makes my blood boil."

"Don't even get me started." Stuart tapped his watch face. "It's early yet. Jorge's contact, Joe…"

"What's his last name?"

"He refused to give it to me. In fact, I suspect his first name isn't Joe at all."

Phyl made a comical face as she sipped her coffee. "Wow, this is strong." She sipped again.

"So, Joe said breakfast is typically three rolls and coffee. And the short guy with Minor – I forget his name – the one I'll be working with at the office, told me that the guys go out at lunch and eat three courses every day."

"They eat out every day? It's cheap here, but I don't think we can afford that, Stu. I thought I'd be making your lunches."

"Not to worry, because you'll flip when you hear this."

Phyl giggled. "What?"

"We have two hours for lunch because everyone has a siesta after lunch, so I might as well walk home. You can do the honors and make me a three-course lunch every day, including the half Saturdays I work. And don't forget the white and red wine and champagne."

Phyl laughed. "Shut up!" She wiped the dessert plate with her forefinger and licked it. "Two hours?" Phyl frowned. "So, you only work another couple of hours after that?

"No such luck. We work till about 7:00 pm. And most don't eat dinner until after 8:30."

Phyl put her cup down a bit too hard, and it clunked onto its saucer, sounding as if it almost broke. A heavy-set woman with hair forced into a brutal bun looked at her almost sneeringly. Phyl smiled at her apologetically. The woman wordlessly looked away. "You mean they finish eating around 9:30? How do people sleep, Stu?"

"Because they have a siesta during the day, they stay up until about 1:00 am."

"Oh, my God. Now it makes sense." Phyl sat back and stared out the window overlooking the brightly-lit boulevard. Darkness had fallen while they were dining, and intense spotlights shone on a large stone monument in the middle of constant roaring, blaring traffic. The statue, which was a soldier on a horse, was surrounded by fountains. She had no idea who it was.

"What makes sense?"

"Now I understand why the whole world seemed out and about on the streets when Minor took us to that godforsaken pension. It was 2:30 in the morning, and yet families were walking around."

Stuart took out his billfold and placed a series of *pesos* on the little plate with the bill. He stuffed the bill into his billfold.

"Souvenir?" asked Phyl.

"I'm not sure what I can claim as a business expense yet, just in case."

"Oh, Stu. That's so smart of you."

"Jorge had mentioned it, though Remington-Rand didn't."

"What would we have done without Jorge? I look forward to meeting his wife and children."

Jorge had left a message with their doorman that afternoon inviting them for lunch at his flat the next day. They were to take a short taxi ride, Jorge saying it was much less stressful than trying to navigate the few blocks on foot. It was best to wait until they became more oriented with respect to the ways of the people and traffic before they made a habit of cruising the sidewalks.

Stuart pushed his chair back and pulled Phyl's chair out as she stood up. She straightened down her light summer dress and her little hat on her sweaty hair and put on her gloves. She picked up her bag and allowed Stuart to lead her out of the crowded restaurant. As they passed other patrons, they saw what everyone else was eating. Everywhere they looked, it was meat, meat, and more meat. Phyl took Stuart's arm as they stepped outside into the sweltering heat. It seemed the night air didn't lessen in temperature from the day.

"Did you notice we didn't get any vegetables? Not even in the soup?" Phyl said.

"You're right."

"In fact, I didn't see any vegetables on any plate when we left the restaurant."

They walked back toward their apartment. They almost stumbled over a mother and child who stopped suddenly in the middle of the sidewalk. Phyl was shocked to see the mother pull down the child's pants to let him urinate. She looked back as they passed. "Oh my god, Stu. Did you see that?"

"What?" Stu looked back as they continued walking and saw the little boy urinate openly, his little penis in his little hand, his mother standing by watching and smiling approvingly.

"Holy Toledo, Jorge didn't warn us about that."

Phyl looked down the street just before they crossed and caught a man in the shadows peeing against the wall of a corner church. She covered her eyes with her free hand. "Oh, Stu. I just saw a grown man urinate against that church wall."

Stuart laughed.

Phyl slapped him on the shoulder. "Don't laugh. It's not funny. It's terrible for a woman to see a man urinate. It's traumatizing. Wait till I tell Jorge."

The crowd crossing the street bunched up at the other sidewalk, and traffic honked at them as they were stuck almost in the middle of the road. Cars and taxis tried to squeeze through the pedestrians. "Oh, how rude!" exclaimed Phyl.

She slapped the hood of one of the taxis. The taxi driver rudely gesticulated at her. "Well, I never!" She moved on and noticed a man in a dark suit and grey hat reach out and grab a young blonde woman's arm and pull her so hard out of the way that her head snapped back. "Oh dear," exclaimed Phyl. She continued to watch and realized something was terribly wrong with the couple. The young woman looked as if she was petrified, her eyes darting at every face that hovered or passed as if beseeching help or acknowledgment. In fact, she was definitely trying to pull against the man, who looked extremely upset with her. He had a rugged face, sharp cheekbones, a pencil mustache and was dressed dapper.

In contrast, the young woman wore a humble shift and rope sandals. He never loosened his hold on her. Phyl tugged at Stuart's sleeve. "Stu, I think that young woman with the man in the dark suit doesn't want to be with him. She looks terrified. I think she's in trouble. Should we help somehow?"

Stuart looked briefly, then away. "Phyl, we don't know the whole story. They may be having an argument. Or it's a father dragging a daughter home."

"No, I have a bad feeling about this," Phyl said, helpless and indecisive. "Oh, the poor thing."

"I really wouldn't know what to do, Phyl. We can't speak Spanish; I don't know if there are any police stations around. I'm too out of my element here to know how to respond."

Sadly, Phyl followed Stuart through the crowd. She almost stumbled over the dirty, bare feet of an older woman sitting at the sidewalk's edge. She had a worn, torn shawl over her head and held a battered tin cup, begging. The woman opened her mouth to speak, speechless, showing only her gums. Phyl tore her eyes away when she heard children's voices rise above the surrrounding insanity. She saw children swarm a paunchy British foreigner stepping out of a taxi across the road. They attacked him with hands outstretched, almost angrily. They wouldn't leave until he put a coin in each child's hand. She leaned more heavily on Stuart's hand and clasped his arm. Stuart looked down.

"Are you alright?"

"It's too much. I crave to sleep because I need a break from this strange nightmare."

Little did she know she was only seeing a glimmer of what was to become of their lives.

* * *

Phyl leaned against the bathroom sink and peered at a shelf built into the white marble of the wall beneath a considerable mirror. She fingered perfume bottles and body lotions with fancy French labels. She picked up an elegant bottle of cut glass and hand-painted flowers and pulled out the glass stopper. She held it to her nose and inhaled the pleasing aroma of exotic flowers. She sighed without realizing it, her eyes closed. "Ah," she said to herself. She looked down to the left of the sink at what she thought was a foot bath with fancy knobs. She looked down at her feet and considered taking her shoes and stockings off to give herself a refreshing foot bath. She looked around, and though she had used a small white guest towel, she felt she needed a larger one to stand on. After seeing the white towels perfectly folded and hung over the brass towel rack, she didn't want to disturb anything. It all looked too perfectly arranged.

She looked around the room. At the end was a tall, frosted window that opened in the middle. The ceiling was at least ten feet, throughout the spacious apartment. The white marble floor tiles were slightly mismatched, giving it a homey feel. There was a grate in the middle of the floor. A sturdy brass shower rod held a white curtain around a white tub of marble tiles. The curtain had a grey strip just above the bottom hem, the same grey as the shadows and streaks naturally running through the marble walls.

She took one final look at herself in the mirror, slid a fingernail along the bottom edge of her lipstick, pressed her lips together, then turned and walked to the door. Her heels clicked sharply into a wide, long hallway.

Earlier, Jorge's wife, Angelica – a blue-eyed and very blonde Basque – had given Phyl and Stuart a tour of the apartment. It was large enough to accommodate all three children, themselves, and each of the four servants and guests. Each bedroom had its own bathroom, and the facility she had just used off the hallway was for guests.

She crisply walked back to a grand dining/living room where the men and Angelica sat at a London-stamped Burr Walnut Art Deco dining set comprised of a long table and matching chairs. They had just been served a five-course lunch by two servants. Twin toddlers played at Angelica's feet while their ten-year-old brother, Georgie, sat in his chair, listening closely to his father speak English to Stuart. The seats were of white brocade, and the arms, legs, and trim were polished to look like gold. Indeed, they shone as such, bathed in early afternoon light that slanted through rich window sheers.

"Oh, it's lovely being able to speak English again!" Phyl exclaimed. She reached her seat and Jorge stood and helped her sit. She nodded at the eldest son, who looked like a tiny version of Jorge with a stubborn blonde streak off his forehead. "And your son speaks such perfect English." She turned to Stuart. "Stu, you should see the foot bath they have in the bathroom. What a great idea! I hope we have one where we're going."

Jorge and Angelica looked at each other curiously. Their eldest son laughed.

"Don't be rude, son." Jorge looked at him pointedly.

His son smiled impishly.

Argentine Riptide

"I never thought of it as a footbath," said Angelica, grinning. "It's called a bidet. It's to wash your," she looked at Jorge, "how shall we say? Your intimate extremities."

"Intimate extrem…" Phyl turned a crimson red.

Stuart burst out laughing. He slapped his napkin against the table's edge, covering his eyes as he laughed, his shoulders bouncing uncontrolled. His neck turned red, and he ended up coughing. Jorge bent over from his position at the head of the table and pounded him on the back, grinning.

Phyl looked down and saw Angelica's well-manicured hand reach out and cover hers. "This is such a pleasure getting acquainted."

Phyl looked up at Angelica. Her ample cleavage and full breasts implied she was still in the middle of nursing the twins. "Thank you and Jorge so much for all your kind hospitality and friendship."

Angelica smiled as she cuddled one of her toddlers clambering to get onto her lap. "It truly is our pleasure, Phyl," Angelica spoke English with a distinct French accent, as did her oldest son, who spoke crisp Spanish with the servants and French with his toddler siblings and parents.

Phyl watched one of the servants return with a large silver pot of coffee on a tray with cups, saucers, and sugar. She noticed that cream was rarely in sight anywhere they went. The servant was a short, stout young girl wearing a crisp black and white maid's outfit.

"Oh, but you would prefer cream, being North American?" asked Angelica.

"Oh, yes, please, thank you."

Angelica turned to the servant. "*Con leche.*"

The young servant nodded and left.

Jorge stood. "Let's move to the living room to sit more comfortably. These chairs flatten my behind after a while."

Everyone pushed their chairs back, and Jorge quickly jumped to Phyl's to pull it out. Stuart caught on, jumped to Angelica's chair, and helped her out. "You didn't have to do that, Stuart."

Stuart looked from Angelica to Jorge. "I didn't want to be upstaged," he laughed.

They moved to the other end of the room to where white couches and armchairs were arranged. Two matching armchairs went with the dining room set, carrying over the white and gold wood motif from the dining room into the spacious white living room. Above the round marble table hung a planet-sized chandelier in crystal. A sizeable glass vase filled generously with white lilies and white and blue hydrangeas, on the table. The walls were white, trimmed with gold edging Parisian-style, which separated the walls into fake rectangles, giving the room texture. At the end, stood a marble fireplace with deeper and darker grey veins than the floors. Above the mantle hung a tall gold-framed and beveled-glass mirror. On each side of the mirror hung brass wall sconces. Tall brass table lamps were spread around the room, all with delicate, large snow-white shades. At this end, another massive window, graced by filmy white sheers and light cream-colored heavy curtains. Side tables were also of white marble, and two ancient landscape paintings hung on two solid walls.

Phyl felt as if she was sitting on a plateau in Heaven. "The whites make it feel cool," she said.

"Precisely. And the curtains are very thick, so when we pull them against the afternoon sun, it can be quite comfortable in here," said Angelica.

The servant came over with the cups and saucers of coffee and a decanter of cream, then returned with a tray of cheeses, fruit, and sweet and savory delicacies. As they sipped their coffee, Jorge looked at his watch. "We will *siesta* before we head out sightseeing, and then get ready for dinner tonight."

""Oh, Papa, may I come along?" Georgie's eyes widened.

"Yes, you can come for the sightseeing, but you will have to sit on your mother's lap."

"I'm too old to sit on Mama's lap," he said, emphasizing the end of Mama.

"Then you stay and help watch over your brothers."

"May I ask where we're going for dinner?" asked Stuart.

"We have a reservation at 9:00 at the Hotel Alvear. Later, we will see the night sights you can't see this afternoon. They don't open until very late."

"Jorge told me that as a woman I should not go out alone. I find that hard to accept," said Phyl, turning to Angelica.

"Oh, he exaggerates. You just can't go out alone after 6:00, though during the day you will definitely get harassed. But after dark? Yes, you will find yourself in deep trouble, which you may never get out of. Either way, it is best to be accompanied by someone, a friend, mother, sister, or maid, during the day. Men are like moths to a flame when it comes to women. And they are not too polite at the best of times, though when they realize you are a *Señora*, their fear and respect for the husbands do sometimes keep them in line. But you never know. Especially if you inadvertently give them too much attention. Then they think all is possible." Angelica took a delicacy. "But, yes, after 6:00, you must stay home."

"It sounds like house arrest." Phyl looked sad.

"Tell them what we saw when we walked around, Phyl," offered Stuart.

Phyl sat up. "Yes, when we left the restaurant the first night we went out exploring, I saw something quite disturbing."

"That would be normal, I'm afraid," offered Angelica. "What, in particular, disturbed you?"

"I'm sure a young girl was being taken against her own will. She looked quite frightened. But we didn't know what to do."

Angelica looked at Jorge, who sat with his legs crossed in his armchair closest to the coffee table. He put his cup and saucer on the table and leaned his elbows on his knees. He clasped his hands. "Unfortunately, Buenos Aires is one of the largest white slave markets in the world."

"White slave?" Phyl's brows knitted. "We still have slaves?"

Angelica reached over and covered her ten-year-old's ears with both hands. "Sex slaves."

Phyl's heart raced. "And everyone knows what's going on?"

Jorge sighed. "We have a solid prostitution base in Buenos Aires. We and Rio de Janeiro are the two biggest centers for white slavery."

"My God, where do these women come from?" asked an astounded Phyl.

"About one-third of the slaves are Jewish as most of these young women are running away from cultural taboos or are widows when they get here. Sex is so blatant you'd think we were in Babylon. For instance, in North Rosario, a nearby city, a very large brothel seats 700 men at a time. They drink themselves into stupors while 50 naked women parade around selling themselves."

"Oh, my dear Lord," groaned Phyl. She covered her mouth.

"Women have no status in our country. We have no passports, no government assistance. We need permission from our husbands to do everything," Angelica added.

"Except have babies, manage the household and servants, and shop to your heart's content," added Jorge.

"So long as you come back to prison from shopping by six, you mean," Phyl said dryly.

"Police turn a blind eye with their hands out for kickbacks. And refugees, who have no other prospects, recognize the massive demand for sex, so it's easy for them to rent a house and create a brothel. Some outdo the others by offering special exotic performances and they can be quite disturbing. The market and brothels are like hungry monsters - they constantly need more young women."

"Young men as well," whispered Angelica, covering her son's ears again.

"Oh, my gosh, I don't want to know all this. What happens to these women? They can't live very long. It's unhealthy, it's destructive." Phyl couldn't believe it. "I mean, I thought we could be pretty immoral with our burlesque houses along Yonge Street in Toronto, and certainly, New York isn't entirely pure, but this makes us out to look like prudes! Are these women *all* refugees?"

Jorge held out his hands. "Yes, refugees from other countries. But also from our own provinces. Poor young girls sent to the city by their families to send home what they can."

Phyl wiped her forehead with the fresh napkin which lay beside her cup and saucer.

"You look tired, Phyl, and I'm afraid we have upset you. You need to rest." Jorge stood up. "Come, my friends, we must retire to our *siestas*. The servants prepared your room for you. We have quite a day and night ahead of us."

* * *

A little refreshed from her *siesta* and having been pleasantly distracted from such upsetting thoughts by being shown a better part of the city earlier, Phyl dressed and readied herself for dinner. She stood waiting on the long balcony by the French doors leading from the living room. The white ornate stone balcony was as long as the entire apartment, and it had separate access points from the other rooms. It had the same marble floor with several grates in the middle for the rain, and daily scrubbing. Looking out the window earlier, she noticed one of the servants throwing a bucket of water over the marble to clear it of the city's dust.

In the balcony's corners, and at each marble column, were potted palms with heavy fronds swaying in the breeze. Oriental pots of exotic flowers, including orange and brown zinnias and prolific pink and salmon-colored roses, added an explosion of color, beautifully contrasted by the bright turquoise and white-striped cushions on the white iron deck furniture. Striped aqua and white awnings hung over certain sections of the balcony, their scalloped edges delightfully dancing and fluttering in the evening's breeze. The sun had just set, and there was a purple haze over the city and bay and the very distant rocky shoreline of Uruguay, which she thought she could almost make out past the distant docks. She heard a ship blow its horn over the honking of cars and taxis and the trundle of streetcars in the downtown area. She stepped closer to the railing and felt a solid wall of heat rising from the pavement five floors below.

Jorge and Angelica's apartment overlooked the grand plaza and park, and a massive stone monument and fountain. Trees and palms dotted the pathways throughout the vast green expanse, and horses and white carriages lined up along one of the broad sidewalks. She smelled a whiff of horse manure. A small streetcar passed below. The wide boulevard was already overrun by people ready for the usual evening gorging, dining and revelry.

Looking handsome in his tuxedo, Stuart stepped out onto the balcony and stood beside her. He looked over the large park and put his arm around her waist. "I see it's important to know where to live. Jorge just informed me that our three-bedroom apartment is on the other side of this park."

"Oh, how wonderful. Which building is it?" She craned her neck to see in the distance.

Stuart pointed to the opposite boulevard where tall white apartment buildings stood. "They're all pretty new, built just before the Crash. Apparently, they're art deco, very posh and modern." He looked at Phyl and noted she had put coloring on her lashes. "You put make-up on, I see."

"I wanted to look like an elegant *Señora*," she smiled and fluttered her eyelashes.

"Well, you always look ravishing."

They turned to see Jorge walk onto the balcony, looking elegant in a tuxedo. It had gotten darker, and the wall sconces on the outside walls, turned on by a servant, started to attract various flying insects.

"Shall we?" He stepped back, motioning them to go ahead of him into the flat. As Phyl passed him, he put his palm on her shoulder. "Phyl, you will be happy to know I just got off the telephone with the building owner across the park from us. You and Stuart can go see your unfurnished apartment midday tomorrow. Angelica will come along. I know for certain you will have many questions she would be more than happy to answer or help with."

Phyl turned and looked out toward the tall apartment buildings about a mile away. Some windows were now brightly lit while big spotlights, directed from below, highlighted art deco details in the stoneware she could see even from this distance. She wondered which building it would be.

"Goodness, I wonder how much something like that will cost to rent."

"I understand you were given an advance in American dollars, though Stuart's wages and commission will be in *pesos*?"

Stuart became upset. "Yes, last-minute change to the contract."

"It was a dirty trick," added Phyl.

"Not to worry." Jorge pointed to his own apartment. "This would cost you less than $100 US."

"Your place? No!"

Jorge nodded at a surprised Phyl. "I'm sure a three-bedroom on one floor with no parking garage will go for less than $40." He pointed over his shoulder. "We also have a back balcony facing a courtyard below, extra rooms for servants, and laundry you haven't seen, plus we have an enclosed parking spot on the main level. If you have foreign currency, Argentina is the place to be."

Phyl looked at Jorge, surprised. "Oh my. Apartments – like, horrid ones and only one bedroom – can go for more than $300 Canadian in Toronto. As a matter of fact," she turned to Stuart. "What was it you paid for the studio flat in Rosedale?" She turned to Jorge. "Though it was quite nice, really."

"I was paying $90 Canadian."

Phyl felt renewed hope. The same $90 would pay for a palace. But they certainly didn't have the reserves to ensure spending that much monthly for a whole three years. What if there was no commission to speak of? She had been a little concerned they would end up living in squalor, but it looked like they could afford something basic that would suit them quite nicely. She glanced back at the distant apartment buildings before stepping into the living room to join a beautifully-dressed Angelica, who stood waiting by the broad white front doors, pulling on long satin gloves which reached over her elbows. The table lamps had been turned on while Phyl lingered over the view outside, and one of the servants had turned on the chandelier. The room shone like a polished showroom.

"Shall we paint the town red, as you say?" asked Angelica.

Phyl reached out for her arm. "Oh, my gosh, yes, Angelica. I'm ready to get so bent with booze, Stuart would have to carry me back to our poor little apartment." She turned to Jorge, who was putting a white satin scarf over his neck. "I hope I don't turn into a pumpkin at midnight. I could swear I'm in a fairy tale," she laughed.

* * *

Jorge drove his white 1935 Ford Model 48 with white-walled tires through the city which pulsed into life at night, rich and exotic. He showed Phyl and Stuart the *Plaza Congreso*, with its fountain shooting almost twenty meters up and ablaze by spotlights. Nearby, towered yet another monument, dwarfing the nearby crowd. Tall, stately buildings stood seemingly on fire by brilliant spotlights. Greek statues peeked over rooftop eaves searching the dark shadows of side streets. On the way to Hotel Alvear, Jorge showed off the hundreds of colorful marques propped like soldiers throughout the streets. Nightclubs with names like *Horacio Coppola, Ton Ton Ton Tonia, Hov La Tia De Carlos, Newark, Pancao*, and the *Titan*. She read more signs on another street: *Santarelli, Libreria El Altonos*, which advertised *Para la Mujer Moderna*. "Oh, I can read that sign. 'For the modern woman.' That must be a clothing store! Oh, I'd love to go there sometime and see."

Angelica laughed, surprised. "You are correct! And we'll make sure you will."

Amid nightclubs stood another massive store with signs that read *Victrolas, Radios, Musica, Pianos, and Discos*. Phyl's neck hurt from peering upwards, around, and side to side.

Finally, they pulled up in front of the Hotel Alvear. Crowds of well-dressed people passed them from both directions, some along the road, staring into the car as the women were helped out. Music wafted out of the front glass doors of the hotel.

"Is that a tango they're playing?" Phyl carefully pulled her hem straight as she stood by while Angelica got out of the car with the help of Stuart.

A valet in a white suit with brass buttons and navy-blue epaulets stood by, waiting to take the Ford away. They carefully snaked through the sidewalk traffic and went up the slate stairs to the hotel doorman. As they entered the large lounge, packed full of men and women dressed to the nines and smoking and drinking in lounge chairs, they were led by Jorge to the far end where the ballroom doors stood open. Rich red velvet curtains draped along both sides of the broad entrance, gracefully tied back with gold rope to large brass knobs embedded into the walls. They saw people twirling on the dance floor before a large band. Each band member was brilliantly dressed in mauves, light greens, and pink and sitting behind pink and lime green partitions that doubled as music stands. A waiter led them to a large round table covered in a white linen cloth and bedecked with pink and mauve flowers and candles. A cigarette girl meandered around a maze of tables toward them.

Phyl allowed herself to be helped to a chair as she looked around wide-eyed. She watched Jorge give *pesos* to the cigarette girl, who eyed him appreciatively. After a polite smile, he looked away, knowing she would flirt. He cast warm eyes on Angelica, who lifted her chin and held her hands together to show off her rings. The scene looked like a Hollywood set Phyl and El always loved to watch and dream about. The waiter offered her a menu and poured champagne. Jorge leaned closer to Phyl.

"After dinner, we will go to a cabaret earmarked for mistresses."

Phyl's mouth dropped. She was appalled. "Are we allowed to go? Do we look like mistresses?"

Jorge and Angelica laughed. Angelica leaned toward Phyl. "It will give you an insight into that part of our culture you like to call immoral, which you are probably right to say it is."

"Buenos Aires is so hedonistic," offered Phyl. She bit her lip and was surprised when Stuart stood up and motioned for her to dance with him. She squealed with delight. Stuart looked back at Jorge as he led Phyl away. "Jorge, please just order for us. We really wouldn't know where to start."

Jorge gave thumbs up and laughed.

Stuart found a spot on the dance floor and held Phyl tightly.

"When did you learn to tango, Stu?" asked Phyl, surprised. They stood still as others floated around them. She looked at them and then down at their feet. "Stu? You're leading, right?"

"I'm thinking," said Stuart.

Phyl laughed. "Do you want me to lead?"

"I'd prefer not, but after watching you closely with that damn Cuban, I thought I had the steps memorized, but now I'm completely out of my element."

Phyl grinned. "Okay, put your man's ego to the side, Stu. I'll lead," she said, as she raised his arm and straightened her back. She counted backward from five, nodding with each number, and then led a stumbling Stu through the basic steps of what should've come across as sensual and seductive but ended up looking like a Charlie Chaplin skit.

* * *

Two hours later, they entered the cabaret Jorge had mentioned earlier. They had to walk into a back alley and go through a dark doorway. Several hefty men were stationed along a narrow, dark hallway into the old building. They were handed dark-colored linens. "What are these for?"

"They're to cover your head," Jorge said matter-of-factly as he placed his over his head.

Phyl held up a hand and waved it in front. "Can you see?"

"Yes. I can see through the fabric, but the point is, you can't see who I am as I walk through. I've arranged a private cubicle where we can take them off. But most patrons stay at the tables and keep their heads covered during the whole show."

"I know who you are," she joked.

"You know what I mean!"

Stuart and Phyl put the cloths over their heads and went through a double door. Inside, a man wearing eyeliner, motioned them to follow past crowds of people with their heads covered. He led them to a private cubicle with a screen facing a stage.

"Why is there a screen?"

"So, no one can see you sitting here," said Angelica, as she carefully sat by a little side table on the inside of the screen. She took off her cloth and instructed Stuart and Phyl to do so. Phyl could then make out more details of the stage. The floorboards were painted a flat black and were quite scratched. One spotlight shone steadily. A chair and a floor lamp were the only props. Including a whip resting on the chair.

She turned to Angelica. "It feels so sinister. I'm a little frightened."

"Well, I will tell you this is definitely highly unusual that we should come with our husbands. Men generally take their mistresses. But Jorge insisted." Angelica wasn't too happy.

"Oh, Angelica. I hope there isn't a lewd show. I wouldn't know what to do. I'd run back to Canada screaming."

Angelica shook her head. "No, not this early in the night. The more serious presentations come after midnight. We'll be long gone before then. I told

Jorge I wouldn't stand for anything that would upset your North American sensitivities, though I also don't appreciate being exposed to garbage."

Phyl sat back, blinking, concerned. "Thank you, I think." She turned to Jorge, questioningly.

He caught her look and shook his head. "I do not frequent these places, but I thought it would be educational to at least know."

Angelica stood, slid her chair closer to Phyl, and sat back down. She leaned into Phyl. "You are wondering, of course, why wives are so tolerant of mistresses."

Wide-eyed, Phyl nodded exaggeratedly.

"People don't marry for love, as North Americans do. As a rule, marriage is a union of two wealthy and influential families wishing to keep their wealth solid. This longstanding custom is what is behind a solid business in Argentina. We are a business society. I understand this is very different from what you are accustomed to."

Phyl nodded. "Yes," she said sadly. She turned to see a waiter in red come into their cubicle with a tray of drinks.

"I went ahead and ordered cocktails, but they are incredibly potent here, so sip slowly," Jorge said as he slightly moved a burning, brass lantern with red cut glass over to make room for the tray.

Suddenly, a crash of symbols and drums announced the arrival of two women in masks and togas on stage. The beat of the drums continued steadily. Phyl and Stuart sat watching attentively. Phyl eyed the whip and saw one of the women pick it up and crack it into the air over the heads of the closest patrons in front of the stage. People called out and screamed in surprise.

"Oh dear," Phyl mumbled, her heart racing.

The woman without the whip stepped off the stage and wandered around, trailing her fingers along the men's shoulders, one table to the next. Heads covered in cloth swivelled, seemingly blindly watching her.

Phyl, feeling anxious, took the shot glass from the tray and eyed the light green syrupy liquid. She wasn't sure if she was going to have the courage to sit and watch without some sustenance of the alcohol kind. She took a sip as she continued to watch the woman searching the audience. The liquid burned her mouth and throat, and she coughed. She fanned her burning lips. Angelica looked at Jorge disapprovingly.

Jorge smiled apologetically as Stuart took the drink from Phyl and tried it. "Wow, that packs a punch! If I finish this, I will miss a month of Christmases!"

Phyl shushed him, then suddenly sat up straight. "What day is it?" she asked, worried.

"It's November 25. A month to Christmas," said Angelica.

"My brother will marry my best friend in a month." She sadly sat back and sighed. "And I'm not going to be there." Her bottom lip trembled as she retrieved a handkerchief from her sequined evening purse. She suddenly felt so terribly miserable. She grabbed back her drink from Stuart and sipped again, hoping that the alcohol would dampen the pain in her heart. It didn't do the trick. She took a deep breath, held up the glass and, as Stuart reached out to stop her, she downed the drink.

She gasped. Then choked as she watched the woman choose a man in a tuxedo and led him up to the stage. His head remained covered as he was positioned on the chair. So far, it looked quite innocent. Phyl relaxed a little. "Well," she gurgled. "No one's naked, that's a plus. This can't be so bad."

As she reached over for Stuart's hand and sat back in her chair a little more relaxed, the two women suddenly allowed their togas to slip off their shoulders to their feet. They kicked the togas away and stood threateningly on each side of the gentleman. There was a twitter amongst the patrons. Phyl almost choked.

"Oh my God, Stuart, they're buck naked. Don't look!"

Stuart, wide-eyed and riveted to the scene, mumbled, "Too late."

Chapter Five

Phyl Rebels and They Get Their Apartment and Maid

Phyl sucked at an ice chunk while she hung over the stone window sill, watching the people and traffic below. It was still early, so rush hour hadn't finished yet, and she enjoyed watching poor pedestrians dodging speeding cars as they tried to cross. Five wide streets intersected at their corner, which was quite a show. Here, traffic lights towered above the intersection, but they had been hanging there for years and never turned on. Despite the chaos, there were surprisingly few accidents. The odd cute little bus would go by. These were called *collectivo*, smaller than the other buses, and only held about ten people. But a person had to dash and jump on board as they never fully stopped. Horns blew at the slightest provocations when people scattered from the sidewalks to catch them. Phyl decided she would never attempt to ride one of them, though they were by far cheaper to ride.

The day before, on a Sunday, she and Stuart had taken a regular bus to the waterfront, where they discovered it felt uncannily similar to Toronto. Many establishments were open, unlike Toronto, with a few stores closed almost apologetically. She was also delighted to find that in this area all street corners were bedecked with mounds of every flower under the sun for sale.

She turned from the window and looked at the card table and folding chairs in their dining room. Claude Jr. and El had bought the set for them as a wedding gift, and they had taken it along, expecting not to be able to buy furniture for a while. Flowers would look nice in the middle of that little table, she thought. She made a face and looked out again. If only she could just nip out and get some. She sighed as she continued looking at the busy streets below.

She loved studying people's clothing and noticed how well-dressed everyone was. She found that clothing in Buenos Aires was expensive, but a badly dressed person was an exception. Even in the working-class neighborhood, which they had passed by streetcar, there wasn't a single person who did not dress with dignity and flair. Because it was summer, most of the men wore light fawn and white summer waistcoats and linens but Stuart's were either all dark and heavy, or white cotton, so they had gone shopping for him the week before. Now he looked like a true local when he left that morning for work.

She raised her eyes and looked over the park toward Jorge and Angelica's place about a mile away. In between, people congregated in the extensive grassed areas from one end to the other. She heard a tango from somewhere and remembered seeing people dancing to it on a working-class street during their outing. A woman was singing a Spanish song, but she couldn't locate her. Phyl looked under the trees. She had learned that the funny fat tree in the park blossomed into white, pink, and red blossoms every December. They were called 'The Drunken Stick' because the trunk looked like a giant beer barrel. Then there was the Jacaranda tree, which she read was new to Buenos Aires. When she and Stuart arrived the month before, the Jacaranda trees were brilliantly in bloom with masses of tiny purple flowers, giving the town a distinct and mesmerizing smell. But those were gone now. There were other exotic-looking trees with flowers she hadn't learned about yet. Then there were the palms here and there - her all-time favorite. The sight of them reminded her of the passion behind her dreams a lifetime ago.

Dreams. Phyl sighed. She never would have imagined that she'd be a prisoner in her dreams.

She stood and looked at their clock on a crate in the corner of the empty living room. It was only nine in the morning. Stuart had left for work in his Panama hat and white waistcoat at 8:00. The office was four blocks away downtown. He wasn't expected back for lunch until 12:30. There was no use in starting his lunch now. There was no room in the ice box to put a prepared plate. She had, literally, nothing to do. She looked at her watch and made a face. Watch, clock, watch, clock. Tabletop.

She went to the front door, opened the three locks, and looked out into the cool hallway. She heard a woman's voice speaking in Spanish at one end. Down the other end, she heard a child speak French. She went back into the apartment and locked the door three times. A young woman was coming to be interviewed for the maid position sometime after *siesta*. Phyl walked to one of the two spare bedrooms. This was going to be the maid's room. Angelica had given them old furniture from one of their maids' rooms and it looked cozy, with a small window overlooking the side of their building. The maid would still have a nice view of the park.

The room between it and the master bedroom, was designated as Stuart's office, though there was just a crate for books, and a cane chair they had retrieved after someone discarded it on the street.

She looked at her watch again. She already knew what she was going to wear that night. They were to celebrate Christmas Eve with a client, a gentleman from Chile whose name was Knause. She knew he spoke English, but his wife didn't, so she wasn't looking forward to it at all. Stuart said the wife was Basque and blonde like Angelica, and he warned her that Knause didn't have a high regard for North Americans. Which might make the evening even worse. So, Phyl was determined to wow them. She hoped they'd play cards so there would be very little talking and much winning by her. Phyl was quite a card shark. And she'd try to mesmerize them with her personality and smile and maybe the guy might buy, buy, buy from Stuart. Stuart had made no sales as yet but a few possibilities were in development. But she knew, already, that gesticulating and attempts to communicate was going to be tiring.

Oh, well, anything for business. But some Christmas Eve.

She imagined El getting ready for her wedding. Thankfully, Phyl would be distracted, as they were invited to spend *La Navidad*, as they said in Spanish, at the Piñiero's beautiful place. Phyl would've felt absolutely depressed if they had to be alone and left to do nothing but think about Claude Jr. and El and the wedding six thousand miles away. Her heart quickened. They should send a telegram! Why hadn't she thought of that earlier? She desperately hoped they'd have time after Stuart came home from work to do so. But what if the telegram office was closed early for Christmas Eve? She started to fret.

Phyl stepped to the glass doors leading onto their tiled balcony. There were no balconies overhead, as they were at the very top of the building seven floors up. This way, they enjoyed direct sunlight the whole day, with a beautiful view of the park and, to the right, the harbor and the distant shoreline. Jorge and Angelica had given them a double seat swing and two canvas chairs. This was where she and Stuart spent their evenings and had their morning coffees. She stood at the railing and looked down, and then at the people again walking along the boulevard and park. She searched to see how many women walked alone. She saw servants and maids rushing to the market or home. Some were out with children in tow. But no *señoras* or *señoritas*.

She sniffed joylessly the smells of car exhaust, horse manure, urine, and sweet flowers. The sun felt nice, which made her feel a little better. She closed her eyes and listened to the noise of the city.

Flowers. Telegram.

"The heck with it," she muttered. She would send the telegram and buy flowers for herself and her hosts. Angelica had told her three vases full were only one *peso* –30 cents. How could she resist *that*?

She left the balcony doors open as she stepped back inside and grabbed her keys, gloves, and bag. She unlocked the door and walked out, locking it behind her.

She hesitated in the hallway. How strange that after just a couple of weeks of house arrest – as there was no one to accompany her anywhere while Stuart worked or while Angelica was busy – she was already programmed to be frightened of going out alone. "How silly." She forced herself to the elevator and pushed the button. She waited fretfully. She pressed her ear against the cool brass and heard a moaning windlike sound but no mechanical movement of any kind. She banged at the brass doors. In ricochet fashion, she pushed the button a dozen times in a row. She considered going back into the apartment. "No, I'm going out." She walked to the stairwell leading down the seven floors.

Her heels clipped and clopped as the stairwell spiraled downward, the skylight at the top showering her with brilliant light. The stairs were very well-kept and clean, and she was pretty happy being in this building. It was still all very new. She hadn't started Spanish lessons yet – they were scheduled for the New Year - so even holding a short conversation with the doorman was a chore. As she descended the stairs, Phyl referred to her well-used Spanish language dictionary and whispered to herself. "*Buenos dias, Matteo. Como estas hoy?* How are you? How are you? *Como estas hoy.*"

She reached the bottom floor and stepped past brass mail slots and walked to the front marble counter where the doorman, Matteo, sat at his post, wearing a Panama shirt and a bigger smile. He nodded as he stood up, grinning, and started walking to the door to open it for her, but when he saw no one was following her down the stairs, his smile vanished. His eyes widened as she approached. She put her gloves on as she stopped, then she adjusted her shoe. She would've worn flats if she had known the elevator wasn't working. She took a breath and smiled. "*Buenos dias, Matteo. Como…?*"

Matteo nervoudly spoke at a fast clip, and she was lost entirely. He pointed at her, up the stairs, outside, shaking his head.

"Um, I'm sorry, *no español*," she laughed. "I'm going for a walk. For flowers and telegram."

Matteo put up his hands and shook his head. He said something about a taxi.

"No, no, I don't want a taxi." Phyl pointed to herself and then made her fingers walk through the air. "I go for a walk." She smiled and walked through the door, not waiting for him to open it, which was his job. She could hear him lament, "*Ayayayay.*"

She pushed forward. She turned to the right to walk to the closest corner where she was determined to cross with anyone going the same way. Strength in numbers against predator drivers. As she reached the corner, a car pulled to the side and stopped. At first, she thought someone was stopping to let her and a nanny with four children cross safely. Instead, a fifty-year-old man jumped out and motioned to her. "*Que linda,*" he said. He jabbered familiarly at her. He pointed to her figure and made a lovely flowing motion. He pointed at her breasts and made a sign saying they were perfect. She gasped and looked around. Her heart pounded against her chest, which she promptly covered with her hands. She saw the maid cast a piercing look at her as she hustled the four children, all dressed alike, to the other side.

The man motioned for Phyl to get into the car. She tried to cross the street after the nanny and children, but he got in the car and moved forward to block her. She banged at the hood with her fist.

"Nuts to you, *Señor*," she blurted as she hurried after the nanny. She reached the other curb, as a younger man in a Boater hat was about to pass her. But he stopped and stared at her as if he was undressing her. She moved on and passed him, blushing, and yet another man in a Khaki hat, slightly older, looked her up and down and stared at her as she hurried passed *him*. She sensed him stopping to take in her behind. By this time, the nanny had led the children off the sidewalk and into the park, so Phyl had to keep going on her own, and she passed two other gentlemen, both wearing Panama hats. They stopped talking to each other and stared and studied her as she passed between them. She heard them turn to follow her. She looked back. They smiled, nodded, and spoke to her in voices that made her feel dirty. She remembered a saying Angelica had taught her. She turned. "*Vaya!*" she yelled. They continued talking to her and following. She stopped and put her hands up. "*No hablo Español!*" she said. "*Vaya!*"

"*Parlez vous Français?*" asked one of them.

"No, no parlez Français! Vaya. Leave me alone!"

Her futile attempt at discouraging the termites only heightened their enjoyment of the chase. They hurried closer, and she scampered backward and almost tripped. She finally yelled, "Scram!"

"Oooo," said one, feigning fear, "Yoo American." He laughed at her.

"I'll tell my husband! *Mio* husband!" She took off her left glove and showed her rings. "*Señora!*"

The other man held his friend's arm and motioned with his head to go. The first blew her a kiss and followed his friend back in the direction they were initially heading. No doubt in search of more prey.

Phyl watched their backs retreat, then looked in the direction she needed to go. There were men everywhere. Groups of maids with children here and there. But men. *Everywhere*. She was close to tears. She turned to the curb, and, reprimanded by blaring horns, she raced across toward her building.

* * *

Phyl couldn't help herself. As Stuart walked through the door, she ran to him and cried.

Stuart was shocked. He gently led her to the card table, looked at the folding chairs, and stepped further to the balcony. He sat on the swing chair with her and maneuvered her onto his lap to cradle her.

"Talk to me. What happened this morning?"

"Oh, Stu. You'll be upset with me."

"No, I won't. I can't possibly think why I should." His face dropped. "On second thought, what on earth could you have possibly done since I left this morning?"

Phyl faced him but couldn't look at him. "I thought Jorge and Angelica exaggerated. I wanted to send a telegram to Claude and El for their wedding, and flowers for tonight." She blew her nose.

"I thought Angelica was busy."

She looked at him wide-eyed. "I went out on my own."

"What?"

"And they were right." She pointed toward the park. "I didn't even get across the street, and a man stopped his car and accosted me. He pointed at my *breasts*. I think he said I had a beautiful body! Then other men undressed me, Stu. They undressed me with their eyes. I felt as if I was naked. I felt dirty, used, insulted, and absolutely imposed upon in a very upsettingly lewd way."

"We were warned, Phyl. They're sex crazed here. They are blatantly whacky over sex. Even at the office, the guys talk so – well, let's just say I could never talk about women in such a low way." He took her hand. "You shouldn't have done that, Phyl. You could've gotten hurt."

"I know, but I didn't believe it. Now I know how that young woman felt. Now I know she had no choice. These men are so forceful. I can only imagine how frightened she must have been."

"What did you do?"

"I told them to scram. I said, *vaya* like Angelica told me. Two men simply wouldn't leave me alone until they saw my rings, and when I said, *Señora*." She held up her hand. She pointed to her rings. "These saved me. Barely. In broad daylight, Stu."

Stuart stood up and looked over the rail at the park. He seemed to be searching for something.

"What are you looking for? Those men are long gone."

"I'm looking for your Christmas present."

"Christmas present?"

Stuart kept an arm protectively around Phyl as he led her through traffic to the park. He marched along the sidewalk, sternly eyed the men they passed, and silently dared them to say something about his beautiful young wife. Some purposely averted his gaze, others looked at him wide-eyed. They knew.

Finally, Stuart took Phyl to a man under a tree with a box and a little sign in Spanish. In the box were three puppies, squirming, playing, licking their paws or each other. He pulled out *pesos* and held them out. The man looked at him and then Phyl. He took the *pesos* and motioned to the box.

Phyl looked into the box and saw puppies of a mixed breed.

"Choose one, Phyl. You should have protection. And if you insist on leaving the flat alone, you have a guard dog with you. I'll make sure we train it well. So, choose."

Phyl chose one with a little cream to its forehead, cream-colored forepaws and golden curls. She picked it up gently, looked to see what sex it was, and cradled it, burying her face into its little neck. She cooed and giggled as Stuart took her elbow and directed her back the way they came.

Phyl rolled up a piece of newspaper and threw it as a ball for the puppy to chase after. She grabbed the puppy to give it yet another hug, cuddle and kiss, and then let it go. Stuart sat at the card table, eating his salad, hard-boiled eggs, and soup, watching.

"I'll call him Tony Junior." She looked up at Stuart from the floor. "TJ for short."

Stuart took another bite. "That sounds great. 'Make you feel even more at home."

"How much longer do you have to work today, seeing that it's Christmas Eve? "

Stuart looked at his watch. "Let's see, back at work at 2:00, but off at 5:00 instead of 7:00."

"Will the telegram office be open after 5:00?"

"I'll slip out of the office this afternoon and send it. It's just around the corner."

Phyl got up off the floor, threw the paper ball again, and sat on one of the chairs. "I'm so confused. Sometimes I think it's beautiful here. I look out at the park and over the water and am so grateful. And then this happens, again." She waved toward the balcony doors.

"Again?" Stuart put his knife and fork onto his plate and the empty soup bowl on top.

"I was just as shocked at that cabaret. I can't get that whole evening out of my mind. And those naked women? It was all so silly, really, but so crude. It really disturbed me. I've never seen a fully naked woman. I don't even see myself fully naked."

Stuart stared at her for a moment. "You know, now that you mention it, neither have I."

Phyl looked at Stuart. She blinked.

He raised his eyebrows and slanted his head. He slowly got out of his chair.

Phyl stiffened up. She put up her hand. "Oh, no. What are you doing?"

"We're sex crazed, remember, us men?"

"Oh, Stu, no, you're not," she laughed nervously.

He came towards her. "Oh, no? Maybe it's in the food," he pointed at the dishes. "Maybe it's in the water or the air we breathe, and it makes men sex fiends."

Phyl giggled. She moved slightly to the other side of the table. "Oh, no, you're not. Stop, Stu."

He widened his eyes and put his hands up. "Stop what, *Señora?* I'm not allowed to see my own wife completely naked but I'm allowed to see a stranger in her birthday suit?"

Phyl laughed, held up her hand, and pointed to her rings. "Stay back, I'm armed!"

Stuart growled, "That means you are MINE!" He jumped after her, but she left screaming and laughing into their bedroom. TJ growled like a little engine and hopped after them. Phyl's screams and laughter echoed through the flat.

Someone knocked at the door.

Phyl kept screaming. "Oh, my God. Let me outta here!"

The door opened suddenly, and a woman stood looking frightened. Wide-eyed, she looked all around, ready to help. She stepped into the apartment, clutching her bag. She looked back in the hallway and held her hand to her mouth, unsure what to do. "*Ayayayay,*" she mumbled.

Phyl, laughing, ran back into the dining and living room half undressed, Stuart, topless, chasing her, and TJ chasing the both of them. Phyl and Stuart saw the young woman and they all screamed.

* * *

"So, did you interview the new maid?"

Phyl made a comical face at Angelica. They had just had their Christmas lunch, watching the twins play with their red balls with white polka dots they received for *Navidad*. "I think we frightened her away. We didn't even get to interview her. She came, and she went."

Angelica tipped her head. "Hmm. Curious. Maybe she was afraid of the puppy."

"Maybe," Phyl lied.

"Well, one of my servants has a sister-in-law in Uruguay whose mother died, and she is looking for a position. Her name is Carmen."

"That would be great." Phyl caught the ball one of the toddlers tossed up at her. She bent down and rolled the ball back to the toddler. The toddler picked up the ball and started licking it.

"I'll arrange for her to come next Wednesday. You can meet her and see what you think. One shouldn't be caught doing one's own wash or floors, Phyllis. It just wouldn't do." Angelica had a habit of pronouncing Phyl's name as "Feelees." "And the shopping should be done by the maid, too."

Phyl sat quietly pondering a maid in her life. She never dreamed she would ever have one.

"And the cooking and mending. And the beds."

"What do I do, then? I can't just sit all day and do nothing."

"You join clubs, play Bridge, shop with me or other friends. You do lunch with other women." She leaned forward and put a hand on Phyl's knee. "But always, always take a taxi when you are alone."

"It means another expense," argued Phyl.

"Your life and dignity are well worth the *pesos*. Converted to American, it costs next to nothing."

Phyl frowned. "So, why wouldn't a taxi driver accost or kidnap me when I'm alone with him?"

"You are paying them for a service. They may look and perhaps say one or two things, but you must treat them like dogs. Do not show kindness." Angelica sat back, pleased with herself for being such a good advisor. "It really is very cheap compared to other cities."

"Oh, my gosh. Stuart and I went shopping the other day. I couldn't believe how cheap shoes, milk, and bread were. But clothing is so high." Phyl took a sip from her champagne and orange juice. "I get confused because milk is sold by the liter, material by the meter, the temperature is in centigrade, and I have the darndest time getting cream for our coffee. When I ask for *crema*, I get sour cream. When I say *fresca*, it's still sour stuff. I could only find real coffee cream in the English department store."

Angelica laughed. "The English department store is a good standby, as you say in English."

"Thank goodness it's there," laughed Phyl. "But other things are so expensive. We sent a telegram yesterday to my brother and new sister-in-law and we paid 12 American dollars for every three words!" She looked at her watch. "Well, she'll be my sister-in-law in an hour."

"Oh, yes. Telegrams are expensive. But prices do go up during holidays."

"No! For Christmas? That's extortion."

"It's business," Angelica said with a shrug. "By the way, how is Stuart doing with his own business contacts?"

Phyl shook her head. "Remington Rand isn't doing too well. Stuart thinks it's very poorly managed. He was appalled to find out you can't do anything without kickbacks. His boss expects him to add kickbacks in the quotes but Stuart wants to make a good impression being the honest American."

"Unfortunately, that's the way it is. I wish him luck in figuring out how to do business and still keep his dignity intact." Angelica looked around for a servant when she noticed one of her twins needed his nose wiped. "That's one of our problems. Business would do so much better if only those who work in it do their best. Good workers are hard to find."

A servant caught Angelica's beckoning. Angelica motioned to one of her toddlers. Then she smiled and made kissing sounds at him while she watched the servant wipe his nose.

"I think it's the heat or men's brains. Too much sex and play. How do you do work when you have two mistresses on the side and a wife and family at home?" She shook her head. "I do not know. Jorge thinks men are just not diligent enough in business. He believes that is one of Argentina's problems and it gets in the way of Argentina becoming an international player in world trade." The toddler, his nose now cleaned, shuffled to his mother. He sneezed as he slammed his red ball onto his mother's lap. The little boy's nose ran again, and this time, Angelica took out her own handkerchief and wiped his nose.

Phyl looked away. Germs. She had been washing her hands consistently since they lived in a world with not enough hygiene and tainted by zillions of germs. She had read in the English newspaper that sickness was rampant, especially sexually transmitted diseases. There were many reasons: the culture, poverty, and the many refugees from other parts of the world who came into the city weakened by their travails and rough ocean voyages. Immigrants were scanned for sicknesses when they arrived, especially for TB, but with such a lack of workers' diligence and leanings to bribery, plus the lack of hygiene throughout the city - public washrooms were filthy, and streets were constantly urinated and defecated on - there were at least 52 TB deaths in the city per day.

She had lost an uncle to tuberculosis in Toronto, and, of course, her own mother died of the Spanish Flu. Phyl was deathly afraid she and Stuart would get sick and possibly die. She wasn't at all looking forward to the coming winter season which started around March. She had recently read that winters were killers for people with compromised health. The rains apparently didn't let up once started and, as a consequence of that and poor air circulation, there was chronic mold and lung problems. She remembered the smell and the wet walls in the pension their first night in the city.

She stood up. "Excuse me. I'm going to wash my hands. I'll be right back."

Phyl went to the guest bathroom and heard Stuart and Jorge's voices. The phone rang, and she heard one of the servants answer it. Phyl washed her hands rigorously, then thought she'd check on the men.

She followed Jorge's voice talking on the telephone. Then, it sounded like he hung up, and he and Stuart spoke again. Stuart's voice had a tone of earnestness though Jorge's was very low. She finally found them in one of the corners of the vast patio outside of one of the guestrooms. Jorge and Stuart sat in canvas chairs smoking cigars, brass phone on a long cord resting on Jorge's lap.

"Hi, fellas," she smiled. She grabbed a chair and sat down. Stuart reached over to touch her hand.

"You, okay?" he asked.

Phyl looked at her hands. "Yes, I just washed my hands. What are you two up to?" She looked at Jorge, who was frowning and put the phone on the floor at his feet. "Everything alright?"

"Jorge just got some terrible news," Stuart said, leaning on his elbows.

"Oh no, what happened?"

Jorge sat back and squinted at the sky. "I just heard from my brother. Our vineyard in Rio Negro burned to the ground last night. Bad timing. Our fruit crops also did very badly this year. We don't have enough insurance to cover full damages for it all. The year, unfortunately, is ending on a bad note for us."

"Oh, my God, Jorge, I'm so sorry to hear that." Phyl covered her mouth. "What a terrible thing to have happened. Anyone hurt?"

"No, thank God, no one was hurt. The buildings and machinery were ruined, but the wine was still intact. We still have product to sell, fortunately. But the crops…" He shook his head.

"How much will that set you back, do you think? The damage by the fire, I mean," asked Stuart. He had gotten quite tanned and more freckled. It made him appear endearing. Jorge looked at him fondly.

"Over two hundred thousand *pesos*."

"Oh my."

"It's quite a setback." Jorge looked at his cigar as he twirled it between his fingers.

"How did it start?" asked Phyl.

Jorge jutted his chiseled chin, his thick eyebrows tightly knitted. "It had been purposely set."

Phyl gasped. She looked at Stuart.

"We are sensing deep unrest again." Jorge peered at his cigar. "An election is coming up."

"Who would do such a thing?" asked Stuart.

"There are Italian immigrants around our *estancia* and vineyard. Now, don't get me wrong. Many are very hard-working and came to this country with skills we desperately need. However, they tend to be members of the *Conservadores*. There are indications they want a revolution."

Jorge tapped his cigar onto a brass ashtray on a side marble column used as a tabletop. "As you know, there's always trouble when it comes to elections. One party will tell voters who already support another party that they have no vote or rights, that they were lied to, or if they insist on voting, they are threatened with violence. The system has many issues caused by those who manipulate the voters. These radicals think Mussolini is, as you say, the last word. It all leaves me with a bad taste in my mouth."

Stuart shifted in his seat and crossed his legs. "I noticed quite a congregation of men outside the newspaper offices yesterday morning and heard them talking a mile a minute. They can get so darn hot under the collar. They remind me of a pot of milk about to boil over," Stuart said as he now studied the end of his cigar. Its embers had died, and he leaned over to retrieve the gold lighter Jorge was holding out for him. "I guess you don't expect much trouble here at your end of the city, but I should think they may pick the parks to cause trouble. At least, from what the guys are saying at the office."

"Oh, dear," mumbled Phyl. "That close?"

"The worst trouble is usually out in the provinces," said Jorge.

"Ergo," motioned Stuart toward Jorge. "Your crops and vineyards."

Jorge slowly, ponderously, nodded.

"You still want me to come and visit?" Phyl felt queasy at the thought of staying at the *estancia*.

Jorge shifted in his seat and sat up straight. "Oh, there is absolutely no problem with the *estancia*. You'll be safe. We have quite a staff running the home and grounds. The cattle are well looked after and managed, and so are the *estancia* orchards. No," he said, shaking his head. "If our own *estancia*, our ancestral home, becomes unsafe, then our country truly is doomed."

Georgie, Jorge's son, ran onto the balcony, his feet outgrowing him in every other way, flapping against the stone porch floor as he ran toward his father. "Papa, Papa. Can we go to the zoo today?"

"It's *Navidad* and closed, remember? But tomorrow we can go, if your Mama agrees."

Georgie looked unhappy and impatiently kicked Phyl's chair. Phyl turned back to look at him. The boy's eyes widened, and he looked away.

"Son, do not be impertinent. Be a good man. Now apologize to *Señora de Redington*."

Georgie rocked on his feet, then in a thin voice, said, "Pardon me, *Señora de Redington*. I did not mean to kick your chair." He held out his hand to shake.

"Women do not shake hands. You take it and kiss the back of it. Remember how I showed you?" Jorge squinted at his son.

Georgie bowed and held out his hand. Phyl slowly held out hers. He kissed the back of her hand and let it go. He bent one more time and then skipped off.

Phyl looked at her hand and considered rewashing it. She smiled at Jorge. "Charming."

"There's a zoo nearby?" asked Stuart.

Jorge crossed his legs, leaned sideways, and settled on one elbow on the arm of the chair. He motioned over the railing. "We have a couple. One in Buenos Aires province, and the closest is at the furthest end of the park. We walk there easily."

Phyl looked at Stuart. "Oh, Stuart, Dad would get a kick out of photos of the zoo. We should go!"

"Do a lot of people go there?" asked Stuart.

Jorge inhaled deeply. "Why yes. Sometimes you can't get in; it's so busy."

"A good spot to disappear into, I would imagine."

Jorge looked at his nails and blinked at Phyl. Stuart looked at her as well. They locked eyes.

"What?" asked Phyl.

Stuart shook his head. "Phyl would have to come along to make it real."

"Make what real?" she asked.

"We're figuring out a safe place to meet with contacts." He turned to Jorge. "You said you could invite American Embassy attachés and their wives to the *estancia* openly? 'Befriend them?'"

Jorge nodded.

"That would help my own mandate," Stuart said.

Jorge grimly nodded again. "Understood."

"May I ask why you need to do all that?" Phyl looked at Jorge. "Or shouldn't I ask?"

"Okay, this is pretty dry and long as an explanation, but bear with me. Here's an example: Ambassador Weddell reported to the Secretary of State that he was communicating with the Argentine Ministry of Finance to establish the cause of a discrepancy found between what Argentine records show as exports to the United States compared to numbers declared to the American Consulate General in Buenos Aires. Argentine numbers show a lesser value than the returns declared by us."

"Oops, that means a couple of things, right?"

Stuart turned to Jorge. "See, I told you she was astute."

"You mean for a lowly woman?" Phyl jested, before Jorge could answer.

"No, you are an astute human being." Stuart pointed to her and looked at Jorge proudly. "And she is my wife." He pointed to himself, grinning.

"Yes, Stuart, I keep saying you are a fortunate man," Jorge nodded.

"Yes, anyway, you are correct. Either Argentine staff are not doing their jobs diligently, or someone is skimming money off the top and hiding it on the Argentine side."

"How are you sure the Americans aren't wrong with their numbers?"

"A valid point. But there's nothing to gain by doing that." Stuart looked at Jorge, then Phyl. "The point is, there are Fifth Column Nazi activities being funded by unknown groups and individuals. In the case of the German schools, the Americans and the Justo administration can't figure out where the money comes from. There's no evidence that it's coming from private sources or from Berlin. We know Hitler's not prioritizing Nazi activities in Argentina right now. He's focusing on his own economy. Selling machinery, armaments, and strengthening his home base. So, it's not in his mandate. But there are at least 150,000 passionate Argentine Germans, almost all of them members of the Nazi party, and they're busy."

Phyl wondered how he knew this. "So, you think someone is skimming to finance the Nazis?"

Stuart grinned again at Jorge and silently, proudly, motioned to her with both hands.

Jorge smiled, tipped his head at Phyl, admiringly. "Yes, it's possible that a Nazi sympathizing Minister – of which there are a few – is skimming funds for Nazi ideology purposes," he said quietly.

Phyl eyed the two men, who were now deep in thought. "So, why the zoo again?"

Stuart eyed Jorge questioningly. "Can I tell her a little more?"

Jorge nodded, closing his eyes for a moment with restrained weight. He smiled gently at Phyl.

"Secret meetings. They asked me to be a conduit for information I gather through meetings and discreetly pass it on. I'm nurturing a potential contract with the Ministry of Finance and they've asked me to check with them if I hear of information that may be helpful." Stuart shrugged slightly.

"That's spying, Stu," Phyl said, her voice cracking. The reality was starting to dawn on her.

"On behalf of both governments, Phyl. Both sides want to know what's going on. The Argentines want to know what officials are upsetting the apple cart. They certainly don't want us to be enemies."

That made sense to Phyl. She realized, then, there were potentially many visits for her to the zoo, whether she liked it or not. But, again, with her father, a zoo keeper, it fit into their *story*. "I could say it's because my Dad is a zoo keeper and I want to go and take photos for him. It's the most natural thing."

"Absolutely correct."

"Just call me Mata Hari," smiled Phyl.

"Actually, I could." He turned to Jorge and leaned closer. "Phyl did a dance for me in mid-attire yesterday, and the maid she had to interview came early and caught us in the act. She ran away screaming," Stuart laughed.

"A dance in mid-attire?" asked Jorge, forcing back a grin. "Now burned in my brain."

"Oh, Stu!" Phyl, flustered and shocked, slapped Stuart's knee and then waved Jorge away before covering her face in embarrassment. "Yes, well, oh dear," she mumbled. "Let's not think about *that*!"

* * *

A month and a half later, with city in a happy and vulgar Carnival uproar, Stuart raised his pen and looked at the letter he had begun to Claude Sr. Phyl had been pestering him to write for a change, as every time they received a reply from her family to her long, detailed notes, they had written asking to hear from Stuart. Having known all along, their letters were probably being spied upon, Stuart thought he would kill two birds with one stone. He would write as a son-in-law but also establish the zoo as a part of their lives. And seeing they were in the middle of Carnival holidays and work had ground to a stop, he had much time on his hands to fill. He wrote to his zookeeper father-in-law:

> Dear Jack,
>
> Phyl says it's damn time I called you something besides "Mr. May" and that you would shoot me if I ever called you "Claude" – so let me know if the above moniker suits you.

Phyl passed from the bedroom with laundry in her arms and disappeared into the kitchen. She and Carmen started to talk together. Phyl in English and Carmen in rapid Spanish. He continued.

> We have been out to the Zoo and tried to get some pictures to send you – I finished the roll today and will mail when they are developed. Didn't have much luck as we waited hours to get a shot at the Big Bull Hippo, which is the most tremendous animal we've ever seen outside of an elephant – its head looks the size of our front door.

> They keep him in a stone dungeon with three big iron bars across the entrance. They also have a wonderful collection of sea-lions – they live off the coast four hundred miles from here, so I guess it's easy to keep them – three little tiny ones make an awful racket.
>
> There is a cross between a kangaroo and a rabbit, and together, with all kinds of animals and birds, they are at liberty to roam around the grass, paths, etc. In their native state, they make for great hunting – I know a Belgian woodworker who would rather hunt than eat – he tells me they hunt them at night because they only come out with the moon. They burrow and live underground. If the first shot doesn't finish them, the little devils go for you – they have four large incisor teeth. And these teeth are strong enough to go through leather and boots. Others of the family attack if one is wounded, so this fellow says it's quite a thrill waiting in the moonlight for one to pop up and not knowing how close beside you the others are. They carry a heavy wooden club so as to finish them off.

Stuart coughed into his hand, then reached for a cigarette, lit it, and rested it on a filled ashtray. He waved at smoke and continued to write, half hearing the Carnival music and drunken mayhem outside. Phyl left the kitchen to go out onto the balcony to observe the orgiastic festivities.

> Another thing they hunt here is a native duck, which flies about 100 yards overhead but is curious and swoops lower when it sees something. The hunters dig trenches, lie in wait, wave something to attract them, and then let them have it. You can't reload fast enough to get all you want – this Belgian and a friend bagged 230 of them in three days.

Stuart leaned back and felt satisfied that any snoop reading this would've fallen asleep by now.

> The fishing is not what you'd like – no small game fish except on a few estates (estancias). They imported the game trout, bass, etc., and they didn't thrive any too well, probably because the owners didn't have anything else to do but hunt and fish. The Argentines think we're crazy to fish the way we do – they can't see the sport and don't understand why we give a damn fool fish a chance to get away, using a silly little silk line, a hook about the size of a hairpin and a flexible rod. When they fish in the river, at the Anglers' Club, or at Mar del Plata on the sea, they use long stiff poles, long clotheslines, and formidable hooks. Also, nets, lights at night. They have all kinds

and sizes of fish. Shellfish, snails, shrimp, catfish, trout, everything in all shapes and sizes. The sport is to get the biggest one you can – a lady we know landed one weighing ninety pounds – they drop the pole after setting the hooks and yank them in by pulling the rope line. Then their partner shoots, stabs, or batters the fish to death – must try it sometime when I get enough money to go. No fishing or hunting around the city except at the Angler's Club - $1,000 (Arg) membership fee. The hunting is about 300 miles inland. Argentines get a laugh out of our artificial bait for fish and decoys for birds – they say our game must be half-starved. They just use a hunk of raw beef or pork for fish.

He stopped, crushed his cigarette, and heard gunshots. People screamed. He heard Phyl say, "Oh for goodness sake." He continued.

Carnival started yesterday – lasts till Tuesday night –they just go crazy – all offices are closed till Wednesday – most stores except the market, which is open Tuesday – and they raise hell – they let off steam because Lent starts right after. It's not safe to go out, especially for foreigners, because anything goes, and the cops look the other way. Well, Jack, write Phyl and me soon. We both feel better since we are settled in our own place, and if we had some furniture, everything would be fine. We miss you all badly.

Best Stu.

PS. We're both losing damn weight because the elevator has been out for a month and a half and we live on the seventh floor. The view still makes it worth the head ache.

"There," Stuart said to himself, "that will do quite nicely."
"What will?" asked Phyl.

She came back from the kitchen where she was instructing Carmen on how she wanted her to wash her dress. The previous sundress had been ruined, and Carmen almost had a heart attack.

"My letter to your father."
"Oh, may I read it?"

He picked it up and held it high in the air. Phyl tried to snatch it.
"Give me!" she laughed.
"Nope, not until I get a peck right here," he said, pointing at his cheek.
"Oh, silly." She stood on her tiptoes and kissed him.

He handed her the letter and sat by as she read it. Carmen started singing a Spanish lullaby in the kitchen, and they heard the tap run, then squeak off, and run again. They listened to the gas stove being turned on; a kettle clunked onto it. Stuart leaned toward Phyl and whispered. "What's she doing in there? I've never heard anyone be so happy about doing the wash."

"She thought I was going to fire her. So, she's relieved I didn't. I bet she's making us coffee without us asking. She's buttering us up, I think."

"I guess she really needs the job, huh?"

"Uh-huh." Phyl finished the letter and nodded. "Dad will like this. But you forgot to mention we save lots of *pesos* on toilet paper because we now have this extremity bath thing called a bidet."

"It escaped my mind altogether." He pointed at the letter. "Good cover-up, huh, using the zoo?"

Phyl looked back at the kitchen as they heard the kettle whistle and subside as it was removed from heat. Phyl nodded. "Great. Couldn't be better, I don't think."

Stuart held up a finger. "By the way, I haven't given you a Carnival gift yet."

Phyl closed her eyes and held out her hands. Since Stuart received all mail at the office, he had Phyl in his power. Each time she knew the mail boat arrived from New York, she would ask him the first minute he got in if there was any mail. If there wasn't, she felt very low. However, if there was, he would produce it with a great flourish, like Leslie Howard doing Shakespeare. Sometimes, when there were several for Phyl, he'd hold some back. If there were three letters, he might give her one each day so that Phyl would have three 'Christmas' presents in a row.

"Wait here," Stuart said. He disappeared into his office and returned with the third delivery. With a flourish, and, yes, just like Leslie Howard, he drew out a letter and letter opener and bowed.

Phyl clapped her hands, took both letter and opener and sliced the top. She took out what looked like a Valentine's Day card with a letter inside. Two photographs fell onto the table. She gasped.

"What is it?" asked Stuart, sitting back down. He looked up as Carmen came in carrying a tray with a coffee pot, cups, saucers, sugar, and *crema*. "Oh, goody. Caffeine. *Gracias, Carmen.*"

Phyl held up one of the photos to Carmen, who shyly took it, smiled, and nodded. "*Linda.*"

"Yes, she's very pretty. That's my best friend," Phyl shouted.

Stuart smiled at her. "Silly, you don't have to shout. It's not that she's deaf. She just can't understand English." Stuart held a finger to Carmen and translated as best he could in his rudimentary Spanish. He was far better than Phyl, as he had no choice but to pick it up quickly in business.

He said it right, because Carmen nodded. "Ah, *si*." Carmen bowed, grinning, and left.

Phyl handed the photos to Stuart. He studied them. One was of Claude Jr. and El, he with a Best Man, and she with a Matron of Honor. The other was of Jr., Sr, and the Groom. The men were in tuxedos.

"Doesn't Claude Jr. look positively handsome? And El looks so sweet."

"Who's the Best Man?"

"Oh, that's a cousin of ours, Thomas. He and his family have a cottage on Lake Scugog."

"I didn't meet him while we fished there."

Phyl took the photos back and gazed at El in her wedding gown. She saw the brown fur had been taken off and thought it was unfortunate as that was the most excellent touch of the entire dress. The neckline had been gathered a little tighter to create pleats. And El wore full-length, evening gloves. She had a little tiara of lace, probably cream, to match the dress. "She's not happy, Stu. That worries me."

"Well, she has a lot to get over, unfortunately."

She put the photo down. "It doesn't look like she's gotten there yet."

Stuart poured coffee and added cream to Phyl's. "Your Dad looks pretty shaven and dressed up."

Phyl stirred with a spoon. "He lost weight. And his hair is much shorter. He looks so small compared to Claude Jr. I think he's shrinking."

"He's getting older."

"It's been barely two and a half months. How could anyone age that quickly, silly?" asked Phyl.

Stuart ignored her. He stood up. "Ah heck, it's Carnival; I'll give you another present." Stuart went back to the office.

Phyl's mouth dropped. "What all are you holding *back* on me?" She complained as she bent over to watch him disappear into the near-empty room.

He returned with another package, held it up, and skipped to her like a little girl.

"You're such a goose," she laughed as she reached out. She felt the package, and smiled. "Our latest newspapers. Goody. Something to devour." She opened the package and took out the papers, carefully folded in threes. Out fell hose and a letter. "Oh, my Lord! Hose! Wonderful thin hose!"

"I don't know why you're so excited. I think your heavy Granny hose is quite becoming on you."

Phyl slapped Stuart with a newspaper. Then she opened the letter and read a bit. "It's from Dad."

"What's he saying?"

"He's asking where all the white folks are." She laughed. "What the heck?"

Stuart chuckled. "Your father is the only person I know who thinks to be white is to have thin, transparent, sickly-looking skin and ghastly pale blue eyes. I suspect, because I tan, I may not count."

"You weren't white from the start. You're American. That's worse."

"Ha ha ha. You know, it would never in a million years occur to me that he would think an Argentine wasn't like us. It's just a cultural and language difference. Hardly any difference in skin color."

Phyl tapped her temple. "But they're different thinking. Heat boils the brain. They're not like us."

"I know he thinks that. Well, tell him that the white *American* colony mostly lives in Belgrano," Stuart said, downing his coffee and requesting Phyl for more, holding the cup out.

Phyl poured him another cup. "Isn't that where we stayed at that awful pension hotel?"

"Yup,' said Stuart. "Tell him Minor, my boss, lives in the *English* colony in a suburb called Hurlingham where they have fancy clubs and riding stables, which takes money. He already knows about the cheap and fast English, electric trains, right?"

Phyl nodded and played with her spoon, tapping it against the cup. Stuart reached out and stopped the tapping. She bent one knee and tucked it under her other leg, showing skin above the top of her hose.

"Careful, you are showing skin above your oh-so-elegant, Granny hose."

Phyl grinned and jiggled her leg. She wiggled her eyebrows.

"I shall ignore that. Also, tell your Dad that WHITE PEOPLE live in apartments in the city as we do and, like US, they stay out of the downtown mess-ups. That's basically what he's concerned about."

"I'm going to mention I met a nice Scotch woman – they're white by the way, haha - the wife of one of your customers, and several American women. I'll also make a point of telling him there are a lot of Canadians down here, he'll feel better about that. And he'll think me hoity-toity because I've been playing Bridge. Did I tell you I bumped into women who were on the HMS Southern Prince?"

"No, you didn't. I should like to hook up with their husbands again. They were all good chums."

"Oh, he'll like this," she said, resting her chin in her hand and raising a finger. "I'll tell him the English are overbearingly snobbish, yet they are the most liked and respected because they invest a lot of money in Argentina." She looked at Stuart questioningly. "Am I right about the investment part?"

"Yup."

"And that the English gave Argentina a nice pretty statue while the Americans gave them a little dinky thing which Agentines hate, so there." She stuck out her tongue at Stuart.

"Why, I oughtta…"

Phyl squealed and jumped out of her chair, knocking it over. She ran off and Stuart ran after her. TJ poked his head in from the balcony, barked, and ran after them into the other room.

Carmen stepped out of the kitchen holding the wrung-out dress. She peeked around the corner, to see into the room where all the squealing, laughter and barking was coming from. She shook her head and stepped out on the balcony, hung the wet dress carefully on a small wash line pulled taut between the door jam and a wooden pole in the corner of the balcony. Oblivious to the Carnival drunken revelry, blatant nakedness, fist fights and gunfire below, she mumbled, "*Ayayayay, loco Americanos.*"

Chapter Six

Stuart's Cough, Naughty Carmen and Phyl and Stuart Get Nervous

Phyl felt herself drawn out of a deep sleep by a pestering strange wheezing sound. She dreamt it was Stuart and imagined herself shaking him though she knew it was just a dream. But in her dream, a monster shook her bed. She opened her eyes, shot up, and looked around wide-eyed. She looked down at Stuart, who had opened his eyes and was listening with curiousity. The roar was deafening. Shadows flitted past the windows which rattled in their frames. "Oh, my God, Stu, we're being attacked!" Phyl threw her blankets off and ran in her socks and flannel nightgown to the living room to look out the balcony doors. Carmen scurried out of her room, clasping at her housecoat, eyes bulging.

It had rained for two weeks, though it had let up overnight, and now there was a sprinkling with bits of sky peeking through grey clouds both of which were blocked from view by a dark mass overhead. The roar subsided and there was light. Phyl and Carmen pressed their faces to the window, fearing to step out onto the balcony.

Stuart walked up to them in his housecoat, pushed them politely to the side, and opened the door.

"Be careful, Stu!" pleaded Phyl.

He stood out in his bare feet. It had been just above freezing for parts of the night, and he shifted his feet uncomfortably on the cold balcony floor. He shivered slightly as he looked around, then back past the top of the building, his breath hanging in the dawn drizzle. A thick mist shrouded the park below.

They listened to the distant roar build again, and as Phyl screamed at Stuart to get back inside, a mass of biplanes appeared overhead, skimming the top of their building. Stuart instinctively ducked and held up his hands as he stared at the bottom carriages of the planes. Cups and glasses rattled in the kitchen, and something fell and smashed to the floor. Carmen scrambled under the card table. TJ ran to her, tail tucked in, his large, dewy eyes searching for answers from Phyl.

Phyl kept screaming, "Oh, my God, oh, my God," and ran out and clung to Stuart. They ducked every time a plane passed.

"Those are British-made," yelled Stuart. "Argentine Airforce. I think they're Avro 626 Trainers!"

They stood thunderstruck while the fleet of over fifty fighters passed. Phyl and Stuart watched as they roared through the mist toward the bay, in the direction of the hidden Uruguayan coast. They were barely visible but Stuart and Phyl could see that they slowly, en masse, turned and headed West up the wide river. Neighbors in the building and across the road screamed and talked loudly as the noise subsided. Below them, people hung over their balconies and windows, pointing and chattering excitedly.

Stuart motioned for Phyl to come back into the flat. He closed the door with a rattle, saw Carmen and TJ under the table, and laughed.

"Don't laugh, that was terrifying," said Phyl, trying to coax TJ out from under the table.

"Oh, just a lot of noise," said Stuart. "Well, that certainly woke us up!"

Phyl pulled TJ out from under the table. He immediately tightened his behind and had a runny dump. "Oh, TJ! No." She dragged TJ by the collar to the balcony and pointed. TJ, his eyes oozing apologies and sadness, continued to empty his bowels. "Carmen," yelled Phyl.

Carmen crawled out from under the table, careful not to get too close to the feces on the floor.

"Well, another scrub with yellow soap. Dang, that dog. Nerves of a noodle," Phyl said, closing the door to the balcony and shaking her head at her dog, who was ready to come back in, tongue hanging. "No, you stay," she yelled. "Go wee-wee, now!" She turned and mumbled, pulling out a handkerchief from her cleavage and wiping her runny nose. "I guess I better get that bucket."

Stuart took a pack of cigarettes and a lighter from his housecoat pocket and lit up. He dragged one of the folding chairs toward the balcony doors. He positioned the ashtray stand next to the chair. He sat down, and crossed his legs, looking out into the sky over Uruguay where it appeared the mist was breaking. The dog slunk to the door and sat, looking obediently and patiently at Stuart through the glass.

Phyl watched Stuart and made a face. "Stu, it must be 5:30 in the morning. A little early for a smoke, don't you think?"

"Huh?" Stuart looked at his cigarette and coughed. "Nope. I don't see the difference."

Phyl disappeared into the bedroom and returned wearing her housecoat and carrying a brown glass ashtray full of cigarette butts. She held it up and counted them with her finger. "These are the cigarettes you smoked last night while reading before going to bed. I know because Carmen cleans this one out every day. It was a clean ashtray when we went to bed."

Stuart frowned. "Okay."

"You're a chain smoker."

Stuart took another drag. "Chain smokers light their cigarettes with the last one. I don't do that."

Phyl wiped her hand over the card table and rubbed her fingers together. She went to the living room wall and did the same. It felt sticky.

Carmen had gotten a rag, pail, and mop from the kitchen and was scrubbing the floor next to the table. TJ whined at the door.

Phyl walked out the door and pointedly looked at TJ, then pointed at his big no-no on the floor. TJ nervously licked his lips, looked sadly at Phyl, and turned away from the doors. He sniffed at his accident from a distance, slunk into the corner, curled up on the wet stone floor, and licked his front paw. Phyl turned her gaze to Stuart and rubbed her fingers together. "It's wet. Even the table surface is wet."

She walked to the plaster wall closest to Stuart and touched it for emphasis. "The walls are wet. Everything feels wet to the touch. This can't be healthy." She pointed at her chest. "Our lungs filter this dank world we live in." She pointed at Stuart. "Your lungs are working overtime with wet smoke. It must stick to the insides like glue."

Stuart made a boyish face. "But, I like it."

"That's too bad," Phyl joked. But she didn't feel lighthearted. She pulled out her handkerchief again, unfolded it and folded it into a flatter shape. She wiped her nose. "If your cough gets any worse, would you consider cutting back?"

He did a curt nod. "Yes, if it gets worse. But the cough is a healthy reaction. It loosens it all up so I can begin anew."

Phyl gave him a dirty look.

TJ barked excitedly on the balcony. Carmen returned from the kitchen with another pail of water, and Phyl took it before opening the balcony door. "What is it, TJ?" She splashed water on the edge of the runny feces and watched most of it run down the grate in the middle of the balcony. She screamed and jumped back at the sight of worms in the feces. She covered her mouth and retched, then quickly emptied the remainder of the water onto the spot to wash everything out of sight. "Ewe!" she whined, jumping away as quickly as possible. Suddenly, she heard the noise TJ had heard a moment earlier and looked up, still grossed out. She gasped. "Stu, quick, a zeppelin!"

Stuart crushed his cigarette into the ashtray, jumped up and hurried through the open doorway to Phyl. "We don't have zeppelins here." Stuart looked out and saw a sausage-shaped airship slowly make its way overhead. He laughed. "That's not a German zeppelin. They fly from Brazil to Germany. They never come down this far."

"Well, what's that, then?" Phyl stepped aside as Carmen splashed another bucket of water onto the deck. Phyl eyed her dog, the drain, the bucket, the floor. She ensured there wasn't a damn worm left squiggling on her property. Then she looked back at the airship.

"That, there, is an Argentine airship bomber. They're much smaller than a zeppelin. They're warehoused thirty miles northwest of here and their only function is to drop bombs."

"Bombs, oh my. I've never seen one before." She thought, how did he know?

Stuart smiled and looked at Phyl before looking back at the airship. He turned and went back in. "It's *El Presidente* Justo, showing off his muscle. Legislative elections are coming up, and I bet he's making sure everyone remembers the power lies with the *Concordancia*. The Radicals are giving him and his cronies a tough fight, and they're stepping up in their threats. So, he's flexing his muscles. Speaking of which, don't forget, we're going to the zoo this morning." He tapped the side of his nose while looking to see where Carmen was.

Phyl frowned. She looked back into the kitchen. "Stu, we've got the Piñieros coming for dinner tonight. I've got lots to do and might need your help. And with the elevator still out, everything takes so much longer. Can you call the landlord again first chance you get?"

"He told me the last time he would drop by when he comes in for business. He lives in Uruguay."

"Out of sight, out of mind." She wasn't too pleased. "Well, it's driving *me* out of my mind. And now," she pointed at a guilty-looking TJ, "I have to find a vet to deworm you-know-who."

TJ barked once.

Stuart made a face. "A vet?" He paused. "I don't want to know, actually." He raised his eyebrows and motioned silently and earnestly toward the kitchen, where Carmen put away buckets and mop.

"Well, I guess I'm not going back to bed, then. I have to make a cake first and …"

"We have to be there at 11:00 this morning."

"Oh, okay. So, that gives me time in the afternoon to go to the market with Carmen. Well, I guess I better get that apron on. I'll put the cake in the oven before I get dressed."

Phyl sent Carmen to buy Swansdown flour and Crisco the day before. She was upset because she gave two perfectly good cake tins away before leaving

Toronto, and now she had to buy a new one – she certainly didn't want to pay for a second. She hoped the damp weather wouldn't ruin its rising. As she sifted the slightly damp flour, she went over in her mind what they were going to eat that night. They said it would be a scorching day, even though it had been near freezing overnight. Fall was slowly threatening the coming, miserable winter, but for now, it was a waltz between heat and freezing, the fluctuation in temperature playing havoc with their health. She was fighting a cold, and even with the five blankets, socks, and hot water bottle, she still couldn't get warm enough to sleep at night.

She knew she would probably move the bridge table and chairs out onto the balcony, where it would be cooler in the evening. That is if the rain held off. After the airship went by, the rain ended a two-week streak, but she knew more was expected within 24 hours.

The menu was to consist of cocktails and olives wrapped in bacon. Dinner was going to be cold ham and lettuce, tomato served on a large platter, Argentine-style, and liberally sprinkled with olive oil and vinegar. Then a leg of lamb, green beans, and baked potatoes. And, if it lucked out, the chocolate cake with cream and finished with mixed fruit. Unending red and white wine, and finally, *Café Despues*, or coffee afterward. She tried to get Maraschino cherries the day before, but Carmen came back saying that a small jar cost *doce pesos*, or twelve *pesos* - the equivalent of $4. She hoped she'd find a sale on them, as she desperately wanted some for their upcoming birthdays which were only one day apart.

Phyl cracked open an egg and slurped it out of its shell into the bowl, but she wasn't fast enough, and it slid down the front of her housecoat and apron. "Oh, f-iddledee!" she cursed. She looked at the splattered egg on the kitchen floor. Another stain to scrub out of the porous, low-grade granite. "Sh-sugar. What an absolutely asinine and stupid day! And it's not even 8 o'clock."

Phyl heard Stuart laugh and cough from the bedroom.

"And put that cigarette out!" she yelled.

* * *

At 10:30 that morning, Phyl and Stuart headed out on foot to the zoo. Fifteen minutes later, they arrived, and Stuart was relieved to see it crowded. Today, being a holiday, there was quite the racket at the gates. Phyl had seen from previous visits that whenever a car drove up near the entrance or wicket, little urchins raced up to open the door of a passenger or driver, all excitedly jabbering away. The point of the game was that whoever was the first one to get to the door had to be paid a few *centavos* – usually ten. If their victim refused to pay, the urchins loudly called for the Virgin Mary to rain curses upon the man.

Stuart hastened to lead Phyl to the ticket wicket, but they had to stand behind a family taking their time buying theirs, and about a dozen urchins ran up to Phyl and Stuart. One tiny boy carried a filthy rag and attempted to polish Stuart's shoes. Stuart paid him a few *centavos* and shooed him away.

"I know a few *centavos* are neither here nor there," Phyl muttered, "but the idea of being rimmed gets me. I get furious and could kill them all."

Stuart looked at her, aghast. "Phyl, they're only children. How can you say that? They can't help their lot in life." Stuart had tremendous patience with them, but Phyl only saw walking germ farms. "Those are harsh words coming from my wife, a supposed pacifist."

"I know. I'm sorry. That's awful. But they give me the creeps. Some people are afraid of snakes. Well, something about filthy, wild children frightens the heck out of me."

Stuart hurried Phyl away from the urchins to the wicket, bought their tickets, and rushed her through the gate. They continued past flower, candy, and novelty stands, run by old Spanish women with shawls over their heads. Their black dresses were traditionally shorter than the fashion, showing filthy bare legs and feet. Phyl held back as best she could away from them but couldn't help see the fly-bitten candy one woman held up, yelling, *"Bonbons, Señora, bonbons!"*

Stuart brought his camera and stopped to take a photo of Phyl, but he was actually scanning the benches within sight. He spied the bench he sought. A man, his face hidden by a newspaper, was sitting with a book on the bench beside him. Stuart led Phyl to the bench, picked up the book, and opened it as he and Phyl sat down. Stuart pretended to read the book and speak to Phyl, but he began to secretly converse with the man behind the newspaper.

Phyl's heart skipped. She could never get used to this sneaking about. She still didn't know what to do. How was she to act? All she knew of the man was that he was a German lawyer who had escaped Germany after Hitler forbade all Jews from working as civil servants and lawyers. Stuart spoke in her direction, and Phyl pretended to listen, nodded, and pretended to say a few words in response. In this manner, Stuart relayed information he had picked up during meetings or overheard at cafés and restaurants during the past week. As well, he passed on information Jorge had shared about the latest brutal tactics used by political parties in the rural provinces, particularly in the countryside near his *estancia* and his vineyard. There was an epidemic of hired rowdy troublemakers doing everything possible to sway voters for the coming legislative elections.

Phyl shifted as her back hurt. She perched on the edge of the bench, afraid to lean back too far because she didn't want to accidentally see the man's face.

"What should I call you?" asked Stuart.

"I go by Bevel."

"Why Bevel?"

"I like the sound of it," said the lawyer. "And I understand you go by Eaglet?" Phyl saw Stuart nod.

"Did you see the airship overhead at that godforsaken hour this morning?" said Bevel. "You do realize Justo is flexing his muscles. To think he floats his bombs over his own city. How unthinkable, how utterly unnecessary."

"That's what I thought. And the fleet of Avros was quite impressive. Kind of a Hitler touch catching everyone in their sleep, scaring them out of their wits. At a very vulnerable time, precisely when they can't think straight. How many heart attacks did he cause? The Radicals are shaking with fear."

"Right, ready with their machetes and pistols. Speaking of airships, pass on to your people that I have proof that zeppelins leaving Brazil spy on France on their way to Berlin. They take detailed photographs, and I have copies of some of them. Hitler is assessing assets for future acquisitions. There are priceless treasures in Paris. Word has it that Hitler wants nothing destroyed in the city." Bevel sighed. "Do you know that that brute has never even set foot in Paris? Or anywhere outside of Germany and Austria? And he dares to think of himself as a cultured man. He is nothing but a dangerous hooligan."

Stuart's face went pale.

Phyl panicked. What the hell was she doing in Argentina spying and hearing such terrible news?

"Keep from being destroyed?" asked Stuart.

"Excuse me?"

Stuart coughed. "You said, *keep Paris from being destroyed*. You're talking war?"

"Make no mistake about it," said Bevel gravely. "There will be war."

Hot tears welled in Phyl's eyes. Her eyes darted. She had no idea what to think. Indeed, this had to be an exaggeration. People dying needlessly, sons sent to war, her brother sent to war, Stuart …

"As well, German Argentines Passports are confiscated when travelling to Germany."

"Seriously?" exclaimed Stuart.

"They receive German passports, as their German roots overrule their birthright as Argentines."

Stuart stared at Phyl. Frightened, Phyl stared at Stuart's face. "Is that legal?" Phyl's blood froze.

"No, the Justo administration isn't sure what to do. They're putting pressure on Ambassador Von Thermann to sort it out. It's a great embarrassment to Argentina."

"A touch arrogant, I would say," croaked Stuart.

"Stinking Aryan superiority," said Bevel. Abruptly, Bevel folded his newspaper, tucked it under his arm, stood up, and walked away.

Stuart put his arm around Phyl, stunned. He looked at Phyl and tried to act calm and collected. He looked down at the dirty pavement and blindly stared at nothing.

"Stu?"

He didn't look at her. He checked his watch and jumped up. He reached for her. "I have to go. Let's pretend to look at the animals a bit, and then leave. You'll have to take a taxi home." He took her hand, gave her a long and tight hug.

She sadly looked up at him. "Was that bad?"

"Very, very bad. It means Hitler's getting ready."

Phyl's chin trembled in fear. "Where does he get this information, Stuart?"

Stuart muttered quietly. "No one knows he's a Jew. He works at the Antonio Delfino Shipping offices as a clerk down at the waterfront. The company's used as a cover for the movement of Nazi spies. He's at the forefront, ear to the ground."

"Oh my God. So dangerous! If they catch him, they'll kill him." She choked. "And you."

Stuart took her arm and strolled with her toward the kangaroo pens. "I try not to think about that."

How dangerous was this goinig to get? Phyl felt bile rise into her throat as she realized they were teetering on an abyss of evil unknowns.

Stunned, close to tears, Phyl took a taxi home. The flat wasn't that far away, but Phyl was so distracted that after a half hour, she realized her surroundings out her window were unfamiliar. She asked the driver, "What road are we on?" The driver looked at her in the rearview mirror but didn't reply. That upset her tremendously. "*Que calle es este?*" she repeated, this time in Spanish, in a furious voice. The taxi driver threw up his hands and mumbled something about *Estados Unidos*, and Phyl gathered he was telling her that because he couldn't understand her accent when she gave the address in Spanish, he got it wrong. She knew the street was miles long, and it looked like he had taken her to the other end of the city.

She said again, "*Ayacucho dos mil sesenta y dos.*" 2062 *Ayacucho*. She suspected he purposely did it to increase his profit. What did he think she was? A stupid, naïve woman? He had taken full advantage of her moment of distraction.

When he finally got her home, and handed her the bill, it was nearly three *pesos* according to the meter. Having made the trip once before with Stuart, she knew the bill should have been about one *peso*. Angrily, she got out of the taxi, handed him a *peso*, and said, "*Este es bastante, nada mas.*" She made a cutting motion with her hand. "That's enough. No more!" She didn't care if he possessed a revolver or had the nerve to pull it in broad daylight. Worse things were in the workings.

She paused in front of her building and looked up at their balcony on the top floor. Not everyone in the building had a balcony. Only the top two floors, but even then, the other tenants had half the size of theirs. She saw the pipe conduit for the runoff through their balcony grate and traced it all the way down the front of the building through the sidewalk, undoubtedly leading to the sewers. She thought of poor TJ and his worms. She thought of those worms under her in the sewer. She thought of dead bodies and maggots.

She took a moment to look up and down the busy street. Grimly, she saw perhaps twenty men and one young woman, a servant. Traffic wasn't heavy, and an old man pulled a cart by hand, leaning forward under the strain. Things clunked inside the cart, covered with a fluttering canvas. A Model A Ford bleeped at the old man, trying to get around. Two other cars puttered past. She looked across the road at the smaller buildings, one or two only about three floors tall. Their height allowed Phyl and Stuart to have a magnificent view of the expansive park, the downtown area, and the harbor. She studied the windows of these buildings and saw the odd female face peering out. Old and young. A child was playing at one of the windowsills. Would there ever be a war on this side of the world, she wondered?

Would that child know war? Needless death?

If there would be another, Stuart said it would remain in Europe and that political alliances would draw other countries into the gruesome fold but will focus their fighting there. Definitely, Canada, as part of the British Commonwealth, would step in. Perhaps the United States. She remembered the planes that morning and how frightening the sound and sight were. How far could *they* fly? Indeed, European countries do not have the wherewithal to fly bombers across the ocean to North and South America. Or do they? Phyl didn't know. But the zeppelin only took 48 hours to get from Brazil to Berlin, she remembered. What if Germany sent a fleet of bomber zeppelins? If the Argentines had smaller airships used explicitly as bombers, could Hitler not do the same with his zeppelins? Could he not bomb Canada?

She suddenly was sick to her stomach. She turned and saw Matteo, the doorman, looking at her concerned through the glass door. She stepped forward and let Matteo open the door for her.

He sensed she wasn't happy. He nodded and watched her walk slowly to the stairs, hunched over her purse. Matteo returned to his chair behind the counter where he had been reading a newspaper and continued to watch her shakily reach for the handrail to pull herself up to the first step.

Phyl stopped, looked at her hand, and wiped it on her skirt. She continued, leaning on the rail, slowly up the spiral staircase.

Matteo listened to her fading steps until he was distracted by a lovely-looking servant girl walking by the front doors. He forgot about Phyl, got up, and stepped through the door to watch the girl's retreating back. Unbeknownst to him, because it would never occur to him that it was even unsettling or strange, all the men scattered over the sidewalks on both sides of the road, and all the drivers driving past, did precisely the same thing. Their eyes were glued to the poor girl as if they were all programmed to do so. As if, they had every right.

Brainless moths blindly drawn to a bright and acred light in the blackness of a lonely night.

* * *

Phyl hustled Carmen down to their district *feria* - the open-air market. Phyl imagined it being akin to a Persian market, with its exotic smells, sounds, and colors, though she had never actually seen one herself and only in black and white in the flicks. But on the outset, it was as close to what she imagined a Persian market could be. But the charm wore off quickly as she discovered she hated being bumped around by hundreds of shouting servants, stinking men, dirty beggars, and runny-nosed urchins. She was forever slipping through rotting fruit and vegetables while being exposed to the sight of maggot-covered intestines, animal sex organs, live octopuses and strange fish of all colors, shapes, and sizes.

Each farmer's stall had its own peculiar sights and smells, and every one of them was filthier than any one of the stalls in Kensington Market back in Toronto; and that said something because they, too, could be pretty disgusting by the end of a market day. But instead of enclosures, brick buildings and dirty windows with tattered awnings as back home, here every single stall was outside covered in stained and torn canvas. And absolutely everything was covered in flies and squiggling maggots. She was forced to watch where she stepped, being careful not to get any on her shoes.

Food shopping with Carmen amid this explosion to her senses momentarily helped her forgo the fear of war. She remembered what Angelica had told her the last time they had dinner. At that time, Phyl had brought up the price of food during their table discussion, and Angelica brought over the record book her maid kept for the *feria*. The book showed that it cost them under five *pesos* daily to feed her and Jorge, their three youngsters, and four servants. But it cost Phyl and Stuart about three for them, Carmen and the dog. Meat was cheap, as were bread and eggs, so, Phyl couldn't see why it should cost them so much when Angelica's maid shopped at the same places and paid only five for nine people, and the Piñieros ate many more courses and drank far more wine and port than Phyl and Stuart did. This left Phyl with the impression that Carmen gypped her. At first, she refused to believe it, but Angelica had said that most servants tried unless the *Señora* was right on the job, and of course, Phyl being a foreigner and unable to speak the language well, was an easy mark. It was what poverty did to people, Angelica said.

Phyl didn't necessarily agree with her because in Toronto, where the Depression was felt more intensely than in Buenos Aires, most of the people she knew, including her own family, lived with hardship and poverty but their pride and morals were intact. They would never steal. Never.

Phyl mulled this over as she followed Carmen to her usual stalls. They trotted along, pushing and shoving through the throng. Phyl got into the swing of things, stretched her arm in front of a dozen other women, hollered and yelled like a local, and got along quite fine. She was learning how to shove and stand with the best of them. The women shot daggers at her, as they did to each other, and Phyl was again reminded of how horrible they could be. They looked at her like they could kill her for no good reason. Phyl paid no attention and, primarily because of her mood, treated them like dirt. It was a fine time to let off steam. Of course, eventually, everyone recognized her as a *Señora*, the mistress out with her servant, so she was sometimes dealt with a little less harshly than if she were a servant herself.

Carmen, sensing Phyl's mood, timidly led her to a stall to buy a leg of lamb. Phyl asked how much, and the woman looked at Carmen first. Phyl noticed in the corner of her eye that the woman got the wink from Carmen, and the woman, unusually subdued for a *feria* stall owner, said one *peso*. Carmen had always written one *peso* in the book for lamb. However, Phyl argued with the stall owner that it was too much and got a much lower price. As they continued shopping at the other stalls Carmen frequented, Phyl found the same reaction from stall owners – first the pause, then the look at Carmen, then the quote of the same prices Phyl knew she had been paying routinely. But Phyl adamantly argued with each one and paid what she should have been paying all along. Carmen looked more frightened as time went on, and when they finally finished and left the *feria*, Carmen was visibly shaken.

Phyl felt satisfied she got the point clearly, and thought she didn't need to be reprimanded on top of it all. She knew Carmen was humiliated enough to never skim from her again. She also figured that Carmen was desperate to keep her job, and Phyl certainly didn't want to have to find another maid, but it was quite a learning experience. As they lugged their wares home, not a word was exchanged. When they unpacked and put everything away, Phyl figured they had gotten enough groceries for that evening's dinner plus three days of food for only two *pesos* ninety. Carmen had been recording that for one day.

Carmen looked ill. *Tough beans*, thought Phyl.

Phyl angrily slapped that evening's menu on the sink and gesticulated she would rest before readying herself for the evening. She gave Carmen a pointed look. Carmen burst into tears. Ignoring her, Phyl left the kitchen and hovered over the card table. After a traumatic morning of 50 warplanes, airship bombers, wormy dog poop, begging urchins, threats of war, abusive taxi drivers, cruel *feria* women, and Carmen cheating on her, she decided to have a stiff drink. She went to the wall cupboard and took out a bottle of port Jorge had given them for a special occasion.

"This is a hellish, special occasion," she mumbled to herself. Phyl flipped the cork, filled a glass, and looked out at the distant scenery through the glass doors while listening to Carmen sniffling in the kitchen. Phyl longed for her family at home. Toronto the Good. Toronto the Clean. Gentle Canada.

She downed the port and shivered. She smiled grimly. On the upside, she was becoming a more assertive, complete woman, on the down side – she sensed hell was galloping toward them.

* * *

Stuart returned home lugging a tall table which he found left along a curb. It was of a strange exotic wood, but when polished up, it looked just that – exotic. They used it as a tall bar by the cupboard in the wall. This was now where they kept their alcohol and glasses, and Phyl happily placed a vase of flowers from the *feria* on top. She found the prettiest ashtray they had and placed it on the bar, a cherry on the cake. Then, she put a pretty little box of cigarettes and a matching lighter at the end. Later, she had Carmen put a pretty bowl of peanuts next to the flowers.

Jorge and Angelica arrived just after dark, carrying a bottle of eleven-year-old port Jorge's father had given him. Angelica presented an armful of beautiful gladioli. Phyl, quite tipsy by the time they arrived, squealed with delight at the sight of both gifts. She hurried the gladioli into the kitchen to give to poor Carmen to put in another vase, then quickly returned offering drinks. She led Jorge and Angelica onto the balcony to sit on their swinging chair and enjoy the city lights. Stuart, having read a paper outside in the evening air by the hurricane lamp while waiting, lit cigarettes all around, and they settled down while Carmen set the card table inside. It was going to rain that night, so no dinner outside.

"The elevator. I remember you mentioning it was out months ago." Jorge squinted through cigarette smoke and waved it away.

"Oh, sorry. It's a hike. We warned you," Phyl laughed apologetically. "But the owner lives in Uruguay and he hasn't come into town to take a look at it."

Jorge tilted his head and looked askance at Stuart. He pointed at him in a jestful fashion. "Stuart, my friend, you are so blind. You have a certain authority you can rely on."

"What do you mean?"

Jorge leaned forward. "I know we're not to speak of anything here, in your home." Jorge motioned around the balcony and apartment, "but next time you go to the zoo, mention this problem. The message will get across."

"The zoo? About the landlord?" asked Phyl, dumbstruck.

Jorge looked at Stuart, concerned. "You haven't been using Phyl, have you Stuart?"

"Use me? For what?" asked Phyl, looking at Stuart, then back at Jorge. She felt giddy, like on a see-saw.

"Well, yeah. We went today. Phyl's come along a couple of times now. I figured it was less suspicious as a husband and wife team." He grinned at her. "She's quite the Mata Hari."

"I know. She said that before. But is she *involved*?"

"Involved in what?" Phyl frowned.

"In the details."

"No, I don't let her do any more than simply come with me to the zoo." He motioned to Phyl with his cigarette. "And I only tell her so much. Just a need to know." Stuart shifted uncomfortably in his chair.

Jorge pondered as he inhaled deeply and leaned forward. "You may want to consider involving her even more."

"Nope. I don't want her to know or do any more than she does already."

"Well, it's too late. She's already involved, Stuart. Just by being here in Buenos Aires with you. Just by being married to you. By going to the zoo and seeing your sources."

"Involved in …? Oh." Phyl clammed up.

Stuart looked thoughtfully at Phyl and nodded. "Okay, next time we do the zoo and I have to follow through to the next contact, Phyl comes along. But only if in safe places. I'm not taking her anywhere in the countryside. It's far too dangerous."

Phyl's heart quickened. What danger? Where was Stu going with this? All she had banked on was palm tress. And now what? She looked at Angelica, quietly sipping her wine. Angelica raised her lids and did a motion of locking her lips with an imaginary key and then tossing it away. Phyl smiled and decided to change the subject. She held up the box of cigarettes to Angelica.

Angelica put up her hand and shook her head. "No, no. I'm cutting back."

"Are you not well?" asked Phyl.

Angelica grinned. "I am going to have another *bambino*."

"Whoa! Congratulations are in order. Why, you old dog, you," said Stuart, standing and shaking Jorge's hand. "How many are you going for, anyhow?"

"I'm going for a soccer team. I intend for Argentina to have the best soccer players in the world," Jorge laughed.

In happy moments such as these, Phyl wished they had a radio or gramophone for upbeat music, but very few people owned them in the city, and to buy either one would have been - at this point in their lives - a frivolous waste of what little savings they had. However, fortuitously the nearby Alvear Hotel played loud live music all evening, and the sounds of the upbeat band added to the celebration. And all-out celebrating, they did.

After dinner, a storm blew in with heavy rains and uncompromising winds. Jorge, sufficiently inebriated, thought he'd go down and check on the car to make sure the windows were closed. He rushed so fast, he almost fell down the stairs. The rains were torrential by the time he reached the car. He tried to start the engine, but it was so soaked the engine wouldn't turn over. Misery upon grief, someone had parked their bus in front of his car, giving him no room to coast the steep hill to pop the clutch. Jorge, almost crawling back upstairs, returned to the flat, thinking the bus would probably be gone by the time they were ready to leave after midnight. A drunk's logic.

They chinwagged, four happy drunks, arguing about the quality of food in North America compared to food in Europe and South America until two in the morning. By then, Jorge felt absolutely no pain, but he went from happy to perturbed when he saw off the balcony that the bus still blocked his car. All four left the apartment, laughing, slipping and running down the stairs, mindlessly waking Matteo. When Matteo popped his head out of his tiny apartment off the front entranceway, Stuart insisted he help him and Jorge push the bus into the vacant lot next door to their building. They drunkenly, valiantly struggled through that venture, with Angelica yelling, "*Vamos Jorge, vamos!*" In truth, even that Samsonite challenge was fun.

At one point, a dirty old beggar struggled in the rain, proclaimed the stormy night, "*Noche mal.*" He held out his hand, wanting money from them. Jorge, soaked to the gills, told him if he was willing to help push, he could have lots of *pesos*, but the old devil disgustedly motioned them away and walked off grumbling, splashing through the puddles, complaining he didn't feel like giving them a hand. Begger's pride on full display. Jorge, usually pretty refined, let out a string of Spanish oaths at him before God Himself. Then - *le piece de resistance* - he conjured up from the depths French swear words. Then in Portuguese. He was having far too much fun being profane.

While they laughed and struggled with the bus and car, the indifferent storm worsened. Thunder rumbled, and lightning cracked. The rain piledrived so hard that they had to run back like drowning rats into the lobby of the building. They watched a veritable river roar down the street, washing away everything ahead of it, but the bus, heavier than the car, miraculously kept the car in place. However, the cinderblock fence adjoining the vacant lot to the apartment building and an old abandoned fountain with a statue of the Madonna, fell and both broke into pieces and scattered across the flooded road.

Jorge and Angelica helped each other back upstairs with Phyl and Stuart almost crawling behind. They decided to give up to the drink some more and wait for the storm to subside. By early dawn, the rain became a drizzle and they looked out to see the neighborhood looking like a war zone. Still inebriated and all four as jolly as heck, they left the apartment with their glasses filled and gravity pulled their bodies downstairs yet again. Jorge took the women, drinks and cigarettes in hand, into his car. The bus had left, and Stuart pushed the car while Jorge took the wheel to pop the clutch as they invested in the incline, averting debris. Stuart almost lost his grip on the car as he splashed along, but managed to jump in before it rolled ahead or over him. In the process, he felt a stabbing pain in his abdomen, and he groaned as he threw himself into the passenger seat. The pain knocked the breath out of him, lasted a moment, and soon Jorge was driving them around to survey the damage caused by the storm. Passing grand homes, they saw policemen on horseback parading up and down. Angelica and Phyl dunkenly yelled at them.

"I guess all the police are to keep looters away from the filthy rich!" slurred Phyl.

Jorge tried to focus on her but gave up as he tried to drive straight. He shook his head, a lock of thick black hair hanging over his forehead. He whipped the hair back with a flick of his head. "No. These are the mansions belonging to our political bigshots. With the Legislative Elections coming up, they are afraid of assassins. The police have nothing to do with the storm."

Phyl's soured. "Jorge, don't say that. You're not serious. That many people want to kill them?"

"Oh, I'm quite serious. Many routinely die during our supposedly democratic and fair elections. Even local elections bring the worst out of people."

"What kind of country is this?" Phyl said disgustedly, unable to pronounce the 's.'

"It's our country. Unfortunately, it's the only one we have," hiccupped Angelica. "Oh, excuse me." She giggled.

"I need to go home," Phyl mumbled, burying her head onto Stuart's shoulder. They sat in the back with cigarettes and empty wine glasses in hand. Stuart shifted this way and that, groaning.

Bleary-eyed, she looked at Stuart and noticed he was green in the face with deep shadows under his eyes. "Are you alright, Stu?"

Stuart winced but didn't answer. Jorge pulled the car over.

"Friend, how are you?" he asked, concerned.

Angelica peered back. She gasped. "Stuart, you look terrible," pronouncing the word as *tereeeeble*.

Stuart held his abdomen, and Phyl, concerned, placed a hand on his tummy. He gently lifted her hand and put it away. "I have this terrible pain in my stomach."

"Is it something we ate?"

"We all ate the same things, and I'm feeling fine. Jorge, how are you feeling?" Angelica asked.

Jorge shook his head and shrugged. "Other than dimwitted from too much drink, I had a lovely dinner. No bad food. Just too much port. Besides, it's been hours."

"We should go home, Jorge," Phyl pleaded, worried. "I've never seen him this ill before."

Later that afternoon, after a short and fitful sleep, Stuart woke and called out. The pain had become so intense he could hardly breathe. Phyl quickly got dressed and had Carmen put a hot water bottle together to ease the pain, then ran downstairs to get Matteo. But he had gone out. The backup doorman was there, and fortunately spoke English, Spanish, and Slovak. He opened one of the vacant apartments he knew had a phone for Phyl to call Jorge, but she couldn't remember the phone number. The Slovak phoned information, but the operator couldn't understand his accent. Then Phyl got on the phone and said, "*Ola, Señora*," and somehow got the address across but was told it was an unlisted phone. The Slovak, who refused to give up, found a phone book, and Phyl looked up the address and found the number anyway. When she finally reached Jorge's house, the maid answered and said something about "*estacion*" and "*niños*," but she couldn't understand the rest.

Phyl ran upstairs and called Carmen to come down to talk with the maid while she stayed with Stuart. Carmen finally returned and told Phyl and an agonized Stuart that Jorge had taken his wife and children to the train station. Apparently, they were going up to the *estancia*, something Phyl forgot they mentioned. With some difficulty, Stuart gave the number of one of the men he worked with at the office. This man raced to an English doctor and brought him back to the flat. After a thorough examination, the doctor announced Stuart had colitis and dyspepsia caused by something he had eaten or drank the day before.

"But the rest of us are fine," argued an exhausted Phyl.

The doctor shook his head. "Had he eaten anything else before the dinner?"

"I had a little something to eat, but I'm afraid I drank too much cold beer. Would that cause this?" Stuart was given pain medicine earlier which took the edge off the pain, and he was able to speak.

"I understand you also drank quite heavily last night, and lasted over a twenty-four-hour period with no sleep," the doctor offered.

"Yes, we were bad little boys and girls last night," Phyl admitted.

The doctor studied her. "You know, too much alcohol can kill you?"

"Well, doctor, we were certainly quite pickled. In fact, I really don't remember what all we did drink. I guess that was pretty stupid, huh?"

The doctor packed his bag, "No comment. You, Stuart, are to stay in bed a full day and remain on a liquid diet for a while, but you'll come around, I'm sure."

Phyl thanked him and offered him and Stuart's co-worker a snack and some beverages. Both declined, anxious to get back to their holiday. Phyl asked that the bill to be sent to her, then, gratefully and sincerely, thanked them again and bid them farewell.

She returned to the bedroom and sat carefully on the side of the bed. "So, tell me about your meal after you sent me home with that taxi driver from Hell?"

Stuart shifted his body and tried to sit up. "If you're implying I was poisoned at my secret meeting, you're wrong. It would've shown up long before my pains started."

Phyl made a face and leaned over to readjust the pillow behind Stuart's back, to settle him into a better position.

Stuart sighed, reached for his cigarettes and lighter on the nightstand, lit a cigarette, and put a hand on his abdomen. "I met this Englishman-gone-Argentine. Very intense individual. It is arranged that he waits at this particular place while I have my zoo meetings. If I had any time-sensitive dynamite information, I had instructions to go directly to him with the intelligence. Of course, he was there, waiting."

Phyl eyed the cigarette as Stuart took a drag. "A Brit turned Argentine? I hear they are the worst Argentines. Is he a Radical?"

"I'm presuming he works for the Justo administration but can't be sure. For some reason, he kept pushing cold beer on me." He shifted on the bed.

"You'll like this, however: He told me that one of the Ministry's departments was looking to do a business deal with me. He said the contract was potentially big, which would mean a couple of thousand dollars for us if I get it, Phyl."

Phyl was elated. "Oh, Stu. That's wonderful!"

"Yes, but - and this will give you an idea of how low people can be where money is concerned here - he told me, in order to get this contract, he had to be interested. Unless there was plenty in it for him, I was to forget it."

"Huh?" Phyl almost sneered. "He's doing that while you pass on classified information?" She blinked. "Wow. That's terrible. That's extortion! But I don't get it. Wouldn't that be a conflict of interest? On the one hand, you have to inform him of sensitive intelligence, and on the other hand, he's extorting you?"

"Well, it makes sense. Because that's a cover, too."

"Oh, yes." She paused. "But he really meant a contract? He wasn't just lying for the cover?"

"No, it was bonafide. That's why there were so many beers. So much to talk about."

"What did you say to him?"

Stuart shrugged. "I had to remain cool, and I said, *Como no?*"

"*Como no?* What does that mean exactly?"

"Slang for, of course. Why not."

"Oh, Stu. No wonder your guts are in a knot. You have to go against everything you stand for in business. You're being extorted and forced to be dishonest."

"I know." Stuart coughed, winced, and took another drag, flicking the ash into a full ashtray next to him. "I'd like to think I get contracts because of my ability to do the job well."

Phyl snuggled closer. "Of course, you do. I'm so sorry. It must make you feel so dirty."

"Well, I'll have the contract details dealt with by Minor. He's my manager, so it's up to him to take care of all that."

"It's one thing knowing the business is done this way, but you don't really think about it until you come face to face with it," Phyl lamented sadly.

"Well, it will be my first contract, and there must be a first time, I suppose," Stuart said sadly. "But to deal with the devil for a few hundred lousy dollars is enough to make anyone sick."

"And here you are, sick! Argentina better not be the end of you, Stu. Your health is far more important." Phyl sighed. "Well, if you don't do it, a competitor will because one man certainly can't change a system that has been going on for years. It's like one missionary trying to Christianize India, and you know that Remington-Rand doesn't care how you get the business so long as you get it. And if you don't get it because of refusing to do the Buenos Aires way with kick-backs, they'll want to know why."

She stood up and straightened out the bedclothes around Stuart. She picked up the ashtray and held it out while he put out his cigarette. "And it's a matter of falling in with the customs or eating bread and cheese for the rest of our lives. It's a difficult position you're in. You have to compromise your American idealism, I'm afraid." She put hand to forehead.

"I know. Like I said, I'll let Minor do the dirty work and get his hands soiled while I keep my nose clean. If he does his end of the work properly, we'll all be alright, but, darn, you're right, Phyl. Any good salesman likes to know he got a contract through his hard efforts and not by buying it."

Phyl sadly smiled at Stuart and gave him a peck on his cheek. "You go sleep now, Stu. Get better." She left with the ashtray and snuck out his cigarettes and lighter while he wasn't looking. She closed the bedroom door behind her, feeling oddly elated.

Later, Stuart did pin down that hefty government contract. Phyl knew it had to lead to more and even better contracts. She thought anew of their dreams of owning their own home. She thought of the color of the outside walls, the little white picket fence. She could imagine a garden and, hopefully, both of the dogs, Tony and TJ, chasing each other in the yard. She daydreamed about wallpaper and materials for curtains and bedspreads. Two and a half more years, and they would be done with Buenos Aires.

But as she was about to empty the ashtray into the garbage can, she hesitated. She felt her heart tugged by a restless soul, and in a very clear and loud whisper, this sacred Presence within her silently asked, *At what great cost, Phyl? What would you pay for such success?*

She froze, in a state of limbo, and pondered on that voice which wasn't a voice. She frowned for a moment or two. She looked around the all too small kitchen as if she expected to see a living form. She slowly and deeply inhaled, gingerly emptied the ashtray, and slammed the lid on the pail. Admittedly, she sensed she missed the fullness of this profound meaning of what she had just heard. Was it a warning? Somewhere in the back of her consciousness, a seed of concern for Stuart's health took root.

At what cost…?

Chapter Seven

April 1936, Jorge, the Clines, and an Opportunity

Phyl sat at her new dining room table. She wore a heavy sweater, had a runny nose, and pondered the letter she was writing to her Dad and K. She had lost a good deal of weight, partly due to constantly fighting a cold – their heat hadn't been turned on yet - but also ever since the shock of the possibility of war, and Stuart's health taking a turn for the worst, she simply was not able to eat. Doing seven flights of stairs for months didn't help either, though the elevator was finally fixed. Jorge was right; Stuart just had to mention it to Bevel at the zoo, and in two days, it was working. That was quite a learning experience.

She blew her nose. Her ears rang because of the constant church bells from the cathedral nearby. Other bells of different tones rang from a distant church simultaneously. The imposing aural onslaught vexed her focus and her nerves were electric. Every once in a while, she stopped writing. She couldn't think straight with the noise and half-listened to their pestering tolls. It was Saturday, Easter weekend, and church services were broadcast continuously in the park, drawing enormous crowds. Every noise echoed throughout the park and over the city. Singing, chanting, and sing-song Latin liturgies climbed to cotton clouds in the crisp vermillion sky. Flocks of birds flew overhead, bombing the gatherings below. Babies cried, and wild dogs barked and whined. Catholic masses had gone on like this since Thursday.

She took a sip of black coffee. Curiously, the milkman didn't leave any milk at their building that morning, so no milk or *crema*. TJ, who lay curled up on top of her feet, shifted his weight, groaned and stretched his skinny legs. Phyl bent down and scratched him gently behind his ear. She was concerned as he still wasn't well. "That's my baby. You sleep," she cooed.

The cadence of the bells changed, and their rhythm went from sleepy *ding-dong-ding* to a cacophony of wild and intrusive notes over and over. Their intensity quickened Phyl's heart, not in a good way. She shakily put down her pen and sat back. She felt anxiety rising into her chest. "How am I supposed to do anything?" she asked openly. She carefully pulled her feet out from under TJ, got up, and flip-flopped over the cold granite floor to the bathroom for a cotton ball. As the cacophony of bells overwhelmed her, she pulled the cotton into two smaller balls and flip-flopped back, putting one in one ear and, before sitting back down at the table, plugging the other ear. The cotton partially filtered the mayhem. She briefly had to remember where she left off in the letter and then smiled slightly at a recent memory. Phyl picked up her cartridge pen and continued writing:

> *Last week, at dance class, I met a Canadian girl and we threw our arms around one another and wept. She is down here teaching in the American school. She went to University of Toronto and belonged to the Parkdale Ladies Athletic Club. Needless to say, this place nearly drives her mad as the Argentine women think we're all cracked, doing athletics etc. They do nothing but eat, sleep and have babies and it's difficult to find anything else to do here. However, she belongs to a club and we are going there to play tennis. She is from Pembroke, Ontario. We reminisced about the Old Mill but stopped as we were both on the verge of tears.*

TJ got up on shaky legs and shifted onto her warm fuzzy slippers again. She wiggled her toes under his belly to soothe him. She continued writing:

> *We took our pup to the vet to deworm. The dog has done nothing but vomit and has had diarrhea ever since. We don't know what to do as he is getting no nourishment. I doubt if TJ will ever grow up. I shall always hate these people for their cruelty to animals. You should see how they treat horses. They are such animals themselves that they have an animalistic attitude towards other animals.*

The pen splotched slightly, and she looked at the nib, and shook it. She pressed the point onto the blotter until she was happy the ink was properly flowing again. She continued:

> *We have been moaning we have had nothing to do. Thursday, Friday, Saturday and Sunday are holy days here. Stu says what a grand fishing trip we could have had and the weather has been beautiful, not too hot, not too cold, and lovely sun. No rain or storm or flooding like just before Lent. But since Thursday we have constant services and bell ringing, as a matter of fact the bell ringing has gotten to be a standing joke with us and are the ugliest sounding bells I've ever heard. The masses are very mournful for three days and on Sunday, tomorrow, I presume they will be joyful because of Easter. It makes*

us kind of blue to think of Easter here. There are the usual eggs on display in the shops but since the fall is coming instead of the spring it is not such a cheerful time. Gosh, Stu and I never know what to do on holidays as the countryside in Argentina is so ugly and there is no place one can go without going nearly to the Andes and that is expensive.

Carmen, her hair split down the middle and wrenched into a bun, walked up to Phyl holding a letter and looking blue. She eyed the cotton in Phyl's ears and politely waited for her to stop writing.

Phyl looked up holding the pen in mid-air. "*Si, Carmen?*"

Carmen looked at her letter and handed it to Phyl. Phyl looked at it but couldn't make out most of it, though she saw it was written by Carmen's sister in Uruguay.

"*Que este?*" Phyl asked a bit loudly.

Carmen spoke slowly in Spanish, and, with gestures, Phyl got the message that Carmen needed to visit her father, who lived in Uruguay. Her *padre* was ill, and he had pains in the arms and legs.

"Sounds like rheumatism," offered Phyl loudly.

"*Si, pero* the boat goes across in *dos* hours," Carmen explained.

"What? You're leaving me *now*?" Stuart had decided to go to the office to work that morning as he was bored at home, but he would be back by lunch. That meant she had to make the lunch and dinner herself. "When will you be back?"

"*No se*," said Carmen. "*Dos dias?*"

"Two whole days?" Phyl suspected Carmen wanted to spend Easter with her family. Rheumatism wasn't enough to go running home for. Phyl looked at her watch. "*Bien.* I hope *su padre* gets better."

Carmen nodded tearfully. Phyl waved at Carmen to go and watched as Carmen went into her bedroom. Every once in a while, Phyl could hear her shuffling about – a bang here, a loud scrape there. Carmen finally returned with a little leather case. Phyl retrieved her warmed feet and walked with her to the door. TJ followed and lay down near the door.

"*Vaya con Dios*," Phyl said, though she wasn't sure she was correctly using the term. But it seemed to get her message of concern across.

Carmen nodded as she opened the door. The volume of the bell ringing increased exponentially as it echoed throughout the granite and plaster hallway. Carmen tearfully headed for the elevator.

"Oh, and if the *crema* finally arrives, ask Matteo to bring it up."

Carmen nodded again and pushed the elevator button. Phyl, crossing her fingers for the *crema*, locked the door against the intense noise and went back to writing.

> *Maybe my checking up on prices at the feria Saturday was too much for Carmen. She announced Sunday she will be leaving. Believe it or not, she is going to get married. There is a mate for everyone in this world, looks or no looks. This is what Carmen said, "Yo voy casarme, yo engo mi mission en vida, hay no usa para me ir de una familia a otra, alrededor, alrededor." (I am going to get me married, I have my mission in life, there is no use for me to go from one family to another, around and around.) Stu and I are amused at the way they take marriage here. They don't marry for love but because the Church teaches them that their mission in life is to marry and have children, hence, poor Carmen is sacrificing herself and it is quite obvious that she is not in the least happy about it since she is going around with a face as long as a fiddle. She is quite right though as there is nothing for a servant but to keep on being one and to be kicked around from pillar to post, she is thirty-five and lost her Mother whom she is still mourning as she quite frequently has a cry and her Mother died two years ago. Marriage might help her forget since with the inevitable batch of children, she will be kept busy. She said she had been "muy contenta" (very happy) with us but felt she should fulfill her mission. So, I now have to go through the whole works of advertising and train someone, cooking, etc. in my inadequate Spanish.*

The bells stopped ringing. Phyl paused and listened for more. Nothing. She sighed, blew her nose, got up, and refreshed her coffee from the coffee pot on a low flame on the stove. She fretted momentarily, looking at the clock, then figured she could still write for a little while. But then she would have to get Stuart's lunch ready. It was quite a letdown. The thought occurred to her she had it relatively easy compared to Toronto; however, she would rather someone else did the cooking and cleaning.

She returned to the table, and picked up her pen. Toronto would not be as upsetting, she thought. There might be some violence at home, but it seemed hidden in the shadows. Cabbagetown and the waterfront past Cherry Beach, where immigrants tended to gather and where crime seemed to be worse, felt far from her family home on the corner at Gerard and Pickering, even though it was just a couple of miles away from the Beaches. Here, however, no matter where you lived, the threat of violence came from all directions, even from the skies. She felt TJ returning with his warm body. She wrote:

> *A customer of Stu's went to Mar del Plata for the weekend. His wife stayed in a house. A week ago, a man came stumbling up asking for the owner's wife who used to live there. It turned out that the owner was a baker and had had to fire a few men owing to business conditions, so Saturday night, about five men, relatives of the fired ones, jumped out and shot him in his tracks. His poor old wife has no one at all. Sunday, this customer of Stu's, went to the morgue to see that everything was in order as the wife was to view the corpse and when he went in, they had the corpse with his heart and various parts lying at his feet. Mr. Duguid (the customer) said he couldn't sleep all week but kept thinking of this awful sight. It just shows you how they do things here. Minor (Stu's boss) fired twenty-one men a few weeks back and if I were him I'd be worried, but nothing has occurred yet.*

She stood up, put her fists into the small of her back, and cracked it. She wiped her nose, feeling worn out. She sat down for a few more lines and felt TJ once again shift on her toes. He sighed.

> *Well, the revolution trouble was kind of fixed up. "The Mussolini of Argentina" is the bird that resigned from the army and started a little revolution but the Argentine authorities stuck him on a boat and sent him down river for a few months to cool off, the charge was resigning from the army which is not allowed, by the time he returns he should have learned his lesson.*
>
> *Love, Phyl*

Phyl finished her coffee and decided to add a few more words.

> *PS I have no cream for my coffee today. There is another strike. And wasn't it sad about the king? The papers here were full of it, and the one English paper printed nothing else. It was so sudden. Now Edward just doesn't seem kinglike. He is so small. They talk about the time he was here. He raised hell with the Señoritas and drank incessantly and snubbed the Argentine nobility refusing their invitations and were they upset!*
>
> *PPSS Went to the American Women's Club meeting, had tea and met new friends. They have a Drama Club! Am going to join.*

There was a knock at the door. TJ didn't jump up or bark. Phyl looked at him, still curled up. Then at the door. "*Si?*" There was no way she would open that door without knowing who stood on the other side.

"Phyl, it's me, Jorge." He also pronounced her name as *Pheel*.

"Oh, Jorge! Just a moment!" Phyl gently pulled her feet from under TJ and pushed her chair back. TJ raised his head to look and then let it flop again. "Oh, you poor thing," said Phyl as she walked to the door. She unlocked it and opened it. Jorge stood smiling almost shyly, holding his Panama hat and wafting perfume. "Jorge! How are you? I thought you'd gone to the *estancia*!"

"Fine, thank you, Phyl. No, just Angelica and the children are up at the *estancia* for the holidays." He laughed and pointed at his ears.

"Oh! Yes, the church bells are deafening," she said as she pulled out the cotton. "Please," she motioned, "Come in. I'm sorry for the way I look. I didn't expect anyone this time of the morning."

"You are a work of perfection no matter your state." Jorge didn't move but looked into the apartment. "Is Stuart in?"

"No, he's at work," she said, blushing, and looked at her watch, "but he should be back in an hour. You're welcome to come in and wait."

"No, no, no, that won't do," smiled Jorge. "A gentleman does not find himself alone with a beautiful woman such as yourself and not be tempted, friend or no friend. I will not put myself in that position. Or you. Have you noticed I am never alone with you?"

Phyl blushed. She thought back. She was about to shake her head but remembered their trip down on HMS Southern Prince. "We were alone on the boat, looking at the moon, and waiting for Stu."

"That does not count, Phyl." He pointed slightly at her. "You have lost weight. Are you unwell?"

Phyl sadly motioned with her hand. "I'm okay. Homesick, I guess. And we're fighting colds. I'm a bit of a prisoner in my own home. I can't walk out without being pounced upon. That doesn't help."

"No, indeed." He scratched his temple. "Could you, please, let Stuart know I came by. I will come back this afternoon."

"How is Angelica feeling?"

"Pregnancy always suits her very well."

"Then you must stay for dinner tonight."

Jorge smiled. "I'm afraid I have plans."

Phyl couldn't help it. She felt brazen. "With your mistress?"

"One of them, *si*."

Phyl gasped and, wide-eyed, made a face to make a point of her disgust, though it was friendly disgust from a friend. "How does Angelica stand this?!"

"She thinks nothing of it," he said sweetly. He put his hat back on, nodded happily, and left toward the elevator.

Phyl closed the door, shaking her head. She went to the table, reread her letter, corrected some spelling errors, and folded it. She was just about to look for an envelope when there was another knock on the door. Thinking it was Jorge again, she went to the door and opened it. A very large man stood in his grey suit, a Boat hat in hand, and a grim face. He wafted perfume while the shine of his hair dazzled.

"*Si?*"

"*Señora de Redington*, is your husband home? I am the owner of the building."

Phyl felt queasy. The last thing she wanted to do was deal with the owner alone. And why, now that Carmen left, are there people at the door? "No, but he will be back soon. May I ask why you want to speak with him?"

The owner's mouth turned down at the edges. "I will discuss the issue with your husband. I will be back." He turned to go.

"Sir, I have been meaning to have my husband ask you to please turn the heat on in the building. It is icy cold here, and we are fighting colds constantly because of the chill."

The owner patiently stared at her between the lids of thick eyelashes.

"We've been using a little heater and just got our electric bill for last month, twenty-one *pesos*, which is, for us, seven dollars. In Canada, we only paid $1.50, and there we had an electric Frigidaire and a toaster and coffee maker. Here we have only the lights and iron, and we've been going to bed every night around ten, so we don't use much light. The gas stove is left on for my maid to warm up, so we pay more for gas." She noticed him getting restless, but she ignored it and continued complaining. "A person needs a darn good salary to live here!"

He exhaled loudly, shook his head, and in a bored tone, asked, "Then why are you here, *Señora?*"

She blinked. "Sir, you are being belligerent. I take offense to that."

"*Señora de Redington*, I prefer to speak to your husband. But I will point out to you that the lease states quite clearly heat is not turned on in the building until June 1st. Your husband signed the lease."

"But that's over a month and a half away."

"It is what everyone does in the city."

They heard the heavy elevator doors open and footsteps coming toward them. The building's owner turned to look while Phyl quickly looked back to check on TJ. He did nothing. She shook her head. Twice people were at the door, and her guard dog was far too sick each time to budge. Now another presence in the hallway. She wondered if TJ was dying.

"*Ola*," she heard Stuart say. She turned and was relieved to see Stuart stand by the building's owner.

The owner nodded at Stuart. "*Señor* Redington, I am here with an issue."

Stuart nodded at Phyl and motioned for the owner to enter the apartment. The owner stepped in and angrily eyed TJ under the dining room table. He pointed at the dog. "He is the issue."

"You came from Uruguay because of our dog? And what do you mean, issue?" asked Stuart.

"I am in town visiting family for Easter. So, I waited to come here to say anything at all. But I have been getting written complaints for a couple of weeks now. You must not bother taking him out for walks as you should. The stairs are no longer the issue as I fixed the elevator."

"Which took long enough, and you only did it because you were pressured by higher-ups," complained Phyl.

He pointed at Phyl but spoke to Stuart, "I think you let him do all his business all day on the patio. Someone is not too careful washing the excrement away," he looked at Phyl, "because it runs out between the balustrades and drips down onto the balcony below and splatters against the windows further down. I'm afraid either you must go or the dog does. You have broken the lease and are upsetting the other tenants."

Phyl was terribly upset herself. She carefully kept the liquid away from the edges whenever she cleaned the tiled balcony. Evidently, Carmen hadn't cared to be so careful.

Stuart stepped close to the owner, which made the owner shift back a bit though he raised his double chin to maintain his air of authority. But Stuart felt he also had a source of power backing him up. He had become quite aware of that.

"Look at my beautiful wife. She needs a guard dog against you Latin men. Our dog doesn't bother a soul. He doesn't bark. He doesn't chew anything to pieces. He's just a gentle dog unless we want him to give someone we *don't* like the right message."

They all looked at gentle TJ sleeping under the table.

The owner pointed at him. "He is not much of a guard dog."

That got Phyl's back up. "I tell you, he is -"

The owner ignored her. In fact, since Stuart arrived, he was only interested in communicating with him, her husband, the man of the house. She was relegated to the nothing scale.

"That filthy dog goes. And that is final."

Stuart's face set. "You want to break the lease with us? We would be happy to break the lease as the place is so cheaply constructed that the walls are cracking, and we have had so much trouble getting hot water and the heat should be up and running for whenever it's cold, not just four months of the year. And you took your goddamned time fixing that elevator. We're paying plenty. I can't see what we get for our money except for a beautiful view." He poked the owner's shoulder. The owner glared at Stuart's hand, then his face. "And if it comes to a decision between our dog and this apartment, we will take the dog anytime and, furthermore, where we come from, we don't throw dogs out in the streets to starve to death." Stuart stepped out into the hallway and motioned for the owner to leave. "So, threaten all you want, but we're keeping the dog. It's your decision. Good day, sir. *Buenos dias!*"

The owner slowly put his hat on his head, eyes glued on Stuart. He tilted his head to one side and slightly smirked. "You *Americanos*, you think you can order us around." He pointed to his own chest. "My family has been here for generations. You only come here to see what you can get out of us." This time the owner poked Stuart's shoulder. "I would be careful, *Americano*. If I have to come down from Uruguay one more time to deal with issues you generate," he pushed harder into Stuart's shoulder, "I may not bother to ask you to leave." He pointed at his own head. "I know people. You can't survive in this country without help. It would be entirely different if I get you alone." He smiled. "Wouldn't it?"

He didn't wait for an answer. He glared at Stuart again, inhaling through his teeth as he looked at TJ, then left, slamming the door.

"Of all the…" started Phyl.

"Well, I told him."

"Stu, what if he sends people like those guys who killed the baker?" Phyl clasped her tummy, and her thumb touched her bottom rib. It felt bony. "I think I'm going to be sick." Phyl went quickly to the bathroom. She got on her knees and retched into the toilet. Miserably, she flushed and watched the water spiral down. She studied the inside of the cool bowl as she waited for nausea to subside. Thank God, it was clean. Carmen was good with the toilet. But she realized she hated the brown-colored toilet seat.

They also had a brown-colored ice box. And brown curtains. Suddenly, she thirsted for more elegance in her life. As another wave of nausea overwhelmed her, she decided she was going to paint the toilet seat and ice box a lovely white enamel and replace the ugly curtains with white or cream material, such as Angelica and Jorge had. Even in her miserable state, she was strategizing: the seat and ice box would need three coats of base paint. And the curtains would need to be sewn – so long as they looked classy. Stuart was working on another contract, so she knew they would soon have the money to make these changes. Slowly, she felt a little better. Phyl wiped her mouth, struggled to her feet, flushed the toilet once again, and went back into the dining room. Stuart was reading the letter she had written.

"You okay?"

"This country is getting to me."

Stuart put an arm around her. "Can I write at the bottom? I want to add some clever repartee."

"Absolutely. By the way, when do I get a Remington loaner again? I'd much rather type than do these massive letters long-hand. I have such trouble with the pen, and my hand hurts."

"We're getting busier, and we need demo typewriters," Stuart said absent-mindedly as he picked up the pen. He wrote:

> *Hello, folks – how is everything? As expected, we found grief and trouble down here, but everything will come out all right in the end. Hope to be seeing you soon but can't say definitely when. Everything has changed so much. Hasta la vista! Love Stuart*

Phyl read what he wrote. "That's it? That doesn't really say anything," she complained.

"Yeah, but next time nobody can say I didn't write." Stuart coughed, took off his coat and went to the bar. "So, we should do something. These holidays get me down."

"Oh, by the way, Jorge came by earlier."

"He didn't wait?"

"He said he didn't trust being alone with me," Phyl said, coyly.

Stuart poured himself a Scotch and offered the bottle to Phyl. She rolled her eyes and nodded gratefully. "He's going out later with one of his mistresses."

"He told you that?" Stuart laughed, shook his head, and poured another Scotch, clean. "It's good making money finally. 'Love having my Scotch. Especially late morning on a Saturday."

"Ice?" Phyl asked.

"Please." Stuart sat on their new cream-colored settee and put his feet on the heavy, round brass coffee table.

Phyl stood bent over in the kitchen with an ice pick hacking at the ice block at the bottom of the ice box. Slivers of ice shattered onto the granite floor and she quickly picked them up and put them in a bowl. She brought them over to the coffee table.

Stuart took out a piece of ice, gently pulled off a dog hair, and dropped it into his drink. He took a sip. "Ah, that'll put hair on my chest," he said, gratified.

"Finally," joked Phyl, taking a sip from her own drink. "And we almost put it in your drink!"

"I bet the folks at home are under the impression that we're toasting our toes under the palm trees instead of taking hot water bottles to bed and sleeping under a mountain of blankets." He sniffed the air. "So, is lunch almost ready?" Stuart looked around. "Where's Carmen?"

"She had to go see her sick father in Uruguay," said Phyl, sadly. Not wanting to deal with the issue of making lunch yet, Phyl sat in an armchair, looked over at her sleeping TJ before settling back. She crossed her legs, slipped off her slippers and straightened her hose. "I know what you mean. It's amazing the ideas we had about this country before we left. I thought it was tropical, but the beginning of Fall is just like at home, except for the rain. Angelica says everyone wears fur coats here, and instead of snowing, it rains all the time, day in and day out. I shouldn't have given El those flannel pajamas."

There was a knock at the door. Stuart jumped up and opened the door to see a smiling Jorge standing with hat in hand. He walked in without an invitation and nodded, grinning, at Phyl.

"Finally, you are brave enough to come in. Finished with a mistress already and getting ready for the second shift?"

"Something akin to that, Phyl. And it was only a quick coffee."

Phyl eyed him. "Awfully quick, I would say."

Jorge looked at Stuart. "Can we talk?"

"Sure, sit. Drink?"

Jorge nodded. "Sure. Anything." He put his hat on the bar and walked over to the settee. He sat down and looked adoringly at Phyl.

Phyl smiled back. "It's so nice to know I can trust you."

"I've been very disciplined. Besides, I have outlets," Jorge said.

"Hmm. I must say."

Stuart walked over with a Scotch for Jorge, threw in an ice chard he checked first for hairs, and handed it clinking to Jorge. Stuart sat in the corner of the settee facing him.

"There's talk of something brewing over in Caballito. We need some eyes on the scene. Just a once over, feel the pulse." Jorge took a sip of his Scotch.

"Okay. Now? Today?"

"Yes, please. Too many people either know me or are related to those who work for me. I can't go. It could mean my life if something goes amiss." Jorge shook his head. "It's so difficult keeping the lid on the hired hooligans."

Phyl looked at Stuart. "Oh, Stu."

Stuart shook his head to indicate there was nothing serious.

"Phyl, he doesn't have to do anything. Just walk through the street, look around. In fact," he shifted toward Phyl, "it would be much more natural on a holiday weekend for a man and his wife to be out for a walk."

"Oh. I don't know," said Phyl. "If you're concerned for your life, why shouldn't we?"

"You have no enemies. I do."

"I'll take you out for lunch there. And we'll catch a movie after," coaxed Stuart.

Phyl looked at the kitchen. "Well, if you put it that way. Anything to get out of cooking. Okay. Deal. I'll get dressed."

Phyl got up and went to the bedroom.

Jorge coughed. "It's best if you take the *subterranneo* all the way to *Prima Junta* station. You walk out into the middle of Caballito that way."

"That doesn't sound so bad. A train ride out and back. We've not had an opportunity to use the *subterranneo*. A subway ride's okay on a day with nothing to do."

Jorge downed his drink. "I'll come back late tomorrow morning and see what you have to say." He got up, grabbed his hat, and put it on. He leaned toward the bedroom door and called out. "*Hasta luego, mi querida mujer.*" He winked back at Stuart. "You don't mind if I call her, darling woman?"

"Not at all. That's precisely what she is."

Jorge was about to see himself out when he stopped. "You don't happen to have a gun, do you?"

Stuart's face paled. "Excuse me?"

"If you do, take it." Then Jorge left.

* * *

Stuart and Phyl stood on an elaborate escalator floating to the lower level. Young boys raced up and down the escalators, yelling "*Mire aquí*" (Look here), playing tag. In spite of the noisy boys, compared to New York, the station was relatively quiet and clean. The platform and walls were shiny red tile with beautiful mosaics depicting exciting scenes. It felt like a quiet, small town on a Sunday morning. It was well-lit and ventilated, and the station sign was marked in substantial neon lights. They were surrounded by men of all ages and sizes. Phyl and Stuart didn't need to wait long before a train silently arrived. They noticed that the cars were made of wood as opposed to steel. "Wow, none of the squeaking and banging you have in New York," said Phyl, impressed.

The automatic doors opened slowly, giving Phyl and Stuart ample time to get on. The car was practically empty, just a few men. It was white inside and trimmed in copper with wicker chairs built for three people each. There were only four sets of these seats in each car. Phyl and Stuart sat down and looked around. Momentarily, the train rumbled slightly and continued to the next station. She could smell a very slight whiff of perfume from the other men.

"The ventilation is wonderful in here," Phyl observed. "And it's remarkable how quiet it is. I can actually hear myself speak."

"The trains are run by a Spanish company, but the work was done by Germans, and the Belgians built the cars. There are two other subway lines - one Argentine and the other English." Stuart and Phyl settled down, looking all around. Stuart coughed and had difficulty catching his breath, enough so that Phyl pounded his back. He waved her away. "It's okay."

"I'm okay. Don't worry about me. Just a tickle in my throat." After a moment, he spoke up. "I'm going to get a gun."

"Huh?"

"Just in case."

"I'm not having a gun in the flat, Stu." Phyl had a pained expression. "Is something going to happen?"

"No, Jorge mentioned it. I've been thinking about it and it wouldn't hurt."

Phyl looked at him, appalled, and then around the car. She blindly looked at ads hanging from the center of the ceiling and on the few spaces between windows and doors on the walls. She was shaking her head when she inadvertently caught a man's gaze. Shocked, she looked away and noticed someone else studying her. Five other men were in the car, and it seemed they were all watching her closely. She looked away and snuggled closer to Stuart, who was watching the blackness pass by the windows, though he was actually grimly watching the reflection of the men watching Phyl.

"I guess a gun wouldn't hurt," she whispered.

He possessively kissed Phyl on the head. "We'll both learn how to shoot."

"Oh, my God," whispered Phyl, as she sunk into the seat in shock.

They stepped into an explosive riot at *Prima Junta* station where rubble and a car were on fire just outside the *subterranneo* gates. Phyl, startled, quickly ran down the steps back toward the trains, but Stuart stood his ground, refusing to leave. Stuart grabbed a young man who raced by and demanded what was happening. In Spanish, and as best Stuart could understand, he jabbered a short explanation quickly before rushing off. Stuart ran back down the stairs to Phyl.

"Where's that gun now?" cried Phyl.

"Phyl, you stay here. It looks like Governor Frederico Cantoni's son is leading the riot."

Phyl oggled at the smoke beyond the top of the stairs. "But isn't he the guy from San Juan province? What are they doing here in the city?"

"Argentine politics, Phyl. I'm going to go over to the other block and see what's happening. Everyone's running in that direction." He started to go, but Phyl grabbed him.

"Stu, you'll get hurt! Please, I want to get as far away from here as possible."

"I have no choice. I have to do this." He ran back up the stairs.

"I'm not letting you out of my sight!" yelled Phyl, as she scrambled up the stairs after him.

At street level, she called out to him. He stopped and looked. He pointed at the station's black wrought-iron entranceway. "Get back in there!"

"No, I'm coming with you!"

Stuart was upset, but he didn't want to waste time arguing. "Okay, stay close." They hurried with other men to the corner and, eyes stinging from smoke, squinted up the street. Police were everywhere, some on horseback with whips and bludgeons, but they were helping rioters set a building on fire. Over the crowd's roar, they could hear the mournful cry of fire engines. Phyl and Stuart immediately saw two red open fire engines rambling around the corner with four men in each.

"Oh, thank goodness," yelled Phyl.

But as they watched, they saw the firemen talking and yelling with the police and civilians, and then they helped the police pour more petrol at the doors of the building. People scrambled out of the building, screaming. Some were covered in black from smoke. Stuart stopped another person and talked at length.

"There's a political banquet going on inside." Something exploded around the next corner and people screamed. Stuart grabbed Phyl, and they ran with the crowd, past the burning building and mayhem, to see what exploded. A woman screeched and cried somewhere. Stuart, again, stopped a young man who hollered that the 86-year-old mother of the politician holding the banquet lived in the house but he wasn't sure if it was the old lady or one of the servants screaming.

People ran into the house, which monstrously rose up in flames faster than the stone building where the banquet was being held. Onlookers managed to drag out an elderly woman and two servants. But the rioters jumped at the servants, one of whom ran off and escaped. They tore off the clothes of the remaining poor girl, scratching and cutting her in the process. They then forced her to walk naked and bleeding down the street.

Phyl was astounded. A sob escaped. Appalled, she saw the poor young woman, with a large rotund belly, trying to cover her breasts and groin with her hands. "What are they doing to her? Where are they taking her? Stu, she's pregnant! We have to do something! We can't just stand by and watch," she cried. She bolted toward the crowd but Stuart grabbed her by the coat and held her back.

"I have no idea what's going on," Stuart yelled, clasping onto a struggling Phyl. As he cradled her face into his chest to prevent her from seeing more, he allowed the crowd to push them toward a police station. The crowd continued dragging and pushing the young woman into the building.

Phyl freed her head from Stuart's grasp and swiveled to see a naked back disappearing under the overhead lights in the hall. Phyl thought she was going to faint. She yanked at Stuart and then slapped at his arm to loosen his grasp. "Let me go!" She pushed him in a rage. Then she grabbed him closer. "I can't take this anymore, Stu. Please, take me home away from this nightmare," she pleaded.

Stuart bundled her into his arms as he fought their way through to the edge of the crowd. Someone yanked Phyl's purse off her arm. She screamed and reached back but Stuart kept pulling her along. They retraced their steps and passed the poor elderly woman's house, now entirely immersed in angry flames, and the stone building, with roaring fires flicking and exploding out the windows.

Phyl shook all the way home. When they finally arrived at their apartment, she immediately crawled into bed and passed out.

* * *

"Thank you for going. I will pass on your eyewitness accounts as you saw them."

The following day, Jorge sat across Stuart and Phyl. Phyl was sick. She sat in her housecoat, huddled against Stuart, holding a moist handkerchief to her face. Dark rings emphasized her bloodshot eyes, red buttons in her pale, white face. She weighed herself that morning. She was 105 pounds.

"Things tend to be twisted by the time they're reported through official routes. As you saw," Jorge held up his hands in despair, "the police and firefighters were just as destructive. I guarantee you that according to their reports, all will be whitewashed so no one will know the truth except those who were there."

Jorge paused to study Phyl. Gently, he said, "Thank you for doing this. We need to know the truth." He turned to Stuart. "I know this is the kind of activity you report to your higher-ups. As you've personally discovered, key powerful figures can cause a good amount of disruption, and they truly get in the way of justice to such an extent that no one knows how to recognize it anymore. So, what you witnessed yesterday was worth more than you can possibly understand." Jorge stood up. "I must go. Angelica will be back tonight with the *bambinos*, and I have an appointment to take care of first."

"Another mistress?" spat Phyl.

Jorge, surprised, looked at her. Phyl was glaring at him with a slight sneer.

"Phyl? Why are you angry with me?"

Phyl covered her mouth and tears welled in her eyes. She looked away, jaw twitching.

"Can I ask you something, Jorge?" Stuart asked.

Jorge sat back down and pulled his eyes away from Phyl and cast them on Stuart's face. "Yes?"

"I thought this Governor Cantoni was the real thing, that he believed in the democratic process."

Jorge shook his head. "Dr. Cantoni is no rose, as you saw. His son started that riot, but I'm sure it was done with Cantoni's blessing if not by his design." Jorge leaned forward and clasped his hands. "When Cantoni was elected a year ago, he sent men down from San Juan to quell a riot, and the things done to the rioters were absolutely unspeakable. The locals are Indian and Italian blood mixed, and he knew they'd do incredibly evil things. A normal person would never think of doing them."

"Like what?" asked Stuart.

"I can't tell you. Phyl would never get over it." Jorge eyed Phyl sheepishly.

"Tell us, Jorge. We should know what kind of people we live next door to in this godforsaken country," Phyl angrily demanded.

Jorge looked sadly at Stuart. Stuart looked at Phyl. "Phyl…" Stuart started.

"I'm not a child, Stu."

Stuart shrugged, looked at Jorge, then looked away.

"Straight out of Franco's book of mass atrocities in Spain. Violence and brutal torture…"

"An example of these atrocities?" demanded Phyl.

Jorge gulped.

"An example," she snapped.

Jorge looked sadly at his hands. "They chisel down small trees and impale people between their legs through their torsos. You know, through their…"

"NO!" Phyl was stunned. She covered her face and shook her head and remained quiet for a moment. She lowered her hands, tears flowing. "Well," she could hardly speak. She wiped at her eyes. "I'm not going to write home about *that* image anytime soon!" Her voice cracked.

Stuart nervously snorted at Phyl's comment and then looked sadly at the granite floor.

Jorge reached out to Phyl but didn't touch her. He looked at Stuart, then Phyl again, who was now hunched over her lap. "This is all very complicated. You are in a convoluted world, Phyl. But try to remember the beautiful aspects of Argentina. It really is a unique paradise. I need you to remember that. I care very much for the both of you and would do all in my power to not put you in any real danger."

Phyl looked up and glared at Jorge with bloodshot eyes. "Is there any other kind of danger?" She spat. "You keep saying you care for us and will never put us in harm's way," she said, sarcastically. "So, why did you throw us into that Hell, in God's name! Lord knows *what* could've happened!" She sprung up and ran to the bedroom and slammed the door.

* * *

Phyl lay in bed for a week, and it took another week before she finally followed the doctor's orders to get up, eat, and take part in 'normal' activities. She was close to a hundred pounds and very weak.

Life picked up, slowly, but this time without Jorge and Angelica. She missed Angelica's company, but had written Jorge out of her life entirely. She realized Stuart still had to communicate with him in an official capacity, but she didn't care how or when. So long as it wasn't in her company, and she didn't want to hear his name ever again.

The good news was that Carmen was back, and though she was still getting married, it was not for a few months yet. She informed Phyl that there was a chance her future husband would want her to continue working for the pay so, as far as Phyl was concerned, there was hope. She even considered enticing her to stay by buying her the official maid's black and white uniform Carmen's always wanted. That would come after the next contract Stuart sold.

Phyl spent a couple of months playing bridge and tennis at the American Women's Club and formed many new friendships. One day, she accepted an invitation for her and Stuart to join an American woman and her husband, Annabelle and Timothy Cline, to spend Independence Day watching the big military parade pass by their beautiful flat situated on a main *avenida*. They sat drinking and smoking out in the cool air and warm sun, looking down at thousands of footmen and soldiers march by to the beat of loud army bands. They were followed by horsemen, carriages with cannons pulled by horses, open jalopies, a World War I steel tank, and a large convertible carrying a waving and grinning President Justo. Men, and some women, were jammed along the sides of the *avenidas*, excitedly calling and waving little Argentine flags. Ribbons and bouquets of flowers were thrown onto the *avenida* as Justo passed. Overhead, the same Avros which traumatized the citizens of Buenos Aires months earlier, passed low, their rumbling props so loud and deep that people's teeth chattered and bones shook.

"Notice the motor vehicles, bought from the Brits, us and the Krouts," yelled Timothy.

"I hear the quality coming out of Germany is excellent," offered Stuart.

"Well, it's part of their focus, isn't it? Rearmament of their army, navy and air force, which is most disconcerting. Hitler's openly breaking every rule in the Versailles Treaty." Timothy leaned in Phyl's direction. "You just missed the massive Nazi rally in Luna Park. Thousands came. They sang German songs, wore Swastika arm bands. Even the local children were walking around afterward doing the Hitler salute. We found it strangely quaint in a surreal way."

"They've been holding rallies in New York, as well," said Stuart. "But Argentina is friendlier with Germany than the U.S. or Britain."

"Most definitely. Argentina remained neutral during the war and openly harbored Germany's assets and ships. And she is still on very friendly terms trade-wise. Germany receives imports of wheat and grain, along with meat, in exchange for military vehicles, planes and arms. Did you know that? They even sent trainers here for the army and air force."

"Why am I not surprised?" said Stuart.

"Well, it's certainly showing in this parade of might. Very impressive, even how disciplined and precise the soldiers march. I didn't know Argentina had such a large army," yelled Phyl.

Timothy Cline yelled back. "Yes, it's probably bigger than you have in Canada, though it's not larger than ours back in the U.S. of A. Quite the display for Independence Day, I must say."

"Which celebration of Independence is this one? From Spain or the war between Chile and Uruguay?" asked Stuart.

Timothy smiled and shook his head. He shrugged. "I can't remember which one."

The sanity-defying parade ended and Phyl watched the crowds disperse along the *avenida*. She spied Jorge. Her face dropped. Stuart noticed. "You okay, Phyl?"

She pointed to Jorge, Stuart looked, and chuckled. "That's not exactly Angelica on his arm." Jorge was attached to a young woman in white heels, a flowery dress, black hair swept into a sexy scoop under a tiny, white cloche, black netting over her eyes. She wore hoop earrings, large enough to throw a baseball through.

Phyl closed her eyes, shook her head, and breathed deeply.

"Someone you know?" asked Timothy.

Phyl smiled. "Yes, well, no one important. You know, I was just thinking, the day couldn't be more perfect for a parade." She drew a line in the sky. "This must be our first sunshine in weeks – what a session of dampness we've had. It sure brightens things up to have sun warming things for a change."

"I hope we have this weather when we go on our trip Saturday," offered Annabelle.

"Where are you going?" asked Phyl.

"We're going for a few weeks around the Caribbean," said Timothy. "Why don't you come and see us off? It's always such a hoot to come onto the ship early and sit at the bar."

Phyl turned to Stuart. "Oh, I would love that! What ship will you be on?"

"The Southern Cross, the one that brings the mail," said Timothy.

"Oh, my. Well, I tell you, if I come on board, you will hardly get me off that ship when they start yelling, All ashore, who's going ashore. Give me a whisky and soda on board, and I'll never leave."

"How long before you go on a ship to go home?" asked Annabelle.

Stuart looked at Phyl. "Um, let me see." He started counting on his fingers. "According to their schedule, I, er…"

Timothy left and momentarily returned with the schedule for the Southern Cross. The two men sat and mulled over the departures. After a few moments, they agreed. "We think two hundred and ninety-nine boats from now, we will be on our boat going home," said Stuart.

"That many? I don't know if I'll make it till then," said Phyl, her mournful gaze dissolving into the advent of a beautiful sunset over the city.

"Yes, that many," said Stuart. He put out his cigarette and picked up his pack. He saw Phyl look at him, at the pack, and then back at the sky. He put the pack back on the side table. He jiggled his leg.

Phyl half-closed her eyes to see the sunset in a different light. The sky turned a blood red with violet streaks across the blue, creating a striking light and aqua haze along the horizon. The sun was a blood orange and red. "I have come to the conclusion, maybe for the hundredth time," she said thoughtfully, "that the sunsets here are like nothing else on earth."

Everyone mumbled in agreement.

Phyl remembered Jorge's comment about how it was also a paradise. She didn't want to remember anything positive about Jorge, so she sat up and shifted into a more comfortable position on a cushioned, white wrought-iron deck chair. "There is a warmth in the air, too. Like Spring, even though we still have winter for at least another month and a half." She shivered and pulled her sweater in tighter. "Except for this infernal dampness, the winter so far has been like late Fall in Canada, hasn't it, Stu?" Phyl sneezed. "Excuse me!"

"Bless you," everyone muttered.

Annabelle, a few years older, noticed Phyl's discomfort. "Shall we go inside and have tea and the lovely biscuits you made, Phyl?" She stood and led everyone into their palatial flat, and spoke as she walked. "Why don't we go to a movie and then have dinner at *La Cabana*?"

"What a superb suggestion," yelled Phyl.

And they did. They went to the *Cine Opera* theatre at four, paid their three *pesos*, and got out at eight-thirty. They saw two Popeye and one Betty Boop cartoons, a film of an orchestra playing William Tell, and a short feature of Jack Denny. Then a newsreel on Hitler followed by another cartoon, in color this time. Everyone oohed with approval. There was a series of shorts and two full-length movies: Trail of the Lonesome Pine and a Ronald Coleman movie, The Man Who Broke the Bank of Monte Carlo. They had smuggled in whisky flasks, smoked throughout the afternoon, and ate Eskimo Pies. Phyl got a back and leg ache from sitting so long and ended up crying her heart out, mostly because of her traumatic experiences rekindled by the sight of Jorge.

Phyl had acquired an ongoing headache of late. It recurred in closed spaces where men's perfumes overcame her. At one point, slightly tipsy, she was roused when she heard great squishes in the theatre - like atomizers spraying incessantly. She turned and saw an usher traversing the aisles pumping what she swore was the cheapest-smelling perfume possible. It surprised her that the people seemed to love and appreciate it. After he finished bleaching the aisles, he took his cloying squishing act to the back. Phyl turned to see the usher smirking and squirting the stuff all over a peer's head, one whose hair was already slicked with stinky pomade.

After the movie, they exited bleary-eyed and inebriated. The downtown streets were so crowded one could hardly circumnavigate. All the café-bars were packed with men and their mistresses or streetwalkers. The city was an inferno of testosterone.

When they arrived at *La Cabana*, they were led to a round table for four by a window. A band played a light-hearted rhumba, which lightened Phyl's mood considerably. After the couples squeezed through the throng of tables and settled down, they ordered cocktails, lit cigarettes for the ladies and cigars for the men, and smoked as they traversed epic menus.

"I kept myself awake all night with stomach pains the last time we were here. I had the *Parillada Mista*, which could have been the problem. So, you may want to stay away from that," Phyl said, reading the cornucopian list.

Annabelle looked at Phyl's menu. "Which one is that?"

Phyl pointed out *Parilladas*. "They're grills about the size of a medium-sized saucepan laid over burning embers served at the table as they are still sizzling – the pans, not the embers," she laughed. "It's portions of meats and innards, but I couldn't bring myself to eat the dried blood, which I always send back sizzling just as it comes. The last time during the night, I fell out of bed and dreamt that a good friend of mine committed suicide."

"Oh, that's awful. Point noted. Stay away from *Parilladas*," said Annabelle to herself.

The waiter came for orders, and Phyl chose wild duck with savory gravy with a dressing of mushrooms and stuffed olives, and liver. Stuart requested a large steak with *Tallarines*, a sort of flat spaghetti in a special sauce. Phyl thought it resembled tapeworms. Annabelle ordered lamb with tomatoes, cucumber, and mint. Timothy decided to go against the grain and ordered, with a glint in his eye and a wink at Phyl, the *Parilladas Mista*. Then they ordered four quarts of wine, both red and white, settled back to enjoy people-watching, and chatted.

"Tomorrow, I am going to a bridge tea and fashion parade at the Plaza Hotel," said Phyl.

Annabelle smiled. "So am I."

"You, too! Oh, great. A lot of our members are going to be there. Good ol' American Women's Club. My life would be utterly empty without it. Though I've spent a fortune on taxis. That's too bad. Buses would be so much cheaper."

"Take your maid along," suggested Annabelle.

Phyl shook her head. "No, I'd rather she be home cleaning and cooking. Stu comes home for lunch so she makes sure he gets his three courses," she laughed.

"We should sit together. Though I'll probably lose my pocket money playing cards." Annabelle took out a black onyx cigarette holder and squeezed her cigarette into the end, then held the holder high.

Phyl put her cigarette out and watched Stuart smoke his cigar. "Are you supposed to inhale?"

"No, but I like to."

Phyl thought of something for a moment and continued. "Stu's joining me after the fashion parade for the cocktail dance." She turned to him. "At least, if he feels up to it."

"Why wouldn't he?" asked Timothy, twirling his cigar between his fingers. He dangled a Yale school ring on his right hand.

"Stu worked all weekend, arrived home Saturday night at 10:30, and I was worried stiff all evening, wondering if he was dead somewhere in a ditch. I swear this place will be the death of me," Phyl swirled her cocktail and watched the liquid play with the lights. "One feels so helpless with no phone, and I still find it hard making myself understood. Anyway, all that work of Stu's is paying off. Stu hopes to get another government contract soon, and this time it will be no flash in the pan."

Timothy patted Stuart on the shoulder. "Well done, old man."

"May I tell them?" asked Phyl, looking at Stuart.

"It's impolite to talk about money," he pointed out, scanning the crowd distractedly.

"Oh, do tell." Annabelle made a quick clapping motion with her manicured hands.

Phyl grinned. "It is a hundred and twenty thousand *pesos* proposition!"

"That's about $40,000. That should garnish you a good commission," offered Timothy.

"Yes, it will. I would feel a different woman if I could look at a bank book with four figures in the credit column instead of four in the debit column," Phyl smiled.

"My client hates our competition, so I know I have it in the bag," said Stuart, still looking at something in the crowded restaurant. "But it certainly isn't because of my skill as a salesman."

"You mean International Business Machines. I can't think who else it might be," offered Timothy.

Stuart nodded. "Yes, another American company who found a loophole. They have their own questionable methods, which I don't agree with." Stuart studied the tip of his cigar. "Yes, International Business Machines. Or IBM, as we call it. My client used to work for them and was fired for something he thought was petty. Now he works for this government department, and he wants to get back at them."

"Well, lucky for you," Timothy said.

"If it does go through, we're going to forget we are a dignified couple and go on a colossal drunk. We've been suppressed far too long." Phyl laughed.

Annabelle leaned toward Phyl. "Wasn't that awful about the milk strike? Three days of mayhem, trains blown up, milk dumped in the fields. Thousands of children affected, some even died."

Phyl noticed Stuart was still very distrated. She searched the room to see who he was looking at so intently.

"That's Communists for you. The Radicals. You get the rabble taking over, and they don't care who gets hurt or dies," said Timothy angrily. "We have too many strikes. Bus drivers. Taxis. Butchers."

Phyl's eyes widened as she spotted Jorge sitting at a table in the corner with the same young woman they had seen earlier. "Jorge," she whispered. "What is he doing here? He's everywhere."

"You know someone here?" asked Timothy. At that moment, the waiter returned with a Godzillian round platter with overlapping dishes of food. Another waiter followed carrying the sizzling pans aloft for Timothy. They parachuted the plates in front of everyone.

"Yes, a friend." Stuart looked at his massive steak and picked up his knife, a murder weapon.

"An ex-friend with a mistress," Phyl said disgustedly. She started to rise.

"You know, culturally, you're to ignore men when they're out with mistresses. To acknowledge the mistress would be an insult to the wife." Timothy carefully put his cigar on the ashtray and sat back from the sizzling grease that spit everywhere from his personal grill.

Phyl paused. "You're kidding me, right? The man does something like this, people treat the mistress like she is worth nothing, and the wife, who is supposedly not insulted by her husband being out with another woman, *would* be insulted if you acknowledge the other woman even though she accepts it all?" She shook her head. "That doesn't make sense to me."

"Phyl, sit down." Stuart didn't look up. She could tell he was perturbed and pretended to focus on slicing into his steak. His dinner plate oozed with blood seeping from the slab.

"Excuse me, I'm going to powder my nose," she lied. Stuart called to her, but she ignored him. She deftly squeezed between tables and past waiters. She stared at Jorge, who eventually saw her approaching. Their eyes locked. He rose as she came to him. "Hello, Jorge," Phyl said tersely.

Jorge slightly bowed, "Phyllis." (Pheellees)

"How is Angelica?" she asked. Then she looked at the young woman. "Oh, pardon me. I'm sorry." She held out her hand. "I'm *Señora de Redington*, though you can call me Phyl."

The mistress, not wanting to be impolite, shook Phyl's hand.

"And, how is Angelica?" She persisted, looking intently at Jorge.

"Er, she's in hospital."

"Oh, the baby?"

"*Si*, it was born yesterday morning."

"A little girl or boy?"

Jorge closed his eyes and took a deep breath. "A boy. We named him Phillip, Phil for short."

Phyl was stunned. "Phil?" she said weakly. She looked around nervously. Jorge had knocked the wind out of her sail with that announcement. She blinked sequentially, then clutched her purse to herself. "Well," she finally said, "that's quite something. I should like to ponder on that." She turned to the young woman. "Forgive me for interrupting." She left without another word.

Shaking, she entered the woman's washroom, entered a closed marble stall, chucked the lid down on the toilet, dropped and thought. "Crazy." Her face collapsed and she cried.

* * *

On Tuesday, Phyl stayed in bed. She was battling the deepest black melancholy. Carmen, who had finally acquired her new maid's uniform and refused to wear anything else, didn't wear a coat to the *feria* last time so she could show it off. So, she had a full-blown cold, and struggled on her feet. By Wednesday,

Carmen got so bad she had to stay in bed, and Phyl had to nurse her. Stuart got the doctor to see them both. Stuart and Phyl were responsible for medical costs for their maid, and poor Carmen was very grateful. Then Stuart caught a cold and had terrible trouble breathing. The doctor ordered bed rest for him, too. But Stuart kept going to the office. He argued he had contracts under development and didn't want to lose momentum.

Then came the day Carmen finally left to get married. It was a toss-up, again, as to whether she would return. So, they had to wait to find out and Phyl wasn't too pleased. A more severe ennui overwhelmed her, adding to her perturbed presence of mind due to housework she had to do on her own.

Within a day, Phyl broke down and hired a woman to do the windows and heavy scrubbing. While Phyl was out on the balcony checking on the glass doors to ensure they were done the way she wanted, a knock came on the door. She called out to see who it was. When she heard a woman's voice, she opened the door and saw Mrs. Minor and her friend Mrs. White from the American Women's Club.

"Oh, hello. What a surprise. Do come in!"

Phyl fussed, throwing coffee, tea, and biscuits together as they chatted. When she finally sat down, they asked if she would consider accepting the office of Chairman for the Dramatic Group, as someone had highly recommended her and told them she was interested in acting.

"Wow," she said, surprised. "I wouldn't know what to do, to be quite honest."

Mrs. White said, "Everything is run by committees, anyway. You're auditioning for the next play, so you're in the right set of mind, and we have so few people acting that you are sure to get a part. We produce a play every month, in the English-speaking playhouse. The plays are very well patronized."

"Well, I don't know. I may be too busy. I've also been offered parts at the Little Theatre Group for later this year. May I ask who recommended me? And how did you know I was planning to audition? You must have been speaking to Annabelle Cline."

The two ladies looked at each other. "Well, actually, it came from outside the club. It was *Señora de Piñiero*. She is a close friend, yes?"

"Angelica Piñiero? How the heck…?"

"Well, we are very glad she did. She told us your wishes to act and how organized you are and full of life and effervescence. And, of course, we agreed with her."

"Well, I don't know what to say. It seems I had nothing to do for so long, and now there is almost too much. When it rains, it pours, I guess."

"Then you will have an exciting winter and spring, guaranteed," said Mrs. Minor. "By the way, if you take over as Chair, you will also be responsible for finding actors for movie productions in town."

Phyl's mouth dropped open. "Excuse me? Like, real movie productions? For the movies?"

Mrs. White laughed. "Yes, if you like that sort of thing. Another film is being produced just outside the city, I think…" She looked at Mrs. Minor. "Next month, is it?"

Mrs. Minor took a sip of her tea. "Production companies rely on clubs like us to help find extras," Mrs. White continued. "It takes nothing to do extra work, but they pay for warm bodies."

"Of course," said Phyl thoughtfully, though she didn't know they actually did. She wondered how on earth Angelica would even know the club was looking to fill that position. Then she thought of Jorge. Was this a gesture of sorts? And if it was, what sinister goal was up his sleeve. But, oh! The movies! She always told El she would be in the movies someday. This was her chance! She wanted to say, yes, yes and yes! But, instead, she said the proper thing: "I will talk to Stuart."

But she knew, full well, wild horses weren't going to stop her.

Chapter Eight

Carmen being bad, the Glamour of Movies, and Back to Jorge

Something strange started happening with Carmen. As if wearing her maid's uniform went to her head, she became bossy with Phyl. Once, when Phyl looked from her balcony down to the park to watch Carmen walk TJ on his leash, she saw her, instead, talking at length with her sister, who was one of Angelica's servants. Carmen's sister was out with the twins and pushing Angelica's newest in a fancy British baby carriage.

She saw they were conversing so deeply, huddled together on a bench near the playground, that the children and dog were ignored. Poor TJ was forced to lay beside Carmen, in the sun and still on his tight leash, while he panted and soulfully watched the other dogs play. Carmen occasionally looked up at their flat, gesticulating and chatting away. Phyl had to crouch out of view and look through the railing to avoid being seen. Sisters talking was one thing; gossip was another. Phyl's heart skipped a beat. Or were they surreptitiously exchanging secret information? She thought of Jorge and Stu's clandestine relationship. Spying?

After Carmen returned, Phyl tersely reminded her she was meant to go out for TJ's benefit and not for the sole reason of blabbing the time away. Carmen responded by sassing her about TJ being a dumb, spoiled mutt and said he should be on the streets like all the other mutts.

Let's just say, Phyl didn't appreciate that and almost fired her on the spot.

The next day, Phyl saw Carmen standing at Stuart's office desk reading some of the papers. Carmen couldn't read English but Phyl still asked her why would she be interested in Stuart's business. Carmen said she was dusting and that she just picked up the paper as it had fallen off the desk. Phyl wondered if all this spy stuff was clouding her judgement.

That night, after Carmen left to go home, Phyl shared her concerns. "Stu, I caught Phyl at your desk. I'm unsure if she understood anything because it's all in English. Should I be concerned?"

Stuart put down the British newspaper, in thought. "Well, a lot of the business correspondence is in Spanish." He blinked and focused on his thoughts a little more. "And some of the contracts are with government departments and officials." He frowned, nodded and put down the newspaper. "You're right. Perhaps they should remain private." He stood up and walked to his office. Phyl followed. He picked up the papers scattered on his desk and glanced over them. He put them down and picked up a leather journal. He held it up. "Did she look through this?"

Phyl shrugged. "I didn't see. Why?"

"This journal is to record my conversations with Bevel, but it's in English." He flipped through the pages. "I could kick myself because I should know better."

"It never occurred to me to hide things. She comes across as completely oblivious to anything outside her little world," Phyl said, leaning against the door frame. "Perhaps you should keep your papers under lock and key?"

"I don't have a drawer that locks. But it wouldn't hurt to have a safe. We can keep the pistol from under the mattress in it."

"How is a pistol going to help us if it's kept in a safe and we need it quickly?" asked Phyl.

"True." Stuart wheezed. He never overcame that nasty cold and still fought a bug. He coughed, took out a plaid handkerchief, and blew his nose. "I'll get one through the office. It should be an office expense. By the way, we have a loaner I can bring home for the time being. No more longhand."

"Oh, goody."

So, Stuart started keeping his paperwork in a safe. It wasn't that large a vault though it took two men and a heavy dolly to get it to the apartment. Shortly afterward, Phyl peeked in when Carmen went to dust. She saw Carmen standing, looking at the cleared desk. Then she saw her look over at the small safe on the side table. Carmen walked over to it, touched the edge, and dusted it with the ostrich feather duster. Phyl fell deeper into an abyss of distrust. Was Carmen spying? Was she passing things on to her sister? Or was she just nosy? She remembered how paranoid Jorge was and finally understood.

One evening, Phyl approached Stuart at his desk, writing in his journal. "Stu, do you think Carmen spies on us?"

Stuart pushed his desk chair back and looked at her, stunned. "That's a hard call. It's too easy to get paranoid."

"Like Jorge?" asked Phyl, tilting her head and making a face.

"Well, he has reasons to be careful."

"And we don't?"

"No, I wouldn't think so. We aren't of the aristocracy with masses calling for our assassination. Or connected to higher-ups who may be on the wrong end of the political guillotine."

"No, but you're his friend and you may know things that would put him in danger. You're also the filthy *Americano* representing a country all of South America thinks connives to have control." Phyl sat on the corner of his desk, as Stuart used to do back in Toronto. "I watched her today and saw the expression on her face when she didn't see any paperwork. I saw her stare at the safe and touch it."

Stuart shrugged and made a face. "Maybe she's never seen a safe before."

"Maybe. I guess also, Carmen might take it as an insult, that we don't trust her

"Well, we don't."

Phyl shrugged.

Stuart sighed. "I go to great lengths to see contacts in secret. I'm careful about talking about sensitive topics in public or on the balcony. Goodness, you and I even whisper in our home. But perhaps it's to be expected. Working for an *Americano* puts a target on her head, and she could very well be tempted by someone to spy on us for a little extra on the side."

"It was never a problem before she got married. Maybe she's getting pressure from her husband. He's a laborer and Argentine."

"I guess we better keep an eye on what's happening with Carmen," Stuart said.

"And her sister. Maybe you should talk to Jorge?"

"It won't hurt to mention it. In fact, it would be a prudent thing to do."

They were uneasy when they went to bed that night. The next day, as if Carmen intended to play the role of the very recalcitrant they feared she was, she sassed Phyl by ordering her around, then whispered under her breath that Phyl was *estupida*.

Shocked and hurt, Phyl fired her on the spot. Carmen left angry, drowning in tears. Enraged, Phyl slammed the door just as the heavens unleashed a clap of thunder which shook the entire city. Within minutes, a wall of rain overwhelmed Buenos Aires. After it subsided, another heavy storm came in that night with curtains of rain. Soaking everyone and everything, it introduced a new leak onto Phyl's head through a crack in the plaster ceiling above their bed. Nearly a foot of rain fell within 24 hours. The ordeals flung Phyl back into the depths of her depression.

The following day, on her birthday, feeling terribly down, she left the balcony doors open for TJ and went downstairs and asked Matteo to arrange a taxi. Glum, she arrived at the Tennis Club just in time for her riding reservation.

She was so distracted, she forgot to hold onto the reigns tight enough. So, when the horse galloped toward an open field, Phyl flailed her arms at the first bounce, with no hold on the horse, and tumbled backward, landing on the back of her head. A young blond stable hand rushed toward her, whistled for the horse to return, and checked Phyl over before helping her back up on her feet.

Phyl was stunned.

"Are you all right, Mrs. Redington? It's a good thing we had so much rain," he said in excellent English with but a slight accent. "That could've been a nasty fall. In fact, that could've been the end of you." The hand was an Austrian immigrant who most of the women thought was a darling. He was dressed in typical Austrian green leather vest and pants with red trim and his hair was tousled from rushing after her and the mare. His clenched jaw and the deep crease between his brows expressed his most profound concern. But his face relaxed as Phyl looked around, patted the back of her mud-covered bob-cut, and frantically wiped the mud off her backside.

"Let me walk you back?" he offered.

Phyl shook her head slowly. "No, I really don't think I'm very hurt. But thank you."

"Well, perhaps it's best to get right back on."

"If I don't, I will never look at a horse in the face again, I'm sure."

He helped her back up in the saddle. She bent over and patted the horse. "Well, that was a good birthday whipping. It shook me out of a miserable state of mind, I tell you," she laughed.

"Shall I tell Mrs. Minor you won't attend her Tea at the Clubhouse?"

"Oh, please don't. I'll be there. I may show up sore and crawl, but there is no way I will miss it. They're off to New York on Saturday. Besides, my husband would never forgive me if I don't attend his boss's wife's last Tea before they leave."

The stable hand nodded and smiled.

"What is your name?" asked Phyl, studying him as she caressed the mare's neck.

"Reiner Weber."

"You speak excellent English. Are you a student and working here part-time?"

He smiled. "I was hired out of Austria to teach at the German school in the city, but I must wait for the new year to begin."

"But you look so young!"

"We start young," he grinned proudly.

Phyl's mare was getting impatient, but Phyl kept a tight hold on the reign this time. She wondered if he was a Nazi. "I hope you don't mind me asking, but are you a member of the Nazi Club?"

Reiner saluted and clicked his riding boots. "I am a proud leader of Hitler Youth," he announced with a definitive nod. It was the same salute she'd seen Germans do in newsreels, but Reiner made it look so elegant. He smiled as he stood proudly, hand outstretched. He was so charming. She frowned, confused. She had never heard of an organization called Hitler Youth. She certainly heard terrible stories about Hitler and his Brown Shirts from the newsreels and Stuart. This sweet young man and the thought of thugs under the same leadership confused her profusely. She blinked and harrumphed.

With a swish of its long tail, Phyl's mare stubbornly cantered back to the field. Phyl helplessly held on to the reigns and waved back at Reiner. She was most concerned as she turned to face forward. He seemed like such a lovely young man. So polite, she thought, finally feeling the horse's rhythm. She wasn't quite sure how to put this Nazi movement into perspective.

* * *

The next day, with Carmen gone and Phyl stiff and in pain from the top of her head to the tip of her toes, Stuart's birthday didn't start off well. Phyl couldn't go out for a nice birthday dinner and dance, so the day ended up with poor Stuart having to eat a humble dinner made by a suffering Phyl – a simple tomato soup, biscuits, fruit, salad, and a collapsed chocolate cake with one candle in the middle. Stuart did his best to appreciate her efforts, finished the light meal, and sat back to light a cigarette. "Dreschler's coming down in April."

"The big boss?"

"Yes. Dreschler's curious as to why we're doing so well. We'll probably know what is what by the time he's finished with us. I think I told you that because I got the Municipality contract, they may keep us here for the next two years."

"Oh, noooo," whined Phyl. "I don't want to spend an extra six months here. We're halfway through our three years. What would I say to Dad? He'll certainly have something to say about that!"

Stuart winced. "Yes, indeed."

Phyl, sitting on a cushion, was dopey from aspirin. "I get the awful sense that the more successful you are in business, the more entertaining I would have to do. You know how I looooove to entertain." She made a miserable face.

"Hmm. This does not bode well for you, I fear. But think of what we could do with that extra money? It would put us years ahead of our schedule. The office is doing really well."

"You mean, *you* are doing well." Phyl scrunched her face. "I guess I have no choice but to entertain the big boss. The Minors are off to New York, so Mrs. Minor won't be on hand to do it. Is Mrs. Dreschler coming, too?"

Stuart nodded. He scraped the dish of chocolate cake with the side of his fork. "It's too bad they didn't come before Carnival. That would've offered some form of lewd distraction."

"What if the movie studio calls me? They should start production any week now."

"Phyl, I'm sorry. You'll just have to cross your fingers Dreschler doesn't expect too much entertaining. But you better hurry up and get another maid. How come it's taking so long to get one, by the way? I appreciate all you do, but I miss my three-course lunches and crave more substantial dinners. Where's my meat?"

Phyl wanted to knock Stuart over the head. "It's only been two days, ungrateful sod. You have no idea how difficult it is to find a new maid, especially when the language is so challenging. *Plus* moving around in this world that forbids me from running out for errands on my own. I have to budget the taxi rides to go to the Club."

TJ, spread out under the table and groaned. Phyl looked down and gently nudged her dog.

"Some guard dog you gave me," she chuckled. "Never barks. How is he supposed to protect me?"

Stuart chuckled. "Well, if you'd stop babying him, he might grow some balls."

"Oh, Stuart," Phyl muttered. "Don't do a Carmen on me."

Stuart saw her misery. Despite a reasonably upbeat attitude, she still looked sickly. "I was thinking I should send you to *Mar del Plata* for a week after Dreschler returns to New York. I'll be swamped and work nights as I have a few new leads. I know the place is crammed just now, and I'm not sure if I would even be able to get a reservation for you, but I could pull some strings."

Phyl knew he meant through Jorge or that Bevel. "I'd love to visit a seaside resort during this blasted winter. It's far enough north to be balmy. But I hear the hotel is costly," she said. "Don't forget about the movie production and my upcoming rehearsals. Remember I landed a part in the Institute's next play? As well as for The Little Theatre Group for the summer?"

"You go from having nothing to do to having a full schedule and an entourage at your Club."

"When it rains, it pours," joked Phyl. "But *Mar del Plata* is tempting. It's supposed to be very posh." She wiped at a crumb on the table. "I wish El could join me there."

"Why don't you ask her? Though I don't think Claude could afford it."

"El hasn't been well lately, and no matter how much I try to entice her to come down, she resists." Phyl sighed. "Anyway, I don't really want to go alone. Too bad. It sure would do El some good."

"She's still suffering from that gout? Perhaps travel is the last thing on her mind. It'd be a shame if you don't take a break, Phyl, because it's going to be a while before I have time off to make our planned trip to Cordoba." Stuart took a drag and attempted to puff out floating smoke circles.

"What on earth are you doing?"

"I saw a kid make these perfectly round circles with smoke, and they floated up and kept their shape. I was really impressed."

"Impressed by smoke circles."

"Quite a skill. I won't feel fully grown up unless I know how to do it. I think it would impress my clients, don't you?" He pointed a nicotine-stained finger at Phyl. "Your health concerns me."

Phyl pointed at herself, surprised. "My health? You're the one wheezing at night."

"It's this blasted weather," Stuart said, subdued.

Phyl fiddled with the edge of the tablecloth, feeling the creeping pain of homesickness. "I want to talk about how we would get back home." Phyl rested her head on the table, looking up at Stuart. "Just for fun, let's plan how we would do it now. Would we go by train instead of by boat? It would be nice to see the other side of South America."

"Okay. Here's my plan," he said, sitting back and crossing his legs. "Cross the Andes to the Pacific coast, take the boat at Santiago – a tramp steamer which takes about fifty days and stops at a couple dozen ports, finally arriving in San Francisco, then a bus across the States to New York." He bent down onto his arms over the table toward Phyl's face. He smiled. "Sounds good, eh?"

Phyl sat up, nodding happily, then winced at the pain of doing so. "Oh, yes."

"But *when* is the question. I would like to spend a little more time in Rio before leaving South America. And I don't know if we should spend all that extra hard-earned bread to make the trip back up that way, though. We'll be going 1,200 miles north of us. But, they say the Pacific coast is a dream. The Nahuel Huapi Lakes are beautiful, too."

"My Canadian friend at the Club went there. She says it's nothing compared to our Great Lakes."

Stuart reached for a cigarette, but Phyl gently put her hand on his, and he sat back. "The trip would be very expensive either way," he said.

"Well, I guess you'll just have to make more bread. And I'll go without a maid for another month. That would save us money."

Stuart took Phyl's hand. "That would be a false sense of savings, Phyl. Please, I beg you. Find a maid. We need to entertain the heck out of Dreschler and his wife." He looked at his empty soup bowl. "And soup and biscuits would never get me promoted." He sat up straight. "And that would be all your fault." Seeing Phyl's expression made him grin and jump up.

Phyl picked up her dinner napkin to slap him, groaning under the pain as she hobbled after Stuart shrilly threatening to clobber him.

TJ barked at Phyl.

* * *

A rotund Dreschler sat back, patted his torso, and clasped his hands over it. "Buffalo wrote that they want you to go with as little delay as possible to Lima, Peru, as there is a hot prospect there." He leaned forward, pushed his coffee cup and saucer to the side, and put his elbows on the needlepoint tablecloth Phyl had bought the first month they were in Buenos Aires. They had just completed a feast fit for royalty, a lamb dinner prepared by a humbled Carmen. "The paperwork is coming down from Buffalo on the ship as I speak, Stuart. We may have it by the day after tomorrow."

Phyl looked excitedly at Stuart. "Wow, Lima, Peru." She thought it would be fantastic to go along, but then she realized she couldn't – not with the movie and two upcoming plays.

"But we have some details to discuss about your contract," Dreschler continued. "You are doing better than we anticipated, but I hope you appreciate that the very nature of being busier means more costs for us. We had to hire that new male typist you needed, you and Minor."

Phyl's insides turned over. She didn't trust Dreschler. She looked at Mrs. Dreschler, who was as round as her husband with tiny white curls. She wanted to change the subject before Stuart got hot under the collar. The company was always readjusting the original contract.

"Keep in mind, Redington, that we have our eyes on you eventually becoming supervisor of the whole of South America, and, of course, there would be plenty pay for it."

"Well, there are others ahead of me, Mr. Dreschler. And also," he looked at a surprised Phyl, who was drilling him beseechingly with her eyes. "The pay would have to be very good for us to be enticed to stay longer." He smiled at Phyl, who nodded in agreement. "But I must admit, I am happy to have gotten four big contracts since I've been here. One of them is the biggest contract our company has ever had."

Dreschler continued. "No doubt you are doing well. You speak fluent Spanish, and you know how the business works down here, which I understand is very different from what we're used to." Dreschler took a pipe out of his breast pocket and held it up to Phyl questioningly. Phyl nodded. He checked the bowl, took a leather satchel from his breast pocket, and proceeded to take shreds of tobacco out. He crumbled some between his fingers. "I don't know how you end up writing it into the books, but it seems to work."

Phyl watched Stuart's expressions. They went from benign to a frown while tapping ash into the ashtray, shifting uncomfortably, and shaking his leg. "That brings to mind something I would like to discuss with you," he said. He looked at Mrs. Dreschler. "But perhaps this should wait until we go to the office tomorrow." Stuart had already shared his concerns with Phyl that he expected Dreschler to try and rip all the profits and pay him nothing, just his salary. This offer of a future promotion sounded more like a diversion from a high commission than a reward for excellent service.

Dreschler grinned and waved at the ladies. "I'm sure you won't mind if us men retire to the balcony, ladies. Let the men chat strictly business while we smoke at our leisure."

Phyl pushed her chair back, as did Mrs. Dreschler. "Can I get you more coffee, Mr. Dreschler?"

"Please, call me Ron. No," he patted his stomach. "I'm quite satiated, thank you."

Phyl smiled. She thought, *I bet you are.* "Mrs. Dreschler and I will sit in the living room and chat." She looked nervously at Stuart and then led Mrs. Dreschler to the living room while the men noisily pushed their chairs back and went to the balcony doors. Mrs. Dreschler picked up her cup and saucer to take away. Phyl reached out. "Oh, don't worry about that. Carmen, our maid, will sort this out in the morning."

"The little wife keeps on about having a maid and cook," said Ron Dreschler, turning back.

Phyl looked at Dreschler and back at his wife. His wife didn't mind being called the 'little wife.'

Mrs. Dreschler responded. "Oh, yes, I would very much like that. We do constant entertaining for Ron's clients and, apart from having the occasional catering company for the large crowds, I wish I had someone, at least, part-time." She followed Phyl to the living room. "It must be so nice having a maid."

"Well," Phyl said, smirking. "It has its moments. I've already fired Carmen once. But I just didn't have the time to find another and, well, easier to work with what you already know."

Phyl finally had given in and rehired Carmen, making her swear that she was not to be nosing into Stuart's affairs. In fact, Stuart had put a lock on the office door. Though somewhat humiliated, Carmen was relieved to return, as her husband had been pressuring her to find work faster than she could.

Stuart opened the beveled glass door to the balcony, and a lively rhumba wafted in from the Alvear Hotel. Phyl wished they had gone to the Hotel that night instead of dining in, but Stuart said that Dreschler specifically asked for a quiet dinner. Phyl watched as Dreschler and TJ followed Stuart onto the balcony. When the door closed, the delightful bouncy music was muffled.

Phyl politely chatted with Mrs. Dreschler, explaining the outrageous Carnival activities and warning her of the blatant sex in the city. Once in a while, she glanced through the glass doors to read Stuart's expression as he leaned over the railing, the lights from the streets below shining upon his face.

She knew that Stuart was very upset about learning that the company diverted the paperwork from his first sale so that it was processed without his signature as the commissioned salesman. By the time it trickled down to Stuart, he discovered that the Buffalo office reaped practically the full benefit without paying full commission. Technical oversight, they said. She knew that Stuart was determined to correct the issue before Dreschler returned to North America. She was worried there would be a scene.

She hoped Stuart would leave it for the office. She was stressed out enough as it was.

On the balcony, Stuart mulled over how to approach the topic. Dreschler was admiring the scenery and listening to Latin music. His fingers tapped to the beat of the bongo drums as he began talking at length about what he read in the tourist rags on the ship down. That gave Stuart time to prepare his approach.

Finally, Dreschler turned to Stuart and brought up the subject of Peru again. "About Peru. You would have to go as soon as you get the paperwork. This lead must not cool down. It's another government contract. These Latin countries are expanding and growing, and I want Remington Rand to have a solid handle on the potential needs of their growth."

Stuart wondered if other strings were being pulled from elsewhere. Expanding his area of exposure would make sense. He didn't know if he should bring up the Foreign Service. After all, Dreschler was his Remington Rand boss, not his top contact for Foreign Affairs.

Dreschler anticipated Stuart having to light a new cigarette, stuck his pipe in his mouth, and lit the cigarette with his gold flip lighter. Stuart leaned on the railing with one elbow and blindly looked at TJ curling up by the canvas chairs. He cleared his throat when Dreschler paused for breath.

"If the company wishes me to go to Peru, then the pay or commission would have to fit the importance of such a trip. I'd have to juggle leads and contracts from here while working there, so it's a solid workload and long days. But, I have to tell you, I have an issue with how the paperwork is filed at head office. The last sale went through without me getting paid full commission because of a technical oversight. The final paperwork didn't have my signature, yet my name was all over it. But no one allowed me to sign it before it was processed and I'm still waiting for it to be corrected."

Dreschler puffed at his pipe, took it out, looked at it, and then stuck it in his mouth again. His head nodded to the music. He peeked to the right at the lit-up Hotel and saw people milling in front. "Yes, well, I'm sure that was an oversight. I wish it was brought to my attention sooner."

"It was. I sent you a letter outlining the issue a month ago but received no reply."

"Dear boy, that had to be an oversight as well. I will look into this." Dreschler removed his tobacco satchel again and put more perfumed tobacco into his pipe bowl. "Now, back to the trip to Peru: It would be an investment, but I have all the confidence that it would pay off with you at the helm."

"How much time do you see me being there?"

"Oh, I would say a good two or three months. It's quite primitive there, and the systems are much slower than here in Argentina." He turned to face Stuart. "Of course, we wouldn't be able to pay any extra for you to take Phyl along, but if you are in a hotel anyhow, you would just need to cover her travel expenses. But it is costly. Almost as expensive as New York."

Stuart looked down at the lit park. Men lingered along the street studying streetwalkers standing under lights. "I'm sure it's stunning there. I hear the mountains are something else entirely."

"Yup, lots of Indians, though. And lots of llamas." Dreschler looked down at the women. "The class of women here is much better than on the streets of Buffalo. Even New York, I see," he muttered.

How would he know? Stuart wondered dryly. "I think the only way up which makes sense is to fly?" Stuart asked, nervously eyeing TJ, who was fidgeting and smelling the balcony floor near the grate.

"Oh, yes. No sense in going by car or boat. Takes too long. A plane is the only way of getting over the Andes. The only other way, I hear, is to go by Rio to Mendoza and then cross the mountains by car, which makes a nervous wreck of everyone. You are driven by natives in rickety old Fords with your heart in your mouth the whole way. After that, you have to go again by Rio up to Lima. It takes nearly a week that way. By plane, you do it in a day and a half."

Stuart winced. "Phyl's deathly afraid of planes," he said, concerned over TJ's mounting focus on the balcony grate. "She'd be frightened for me, too. The other day a Pana passenger plane went down going north up the East Coast. Eleven people were on board, all dumped into the ocean and killed. Shark bait. Several of the husbands of the women in Phyl's Club were on that plane. All American."

"That is a true tragedy," muttered Dreschler as he turned to face the balcony doors and happened to look just as TJ spurted diarrhea over the grate in the floor.

* * *

Two days later, after the Dreschlers left for Uruguay, Mildred Spright, the Englishwoman who was the head of the Little Theatre Group, called with Phyl's schedule for the movie production. Movies were being produced in Argentina on the same grand scale as in Toronto. In fact, when Phyl was 12, she saw Mary Pickford when she came to Toronto to revisit her birthplace on University Avenue and to drop by a movie set in one of the abandoned factories near Fort York. It was like seeing the Queen in person and Phyl never got over it. It was all over the papers at the time. Over the years, along her travels to and fro from work, she occasionally saw signs of production underway either in the city's side streets or in abandoned factories down by the Canadian National Exhibition grounds. But seeing the tell-tale signs of movie sets from the outside was one thing; being on the inside was yet another. She didn't know how she was going to control herself on set the following day.

At 4:30 the next afternoon, Mildred met Phyl in a taxi. Mildred was to chaperone Phyl for the duration of her stint on set. Matteo, who had just gotten a nice new wine-colored uniform with brass buttons and a cap, nearly broke his neck helping Phyl hurry through the door and to the taxi. He grinned with pride as he stood on the curb, especially when Phyl and Mildred commented on how *hermoso* he looked. Life was good.

They were to be on set by five. They sat nervously in the taxi, watching the cityscape go by. The streets, always so raucous, were strangely tame as most people had their *siesta*. She watched street cleaners with old, broken-backed horses and buggies scrape debris and horse manure off the quiet cobblestones.

The taxi reached the city's outskirts and arrived at the gate of the movie set on time. They got out and nervously approached a gentleman, who checked their names on a list. From there, they were led into a small dark building where a ballroom had been constructed. Phyl's stomach felt queasy as her eyes adjusted to the gloom and looked around at what looked like an actual ballroom with round tables, candles, fancy chairs, and a stage for a band.

Some band members in costume milled around tuning their instruments. People were chatting and laughing in corners and at wooden tables. There were scrapes and bangs as the crew adjusted tripods for lights and moved around wooden boxes for supports for more lighting. The ballroom walls were fake, hand-painted to look like fancy wallpaper and trim, and there were sandbags everywhere, keeping everything in place. There was a musty smell of dust and grease paint, mixed with heat. She heard rapid-fire Spanish everywhere.

Phyl was relieved that Mildred spoke fluent Spanish and that she could rely on her to follow directions. Her heart beat so hard she thought she would faint. How would Phyl remain sophisticated and pretend this was normal for her? How would she keep from gawking and looking like a silly young girl? Phyl looked around, wide-eyed, trying to spy on the movie stars, though she wouldn't have been able to recognize them anyhow. But surely, there would be an air about them, and they would be surrounded by an entourage. She thought, *I dreamed of this.*

Abruptly, they were directed away from the ballroom to a young woman who stood in the deep shadows. She had papers in her hand and addressed Phyl, who looked in turn at Mildred, and Mildred answered. The girl frowned and pointed at Phyl and complained about something.

Phyl looked questioningly at Mildred. "Is there a problem?"

Mildred looked at Phyl as the girl continued to speak, and she waited for her to stop. "She says that you obviously do not speak Spanish and wondered how you got a role."

Phyl shrugged. "Because I got it through the Little Theatre Group. Right?"

"I told her, but she said it was unusual. They only take Spanish-speaking actors because they need to understand directions." Mildred looked back at the girl. The girl looked at Phyl, said something to Mildred, and left. "She said to wait here."

Phyl got nervous and looked around, hoping people weren't watching, but they were. "Oh, Lord."

The young woman hurried back, marked their names off the list, and said something to Mildred as she led them to a table where a pile of evening-wear costumes waited to be sorted.

"What did she say?"

"She said the director said to let us in. Quite peculiar. I don't know the director. Do you?"

Phyl looked to where she thought the director was. A man with glasses stood with a blow horn. She shook her head. "Nope."

"Well, someone pulled strings for you," said Mildred. "Let's see. We need an evening outfit."

Phyl spied the pile. She and Mildred had fun finding something that would fit Phyl's slight body. Mildred teased Phyl by finding the most revealing ones and holding them up to her. Phyl laughed nervously, still feeling unwelcome, which added to her discomfort. She shook off the feeling as she looked for something she wouldn't regret wearing on screen. Not that she expected anyone at home to see her. She knew the movie would only be distributed through South and Central America, Mexico, and Spain. She thought just as well, as no doubt she'll probably act like a corpse and forever regret being on the screen.

After she put on a suitable outfit, they were led to the makeup and hair tables, where Phyl was told to sit in front of a makeshift mirror with very bright bulbs attached on three sides. She looked around at other actors. Men and women were sitting together; some half-dressed, looking accustomed to what they were doing, walking around in open dressing gowns, showing enough skin that Phyl had to divert her eyes. She and Mildred couldn't help but giggle nervously at the amazingly loose morals that prevailed.

Phyl didn't know how much Mildred was getting for her role as her chaperone, but she read on her talent slip that she herself would receive ten *pesos* a day. She couldn't wait to write to El that she was finally a professional actor! She tucked her talent slip into her bag watched over by Mildred.

Phyl saw a young woman, with hair tortured tightly into a braid, put about an inch of brownish-green makeup on every part of her that showed from under her evening dress. Her face, arms, shoulders, hands, and even her cleavage. Her lips were painted with a brush and almost black. The makeup was so heavy that Phyl wondered how the young woman could smile or talk. The mascara was thick on her lashes, and her eyebrows and eyelids were heavily penciled. Then the actress was given a set of artificial lashes by a make-up lady that reached her penciled-in eyebrows. When the young woman tired of Phyl watching, she complained to the make-up lady, who said something to Mildred.

"We're bothering her, apparently. Best not stare at her," Mildred said.

"Oh," said Phyl, looking away. "Who is she, anyhow?"

Mildred shrugged as Phyl's hair was slicked into place with pomade, before she was made up as heavily as the young actress but without the eyelashes. Phyl and Mildred then had to sit by a long table with other actors and wait. And wait. And wait some more. Mildred reminded Phyl that every time she ate, drank, or touched her face, she was to be careful not to smudge anything. Between her hair being plastered, the makeup on her face and her body feeling so thick she thought it would crack, Phyl had no idea how she was to move, sit or talk. She was surprised at how tired she already was just by getting ready and waiting. The acting hadn't even begun.

As they watched the goings on, they saw the same young actress saunter around as if she was in her element. She appeared to be about 18 or so and spoke only to those who mattered, ignoring all the *underlings*. It was apparent she had no interest in the lesser actors or crew. In fact, she was downright rude to most. At one point, Mildred said she overheard her cuttingly call one of the extras a *vaca gorda*, or fat cow.

"That's not very nice," said Phyl. She sat with her back straight as a ruler away from the table's edge. She wondered how she would scratch an itch on her cheek when there was an inch of grease paint over it. "Can we find out who she is?"

Mildred turned to one of the other background actors and asked. One person knew, laughed derisively. "Eva Duarte," Mildred passed on. "Apparently, this is her third movie, and she's the mistress of one of the ministers in charge of movies in Argentina. Eva Duarte's boasting she'll have her own radio program. This lady told me she's very anti-American so we should stay out of her way."

Phyl eyed the young woman. She had brown hair, a mousey face, and wasn't necessarily beautiful, but the all-around effect was pleasant. In fact, it was more her presence that seemed to imply she had something that may catch the camera's eye. She evidently had a speaking role but effused an unapproachable air. Unless one were the director, Phyl noticed, because then she was quite amenable. At one point, she must have heard that Phyl was supposedly American because Eva Duarte looked straight at her and gave her a dirty look. The look that Argentine women reserve for her at the *feria*.

"Well, I'll stay out of *her* way," laughed Phyl.

Around eight o'clock, they were called to fill seats at the dining room tables in the fake ballroom. Phyl was directed to sit with another woman and two men at a round table. They were to pretend they were two couples dining and watching the dancers on the ballroom floor. Phyl started to sweat and didn't know how to dab away the moisture beading on her face. She couldn't understand the others at her table very well, as Mildred wasn't allowed on the ballroom set, but she did understand, through a word or two and motions, that she was to dab with her handkerchief.

"These hot lights feel like they are giving me a sun tan," she laughed, but the others didn't understand. They smiled politely and nodded.

Phyl understood they were directed not to look at the camera or crew but to sit pretending to enjoy the floor show. So, they sat amidst general disorder and ongoing shuffle. The band started playing when someone yelled *rodante!* Then the scene burst into life at the sound of *accion!* Nobody knew exactly what they were doing, but they did it anyway and ended up having to do the scene about a dozen times until Phyl felt she would scream. During the first take, when the camera focused in her direction, she was so nervous, she dropped a glass, and the director called *cortar!* She apologized but then was told as best her peers could not to even apologize. No one was interested, and it was best to move on.

After finally getting home around 4:00 and catching about three hours' sleep, Phyl got up with Stuart. At the table, he asked how it went.

"Stu, I had no idea just sitting and waiting to act could be so tiring. It was so exciting! But something weird happened. It looked like they wouldn't take me when we got there."

"Why's that?"

"They only take Spanish-speaking actors for practical reasons, directions, and all that. But the director told them to take me. Do you know the director?"

"I doubt it. What's his name?"

"I don't know."

"I can't help you there. It certainly wasn't me. By the way, would you do something for me?"

Phyl yawned and widened her eyes to feel more awake. "Sure."

"If Mildred overhears anything of interest, ask her to share it with you?" Stuart stood up from the table and checked to ensure he had his billfold in his pocket.

Phyl thought about it for a moment. "You mean, like...?"

"Yeah. You know."

"Yeah, okay. Will do."

He kissed her on the forehead, looked closely, and scratched at a bit of brown makeup she didn't clean. "Thank you. You just never know what a tidbit of information loosely shared could lead to. Actors hanging around sets tend to talk and observe. Just a thought." He smiled at her. "Have a nap sometime before you're off again tonight. Break a leg." He winked at her before picking up his briefcase. "I don't mean that literally." He opened the door and left.

Phyl put her foot on the edge of her chair and rested her chin on her knee. She was so tired she could hardly move. She looked at the mantle clock at the bar and decided to return to bed for a while. "Get some beauty sleep for my next big six-hour wait to do something," she muttered.

And listen to what Mildred had to pass on from overhearing chatter, she did: A rumor of an uprising here, a murder there, which actress was going out with what general here. Who was a member of the Nazi Party and which government official put money into the movie, or which one of actors was hired to double for an official. Eva Duarte's ongoing diatribe about how famous she was going to be.

During the remainder of the week, Phyl learned much about filmmaking. She found it hard to believe that everything Phyl watched being made could end up looking alright on the screen since nothing was done in continuity. It was all pieced together according to some big plan. The death scenes were done before the birth scenes, and the goodbyes were filmed before the hellos. But Phyl was thrilled and wondered how she could wrangle a small speaking part. Not speaking Spanish made that a non-starter. However, she could still dream. Generally, the experience was so intense that her nerves were strained by the end of the week. She didn't know how professional actors could stand it. She worked from two, three, or four in the afternoon, according to when they wanted her, usually right through till early morning. Finally, the last day she left the studio at four, arriving home just as dawn broke.

Crawling into bed that last stint, Phyl decided she preferred stage over movie-making anytime. Theatre felt more genuine compared to film. She was sure of one thing, however: People in film must only be there for the money and not for the love of acting, since there wasn't much satisfaction in doing one teeny thing a dozen times, then going on to some other teeny part from an entirely different part of the story, and repeating the whole process.

Her stomach rumbled. Phyl had eaten something on set that didn't sit well. She loved her cheeses, and they rarely had it at home because Stuart didn't like cheese. So, on the last day when she saw the catering table had an unpasteurized cooked cheese absolutely marvelous on a piece of rusk, she ate to her heart's content, as much as she dared under the watchful eye of the assistant director. Phyl managed to ignore her stomach's rumblings and slept until 11:30. When she awoke, she had no time to think as she rushed to get ready to go downtown to meet Stuart and a Belgian client who was taking them out for lunch. She didn't eat much there as she didn't want to worsen her upset stomach. The client invited them on his yacht to go sailing for the weekend to Uruguay, and Stuart jumped at the chance.

After lunch, he and Phyl hurried down to the *Comisario*, or the Commissioner, to see about getting *cedulas*, or passes, for Uruguay. Due to the crowd and the Latin system of slow manipulation, it took from two in the afternoon until half-past six, standing in the broiling heat, waiting for their passes. The outside temperature was over 100 degrees, and everyone moved glacially. The Commissioner's people would write a line on their paperwork, swallow a cup of black coffee, take a sip from a glass of water, and write another line. Then they'd have another coffee. While waiting, Phyl continued to feel worse. Strange knife jabs in her stomach, sensations one would get after taking too many laxatives.

She started to panic. When her paperwork was done before Stuart's, she hurriedly left him and rushed home by taxi, ferociously fighting what she thought was the inevitable explosion. By the time she got home, her body couldn't expel anything but gas, and intense fatigue overwhelmed her. She crawled into bed, hoping a couple of hours' rest would help and she would still be able to pack in time to leave for the evening's sailing trip. But after being in bed an hour, she began a terrific fever. By the time Stuart got home expecting her to be packed, Phyl's forehead felt like a furnace. Stuart gave her an aspirin which made her sweat and feel worse. Then he hurried down to the lobby and called the doctor, who came within an hour to find that her fever had broken. The doctor decided to give her a great dose of Epsom Salts and announced it was pretty evident she would not be able to go anywhere for a while.

All night, she sat drenched in perspiration on her sparkling new white toilet seat as her body expelled from both ends. Saturday morning, she was a dish rag. Her stomach, back, and sides ached so much she could neither lie down nor get up. Stuart thought he might as well go to the office. When he returned that afternoon, Phyl was sleeping. At six o'clock, she awoke with the most terrible pains she had ever experienced in her life. Every ten or fifteen minutes, she was doubled up, startling Stuart with her screams as if she was giving birth to quintuplets. This lasted off and on for thirty-six hours.

The doctor returned Sunday night with laudanum, and she was left as limp as a dress shirt on New Year's Day morning. He explained to Stuart that the trauma and pain were caused by simple gas but that her intestines were so inflamed they couldn't stand the slightest pressure. Anything going through her innards, including gas, felt like glass splinters. After Phyl's body calmed down, the doctor gave her charcoal mixed with water - like taking mud. The charcoal absorbed the gas, and she improved after the first dose. She now teetered on 96 pounds, weak as a kitten. She couldn't eat anything but soups and cream of wheat made by Carmen, who had become likable of late.

She was heartbroken. She would have loved to have gone on a beautiful sloop, feasted her eyes on the Uruguayan coastline, and toured the country. As a bonus, the client was even kind enough to invite TJ to come along. But after further thought, she realized she wouldn't have wanted to be caught on a rocking boat in the middle of the ocean with two men and absolutely no privacy in such an embarrassing situation. And TJ would probably have had his own bouts of diarrhea to boot on that beautiful teak deck.

She was relieved she didn't have to endure that comedy of errors. She went from an imagined star to a humbled, groveling dishrag within a week.

So much for fame and pride.

* * *

A month later, three pounds heavier, Phyl sat down to write after making a batch of delicious coffee rolls liberally endowed with nuts, raisins, and cinnamon. They smelled heavenly, and it helped to return her to a perky mood and anxious to share - and dare to boast - of all the great things she'd been doing.

Dear Dad and K,

Well, I'm really busy with the Club. We had the first meeting, which I had to plan, and Tuesday is the big General Meeting at which I have to speak. But the thing that's keeping me the busiest is that I was given a grand part by the Buenos Aries Comedy Company for a play being staged in September, so I have to work like a nitwit at rehearsals. I'm in a panic for fear I shouldn't be able to justify the confidence they placed in me as they have given me the female lead. Two men are in the leading parts. Added to this, Carmen, who doesn't live with us anymore, comes in only half days, so I have enough to do and there are the bridges and teas which I am avoiding as much as possible, but I have a nice girlfriend, Vivienne, whom I don't want to lose so I have to be sociable.

In December, we'll have been here two years. Stuart is always getting ideas that we'll be leaving in a couple of weeks but he has thought this so often. He has trouble with the company and there have been some hot letters. It is just that the company can't bear to see a man make money. Stu has been working towards his third year, and according to his compensation plan, he had prospects of making $9,000 commission (American) before coming back. This would've made the whole trip worth the effort. But Buffalo changed his contract in midstream cutting his commission. They make just as much profit on the business but he gets less. In fact, Stu snagged a total of 200,000 pesos in contracts, but it didn't get counted in, and he's out of $600 commission.

    Phyl thought perhaps she'd include copies of the correspondence between Stuart and Ron Dreschler after Ron returned to Buffalo. It was far meatier content, and it would make her feel better by getting back at Dreschler for what he did to them at that last moment in New York.

    Phyl got up, took a key out from underneath a bottle of Sherry at the back of the bar and went to Stuart's office door. She unlocked it and went to his desk to look through the papers. She found what she sought and returned to the dining room table. She straightened out the letters and read them anew.

    The other letter was Stuart's reply to Ron Dreschler. She absolutely loved it when Stuart raised his hackles. He was so good at communicating frustration.

    The door opened, and Stuart walked in carrying his briefcase and roses. He wore his heavier suit as they were still on the edge of winter. He took his fedora off and put his keys on the bar.

    "You're home early," said Phyl, surprised. "That's for me?"

"No, for Carmen," Stuart smiled. "I find her irresistible."

Phyl got up and slapped his shoulder, happily taking the large bouquet. "It's not my birthday, nor our anniversary." She sniffed the beautiful aroma.

"Nope. Lots of good news all around, so, I thought I'd come home early and celebrate with my little wife, as Dreschler likes to say."

"What's there to celebrate?" Phyl put the roses on the table, kissed him, took his jacket, and shook it. She folded it and put it over one of the dining room chairs.

"Well, I should give my wife roses every day. She's so domestic all of a sudden. When have you ever folded my jacket, never mind helped me with it?"

"Gotta do something for my pay," she jested.

Stuart eyed the coffee rolls and sat down. He picked one up and licked it. "I heard that Rand's sister's husband has been brought from Toronto and put in place in Buffalo. Dreschler is on the way out."

Phyl's mouth dropped open. "Noooooo."

"Yeeeeees. And Schuler graduated to Dreschler's job as head of all export and vice president. He and his wife are on their way down and stopping in Rio."

Phyl picked up a coffee roll and broke off a little piece. "Wow. Did you pull strings?"

"I told them that if there were plans for me to spread out, like a trip to Peru, the company had to make it worth my while. And, yes, I did mention my company problems to my contacts." He shrugged.

"Well, it sure makes me feel grand to be married to someone so powerful."

"It may be just a coincidence," Stuart said as he crammed a massive bit into his mouth, then grinned at her, open-mouthed, exposing its mashed contents.

"Oh, stop!" Phyl laughed, covering her eyes. She dropped her hands. "Rand's sister sure knows how to take advantage of Remington Rand. They're having a grand time on Remington if they stop at Rio." She popped the piece of roll into her mouth and admired the remainder. "I guess I'll be entertaining them. Little did I know that someday I'd have the pleasure of doing so for my old boss and his wife."

"Well, that's not all. I snagged an excellent contract this morning for 140,000 *pesos*."

Phyl clapped her hands, dropping the roll on the table. "Oh, Stu! How wonderful."

Stuart dipped into his briefcase, "I have some mail for you."

Phyl squealed because it looked like a newspaper, which usually meant hose. "I sent money for hose, but I'm never sure if the money gets to K." She hastily opened the large envelope, opened the newspaper, and out fell three flattened pairs of beautiful hose.

As Phyl ran her hands through one of the sheer hose, Stuart chewed and reached for her letter and envelope. He noted that the copies of the Remington correspondence were in the envelope. He looked up.

Phyl saw what he was looking at and frowned. "Is that okay?"

He nodded. "Sure," he said. "But I'd like to keep copies. Here, I just want to add my own little note. 'Save me writing." He took the pen, her letter, and along the sides of one of the pages, he wrote:

> *PS. Hello folks – I've just had my domestic wife's coffee roll, so I have enough energy for a howdy do – this Christmas, the Redingtons may be in Peru, Argentina, Uruguay, or Canada – here's hoping it's the latter – we're fed up to the teeth. Can't tell you how much we miss you – and the fishing. This is a swell country to be from, as far as possible. So long for now. What do you think of the budding movie star I've got for a wife? Stu*

Phyl read his note. Her mouth dropped. "We're going away for Christmas?"

"It's part business, but you're coming along. I hated being gone so long without you last time. Besides, with this new contract, we'll have enough money to extend that trip to a lovely vacation for ourselves. Your health still isn't back. It'll do you good."

Phyl smiled sweetly. She got up and sat on his lap. "Thank you." She kissed him, and he smiled. She looked at him coyly. "I got another compliment today."

"*Another* one!"

"A backhanded one. Today a bird came to inspect the stove, and he promptly called me *Señorita*. I promptly told him I was a *Señora*."

"You sure told him off."

"Uh huh, one must preserve one's standing. Then later, when I went shopping with Carmen, I went into a market. I said, *Buenos dias*, and the young server returned with a *Buenos dias, Chica*."

"That was *chica* of him," Stu grinned.

Phyl slapped him again and got up.

"Ouch."

"Wus. Well, I immediately called the manager and raised hell." She put her hands on her hips. "I asked the boss did the boy think he was addressing a servant and that to kindly remember I was a North American, and where I come from, women are accustomed to respect from men – let alone boys."

"Well, you told them off."

"So, you see, I have some amusement in a day."

Stuart stood up, went to the bar, and poured two scotches. He handed one to Phyl.

"So early? I can make coffee."

Stuart shook his head. "No. You'll want this scotch."

"Uh-oh." Phyl took the glass and sat down as Stuart returned to the table.

"You may not like this. We must pick up again with Jorge and Angelica."

Phyl pursed her lips.

"I've been reminded by Bevel to keep a full communication loop going. We need to spend more time with Jorge. I can only do so many coffee chats. But it's obvious to the entire world we're not socializing with them. And Jorge doesn't feel comfortable about always meeting me in town. We have to start going to the *estancia* and spend some time at their flat for dinners."

Phyl slumped into her chair. "Jorge frightens me."

"It's not him you are afraid of, Phyl. It's the fact that you are involved. And I'm sorry."

"I'm afraid I may not have what it takes to be a Mata Hari after all," Phyl said sadly. "Though, I do miss Angelica. I occasionally hear what she's been up to through Carmen and her sister."

"So, you know she's expecting her fifth child."

Phyl smirked. "Busy Jorge."

"It's what they do. Have babies." Stuart looked at her pointedly. "And one day for us. Soon."

Phyl did a curt nod. "I know. I'd rather wait for the house, though."

"Hmm. So, let me bring you up to date. The war in Spain…"

"Outside the newspaper office today, there were so many Spanish cheering and hissing that Carmen and I were frightened stiff. I don't understand the fools; they'll fight and lose their lives when they don't even know what they're fighting for. That Franco is just like Mussolini and Hitler."

"That's kind of the point, Phyl. The Spanish here are rearing to fight an overseas civil war and are looking for fights here. Argentina has Germans and a strong Nazi political base. Hitler's put a lot of his own military power behind Franco. And we have the Italians who predominantly lean toward Mussolini. Buenos Aires seems to be a small, but just as dangerous, mirror image of Europe. I'm getting anxious. I'm not garnering the information I need to pass on. Everyone – the British, Americans, and the Justo Administration – is concerned that there will be a runaway situation on top of the usual upheaval."

Stuart broke into a cough, took out his cigarettes, and lit one. He looked for his ashtray.

"Stuart, you haven't given yourself a chance to get over that cough. Why smoke?" Phyl got up and returned with a clean ashtray from the kitchen for him anyway.

"I cough when it's too long since my last cigarette," he joked. He took a drag. "That's better." He put the pack of cigarettes back into his shirt pocket. "Another thing, Minor's son has diphtheria. I didn't realize there are no quarantine laws here. Minor came to the office and admitted to allowing the other two children attend school. I thought I'd keep my distance even though we're inoculated but you're so weak. I'll do some work here at the flat."

Phyl frowned. "I've accepted an invitation to a bridge game this Friday, and Mrs. Minor will be there. I'll definitely stay a good distance from her, and I'll keep my fingers out of my mouth."

"You mean these fingers?" Stuart said, pulling her hand to his mouth. He sucked on her fingers.

"Stop," she said, staring at his eyes. "I want to finish the letter."

"Go ahead," he jested, sucking. "Who's stopping you?"

Phyl threw her head back and laughed heartily. She pulled her hand out and wiped her fingers on her hips. "And you just saw Minor and his diphtheria germs? Thank you very much!"

"Speaking of Minor, let's get back to Jorge."

"Do we have to?"

"Yes, Angelica is in hospital as we speak. Jorge has invited us to come next Sunday to see the baby. And then he and I will talk at length. It will be a full day's visit. I think the British attaché and his wife are also invited for later that night."

Phyl suddenly didn't feel quite right. "Excuse me," she muttered as she stood and walked away.

"Where are you going?"

She looked at him comically. "I'm visiting my favorite pristine, white toilet seat as it seems home to me lately. The mere mention of Jorge is a perfect laxative."

"Well, try not to monopolize that pristine white seat. I don't favor the grate on the balcony."

Phyl laughed as she locked the bathroom door behind her.

"And why are you locking the door? You don't trust me?" he called.

"Absolutely not!" she yelled back.

Chapter Nine
Late 1937, the Piñieros, Locusts and a Close Call at Sea

The following week, Phyl rehearsed every night until about 11:30. The play didn't go as well as expected for the first few rehearsals because two cast members stayed away with colds. Phyl was told this was inevitable. People get together, emote together, get sick together. Better to get it out of the way before the serious rehearsals. The weather, a typical Argentine winter, had been extremely damp, rainy, and cold, but Sunday, the day of the big reunion with the Piñieros, was predicted to be pretty mild.

Sunday morning, Stuart came out of the bedroom coughing.

Phyl was putting a ribbon on the gift she and Carmen had picked up for Angelica's new baby – a handsome-looking sweater. She looked up, feeling somewhat drained herself, but concerned about Stuart.

"You've never really got over that bad cold. You were wheezing again during the night."

He waved her away. "Oh, I'll be fine. It's just a tickle."

"No, it isn't. I'm so afraid you may have inherited your Dad's lung problems. If you quit —"

"Are you ready?" Stuart asked, cutting her off.

Phyl sighed. If only he would listen.

"Phyl, I'm sorry. I just want to get going. Are you almost ready?"

She looked at him sadly. "Truth be told? I feel like I'm going into the Lion's Den."

Stuart held her. "One step forward. In just over a year, we'll be home. Not much longer."

"If we survive." She jabbed him in the shoulder. "If *you* survive."

"Come, let's go down and have Matteo grab a taxi. Or do you want to walk?" He looked out the window at the sky. It looked overcast, but it was a pretty good winter day.

"With our luck, this fair weather will change into a cyclone midway. Taxi would be nice."

Phyl felt unsettled as they took the rickety elevator down, but she perked up when they were greeted by a grinning Matteo, who looked just as proud as the first day he was given his official burgundy uniform. She knew Matteo's wife polished those brass buttons every day.

A few minutes later, during the taxi ride to the Piñieros, Phyl sadly watched as they passed the park and the crowds immersed in their Sunday activities. Couples danced the tango out on the grass, a gramophone belting out as best it could, playing a tinny version of the fad. She wasn't sure if it was her imagination, but this version of tango looked more abrupt, ruder, harsher, more stylized, but just as beautiful and mesmerizing. She tore her eyes away and looked at the bare trees and drooping palms. How many times would they have to go to the Piñieros? she wondered. How many more dinners, how many more coffees? Would she be able to get out of going to their *estancia*?

Just as they entered the Piñiero's flat, the sun broke through the clouds and poured through the windows and the balcony doors; it took Stuart and Phyl by surprise. "Well, is this a different planet? The world out there was miserable," Stuart said, as a servant took his jacket and Phyl's coat. Down the hall, they heard a stampede coming their way, and Phyl turned to see the four-year-old twins run toward them ahead of twelve-year-old Georgie, as if they were long-lost family. The twins clung to Stuart's legs, grinning up at his face. Stuart messed up their hair. "*Ola amigos!*"

"*Ola Americano!*" laughed one of the twins.

Stuart shook Georgie's hand who curtly nodded with a smile. He glanced at Phyl sideways.

Phyl held up her arms. "Georgie, it's been so long! You've grown so tall!" Georgie stood almost eye to eye with Phyl and allowed her to hug him.

One of the twins pointed at Phyl. Shyly, and with a finger in his mouth, he said, "Who's that?"

"That's Auntie Phyl, don't you remember?" Stuart asked.

The child shook his head with flare, keeping his eyes on Phyl.

Stuart pointedly looked at Phyl.

A servant led Phyl and Stuart to the master bedroom, where Angelica looked healthy and plump. She sat in bed surrounded by pink pillows, luxurious-looking blankets, and linens. She was the vision of a queen in a pink negligee and bed jacket, ready to receive them. Another servant was taking her empty coffee cup away as they walked in, and Angelica's young toddler, Phyl's nameskake Phil, shakily stood, holding onto the bed skirt, drooling and dancing on the spot in his bare feet.

"Ah, a born tango dancer," joked Stuart while Phyl reached down and patted the toddler's behind.

"Well, *ola, bambino*. I've only seen you from my window, and you were always in the baby carriage," said Phyl. The toddler looked up at her and put a finger into his drooling mouth. He grinned, showing a few teeth and a runny nose, and Phyl had to look away.

Angelica laughed, reached out with her arms, graciously and happily hugged Phyl, accepted the gift, and invited them to sit. Phyl caught sight of a glamorous-looking bassinet in front of the bedroom settee. Phyl and Stuart grinned at Angelica before tiptoeing over to peek in, and they saw the new 10 ½ pound boy with a shock of black hair and long thick black eyelashes.

"Oh, my, what a beautiful boy!" exclaimed Phyl.

"He was two and a half weeks overdue," said Angelica.

"A chip off the old block. Where's the old man?" asked Stuart.

"In his office. Please, feel free to go. Phyl, come and sit by me." She patted the bed next to her.

Phyl watched Stuart leave and then walked over to the bed. She sat down and smiled at Angelica.

"Friend, we missed you. I hear you are quite the actress now. Movies and theatre? When is the play opening?" Angelica's dimples in her cheeks had deepened, and an extra laugh line or two were indications of time passed since their last visit – of course, including two additional children.

Phyl smiled sheepishly. "Oh dear, you know? Well, the first play comes off a week Thursday night. Eleven days!"

"Oh, wonderful. We'll both try to be there. Though I know for sure Jorge will be going. But what do you mean, *first* play?"

Phyl scratched her nose nervously. "I'm in a second one, with an opening night a month later."

"Oh, my! When it rains, it pours with you, Phyllis (Feelees)! And are you ready?"

Phyl shrugged. "I'm a nervous wreck as I take everything seriously and want to make good on my first real opportunity." Phyl scratched at the back of her hair. "This first outfit is more professional than amateur, as the public pays well to see us. It looks promising, in any case." She shifted to get a better seating on the bed. "The play is hilarious, and we have a great cast."

"Do you get paid like a professional?" Angelica smoothed down the hairs behind Phyl's head.

"We get a cut of profits which are unevenly distributed amongst the cast. But with the rental of the theater, the scenery, advertising, and all that, well, there probably wouldn't be much left. But I know it will pay my taxi fares to rehearsals anyway."

"Do you find it's a lot of work?"

Phyl laughed. "Oh, yes. Memorizing! And I have four quick changes. That's my biggest worry."

"Oh, that'll keep you on your toes," laughed Angelica.

"Absolutely," Phyl said, smiling down at her hands. She felt shy. "I love it, of course. Though there's jealousy towards a newcomer and plenty of remarks made to get me flustered."

"How unfortunate."

"Yeah, it bothers me." Phyl played with the lace of one of the pink pillows. "I am sensitive, but I try to remain professional. I say, Angelica, my voice carries better than any of them, even though my knees shake the whole time. I can hear my voice bouncing off the end wall."

"Oh, I'm sure. I've heard your outside voice."

They both laughed. Phyl looked at Angelica and sighed. "I think everyone we know is coming to see the play. Probably with the secret hope that I won't know my parts." Phyl smiled sheepishly.

"Oh, I'm sure they won't. They'll want to wish you the best." Angelica's eyes sparkled, and she cocked her head. "And how did the movie go, by the way?" A servant came in with a coffee and biscuit for Phyl. She took them as Angelica chatted rapid-fire Spanish to the servant before the latter left the room. Angelica turned to Phyl again. "Sorry. Something to do with dinner tonight." Angelica sat up straighter. "Did you like being on a movie set?"

Phyl laughed. "I feel quite the Garbo. I could tell you so much now. I didn't know what to expect. The movie's out, but I haven't seen it yet. But then, they probably cut all my parts anyways. But," she held up a finger, her eyes twinkling. "there are stills in a few shops, and there am I, ha! With a cigarette in a fancy holder in my hand."

Angelica reached for Phyl's hand, looking concerned, and she was about to say something, but the baby started to fuss. Phyl turned to look. "Don't worry. A servant will come and get him for me."

Phyl relaxed and, precisely as Angelica said, a servant entered the bedroom and went to the bassinet. She picked up the baby and rocked him, which made him settle down. Phyl looked back at Angelica, who was still holding her hand. On the other side of the bed, the toddler suddenly fell on his behind and cried. The same servant walked to the toddler and spoke softly at him. She reached down to his chubby arm and pulled him back to his feet. She led him to the bassinet, gave him a squeaky toy, and started rocking the baby. Every move was watched closely by Angelica. She finally turned to Phyl.

"You have lost so much weight, Phyllis. I am most concerned about your health. Jorge keeps me up to date every time he sees Stuart. I hear you have not been well."

Phyl watched the servant put her finger in the baby's mouth to keep it still. "Oh, my nerves are shot. And I have this rheumatism, and the doctor wants me to have an examination again. I don't want any more injections – I had these special injections that seemed to help a bit. Otherwise, I feel great. There's another movie production soon, but Stu won't let me do it because I'm struggling physically. He says it's too much of a strain till three or four in the morning, and with all the other things I'm into, he's afraid I'll have another attack of pneumonia. I suppose he must wear the pants."

"Yes, I know. Jorge was also very concerned. He said the movie took a toll on you."

"Yes, well, it did." Phyl felt a little uneasy. "Jorge knows a lot about what I've been up to."

"Oh, he cares very much. He knew you wanted so much to be in a movie. He's a big investor in movie production in the city; did you know that?"

"No, I had no idea." Phyl stood up. She remembered the director on set, not hesitating to approve her as part of the background cast. Now everything made sense. But she wasn't sure if she liked being part of a plan, even if the goal was to fulfill her wishes.

The baby fussed again, and the servant brought the baby to Angelica. Angelica lifted one side of her bed jacket to expose a bulbous breast and the baby immediately latched on to the large pink nipple and suckled. Phyl had never seen anyone nurse a baby before. She looked away.

"I love your dress, Phyllis," Angelica said as she looked down at the newborn. "Did you have it tailor-made?"

Phyl pulled out of her deep thoughts. She looked down at her dress. "Oh, yes, I did. I lost so much weight I had to have a few things made. Everything I try on now just hangs on me and makes me look like a scarecrow. So, I saw this plaid wool at the *feria* and knew right away that it would make a stylish dress. I added the deep brown velvet collar and cuffs – like it? I designed it."

"Love it. You should wear it when you come to the *estancia*. Though you would need to pack some riding and hunting clothes. Stuart says you are coming finally?" Angelica looked at Phyl hopefully.

Phyl smiled politely. "When is that?" she asked, concerned.

"Oh, certainly not until after your obligations are met," laughed Angelica.

"Can't wait," Phyl said, not feeling the smile but hoping she sounded sincere.

There was a pause as the women listened to the baby suckle.

"So," said Angelica, still looking down at her newborn. "Tell me why I haven't seen you for so long. I can guess. But I need to hear it from you. What exactly happened?"

Phyl was surprised at Angelica's directness. But then she should have expected it. Angelica was not one not to live in the moment of truth, unless diplomacy demanded otherwise. Phyl played with the material of her dress for a moment as she thought about her pain and what caused it. Tears threatened. She took a deep and ragged breath.

Angelica placed a gentle hand on Phyl's arm.

Phyl saw a genuine look of concern and love on her friend's face. She looked around the lavish surroundings as she searched for words. She swallowed hard. "Jorge put us in a bad position."

"And what position was that?"

"A dangerous one."

Angelica did not respond for a moment. Phyl searched her face for any kind of expression.

"And did you get hurt?" asked Angelica.

Phyl blinked and thought back. "Well, no."

"Did Stuart get hurt?"

"No."

"So, what is the problem, exactly?"

"I saw things. Terrible things. I was frightened."

Angelica pondered Phyl's words.

"So, from what I know, Jorge asked for you to go and witness events which, if he were to go, certainly meant his death. And his presence would've affected the course of events."

"Why did he have to go to begin with?" asked Phyl quietly.

"You know how these things go, Phyllis. Both my husband and yours are in difficult and compromising positions. They are part of a larger picture for the good of the whole." Angelica paused and kept a steady gaze on Phyl's face.

Phyl's face dropped.

"To be here is to know what is truly going on. If you have a problem with what you saw and experienced, perhaps you have to put things into perspective. This will not end. You will see more. You will experience things you will not like. Simply by living here, in Argentina, in this city. You have to wake up, Phyllis. This is the world we live in. I so appreciate you in my life. I don't feel as lonely. My other friends do not understand the subtleties, the potential loss. I don't know why they don't take the time to understand the real world. But I do. My family has been here for generations. So has Jorge's. We do not want to see this country fall apart for good. You and Stuart understand."

"But the violence. How do you live with that, Angelica? How can you bring children into this?"

"I bring in wonderful human beings who will strive to make it better." Angelica said, with an air of pride and authority. "They will have big shoulders."

Phyl felt like an ass. A cry-baby. "Shoot," she whispered. "In Canada, we don't have to live in a terrible nightmare like this."

"You're not in Canada, anymore, Phyllis. You are here in wonderful Argentina. You are riding the wave of history in this exceptional country of mine. Stuart is here for a reason. And so are you. Now find the strength to fight alongside him."

Phyl faced a fork in the road. She could choose to take offence, walk out the room and never come back. Or she could take Angelica's very clear and harsh advice to become a stronger, wiser woman and to face a world that needed oversight. A world that needed help from whatever source it would come. She shook her head. Then she nodded. "You're so, so right." She clenched her jaw and stood up. She straightened out her dress. "I will do that. Sorry."

Angelica gently switched the baby to the other breast. She smiled sweetly at her child. She looked at Phyl, continuing to smile. "Good."

Phyl smiled back. "Good."

"Well, onto other things," laughed Angelica. "I'm so relieved the election is over. President Justo was a very bad boy. He certainly kept his security forces busy on election day, but we think Ortiz may be good to us when he takes over next year. He's certainly the favorite of British interests. And Castillo, his running mate, is an ultraconservative, thank goodness. I will sigh with relief once they take over."

Phyl sat in the armchair, ready to pick up from where Angelica led. She nodded. "Women don't vote here yet, do they?" she asked, finally shedding the negative side of her. "In Canada, women have been voting since 1917."

"No, but I do hope that changes, though I suspect that when women do get to vote, they will end up voting as their husbands tell them to. However, I certainly would vote for what both Jorge and I believe in. Our politics affect our entire business and that of my father's. We always seem to be on the brink of losing something since the beginning of the Depression. Life has changed so much since my childhood. I don't recall my father having so many worries about everything losing value or investments not generating returns. Jorge is forever scrambling for other means of solid investments."

A servant knocked on the door, and Phyl understood that lunch was ready. Angelica held the baby out for the servant to burp. "Phyllis, you go and join the men for lunch. I will have a short nap if you would excuse me. After lunch, Jorge's brother, Diego, will drop by, and he and Jorge will take you and Stuart to the *Exposicion Rural* for the afternoon. I will join you later at dinner."

Phyl's eyebrows raised in surprise. "Oh, like the Royal Winter Fair in Toronto."

"Does your Fair have horses, cows, sheep, goats, and dog shows?" asked Angelica.

"Yes, exactly, and lots of manure and sculptures out of butter," Phyl laughed.

"Well, we don't have greasy sculptures; they would melt immediately," Angelica chuckled. "But there's lots of manure. I gather you have a stomach for that sort of stench."

"Oh, I love it. Brings back happy memories. Deep down, I'm a country girl." Phyl stood up and smoothed down her dress again. "You have a good rest," she said as she followed the servant cradling the baby down the bright hallway toward the livingroom.

Lunch was a generous serving of young partridges cooked in wine and herbs, followed by a cheese tray. As they were finishing, Jorge's brother, Diego, walked in, said hello, and sat down for a glass of red wine to chat before Jorge finally looked at his watch and announced that it was time to go. It was such a lovely day, the sun being surprisingly warm for the winter day of July, they decided to walk to *La Rural* at the far end of the large park.

Phyl leaned on Stuart's arm as they sauntered, while the men smoked cigarettes. Phyl had started to cut back of late, not liking the effect of cigarette smoke and humidity on Stuart's lungs. She issued a sympathetic cough. Stuart patted her on the arm.

The closer they approached the *Rural* buildings, the thicker the crowds became. The music of a beautiful tango echoed through the canyons between buildings, and they saw people dance in the open square by a large monument. "This is exciting," said Phyl, squeezing Stuart's arm, her nostrils twitching at the smell of manure in the breeze. "Doesn't this smell like the Royal Winter Fair, Stu?"

Stuart sniffed the air. "I think I smell a slightly pungent aroma. Good healthy stuff," he said, laughing. "Reminds me of home in Wilkes-Barre."

Jorge slowed down to walk in tandem with Stuart and Phyl. "Every year, breeders come from all over the country to show their livestock. Diego and I sometimes show our bulls and cattle."

"And sheep," yelled Diego.

"But today, we hope to find a prize bull." He pointed to both sides of the large pavilion. There are other buildings, but today we're just concerned about cattle, sheep, and bulls. Although, later, if you like, we'll take a look at the horses."

"Oh, I would love that!" exclaimed Phyl.

Diego, who was a couple of inches taller and two years younger than Jorge, and no less handsome, half turned back as he watched a young woman walk by on the arm of an elderly man. He made an approving face. "I need to buy sheep," he said, distractedly. Diego flicked his cigarette butt to the side and stuck a toothpick into his mouth.

"Yes, and Diego needs sheep. And our old bull, which has done a very good job over the years, by the way, is getting on, and we must replace him. Though we're considering insemination within the next few years for more control over stock quality."

"How much does a prize bull go for?" asked Stuart.

"A prize pedigree bull? It can go from 3,000 to 8,000 British sterling pounds."

"Oh my," exclaimed Phyl. "Just for one bull?"

"Well, yes. When you think of all the *bambinos* he makes, a bull is always one of our best investments," grinned Diego.

"That's a lot of bull," laughed Phyl.

As they passed the massive monument and dancers and approached the grand front entrance, they heard more music from one of the side pavilions. In front of another entrance to the right, south of them, they noticed a gathering of young people, all wearing armbands. Tables were set up with leaflets, and large swastika flags were erected on poles behind them. Phyl was surprised to see Reiner there, handing out leaflets.

"Nazis," muttered Stuart.

Another group of young people, further along, also stood with leaflets, and surprisingly, unusually, a few young women were handing them out, too. This group had a large painted sign behind them that read, "*Alianza de la Juventud Nacionalista.*"

Jorge stopped to look at the displays within such a short distance. "I heard of that new *Alianza.*"

"Yes, as I have, though I haven't seen any of their handout material," said Stuart. "I heard it's an extension of the Argentine Civic Legion." Stuart started walking toward them.

"Where are you going?" asked Phyl.

"I want to read what they have to say," Stuart continued. Jorge followed.

Diego stayed behind and looked at the dancers around the monument. He looked at Phyl. "Would it be inappropriate to invite you to a dance, *Señora de Redington?*" He held out his arms.

Phyl's heart quickened. Any chance for a dance was welcome. She eyed the other dancers. They were so quick on their feet, so precise. So very serious.

Then she looked at Stuart walking away. Then over at Reiner. She shrugged and nodded happily. "I would love to. I'm sure Stuart won't mind."

Diego led her closer to the other dancers and immediately put his palm securely against the small of her back, forcing her into a ramrod posture. "You are like a little flower in my arms."

"Now, Diego. Behave yourself. I am a *Señora*."

"If I didn't know, I wouldn't have believed it," he said. He suddenly dipped Phyl backward.

"Oh!" she exclaimed, but she loved the sensation of being under control.

Diego led her through provocative steps. Occasionally, Phyl looked at Jorge and Stuart talking to the young people at the *Alianza* table. Before the dance was over, Jorge and Stuart walked back to her and Diego while they were perusing leaflets they were given. Stuart looked up and caught Phyl's proud look. He grinned, lifted his finger, and wagged it as if saying, 'Naughty.' She stuck her tongue out at him.

Diego led Phyl back to the men. He looked at his brother questioningly. Jorge looked at him and held up the leaflets in his hand.

"Another fascist group." Jorge slapped the papers. "They reject liberalism, parliamentary democracy, and communism, and they claim to be concerned about the needs of the masses."

"Same old, same old," said Stuart. "Did you notice they also used the Nazi salute?"

Jorge nodded. He looked back at the two displays. "I sense there is a strong streak of Nazi philosophy in the *Alianza*." He looked at a leaflet. "Very anti-Semitic."

"Oh, dear," said Phyl. Stuart handed one of the leaflets to Phyl. "This is all in Spanish."

"Sorry," Stuart pointed at the bottom of the page. "*War against the Jew. Hatred towards the Jew. Death to the Jew.* And the Legion's women's section is called *Agrupación Femenina de la LCA*." He held up the other leaflet. "Apparently, these young women help the poor and establish social peace."

"Strange juxtaposition. On the one hand, these say death to the Jews; on the other, they promote peace." Phyl looked at the young women standing by the table. A group of young boys stood nearby, curious and ogling. Then she looked at Reiner again. He spotted her and waved. She waved back politely.

Stuart looked over. "Someone you know?"

"Stable hand at the Club."

Stuart frowned. "One of those Nazis work at the Women's Club," he muttered to Jorge.

Jorge's eyebrows shot up. "That would make sense. Much to garner from the wives of foreign executives and political diplomats."

Phyl's heart skipped a beat. Her blood ran cold. All the times the women chatted freely as they readied to ride! Quite sensitive subjects were shared, if she were to be honest with herself. She felt rather disturbed at how blind she and the others were.

Jorge angrily scrunched the leaflets into a ball in his hands and threw it onto the pavement. "These damn moles are in every goddam corner of this country." He turned to Phyl. "Apologies for my harsh words. Nazism and Fascism worries me to the bones. We wouldn't fare well either way."

Phyl knew what he meant as she followed the men toward the main entrance. Jorge stopped, allowing Phyl to catch up. Stuart and Diego continued walking ahead. Phyl swallowed, looked at Stuart's receding back, and cleared her throat. Jorge looked at her questionningly.

She looked down at her shoes. "May I ask you a question?"

Jorge ran one hand along his pomaded hair. He smiled. "Of course, Phyllis." His eyes danced.

Phyl hesitated. "Did you get me that job on the movie set?"

Jorge frowned and studied the end of his cigarette. "Yes," he said, looking at her. "I happen to be a major investor in the two being made this year, and you were having a hard time doing nothing. I thought it would give you a lift."

"Well, then. I thank you." She felt sad. Remorseful. "And I'm sorry," she whispered. "I'm sorry I stopped seeing you and Angelica." She looked up at him, her eyes watering. Her chin quivered. "I'm so sorry," she whispered.

Jorge looked over at the men who stood waiting at the top of the stairs watching other people entering the stadium. He scratched his brow. "I understood. I know it's all quite unnerving for you." He smiled slightly and looked concerned. "I understand Stuart won't let you do the next movie?"

Phyl shook her head. "He doesn't. After the last one, I was over-exhausted and very ill for a while. I shouldn't complain. I'm about to have two plays open in sequence in the next two months. I'm still able to sharpen my thespian incisors."

Jorge laughed. "You have such a way with words, Phyllis."

Phyl smiled.

"But the information you came back with from the other actors on set – well, it was helpful."

Phyl brightened up. "Oh, I didn't know that. Really?"

"So, I will ask Stuart to allow you to do the second movie." He squinted his eyes and gave her a gentle look. "So, you can continue to talk through all those hours of waiting. Would you like that?"

"Oh, yes. I would love that!"

Jorge gently took her arm and led her to the entrance to join Diego and Stuart. "There is a young woman in particular you mentioned. Eva Duarte. She is also fascist-driven. Young but ambitious. She will be in the second movie."

"I remember her. Quite bossy." She laughed.

"And also, by the way, I've just invested in an apartment building closer to our flat. I know you've had issues with your landlord, whom I know quite well. He's been looking into your background and has a chip on his shoulder. Apparently, Stuart gave him an earful?"

Phyl looked at him, surprised. "How do you know that?"

"Stuart told me." Jorge flicked his cigarette to the side. "He's dangerous. He's going to give you trouble and is much too inquisitive. You have to move. You will have more security and privacy. I will be in control, and you know I always have your best interests in mind."

"Would we still have a view of the ocean?"

"Absolutely. I can make sure of it."

The thought of packing and moving did not sound enticing to Phyl. But she remembered the landlord's threat. She looked at Stuart, wide-eyed, as they continued to walk. Stuart stepped toward them, concerned. As they approached, Stuart held out for Phyl's arm. She took his arm.

"Are you alright?" he asked. He looked at Jorge. "Everything okay?"

Jorge smiled at Stuart. "I made her a proposition."

Stuart gave him a "look."

Jorge made a face at Stuart. "Not that kind of proposition." He waved at him. "Come, let us go in. I'll explain." He turned and led them into the shade of the archway and moved along with other patrons entering the stadium. A wall of pungent manure aroma slammed their senses.

Stuart blinked and coughed. "Okay."

An uncompromising breeze tossed debris and leaflets around their feet and into the corners of the entranceway. Phyl shivered at the sudden drop in temperature in the shade of the archway. But she wasn't sure if it was the sudden drop in temperature that caused such a rattling stir in her bones or the mounting fear of unstable changes approaching. She took a deep breath and shrugged. She reminded herself they only had a little time left in their contract. Surely, before she knew it, they would be back in North America and all the mayhem, violence and fear would be far behind them.

Little did she know. Adventure? Ask and ye shall receive.

* * *

"Last year, General Juan Molina reorganized the militia based on the Nazi Party. He likes to see himself as an Argentine Hitler."

Jorge swilled the last red wine in his wineglass and held it against the chandelier's light above the dining room table. "This is a lovely batch of wine we made. Thank goodness we didn't lose it in the fire."

He sniffed the wine and downed the remainder, tilting his head back which loosened the short hair at the top of his neck. He placed the glass back on the marble tabletop and smoothed down his hair. "Molina believes in destroying the oligarchy in Argentina."

"And that is us? The oligarchy?" asked Angelica, sitting at the other end of the table. A servant took away her plate and utensils and brushed crumbs away with a silver brush and dustpan.

"It certainly is."

"I don't know how to stay on top of all the information we're gleaning and passing along," said Stuart, playing with his fork. He coughed into his fist. "The names keep piling up. And it's unsettling how deep the Nazi influence actually is."

"Indeed. It *is* amusing how deeply Argentines hate Americans, while they sneer at the British who have invested extensively into our infrastructure and transportation, yet there is very little alarm at the growing German influence in politics and culture. We have a young soldier, Juan Perón, who served in Chile as a military attaché. His wife just passed away, so he is investing all of his time and energy into studying the military in Germany. He deeply admires Hitler's philosophy in hard training. This is fairly unsettling, but Germany's army is quickly becoming the largest and most advanced in the world. Interestingly, he also wrote and published his own political philosophy."

"You mean, like Hitler did with his *Mein Kampf*?" asked Phyl.

Jorge blinked. "I suppose with the same motivation of possibly running for office, getting people on board. I did hear, Perón is being groomed by the military for potential leadership. But I would hope he is not as radical and his book not as misdirected as the Fuhrer's. I can't help but see Hitler as unhinged." Jorge looked up at the ceiling. "Learning to become such an expert on Germany's military could become his calling card when he decides to run for office. He's an outstanding boxer, by the way."

"Oh, yes?" perked up Stuart.

Jorge continued. "Another flag popped up. We suspect that Dietrich Niebuhr, the German attaché, is a Nazi spy. He served in the German Navy and then as a civilian in the *Abwehr*. He also worked for the Dutch shipbuilding firm *Ingenieur Kontor für Schiffsbau*."

"But that's not Dutch. It's actually German," interrupted Stuart.

"Precisely. It's a very bad cover."

"What do they think we are, stupid and unsophisticated?"

"Their arrogance only surpasses their audaciousness." Jorge shifted his position and cleared his throat. "Neibuhr was promoted to Commander and is now the naval attaché to Argentina, under the pretext that he is the only German upstart who is fluent in Spanish. I think it's part of a grand plan of infiltrating our government. He's been aggressively lobbying us to buy German ships and equipment."

"He's been quite successful at it, I hear."

Suddenly, everyone was startled by a massive bang against one of the balcony doors. Angelica and Phyl screamed. Down the hall bangs reverberated against other windows. The baby wailed, soon joined by the toddler twins. Servants scrambled.

"Oh, *Dios mio!*" Angelica held her hand to her breast. Wide-eyed, she looked at Jorge.

Jorge and Stuart pushed back their chairs and rushed to the balcony. Jorge pushed in the light switch, and light flooded the area outside the balcony door. Movement caught their eye, and they both looked down at a massive locust lying on its back, its legs kicking in the air. Another hit the glass as they stood, and the men jumped back.

Phyl stood up but stayed at the table. "What is it? How can anyone throw something so high?"

Stuart turned back and grinned. "Nobody's throwing anything. It's a monster grasshopper." He motioned at her. "Come and see. It's simply biblical." He cleared his throat loudly as he waited for her.

Phyl and Angelica hurried to the balcony door. More bangs made them squeal as a wave of locusts hit the windows. The four watched as the steady barrage flew against the walls and windows. In the circle of light on the balcony, the creatures – writhing, wriggling, and kicking – piled up quickly.

"Oh my god!" yelled Phyl.

"*Langostas,*" whispered Angelica.

"They're huge! Almost as big as lobsters!" exclaimed Phyl.

"We have them every seven years or so," said Jorge. "A cloud of them falls over Argentina. They congregate in the parks, like the one below, eating grass and shrubbery. Our lights are attracting them."

"You can't go home in this," said Angelica.

"Well, we have to eventually," laughed Stuart. He looked down at the pile of locusts on the balcony. "We'll be fine. We'll take a taxi."

Angelica led Phyl to the living room. "Let's change the topic to something more pleasant, shall we? Enough about spies and Fascists and Nazis." An exceptionally large bang against the window. Phyl whipped her head around and stared at the door in fear. "And *Langostas*," Angelica laughed. "I'm tired of it *all*. I want to hear about your quaint family now. How are they doing?"

Phyl was relieved to talk about normal things. "Well, my Dad is doing fine. So is K. El's been sick, however." She sat on the arm of the settee and crossed her arms and legs. "There's some health issue she's been struggling with, but they bought a new house and are moving away from where they are near Dad and K. It's a much bigger house, so I hope they can afford to hire help if El's still struggling."

"Is she still working?" asked Angelica, raising her voice above the noise at the windows.

"Yes, Claude's letting her work. They were saving up for this house," Phyl shouted as she stood up and moved to the middle of the white settee. "But I guess she can stop now. Maybe start a family."

"Maybe start a family? That is such a strange concept. Here you have babies right away, and when they come, they come. We don't control it and hold back."

"I know," smiled Phyl, "but we're not Catholic."

"And you? Are you waiting for a house back home?"

"Absolutely! Then we'll start our own family," piped up Stuart.

Phyl pursed her lips and gave a small smile.

"God willing," said Angelica, smiling, looking at Phyl curiously.

"Yes, as you say, God willing."

"And your in-laws?" Angelica grabbed a gold pillow, punched it, and dropped it on the white carpet at her feet. She lifted her feet and placed them on the pillow. "How are they doing? The hotel is doing fine? Better, I hope."

"Mr. and Mrs. Redington both had pneumonia last winter." Phyl made a motion with her hand. "Well, *their* winter was while we had our summer. My father-in-law has had it four times now."

"I'm so sorry to hear that. How old is he?" Angelica turned to Stuart.

"Dad's 78 years now," Stuart answered. He coughed and faced Jorge to talk as they continued to watch outside.

Angelica looked at Stuart thoughtfully. Another deafening bang made the women jump in their seats again. Angelica covered her breast. "That is so unsettling."

Phyl laughed.

Angelica frowned. "I noticed that Stuart is always coughing and clearing his throat. Does he have a tendency for pneumonia like his father?"

Phyl blinked and looked back at Stuart. "Oh, Lord. I hope not. I think it's because of too many cigarettes and this awful humidity that never seems to go away. I've been struggling, too. I don't know how people live here all their lives and not die of consumption."

Angelica raised her eyebrows. "Many do. Every day."

Phyl, surprised, looked at Stuart.

Jorge and Stuart came over and sat down. A servant appeared with a tray. She placed coffee cups and saucers on the table and poured while everyone watched. When the servant left, Stuart poured a little *crema* into his coffee.

"Phyl," he said. "I forgot to tell you, we're finally going on our sailboat trip to Uruguay. We have time between your two plays, right?"

Phyl, surprised, shook her head. "No, after the first play is finished, I'll still have rehearsals for the second."

"What about this coming weekend? Do you have rehearsals?"

"No, not this weekend. Can't we go after both plays are finished? The weather will be better."

"A sail to Uruguay. How lovely," said Angelica. She turned to Jorge. "I don't think I've ever been on a sailboat."

Jorge shook his head. "I don't think you have. I have, but not very often. Contacts in Uruguay. The same ones you'll meet on your trip," he said to Stuart.

Contacts. Phyl was taken aback. She looked down at the rug, confused. Sadly, she realized that everything they ever did had something to do with Foreign Service. She sat back, somewhat deflated.

"You should have a grand time," offered Angelica.

"We will," said Stuart. He turned to Phyl. "We'll go this weekend. I don't want to put it off."

"Because of your contacts?" asked Phyl.

Stuart sighed and nodded.

Phyl crossed her arms. "Well, I guess I have no choice. With my luck, it will be a rough crossing. I'll probably be sick the whole trip and spend my time feeding the seagulls."

"Well, that's not a very pleasant topic for conversation," Stuart said.

She cast him a wary glance. "Well, I guess I'm not feeling very pleasant at the moment."

That night, the temperature rose to its highest ever recorded for the winter season. By the time Phyl was ready for bed, she was soaked with perspiration. Lying in bed was unbearable.

"Let's move the bed out on the balcony for a romantic night under the stars," joked Stuart.

"Absolutely not! Not with an Armageddon plague of locusts going on out there," Phyl retorted.

"Oh, come now. Where's that girl who loves a northern Ontario camping trip and pinecones sticking into her vertebrae? Those things are already dead or moved on." Stuart looked out the window and turned away to get a broom. "I'll clean the cadavers. It's much cooler there, and the sky's cleared up." He turned to her and wiggled his eyebrows. "And it's a full moon."

Phyl snorted and walked up to the window and pressed her nose against the glass. She saw a blanket of *langostas* and studied them, looking for signs of life. There didn't appear to be any. She eyed Stuart gingerly stepping onto the balcony to shovel carcasses over the edge. TJ happily sniffed through them and tossed the odd one into the air. Phyl gagged.

The moon shone as if it was day, and the thought of sleeping under the stars was a very tempting proposition, but she waited until Stuart was finished before she dared step out to see for herself. She looked around and inhaled the ocean air.

"What do you think?" said Stuart. "Shall we?"

Phyl looked at the balcony below them. She looked up at the sky and over at the park in the gloom. "I guess they stopped attacking us." She nodded. "Okay. I'll pretend we're in Algonquin Park."

"That's the ticket," said Stuart. He disappeared indoors. Phyl heard squeaking and scraping of heavy furniture. She helped him tip the bed, covers and all, through the balcony doors and into place.

They finally retired for the night under the stars, but after an hour of deep sleep, a wayward *langosta* bumped into the wall above Phyl and plopped on her head. She screamed, scrambled out of bed and frantically knocked it off the bed covers. She squinted angrily at Stuart who continued to snore. She panicked but remained standing, bracing herself for another random visitor, but after twenty minutes, falling asleep standing up with her arms crossed, she slowly lowered herself onto the mattress and covered her entire body and head with blankets.

Minutes later, she felt a breeze on her face and realized the blanket had slipped off. She opened her eyes and looked cross-eyed at a set of beady eyes and antennae. Phyl didn't remember how she ended up inside the flat; she was that quick, then she almost fainted at the sight of several more in the midst of death throes on the floor. She chased one still quite alive with a shoe but couldn't kill it, even though she pounded it as hard as she could. At three o'clock, she woke Stuart by holding his nose, and begged him to push the bed back inside. He turned over and promptly fell back asleep.

At 7 o'clock, Stuart, with a silly grin, woke her up where she was sitting sleeping on the toilet.

"Good morning, sunshine. Rise and shine. Time to make the lord and master his breakfast."

"If you say lord and master one more time, I will divorce you," she groaned, looking fearfully at the granite floor as she shuffled to the kitchen.

"Someone's cranky this morning. Not enough beauty sleep?" Stuart joked.

Phyl flew at him and smacked him on the nose with the identical shoe with which she pounded the monster grasshopper from hell.

* * *

Friday mid-afternoon, with white cumulus clouds climbing into the heavens and a bright clear sun, they climbed on board the fifty-foot teak and mahogany sloop belonging to Stuart's Belgian client and contact, Addie Dimsdale. TJ refused, at first, to get on board but eventually succumbed to pushing and pulling, finally scrambling down the cockpit ladder to be under the watchful eye of a servant of Dimsdale's. Dimsdale and Stuart untied the dock lines on the stone wharf at the Yacht Club Argentino and hopped on board to putter past the other yachts moored in the bay. Once cleared, they hoisted full sails and set out to cross the broad and rough stretch of the mouth of the Plata River. The ship rocked and dipped through the waves. Swells came in from the South Atlantic, causing the ship to rock and roll like a Roly-Poly Doll.

Seabirds dipped into the white caps and floated midair above their heads. Spray stung Phyl's face. She squinted around, trying not to give into seasickness. After two hours, Phyl saw nothing but an endless stretch of white capped water. As expected, she did *feed the seagulls* over the side and was kindly instructed by Dimsdale, that once they saw the Uruguayan shore in the distance, to focus on something on the distant shore to help settle her stomach. It helped somewhat, but she still ended up lying on her side along the lee side deck, holding onto a stanchion with one hand and a rail with the other, ready to toss without getting up.

As they came due south of Sacramento, Dimsdale laid out a new course to go up the coast toward the mouth of the muddy Riachuelo River. Finally, the swells lessened despite strong winds. Hot air occasionally wafted over them from inland. The temperature change made them sweat in their heavy sweaters, and they took them off.

However, hours of chop and swells yanking at the tow rope of the rowboat towed astern eventually did its job, and the rope snapped. Dimsdale immediately instructed a surprised Stuart to take the helm while he retrieved the boat hook and stood ready to grab hold of the rowboat. He rolled his arm motioning this way and that, pointed and hollered directions back at Stuart as he tried to tack the boat to head back to the rowboat. In the first two attempts, Dimsdale tried to snatch any part of the boat or rope, but they were either not close enough, or they shot past before Dimsdale had a chance to even touch the runaway, bending as far as he could over the railing.

Stuart was not a seasoned helmsman, and a massive gust of wind accosted their sails and hit their bow; the yacht suddenly heeled onto her side, at which point Stuart overcorrected the tiller and the yacht jibed, with the boom whizzing past Phyl's head, who fortunately was cowering in the cockpit. Phyl screamed and hung onto the trim as if her life depended on it. Dimsdale grabbed a teak rail on the cabin top just in time, though his feet were flung from under him. For a moment, he hung on for dear life. All were deathly afraid of capsizing while TJ, whining, was helplessly thrown back and forth down below. The servant cowered in the cabin as he watched dishes crashing out of the cupboards over TJ.

After the last attempt, during which time they took on water and almost lost Dimsdale over the side once again, he successfully hooked the rocking rowboat, awkwardly pulled and dragged it to the side, and cumbersomely jumped into it to grab what was left of the towing rope. He yelled at Phyl to take the rope while he looked for a way of splicing it to another line. Phyl held the rope, praying that the rowboat wouldn't capsize with Dimsdale and leave them helplessly on their own. But Dimsdale managed to reinforce the rope and climbed back on board. He drifted the rowboat to the stern and tied it.

After Dimsdale took over the helm from a relieved Stuart, another swell broached from the stern, smashing the rowboat into the boat, and the newly-repaired rope immediately broke again at another spot in its weave. Stuart and Phyl argued with Dimsdale not to risk their lives by repeating the dangerous process. Dimsdale accepted the mutiny and had no choice but to let the boat go adrift. But something about it didn't sit well with him, and he swore that someone had intentionally cut into the rope.

Phyl and Stuart looked at each other. Phyl leaned into Stuart's ear and cupped her face so that he could hear her over the roar of the wind. "I thought we were just going out for a nice sail."

He yelled into her ear. "We have to pick up a package."

Phyl glared at him. She got up, went down below and hugged TJ tightly as she securely positioned herself into the corner of a settee and fumed.

Dimsdale finally tacked into the mouth of the river and the intense noise and mayhem lessened considerably. Dimsdale started the engine and called for Stuart and Phyl to drop the sails. Phyl stiffly clambered back up the cockpit ladder and helped Stuart loosen the halyards, pull the sails down, and bundle them up as they continued motoring up the river toward Riachuelo. It was dusk by the time they maneuvered the sloop through the narrow channel lined with jagged rocks jutting out like sea monsters. Phyl's nerves were shot, trying to watch the threatening shoreline, as Dimsdale's flashlight wasn't strong. However, the lights of the town helped direct them to a broader section of the putrid water, where they passed peacefully moored boats toward a dimly lit town wharf.

Stuart and Dimsdale tied the boat. Stuart helped a stiff and shaking Phyl down onto the wharf and physically lifted TJ and handed him to Phyl to be taken for a well-deserved doggy break. Staying within pools of light from lamp posts, Phyl took a few deep and shaky breaths as she held onto TJ's leash. She was physically drained, and the whole world rocked as if still being tossed on the ocean. After TJ had his fill of doing his deeds and sniffing the foreign territory, Phyl returned with him, and they untied the boat to shift to an appropriate spot to drop an anchor.

After a fitful sleep in their cramped bunk, Phyl and Stuart woke stiff and sore. Stuart was badly sunburned from the sun and wind and had already started to peel by the time he sat down for breakfast. Phyl, on the other hand, was deeply tanned.

Within the hour, they watched a nearing rowboat dodging floating garbage, and two Latin-looking gentlemen acknowledged them and asked for permission to climb aboard. Phyl stayed on deck with TJ and the servant while the three men went below to talk. She gathered from the tone of their voices that the exchange of information was very enlightening. She peeked and saw one of them give Stuart an official-looking pouch. From what Stuart had told her the night before, she knew it was diplomatic papers to be taken to the American Embassy in Buenos Aires. Apparently, sending important documents to Buenos Aires by air or boat was becoming more of a liability, and though the sailing trip was rough and far, the exchange ensured the pouch would get to where it was going without being stolen and photographed. Phyl thought there must be dandies of secrets in that particular pouch.

It smelled like danger.

Phyl distracted herself from unpleasant thoughts by picking up binoculars and looking around. She spotted Dimsdale's rowboat among the rocks further back from where they had come the night before. When the meeting ended, and Dimsdale finally raised his head from below, she hurled the news at him. He grabbed the binoculars and spotted the boat. He broke out in a grin. One of the men helped him retrieve his rowboat by rowing over with theirs as the others cracked open the rum and waited.

Later in the afternoon, after the men left happier than when they arrived, they left the servant on board to watch the yacht. They took TJ with them to shore, where Dimsdale had a driver take them to a small ranch he owned just outside town along the waterfront. There, they had dinner with the family who ran the ranch. They were good-hearted *Campañeros* – people of the country.

The overall experience thoroughly unsettled Phyl, however. Though they were good, kind people, she would've much preferred them cooking over a camp stove and sharing a meal out in the open than to eat in a dirty mud house, out of dirty dishes, off a dirty table, and prepared with dirty hands with dirty pots. Everyone had dirty faces, dirty fingernails, and dirty hair. Their clothing was so dirty they looked stiff. Cleanliness was not a priority, and she looked at everything before stepping anywhere or touching anything. Nothing, it seemed, was cleaned or swept. Everything was built of dried mud, including the walls, floor, stove, and oven. There was loose dust on everything. Food and pots were simply planted onto the dirty table along with two rough loaves of bread from which everyone grabbed chunks with their dirty hands to dip into a stew. They all ate from one pot and drank bottles of strawberry wine, which was the cheapest wine in town.

Phyl decided to let TJ hang outside to chase cows and pigs and climb in and out of boats. He seemed delighted that there were children to play with. She watched from the dirty window when someone suddenly came banging on the door to announce that one of the neighbor's mothers had died. When Dimsdale asked how she had died, the man told them it was because she had bathed the day before.

Phyl laughed. Then she looked around and saw that everyone stared at her angrily. She looked at Stuart aghast. "They're not serious. They're saying she died because she took a bath? Was there a snake in it or something?"

Dimsdale asked for more information, and he translated. "They have a saying, *de golpe*. It means a bath all at once. In other words, she bathed her whole body."

"*De golpe*? And that's a bad thing?" asked Phyl.

"They believe the cleaner you are, the sicker you'll be. A full bath is a death sentence."

Stunned, Phyl was quiet for the rest of the visit. When they returned to the yacht, she asked if she could use fresh water for a sponge bath. When she went down below to get a cloth and towel from the servant, Stuart, who had already broken out the rum, yelled after her. "Don't go *de golpe* on yourself, or we'll have to throw your carcass into the rowboat and tow it back."

"And let the rope snap," guffawed Dimsdale.

"Right, and we won't go after you!" added a gleeful Stuart.

Phyl sneered. "Hardyharhar."

After an early start back to Buenos Aires Sunday morning, they went down to the mouth of the river and started putting up the sails, only to find the wind was right on their nose, and they simply couldn't make any headway. Dimsdale had no choice but to turn back and anchor partway up the river to wait. The weather didn't calm until early Monday morning, just before daybreak, when they finally left to find perfect sea conditions though the wind was still on the nose, forcing them to take a long tack upriver on the first leg of the journey.

Phyl cradled TJ on her lap. The sun was brilliant and warm on the face though the winds were cold. She wore layers of clothing and precariously held a mug of what was hot chocolate, now cold, in her other hand. TJ erupted into a series of barks. Phyl looked around, perhaps it was a seabird catching his attention. Then she heard it: a buzzing sound. She sat up straight just as Stuart and Dimsdale noticed the sound. Momentarily, they saw something in the sky coming toward them.

"A plane," yelled Dimsdale.

Stuart watched it thoughtfully. "A private plane? It's small."

"Yup," said Dimsdale. "Stuart, go down below. Make it look like a couple here in the cockpit."

Stuart got up and went down below to peek out the porthole.

Dimsdale and Phyl stayed in place and pretended nothing was amiss. As the plane came closer, its props sounding more distinct, Stuart yelled out it was coming straight at them.

At this point, Phyl couldn't help but twist to see.

"Holy cow," yelled Dimsdale, as the plane dipped and barely missed their mast, knocking the wind out of their sails.

Phyl ducked and covered TJ, who barked and snarled at the plane.

Phyl shaded her eyes to watch it recede, wondering if it were to come back, and if it did, she was going to scurry down below. She thought of guns and bombs. She quickly glanced to see where the rowboat was and was relieved to see it still towing behind them.

As if in answer to her fears, the plane turned around and headed for them.

"Oh my God, should we jump overboard?!" she yelled, ready to jump with TJ.

"Stay put!" yelled Dimsdale. "Stuart," he yelled down below from the tiller, "Get the rifle!"

"RIFLE?" screamed Phyl.

Stuart appeared with a rifle and handed it to Dimsdale. "Take the helm," Dimsdale yelled as he hurried forward and climbed on top of the cabin, leaning against the mast. He held his arm straight out aiming the gun at the oncoming plane.

Stuart took the tiller before it went out of the control. Phyl quickly cowered against Stuart by the tiller as she watched Dimsdale focusing on the oncoming plane. She could swear she felt a cushion of air hit them before the plane buzzed overhead. Dimdale took a shot. Phyl screamed.

"Did you get it?" yelled Stuart.

Dimsdale shook his head. "I wasn't aiming at it, just a warning shot. But I'll damn well shoot it next time it comes around."

Phyl watched the plane recede, her heart pounding and her mouth dropped open in fear and suspense. Her eyes started to water as she refused to tear her eyes away from the image, "Don't come back," she whispered. "Don't you dare come back!"

They watched it do a figure eight in the distance and then turn toward what must be the small airstrip in Buenos Aires itself.

Phyl burst into tears as Dimsdale jumped off the cabin and returned to the helm. He gave the rifle back to Stuart and Stuart wordlessly took it back below.

"Well, there's not much to say about that," said Dimsdale, "except that losing the row boat was not a coincidence. If he had hit us and we had no rowboat, we would have been a dead Canadian, American, Belgian, servant and dog." Dimsdale looked around the horizon. "He's not coming back."

"Did you catch any identifying numbers or letters?" asked Stuart. "I didn't notice any."

"No, but then that in itself has got to be a clue," sneered Dimsdale.

"How long before we're home?" asked a tearful Phyl.

Dimsdale looked at his watch. "Unless the winds change, I'd say six or seven hours at least."

"I'm going to be sick," Phyl announced, and she fed the fishes and the seagulls with a vengeance.

By the time Stuart and Phyl walked through their front door it had taken them twelve hours from leaving their morning anchorage.

Phyl headed straight for the bathroom, ran a bath, and let herself soak in a mountain of soap bubbles. She wasn't in a good frame of mind. She could hear Carmen rustling up a good meal with clean dishes using a clean tablecloth in their very clean flat. She looked around the clean bathroom and saw the clean white toilet seat. Then she raised her shaking foot and looked at her clean toenails. She still felt nauseous because the whole bathroom rocked as if she were still on the boat.

She jumped when Stuart rapped sharply at the door.

"WHAT?" Her heart pounded.

"Are you doing that *de golpe* thing again?" he yelled.

Phyl could hear Carmen laugh. It soothed her soul somewhat, but dying from *de golpe* was far from how she thought she was going to die that day.

Chapter Ten

Thespian Dreams, Weary Phyl

Phyl stood in the wings waiting for her final scene on the final performance of her second play. She fretted about the brown grease paint on her woolen plaid dress with the brown velvet collar and cuffs. She was required to provide her own costumes and she chose a white summer outfit, a black evening dress she had worn for many dinners out, and her tailor-made plaid dress that Angelica admired so much. But she hoped Carmen would be able to get the stain out. It was her favourite outfit.

Off stage, she peeked from behind musty stage curtains to the far end of the front row of the dark auditorium. She saw patrons having a grand time. The sight warmed her soul. She so thoroughly enjoyed both plays she didn't want to stop acting, so she had already auditioned for a production scheduled for the following season. To her dismay and surprise, however, she didn't get *any* part. She had cried about it. At one point, she blamed Jorge and Stuart, because she being in plays upset *their* plans.

Jorge had been pressuring Stuart and her to come and visit his *estancia* for a very long time. So, not surprisingly, Stuart announced they were going the following Thursday for 15 days. He had already planned out the trip. They were to go by train to *Rio Negro*, leaving Buenos Aires at eight in the morning to get in at eleven the following morning after changing trains in *Bahia Blanca* during the night.

Phyl didn't feel comfortable about staying that long, but Stuart's argument was she needed to be in a healthier climate. As well, he had just gotten over his battle with asthma coupled with chronic bronchitis so he hoped the drier climate would help him break the nasty bug. The night before, he slept for only an hour and woke up choking, coughing and spitting. This went on for hours and neither of them could sleep. After a while, they gave up trying and played cards at three in the morning. They were dish rags by the time the sun rose and Stuart's eyes were inflamed and running. He left for work even though he looked like he had done an all-nighter. Which he, in essence, did. Out of necessity, they had a long siesta after lunch, but Phyl still felt drained. She had to be fresh for that last night's performance.

One positive outcome of such a dreadful night, however, was that Stuart finally announced he was giving up smoking. He put out his 'last' cigarette with a flair while she was beating the pants off him playing cards. Being practically a chain smoker, Phyl half expected his good intentions to peter out as soon as withdrawal symptoms hit with a vengeance the next day or so, but she was pleased he started to see it her way.

Her train of thought was suddenly broken by laughter in the audience. She smiled, noting that each audience was different and though there were funny lines in the play, sometimes simple words spoken in a certain way – though they were meant to be serious – could spark the audience's tickle bone. She looked at her fellow actors on stage and noted the sweat beading their foreheads. She then looked at the dusty-looking rug on the stage and the worn furniture. Funny how, if you weren't looking too closely, you couldn't tell how run down and overused everything was when seen from the audience.

As was the first play, this production was an English murder mystery spoof, with its mishaps, slapstick, and innuendos. Like Phyl, the cast were sad to see their play come to an end but looked forward to the party later that night. Unfortunately, she wouldn't be able to stay long. Stuart simply wasn't up to it and it certainly wouldn't be right for her to remain on her own and go home unaccompanied.

She jumped when a tap on her shoulder brought her back to earth. It was the stage director with a clipboard. He motioned she was about to go on. She nodded, straightened out the long narrow skirt of her dress, and tucked the black handbag under her arm. She pulled at the black gloves and repositioned her black cloche on her sweating head. Beautiful dress or no, wool is always a bad choice under the hot lights and backstage where hot bodies continued to shed wave upon wave of heat; it was almost distracting. But it was her choice for this scene. It looked so darn like an Edith Head and Hollywood-inspired outfit.

Her cue. She floated onto the stage and greeted the two male actors in her reasonably good British accent. She only had four more lines before the what's up of the murder mystery was to be solved. She milked every word. And before she knew it, they were standing hand in hand with the rest of the cast bowing to a standing ovation. *Bittersweet*, she thought. Oh well, at least she had the next movie production to look forward to the following month.

Later, milling among her fellow thespians, all still in make-up and costume, she hugged and chatted with everyone, and promised to keep in touch. She and Stuart left within an hour when he started to really suffer — both from his cough and congestion but also from nicotine withdrawal. *Everyone* at the party smoked and it was unbearable for him.

In the taxi, Phyl reviewed what was to happen in the next little while. The first Thursday of the next month was the start of shooting for the new movie production – from nine in the morning until five at night, which she thought was much more sensible.

As the streetlights passed, rhythmically lighting up the interior of the cab, she turned to Stuart. "Do you know if Jorge had any influence on the scheduling of the shoots with this next movie?"

"What do you mean?" Stuart coughed into his fist and sniffed.

Phyl caressed his cheek. "Oh, you poor thing. Well, we're shooting during the day now."

Stuart shook his head, looked out the passenger window and jiggled his legs. "I'm also scheduled for several close-ups. Isn't that fabulous?"

"Absolutely."

"I asked again if I could have a speaking part, but I can't because of my accent."

"Well, your Spanish has much improved. You have a very good teacher."

"Oh, that brings something to mind. Someone asked me to give drama lessons."

Stuart looked at her curiously. "But what do you know about acting? You've only ever done two plays and only background in one movie."

She looked away and shrugged. "I don't care. My Spanish teacher made me a proposition: I get two lessons a week in Spanish if I, in return, give her son, who is stage struck, two acting lessons a week. She costs us twenty *pesos* a month, Stu, so I have nothing to lose." She looked at him sideways, wondering what was wrong with him. "You should be proud of me. One way or another I've gained through my thespian endeavours. I earned taxi money from the plays, am getting free lessons basically from the exposure, and, of course, the ten *pesos* a day I get for being in the movies."

Stuart broke out into a cough and Phyl patted his back and waited until the cough subsided. "Well, now," he finally gasped, "Because of my little wife, we're finally rolling in the money."

When she studied his face, she was relieved he meant it in good humor. She slapped him gently on the shoulder as the taxi came to a stop at their building. Matteo came out and opened their doors. He giggled at Phyl's funny make-up and motioned at his own face. Then he tipped his cap and ran back to lead them through the open entranceway.

"You're leaving the door open tonight?" asked Stuart.

Matteo nodded, smiling. "*Sí*, the air is *perfecto*."

"Good idea, help get some air flow going." Stuart started coughing again and had to stop walking for a moment. Matteo jumped ahead to the elevator and pushed the button. When the door opened, he held it until Phyl helped guide Stuart into the elevator.

"*Gracias*, Matteo," smiled Phyl.

"*Buenos noches*," wished Matteo.

Phyl watched Matteo go back to his post and yawn before the brass doors cut him from view.

At their flat, TJ greeted them with wagging tail. Phyl scooped him up and cuddled him while he tried to lick the grease paint off her face, but she wouldn't let him. She giggled as she put him down.

"I'm going right to bed, Phyl. I feel unwell." Stuart struggled to the bathroom to get ready.

"I'll get this war paint off then. 'You want anything hot to drink?" Phyl asked.

No answer from the bathroom but she heard the tap running. Phyl walked into the bedroom with TJ at her heels. She took off her shoes and hose, then carefully peeled off her sticky woolen dress. She hadn't bothered to lug all her things back from the playhouse. She and Stuart were too exhausted. She planned to have Carmen go back with her the next day to retrieve them - all left hanging around her make-up station for the night.

Oh, she was going to miss that dressing room and the wonderful make-up lights. Yes, indeed, the acting bug had bitten hard. She and Stuart had finally gone to the cinema the week before to see her first movie performance. She was so nervous as they walked into the cinema, she thought she was going to faint, but somehow, she settled down and, once the movie started, she scoured every group scene she knew she was in. She was mildly surprised she didn't look as bad as she expected even though the poor star looked terrible. Compared to Hollywood standards, the movie was pretty awful but Phyl was so proud and wished everyone at home could see her. What a hoot! That night she wrote El all about it for the next day's post, reminding El how she told her that night on the streetcar so long ago, that she knew in her bones she was going to be up on that proverbial magical screen. Well, even if it was just as a humble background actor.

Interestingly, she thought Eva Duarte managed to come off looking the innocent character she was to play. Funny how such ugly demeanor in real life could come from that bright-eyed young face on that screen, she thought. She heard a rumor that Eva Duarte had gotten a part for a radio play, but not having a radio, Phyl couldn't find out how well or badly she'd be. Secretly, she hoped she'd be a flop.

She slapped herself on the hand. Oh, that's so awful of me, she thought.

Phyl sighed with satisfaction as she sat at her make-up table and lathered cold cream onto her face. She felt like a regular professional now. She looked over at newspaper clippings she cut out about the first play which she intended to send along with the play's poster to her Dad and K. She was holding out to see what the reviews were in the next week's English-speaking newspaper. She also put a program aside to go along with the rest of the package. She hoped the reviews wouldn't say anything awful about her. If they did, she would never get over it. How would she face all her friends at the Club? They devour the newspaper like it was manna from heaven.

Suddenly, she heard a car squeal its tires outside and come to an abrupt stop. She heard a dog cry out in pain. Then eerie silence.

"Oh, dear, TJ. Someone just hurt a doggie," she said looking down at her feet. But TJ wasn't there. She got up and knocked at the bathroom door and scanned the dining room floor. "Stuart, did you hear that? I think someone hit a dog outside."

Stuart slowly poked his head out the bathroom. "What did you say?"

Phyl looked around the bathroom. "Is TJ in here?"

"No."

Phyl turned and whistled as she walked past the bar. She stopped and panicked when she saw the door to the flat ajar. "Stuart, you didn't close the door behind you!"

Stuart stepped into the living room and looked at the door. "What?"

"TJ! The door! Oh, Stuart! I hope Matteo has that door closed downstairs!" In her dressing gown and bare feet, her face still half covered in cold cream, she ran to the elevator and frantically pushed the button several times. Frustrated, she slammed the brass doors and ran to the stairs, scrambled down the seven floors in record time, and barged through the front lobby. The door was ajar and she could see Matteo in the street. She ran out into the night, down the stone steps and onto the sidewalk. She stopped.

Matteo was on his knees cradling a limp TJ. He looked back. "*Señora, lo siento mucho.* I'm so sorry. *Me quedé dormido y él pasó a mi lado. Si tan solo lo hubiera visto.*" He had fallen asleep and hadn't seen TJ in time to stop him.

Later, all she could remember was little TJ's head hanging loosely as she desperately grabbed him and cradled him like a newborn baby. That, and her own scream and cries echoing across the park.

Stuart caught up and bent over Phyl. He pulled her cradling TJ and practically carried her back into the lobby. He took TJ's limp body from her and put his other arm around Phyl's thin shoulders.

"My baby," she cried, her voice sounding like a little girl's as she weakly shuffled along with him toward the elevator.

Stuart let out a soft sob. Not for TJ. But for his wife's broken heart.

* * *

In the kitchen, Carmen and the laundry woman were chewing the fat so darn much Phyl couldn't hear herself think at the dining room table. They sounded like a couple of machine guns. She had a headache, was miserable and her heart ached. She missed her darling TJ so much. In panic, she couldn't shake the feeling she was late feeding him and that he was sitting beside her wondering why.

She scratched the pin curls under her scarf. She was still in dressing gown and slippers even though half the day was gone. The vet had come in the early morning to take poor little TJ's body away wrapped lovingly in his favorite blanket. He had politely informed her that they were probably going to cremate TJ that afternoon. She burst into tears at the thought and allowed herself to sob until she felt pain subside somewhat. Oh, her poor little TJ.

She didn't go to the playhouse that morning, she simply didn't have the will. So, she waited until Carmen arrived and immediately sent her by taxi to retrieve her things. Quite frankly, she didn't care if she'd left everything behind, but that would've been terribly impolite for the others who needed to clear out the playhouse. Truth was, nothing seemed to matter now. The pride and joy she had felt in a job well done on stage evaporated like a bubble in a stiff wind.

The laundrywoman arrived not long after Carmen left. When Phyl let her in, the woman nodded at her, then looked at her queerly before heading into the kitchen. She was elbow deep into suds at the sink by the time Carmen returned. Phyl instructed Carmen to hand her laundry from the play's performances to the woman. Carmen stayed beside the laundrywoman to chat while she peeled potatoes with a knife, sitting on a stool. Phyl heard the odd potato plop into the big pot on the granite floor at Carmen's feet. The women seemed quite content, no doubt discussing the latest events of the Redington soap opera and knowing darn well she wouldn't be able to understand their rapid-fire Spanish.

Phyl craved peace and quiet to nurse her broken heart. She shook her head and groaned under her breath. Everything in her body ached — her teeth, her sinuses, her ears. She felt so miserable. She took out a handkerchief and wiped her eyes and slunk away to sit on the balcony.

She wasn't up to leaving at eight the next morning for *Rio Negro* with Stuart and Jorge. At that moment, Stuart was still in bed with bronchitis, asthma, and on top of it all, gripe. The minute he got into bed after poor TJ's demise, he had an asthma attack, and after coughing for two and a half hours and nearly choking to death, Phyl, still reeling from TJ's accident, became alarmed and ran down to Matteo still terribly upset he had allowed TJ to escape. She begged him to get a hold of their English doctor, but Matteo couldn't get through on the phone. So, he called a Spanish doctor he knew who came over and gave Stuart an injection of adrenaline. The asthma attack passed but he still had a bronchitis cough. He had to remain sitting up as the cough was worse lying down.

"Phyl!"

Phyl could hear Stuart calling her through the open bedroom window. She didn't move and cast her watery eyes sadly over the park to the water.

"Phyl!" She heard him cough.

Slowly, painfully, she dragged her eyes from the comforting distance and struggled to her feet. She shuffled into the flat like an old woman. The chatter in the kitchen stopped and she looked briefly in that direction. Both Carmen and the laundrywoman were looking curiously at her through the kitchen door: Carmen with knife and potato in midair, the laundrywoman with arms in bubbles past her elbows. Phyl blinked and continued to the bedroom. She opened the door and peeked in. Stuart was sitting up, unshaven, his striped pyjamas rumpled and stained on the front, and his hair stuck up in all directions. He was shaking his legs and didn't look good.

"Yes?" Phyl asked.

"I need a cigarette."

If anything would kick Phyl out of the depths of despair it was this. She straightened up. "No, Stu. Look at you. You can hardly breathe." She walked in and sat on the bed. "And I don't think we should go to the *estancia*. I'm too miserable and look at you." She motioned to him. "You can't travel 1,200 miles on a train like this."

Stuart did a funny motion with his hands and frowned. "Phyl, give me a cigarette."

"No."

Stuart looked feebly around the bed and at the nightstand next to him. "Phyl, there is a practical reason why you should give me a cigarette."

"What possible practical reason could there be? To quicken your death?"

"You're exaggerating. Phyl, help me."

"I *am* helping you."

Stuart looked at the open door. "Why'd they stop talking?" he asked.

Phyl got up and closed the door, but not before she saw Carmen and the laundrywoman peeking around the corner from the kitchen. They disappeared and the chatter continued. She returned to the bed and straightened the bedclothes. She didn't want to look at him.

"Listen, Phyl. Apart from the fact that we could both do well in a drier climate, we've suffered with very little sleep and you have been on the run for months and not getting any better. Look at you. You're skin and bone. I need you to fatten up a bit, otherwise I don't think you could last another winter."

She sat back down.

"And if you're scrawny, I wouldn't want you as my *Señora* anymore. Unless you give me a cigarette. Then I'll keep you even if you grow fat and a very long beard."

"No."

"I'm not joking. I need a cigarette. Look at me."

"I am and I'm really frightened, Stu."

"I cannot fight two major things here. I have to get better, but I'm wracked by withdrawals on top of it all. Give me my cigarettes. I will be able to relax and focus on getting better."

"Stu, listen to yourself. What an idiotic argument for getting your cigarettes back."

"Think about it. Withdrawals are a major issue to combat. I only have so much energy here."

Phyl looked at him, not knowing what to say.

"Have Carmen feed me lots of good broth from bone and marrow. I promise you, you will see me get better." He nervously scratched his day-old beard. "And you will see, you will be happy we went. You will be surrounded by all that nature. Think about it. Sleeping in. Lounging by the pool..." He looked at his watch. "It's early afternoon. This evening, I will be better. Well enough to go in the morning."

Phyl got flustered. She really didn't want to ask why it was so darn important to go, she didn't want to know. "It's a very long trip, Stu."

"We'll take a sleeper."

Angelica had told her so much about the beauty of the *estancia* and its tens of thousands of acres and she had always secretly wanted to hunt for ostrich just so that she could write home and brag about it to her father and brother. But now that wasn't so important anymore. She took a deep breath. Why are you so stubborn about us going? And don't tell me anymore about how good it will be for us. I want to know why it is we have to go at this *exact* time."

"Get me my cigarettes, and I'll tell you."

Phyl, upset and impatient, got up, opened the door and went to the bar. She reached in between the bottles and took out a package of cigarettes and Stuart's lighter. She also picked up the ashtray on the bar counter. She brought it all back to Stuart who perked up when he saw what was in her hands. She handed over the cigarettes and lighter and placed the ashtray on the nightstand. Stuart shakily shook out a cigarette from the package. He stuck it into his mouth. Phyl took the lighter from him and lit the cigarette. She then reached over for the package and squeezed out another cigarette for herself and lit hers. They both sat smoking quietly for a few moments. Stuart sighed loudly.

"Wow. That's better." He flicked the cigarette against the ashtray and shifted his body. She got up and fluffed the pillows behind him before sitting back down. "Okay, now I'll tell you why we have to be there this coming week. There's a major gathering of Nazis at Jorge's German neighbor's estate, including the German Ambassador Thermann and his wife. Apparently, this Dieter guy, the neighbor, is at the top of the German National Socialist Labour Party. We have to monitor things from Jorge's place."

"And so how exactly are you and Jorge going to monitor things?"

"Sneak up to the estate and take photographs. By the way, where's my gun?"

Phyl dropped her cigarette.

The next morning was lovely and warm when they arrived at the train station. Jorge wasn't there as he had to leave the day before for *Rio Negro* for *business* reasons, so Phyl and Stuart quietly enjoyed each other's company, settling down in the train compartment, and watched the countryside go by. Phyl occasionally stole a glance at the duffel bag at their feet with the gun and camera equipment.

Passengers chatted, slept and read. Stuart wore a red and black plaid woolen scarf around his neck and seemed comfortable enough, especially after a bowl of hot soup followed by a double scotch and a cigarette. A few hours later, as if by magic, at a higher elevation, Stuart's chest cleared up.

"You're breathing easier!" exclaimed Phyl.

Stuart coughed into his hand, and nodded. He had color in his face. "I feel better already." He readjusted his scarf before reaching to hold Phyl's hand.

"Uh-uh," she joked, "No way. Not until you wash that hand of yours. You just coughed into it."

"But you kissed me this morning and I felt even sicker then," he said, looking at her forlornly.

"Don't hold that against me. Wash," she demanded, pointing behind him.

Stuart made a face and looked back up the aisle and saw a sign, "*Baños Públicos.*" As he did so, a rowdy group of boys appeared at the end of the jostling car. They slammed the door shut behind them. The first ones noticed Stuart. One laughed and pointed. Phyl heard them speak in German.

"I think they're making fun of your scarf."

Stuart looked at the fair-haired hooligans. "I recognize two from the Nazi display at the *Rural.*"

"Well, they seem to remember you. I think they think you're their friend. Because you showed interest, maybe?" asked Phyl, feeling somewhat nervous, watching them ingratiating themselves into vacant seats and bothering passengers. Some passengers stood up and moved further away.

"Maybe. They mentioned they went to one of the German schools in town."

"What are they doing on this train? A school trip, do you think?" Phyl didn't like their mounting interest in them. They were openly looking at them. They suddenly burst into song. One stood on a seat and led them like a conductor. They grinned as they sang.

> "*Deutschland, Deutschland über alles,*
> *Über alles in der Welt,*
> *Wenn es stets zu Schutz und Trutze*
> *Brüderlich zusammenhäl.*

"What are they singing?" asked Phyl.

"The German Anthem," said Stuart, grimly. They both looked around at other passengers who had all stopped what they were doing. Some were perturbed, a few frightened, but mostly just curious.

One of the young men stood and did the Nazi salute. "*Heil, Hitler!*" The others followed suit.

Stuart sat up straight and faced Phyl. He was very upset. He shook his head.

"Where do you think they're going?" asked Phyl, facing away from the hooligans and shifting closer to Stuart as she pushed the heavy duffel bag further under their legs.

Stuart put an arm around her shoulders. "So, *now* you come close to the sicko."

Phyl weakly slapped him on his chest.

He grabbed his chest and made a face. "Oh, my poor chest."

Phyl grinned. "Silly."

Stuart coughed and leaned closer to her ear. "I have a fairly good idea where they're going."

Phyl looked at him questioningly.

"The German guy who owns the *estancia* next to Jorge has more money than God and we suspect he's financing a good bit of what goes on in the German schools. He's been holding large informal gatherings at his place and giving Jorge stress by bringing people onto Jorge's *estancia* claiming the hunting is better on that side."

Phyl turned to look up the aisle. One of the hooligans winked at her. Perturbed, she turned back. "One of them was just fresh with me!"

Stuart angrily looked back. The young man quickly looked away. "Do you want me to do something? Just give the word."

Phyl shook her head. She thought for a moment and frowned. "They're part of this gathering at this German guy's estate, you say?"

Stuart coughed. "Most probably."

"Stu. You're not going to do anything stupid, are you? They're just boys."

Stuart lowered his voice. "I promise. Just a few photos."

She crossed her arms and angrily sat back. "Well, I'm going to stop caring what you do from now on. I'll think about myself for a change. I'm going to sleep in every morning like Angelica does because, thank goodness, I won't have to make the idiot lord and master his breakfast every darn morning."

"Now, that's what I want to hear." He frowned comically. "I think."

"So, what exactly are you and Jorge going to do? Just take a photo of people coming and going?"

"Jorge wants to catch this guy in the act of trespassing. The guy's obviously not listening to Jorge's *majordomo*."

"Major who?"

"*Majordomo*. Remember? That's what they call the guy who runs an *estancia*. Or head butler."

"Okay."

"And the German ambassador, Thermann, is going to be there with his wife."

"Yes, you said. I don't know much about the German ambassador —"

Stuart put a finger to his mouth for her to lower her voice.

She whispered, "But some of my friends at the Club met his wife. One of them said that she dressed up like a Greek goddess for the Berlin Olympic Games back in '36. Did a big do. Fancy dresser. Weird lady with weird ideas. She's quite bossy, apparently. They joke the wife tells *him* what to do."

"Yes, that's the problem. She is a vicious Nazi with tunnel vision." Stuart looked around at the passengers. He leaned closer. "We should be careful what we say. You never know who's listening."

She looked past Stuart out the window. "My goodness," she said, "I think we're in for a very interesting stay at this *estancia*. Can't we simply do things for the joy of doing them anymore?"

"Nope," said Stuart. "Not while we're here in South America on American dimes, we can't."

"America is gonna owe us big time. They better appreciate what we do."

"Who are 'they'?"

"You know very well who 'they' are." Phyl crossed her arms again and pouted, took one more look back at the hooligans and was again winked at. She gasped and turned back. "For goodness sake!"

They were met at the train station by the *estancia's majordomo* who took their trunks and luggage and opened the door of the ranch's jalopy.

"Goodness, this car has seen better days," said Phyl.

The *majordomo* spoke English with a thick Spanish accent. "The roads they are almost non-existent at times," he explained. "But you will see very soon. There will be some very rough stretches, and you will bounce *mucho*."

"Oh, wonderful. A circus ride," quipped Phyl. She saw the hooligans assemble in front of the train *en masse*. Several fancy cars with little Swastika flags rolled to a stop along the road in front of the platform. Drivers in chauffer uniforms with Swastika armbands, jumped out and stood ramrod beside open doors. "Goodness," Phyl whispered.

Stuart turned to look. "Hmmm. You'd think we were in Deutschland."

The *majordomo* threw the hooligans an angry look before closing the doors after Stuart and Phyl. "I smell *mucho* troubles," he muttered, getting in behind the wheel. He started the jalopy and put it into creaky gear, threw up a cloud of dust and pulled away from the busy station.

Soon they were passing through flat countryside surrounded by distant, arid hills. There meandered streams and saw hundreds of wild ducks, egrets, herons, wild geese, and *bandurrias* with their broad wingspans and trumpet-like calls. *Chimangos*, a bird of prey with yellow heads and black streaks down their sides, were everywhere. There were wild swans in one of the rivers. Once in a while, the *majordomo* had to slow down to carefully find a way around deep ruts, holes, rocks, and the odd carcass of some animal along the dusty road.

They were pleased to see Angelica waiting on the stone terrace in front of the house with cocktails ready. They disembarked, dust-covered head to toe, and finally settled into lounge chairs, looking out to the hills beyond. Cattle spread out as far as the eye could see. After drinks, they unpacked and took a *siesta* to get refreshed. Angelica arranged for an outdoor barbeque in Jorge's honor who had arrived unexpectedly from his business trip during their *siesta*. Three lambs were slaughtered and roasted over spits for hours before they were joined by folks and friends from a ranch called *Ventana*. The word meant *window* and the ranch was named after a nearby mountain in the district of *Sierra de la Ventana* which had a natural square hole that looked eerily like a window to another world.

Argentina is a window to another stranger world, thought Phyl.

With no rain for three weeks, the ranch was parched. Everyone talked about it, as everyone's ranches so depended on it. Sitting inside the open living area later that night, they got quite inebriated and expressed concerns over their crops and cattle.

"When you have 1500 head of cows and horses to graze, rain is crucial, life-giving," Jorge pointed out. Their friends shared stories of past droughts and emaciated corpses of cattle and horses. Jorge motioned to some of the chairs they were sitting on. "That's where those horns came from. My grandfather lived through one of the worst droughts this country had ever seen. He commemorated it by creating furniture out of the horns and bones of a few of his cattle and bulls."

Everyone shifted to look at the chairs they were sitting in. Leather over bones and massive horns for back rests.

"Charming," mumbled Phyl, as she fingered her bone armrest. She couldn't wait to write about *that* to her father and brother.

As if by coincidence, shortly after, rain came down in torrential curtains. The noise was deafening, and everyone so elated they let the children run out into the pouring rain. One or two adults did the same. The servants stood by and smiled.

Everyone else was drawn mesmerized out of the house to stand under the massive awnings over the patio. As they watched the rain and the people and children frolicking, Jorge hollered at Phyl, "So, what are your plans while you are here? Going to write the great American novel?"

Phyl laughed. "I'm no Hemingway, believe me!" she yelled. "Although there is certainly enough to inspire a person everywhere one looks." She motioned to the rain. "Even this is memorable."

"Wait till you go ostrich hunting!" exclaimed Georgie, who now at 13 towered over his father.

"Oh my! I don't know if I have the heart to shoot an adorable ostrich!" laughed Phyl.

Stuart went back through the open patio doors inside and sat down in a chair. "We'll do nothing but ride, fish, hike, and swim in your pool with your kids," he said, watching the rain run off the edge of the awning.

The twins, soaking wet, squealed as they returned and happily climbed onto his lap, soaking him and accidently kicking him in the stomach. It knocked the air out of him, which made the twins laugh even harder. He viciously tickled them.

"Well, I have something that might keep Phyl busy," yelled Jorge, mysteriously.

Phyl looked at him curiously, then at everyone else. Most guests were scattered off, some on the outside terrace under umbrellas, or back in the living room talking and drinking. She blinked at Stuart.

"Don't look at me," laughed Stuart, as he wrestled with the twins.

The rain subsided suddenly and everyone looked out into the dark past the terrace.

Jorge turned and made a motion to a waiting servant at the patio doors. The servant disappeared and momentarily returned carrying a wire-haired puppy with button eyes in his arms. Everyone stopped talking when they heard a squeal, and turned to see Phyl jump up and joyfully run toward the puppy.

Stuart looked at Jorge, who looked at him knowingly. "Well, I guess our old Phyl is back."

"*Gracias a Dios,*" said Jorge, smiling, as he let Phyl gently take the puppy out of his arms and, with children laughingly following her, scurry back to her chair for cuddles.

The next morning, Phyl and Stuart went horseback riding with Jorge, Diego – who had arrived during the night – Georgie, and the *majordomo*. After an hour's riding, Phyl spotted three red foxes on the side of the hill.. Georgie got one with a .22 but it got away. She was sorry she had yelled when she saw them because the one that was shot was wounded and probably crawled into a hole to die a slow, agonizing death.

Along the way back, they spotted a flock of ostrich and Georgie dropped one at about 200 yards. Phyl watched with bated breath as she realized Georgie had to be very careful not to shoot any of the horses or lingering cattle by accident, never mind any of the riders. The *majordomo* and Georgie got off their horses and proceeded to tie and cart the bird back to the *majordomo's* horse. The *majordomo* threw it over his horse's rump and tied the ostrich down. Feathers dropped and floated in the wind. Phyl again felt a twinge of regret. After having been brought up on camping, hunting and fishing by her father, killing animals was never something she worried about. But on these lands with these beautiful creatures who didn't really know how to run away fast enough, she had tugs of remorse.

They moved on, swiping at flies and bugs at their faces.

"Look down as we cross this field. See the holes? They're from armadillos. One's horse could break his leg if he steps into one of those," warned Jorge.

Phyl went cross-eyed looking out for holes in the tall grass. "Where are they?" she yelled out.

"Armadillos come out at night. We call them *peludos*," said Diego. "They are a pest and have the fields so full of holes they are a constant danger. They're best hunted on a full moon."

Phyl kept her eye out until they left the flats. They eventually arrived at a pool in a broad river. As they approached, thousands of ducks rose en masse from the marsh and surface of the water. They had no hunting guns with them, other than the one Georgie had, so they decided to come back the next day by car, hopefully to catch the next week's provisions. They decided to head back. Diego pointed out to Phyl that they were close to the German neighbor's property along that side of Jorge's *estancia*.

That night, once Phyl and Stuart got over the stiffness from riding by taking piping hot baths, they had a good night's rest. The next morning, after a massive breakfast and a good play with the puppy, they all climbed into two jalopies armed with an artillery of hunting guns. On their way back to the river, they stopped here and there briefly to hunt whatever they came across. This time, they caught ostrich, red fox, guanaco, deer and wild goat. The *majordomo*, Georgie and Diego tied the carcasses to the side and tops of the cars. At one point, as they bounced through a field with tall grass, there were suddenly so many partridges that they ran right under their wheels. They had to slow down to give the birds fair warning, but didn't shoot them, as they preferred to wait for the hordes of ducks they saw the day before.

They heard a gunshot in the distance. Looking ahead, they saw hundreds of duck and geese rise above the trees and bushes. "Someone is beating us to it," yelled Jorge angrily.

"Well, it ain't any of us!" Stuart said sarcastically. "We're catching your Nazis in the act."

Phyl looked around desperately. She didn't know if she should hide or come along.

Jorge looked miserably at Diego. "Stuart's right. Our neighbor, do you think?"

"Most certainly," answered Diego, turning in his seat. He looked at Phyl and Jorge. "Perhaps it's too dangerous to go on?"

Jorge readjusted his Panama hat. "Nope. I want to catch this neighbor of ours in the act."

"Oh dear," muttered Phyl.

They stopped at the edge of the bushes and turned off the ignitions. They heard horses neighing and people chatting. It was obvious whoever they were heard them coming by car a mile away. And it didn't frighten them off. Which was somewhat disturbing. They slowly walked around the bend. Phyl hung back with her heart in her throat. They saw the German students making a muddy mess of the shoreline and the riverside.

Jorge strolled toward the students and motioned to them with the shotgun briskly. "You are trespassing. This is my land. Out!"

One of the young men laughed and said something in German that made the others laugh. He turned back to Jorge, while eyeing Stuart and Phyl. He winked at Phyl. "We were told we could hunt anywhere we like," he said insolently, responding in English.

"Yes, on your host's property," Jorge pointed in the distance past the trees. "But this is my land."

"Oh, but this is such a lovely spot to swim," piped another young man. "There is nothing like this lovely cove on his property, at least, not that we know of." He grinned as he started to take his clothes off. Then he stopped midway as he stared at Phyl, his grin fading.

Phyl frowned. "Reiner?" she said, voice cracking.

Reiner was about to say something when suddenly, another horse broke through the surrounding bushes and Jorge's German neighbor appeared. He stilled his horse as he saw Jorge and the rest of his party.

"I told my guests they could shoot and swim here." The German wore a long Austrian Tyrol coat over leather pants and hiking boots. "They are not causing any problems, Piñiero."

"We came here to hunt our own duck and geese. Now they've been frightened away by these oafs." Jorge was angry. He walked up to the neighbor's horse and held it by the reign.

Phyl looked around. Indeed, there wasn't a single bird in sight. As she turned to look back, Reiner still stood half naked while two of the German students disrobed entirely and waded into the river. Phyl gasped but couldn't look away from their dimpled white rear ends disappearing into the muddied waters.

The German pointedly patted his shotgun hung near his saddle, laughed at the boys, and ignored Jorge and their party.

Diego went to get his shotgun out of its holder but Stuart put his hand on Diego's. "You do that, Diego, and I have a feeling there are going to be a few accidents. Let's go."

"I'm telling you now, I need you to leave," Jorge demanded of the German.

"My dear friend, look at these young men. You can't fault them to want to enjoy this beautiful part of the river."

Jorge's nostrils flared and his jaw set.

"Jorge, perhaps we'll let these fine young men have their swim." Stuart stood by with Diego, ready for a fight if necessary.

Phyl inched closer to Georgie, who stood watching, mesmerized. She and Reiner continued to exchange glances.

Jorge finally let go of the horse's reign, turned on his heel, and walked back to the group. "Have your own way, Dieter. But this is the last time. You want a swim hole, dig your own."

Dieter put his gloved hand over his saddle and continued to smile. "Who knows, Piñiero, this may one day be mine anyhow. I think I will wait before I start digging up a perfectly lovely river."

Jorge pretended he didn't hear, but everyone saw the black storm crossing his face. Phyl couldn't take her eyes off him as he passed wordlessly. Everyone quietly followed him back to the cars as they heard the German students laugh and splash. Diego put a reassuring hand on his brother's back.

"Another day for this battle, brother. Another day."

"It can't come fast enough," Jorge sneered, looking at Stuart. He looked to be in a killing mood.

Stuart studied him quietly, obviously disturbed and deep in thought.

As they left the river, Phyl looked back at Reiner, who watched them go. Then she turned to Jorge. "That was so arrogant of them, Jorge. That Dieter acted as if he owns everything."

"That's what you get with these Nazis. They have plans to own everything, and act as if they do."

"That's okay, Jorge. I think I have a plan," said Stuart.

"Stu," said Phyl, worried. "One of the young men is Reiner, the stable hand I told you about at the Club."

"The one who I said probably was spying on you women?"

Phyl nodded.

Stuart shook his head at her. "Well, I don't mean I'll hurt them. At least, not today. Not tomorrow either. This would take some time to set up." He looked at Jorge eyeing him. "We have much to talk about. Something's forming in my head and I think I know who to contact for help." He sat back and took a deep breath. Phyl noticed he didn't cough. Stuart closed his eyes and sat rocking with the car.

What was going through that head of his, she wondered?

Stuart opened his eyes and tapped the *majordomo's* shoulder. "Can we go any faster? I have to get my equipment ready and make a few calls. And Jorge, I want to set out before daybreak. I'd like to find a good hidden spot as close to Dieter's main house as possible."

Jorge nodded and every so often looked back. They could hear the occasional gunshot, even over the engines.

Later that night, on the terrace with drinks, Phyl lamented. "I could swear they were going to kill us, so I was glad we hotfooted it out of there."

"We'll try hunting ducks tomorrow again if you like," said Diego.

She shook her head, puffing nervously on a cigarette. "Uh-uh. I'm not going anywhere near that river. Besides, I won't rest until Stuart and Jorge come back from whatever it is they have to do."

Stuart looked at Jorge pointedly. "I'm going to bed now so we can start off early." He stood. "Don't worry, Phyl. What I said about getting back at them. That's not for tomorrow. We're just taking photos. Okay?"

Phyl took a drag from her cigarette without taking her eyes away from his.

Jorge looked at Stuart thoughtfully. Then he looked at Angelica nursing a vodka martini. She had picked up smoking again, even though she was still breastfeeding. She stared at Jorge.

"We'll go armed in any case."

"How do we lug the guns and ammunition along with my camera equipment and binoculars? We don't want to bring any attention to ourselves." Stuart looked as if he was calculating the weight to carry.

Jorge turned to the *majordomo*. "I need you to hide guns and ammunition at the junction of the bridle path closest to Dieter's property line. You know that hollow tree?"

The *majordomo* nodded thoughtfully.

"Only you do that. I'm not sure if I can trust all our men."

The *majordomo* got up and left.

He turned to Stuart. "I'd like to see if he camped guys along *his* land as security."

"How far to Dieter's main house from here?"

Jorge tipped his head. "About three kilometers."

Diego piped up. "I'll go ahead as scout. I can track them if they're around."

"Thank you," said Stuart.

Phyl, cuddling the puppy, sat up in her willow chair. "Why would you leave us like this?" Her voice cracked. "What if they come *here*?"

Stuart paused, looking at the children playing around them.

Georgie, who sat with the adults, listened intently to their conversation. "Don't worry, Auntie Phyl, I will protect you and *Maman*," he announced proudly, padding a revolver in its holster.

"Oh, my goodness," Phyl whispered. "Babes in arms."

The following morning, long after Diego, Jorge and Stuart left on their mission, Angelica talked Phyl into going with her, the *majordomo*, the three boys and a servant for a picnic but instructed they take along old double-barreled carbines, just in case. These were handed down by Diego and Jorge's father, each one beautifully hand-carved and oiled with pride. They also took along a couple of .22 automatics for Phyl and Angelica. Georgie had his revolver. When Phyl protested she would never use a gun to shoot a person, the *majordomo* reminded her they were there just in case they wanted to bag a duck.

"Oh, well, in that case, okay," answered Phyl, somewhat embarrassed. However, secretly she felt that shooting and killing something was the last thing she would want to do in such stressful times.

They set up for a picnic on a lovely knoll. After some good food and drinks, they left the servant to guard the food, and went for a hike up one of the rocky hills. Their legs were covered against rattlers as they climbed, carrying guns and ropes, looking for guanaco and deer. They were about 1200 feet above sea level, but the hill they climbed was yet another thousand feet. They started to feel the physical exertion upward – especially Phyl and Angelica, hot and not in very good physical condition or health.

When they got to the top, they were exhausted and all they had seen were two rats. When Phyl finally stopped to look around, she gasped at the sight of the magnificent Argentine countryside, which stretched, it seemed, to the bottom of the heavens - a giant dome of majestic white clouds in an endless blue sky. Hordes of cattle spread out among the grasses. Pockets of ostrich raced willy-nilly. Massive flocks of birds rose, cartwheeled and floated on the winds.

"Paradise," she whispered, the gentle breeze on her face. She closed her eyes and lifted her chin to the sun. She inhaled deeply and felt transcended. Why did she get so upset about every little thing nowadays? she wondered. Why didn't she stop to see the beauty of Argentina more often? Why was there always so much to worry about?

She heard the scrape of boots and stones and turned to see the others heading back down the hill. She took one last long look, turned in a circle, and memorized the glory around her. With a lifted heart and lightened spirit, she carefully made her way down.

When they finally returned to the jalopy, the servant told them there had been a flock of about 200 ostriches near the car – no doubt attracted by the smell of the food - before they were frightened off by the group's noisy chatter and laughter coming down.

As they made their way back to the *estancia*, Phyl surrendered to the rough ride and recounted the day's events from the day before. The arrogance and disrespect shown by those young students did not bode well for the future. It certainly was a shock to see Reiner but after much thinking, she was no longer surprised. And what was it Stuart had in mind anyhow? And would he and Jorge get caught and if they did, what would this Dieter and those students do to them?

At one point, Angelica reached out to her and told her not to worry, that Jorge and Stuart wouldn't take silly chances. But Phyl couldn't relax and was close to tears until they arrived home tired, dusty and sunburned. As they climbed up toward the main house, to her intense relief, they found Jorge and Stuart sitting on the terrace enjoying the setting sun, smoking and having drinks with little Tony at their feet, who was chewing on a dried pig's ear. Phyl ran to Stuart and hugged him tightly. He stood up and grabbed her in a bear hug. She cried and he comforted her, smoothing down her bobbed hair.

Not too early the next day, a relieved Phyl scrambled with everyone into the two jalopies to head out to the *Ventana* estate as guests this time. The elderly *Señora* owner, whom Stuart and Phyl had met the first night they arrived at

Jorge's, was the daughter of Ernesto Carlos Tornquist, one of the most important 19th century entrepreneurs in Argentina. He had played a key role in linking Argentina with international trading and financial systems and consequently, the *Señora* was one of the richest women, if not richest, in Argentina. Yet she was one of the most generous and sweetest people Phyl and Stuart had ever met. The luxurious old house built by the Tornquist patriarch was, itself, situated on a hundred acres of clearings, gorgeous trees and bridle paths. There was an excellent tennis court, a green-tiled swimming pool similar to those found in Hollywood and there was a miniature pond complete with swans and other waterfowl. A stream ran down from the hills, winding its way through the property and under elegant and picturesque oriental bridges from which Phyl could look down and see trout swimming in droves. She would've loved nothing more than to fish but fishing was not allowed near the house.

Their grand hostess had her two daughters and grandchildren – about sixteen of them – staying for the summer. Each child had his or her own horse, fishing tackle and shooting equipment. The eldest boys carried their guns and revolvers on their hips like *gauchos* but, unlike Georgie at home, the Tornquist boys had to remove theirs before they entered the main house.

At tea time, they were led into a palatial dining room with a long table set for twenty-five where they were served tea from a beautiful silver service. Toast and home-made butter, including the ranch's own pine-flavored honey, and a variety of cakes, were served by a white-coated manservant. After tea, Phyl was taken by one of the girls to one of the dozens of bathrooms to change for tennis. The bathrooms consisted of dressing rooms and guest supplies of powder, combs and other female necessities. Along the route to the washrooms were racks of water polo mallets, tennis rackets, fishing rods and tackle.

After tennis and *siesta*, Phyl and Stuart climbed into old jalopies with a few of the children to drive to a nearby river to fish. But they refused to bite, which frustrated Stuart to no end. Finally, with the last cast, he landed a three-pound salmon trout. They brought it back for their elderly Tornquist hostess and by this, cocktails were laid out on the spacious veranda which overlooked a small lake with the hills in the distance.

Throughout the entire visit, Phyl was aching to ask how Jorge and Stuart's secret mission went but neither offered any clue as to what they saw. She sensed things were best left unspoken. At least they returned safe and sound.

She wondered how long that would last.

Stuart and Jorge waited a day to see if there were any waves from their spying. When nothing followed, they felt safe enough to leave Phyl and Angelica behind to go to Buenos Aires with the negatives Stuart had taken of the prestigious gathering at the German neighbor's *estancia*.

Angelica, Phyl and the children were invited yet again to *Ventana* to swim, play tennis and have tea. On the way home after dusk, Georgie drove the jalopy. Angelica and Phyl sat in the back. Safer. It was getting dark, and the headlights were so old and weak, they couldn't see twenty yards ahead. As they came around a bend in the dirt road, they spotted a group of cows in the way. The brakes failed and they piled into a sleeping cow. The jalopy fared better than the cow, as they had rumbled right over the poor thing, got stuck on it, and killed it. Angelica, shocked, yelled at Georgie.

"Angelica, it's not his fault. The brakes went." Phyl looked back at the other jalopy catching up to them. She saw the *majordomo's* shocked expression when he saw the jalopy's rear end sticking up over a fat cow. "And what a stupid spot for a cow to sleep! Honestly! How dumb is *that*?"

Georgie had tears in his eyes. He allowed himself to be squeezed between his mother and Phyl as they each held a twin on their lap in the second car. They waited as the *majordomo* took a flashlight to look under the jalopy atop the torn-up cow. Cattle hung back in the dark. It was an unsettling sight.

The *majordomo* called but Phyl couldn't hear. She turned to Angelica. "What did he say?"

"He said the cow was already dead. He was shot," offered Georgie, surprised.

Phyl saw the *majordomo* pull the brake line to study it, frowning. He clambered down the dead cow, and returned to the car. "I will come back and clear this up in the morning. We'll get a truck and tow it back," he said, pointing the flashlight at the surrounding bushes. He looked terribly angry and obviously searching to see if anyone was secretly watching.

They manoevered around the cow and stalled jalopy and headed home. It was ten o'clock before Phyl was settled in with little Tony in bed. She couldn't get it out of her head that someone would fiddle with the brake line and leave a dead cow in their way. She thought grimly of the children and how worse it could've been. She couldn't wait for Stuart to return.

On Jorge's return from the city the next day, the *majordomo* took him to the car shed to show him the brake line off the jalopy. Phyl watched from the terrace, smoking a cigarette with Angelica.

"Oh, happy news," said Angelica. "I am going to have another Piñiero."

Phyl stared at Angelica, shocked. She looked at her cigarette. "Then you shouldn't smoke, Angelica. It's not good for the baby!"

Angelica waved her away. "Just for now. I'm a wreck. It's calming my nerves." She motioned to the shed with her chin. "I don't like all this what's going on."

She suddenly burst into tears and Phyl, stunned for a moment, finally held her friend. She rocked her gently. "It's okay, Angelica. You have lots of help here."

Angelica pulled away and wiped her tears. She pulled herself together, making sure the children, and more importantly, the servants, didn't see her weakness. "That's the problem. We think someone on the staff is sharing information about us."

"You mean you have a mole?" That was too close to home. It also meant everything she and Stuart did was closely watched. She took a deep breath, going over the days spent there so far. Had they done anything compromising? Did they speak too loudly about things which should not be overheard? "Well," she said, with a downturned mouth, sharing Angelica's angst. "Isn't life grand in Paradise?"

* * *

Two weeks later, Phyl had lost more weight. She weakly hunched over the dining room table writing another letter home. The new little Tony lay curled up half on her slippers, like the old. The building shook as six American made bombers flew overhead for the third time that day. It was a couple of days before the swearing in of the new Ortiz government. Phyl laughed at herself. All the fuss over the inauguration, with parades, national songs, and large gatherings in the parks; it was like a total farce. *She* knew that everyone *else* knew the votes were manipulated in the election. Everyone acted oblivious to that fact, and Phyl thought that all Argentines were the greatest bunch of actors she'd ever known.

Nothing appeared to have order. Nothing was dependable. Nothing was safe.

She wiped her forehead and felt as if pressed by a hot flat iron. The temperature was above 90 but the humidity made it much worse. They were to go to Jorge's that night for dinner, the first time since their stay at the *estancia*. She was tempted not to go but Angelica was still out at the *estancia* with the children and Phyl and Stuart were going to hear about Jorge's new mistress.

She couldn't help it. Phyl didn't want to miss *that*. She sadly reread the letter she was writing.

Friday, February 18, 1938

Dear all,

The prodigal daughter is returning. The doctor advised that I don't spend another winter. I had a breakdown and I've been in bed with tonsillitis.

There's a lot I can't talk about here but this place is killing me.

So, Stuart decided I come home and have the benefit of the summer there and skip the damp winter here. Sailing on the Southern Prince on 7th May – if all goes well with documents, the consulate, etc. The lease is up on the apartment in months and we must decide as to furniture, what I shall take to keep at home (home, how wonderful that sounds), what I shall leave for Stuart to sell, etc. I'm having nightmares: they're muttering they need him for another three years! It's starting to feel like I'm caught in an Argentine riptide and I won't know how to get out of it if we don't call this quits. People die in riptides.

Stuart's family will meet me in New York and I will stay in Wilkes-Barre for a few days. I'd love to have some of you folks meet me in New York but it would be a waste of money. Stu's mother will want to know about him, etc. There's no point in coming to Toronto and then returning to Wilkes Barre. It is going to be very funny to hear everyone speaking English again.

I have visions of myself getting mixed up with customs, labels, tips, steamship tickets and heaven knows what. Hope I don't get stranded in Trinidad. The boat stops at Santos, Rio and Trinidad. One of the company men will meet me in New York and help me with all the junk. It's going to hurt to see Buenos Aires receding after two years of cussing it up and down.

I am miserable leaving Stuart and worrying how he's going to be. But he insists that one in the family is enough to suffer through another Buenos Aries winter. We have an abundance of friends here who have all promised to take good care of him and I'm sure they will. I am feeling mighty blue.

Lovingly, Phyl

PS. I will be able to take home little Tony to meet Tony Sr.

Chapter Eleven
Here We Are Again and War

"Stuart, NO WAY! How *could* you?!"

Phyl flung open the door and stormed out of her in-law's penthouse into a gloomy hallway. Her nostrils twitched at the mustiness lingering in the air as it did on rainy days such as today. It was winter. It snowed heavily, but today they had freezing rain for the most part. Three years before, in '36, the great Susquehanna River flooded twenty-two feet. The bottom floor of the hotel was under five feet of water. The Redingtons, like all of Wilkes-Barre, had a heck of a time getting rid of mold; an unfortunate testament to the flood's long–term physical and economic damage. This was in addition to the devastating losses caused by the Depression. Like most of the United States, Main Street was still very much afflicted with sad, empty, ragged storefronts, a town with struggling families left to survive as best they could.

Mr. and Mrs. Redington were close to the end of all they could do to save the hotel from foreclosure. Stuart and Phyl gave them $150 US – 900 *pesos* – a substantial amount of money to them, but a drop in the bucket of what the Redingtons owed the bank. That was the Redington's crisis. Phyl was facing her own worries.

Stuart had reneged on their agreement and accepted a second three-year term with Remington-Rand for the Buenos Aires office.

Phyl raced down two sets of stairs, her steps echoing off the walls. She banged through the door and scurried along the carpeted hallway, crying. She couldn't hold back tears. It had been such a roller coaster ride since she arrived in May of last year. Being away from Stuart for those six long months had been difficult, but their plans for the future were the carrot on the stick, that made it all worthwhile. They had agreed to build toward a future here at home, in North America. This is what kept her going. It was her focus. Her passion. The plan was filled with her many dreams of a bright and happy future.

She body-slammed her hotel room door open with a ferocity, she did not realize she had. She didn't care if her in-laws or guests could hear. The hinges loosened in the door frame, walls shook, and windows rattled. She stopped and wiped her nose and stared unseeing toward the windows.

She reflected on the brightest highlight of those six months: El and Claude Jr. had a baby boy, and named the precious after Stuart. Phyl was elated to live with them during her stay in Canada and watch this little baby grow. Holding the child broke through all those fears she struggled with about children. She was finally anxious for Stuart to return so they could create their own little family.

When he finally did return from Buenos Aires, Claude Jr. and El extended the same invitation to him to stay. Oh, it was fun and heavenly being all together under one roof. In fact, sharing the costs, there was no real point in hurrying to buy a home as they could save even more toward a deposit. They just needed to sort out one unknown: Would they set up a home in Toronto near her family, or would they settle in Kingston, Pennsylvania, from where Stuart planned to commute to the New York office?

Not in any corners of their brains was Buenos Aires *ever* an option.

But, after Stuart resumed working in the Toronto office, Remington Rand pressured him for an extended contract. Phyl wasn't worried. She knew he'd give a definitive no as Stuart and she were on the same page. Even when the American Foreign Service raised its ugly head again and pressured Remington Rand and Stuart, he didn't budge. But today, Stuart returned from the train station, having gone to one of those bizarre meetings in Washington while Phyl and her in-laws were enjoying a rainy day, listening to the radio. He didn't even offer a preamble; he just blurted it out. All the more reason why Stuart's unexpected announcement was such an incredible shock.

She felt she had been kicked in the solar plexus. She just couldn't allow him to explain.

She felt rage, hurled herself onto their bed, and sobbed into the bed cover. She knew Stuart would follow her to the room, to console her, explain the reasons, cajole, argue, and persuade. She didn't care. She didn't want to see his face. She wasn't going to budge.

She would divorce him.

With a start, she stopped crying. What an awful thought *that* was. How could she even *think* that? But returning to Buenos Aires was like selling her soul to the devil. *Again.*

She took a deep breath. She felt so helpless. She grieved at the thought of losing three whole years she could be sharing with little Stuart, years during which their children could be playing together.

Another demon poked at her heart. They had no luck in trying during the few months since Stuart's return. She was only 26, so it couldn't be her age, though she had been so feeble her monthly had stopped in Argentina. Still, it continued after she gained a couple of pounds on the ship coming home.

Expected, there was a gentle knock on the door. She heard the door open. Suddenly, a small body hurled itself onto her back and frantically licked her ear. She gently pushed little Tony away and lifted her head, sniffling. She pushed herself up on all fours and let her head hang as a tear rolled down her nose and dripped onto the bedcover. She wiped her eyes and nose and sat back on her haunches.

Stuart's strong hands wrapped around her shoulders from behind. He moved next to her. He didn't say a word but breathed heavily, his lungs wheezing softly.

She shook her head as she covered his arm. He burrowed his nose into the back of her neck.

"I don't know if I can do this. In fact, I refuse to go. I can't. I just can't."

He gently turned her around. She leaned against his chest. He pushed her away slightly to look at her. He wiped her face and pushed her hair back. Tony jumped on both of them to get into the group hug.

"Stop, Tony. Sit." Stuart demanded.

Tony sat back and watched, panting. Out of frustration, he clawed at the bedcovers.

"I knew you were going to be upset, and I sat on the train agonizing over how I would tell you."

"You might as well have said the world stopped turning and the sun's not coming out tomorrow."

Stuart let her go and sat on the edge of the bed. He clasped his hands and hung them between his legs, and leaned forward over his knees. He stared at the worn carpet.

Phyl sniffed, slowly struggled up into an upright position. She sighed and walked to the window. She looked over the frozen Susquehanna River toward Kingston, where the in-laws had their home still rented out to keep them afloat. Barely. She looked north of Kingston over the snow-covered farmers' fields and a solitary estate home. Stuart and Phyl had just bought a little three-acre building lot. Slightly rolling, old farmland. The sun was setting over the land, and the sky was a brilliant pink fading into turquoise, painting the snowy landscape robin's egg blue. She thought of the sunrises over blue waters from their flat in Buenos Aires. It occurred to her that the world is beautiful no matter where you were.

"So, now we have to accept a tough reality," Stuart said.

Light from the window shone on his face, heightening the blue in his eyes. The pink in the sunset enhanced the blush on his cheeks. He looked so innocent. So scrubbed. So beautiful. He still sported a pencil mustache and slicked, dirty blonde hair. A tendril hung over his forehead as if to suggest that even he was not perfect. He was such a fine specimen of a young man.

It's no wonder *they* wanted to keep using him. It's no wonder *they* wouldn't leave him alone.

She thought, it's no time to die. No time to die.

Tony jumped off the bed and trotted to her, tail wagging. She scooped him up and sat in the armchair in the corner.

"All right," she said. "Talk."

She squinted out the window at their lot in the distance. So close. Yet so far. She remembered how beautiful the panoramic view of the river and the city was from there. They specifically chose it because it was high enough to be out of the flood plain. Their boot prints had barely been blown away from when they paced it the day before to see where their future house would stand: Here will be a shed, there a garden, next to it the driveway. They had no construction timeline, but it was a beginning. They had their land. They could envision their home. Their purchase thrilled Stuart's parents. Her father, on the other hand… They had to assuage him by saying that Stuart would have to work out of the Toronto office, probably for many years. Claude Sr. calmed down when he heard this.

Phyl told her Dad she didn't want to miss little Stuart growing up. And he believed her. Because it was true.

"I have nothing more to say," whispered Stuart.

"I want our children to play with El and Claude's children. I don't want them growing up with a gun and holster like Georgie."

Stuart took a deep breath. "So. Are you saying…?"

Phyl put up her hands and shook her head. She let them drop.

Stuart looked away.

"Give me one good reason why we should return," said Phyl.

"Well, they've offered a raise and a higher commission rate."

Phyl looked out the window again. She frowned.

"Perhaps we could build the house once we're finished. Not just a down payment. No mortgage."

She picked at her brown tweed skirt. "By selling our souls," she said quietly. But, prudently, it made sense. On paper. On her body and his, however…

Stuart unclasped his hands and stretched his arms above his head. He let his upper body drop onto the mattress. His legs hung over the foot of the bed. He stared at the ceiling light where a spider web floated in a ghostly breeze. Belgian lace in the sunset. "There's something else," he whispered.

Phyl turned to him. Tony jumped off her lap and curled up on her feet.

He sat up to face her. "Do you remember back at the *estancia* when I said I had an idea to get back at that Dieter, Jorge's neighbor?"

Phyl's eyebrows shot up. "Yes. With those Nazi hooligans."

"I sowed the seeds, and things have developed into something quite…large."

"Oh? Can you tell me?"

Stuart got up and walked around the room, looking up in the corners and behind the lamp.

"Silly, no one's listening."

"You'd be surprised what they can do now, Phyl. They showed me things. I would be using and relying on some of them when we get back."

"Well, whisper it to me, though I think it's silly."

Stuart walked over and leaned over her. First, he kissed her on the mouth. Softly. Slowly.

Phyl closed her eyes.

Stuart bent further so that his mouth caressed her ear. "We've set up a conspiracy, making it look Nazi-driven. It's my comeuppance. With love from the British Empire and the United States of America."

"Huh?"

"We're going to make the Nazis put their money where their dirty, big mouths are."

Phyl pulled away and shot a look of wonder at her new husband. A man of intrigue. She felt a surge of power pass through her groin. Her heart quickened. "Okay, that gets my attention." She thought for a moment. "Stu, I want to talk to Washington."

He stood back. "What do you mean?" he asked, looking deeply into the beautiful eyes he loved. Her blue eyes, her deep blue pools.

"I'm not a piece of flotsam floating around whatever swamp they plop you into. I'm an extension of you. I've sat on benches at the zoo, for crying out loud, while you had pseudo-conversations with contacts. I've seen brutal things. I am affected by all you do. I demand to speak with them."

"I doubt they'll meet with you."

"Oh yeah? Tell them it's not an absolute, concerning another three years in Argentina. I might consider it *if* they meet with me."

Stuart swallowed. He cocked his head and took a deep breath, "The worst they can do is say no."

"And if they do, we're at an impasse. Aren't we?"

"I'll call in the morning."

Phyl stood up and looked out the window again. The sun was setting fast. She was tired of not being part of the planning of their lives, of their marriage. That helpless feeling ate at her very soul. She was intent on getting rid of the awful feeling. She was going to give them an earful. Whether they listen or not, she didn't care. In fact, she expected they may not even see her. But it was worth the try. Whatever was to happen, she and Stuart were doing it together – not one doing it and the other following under duress. If they could talk Stuart into it, then she could think of ways they could sway her, too.

She had plans.

* * *

Seven months later, Phyl, upset, reviewed what she had typed on the Remington Rand loaner.

> CALLE PENA 2418 7
> Buenos Aires, Argentina
>
> Sunday, April 30, 1939
>
> Dear All,
>
> Well, here we are two months in Buenos Aires, and Stu is flat on his back again. He celebrated our entrance into the new apartment with asthma attacks and a good session of bronchial asthma. Then he was home for two weeks and got rid of asthma but continued with the bronchial cough, high temperature, and chills, and he came close to pneumonia. He has been in bed a week, and is very weak. The medicine chest is full of adrenaline and cocaine, but we use it only when absolutely necessary. I put mustard poultices on etc. Believe me, it is no joke, what with bed-pan and all. I don't think I'll ever be a nurse. The doctor is German and is quite good, but a couple of good purges which I gave him have done more good than all the dope prescribed. When he gets better, it means another session in Cordoba, but if he continues to be sick, it's back to North America. It isn't worth the effort. He coughs up blood. The doctor says it's lesions. The point is that this might lead to TB...

Their new maid, Mercedes, shuffled into the living room struggling with a willow basket of wet wash. Smiling, she told Phyl she was going out on the roof to hang the laundry. Phyl had never seen such a happy maid, and she knew it had absolutely everything to do with the new washing machine – a gem not found in every household in Argentina. Phyl was proud to have arranged that with Washington.

She watched Mercedes leave then continued to type. Phyl sat on a couch in a near-empty apartment. She continued to pound the keys.

> For weeks, our furniture has been in customs. Fortunately, my friend, Vivienne, brought my towels, sheets, and pillowcases. I have four of each, but they don't go far when anyone is sick. We got a Davenport

bed from Jorge, and Stu sleeps on it while I pile the big pillows and cushions from it on the floor for myself at night. We have chairs and tables which were in storage and a few lamps.

The fool company dispatcher declared our stuff secondhand, and when they inspected it and found the new radio, bedroom suite, chesterfield, and two telescopes, there was a devil of a mess, so that's why the stuff is still in customs. Heaven knows whether we'll see it all again. There's a ban on American goods. We can't even buy American cigarettes. Not that it matters to us, as Stu hasn't smoked in three weeks. Please persuade Roosevelt to pass a law allowing trade with Argentina for meat. Otherwise, we'll never get our furniture.

Phyl stretched. She popped a button on the front of her blouse, looked down, and buttoned it again. She gained weight in Toronto and Wilkes-Barre, and now her clothes were tight. She looked through the patio doors across their oversized balcony. They were on the ninth floor of the building Jorge owned. Looking straight out, she could see part of the building he and Angelica lived in. She continued:

The apartment is gorgeous, but we haven't been able to enjoy it. The heating is going to be the same here as everywhere. Jorge owns it but has no choice. There are general restrictions. We've had very cold days and about three hours of heat each time. It doesn't go on officially till May 15.

Before we left, Stuart had trouble with the company again and had to jump on the train several times to go to New York for meetings. He finally signed the contract at 5:00 p.m. Friday, and we sailed at midnight. A re-enactment of the first trip. He nearly resigned but finally got confirmation and feels he can make it worthwhile on this arrangement. Friday afternoon, we bought: R.C.A. 12 tube radio (the best), one studio couch Chesterfield combination, one bedroom suite in Maple, one bedspread, one set Roger's Silver Plate, bath towels, leather hassock, shower curtains, one Sunbeam Mix Master, one automatic iron, one glass coffee maker, one dozen and a half hose, two pair of beach sandals, one pair evening and one pair street shoes in black and flannel house coat, golf set for Stu, shorts, shirts, pajama, and telescopes (don't ask). Are we not the phenomenon of this age?

We finally got away to the S.S. Uruguay in a state of nerves. The trip was rough, although we didn't get sick. It was a fine ship with all the equipment.

Tell Claude we had a narrow escape with a champ asleep at the wheel at 11 o'clock in the morning on the way to New York. He woke with a start when he saw he was heading right to us. We were doing 60, and he about 50. What a fright, we nearly went over the bank trying to avoid him.

I put on five more pounds, eating Claude's chocolate, and enjoyed it, too.

Their new phone rang. Tony appeared from nowhere, barking frantically. Phyl jumped in her seat, not used to its harsh ring. She ran to the phone.

It was her Canadian friend, Vivienne, also a member of the Women's American Club, calling to tell Phyl there was a big do on the following Friday to meet the new American Ambassador's wife. Stuart had told her it was coming up. She thanked Vivienne, told her she was coming, hung up, and stood staring at the wall. It seemed events were on a roll once again.

Phyl was aware of the upcoming swearing-in of the new American Ambassador, Norman Armour. Stuart had met him in Washington and Ottawa, where Armour served on a diplomatic mission as Envoy Extraordinary and Minister Plenipotentiary. Stuart took Phyl to meet Armour and his wife, Myra Seregueievna Koudashev, a Russian princess. Mrs. Armour was anti-communist, anti-fascist, and anti-Nazi. Phyl was mesmerized by how she and Norman met, in the wake of the 1919 Russian Revolution, when Armour helped her escape for her life by taking her across the Finnish border disguised as a Norwegian courier. They were strong supporters of peace and unity, and intensely disliked rebellion.

When Phyl met them at their home in Ottawa, she liked Mrs. Armour instantly for her down-to-earth graciousness. Phyl returned to Toronto, gloating to her Dad and K that she had met a real princess.

Now, back in Buenos Aires, with Stuart sick and unable to do a secret drop for the ambassador, Phyl and Myra, had to do it in Stuart's absence. She was looking forward to seeing Myra again and giving her something precious under the guise of the Women's American Club gathering.

Phyl walked to the bedroom door, knocked softly, and entered. She gently closed the door behind her and allowed her eyes to adjust to the gloom. She had closed the drapes against the daylight to enable Stuart to sleep. She stood listening to Stuart's soft rasp. "Are you asleep?" she asked softly.

"How can I sleep with that racket?" he roared and coughed.

Phyl laughed. "It was Vivienne. The reception is this Friday."

Stuart looked at her over his shoulder. He coughed again. "Good."

She sat on the daybed and played with the blanket.

He reached out for her. "You'll do fine."

"You think?"

"You're doing one simple thing."

"Remember. Mata Hari, I am not. No stomach for it."

"*Señora Mata Hari de Redington.*"

Phyl laughed, lay down, and allowed him to wrap his arms around her. Tony scratched at the door. She got up and let Tony in. He jumped onto the bed. Phyl lay back down.

Tony farted. Phyl giggled. So did Stuart. They waved away the foul air.

"Ew!" laughed Phyl.

"That was a killer. What did you feed him?"

Phyl laughed. "I don't know. He's always eating the strangest-looking bugs out on the balcony."

Stuart laughed and coughed again. She reached and patted the top of his head.

"You've become quite the pillar of strength," he whispered into her ear.

"Hmm. You think?"

"Oh, definitely. You used to whine a lot."

"A crybaby?"

"Yes. It drove me nuts. But you were a beautiful crybaby."

"Hmm. And now I'm not?"

"A crybaby?"

"Beautiful, silly."

"No. You are now ravishing."

"That's more like it."

"And here you are in an apartment supplemented by Uncle Sam. You talked him into giving you a washing machine, furniture of your choice, spending money, and investing in a bond."

"So, I'm an extortionist." She smiled.

He kissed her on the neck. She coyly touched his lips. "Don't you dare cough in my face."

"So, let me look at your compact, and we'll see if my idea will work."

Phyl went to a crate in the corner. "I'll sure be happy when we have some furniture here."

"It'll come. Right now, do you have it handy?" Stuart groaned as he leaned on one elbow.

"Give me a sec," she said. She retrieved a zippered, woolen satchel. She opened it and walked to the light of the window. She rummaged through the bag and pulled out a gold square compact. She flipped it over and looked at both sides. She walked to Stuart and handed it over. He looked it over, opened it, and returned it. She held it upside down. Nothing came out. She left the room. She returned with a sharp-edged knife and pried at the casing inside the compact. It flipped out, shedding flakes of powder.

"Shoot," she said.

"That's okay. We'll get you a new one," said Stuart.

Phyl took the powder casing out of the compact. Stuart motioned to his leather briefcase leaning against a wall near the window. Phyl brought it to Stuart. He opened clasps, dipped into a side pocket, then into another side pocket. He retrieved microfilm and placed it in the compact, and snapped the lid.

"Good," he said. "We've got something here." He held it up. "This is what you give, Myra."

"Will she know what it is?" asked Phyl.

"Myra knows she's collecting something from you and will give it to Norman. She doesn't know what it is or what it's for. Norman will be expecting it. You don't need to worry about another thing."

"Can I know what's on there? I mean, can I be killed for this?"

"At a woman's gathering?" He paused as if to reflect. "Nah, no man in his right man would immerse himself in a large crowd of women gabbing away like hens."

She gave him a dirty look.

He shook his head wearily and smiled. "People *have* disappeared," he said, "but they are usually troublesome individuals. Besides, we're dealing with a bunch of Nazis scrambling to get Hitler's attention. They're so caught up in their espionage and lies that they're far too myopic to even consider women doing *our* dirty work." He motioned to the compact. "Just know this represents over a year of work. So, please, guard it with your life."

"A tiny thing like that?" she said, looking at the compact in Stuart's hand. "With my life?"

She reached for it, and he pulled his hand back.

"Nope, I'm going to sleep on this until Friday." He tucked the compact into the pillowcase and lay back. "And now I need a little comforting." He coughed but didn't cover his mouth.

"Stu!"

He coughed into his hands and reached out to cradle her face.

She jumped up, squealing, and ran out. "You wash those hands before touching me!"

"How the hell am I supposed to do that? I'm an invalid."

Phyl stood in the living room, smiling, listening.

"Okay then, I'll let Tony lick my hands clean," he yelled.

Phyl's eyes widened, and she hurried to the bathroom for a face towel. "NO. Don't you DARE."

* * *

"What a brawl these club things are," said Vivienne. "A giant gabfest"

Phyl laughed. "That's funny. That's what Stuart called it." She looked over the 200 women gathered in the bright reception hall and tried very hard to see Myra, Ambassador Norman's wife. She needed to catch her eye so Myra could call out for her. It was arranged this way, but it was hard to make eye contact. "Darn, our guest of honor is always surrounded by at least fifty women at a time," Phyl complained. She clung to her handbag and covered her hand with the other.

Vivienne offered Phyl a cigarette. Phyl looked down at her purse with the compact and wondered if she should take out a lighter.

"That's okay, I've got it." Vivienne picked up a monogrammed book of Club matches from an ashtray nearby and lit both cigarettes.

Phyl met Vivienne at a dance class the first year Stuart and she were in Buenos Aires. When they met, they threw their arms around each other and cried with homesickness. Vivienne was born in Pembroke, Ontario, attended University of Toronto, and belonged to the Parkdale Ladies Athletic Club. She had come to Buenos Aires on an adventure and taught at the American school. She was strong, independent, and well-educated, which meant she was opinionated. Phyl loved that about her. She turned to Vivienne and touched her long red hair.

"You're wearing it down today. That's quite risqué and somewhat of a waste on all these women." Phyl took a drag, then tore her eyes away to look around. "The only men here are the photographer from the society page and that guy playing the violin who no one is paying attention to."

Vivienne looked at the violinist. "Oh, I don't know, I think he's kind of cute." She searched through her purse. "Besides, you never know. I just may end up on the cover of the society page. Now, where's my compact?"

"Why? Why do you want a compact?" asked Phyl nervously.

"I want to look my best," she said, grinning and fluffing her hair. "Can I borrow yours?'

Phyl shook her head. "I don't have one."

Vivienne pouted and looked for a mirror on a wall, saw a small one near the door, and stood in front of it, primping.

Phyl smiled and looked at her friend. Vivienne wore a tight black dress, shoes, and a white fluffy-neck collar. Her hazel eyes sparkled, and she had freckles all over her face. She didn't wear make-up. Her red eyelashes and eyebrows were eye-catching, especially in a country where the women were 95% brunette.

"Well, I'm going to get a cup of tea or coffee," Phyl announced nervously. "Where do I go?"

Vivienne stretched her neck and pointed. "That end is the coffee, and at the other end," she said, "is the tea."

"Thank you, Madame. Want some?"

Vivienne shook her head. "No, I'd rather wait to be seen by that photographer and be photographed elegantly posing."

"Oh, so posh."

"Absolutely, my darling," quipped Vivienne.

Phyl squeezed through the throng, looking to see if she could catch Myra's face. At some point, she saw the cloche hat Myra wore. Unfortunately, Myra was small and petite, just like Phyl, and it was difficult to see her clearly.

Phyl went to the coffee end and saw that the sandwiches, cream cakes, and cookie platters were a little on the dwindling side. She picked up a plate, poured herself a coffee, and perused the bits of food. She chose a small ham triangle sandwich and one chocolate cookie. She turned, and someone bumped into her. She spilled some coffee onto her plate, and the front of her frock. She looked back at the table for a napkin, took one, and brushed down the front of her dress. She picked up her cup to take a sip, and was bumped again. She wiped her front again and quickly took a healthy bite of her sandwich just as three women approached her.

"Oh, Phyllis, did you get your furniture out of customs yet?"

Phyl's mouth was full, and she quickly tried to chew enough to answer.

"Did you enjoy your trip back to Canada?" asked another, without waiting for Phyl's reply to the first question.

Phyl nodded and desperately smiled, chewing feverishly, pointing to her mouth.

"You should give us a ring sometime; I want to hear all about it," said the third.

Phyl finished chewing and swallowed hard just as the women moved on. Phyl sighed. She wiped her mouth. She put plate and cup down on the table and turned to face the crowd. "Well, here goes."

"Excuse me," she said. "Pardon me." She pushed herself through the throng toward Myra and her entourage. Eventually, she made it so she could see Myra's face clearly. Phyl waved discreetly, trying to catch Myra's attention. Myra looked in Phyl's direction as she talked to a very attentive group of ladies in hats and gloves. Myra brightened up.

"Oh, ladies, you must pardon me. Could you please direct me to the powder room? I would like to refresh myself," said Myra.

"I'll take you there," keenly offered one of the ladies.

"No, I will," said Phyl. "Hi, Myra."

"Oh, Phyllis, how lovely to see you again." Myra grinned graciously at Phyl.

The women around them stared at Phyl. "You know each other, Phyl?" asked one of the ladies.

Phyl waved in the air. "Oh, yes, from way back. Back home in Canada."

"Oh!" said another, surprised. The ladies watched attentively as Myra excused herself and took Phyl's arm and was led to the lady's room, to have a cigarette in peace on plush chairs. Two ladies were in the stalls, and Myra chatted as Phyl reached into her purse. She took out the compact and handed it to Myra just as Vivienne walked into the washroom.

Vivienne stopped, looked at the compact in Phyl's hand, and frowned.

"Oh, I was just borrowing this from Mrs. Armour," Phyl choked.

Myra took the compact and put it in her own bag. She reached out for Phyl's hand. "Good to see you, Phyllis. Funny to meet again on the other side of the world."

"Yes, isn't it?" smiled Phyl, catching Vivienne's look as she went into a stall. "I'm sure you have a lot of settling in to do at that beautiful big place. How are things with you and customs?"

Myra shrugged. "Customs? No problem at all. We're diplomats. We get preferred treatment." She frowned. "Why?"

Phyl leaned closer and lowered her voice. "Well, our things have been held up at customs for over six weeks now. It's frustrating, Myra. I'm totally depressed over it."

"What? Well, that's absurd! Leave it to me, Phyllis. I'll pass that on to Norman, who'll arrange it with his secretary."

"Thank you so much!"

A toilet flushed, and Phyl gathered herself together. She wanted to be out before Vivienne stepped out of the stall. She smiled at Myra. Myra winked and grinned.

"Good news. Our furniture is being released," said Stuart at breakfast three days later. He had been in the office the day before and received a call that all was ready to be delivered.

"I know."

"What do you mean, you know?"

"Well, I told Myra, and Myra told Norman, and he spoke to his secretary, who spoke to someone who arranged it. Easy-peasy."

"Well, look at you." Stuart sipped his coffee. "I can finally get that radio and antenna up."

"Oh, goody. I'm looking forward to listening to my favorites, like Charlie McCarthy and the Lux Radio Theater."

Stuart wiped his hands of some grapefruit. "Well, don't forget why we were given that radio. I have to listen in on secret code stuff, same old, same old. So, I may have to put on some boring BBC." He pointed a finger at her. "That takes priority over Charlie McCarthy."

"Hmm."

"By the way, thank you for passing on that microfilm."

"Don't mention it," she smiled. "Back to the radio."

"Hmm."

"Well, I think I'd like to hear Eva Duarte on her new radio program. I'm hoping she's terrible."

"You really have something against her," he teased.

"Well, there's something about her that bothers me. Competition, maybe."

"Such a supportive female, you are."

"Hmm. Well, I can't wait to get Schenectady, either. We can listen to what your parents listen to every night."

"No, thank you."

"Oh, I didn't mind it at all. In fact, it became quite the routine. Supper and then sitting around the ol' radio. Listening to all the terrible things going on in Europe." She pushed her chair back and picked up her coffee. "Oh, Stu. It will be so nice to hear English whenever we want."

"Oh, that reminds me," said Stuart, reaching into his vest pocket. "A letter."

Phyl squealed and took the letter. She picked up her knife, wiped it off with her napkin, and sliced open the end of the letter. A photograph fell out. Her eyes moistened and she smiled.

"What?" asked Stuart.

She held it up. It was their baby nephew, little Stuart. Stuart Senior nodded and grinned.

"Doesn't he look like me?" she asked proudly, holding the photo beside her face.

"Why should he? He's not yours. At least, I don't think so."

"No, but I would be insulted if he didn't look a little like me after he looked at me across the table three times a day for nine months while I was there. *Some* resemblance has to rub off."

"It doesn't work that way."

Phyl ignored him and read some of the letter. "Oh, they saw the King and Queen when they stopped in Toronto!"

"More royalty rubbing off on the Mays. You guys are shooting up in the world," quipped Stuart. He wiped his mouth with his napkin, threw it on the table, and got up. "Gotta go. Be good." He bent down and kissed her.

She grabbed his lapel. "Stu."

"Yeah?"

"I'm so glad you quit smoking."

Stuart smiled and pretended he would cough in her face.

"Not again! DON'T YOU DARE."

* * *

Two weeks later, Stuart slammed the door as he entered the flat. Phyl and Tony came rushing out of the kitchen, surprised.

"Are you angry?" asked a concerned Phyl.

"I'm bloody mad," Stuart swore. "The guy next door, you know, the one who owns the next building. He has ten floors, right? A *huge* building. He could put his radio antenna anywhere he wants. But, noooo, he installs his antenna so that it swings between the buildings, EXACTLY where I planned to hang mine."

Phyl looked confused and blinked. "So, isn't there tons of room up there?"

Stuart sat on their new couch and slammed his legs on a sturdy, new coffee table. "To get the height, you need to have a strong base. The winds off the water are strong, so you need to also have spring lines to secure the line holding the antenna. It means anchoring here and there. I don't want my things fouled up with his." He coughed.

Phyl frowned.

"The guy has a new Marconi set.

I'm sure he didn't get in touch with Jorge for permission because Jorge knows we need this radio set up for both our sakes." He got up and went to the phone.

"Is Jorge home?" asked Phyl.

"Not sure. I'll give him a call."

He listened to the phone ring, and when a servant answered, he spoke in Spanish, asking for *Señor* Piñiero. He wasn't home. He hung up. "We may have to go the lawyer route. I threatened him with that, but he didn't budge." He angrily returned to the couch.

Phyl went to the balcony and looked up to the roof where the laundry was hung. Over to the side, she could see a shadow of something suspended between the buildings. She could hear the radio blaring from the other penthouse next door. She went back in.

"Why does it have to be suspended between the buildings? Why can't you just put up a pole?"

"Well, first of all, he's attached the wire to Jorge's building without his permission."

"But you were going to do the same to his?"

Stuart shook his head, "No. Jorge had informed him he needed to suspend an antenna and he said fine. Apparently, he owes Jorge big time. But as soon as he found out it was for an American, he skedaddled out and did this."

"Stu, why are you so upset about this? Are you okay? Just get a pole."

"It costs more money, and not only that, it is an obvious structure. It might as well yell out, 'Hey, there's an American foreign service stooge with a radio to listen in on code in this building.'" He put his hand to his chest.

"Well, I'd leave it to Jorge."

"What the hell do you think I'm trying to do?" he yelled. "The man isn't home."

Phyl's chin trembled. Mercedes was at the *feria*. Mercedes was now a full-time live-in housekeeper, and they were rarely alone like this. But she didn't like to be treated this way, even though she knew Stuart was stretched health-wise and mentally.

She walked to the front door, took the dog leash from the hook, and clucked her tongue to beckon Tony. Tony scrambled to her, sat still while hooked to the leash, and happily waited for the door to open.

"Where are you going?"

"I'm going to walk Tony."

"On your own? You can't do that," he snapped. "We go together."

"Watch me," she said. "And who gives a shit." She left.

* * *

Stuart stood between the open balcony doors in the middle of the night, looking into the viewer of a telescope. Phyl sat in their armchair with a floor lamp turned on next to her. She flipped through a magazine while Tony slept on her lap. The Toronto Symphony Orchestra played Mozart's Piano Concerto No. 23 in A Major on their new radio.

"It sounds like the orchestra's right next door. It's so beautiful, Stu. What a thrill to have a radio."

Stuart focused on what he was looking at.

"And ever since you got that antenna up and we get home stations, it's so much better than constantly listening to tangos and advertising on the latest headache remedy or cheap furniture sales. Or," she sat up to mimic a promoter, "'*Porque usa Usted Febeco, m'hijito? Porque limpia bien y es el major, Papi!*' They're always cleaning with *Febeco*, the worst cleanser I've ever used. And why would a father ask his son why he uses *Febeco* to clean? The maids and wives use it, not the men. Why don't they advertise with women promoting products?"

"Because the money comes from the men," mumbled Stuart. "Women legally do not exist."

She turned to him. "Well, as a man, do *you* ever use the cleaners?"

"I wouldn't touch the stuff."

"I rest my point." She noticed he was distracted. "What ya lookin' at?"

"A message from Jorge." Stuart grinned. He stood up and waved frantically at Jorge in the distance. He keenly looked back into the viewer for a response.

"You boys."

Stuart gave a thumbs-up directed to Jorge. He looked again to confirm Jorge saw his gesture. Satisfied, he backed off. Stuart was in a good mood. He directed the telescope to the night sky and looked. "Beautiful," he whispered.

Phyl stood. Tony rolled off her lap. She walked onto the balcony and wrapped her arms against the cold air. She looked up at the stars and the moon. The breeze off the water was cool.

Stuart motioned to the viewer. "It's a Waxing Gibbous Moon tonight."

"A waxing what?" She stepped over and squinted into the glass. She gasped. "Oh my God! It's like we're sitting in an observatory. The moon's right in my face."

"Precisely. Isn't it wonderful? Can you imagine going up there?"

"To the moon? Would that be possible?"

"One day, I don't doubt it."

She looked again. "It looks just like the plates we see in an astronomy book. I can see all the craters and volcanos as clear as can be."

"Well, they're not volcanos. What you see are the effects of eons of meteor strikes."

"Well, I've never ever seen anything like it. I can actually see a mountain sticking out the side, like strands of spun glass sticking out from the surface."

Stuart took out his cigarettes, took two out, and lit them. He tapped Phyl on her back. She looked up and hesitated before accepting hers.

He took a deep drag. "I know, I know. But I've cut back considerably. I used to be a chain smoker, remember?"

"Yes, that's why so many problems," she pointed at his chest.

"Well, to be fair, it's the climate here."

"I don't stay in bed with near pneumonia," she protested.

"And I think I'm only going through a pack a day now, maybe."

Phyl opted not to say anything. She hated to argue.

Stuart put his arm around Phyl and led her to the balcony railing to look over the lit park and distant, dark waters. They could see lights along the shore of Uruguay because they were so much higher on the ninth floor. Music continued to play from the living room. "Isn't this a perfect moment?" he asked.

Phyl nodded, smiling.

"Gorgeous view. Even nicer than the last one we had," Stuart added.

"You're in a better mood."

He nodded. "Hmmm. Wait till the papers come out tomorrow. You'll see why."

Phyl cocked her head and looked at him in wonder. "You are such a mysterious guy." She stood on her tiptoes and kissed him. Love was there between them, no matter what. No matter where.

* * *

"Is this an April Fool's Day joke?" Phyl looked at the New York Times.

"Nope, it's for real. And you're going to see this plastered on the front of all the other newspapers." Stuart took a bite of his burnt toast. He picked up his knife and scraped off charcoal.

Phyl looked at Stuart's toast. "I know. Mercedes still doesn't have the hang of that new toaster."

He shook his head, chewing. "Not to worry."

Phyl straightened the paper and read. "*Nazi Plot to Seize Patagonia is Aired.*" She squinted at the smaller type. "*Spy Document is Published in Buenos Aires Calling Rich District No Man's Land.*" She took a sip of her tea. "*Germans Charge Forgery, Argentina, Not Satisfied with Denial, Holds Informer, Orders Investigation.*" Her mouth dropped open. "Oh my gosh, is this for real?"

Stuart grinned. He motioned with his knife. "Read on, fair damsel."

She read the following:

> *The annexation of Patagonia by the Third Reich is one of the objectives of the present Nazi penetration of Argentina, according to a secret document published here last night.*
> *The German Embassy charges that the document is a forgery, but the statement that it gave out this afternoon to prove the forgery was not considered to be conclusive by Argentine authorities.*
>
> *The document purports to be a dispatch to the colonial office of the German Reich, signed by the counsellor of the embassy and the chief of the German National Socialist Labour Party in Argentina."*

"Isn't that the Dieter guy who was so arrogant? Jorge's neighbor? He's the counsellor, right?"
"Hmm."
She continued to read.

> *It details plans for organizing Nazi espionage in the six Argentine territories that comprise the southern region of the South American continent, formally known as Patagonia.*
>
> *The Argentine Foreign Office announced today that all departments of the government are investigating the authenticity of the document.*

Phyl looked up. Stuart motioned at the paper. "Read on, don't stop," he said proudly.

> *Argentine newspapers have been urging the government to investigate Nazi activities in Patagonia. Some time ago, German schools were closed in the territory of The Pampas because pupils were taught allegiance to Chancellor Hitler instead of Argentina and because German instead of Spanish was used.*
>
> *There have been persistent reports of Nazi activities in many parts of Southern Argentina, including a supposed Boy Scout rally—"*

Phyl looked up again. "The kids on the train."
Stuart nodded and shook his head. "The kids, yes, but they make it sound like an innocent Boy Scout gathering. Hitler Youth is not Boy Scouts, excuse me."
Phyl continued.

> *—Boy Scout rally that turned out to be a concentration of the Nazi youth movement.*
>
> *The investigation began today. However, it is limited, so far, to the question of whether or not the published document is genuine. The German embassy statement given out this afternoon says that the German Chargé d'Affaires, visited the Foreign Office this morning and made a formal complaint against the newspaper and asked the Argentine government to undertake the fullest investigation. Foreign Office sources denied that any such protest had been made by the Chargé d'Affaires and said that his only protest is of innocence.*

> *The photograph that was published carried twenty-seven enclosures, including six maps obtained from the Argentine General Staff Office. The dispatch stated that espionage contacts were established in the Argentine Ministries of War, Marine, Agriculture, the Coast Defense Headquarters, Bureau of Mines, Argentina official Petroleum Corporation, the Standard Oil Company, and the Bank of the Nation.*
>
> *It describes Patagonia as only sparsely settled, which is true.*
>
> *The Argentina government, it says, has never established its administration over the district in the manner required for the occupation and colonization of any territory, and therefore, the territory can legally be considered a No Man's Land.*
>
> *It is, therefore, suggested that it be occupied as a German colony.*
>
> *The district mentioned in the dispatch embraces the territories of The Pampas, Neuquen, Rio Negro, Chubut, Santa Cruz, and Tierra del Fuego, or all of Argentina south of the Rio Negro to Cape Horn. The Germans own large sheep ranches in this district, which also includes Argentina's famous petroleum fields at the Comodoro–Rivadavia."*

Phyl sat back and dropped the newspaper onto her plate. She covered her face and started to cry.

"Why are you crying?" asked Stuart.

Phyl wiped her eyes. "They planned to take over Jorge and Diego's land in Rio Negro. How can they do that!?"

Stuart went around the table. "Where's Mercedes?"

Phyl motioned to the kitchen.

Stuart whispered. "It's not true. Don't worry. " He pulled back to look at Phyl's face. He smiled at her tears. He put a finger to his lips and looked at the kitchen. "I'm sure the Nazis have been thinking of doing precisely this for their *Lebensraum*. But this is *our* doing. I wrote this and we had it forged. It's the comeuppance I began planning back when we had that run in with Dieter."

Phyl blinked through her tears. "Oh. And the photographs?"

"Mine. We planted the article in the New York Times after the documents were handed to Ortiz by a patsy a few days ago. We anonymously released the information to *Noticias Graficas* two days ago."

"But I think I saw something in that article written in Germany about doing this precise thing back in 1937. This plan of theirs has been in the workings for a long time." She went to get the newspaper.

Stuart put his hand on hers. "As I said, they did talk about it. But these documents are all planted. All made up. All forged. And what was their secret plans are now exposed."

"What if they find out it was you? Couldn't they kill us?"

"No. They're blaming the Jews and Freemasons. No mention of Americans or Argentines."

"Oh, dear. The poor Jews. They're blamed for everything. Who is this 'patsy' as you call him?"

"A poor schmuck named Heinrich Jürges. He has a big, massive hate-on for the Nazis and has a grudge. Something to do with the death of his mother back in Germany. He's safe. Besides, he doesn't know the chain of command here. Dozens of people are involved, and just as many departments in the States, here, and Brazil."

"Why Brazil?"

"Keep reading." He sat down as Mercedes came in with the pot of coffee. Phyl quickly wiped her tears and picked up the Times.

> *Police took into custody Enrique Jurges, whom they described as a former Nazi and friend of Captain Ernst Roehme, Storm Trooper chief of staff, who died in Chancellor Adolf Hitler's blood purge of June 30, 1934.*

Phyl waited while Mercedes topped up her coffee. "*Gracias.*"

"*De nada.*"

> *Jurges, held incommunicado, was reported to have sent copies of an espionage plan to President Roberto M. Ortiz and to the newspaper Noticias Graficas. It was disclosed that Señor Ortiz received his copy on March 20 and that a police investigation was underway when its contents were published by the newspaper.*

Phyl read to herself for a bit. She read aloud again. "It says here that the Argentine government has received many complaints of Nazi activity in southern Argentina, but this was the first instance in which written proof had been submitted to support the charges."

He gave her a warning look, picked up his knife, and hacked off the top of his boiled egg. He leaned out of the way as Mercedes poured more coffee into his cup. "*Gracias, Mercedes.*"

"*De nada.*"

Phyl and Stuart thoughtfully watched Mercedes disappear into the kitchen. Then they turned to each other and held hands.

"The pictures. I did that with Myra back at the club?"

Stuart's eyebrows shot up. "You certainly did. You did a mighty fine job for the sake of good ol' US of A. But, sorry. The compact didn't survive. Consider it the sacrificial lamb."

She kissed Stuart on the nose. "This was worth a hundred compacts. But you owe me a new and very expensive replacement." She sat back and tapped her lip with her finger. "Perhaps one with a diamond in the middle."

"What do you think you are? Royalty?"

"I might as well be. I've been climbing up the hoity toity ladder, don't you know."

* * *

Five months later. Phyl and Stuart sat by the radio, enjoying the music on CBC, the Canadian Broadcasting Corporation. Phyl held up a little half-finished sweater for little Stuart.

"Look," she said, smiling.

Sitting under the corner reading lamp, Stuart looked up politely, smiled, nodded, allowed a sparkle in his eye to escape. He returned to reading the newspaper.

Phyl flattened out the blue handwork over her lap and measured with her finger how many more rows she would have to knit.

An announcer interrupted the radio program. Phyl's heart turned to ice. Britain had proclaimed war on Germany days before, and everyone wondered if Canada would follow in Britain's footsteps. An interrupted program under the circumstances, was foreboding.

> *We will take you now to Ottawa. The Prime Minister of Canada, the Right Honourable William Lyon Mackenzie King.*
>
> *For months, indeed for years, the shadow of impending conflict in Europe has been ever-present. Through these troubled years, no stone has been left unturned, no road unexplored in our patient search for peace. Unhappily for the world, Herr Hitler and the Nazi regime in Germany have persisted in their attempt to extend their control over other peoples and countries and to pursue their aggressive designs in wanton disregard of all treaty obligations and peaceful methods of adjusting international disputes. They have had to resort increasingly to agencies of deception, terrorism, and violence. It is this reliance upon force, this lust for conquest, this determination to dominate throughout the world, which is the real cause of the war that today threatens the freedom of mankind.*

Stuart reached out for Phyl's hand. She dropped her knitting to the floor and clung to him.

> *This morning, the king, speaking to his peoples at home and across the seas, appealed to all to make their own the cause of freedom, which Britain again has taken up. Canada has already answered that call. On Friday last, the government, speaking on behalf of the Canadian people, announced that in the event of the United Kingdom becoming engaged in war in the effort to resist aggression, they would, as soon as parliament meets, seek its authority for effective cooperation by Canada at the side of Britain.*

"Oh my God, Stu," Phyl cried. She covered her mouth in shock.

> *In what manner and to what extent Canada may most effectively be able to cooperate in the common cause is, as I have stated, something which parliament itself will decide. All I need to add at the moment is that Canada, as a free nation of the British Commonwealth, is bringing her cooperation voluntarily. Our effort will be voluntary.*
>
> *The people of Canada will, I know, face the days of stress and strain that lie ahead with calm and resolute courage. There is no home in Canada, no family, and no individual whose fortunes and freedom are not bound up in the present struggle. I appeal to my fellow Canadians to unite in a national effort to save from destruction all that makes life itself worth living and to preserve for future generations those liberties and institutions which others have bequeathed to us.*

Stuart turned off the radio. Phyl stood up and walked to the balcony doors, and opened them. Tony followed and sniffed at the grate on the floor.

In Argentina, though it was September, spring was just setting in, and flowers had begun to blossom. They filled the air with renewed life. She looked at the lit windows in the buildings around the dark park and down well-lit streets. Were others listening in on what was happening in Canada and Europe? Or were they listening to Spanish radio plays and silly commercials about *Febeco* cleaners? Were Stuart and Phyl the only people who had just heard history in the making? She knew she would never forget the smell in the air, the feel of the breeze, the noise in the street below. She would never forget the moment when her world collapsed.

Until that day, the Patagonia Affair had immersed Phyl with intrigue and sharp amusement, but suddenly, it all seemed insignificant in the shadow of this threat closer to home. She burst into tears at the railing and allowed Stuart to hold her and lead her back into the flat.

"Oh my God, Stu. Will Claude have to go to war? What if he never comes back? El could become a widow, and little Stuart'd be without a father. Oh, how awful. And we're stuck down here."

Stuart rocked her. "We don't know if Claude would have to go and fight, Phyl. Don't start thinking of things that may not happen."

"I mean, World War I is still so very fresh. How can the world let this happen again?" She was devastated.

"We've been watching it coming for years, Phyl."

"I know, but to have it actually happen!"

The phone rang, and Mercedes came and answered it. She turned to Phyl, concerned. "*Señorita* Vivienne," she shyly announced.

Phyl ran to the phone.

Stuart watched Phyl talking at length, frightened. He picked up his paper and reviewed what he had read earlier. On the 1st of September, the Argentine government proclaimed its neutrality in the conflict, and on the 3rd of September, the diplomatic representatives of the United Kingdom and France informed the Argentine government that their countries had proclaimed war against Nazi Germany.

Phyl said goodbye to Vivienne and hung up. She walked to the living room. "Vivienne is very upset."

"Hmm."

"I'm going to bed."

"Okay." He looked at her curiously.

"Will you come with me?"

Stuart threw the paper onto the coffee table and stood. "Absolutely."

She climbed into bed in her clothing. Stuart watched her curl up into a fetal position. His heart broke. He climbed in beside her, covered them both with the bed cover. He wrapped his arms around her. Tony jumped onto the bed, curling up at their feet. Phyl cried herself to sleep in Stuart's arms.

The next day, they heard that the Canadian Parliament had convened and that it was almost a unanimous vote — Canada officially proclaimed war on Germany.

"Will the Americans get involved?" Phyl had a haunted look about her.

Stuart paused and shook his head. He looked at his watch. "I really should be going." He got his briefcase.

Phyl turned in her armchair and watched him walk to the door. "Stu?"

He turned. He took a deep breath. "Don't worry. From the beginning, the United States' policy is to stay out of the conflict."

But Phyl couldn't fully believe that. "And if they *did* join in the fight, are we supposed to return to the States? Would you be called for military service, even from here in Argentina? And if not, would you feel you have to enlist?"

"I don't know how to answer your questions." He stood momentarily before stepping back to Phyl and kissed her on the forehead.

She watched him leave and sat and stared at the door. She felt like they were caught in a web, and a hairy spider sat in a corner, watching them. Argentina claimed to be neutral, but too many seemed to ignore the proverbial white elephant sitting comfortably in the room. In her mind's eye, the elephant wore a Swastika.

The Nazi Fifth Column wasn't going anywhere. To her, the enemy was watching, calculating, sharpening its fangs right under their noses.

Chapter Twelve
Graf Spee, Reiner and Throwing Up

The radio was set short-wave, tuned in all over the world. Stuart sat by the hour hunched over, the volume low, not to wake Phyl. He smoked endless cigarettes and drank pots of tea until the early morning hours. Phyl could tell how bad the foreign news was overnight by looking at his bloodshot eyes. His concern was Germany's battleship, the Admiral Graf Spee, hunting and sinking nine merchant ships totaling 50,000 tons.

By a miracle or design through its commander and captain, Hans Landsdorff, not a single life, German or ally, was lost. The British Navy frantically pursued her with no success. Winston Churchill, First Lord of the Admiralty, sent a fleet to hunt it down with no success for months: The Graf Spee was elusive and brilliantly commanded. Then, one fateful day, Landsdorff surrendered to temptation, and the Graf Spee sunk two ships within hours off the coast of Africa, leaving a trail in the direction of South America. The British Navy guessed she was heading for the busy shipping lanes outside of Uruguay, and by the time the Graf Spee came in sight of the River Plate, Churchill had his fleet waiting, guns drawn.

Just after six on the 13th of December, 1939, Phyl was thrown out of bed as Buenos Aires shook from the roar of cannons. The explosions tore apart the early morning, echoing across the River Plate estuary, hills, and countryside. Phyl saw smoke over the distant horizon, and flashes reflected off the low hanging clouds.

"Stu!" she screamed. She hurried into the dining room. Mercedes, frantic, ran out of her bedroom. Stuart beat them to the balcony, trained the telescope onto what now were horrific and angry plumes of smoke curling over the horizon.

"It's the Graf Spee. It's closer to Montevideo than us, I figure. Boy, Uruguay's getting an earful."

"Well, my ears are splitting!" cried Phyl, tightening her nightgown. She shivered with fear.

"Churchill's been looking for her for months. There's been code all night; they suspected she was heading this way." He turned and looked at Phyl. "Are you okay?"

"How can you ask such a thing!?" An explosion rattled the windows and doors. Phyl jumped, her eyes dancing wildly. "Are they going to bomb here, too!?"

"No, she shoots at ships, not neutral territory." He shook his head in wonder. "I have to admit, those wily British. They knew she'd come here." He looked at Phyl. "Are you cold? You're shivering, and it's already sweltering."

Phyl shivered, jaws clenched. She turned to see Mercedes standing behind her on the balcony, crying quietly. Phyl asked her to make a pot of coffee. Mercedes rushed back into the flat, and Tony, frightened by the noise, meandered out, perplexed, his tail at half wag. He looked at Phyl as if to ask if everything was okay.

"Shhh. It's okay," she said, motioning for him to come closer. He dipped his head and panted as he came to her, allowing her to pick him up.

"Phyl, you are watching history in the making," continued Stuart excitedly. "This is officially the first naval engagement of the war between British and German ships. Right here, under our noses. One of those moments in life you will never forget. The kind when you say, I remember when."

"I can do without that privilege, thank you very much," she said grimly, wrapping her arms around herself, more from nerves than anything else.

Stuart went in and turned on the radio. Phyl followed and sat on the couch. The English channels had already interrupted their regular programs with a special bulletin. Mike Fowler, an American journalist evidently standing on the Montevideo waterfront at that very moment, was reporting live on air.

> *Shortly after daybreak on this morning, Wednesday, the 13th of December, the British ship Ajax sighted a plume of smoke to the north. The Exeter was sent to investigate and, at 6:15, signaled, "I think it is a pocket battleship!" It was the elusive German battleship, Graf Spee. It looks like the heavily outgunned British ships are pursuing her. The Exeter appears to be coming from the south, while the other two from the east.*

Pale, Mercedes arrived with the pot of coffee and tray. She poured two cups. "Mercedes, *adelante, tómate un café también*. Pour one for yourself."

Mercedes hurried back and returned with a third cup and saucer. She shakily poured and sat respectfully away from Phyl and Stuart, her cup and saucer rattling. Phyl appreciated the extra comfort from another soul. This affected them all.

> *Instead of keeping his distance and picking off his attackers at long range, Captain Langsdorff of the Graf Spee decides to close in. The*

> *British guns are opening fire at maximum range, and the Graf Spee is responding by dividing her salvoes against both groups of ships.*

Phyl finished her coffee and tore herself away to get ready for the day. The apartment shook and rattled continuously as she walked into the bedroom. She stopped and put a hand on her chest, feeling ill, but she shook it off. Her ear tuned to the radio as best she could in the other room, she returned dressed. She sat near the radio. Mercedes was gone.

"Where's Mercedes?"

Stuart shrugged, his ear to the radio speaker, occasionally looking up at the horizon through the glass doors.

> *Graf Spee has now turned all her firepower against the Exeter, which has eight-inch guns. Grave damage is being inflicted by Graf Spee's eleven-inch guns from the turret on her bow. Massive geysers of ocean water tower over the ships with each salvo.*

A massive explosion rocked their apartment, and the windows rattled so hard Phyl could swear next time they would shatter.

"Well, this will go on for a while, I'd say," said Stuart, standing up and putting the volume down. He stood at the doors and gazed at flashes ripping through angry billows of pitch-black smoke reaching up into the heavens.

"Dear God Almighty," whispered Phyl. "Do you have to go to Uruguay to look into this?" she asked, frightened.

Stuart shook his head. "No, it's up to the British. I can only observe, though Jorge may want to hop on the ferry and go over and take a look. We'll be able to see better in Uruguay."

The fury lasted just over an hour, and when it seemed the Germans were winning, the Graf Spee broke off the action. The radio said it looked like it was limping to Montevideo for emergency repairs in the neutral waters of the port.

Shocked and distracted, Phyl and Stuart went on with their day as best they could. It was late that night when everyone knew the Graf Spee, scorched and pockmarked by shell blasts and taking on water, had taken two dozen hits in the battle. There were holes at her starboard waterline, her control and fighting towers had been damaged, and a gun tower on the port side had been torn off. Neutrality laws permitted the vessel to stay in the port for 24 hours, after which she would be forced to leave and face the British again. It was announced that Langsdorff had tried to negotiate an extended period, necessary to repair the damage and be seaworthy enough to return to Germany, but Uruguay refused.

Everyone felt queasy knowing the two British cruisers stood off at the mouth of the River Plate waiting for reinforcements.

Three days later, seven more cruisers joined the waiting ships.

Phyl and Stuart heard Captain Langsdorff had buried his dead, placed the wounded under medical supervision, and freed his British prisoners. Then, it was announced that he ordered his damage control crew to start repairs on the battered ship. Langsdorff requested at least fifteen days to complete repairs once again, but the Uruguayan government gave him only two.

Everyone knew it was impossible to do all that he needed in just two days, and it was reported that after discussions with Hitler in Berlin, he had most of his crew transferred to the Tacoma, and sent the Graf Spee off with a skeleton crew, her battle colors hoisted, to be destroyed by their own hand and sunk in twenty-five feet of water.

Stuart decided to go with Jorge across the river. There, near Montevideo along with thousands, they silently stood at the riverbank to watch daylight fade and a glorious sunset bathe the last throes of the sinking Graf Spee.

In the middle of the night, Phyl, Stuart, and Jorge listened to an eyewitness account from one of the sailors on the ship named Ajax. He described what it felt like during the battle.

> *We were closed up and loaded, ready for whatever might come. Then we received the news that she had sailed, and we could hear the Yankee broadcasters describing us as the suicide squadron with our little 'pop-guns.'*

Later, a London Daily Telegraph correspondent reported on the explosion and consequent sinking of the Graf Spee,

> *At that moment, the sun was just sinking below the horizon, flooding the sky in which small gray clouds floated lazily, a brilliant blood-red. It was a perfect Wagnerian setting for this amazing Hitlerian drama.*

Days later, the news reported that in the early hours of December 20, Captain Langsdorff shot himself in the head. Later that week, he was buried with full naval honors in Buenos Aires.

Graf Spee sailors, now forced to stay indefinitely, overran the city of Buenos Aires, adding to an already tumultuous nightlife. Very soon after the Battle of the River Plate, the USS Helena, a newly-built light cruiser from the States, was on a shakedown cruise and arrived in port for training, though many suspected the Americans simply wanted to remind the Nazi contingency of their presence. Consequently, American and German sailors co-mingled with no qualms of becoming fast friends.

Stuart, Phyl, and Jorge dropped by the docks to see the USS Helena on their way to the American Club for a buffet dinner and dance in honor of the ship's officers.

"Wow, that's some boat," said Phyl, looking at its length.

"That's no boat, Phyl. It's a ship." Stuart gave her a funny look.

She kept her hand on her hat to keep it from blowing away in the onshore breeze and slightly sneered at him. "Ship, then." They stood under the towering, high bow of the ship and were surrounded by wandering sailors from both the USS Helena and the Graf Spee, who all seemed to be chummy together.

"It's about two city blocks long and carries six planes, and I don't know how many guns," offered Stuart. He stood with his hands in his pockets, gazing at the turrets. He ignored the young sailors walking around them.

"I don't know very much about boats, but I suspect with this war and being a neutral port, we will have a crash course on battleships," said Jorge.

Phyl looked with disgust at hundreds of butts strewn and ground into the grimy cement. Sailors, bystanders, and streetwalkers walked over them, through grimy oil-covered puddles. Phyl shivered at garbage clinging to the edges of the wharf and surrounding building walls. She checked her gloves to make sure they were clean. She squinted at the surroundings, the overhead cranes, the trucks. Her ears rang. The noise was deafening, but the excitement of a new and massive battleship sitting so gallantly and majestically in the sun captured her imagination. "I can't imagine living on a ship like that with thousands of others. What a different life that is."

"You said it," said Stuart. He looked at Jorge and stepped closer. He motioned with his chin. "There's talk that Japan may get into the war. I wonder if the USS Helena is using that as an excuse to hang around?"

"They'd be better off closer to the Panama Canal."

"True, but they wouldn't be able to lounge there at length as they can here in the neutral zone." Stuart looked at his watch. "It's time we left, or we'll arrive late for the buffet supper."

Phyl laughed. "God forbid we miss the food."

"Well, I want to get in early to speak with some officers."

"You've got all night to talk to them."

"Once the dance starts, there's no sense in trying to talk."

Jorge saw a line-up at the road and main entrance to the docks. He motioned with his head. "Shall we get a taxi for the American Club, then?"

"Are you coming along?" asked Phyl.

"He's not a member of the Club, so he can't get in." Stuart took out his billfold and counted his *pesos*.

"Not even as a guest?"

Stuart looked at Jorge, questioning. Jorge held up his hands. "This is your area of expertise. I have mine. Right now, I have a date."

"Oh, that's too bad," said Phyl sarcastically.

Jorge scratched the side of his face, frowning.

Phyl cleared her throat as she tried to keep up with them. "I think you'd enjoy talking to them, Jorge. Besides, you are such a good tango dancer, and Stuart hates to dance the tango. Anibal Toilo Pichuco's Orchestra is playing tonight. His tango keeps you on your toes. I listen to him on radio in the afternoons."

"I would love nothing more than to dance with you, albeit under Stuart's watchful eye."

Phyl laughed.

"But that's okay," continued Jorge. "The taxi can drop me off at my flat on the way to the Club." He gave her an appreciative look.

"What about your date?"

"I'm getting *ready* for a date."

"Geez, I hate it when you admit to seeing one of your mistresses."

"Well, it bothers you more than my own wife." He smiled at her. "Looking fine today, Phyllis."

Phyl smiled. "Thank you, Jorge."

This bothered Stuart. "Come on, you guys." He sidled closer to Jorge. "Stick to your mistresses, Buster."

Jorge looked at him in surprise, then humbly nodded in agreement. He shrugged. "Of course. I wouldn't think of it." He blinked several times. "You know by now you shouldn't worry."

Stuart motioned they hurry to the entrance.

Phyl's hat blew off, and she ran after it, while the men walked ahead unaware. A young sailor broke from a gathering of USS Helena and Graf Spee sailors. He ran to help her with her hat. He picked it up, brushed it off, and held it to his nose to smell its aroma. He grinned. He held it out to her, but when she went to retrieve it, he pulled it back teasingly.

"*Buenos dias*, sweetheart. Aren't you a looker!" The American sailor oggled her appreciatively.

Phyl didn't say a word and stood holding out her hand impatiently.

The young sailor turned and motioned to his friends, who all gathered around Phyl. They discussed her most admirable features in detail. She nervously looked toward the entrance, where she saw Jorge and Stuart squabbling with a taxi driver. She looked at the young men, who all couldn't have been more than eighteen or twenty, some wearing Graf Spee uniforms. Another stepped closer and looked at her with twinkling eyes. He wanted to hold her middle, but she pulled away. She nervously glanced toward the entrance.

"Aren't you *Schön*," he said with a thick German accent. "*Schön* enough to hang up above my bunker," he said.

"Don't talk like that about her," another said, evidently American. "That's rude."

The young German turned. "Why? She's Argentine and they're sex-crazed. She doesn't understand a single word I am saying," he turned to Phyl. "Do you, *Schatz*?"

"Shall I call my husband, who is right over there?" She pointed to the dock entrance the same moment Jorge and Stuart turned back to see where she was. Stuart whistled and motioned for her to catch up. He glared at the young sailors.

The German sailor's face paled. "*Ach, du lieber Gott*, she's English!" He motioned to the American to return Phyl's hat.

"Scram BOYS," she yelled with satisfaction. As they rushed off, she secretly smiled and hurried to Jorge and Stuart.

In the taxi, Jorge sat up front and Stuart and Phyl in the back. She took her gloves off. "The American sailors seem to prefer the company of the Graf Spee sailors to the English ones, I notice."

"Yes, it's upsetting the English. They're making quite a fuss about it," said Stuart.

Phyl looked out as they passed monument after monument. "There is no reason why the Americans shouldn't chum with whom they please since they're completely neutral. The Graf Spee boys are really just a bunch of children."

"Did they bother you?" asked Stuart.

"The usual lewd remarks. This time, a snot-nosed German," said Phyl, shaking her head.

"Yes, they are very young. I think their inexperience is the reason for the loss in the battle. It certainly wasn't their captain's fault. They lost a good man." Stuart reached for Phyl's hand.

She took his hand and watched various sailors carousing in the streets. "I wish Canada didn't belong to the British Empire. They're always in a fight. Why can't we be completely independent and let Europe do what they want? My God, they might as well give in to Russia now, then Russia can take Germany. By that time, Japan will be fighting someone else. We in North and South America settle our troubles more or less amicably, why can't they?"

Jorge turned. "Speak for yourself, North Americaner. We in South America have our own peculiar problems." He gave her a look.

She nodded. "Ah, yes. Well, at least you don't use battleships and bombs to settle elections."

"People still die," added Stuart.

"Not in the thousands," said Phyl. "Or in the millions," she added sadly. "And why should our boys go over and lose their lives or come back broken, having to start all over again? All this propaganda about crusading and fighting for civilization gets me upset. The whole darn thing is purely commercially driven. Either someone wants the other's wealth, or the other wants theirs. It's all so hypocritical."

"It's the Human Condition," said Jorge. "You can't go anywhere where this isn't so."

"I'd rather live on a farm and forget it all," Stuart said. He looked at Phyl. "How would you like to live in Alaska?" He grinned.

"Ye gods!" exclaimed Phyl. "With my luck, I would be eaten by a bear. I'd much rather take my chances with the turmoil of real life and squeeze in a bunch of eating, drinking and making merry."

"You're a true hedonist," laughed Jorge.

"You should know, with all your mistresses."

"Now, now, Phyl. Time to behave yourself. We're about to rub shoulders with the elite of the expatriates."

"You mean getting drunk and high on the calamities of the day?"

"Point taken. Let's get bombed tonight," said Stuart.

"Deal," laughed Phyl. She gazed back at the sailors and prostitutes gathered in front of the USS Helena. "So long as it's the alcohol kind and not the other."

* * *

Phyl felt underdressed for the dance. But was having so much fun by the time the buffet supper was cleared away she didn't mind one bit. There were so few women in the room, each female was a beacon of beauty and delight for the men crammed into the Club. The officers and guests of honor were handsome in their full blue dress uniforms.

Phyl peered through the thick smoke in the hall. While enjoying the orchestra, she half listened to Stuart's conversation with Lieutenant Richard Washbourn from New Zealand. He served as a gunnery officer on the HMS Achilles, one of the ships that battled the Graf Spee. He was sharing their table.

"I wasn't as dead as I had first surmised."

Phyl turned to Lieutenant Washbourn. "You thought you were dead?"

"Certainly. Everything shattered around me at one point, and I had shrapnel in my midriff. Later, I noticed holes in my legs. So, it certainly was a close call. It's actually a miracle I'm still alive. Someone's prayin' for me."

"Tell us more," said Stuart. He leaned toward him, elbows on a wine-stained linen tablecloth.

Washbourn pondered what to say next. "Well, the Hun was under the usual delusion of their own naval superiority, and they came at us full force for the first ten minutes, which was just what we wanted to get into for good effective fighting range with our own cannon."

"That's quite a pounding you left yourself open to," offered Stuart, listening closely.

"You better believe it. And, thereafter, when we showed no sign of conforming to *his* expectations or bolting from his undoubtedly superior force, Langsdorff turned around and bolted himself, and never again showed any inclination for a fight."

"What did you think at the time?"

"We thought he lost the stomach for fighting, but then we saw she was quite damaged. This bloke, Langsdorff, ended up being sensitive. Could be he didn't want any more lives lost."

"Hmm. So, what happened then?"

"We engaged him hotly, having the superior speed, for nearly an hour and a half. Poor old Exeter, having the bigger guns and therefore being the more dangerous foe, received the benefit of Langsdorff's attention mostly for the first three-quarters of an hour, and she was unlucky. It was gratifying to hear that she was still afloat at the end. I didn't for a moment expect to see her alive."

Another New Zealand lieutenant at the table, whose name Phyl didn't catch, jumped in. "To understand the significance of the battle, it is important to know that the Graf Spee embodied all that was aggressive and powerful in the German war machine. A huge warship with advanced technology and armor-plated defense, it boasted 11-inch guns that could send deadly artillery shells nineteen kilometers."

"Wow," offered Phyl.

The lieutenant smiled gleefully at her.

Lieutenant Washbourn picked it up from there. "The problem was that the three warships were outgunned, you see."

Stuart nodded and motioned with his hand. "That was quite apparent."

"Yes, and the Spee liked to fight from a distance - where its bigger shells could destroy the enemy but where the 6-inch and 8-inch shells of the British either fell short or bounced off the German armor."

"What a discouraging sight that must have been," said Phyl. "Did many die?"

"Indeed. The Achilles lost four sailors, with nine wounded. On the Ajax, seven died, and five wounded, while the Exeter suffered sixty-one deaths with twenty-three wounded. The Graf Spee lost thirty-six sailors, and sixty were wounded."

"Oh, dear."

An exuberant sailor, dancing with one of Phyl's friends, suddenly crashed into the back of Lieutenant Washbourn, who turned fists raised, ready for a fight.

"Sorry, Lieutenant," yelled the sailor, as he swept the woman back into the dancing throng.

The lieutenant laughed and returned to the other lieutenant. "So. Did you see how, when everyone did the Hitler salute at the graveside, Langsdorff proudly did the naval hand salute?"

"The man had depth," offered the other lieutenant.

At that moment, Vivienne, sashayed from the edge of the dancers to their table, her red hair coiled around her head. She smiled graciously at the handsome men in uniform and nodded at Stuart.

"Hi, Vivienne," smiled Phyl. She got up and pointed to the lieutenants, who stood up politely. "Gentlemen, this is my Canadian friend, Vivienne Beatty. Vivienne, this is Lieutenant Washbourn, and this is?" She looked at the young man. "I'm sorry, I didn't catch your name."

"Sam. Sam Windsor," he said, wide-eyed at Vivienne. "Lieutenant," he added proudly.

Vivienne smiled beautifully and shook hands with both. She threw a second, preferred glance at Sam Windsor and turned to Phyl. "Sorry, Phyl, darling. I have a whole herd of clothes which I was going to send to family, but I've decided to send them to the Red Cross for those poor souls in Europe. I thought perhaps you might have some. We could take it together. We'll need a taxi to take it all, maybe Monday. Everybody here seems to be collecting for something," She sadly looked at the officers. "Are you British? You have a funny accent."

Windsor: "No, we're New Zealanders."

"Oh, so you're not from England."

"Are you alright?" asked Phyl.

"Oh, I'm simply heartbroken. My sister's boyfriend left for England. He's at the Cliffs of Dover training as a pilot." She motioned at the officers. "I thought they might have been at the Cliffs of Dover."

Windsor shook his head. "No, we've never been."

"Pilot, you say?" asked Stuart. "The odds against pilots lasting are already rather grim, I hear."

"Stu!" Phyl looked at him as if he was a brute. "She didn't need to hear that."

He looked surprised and raised his shoulders. "They are. Unless he's smart enough to stay put as a trainer."

"Tell him to shoot himself in the foot. He'll stay put then," Lieutenant Washbourn laughed.

Vivienne frowned sadly.

Washbourn: "A lot of men have left Argentina for Canada to train as pilots, I hear. They'll also probably end up in England."

"Yes, for the RAF," said Windsor. Suddenly the band jumped into their version of *When the Saints Go Marching In*. He stood up and offered his hand to Vivienne. "Care to dance, Miss Beatty?"

Vivienne brightened, and a hopeful glow slowly appeared in her eyes. "Yes, I would love that, Sam." She smiled as Windsor led her to the dance floor, squeezing past groups of standing officers in deep conversations with dancers. Every single man watched Vivienne walk by.

Phyl sat down, deflated. Stuart reached out.

"You okay? You look pale."

She shook her head. "Oh, I can't stand the thought of young men going out to a sure death." She covered her eyes. "Stu, I'm so worried about Claude Jr."

"Remember what the doctor said. If it gets too much, get away. Be careful of your nerves, Phyl. I don't want to lose you."

"I can't go. And I don't want to leave you. You're sick most of the time, Stu."

"Ah, you're exaggerating," he smiled. He squeezed her hand for a moment. He picked up her glass and handed it to her. "Drink. Be merry. Relax those nerves. And seriously, consider going to Mar del Plata for a break."

"No, I think I prefer Cordoba."

"Then go there for a week. I don't care. It will do you good."

"Bad time of year to cut it so close, Stu. Besides, all the hotels are probably filled." She accepted a cigarette from Stuart.

"I hear Cordoba is beautiful," said Washbourn. "But they have a TB scare there right now. Not safe."

Stuart turned to him. "You're right, they have that TB Sanatorium. I bet everyone's living like inmates in town."

"Oh, Stu. Yeah. I can't go there and be exposed to that. I'm too run down. With my luck, I'd get it the moment I arrive."

"Well, then, it's Mar del Plata. I want you to go up at the end of the month. I want it to be a complete rest. Take walks, swim a bit, go horseback riding. The air is dry and clean. Doctor's orders." He looked into the crowd and spied Vivienne's red hair, a pearl in the crowd. "Take Vivienne, if you like."

"But I hate the trip. I'm sure Vivienne would hate it even more than I. Twelve hours by train and then another hour or so by bus."

"A Scottish friend of mine just dropped 100,000 *pesos* in the roulette casino at Mar del Plata," said Washbourn.

"Oh, my gosh!" Phyl leaned on the table, feeling a little better. "I like to gamble, but that sounds crazy."

"I think that friend could arrange for someone to drive you up to *Valle Hermoso* from the train station by one of his employees. It would be much nicer than the bus ride. The driver would be a native, probably, and I know of an English man who could accompany you."

Phyl looked uneasily at Stuart, who turned to the lieutenant. "That won't work here. Women aren't left alone with strange men. The Argentine culture's quite different, you may have noticed."

Washbourn blinked and shifted uncomfortably. "I did, actually. If you pardon the expression, it's a bit sex-crazed here. The men are going crazy."

"Hmm," said Phyl, looking around at the younger men.

"I heard that the big house, as they refer to it, in Rosario, is the white slave deposit for Argentina," added Washbourn. "But you'd be safe, if you would pardon my talking of it. They don't dally with English or American women in that business. It's too risky. Women from the poor sections of Europe are taken there. My friend saw a poor little thing, obviously from an immigrant ship, being rushed through and she was frightened to death. I could kill the men responsible for this type of business. I have six sisters back home in New Zealand. I'd hate to see anything like that happenin' to them."

Phyl looked at him thoughtfully. "Well, if it isn't young men being slaughtered ultimately for wealth, it's the poor little girls being sacrificed for the pleasure of young and old men alike, also for wealth."

"What a world," said Stuart. He shook his head in disgust. "I need a stiff drink after all that. Washbourn, you protect my beautiful little wife with your life from all these ogres while I get us a round of stiff drinks. We need to celebrate something."

"What are we celebrating?" asked Phyl.

He took her chin and kissed her forehead. "You, Phyl. I'm going to celebrate you."

Phyl's eyes filled with tears of gratitude. She watched her hero Stuart struggle through the crowd to the crammed bar.

* * *

Two months later. The war was temporarily and gratefully forgotten by lustful and riotous Carnaval revelers who kicked in with a vengeance. Usually, Phyl and Stuart left town to let the out-of-hand crazies hurt themselves and destroy parts of the city. This time, Phyl and Stuart craved an opportunity to let off steam.

On the first day of *Carnaval*, they spent the day at the Club, then at night, invited Jorge over to the flat for dinner. Angelica wisely left the city for the *estancia*, so it was just the three *amigos*. After dinner, feeling a little sotted after more than a few good quality scotches, they went to *Les*

Ambassadeurs, where everyone was going nuts wearing goggles and squirting perfume over everyone else.

The three amigos entered the ballroom crammed with half naked and brightly-dressed party animals and stood grinning and watching.

"What's with the goggles?" asked Stuart.

"Oh, my God," yelled Phyl, pinching her nose. "I don't want to get soaked with cheap perfume!"

"I don't think you have a choice," quipped Jorge, laughing.

"This whole place stinks, and I'm already getting a big headache from the fumes." Phyl squinted her eyes against the sharp, acrid air.

"We should get goggles. We have to protect our eyes," said Jorge, looking around. He saw a young woman in a revealing Carnaval costume carrying a shoulder-strap tray of goggles. He motioned her to come over.

"*Quantos?*" he asked as he pulled out his billfold.

"*Cincuenta centavos,*" yelled the young woman.

"Fifty *centavos*! Burglary!"

Jorge bought three pairs. Just as they were pulling them on, a young man came by and squirted an eyeful of the stuff into Phyl's face. She squealed and covered her eyes.

"Oh, my God, I'm going to go blind!"

Stuart held her until she overcame the pain.

"Right," she said, pulling her goggles over her eyes. "I'm going for revenge. But first, where do we get those squirt bottles? And I need a stiff drink."

"Good call," said Jorge. He left and quickly returned with a large bottle of Champagne. They found a table, drank the wine, then switched back to scotch at Stuart's insistence.

"You Argentines have an amazing idea of a good time. You're either so formal it hurts, or you're completely wacky," yelled Stuart. People screamed and laughed around them. Some women, half undressed, wore towering, massive headdresses. Something popped, and something else smashed.

Phyl and Stuart looked around to see what smashed just as Jorge jumped and squirted perfume down the back of Phyl's dress. Phyl shot up screaming, and retaliated by squirting into Jorge's mouth while he laughed. He spit and cursed, grabbed Phyl, and dragged her to the dance floor.

"I'm kidnapping your naughty wife," he yelled drunkenly at Stuart.

Stuart was stunned. He looked around at the mayhem through his goggles askew on his nose, stained with perfume droplets. Surreal, he thought.

He watched stupidly as Phyl danced a frantic tango with Jorge. He frowned and took off his goggles and focused at them. She was outstanding. When did she get so good at tango? A strange sensation rolled over him and he grabbed his chest. He wasn't happy. He decided Phyl was having far too much fun with Jorge. The same Jorge who wasn't satisfied with a wife and two mistresses, he thought grimly. "He has to go after my wife, too," he muttered. He downed his scotch and evaluated the room. Suddenly, he was squirted from the back, and cool perfume dribbled down his hot spine. He felt the hairs on his back flatten and pop from rolling droplets. He glared at the next table, and saw a woman looking at him, grinning and showing off her squirt bottle. She winked. Almost dirty.

He straightened in his seat and looked down at the goggles in his hand. Then he looked at Phyl on the dance floor doing a seductive turn, hooking her heel around Jorge's calf. He chewed on his tongue. His nostrils flared. He grappled with an ache in his heart. "That's it," he said aloud, drunk. He stood and turned to the other table. The tramp, heavily made up with tight, black hair slicked back, looked at him expectantly, hungry.

He didn't even ask her to dance. He simply grabbed her, bodily lifting her from her chair.

She squealed excitedly. She was Spanish but spoke English willingly. She was all eyes for Stuart while he forcefully steered her onto the dance floor close to Jorge and Phyl. He stepped on her toes in the process. She didn't seem to mind or too drunk, anyway. Phyl and Jorge in their silly goggles grinned at each other. They were far too happy for Stuart. He watched like an eagle as Jorge dipped Phyl back, back, back. It looked too suggestive, too sensual.

"You are an excellent dancer," the woman lied to Stuart, trying to grab his attention.

"What?" Stuart looked into her upturned face. She had a discolored tooth. He couldn't help but look deep into her inviting cleavage. "Oh. I'm actually all left feet," he yelled at her, craning to see Phyl. Not to lose sight of her.

The woman looked down. "You have two left feet?" she asked incredulously.

"It's a saying we have," he said impatiently. "Never mind."

"Do you live in Buenos Aires?" she asked, batting her eyes at him like two telegraph keys.

He did a double-take. "Yes," guardedly.

She pushed herself against him, squashing her breasts against his chest. "You are very handsome. I would like a handsome man in my life." She grabbed his behind and pressed her pelvis against his.

He gasped. His eyebrows flared.

"You see, I am very lonely and bored. I would like very much to have someone like you to entertain me. How would you like to establish me in a little *garçonier?*"

"You don't waste any time, do you!"

"Life is short, no?" she said, beaming at him, her breasts out like headlights.

He propelled her back to her table. Without a word, he turned and fought to the bar. He stood, drank, moped and poured and drank more. After a few minutes, he cursed the winds. He grabbed the closest woman and tangoed, allowing only one dance before forcing himself on another and another. Each time, he was gustily propositioned.

Later that night, there was a terrible thunderstorm. The air was electric. The rain came down in merciless sheets. Lightning flashed continually. Thunder roared almost instantly after each flash.

Phyl sat at her dressing table. She put bobby pins into her hair, creating little pin curls. She had such a fabulous time and was still quite drunk and humming quietly.

Stuart was also quite inebriated, stung by an evening's pang of jealousy. He ground his teeth. He sat on the edge of the bed watching her.

She noticed. Her arms froze in midair. She raised her eyebrows. "Are you okay?"

"Why shouldn't I be okay?"

"Okay. It's just that you don't normally sit there and watch me. It's weird."

"Weird, is it?" He sucked his teeth as he stared at her craven image in the mirror. "Do you do this every night?"

"Well, yes. I have since the day we married, I'm pretty sure." She looked at him. Curious. She put down a bobby pin and turned to face him. She sighed deeply. "Talk to me."

"I forbid you to dance the tango." He looked away like a little boy.

"Excuse me? You *forbid* me?"

"Yup. No tango. You look ridiculous dancing the tango."

Sneaky tears stung Phyl's eyes. She blinked them back. "What do you mean? How can you say that? Everyone dances the tango like I do."

"That's the problem. It speaks sex and more sex. I might as well watch naughty things, Phyl. I mean, really naughty things. It disgusts me when you dance. All the men watch, and I know very well what they're thinking." His nostrils flared. He wanted to walk away, but like a magnet, he couldn't leave Phyl. He had to poke some more. "Filth. I'm so disappointed in you."

"HUH?" She stared at him incredulously. Her eyes darted around the room, trying to make sense of everything he said. Was she really disgusting? But that can't be. Everyone dances the same way. She thought she was so good. And sex never entered her mind while dancing. She frowned. Well, she felt sensual, she thought. Her frown deepened. But the song and dance *is* very seductive.

Why dance it if you do not feel it? "But I don't think about sex when I dance. I just feel what I'm supposed to feel."

"Yeah? And what is it that you feel, huh?"

"Well, sensual."

"I rest my case." Stuart grabbed his pillow and yanked the blanket off the bed. He traipsed to the bedroom door and turned to a surprised Phyl. "I'm sleeping on the balcony. Have fun with your sensual thoughts. And if you dream about Jorge, I'll kill him." He left, slamming the door behind him.

Phyl heard Mercedes through the wall. "Ayayayayay."

Phyl covered her face and bawled.

* * *

Four days later. The streets were finally cleared of litter, costumed folk and parades. Stuart and Phyl were dizzy with colds and still upset with each other. Hardly shared four words since the dance. Mercedes, as a result, was also much quieter. So was Tony. Everyone felt the tension. The pain.

That morning, they sat together, nursing hot tea at the dining room table. They carefully ignored each other, though neither wanted to leave. Stuart didn't shave. Phyl still had pin curls under a headscarf. Neither cared how they looked. She reviewed a letter from Canada received the day before. He read a copy of the New York Times, sent along with the letter. Outdated but still most informative.

Stuart glanced up guardedly and cleared his throat. He coughed, took out a cigarette, and lit it. "I didn't tell you that Schuler's coming again with his wife." He rubbed at the nicotine stains on his fingers. "You know that he's Rand's brother-in-law, right?" Stuart asked, pretending to be immersed in the paper.

"Yes, he married into the company, the smart sod," she said, reading, careful not to encourage a conversation. She shifted away from him. She held the letter higher and continued to read it intently.

"There will be some changes for the good. Schuler likes me. We'll have to have them and the Minors for dinner. Many, many times. I know you don't relish the thought."

"Many, many times?"

"Yup. Lucky you."

"Lucky me. How long are they staying? We're supposed to get away the first week in March down to the Piñiero *estancia*. Jorge says a new trout stream has just been discovered close by. I want to catch a damn fish!"

"Your fish will have to wait. They'll be here for seven long weeks."

Phyl started to hyperventilate. She picked up her coffee cup. It shook like a leaf in her hand.

"Don't worry. Hire a cook if you feel you really need to." Stuart hoped it sounded like an insult.

Phyl's bottom lip quivered. "Why are you so intent on hurting me?"

Stuart felt truly ashamed. He took a deep drag of his cigarette and blew the smoke toward her.

She waved it away angrily. "Stop it!"

"Make me."

"What?"

"Make me. Stop me. How do you propose to make me stop?" He took another drag and blew more smoke at her.

"Stu, what happened to you? It's me, Phyl, your wife." She stood up and grabbed his face. "God, I love you, Stu. How did you forget that?"

Stuart gulped and stared at her. The cigarette suddenly burnt his finger. He butted it out and grabbed her. He hugged her so tightly she could hardly breathe. He picked her up and hurried her to the bedroom. The door slammed behind them.

Mercedes popped out of the kitchen and saw the closed bedroom door. She heard Phyl squeal. She made a face, removed her apron, picked up her purse and net bags, and left the apartment.

At the elevator, she kept hitting the button. The elevator wasn't fast enough. She heard another squeal from the flat. "Ayayayayay!" she flung a string of curse words at the elevator. Still it wasn't fast enough. She grunted as she gave up. She covered her ears and raced for the stairs.

* * *

Phyl sat alone near the radio. She listened to Eva Duarte do a rendition of Marie Antoinette. Badly. Phyl's heart sang. The program cut into a brash commercial while Stuart came in from his office. "Oh, my goodness, Stu, when are we getting our summer holidays? I'm so worn out! The Schulers have been here for almost two months, and they've completely drained me."

"I think the Schuler's are first consuming all the scotch in the city before they go. I think their motto is *We drank, We conquered*. I've never seen people put away so much whiskey," said Stuart as he looked around for his lighter.

"Thank God for the Minors. She's done most of the entertaining, and they certainly went out of their way to make sure we didn't get out with the Schulers alone too often. Poor things, they'll both be fit for the hospital when the Schulers finally leave. When *are* they going back to Toronto?"

Stuart looked through papers he pulled from a small coffee table and found a calendar. "A week today. You know, we will have been in this apartment one year on the 15th of this month. Can you get your head around that?"

"Can we finally go on our holiday to Mar del Plata on the 15th then? Like an anniversary holiday?" Phyl stood up and lowered the volume on the radio.

"I'll check at work and with my clients. I think we deserve it. And I can always go back to town by train if necessary. But we'll be getting there in the rainy season, and I'd really like to drive so I can take my fishing tackle."

"I don't care. So long as we get away." The commercial stopped, the program returned. Eva Duarte's shrill voice.

"By the way, Angelica and Jorge invited us out—"

"Shhh! She's back! Sorry, Stu. I want to listen to this!"

Stuart made a face and looked at his watch. He was to listen to BBC within the half hour to receive a code. "I don't know what the attraction is about this Eva girl."

"Shhh." After a second, Phyl turned to Stuart. "We keep an eye on her at the Club. She's always with some Minister or other important person. This woman's a bulldozer."

"You don't say," said Stuart. He sat down and looked at Phyl thoughtfully leaning toward the radio. He listened to Eva Duarte. Perhaps, instead of just focusing on gathering information on dominant male actors in the political scene, he should also be watching the females who have a growing influence on key decision-makers. He made a face and raised his eyebrows. As he chewed his lip, he looked toward the kitchen, then sauntered off in search of chocolate cake left from dinner.

* * *

It rained heavily and steadily for four days. Driving the almost non-existent roads to Mar del Plata was almost impossible. Deep mud puddles mined the route, so numerous they had to stop frequently to strategize how to get around them. At one point, they came upon a couple who were in the midst of moving to a new home. The couple's truck was stuck in a mud hole so severely they couldn't do anything but wait until a truck came by.

Phyl and Stuart stayed with them. When the rains subsided, they helped them remove all their furniture and set up temporary shelter in the middle of the *pampas* with the sky for a ceiling. This way they all had some comfort until, hours later, a truck with chains did finally come by. Stuart and Phyl helped the couple pile all the furniture back on their vehicle once it was pulled out.

Waving the grateful couple on, Phyl and Stuart continued their trek. They eventually arrived at the resort in Mar del Plata. Unfortunately, having been drenched for so long in the rain, Stuart's bronchitis and asthma returned with a vengeance. He spent the first week of their holidays in bed.

The mornings were frosty. The days sweltering from an intense sun. Stuart improved after Phyl found a doctor who could come to help. They lamented that Stuart's demise with his lungs had cost them some marvelous horseback riding and fishing.

Argentina celebrated another Independence Day and a very weak Stuart insisted on going along to sight see. He bought Phyl little Argentine and British flags and, once back in the room, said, "You better make the best of these because this is probably the last time you'll ever see these dual flags, now with the war going on."

"Aren't you being cheerful!" complained Phyl.

"Well, just saying."

Phyl looked into the corner of the resort room at Stuart's fishing tackle and box in a heap. "We made a laughingstock of ourselves carrying the fishing tackle and box into the resort. Where did you think we were going to fish?"

"I honestly thought there were fishing streams nearby. Wishful thinking, I guess." Stuart threw the book he was reading onto the couch and stood to look at his tackle. "No one here fishes for sport."

"Well, in a country where they use dynamite to catch supper, I can see how it would look a bit underdone."

Stuart walked to the corner and picked up his tackle, rod, and box.

"Where are you going?"

"I'm going to throw out the line and practice on the front lawn," he muttered, juggling everything in his arms.

"Is that wise bringing attention to yourself like that?"

"No one knows us here." He swished his rod in the air like a swashbuckler.

"What if we were followed here from town?"

Stuart looked at her thoughtfully. "Okay. Let's go. We'll head up to the big dam in Santa Rosa. There's a new powerhouse I need to see, anyway. Maybe there's some fishing there."

"How far is it?"

"About seven hundred kilometers. We go up another two thousand feet in elevation, so you may want to take along some warm clothing."

"Oh, my God, Stuart. We'll have to stay overnight, right? The trip would take the rest of our holiday. We might as well pack everything."

"Right. So, pack your bags. We'll go back to Buenos Aires from there and it better be with some damn fish."

Stuart drove a full day. They came to a section of the Sierras called Santa Rosa- the color of the dried pampas – brown, grey, dotted with green. They arrived at a big dam and powerhouse. They parked the car in the afternoon heat and walked onto the massive broad dam. Torrential waters thundered into the valley creating a swirling mist. On the other side, a peaceful deep lake. Stuart had his camera, carefully hung around his neck. He looked down into a majestic valley, then looked at the powerhouse, attentively listening.

"I should've known you were here to spy," said Phyl grimly.

"Not at all. I'm just going to take photos of you and the view. This fascinates me. This was built to supply electricity to the valley, but the turbines aren't running." He looked at the water on the calm side. "Anyway, I read there are fish in the dam called *Ted Jerrys*. They're supposed to be delicious but small. Let's drop a line in with a worm."

"Both of us?" asked Phyl, getting excited.

"Absolutely."

They scrambled to the car and took out their tackle. They threw out hook and worms, and though they had a few nibbles, they didn't catch anything. After a while, Stuart spoke up. "The fish aren't educated enough to know what worms are, I guess."

"I think I see salmon."

Stuart looked into the water. "There's an interesting salmon hatchery upriver. I guess when the fish are old enough, they're dumped into the river, but no one is allowed to fish them for several kilometers."

"How do they control such a thing?" asked Phyl, dipping her hook into the water without a worm, just because.

"Naturally, a thing like that can't be controlled." Suddenly, they heard a different kind of explosion over the roar, further downriver. They turned to see a plume of water rise into the air, sparkling like a tower of diamonds, then crash back into the river. "Oops, looks like the hillbillies just put a few sticks of dynamite in for supper."

In the distance, they saw people wading into the river to their hips, scooping large baskets through the water. A few formed a bucket brigade and hauled in basket after basket of fish.

"Geez, life is cheap. Poor fish. What a waste," Phyl muttered. Suddenly, she saw a flash of light up into the hills. She stared. It continued to flash.

"Yup, life is cheap." Stuart started packing his tackle box.

"Stu."

"Hmm?"

Phyl turned her back to where she saw the flash of light. "Don't look now, but I think I'm seeing a flash of field glasses. Trained on us, I think."

"Really?" joked Stuart. "Someone is spying on us, do you think?" He grinned. "Shall we check it out?"

She thought, *When did Stuart become cavalier when in danger? Was he always like this? Had he covered it up all along?* "How? It's somewhere in the hills," Phyl glanced downriver into the hills. She couldn't see the flash anymore. She looked back at Stuart. "It'd be like searching for a needle in a haystack."

"Not necessarily," Stuart gathered his things. "Let's go see what we can find."

They packed their car. Stuart drove full speed down the hill, along a dirt road, a trail of dust clouds behind them. They headed around a corner. Stuart slowed down and spied motorbike tire marks in the dirt. He stopped, backed up, and followed the tracks into the bush. Not far into the wild grasses, a motorbike was parked against a rock at the base of a hill. They stopped and jumped out of the car. They approached the dusty, German BMW. With a swastika roughly painted on it.

"They're everywhere," said Phyl thoughtfully. "Do you think someone's up to no good with the dam? Or do you think they were spying on us?"

Stuart took a deep breath. "I wouldn't put it past them. If they were thinking of taking over, they'd want to have security, always keeping an eye on the dams."

Phyl circled. "Oh my God, we're in no man's land, right? We're in Patagonia."

"Yup."

"But I thought you and everyone else made that up about Patagonia and *Lebensraum*."

They heard a rustle not far off. Stuart looked at her and put a finger to his lip. He took a quick photo of the bike and tire marks. "Just in case," he said in a low voice. He stood up straight. They waited and listened. The distant roar of the dam and cascading water hung over the valley, but they clearly heard a branch snap. They twirled in its direction. Stuart motioned to Phyl to follow him.

Stuart pushed aside branches, then stopped to listen. Another cracking noise. In a slightly different direction. He cautiously led Phyl through thicker brush. Suddenly, put a hand back on her midriff. Stop. They saw a clearing at the edge of a cliff. Standing in front of them, staring in surprise, was a young man in a brown leather jacket with field glasses around his neck.

They all stared at each other.

"Riener?" yelled Phyl.

Reiner, openmouthed, pulled out a gun and held it out straight at them. It shook in his hand.

Phyl gasped. "Reiner, it's me! *Señora de Redington*!"

Reiner cleared his throat nervously. He looked at Stuart from top to bottom. Then he looked around, obviously seeing no escape.

Stuart looked around, smiled and shook his head.

Phyl looked at the shaking gun in Reiner's hand. She could not believe he would ever hurt her. Then to Stuart. She couldn't believe he was smiling. Who was this typewriter salesman she married? She raised her hands. "Reiner, it's me. Let's just talk."

Reiner took a step back.

Stuart saw Reiner was very close to the edge. He held up his hand as a warning. "Stop!"

Reiner shot in alarm, but the gun recoiled; the bullet barely missed Phyl and Stuart, and Reiner, in shock, took one more step back. But the edge was unstable and gave under his weight. He flailed his arms, and lost his footing. Wide-eyed, he screamed and helplessly slid with the rocky ledge. Then he vanished, his scream echoing through the valley lost in the roar of the dam.

Stuart and Phyl stared at nothing, stunned.

Phyl gasped. "Oh my God!" Phyl rushed toward the edge, but Stuart held her back.

"Careful." He stepped toward the edge and leaned forward to look down.

Phyl got down on her hands and knees and crawled to Stuart's feet. She held onto his legs as she leaned forward to look down. She gasped. It dropped over two hundred meters into white water and rocks. No sign of Reiner. She groaned, flattened onto her stomach, and crawled like a snake away from the killing edge.

Stuart helped her up. He led her back through the brush. They stood looking at the bike, then around to see if other people were nearby. They looked at the hills and back from where they came. They looked at each other, faces drained of color.

"Well, that's the stupidest thing I ever did see in my entire life," said Stuart.

Phyl's face shriveled into a cross between a cry and a laugh. Tears streamed down her face. Her mouth was fused shut. She blinked like an idiot.

"Are – are you crying or laughing?" Stuart asked stupidly. Then, his face collapsed as he tried to control himself. He giggled. He squeezed his eyes shut and covered his mouth.

Phyl laughed uncontrollably. Then she covered her face, and laughter slowly turned into sobbing. She fell to her knees.

Stuart stood, still laughing. He shook his head, stopped laughing, and rubbed his eyes – hard. He waited and stood swaying, holding his face. They were, for this brief moment in time, quite insane. She wondering who she had married. He wondering if she was as crazy as he.

Phyl wiped her eyes and nose with the hem of her blouse. She brushed herself off. She sniffed. "Right. We should call the police, Stuart." She took a deep breath and looked around. She nodded stupidly. "We have to find a phone. Call the police."

Glassy-eyed, Stuart looked at her, his watch, and the sky. He shook his head. "It's war, Phyl. Shit happens." He grabbed the bike, and pushed it further into the brush.

"What will you do with the bike?"

Stuart studied the bike, saw a leather pouch off the side seat. He pulled out something wrapped in brown paper and an envelope. He opened the package. It was a sandwich of black bread with sausage. He smelled it.

"We're NOT going to eat that!" screamed Phyl.

"It'd be a shame to waste," said Stuart, matter-of-fact, and took a huge bite. He was suddenly very hungry.

Phyl gathered her senses. Took control. And primly stepped forward and leaned on the rear of the bike. "Help me push."

"That's exactly what I thought." He slipped the envelope into his back pocket, put the sandwich back into the pouch, and grabbed a hold of the handles.

They pushed and pulled it hard enough to roll it forward, balanced upright on its wheels. They watched it slowly roll over the rocky edge. They stood silently, listening for a splash.

After a surprisingly long time, they heard a splash.

"Right," said Stuart.

They gathered branches and walked backward, brushing away tracks and footprints until they reached the car. Stuart climbed in, started the car, and moved it onto the road into old tire tracks. Phyl brushed the tire tracks leading from the bush to the road. She threw her branch off to the side, and wiped her hands. She pushed her hair back, turned, and straightened up. With chin up in the air, she stepped into the car. Now she truly was Mata Hari.

Stuart put it into gear, and yelled. "We'll come back tomorrow. Better fishing, I betya. In all ways." They raced out of the hills.

Phyl rolled up the window against the dust and dirt, surprised at his suggestion of returning. She started to yell at him when a big fat fly flew into her mouth. She sputtered, spit, coughed and hacked. The fly flew out and landed on the dashboard. Phyl tried to smash it but missed. She hit the dash again and again in anger.

"What are you doing!? Stop!" Stuart screamed. He slid to a sudden stop in the middle of the road.

"I don't want to come back tomorrow!" she yelled. "How can you say such a thing? We just saw a young man die! Someone I *know*! And you say we do nothing?!" she squealed. "I never want to come back here again. I will have nightmares about this for the rest of my life."

"We have to come back. Make it look like we're just fishing. Besides, I want to see if any activity will occur between now and then."

"Stuart, you are going crazy. Don't you have at least one empathetic bone left?"

"We'll need a place for the night. I noticed something on the way here."

During the hour's drive, Stuart didn't say a word. Phyl did nothing but cry.

They came to a small village, seeking a room for the night. They found a house with rooms for rent. Filthy rooms. No indoor plumbing, the washroom an outhouse with a hole in the ground, no bench to sit on, and no paper.

Phyl sadly stood looking at the hole. She took the hem of her blouse and yanked at it, tearing away a strip. She gulped and closed the door.

Later, she stood looking at the room. Phyl was deathly afraid of bed bugs, and the room and furniture were so filthy she opted to sleep in the car. Stuart wasn't happy about it but managed to park the car against the wall near their own window so he could keep an ear open for her.

During the night, Phyl awakened with a start. She heard a scraping around the car. She looked out of the passenger window. A dark form was peeking into their room. She immediately dropped out of sight and listened intently, her heart beating a mile a minute. She thought the individual would look into the car and see her, so she lowered herself into the gloom as far as she could and screwed her eyes shut. Eventually, there was no longer any noise, and no sign of the individual.

She froze in place until dawn. Then scrambled inside and woke Stuart to tell him of the stranger spying through the window.

"We're definitely going to give fishing another try," announced Stuart. "There's something there we're not supposed to see."

"Stuart! No way!"

"Did you get a good look at him?"

"No! I was deathly afraid, Stu."

"Think. You had to get some impression. Old guy? Young guy? German, Argentine…?"

Phyl bit her lip and frowned, actually thinking. She shook her head and said, "I did get the impression it was a young, slim guy with a leather jacket."

"Good. That in itself helps. We have to go and follow up on this, Phyl. I need to know, number one, if we will be followed on our return, and two, if we can see anything strange."

"Well, you don't think being spied on is strange enough? And what of the turbines not working? It's almost as if the dam was built for something in the future, not for something that is built now."

Forgoing breakfast, Stuart checked the car out. He discovered the brake fluid had been drained. "Yeah, Phyl. This is getting out of hand."

Phyl sat in shock while Stuart left to get the car fixed. "Next time we go anywhere, we should come with the gun," Phyl muttered, her arms crossed in anger. "Better yet, make that an entire arsenal."

* * *

"Do you really need to go to that German Club? Is it far from the city?" asked Phyl. Back in their apartment, she helped Stuart with his business suit jacket.

He adjusted his lapels and shoulder pads. "It's about forty-five minutes by train from town. I'm meeting this guy at the Club Teutonia, and I have two reasons to go. I see a potential contract with his many businesses, plus this German is rather an important person. I believe he can help me with what we saw at the dam."

"You're not going to tell him about Reiner, are you?"

Stuart simply made a face at her.

"Do *I* know him?" she asked.

"No, I doubt it. His name is Von Rintelin. A very bright guy."

Phyl looked at the clock, then out a window at the weather. The sun shone brilliantly, and the distant waters of the River Plate sparkled merrily. The window was slightly frosted. It was May in Argentina, the beginning of winter. "It is now just 9:30, so you're a bit early. And it's too cold to stand waiting on the train platform. But if you wait too long before you leave here, you'll get stuck in the morning's parade."

"Another Independence Day."

"Lord knows which war. I've lost count." She handed him a scarf.

He shook his head. "I won't need that."

She let her hand drop, still holding the scarf. "Stu, your chest." She held it up again.

This time, he took the scarf and wrapped it around his neck. He coughed. She ran to the bathroom and got a small cobalt blue glass jar of Vick's Vaporub. She opened it, dipped two fingers into the jar, and smeared the gel on Stuart's throat.

"I'll smell up the train, and it will empty of people. And no one will come near me at the Club."

"Too bad, I want you to outlast this damn country and war," she insisted. She patted Stuart on his back as she walked him to the door. He turned.

"What are you doing today?" he asked.

"I'm going to the Club with Vivienne. A few ladies went to a Tea last week at the German ambassador's residence. His wife is drumming up support for the Graf Spee sailors who could use cash, everyday toiletries, cigarettes, and such. As if we, at the American Club, would give them money, honestly! But Vivienne and I want to go and spy."

Stuart kissed her on the nose. "Perfect. Two Mata Haris. Let me know what you find out."

Phyl saluted and stood ramrod straight. "Aye, Cap'n."

* * *

Phyl and Vivienne sat in a taxi stranded in the middle of a crowd gathered along the road to watch the military parade pass. They had no choice but to wait for the parade to pass. "These Argentines, any excuse for a show and holiday, even if they have to stand and freeze." She jumped in her seat as a group of runny-nosed youngsters slammed against her window, begging for *pesos*. One of them blew a fart noise against the glass and smeared of snot. The driver swore at them and they fled.

Phyl studied the driver's eyes in the rear-view mirror. It didn't look like he understood English. She looked around at the people standing by. It felt safe to talk. Vivienne thought so, too.

"I wouldn't want to be standing out there watching," Vivienne said quietly. "The only parades I'll freeze to watch are the Canadian Field Artillery back in Toronto."

"Or the Santa Clause Parade down University Avenue," Phyl added.

Vivienne nodded and smiled.

The ground shook, as massive cannons trumbled by, their barrels looming threateningly over the crowd. They saw the tops of the tanks and trucks. People cheered and jabbered away in ricochet Spanish.

Phyl lowered her voice and leaned into Vivienne's face. "The British are doing all they can to get the Americans into the war, Stu says, and the Germans are feigning innocence."

Vivienne looked out the window and shook her head. She wore a purple cloche over her red hair. Stunning, thought Phyl. Vivienne turned back to Phyl. "What does your family back home think?"

"They feel the Americans should immediately rush to Europe with their airplanes, ships, money, and men. Just like us. I suppose on account of how they got out of the last war, they're getting a hard time from everyone. But I fully expect they'll be into it in six months. The King and Queen's visit was very timely, to say the least. Dad wrote the whole country stood behind them. Royalty going personally to the colonies certainly does the trick." Phyl studied Vivienne's face. "We read that they finally rounded up the spies working for the Germans in England, by the way." Phyl looked at the driver and spoke louder. "They should put them in front of a firing squad."

"I agree. In my opinion, anyone who is a spy and takes money to the detriment of his own country is about the lowest thing there is. I read a very good book about something like that two years ago. It was called 'The Dark Invader,' by Von Rintelin."

Phyl's ears perked up. "Von Rintelin, you said?"

"You've heard of him, then?"

"By coincidence, just this morning."

"Well, you must know that during the First World War, Von Rintelin blew up munitions so they couldn't be sent across the Atlantic to help the Germans."

"So, he worked against his own country," said Phyl.

"Yeah. Under different names through front companies. He used his own money to back American operatives and did crazy things like use the SS Friedrich der Grosse as a base. Ha!"

"Is that a ship?"

"Yes. A German ship anchored in New York harbor at the time. The audacity!" Vivienne laughed. "He made his own explosive devices and no one knew. According to the book, he wasn't too happy about how Germany treated him before the war."

"Vindictive."

"Yeah, right. Crazy, huh? It's a miracle they didn't shoot him. I don't know how he's still alive. He helped the allies, in any case." Vivienne shifted impatiently. "When's this parade over?"

"Tell me more about this guy. Where is he now?"

"Von Ritelin? He's here. I heard on the radio that he was arrested early this morning on spying charges. Again." Vivienne turned to Phyl. She did a double take. "Are you all right, Phyl?"

Phyl suddenly felt ill and frightened for Stuart. He was with Von Ritelin! Strains of patriotic music wafted over the crowd.

Vivienne forgot about Phyl and strained to look past the people. "Finally," she said. "The parade is coming to an end. The bands are coming up. They're usually at the end with the planes screaming overhead." By coincidence, a hundred and fifty Argentine Air Force planes screamed overheard, rattling eardrums.

In panic and fearful for Stuart, Phyl was deaf and blind to them. Before she realized it, she vomited onto her lap.

"Oh my God!" yelled Vivienne. She scrambled to get her handkerchief and pulled a silk scarf from her bag. "Phyl, you're pregnant!"

Chapter Thirteen
El, Dad Redington and Perón

"So, false alarm?" asked Stuart. Early morning. On the radio, a quiet rhumba smoothed the start of day.

"Not even close," Phyl said, shaking her head. "It had nothing to do with being pregnant." She watched as Stuart disappointedly went back to reading the newspaper. "As I said, I was physically and mentally shocked. I thought you'd been arrested along with what's his name."

"Von Rintelin, poor guy." Stuart kept reading.

"Yes, him." Phyl wasn't happy. "My goodness, what would've happened if that man didn't slip you that note on the train? You could've stepped into a trap."

"I doubt it. But I certainly didn't want to take the chance. Protocol says to ditch when there's any sign of trouble, so I got off and returned as soon as possible, though I slipped into a store to make it look like I was making a cold call on business first. Just in case I was being followed." Stuart coughed and hacked for a moment. He returned to reading.

"You don't seem too concerned about that man."

Stuart turned the page. "It's all part of the business. He's probably fine. Routine pick up, questioning."

Phyl started to feel a little depressed about that dining room table. They always seemed to sit there feeling glum. She pushed her chair back, the legs scraping the granite floor, and took a deep breath. "Well, I'm getting dressed."

"What's the plan?"

"I'm going with Vivienne to the Alvear. We'll have tea and hope we catch a glimpse of Errol Flynn. He checked in last week."

Stuart was amused. "And what will you do if you see him? Accost him?"

"That swashbuckler? No," she chuckled. "I hear he's a pervert. But I still would love to meet him. At the least, cast my eyes on him in real life."

"Well, if he's a pervert, he's in the right city then." Reading. "Don't embarrass me by grabbing his legs and kissing his feet."

Phyl stood up and blinked. She suddenly felt quite ill again. "Stu, that boy. Reiner. I can't stop thinking of him. His body rotting away and no one other than us knowing. He has a mother somewhere."

"I informed those who should know."

"Will there be repercussions? Will they look for him?"

Stuart picked up his cigarette from the ashtray and took a drag. He pondered. Squinted at her. "Don't waste your time thinking about it, Phyl. You're already on the verge of another nervous collapse."

Phyl put a hand on her stomach and the other on her chest. She patted both. "It hurts, Stu. I can't seem to put it to the side. I have nightmares about it."

He put the paper down and stood up. "Well, Toscanini's in town with his orchestra. They're playing tomorrow night, if you want to go. A nice distraction."

The thought of good entertainment lightened her heart a bit. "That's interesting. So far, we've had Jascha Heifetz and Fritz Kreisler come. You know that Jean Sablon, the Frenchman who used to sing on the Chase and Sanborn Hour? He's here, too. If we keep this up, we'll have some good English plays and musicals to go to."

"I know, but it's an ill wind. The war has sent all the European celebrities down here. The city is teeming with them."

"I don't think they'll find much peace, though. Everyone, except, of course, the Argentines, is a nervous wreck over this war."

"With so many pro-Nazi Germans and pro-Fascist Italians here, they *should* be nervous." Stuart stood up, folded the paper and placed it beside his breakfast plate. He walked past Phyl to the hook by the door and grabbed his coat. It was August and still quite chilly out. "I'll leave you to the paper. It's that new one, the *Campero*. Your Spanish is good enough for you to understand, right?"

"Yes, but just like the English papers, it's just propaganda. Even these Spanish papers are either for one side of the war or the other, so all I can do is read between the lines for a bit of real news, and even then, I don't think I'll ever figure out all that's going on."

She waved in the general direction of Europe. She pushed her chair back, struggled up and walked to Stuart to adjust his collar. "And it's not always so pleasant going out. Constant fights between English and American, German and English, French and Dutch. The English glare at the Germans and tell the Americans they should be in the war, too."

She stood on her toes and kissed Stuart on his freshly shaven cheek. "And the Americans get furious and say they can't see why they should send their men to fight when the English can do it themselves, and so it goes on."

"Don't forget we're going to the zoo tomorrow. You up for it?" he asked.

"Piece of cake."

"Your favorite saying. That's my girl." Stuart checked his pockets for cigarettes, looked over at the table and spied them. As he went to retrieve them, the doorbell rang.

Mercedes popped her head out of the bedroom. Phyl shook her head at her as she opened the door. Phyl looked at a short young man in round glasses wearing a police uniform.

"*Sí?*" asked Stuart, as he walked back to the door.

"*Discúlpeme señor,*" the young man said, smiling broadly.

"*Sí?*"

"I hear you speak English. You are English?"

"No, American," said Stuart, looking at him sideways. "Can I help you?"

"Ah, *sí!* I have it here," said the young policeman, searching in his briefcase. "A *forma.*"

"Another form?" piped up Phyl. "Is this another fundraiser for a political party?"

"No," he said, slightly taken aback, "It's a *programa* for your own interest. It's to make'a the arm of the law stronger, and it would be *muy bueno* to subscribe to it by paying each month. You can pay as little as a *peso.*"

"Each month?" Phyl glanced at Stuart.

"Well, I better go," Stuart said. "You take care of this, Phyl."

"Oh, but I'd rather you stayed."

"Mercedes is here?"

"Yes, but —"

"Then you're okay." Stuart put on his hat and looked at Phyl as he was about to walk past the young policeman. She gave him a look that could kill, and he frowned. He stopped. He yawned as Phyl read the form from the young man.

"And what is it we get for this *peso* a month?"

"*Proteccion.* We are in a state of siege."

"State of siege. Such big words for a little guy like you." She turned to Stuart. "How do you like that for extortion? Talk about the Chicago gangsters." She looked at the policeman and held up the form. "This was signed by the commissioner, even. That's something Toronto people would never tolerate, you know that?"

"Toronto?"

"Where I come from in Canada." She pushed the form onto the young man's chest. "We're not going to sign up." He took the paper back.

"*Pero*, you don't know when your neighborhood has undesirables with violent intentions."

"We already have them. And you're the police. You should already be protecting us." She cocked her head. "Are you making all the poor little grocery shops, butchers, and bakers in this neighborhood pay for this extortion?"

"*Si*. It's for everyone's benefit," the young policeman said dryly, looking at Stuart, wondering why the man of the house wasn't doing the ordering.

Stuart motioned with his head for him to listen to Phyl, then glared at him pointedly for good effect. "Right, you heard the *Señora*, we're not interested."

"*Pero*—"

"*Gracias*," said Phyl. She waved goodbye and closed the door in his fresh face.

"I know. It might as well be Toronto criminal scum," he agreed. He pursed his lips. "Perhaps it would've been better just to play along. Not bring so much attention to us."

"So, do you think they'll do something to hurt us?"

"Oh, I doubt that. At worst, just bothersome things." He paused. "Best stay home for a while. I wouldn't trust them." He paused. "And maybe not send money through the post to Canada."

The music stopped on the radio and an announcer spoke in clipped Spanish. The news. Mercedes walked through the dining room to the master bedroom, humming. Tony at her feet.

"The very tone of voice of that commentator makes me nervous. They always get me upset."

"Now, I really have to go." Stuart gave Phyl one final kiss and opened the door.

Phyl held him by the coat. He turned, questioning.

"You're safe down here if the States should go to the war, right?"

"Yes, Phyl." He patiently looked at her.

"And when we return by ship, I wonder if Americans are safe. The Germans sunk the SS Uruguay in May. I have so many nice memories on that boat."

"Stop. You're getting yourself all riled up. Settle yourself down. Errol Flynn will never look at you with dark circles under your eyes. And if you do insist on accosting Errol Flynn, you better stick to Vivienne's side and never find yourselves alone as targets. Okay?"

Phyl made a face but nodded.

"Do fun things today." Stuart shut the door behind him.

Phyl looked at the door, listened to his footsteps echoing down the hall. Her insides weren't feeling right. They weren't behaving. Like Stuart. Like her. Maybe, she thought, her insides knew something she didn't. Mercedes hummed in the next room. Mercedes was oblivious to what was going on outside of the neutral zone. Perhaps ignorance was, indeed, bliss. Or denial.

* * *

Phyl and Vivienne walked past the newsstand at the hotel lobby entrance. Phyl stopped and picked up a magazine. Vivienne walked back, curious to see what Phyl bought. Phyl showed her the cover of *Mundo Argentina*.

"Look. It's that young actress I told you about. Eva Duarte."

"She looks younger than you described," said Vivienne, looking at a picture of a plain brunette. She shrugged. She was not impressed.

"Oh, that's her. I don't think she's quite twenty. She has this strange combination of knowing what she wants yet at the same time very distant. Outgoing yet withdrawn. As if she's playing her cards carefully." Phyl put the magazine back. "You know, I look at actors like her and think, geez, I can do better than that." Phyl sighed. "I listen to her on the radio and she's so shrill. If only I was fluent in Spanish because I think I may have a chance of getting speaking parts. And if I had by now," she shrugged, "who knows. I may be on this cover instead of her."

"While I admire your outrageous self-confidence, I doubt that, Phyl. You're a foreigner. On an Argentine magazine? Never."

"But you never know…"

"Keep dreaming, girl!"

Vivienne led Phyl to a stuffed loveseat.

Phyl picked up a discarded newspaper off an elegant sidetable. "The Truth," she announced. She flipped pages. "It's an Australian paper." She looked at people lounging – primarily reporters - in the lobby. She looked down and did a double take. "Oh, Vivienne, here's something on Errol Flynn."

Vivienne, smoking from a cigarette holder, a sharp eye on the elevator doors. "What does it say?"

Phyl hunched over the newspaper, reading aloud:

"Errol Flynn Invites Nazi to Duel!"

"Oh, my goodness! The swashbuckler is alive and well," laughed Vivienne. Phyl continued to read aloud.

Angered by a sneer at his 'synthetic courage,' Errol Flynn was not accepted, and perhaps it was as well for the Nazi, for Flynn is a good boxer, as well as a first-class fencer and pistol shot. Flynn's arrival in Buenos Aries was reported by 'El Pampero,' a strongly pro-German newspaper, with slighting references to his film portrayals. 'The time is not propitious,' the newspapers said, 'for the arrival in South America of an actor whose plays are based on fantasy.'

"That's silly. Of course, they're all based on fantasy," clipped Vivienne. Phyl continued:

> *A sneering comment on the taste of United States film fans and the parts played by Flynn caused Errol Flynn to send a letter to the editor."*

Phyl grinned. Vivienne laughed.
"This is what he wrote back." Phyl read.

> *From the safety of your office, you complain of my synthetic courage,' he wrote. 'I agree that there is no doubt regarding your own courage. Therefore, the remedy is simple.' Flynn went on to invite the editor to his room at his hotel and bring all the arms he wanted. 'Then we will lock the door,' he said. 'If you open it before I do, I will kiss the ground three times in front of your office. If I leave first, then publish in your paper that for once a Nazi hero had the courage to meet a contender on an equal basis.' Flynn waited in vain in his room for the editor to turn up!"*

Suddenly, a raucous at the front doors. They looked up to see two hotel employees trying to prevent a crowd of banner-carrying men from entering the hotel. The intruders' demanding voices and proclamations echoed through the lobby.

Phyl read the banners. "*Accion Argentina.*"

"Crazy," said Vivienne, nervously looking for a way out if things got ugly. Everyone in the lobby froze. "Do you see any sign of guns?"

Phyl watched the men march past the hotel employees and fill the lobby. "No," she said, wishing she had taken their pistol in her purse. She jumped when the flash and pop of reporters' cameras, which were poised and ready for Errol Flynn, filled the room.

"Who are they? Should we be worried?" Vivienne looked pale.

"We should go." She led Vivienne out a hallway to the back exit. Phyl sadly looked to the windows above. "Oh, what a shame. He may be listening to music or drinking himself into oblivion."

"Or getting over a hangover. I heard he partied hard last night."

Vivienne yelled. "Hey Errol, lover boy! Look outside! Yoo hoo!"

A curtain moved aside and a handsome man with a moustache grinned down at them from the window. Phyl and Vivienne screamed heartily.

Phyl laughed and pulled Vivienne into the street. Dodging traffic, hand in hand, they hurried across to a café. They rushed into the smoke-filled restaurant and found two seats at a small round table by the window. "Oh my god, that was wonderful! Let's watch the front of the hotel and see if we can catch him," howled Phyl.

Vivienne pointed to where they saw him. "Oh, I bet he's with a woman. It looked like he was still in a robe!"

They sighed in unison. Phyl focused on the crowd from the *Accion Argentina* group spilling out the hotel's front door. A few knocked over a large, beautiful, potted palm tree. "I know about those guys. Stu told me about them. The initial manifesto of *Accion Argentina* was drafted by ex-president Alvear. It's a bunch of intellectuals, journalists, artists, and politicians with over 300 chapters across the country."

Vivienne was puzzled. "Boy, you seem to know a lot of trivia. What do they do?"

"They organize political meetings and protests, make propaganda posters, and hand out leaflets. I guess they're here because of all the press hanging around for Errol Flynn. They want exposure."

"What do they stand for?"

"Exposing Nazi activity," Phyl said, saddened. She thought of Reiner falling off the cliff. She looked around the café. "I'm so sick of this Nazi garbage."

"Speaking of presidents, Ortiz is really sick, I hear. Castillo is covering for him."

"Stu says he's blind now."

Vivienne gasped. "Castillo?"

Phyl shook her head. "No, Ortiz."

"Well, how can he be president if he's blind?"

"Exactly. That's the problem." Phyl looked around impatiently for a server. "Stu is suspicious because Ortiz is pro-Allies and Castillo stubbornly neutral. Stu thinks having Castillo call the shots, or rather not be *able* to call the shots, emboldens the Nazis because most of the military lean toward Hitler. Castillo doesn't seem to have power against the army. So, Stu thinks he's being set up."

"Well, that's silly. How can someone make someone sick as part of a conspiracy?"

"You just never know, I guess." Phyl saw a bright-eyed server approaching them, his perfume preceding him. "Oh dear." She quickly took off her gloves to show off her wedding ring. "You'd be surprised what the British and Americans can do," whispered Phyl. She bit her tongue, surprised she even said that.

"Oh?" said Vivienne, suddenly even more interested. "Why on earth would you know that?"

Phyl's heart skipped. She had forgotten about her secret life and not to mix the two. She diverted back to Castillo. "If Castillo didn't have all this opposition, I think he would go the way of Ortiz."

"He would join the Allies if he could, you mean?" asked Vivienne.

"I'm not sure. But Stu says that if they did, Ortiz and Castillo would be deposed in a military coup. Many believe the United States is pushing Castillo into the war."

"For crying out loud. Why the Americans and not the British? I thought the Americans didn't care. And you'd think the British would do that to get more people on their side," quipped Vivienne, taking out her cigarette holder.

Phyl shook her head, watching the waiter being held up by another patron. "No, Britain likes Argentina staying neutral so she'll keep supplying beef and wheat for British soldiers."

Vivienne looked at Phyl closely. "That makes a lot of sense. Of course. There you go again. How come you know so much about this stuff? Are you a student of politics?"

"I guess you can say that. Never thought of it that way."

The server finally arrived. They ordered coffee in a no-nonsense way, as *Señoras* were expected to do, discouraging any freshness from the young man. However, they couldn't control his lingering gaze, especially at Vivienne.

"*Ahora, por favor*," Phyl demanded, snapping her fingers.

* * *

A month later.

Angelica and Jorge lounged on Phyl's balcony. The weather was finally spring-like and warm enough to deliver a pleasant late afternoon. The sunset, a canvas to the building, cast purples and blues over the already beautiful view.

Stuart nursed a scotch. He tapped his cigarette onto the standing ashtray beside him. The ashtray was of thick brown glass cradled on the top of a very ornate, sturdy willow-branch stand. It was already overflowing. Phyl had been eyeing it restlessly.

"At the beginning of the war," began Stuart, "the Communist Party was tight with Soviet Union policies. They wanted neutrality and hated British influence. However, Russia signing the Non-Aggression Treaty with Germany and then launching Operation Barbarossa makes them pro-Nazi."

Jorge scratched the back of his ear and smoothed his hair back again. "War makes for strange bedfellows here in a neutral zone."

Phyl piped up. "You know, we haven't received any letters on the mail boat for a long time, and I'm beginning to wonder if that young policeman extortionist told the postman not to deliver anything. It would be a dandy way for him to get back at a pair of foreigners."

Stuart: "Hmm. Could be."

"It's been a whole month since we received *any* letters. I'm getting worried."

Angelica lifted her glass of wine off a wrought-iron, glass-topped table. "How is the family, by the way?"

"Well, last we heard when we *received* mail, we heard El still wasn't doing well. I wrote her that she should get a maid. It certainly cost no more than the doctor's bills they must have. With a maid, she could rest and devote her time to little Stuart. Eleanor must be run down, or the doctor wouldn't have prescribed rest as a cure. I could understand if Claude was out of work. Then I could see the point of her still working, but she just goes on in this ridiculous way. I wish I were home so I could go up there and help out. Believe me, I'd see she got into bed and stayed there!"

Stuart chuckled. "My Mother Theresa."

"Well, I hope she improves after some time at the cottage." She turned to Angelica, "They vactioned at the cottage on Lake Scugog. Though I can't see that she would've had much rest because children are work no matter where you go."

Phyl reached to Stuart for a cigarette. He shook one out for her, lit it on the tip of his cigarette, and handed it to her.

She took a drag. "As if I'm a voice of experience," she chuckled. "She'll probably pay no attention to my advice anyway."

Jorge crossed his legs. "What do they think of the war up there in Canada? They must already have lost friends and perhaps family. The economy must certainly be affected."

Stuart: "They're human and really not sure what they think. They seem to twist things any matter of ways, according to their mood or what they heard on the radio. One day, the French are the beloved Allies, and the next day, they are traitors. The same goes with a Belgian or a Dutchman."

"Oh, but England never lets any of them down, oh no!" said Phyl sarcastically. "I see it very differently. Not nice of me, maybe, but I think the British empire, wonderful as it is, was built by fighting and taking what they wanted. Just like the English people here, they think everything German is evil. They seem to forget that their own beloved Queen Victoria married a German and that the King has German blood. I don't understand why people have to be so narrow-minded with such short memories."

Phyl took a sip of her white wine. "I could go on harping on my point of view indefinitely, so I better close down the broadcast now."

Angelica laughed. "You are very outspoken, Phyl. We're used to it."

"It's one of the things we admire of you," added Jorge. He turned and smiled at Angelica, who warmly smiled back.

Phyl thought how odd that Angelica could be so doting on her husband, who spends so much time away on business and entertaining mistresses. So, per protocol, Phyl smiled lovingly and warmly at her own husband.

Stuart chuckled and took a drag.

"What worries me is the destruction of foods when so many are starving. We have an overload of food for the international market, which we can't get rid of due to the blockade," said Angelica sadly.

"The Lord must tear out his hair sometimes when you think of all the food he puts on earth for the poor folks to eat, and then somehow half of them starve to death while the other half burn the food up." Phyl settled into her chair. "In the meantime, the *peso* just drops and drops."

Phyl was on a roll. She raised her hands, cigarette between fingers. "We now have to pay nearly five *pesos* for one American dollar, and when we first came down here, it was three. When it comes to buying American money to go home, we may have to use up five years' worth of savings."

She looked sadly at Stuart.

He bent forward to grab an olive. "I know what you're thinking, Phyl. We should never have accepted this work arrangement again, but you know how it was hanging around New York for two weeks and fighting contracts. It wears a guy down."

She touched Stuart's knee. "I know, Stu. Sorry. That wasn't meant as a criticism of you."

"Besides, there were other aspects to this arrangement, and we did get benefits to that end."

"True."

The doorbell rang. Stuart looked at his watch. "I wonder who that could be."

Mercedes hurried to the door with Tony at her feet. Phyl saw a delivery boy with a telegram.

"Telegram," she muttered.

"Oh?" said Stuart.

"*Un telegram, Señor*," said Mercedes, sadly. Telegrams were always bad news these days.

"*Gracias.*" Stuart took the envelope, and retrieved a cocktail knife from the table. He opened the telegram and read. He sighed deeply and covered his eyes.

Phyl held out her hand. "Stu, can I see? What is it?"

Stuart handed it to her.

She read it and gasped. She covered her mouth, sprung up, and ran off the balcony.

Jorge and Angelica looked at Stuart questioningly.

"Bad news, I'm afraid. Sister-in-law died on the operating table."

Jorge: "You mean, El? Phyl just spoke about her."

Angelica covered her mouth in shock. "Oh, what a tragedy! Her poor little son!"

Stuart stood up. "I'm sorry. I'm going to have to go to Phyl."

Jorge and Angelica stood up. "We'll go. We're very sorry. Let us know the details when you get them, friend," said Jorge as he led Angelica into the flat.

Stuart closed the door behind their friends. He listened to Phyl's sobs in the bedroom. Mercedes stepped toward Stuart with a questioning look.

"*La cuñada de la señora murió en Canadá*," he explained.

Mercedes covered her mouth in surprise and nodded. "I'm making a *café crema*."

"*Gracias*, Mercedes. Though I think it will take much more than *café crema* to bring her back from this abyss," Sadly, Stuart walked to the door and momentarily stood listening to Phyl crying before knocking gently and entering the room. Tony followed at his feet, dragging his tail.

Slowly, the door quietly shut on a major part of Phyl's life, as if on its own.

*   *   *

Phyl sat at the table. She clutched a handkerchief struggling to write a note by hand. She had dark circles under her eyes. She was pale and sickly. She grieved with a broken heart. She wrote:

September 18, 1940

Dear K,

We were brokenhearted when we received the cable – what a shock! I could hardly talk when I read it. I had just written El begging her to see several specialists before being operated on. I feel terrible, too, because I renewed my regular balling out at her, telling her that she must take care of her health, imploring her to get a maid, etc., but now it's too late. I feel so helpless. If I could only be there with Claude to comfort and help. I feel if I had been there, I would've forced El to stay in bed as prescribed, but I suppose she shouldn't have liked the interference. It was God's will, but it is so hard to understand why He takes people so young. Are there not enough deaths with the war!? My heart aches for Claude, for El's people, for all of you, and for us, too, because we looked forward to the day when we could visit and have them visit us for odd games and bridge and so on. I have memories of the walks we took in the ravine, of evenings we listened to the radio, had hot milk or chocolate at night.

Claude will need you and Dad more now than ever, K. Don't neglect him, Dad has often wished he could live his life over again. He knows the mistakes he made when my mother died and what should've been avoided. He has a living picture of himself, his same tragedy all over again.

Stuart and I have written saying that we would love to take little Stuart and bring him up. I don't know how Claude would feel about that. At this time, we realize what it really means to be away from the only people who make life matter. I still don't see what else we live for if it isn't for our husbands, wives, children and families. There is a land of the living and the land of the dead, and the bridge is love. We are immortal so long as those who love us live.

You will understand me, K, when I say that I don't want to see Claude's child brought up as we were, by one and then the other. A child must have a steady environment, the same ideas, the same sense of values, the same objective, not first one idea and then another and one has no particular philosophy about life. I feel sure El's parents will want to take Stuart. But they are not young.

It was such a tragedy about El. I can't understand what could've happened if the operation was successful. Her heart must've been in a weak condition through so many attacks of pneumonia combined with goiter.

Oh dear, none of us look forward to a very merry Christmas this year.

The phone rang shrilly. Mercedes rushed out of the kitchen to answer it. "*Señora, soy es el Sr. Redington.*"

Phyl saw Mercedes hold out the black earpiece of the phone. She sniffed and pushed herself away from the table. "*Gracias*, Mercedes." Phyl held the phone to her ear. "Hi, Stu," she whispered.

"You, okay?"

"I just finished the letter. I hope we'll be ready for the mail ship in the morning."

"I'm sure we will. Listen, I just got a telegram from Marita. Dad's in hospital."

Phyl gasped. "Oh, no. What happened?"

"It's his lungs. He's having difficulty breathing."

"Oh, Stu. Pneumonia?"

"I don't know any more details except that she said it's bad. She'll keep in touch."

"I'll pray for him." Phyl wiped her nose with the handkerchief and sniffed.

"You don't believe in God."

"I say that and yet I do. I believe in good thoughts. I'll still pray."

"I expected to have this bad news in a year or so as Dad is eighty years old and has pneumonia regularly every year; his body can only take so much. We're leaving in such a short time back to the State that I was hoping to see him again."

Phyl bit her bottom lip. "So, Marita doesn't think he'll pull through?"

"It sounds it. I wish I could be with Mother in her trouble."

"Yes, just as I want to be with Claude. I totally understand. You feel everything so deeply, Stu. Just like me." She looked around to see where Mercedes was. She could hear her humming in the kitchen. "Being there, one has practical things to do to help, but at this distance, there is nothing to do but sit and think and grieve, and it's terrible. I can't handle any more grief, Stu."

"I understand."

Phyl listened to his breathing for a moment. "We need to get away. I can't stay cooped up in the house like this, and I'm not in the mood for endless Teas and Bridge games at the Club. Can you take time off? We can go to the *estancia*."

"I'm afraid I can't, Phyl. Minor's out of town for a month, and I cover for him."

"Can you ask him to hurry back?"

"You know, he's always been a little jealous of our friendship with the Piñieros as they're one of the biggest and richest families here, and he knows very well that Argentines, as a rule, never make friends with foreigners like us, let alone invite them to their home and on trips. So, it isn't likely Minor will rush home to give us a holiday with the Piñieros. But you should definitely go away on your own."

"I won't go without you."

"Don't be silly. I'll give Jorge a call. It is always what the doctor orders for you, and they want you to come."

Stuart hung up. The weight on Phyl's heart was so overbearing she grabbed her midriff and bent down. She returned to the table, and wrote a postscript about Stuart's father in hospital on the letter, and signed it. She kissed it, folded it, and put it in an envelope. With a shaking hand, she addressed it and sat back. Tony hurried up to her chair, as if he knew. She picked him up like a baby and hugged him tightly. She rocked him from side to side, silently, miserably. She looked at the envelope on the table for a very long time, as if it were a murderous knife to the heart.

* * *

The trip to Patagonia by rail, to the *estancia,* was pleasant. Jorge and Angelica, four children, and three servants came along. Jorge's family passed a lot of business on to the railway by transporting wines, wool, fruit, and cattle, so they were treated quite royally. They had an entire coach to themselves, complete with a living room, refrigerator, a bath, and even a fireplace.

Usually, Jorge stayed in town and handled the business, while his brother Diego ran the *estancia*. This time, Diego stayed in town because their mother was ill, and he hadn't seen her very much.

Jorge joined Angelica to watch over the ranch. Phyl and Angelica planned to spend the month together, even if it ended up that Jorge couldn't stay the entire time.

The following day, the train passed the gully near the great dam and Phyl sat at the window frantically studying the river below. Against all odds, she carefully scanned the shoreline for any sign of a body or clothing. It had been a little while, but she thought perhaps there would still be some sign, some proof of poor Reiner.

The train passed the dam, beautiful, grand, blindingly white in the nova sun. The waters sparkled and danced in a stiff breeze. She saw where she and Stuart had stood and fished. She didn't realize the train tracks were so near to the dam. Anyone could've seen them standing there fishing. Her heart trembled under the tension. She closed her eyes, a deep breath. One of the servants offered Champagne, and she turned and willingly downed it and asked for more.

She knew they were near their destination when she saw sparkling irrigation channels in the distance and the horizon was dotted with cattle and sheep. She looked at the grand dome of the sky and swore the colors were different, more intense, more brilliant, than in the city.

They finally slowed down and creaked into the station. Amidst the spewing black smoke and raised twisters of dust, sand, and tumbleweed, they saw the *majordomo* and another servant waiting beside the *estancia's* two jalopies at the end of the platform. One jalopy was for the packing trunks, the other for Phyl and the family, though the twins wanted to go with the trunks to sit on top for an adventurous ride. Everyone was giddy and happy, anxious to enjoy every glory of their stay.

"Oh, my God. It's good to be back," said Phyl, bright-eyed. She smiled weakly.

Jorge put an arm around her frail shoulders and squeezed tightly. "It's good to have you here."

"Absolutely," agreed Angelica. "Right, children?"

The children cheered and hugged Phyl before jumping into the cars. Georgie grinned at her.

After an hour of discomfort and being jostled by the terrain, they approached the *estancia's* main buildings in the heat of the day. Phyl took a deep breath and felt life finally pumping through her veins. The beauty of the surroundings and the promise of a fantastic stay with livestock, wildlife, fishing, and riding brought back all the amazing goodness she felt when visiting. It was like coming home.

Once settled and unpacked, she ran the bathtub. The water ran like blood. It used to startle her, but she knew enough now that they must have had a good rain the week before, and the sands had washed down from the hills into the cisterns. Getting used to bathing in this water took a while, but it washed her clean, regardless.

Dressed and refreshed, she stepped out of her room onto the terrace. She looked out on the surrounding fields. Thousands of Lombardy poplars swayed in the wind, marking off every field. The rivers running through the *estancia's* acreage were full of salmon and trout this season, so she had all the tackle she needed and more in case Stuart was able to join them.

Angelica stood outside by their large bricked oven, talking to the servants about dinner. As if reading Phyl's mind, she came over and asked, "Are you going to fish tomorrow? The children would like to come along. And, quite frankly, I wouldn't mind starting our stay with a picnic beside a cool stream in the shade of the trees."

Phyl laughed. "That's a deal!"

"Well, we'll do nothing tonight except eat, drink, and go to bed early."

Phyl took a deep, deep breath. "Absolute music to my ears."

The following day.

They saddled the horses with thick sheepskin for comfort, as they were going a distance. After two hours of riding, they found themselves beside a fishing hole surrounded by poplars, beech, and cyprus trees. They crossed to the other side, where the fishing hole was deeper. Phyl's horse put his hoof in a hole and instantly, Phyl was submerged, hanging onto his mane for dear life. It was a swift, deep current, but the horse was a good swimmer and brought Phyl out safely on the other side.

Once everyone was settled and Phyl peeled off a few layers of clothing to dry in the sun, they set up the picnic and took out the tackle. Phyl showed

Angelica how to use the new reel Stuart had given her, and helped her cast a dozen times in quick succession but with no luck.

"I thought by the stories Jorge told me on the train that they'd be clamoring for the old spoon before we had a chance to even get it hooked to the tracer," complained Phyl.

"Well, I'm not having trouble," said Alejandro, one of the five-year-old twins, pulling in a rope with a hunk of meat on the hook. He threw it out again with a splash and plop after pointing to three little perches he had flopping amidst a few rocks he used as a tiny catch basin in the grass.

"Rub it in, Alejandro, rub it in," Phyl laughed. She picked up her reel and cast. It zinged and sang as the hook flew into the distance and into the depths. "Well, my casting is pretty hot if I do say so," she yelled over the rushing waters. "But it kind of makes me mad how even with a casting rod and reel, nothing's biting at your Mom's tackle. And there you go, Alejandro, catching fish hand over fist. I just hope you don't catch a huge *Criolla* fish. It'll pull you right in and gobble you up!"

Alejandro's twin, Luis, laughed. "You can only catch *Criolla* in the ocean, silly!"

"Don't you call her silly, Luis. That's rude," admonished Angelica. She slowly and carefully reeled in her line.

Phyl laughed. "That's okay. They're winning the contest of fishing. Geez. A chunk of meat on a rope. Not even a hook!"

Everyone laughed.

"A local farmer took in an enormous salmon and dozens of trout and *pejerrey* the other day, but we had not even a nipple," offered the *Majordomo*.

Phyl nearly fell into the river laughing. "You mean, *nibble*." Everyone else got the joke and laughed heartily. Time passed. They drank and ate, and the twins eventually stopped pulling in fish and went for a swim.

It didn't get dark until nearly ten that time of year, so they waited until what would normally have been after tea, packed up, and returned home for dinner at ten.

The next day, Phyl went for a swim in the pool, and spent some time riding her favorite Arab steed on the old sheepskin. She played three sets of tennis with Angelica. By the time they retired for afternoon cocktails, Phyl was rejuvenated.

"I'm beginning to recognize the old figure that was once mine." Phyl slapped at her thighs. "I think I see the difference already."

"You are tiny regardless, Phyl," Angelica said, grabbing a handful of her midriff to make a point.

"Yes, but being tiny, it doesn't take much weight to look overweight," Phyl laughed. She took a cigarette from a marble box on the table next to her. One of the servants hurried over to light it.

"*Gracias*," she smiled. She sipped her cocktail and looked over the fields in the afternoon sun. "It's so beautiful here, Angelica. It's heaven."

Angelica scanned the vista and nodded slowly. "Yes, it is quite beautiful. We are quite fortunate."

"I should like a shot at the ducks tomorrow but haven't the heart to creep up on them because they're so trusting. Even when they swim in the canals and a sure shot, it just wouldn't be sporty, would it? And if I do shoot and kill them, and they're in the river, I'm not a good enough swimmer to figure out how to get them out of the water, though maybe I could train my horse to be a retriever."

She took a long drag of her cigarette, tilted her head, and blew the smoke up toward the striped awning above her head. A little bird was perched on one of the supporting arms. "The bird life is wonderful here – herons, storks, cranes, and emu roaming around the fields." Phyl sighed, shook her head in wonder, and downed her cocktail. She held up the glass just as Jorge joined them from the house.

"Empty glass. That's not allowed," joked Jorge. "We have a famous local dandelion wine you should try. Or our own peach and elderberry wines. Whatever you would like."

"Ooooh. Give me dandelion. Dad tried to make it once. It was potent!"

Jorge turned to a servant and ordered him to bring dandelion wine.

"Dad tried out the dandelion wine and had to be put to bed. He didn't believe it could be so strong," laughed Phyl.

"Well, you will have to write your father for the recipe. If it's that good," said Jorge, smiling. He sat next to Angelica, took out a pack of cigarettes, and lit one.

"Why don't you use the cigarettes on the table?" asked Angelica.

Jorge held up his package. "These are Turkish. I prefer them. Great taste. True cigarettes."

"You mean a faster track to a hacking cough," said Phyl.

Jorge offered the lit one to Angelica, who shrugged and took it gladly. He lit another and handed it over to Phyl. She held up hers to show she was still smoking. He put the cigarette into his own mouth and took a drag. He pulled tobacco off the tip of his tongue before speaking. "Your dandelion wine recipe must come from the native Canadian Indians. It's how it was created here, by the natives."

"Actually, I didn't know you had dandelions in Argentina. I've never seen them here." Phyl watched the servant return with a couple of bottles of what she assumed was the wine. The servant opened a bottle and poured a fresh glass. He went to hand it to Jorge, but Jorge motioned toward Phyl. Phyl gladly took it from the servant, sipped it, and inhaled the aroma. She coughed and everyone laughed. "Whoa," she exclaimed happily. "That's strong!" Her eyes watered immediately, and she wiped at them.

"Our dandelions are more potent than your Canadian ones. As is our fruit," claimed Jorge.

Phyl adamantly shook her head in disagreement. She was getting inebriated. "Oh, no! There's no way your fruit nor your orchards can compare with our Niagara Peninsula produce. I have been in this country for six years and have yet to taste a lovely, sweet, ripe peach. They are picked green and never seem to ripen. The ones in the markets are like hard little stones with no flavor. The pears are inferior but somewhat better than the peaches. I never get a bite of a hard, juicy apple. They are always mealy here. Even the ones here on the *estancia*. The plums are good, though." She pointed at Angelica. Then she looked at Jorge again. "The melons are always half green and tasteless in the city."

Jorge raised a finger to protest.

Angelica laughed aloud. "Here we go again."

Phyl didn't give Jorge a chance. "As you Argentines live mainly on meat, things like fruit and vegetables — which are far healthier than anything else, but you don't care about that — don't worry you, and that is probably the reason for the inferior quality of the fruit."

"The fruit is small and hard because the people like it that way."

Phyl almost choked and laughed.

"And they don't eat vegetables, so don't focus on them because meat makes one stronger," argued Jorge. "Much stronger than vegetables ever can."

"If Canadians saw how puny your fruit was, they'd die laughing!"

"Uh oh, life never gets boring between the Piñieros and the Redingtons. Get ready for a good three-hour argument!" yelled Angelica, also inebriated.

A servant suddenly appeared from the main house. He walked to Jorge with a piece of paper on a silver plate. Jorge took it and looked at the front. He looked at Phyl. He held it out. "It's for you." He glanced at Angelica, who looked back at him, frowning. They watched as Phyl took the envelope and opened it.

Phyl's face paled, and she covered her mouth. She shook her head. "It's a wire from Stu. His Dad passed away." She looked up. "I have to pack and take the next train back. Stu's probably all cut up. He needs me. Oh, how I wish we could just fly. It will take a whole day and a half just to get home to Stu!"

Jorge looked at his watch. "There's a train early this evening. If you pack now, we'll make it, and you'll get to Buenos Aires by 10:30 tomorrow night."

Phyl jumped up and ran to her room to pack.

* * *

Weeks later.

"If Mother has left the hotel and gone with Marita to Washington, then they will forward our letter there," said Phyl.

She and Stuart rode in a taxi to the zoo

"Well, I hope she won't stay around the hotel to add to her grief. Everyone's so used to Dad going on the warpath, yelling, and banging his cane. It will be terrible without him. You know, he was in hospital with pneumonia for two weeks before he passed." Stuart was pale and glum. He rearranged his jacket and adjusted his tie.

"I hope the war censor office in Trinidad doesn't hold up our letter. Heaven knows nothing is censurable in it, but I guess it takes time for an army of people to read all the mail going through to the States and Canada." She reached for Stuart's hand. "Goodness, I hear they may no longer have silk stockings in Canada. I just might have to stay here and not return with you." She tried to laugh. Her smile suddenly disappeared. "Of course, I'm only joking. I wouldn't dream of letting you go without me."

"Oh, must tell you something funny," said Stuart. He looked out the window. "Though, of course, saying something funny at a time like this almost feels sinful."

"I know. But do tell." This made Phyl happy. Anything to lighten their moods.

"You know the motion picture The Dictator with Charlie Chaplin?"

"Oh, yes! I so want to see it!"

"It's *banned* here. They're afraid of riots by the Italians, but it's showing in Uruguay. So, how about we go over to Colonia, Uruguay, and see it?"

"Oh, Stu, the trip takes 2 1/2 hours across the river," argued Phyl.

"Yeah, but it's like going to Niagara from Toronto. Just think, it would be the first time we have to have our passports just to see a movie." Stuart smiled at her and winked.

Phyl smiled with her eyes. She frowned. "Stu, just imagine when we finally go home. It will be weird to go to Claude's and not have El there."

Stuart nodded thoughtfully and squeezed her hand. "And I also have a terrible loss to face. The hotel won't seem at all the same without the banging of Dad's cane." He sighed. "And, of course, it's still in financial straits. There is much to do."

"I don't envy you."

Stuart patted her hand. "I know." He suddenly grabbed the leather strapping hanging by the window as the taxi did a tight turn, almost on two tires.

Phyl hung on. "You know, there was a moment at the *estancia* when I was coming up from the river, and Angelica was coming down the hill with a fishing rod in her hand. As you know, she's short and blonde and has gotten rather chubby, whereas El was tall, blonde, and skinny, but just then, in the twilight, with a fishing rod and all, she looked the image of Eleanor coming down the hill."

"No," whispered Stuart.

"Yes, and Stuart, I stood stalk still and gasped."

"Goodness."

"It's funny that Angelica so loves fishing, which is unusual for an Argentine woman."

"For sure."

"She even got up with me at dawn, and we decided we'd have whiskey and hot water for breakfast and left Jorge and Diego dead to the world." Phyl shook her head and laughed. "I'm so very happy we have Jorge and Angelica. They're the family we don't have down here."

"I never thought about that. I'm glad you feel that way."

"I do," smiled Phyl.

"But they have their own sad loss to deal with. I don't think Jorge's mother was very elderly."

Phyl looked at him sadly and shrugged.

Stuart shifted on the seat and sighed. After a moment of contemplation, he changed the subject. "You know, I am weighing the pros and cons as regards our trip home. We might come by West Coast instead of East for obvious safety reasons."

"You know what I'm afraid of?" She looked up at Stuart with sad, wide eyes. "I'm frightened they'll nab you off for conscription as soon as we step foot on American soil." Phyl's voice cracked. "I have nightmares of you being in uniform and fighting somewhere in France or Belgium."

Stuart let go of her hand and put his arm around her frail shoulders. "I wouldn't worry about that. I'm already filling a role on paper. I'm already doing my duty."

"I hope so."

"Damn right."

They neared the zoo.

Thousands of people milled both outside and inside the pungent-smelling, noisy zoo. Phyl and Stuart fought through urchins to pay their ten *centavos* each. Then they rushed through the crowd to the zoo's center to a new arrangement of tables and chairs near the chimpanzee and wildcat enclosures. Both were upgraded to large pits surrounded by high cement walls and tall wrought-iron fences curved above. One chimpanzee hung onto the rails of the high fence, screeching as Phyl and Stuart approached. Adults and children laughed at the chimpanzee. Some threw peanuts at it. The monkey, in turn, threw feces down into the crowd, making them all scream.

Stuart saw a half-empty green bench at the back of the garbage-strewn seating area. On one end sat a bearded gentleman in a Panama hat smoking a pipe and reading a newspaper. What looked like a folded coat lay on the remainder of the bench.

"Pretend you have something in your shoe, Phyl," Stuart whispered.

She looked at him and stopped. She stomped a foot and leaned over to touch her shoe. She motioned to Stuart to allow her to lean on him while trying to remove her shoe. He pretended to look around for a spot to sit and motioned her to go to the back of the seating area.

Stuart led a limping Phyl between occupied tables and benches to the seated gentleman and asked if they could please sit. The gentleman lowered the paper, looked at Phyl balancing on one foot, removed his coat, and placed it on his lap. Under the coat was a large envelope. Stuart immediately sat on it and looked around. They were surrounded by people, and no one appeared interested.

Phyl leaned over and took off her shoe. She pretended to shake out a pebble.

"This is like being an extra on a movie set. I pretend I'm doing something while you do the talking elsewhere," she giggled.

Stuart smiled and nodded as if enjoying the conversation.

"You're late," said the stranger. He was a gentleman Phyl had never seen before. She could tell he was American. Perhaps New England.

"Yes. Sorry."

"There are codes in that envelope. Please pass it on to the American attaché. I understand you have a meeting with him tomorrow. Selling typewriters."

Stuart leaned over and kissed Phyl. Phyl hugged him. "Yes," he said.

"Condolences, salesman. I believe they are in order for both of you."

Phyl gasped. She put her shoe back on and pretended to look for something in her purse.

"Yes, correct. Thank you."

"You may want to pass a few things on when you meet in Washington."

"Okay."

"We're keeping an eye out on an upstart. Someone who's been groomed by Nazi-leaning factions within the military. His wife died years ago, then was shipped off for training in Europe, particularly Fascist Italy, with time in Berlin with the Nazis. He just returned last week and we hear he will help lead another military coup soon."

"Already? We only just had Ortiz take over a couple of years ago."

"He's useless to us. Too sick."

"What about Castillo?"

"His hands are tied. The very factions who are grooming this bright upstart are the same who are threatening Castillo to stay in line. It's not good to have a family you care about in this day and age while wearing a leadership hat. Not with these animals who have no qualms about getting what they want. Castillo's too much of a family man. He has his own priorities. It's a shame. He's an excellent and capable diplomat and leader. But I think he feels the pressure."

"From the Nazis?"

"Yes. And his own people who are Nazi sympathizers."

"They don't ever suspect us trying to manipulate them, do they?" asked Stuart.

"I certainly expect it always worries them we would and do. But we can't at the moment. The Brits have their hands tied and are trying to keep a balanced head. They do not want us to upset the applecart, which is barely stable. They want the food supplies for their fighting men to keep coming."

The man sucked his pipe and looked down at the paper. He took his pipe out. "Of course, the Brits are getting it from all sides, at home, in the air, on the ground, on and under the waters, and no one seems to look out for them." The gentleman smirked. "Did you know they're letting merchant ships get sunk by Nazi subs though they have intelligence of them lurking below? They don't want the Nazis to know *they* know. Oh, the damn sacrifices of war."

"Can we back track? Can I know more about Perón?"

"Yes. Perón. Juan Domingo Perón. He's elevated to Colonel and is a member of a secret military lodge called the *Grupo de Oficiales Unidos*. They're looking at long-range goals. The coup won't be until they see what Castillo can do for them. Another year or so. But if the coup goes their way, it may mean we're completely kicked out of Argentina."

"We, the Americans?"

"Yes. And warning. When you return to Washington, salesman, your place here in town will be used for Embassy purposes until you come back."

Phyl gasped. "Is he implying we're coming back *again*!"

Stuart motioned for her to be quiet, smiled and nodded.

The man folded his paper, sat up, and looked into the crowd. His demeanor changed. He took the pipe out of his mouth. "Hell, I've been spotted."

Phyl's heart skipped. She glanced around from under her lashes. She only saw the backs of young and old around her. "What do we do now?"

"You, madam, sit still. You, salesman, there is a snake enclosure to the right. Open the small gates to let them out. I'll open the back gates to the chimpanzee and wildcats. Between them and the snakes, the consequent riot should cover us when we escape with the crowd." The man was just about to get up when Stuart cleared his throat.

"Wait," Stuart whispered harshly. "How do you know they don't know where we live? How's escaping in a riot helping?"

"This is not someone who knows you. But this person has been on my tail for the last two weeks. I thought I got rid of him."

"Gotten rid of?" spit Phyl. She covered her chest with her hand in fear.

"Shhh," hissed Stuart.

"Nothing to do with you. Quick. The snakes." He got up, ripped off his beard, and threw his Panama hat into the bushes behind the bench. He deftly pulled out a fedora from under his arm. He punched the fedora into shape and slipped away through the crowd in front of them, slapping the hat onto his head.

Stuart passed in front of Phyl. "Sit tight," he hissed and hurried away.

Phyl sat nervously, rubbing her gloved hands. She looked around wide-eyed. She craned her neck to look around. Elephants continued to call, lions continued to roar, and hyenas continued to bark. Babies cried, women laughed, men yelled. The usual roar. Suddenly, the smell, which she never minded as it reminded her of the zoo at home, was too much of an onslaught on her nostrils. She held the back of her gloved hand against her nose and mouth and waited. She could hear a different kind of murmur running through the crowd almost imperceptibly at first. Suddenly, there was a scream. And then another.

Phyl stood up on the bench and looked frantically through the crowd. "I hate snakes," she cried to herself. She heard feet stampeding, and saw heads of people running in the direction of the gate. To the left, she heard chimpanzees screeching. She spotted two chimps climbing up into a large tree nearby. She screamed. So did other women. She heard wildcats crying. As she shook in fear, she felt her arm grabbed. She screamed and jumped before looking down at Stuart.

"Quick, seven snakes escaped." He helped her down, and they moved with the panicked crowd.

"Are they poisonous?" she asked, trying to keep up with him, frightened to death.

Stuart shook his head. "This is a zoo. They wouldn't have these snakes so easily loosened through doors. Still, it's best to get away. Clear out. I don't want whoever that is after the guy to know where we live and find out who we are."

They rounded a bend in the park along with the surging crowd. They stopped to help a little boy get back to his feet and be reunited with his parents. Then, they continued running. Comically, as Phyl kept pace breathlessly, she looked over at the rhinoceros enclosure and saw a couple copulating. She laughed, despite herself, and knew she would never forget that image.

They walked halfway home and found a taxi for the remainder. Phyl dabbed her forehead with a hanky. Stuart started coughing as soon as he settled in the cab. Phyl banged on his back. Stuart got control of his hacking and settled into somewhat normal breathing, Phyl looked back to see if anyone followed.

"I hope they catch those snakes and cats. I don't think the chimpanzees will hurt anyone, but I remember the snakes. The smallest is seven feet long. I'm so glad we live on the tenth floor. I'd hate to see one under our bed tonight," she said.

"These are jungle snakes. They have absolutely no problem finding ways of climbing outside buildings," Stuart said dryly.

Phyl turned to him, appalled. "How can you say such a thing!"

"Well, it's true. They're Amazonians. They could climb anywhere. Especially if they're hungry."

Phyl hit him with her purse while Stuart laughed aloud.

Chapter Fourteen
Going Home, Coming Back, Ortiz and Gay

"I feel as if I'm caught in an ongoing horrific riptide. A never-ending dream."

Phyl fretfully scanned the Atlantic waters for German periscopes. She must have done so a thousand times. Every change in the rumble of the ship or angle of the bulkheads, any change in the demeanor of the crew – she was deathly afraid it meant they'd be torpedoed.

Stuart put his hands over hers, white-knuckled, clenching the railing as if it was a life preserver. He snuggled his face into the back of her hair. "I know. An Argentine riptide."

"A huge one with sharks and all. Always back and forth. And here we are, returning home again, taking our lives in our hands in waters full of Nazi submarines and possibly mines. In fact, we're probably going over Allied shipwrecks this very moment, thanks to Hitler."

"A sobering thought, I must say." Stuart pressed his cheek against hers. "However, we have no control over the fact we can't stay in Argentina longer than three years at a time and we have to leave. You know that very well."

"I do, but it's still come back, go there, come back again. Though this time, it's different, I guess. At least we know for sure we're turning around to come back to Buenos Aires. Last two times, we thought that was it. Surprise, surprise. Argh. Again, through dangerous waters."

"Unless the war comes to a miraculous end during the one month we're in North America."

"Dream on," Phyl said.

She turned within the circle of his arms and leaned back against the railing. The breeze off the crashing waves below blew up her pant legs. The hem of her pants flipped and flopped frantically under the pressure. She put her head on his shoulder. She stared at the saltwater pools on the well-scrubbed teak deck of the ship. An exceptionally high wave crashed and flowed by the ship's hull, causing a tower of sparkling water to crash through the railings onto the deck. The back of Phyl's pants and top weren't spared. She squealed with surprise.

"Thanks to you, I'm dry," laughed Stuart.

He led Phyl away from the railing. They wobbled to the doorway into the belly of the ship.

Phyl reached back and pulled her wet pants off her skin. "I'm feeling very emotional, finally going back to little Stuart and you having to see your family and no Dad."

They hurried through a hallway into their cabin. Phyl shivered. She reached for her housecoat on the hanger inside the little steel bathroom door.

"Gosh, getting our passports renewed was an ordeal this time."

"It's war, Phyl. Everything is more complicated."

"Yeah, but all that red tape, two weeks with pictures taken and fingerprints, and you having to go to the British Council to be visa'd to enter Canada, and I to the American Council to be visa'd to enter the States. I thought that renewing our visa business would be as simple as it used to be, but now it is actually more trouble than taking out an original passport. Being forced to decide between a tourist visa or a permanent resident when really not knowing at the time. Am I dreaming? We *are* going back, yes?"

"Like I said. We *are* going back. Read my lips. What we did was the wisest move, keeping everything put: the apartment, furniture, and car. Believe me, Phyl, there's a very good reason we will be coming back. Too much going on out there, and I have too many contacts to simply let go." Stuart lay down on his bunk, looked at his watch. "Far too much going on." He paused, thoughtful for a moment. His stomach growled. "I'm hungry. Let's get a snack and coffee."

"Well, it's got to be really worthwhile because we are not saving anything due to the exchange, which has cut a third off your salary, and it's wiped out a third of our savings converting the money into dollars. And what's this about having to take out a Certificate of Good Conduct to get back into this country? What do they think we are, criminals?"

"Well, they heard what a pest you've been," Stuart joked.

Phyl threw a towel at him. He grabbed it in midair and tucked it under his head for support.

"And then there is that other little doohickey we had to take out to allow us to land in Trinidad since it's also a war zone." Phyl shook her head and entered the bathroom but left the door open. "Each of these jolly little papers cost money!" she yelled. She poked her head out. "Our money is disappearing."

Stuart threw the towel back at Phyl. "Money, money, money, that's all you worry about."

Phyl popped back into the bathroom and undressed. She reappeared in her housecoat with the belt tied tightly. She walked to the closet and pulled out a small suitcase. She threw it on the other bunk and looked for something to wear. Stuart watched, then looked up at the porthole above his head. Spray splashed against it, leaving sparkling diamonds on the outside.

"This isn't a bad ship, the Argentina. Big boat."

Phyl took things into the bathroom to dress.

"Oh, why do you always have to go into the bathroom to change. Let me see you!"

"No!" yelled Phyl. She closed the door and locked it.

Stuart felt the ship rock. "Well, I'm glad we chose a nice room up in the bow. It's great having three port holes and good ventilation; otherwise, it could be like Hades." He looked at the dressing table and wardrobe. The bathroom had a tub and shower, very nicely fitted. "Wear something nice," he yelled.

Phyl opened the door and looked at him. "Well, with so many people on board we know from the city, I'm quite reminded of what Argentina has taught me - that appearance is half the battle."

She walked out wearing a tasteful light pink pants set, wide-legged, wide-sashed, with a cream-colored blouse and high collar.

"Much too nice. You look suspicious, like a jewel thief or something, too glamorous for words."

"Oh, you. You'd say anything to get me out of these clothes."

Stuart went to jump up. Phyl giggled and ran out of the cabin, slamming the steel-rimmed door behind her.

* * *

Weeks later, Phyl stood on their land in Kingston, Pennsylvania.

She took a deep breath as she looked over the poured concrete foundation of what would become their future home. She smiled, imagining the rooms, the shrubbery, the flowers, the driveway finished. She looked across the Susquehanna River and could make out the top of the Redington Hotel. Stuart was meeting with his brothers at the bank in town that morning, so she thought she would go with Marita to look at her and Stuart's long-term dream in the making.

"It's going to be beautiful," said Marita. She wore a navy-looking outfit with a broad white collar and flap at the back. A fun summer dress with a thick light blue stripe and red wooden buttons down the front. "Where's the nursery going to be?" she asked, looking at the foundation.

Phyl squinted into the sun, then at the foundation. She pointed to the opposite side. She looked down at the dry grass below her sandaled feet and pondered on future children. Still no luck. But the doctor told her that nerves often influenced conception. He said as soon as their lives settled down, everything would change. But when would their lives settle down? That was the million-dollar question. If it wasn't the Depression, it was a new culture and climate. Then, if it wasn't family tragedies, it was Stuart's ongoing battle with bronchitis and pneumonia. And if it wasn't the war, it was Stuart's ongoing unofficial role as a G-man and all the nerve-wracking things that came with it.

"We better get back. We have to catch the 5:00 train for Washington, and I wouldn't mind having a late lunch first."

Phyl nodded. Marita had an apartment there. Mrs. Redington stayed with her to escape the hotel's problems. Unfortunately, no one expected any money to be left over from any sale even if they could sell. In the worst-case scenario, she walked away and let the bank take over. Well, at least Mrs. Redington had their home in Kingston. Phyl looked to the west. She could make out the brown roof of the Redington rented house. "Right. Is there anything your Mother would want from her penthouse?"

"Good point. I'll give Mother a call on the hotel phone later and see. For now, we have the odd perks like access to long distance." Marita led Phyl to her father's car, a black 1938 Buick. She opened the driver's side door. "Life's kind of different, isn't it?"

"It sure is."

"I mean all around. Even poor Claude has his little son." Marita sat behind the wheel, Phyl on the passenger side. "How is he doing?"

"He has a housekeeper."

"A housekeeper?" Marita looked concerned.

Phyl noticed. "I hope to meet her soon and check her out. Apparently, she's very good with little Stuart."

"Oh, that's good."

Phyl looked at Marita, who was sitting, deep in thought. "I wouldn't try to complicate things any more than they are, Marita. The last thing Claude can handle is you entering the picture. He's not even sure if he'll be called to fight. Or if he's keeping that house. I doubt he'll have room for someone new in his life at this point."

Marita nodded and started the car without looking at Phyl. She backed out of the dirt drive.

"Well, here we are in Boomtown. I think everyone and his brother are in Washington," said Stuart.

They sat down to dinner at Martin's Tavern on Wisconsin Avenue. He looked out the beveled window at the old buildings across the way. The sun was starting to set, and the light enhanced the brickwork and shutters of the old New England architecture. "You should see the messy, tiny room we have for the small sum of seven dollars per day," he said sarcastically. "We wouldn't pay three dollars any other time."

"It's Washington," said Mrs. Redington. "And it's wartime. Everything is expensive here."

"Why take an apartment here then?" asked Phyl.

Marita looked at Stuart. "Stuart was able to get us a deal on this larger one, and there certainly wasn't anything in Wilkes-Barre." Marita butt out her cigarette. "Though I still can't figure out how Stuart has that much influence."

"I don't have any influence. I just know the odd person," he said.

"Well, that odd person allowed us to find a very upscale and affordable flat."

"I'm afraid I've been spoiled with so much room with the penthouse. But this particular apartment is quite nice, don't you think?" said Mrs. Redington to Phyl.

"It certainly is a beautiful apartment."

"The only thing is we only have three bedrooms. So, it was either the couch or floor for you two."

"That's okay, Mother." Stuart tapped his cigarette on a metal ashtray. "It's just a few days before we have to go to New York. And then I'm spending time back at the family hotel anyway while we sort out your papers. Just another week or so. Then we'll have the movers come in and take what you decide to keep. Storage is already set up in town for when you decide to live in Kingston again."

"It's a better distraction for me, being here. Too fresh a memory staying in Pennsylvania." Mrs. Redington carefully spread out the linen napkin on her lap and patted it. "It is certainly a beautiful city. A combination of European and North American architecture. It's just marvelous; one certainly sees where a lot of the people's taxes go. There are gorgeous wide boulevards and parks, but it's impossible to see much of it on a weekend. It's too bad you're going to New York on Monday. At least I can come back and take my time being a tourist? You probably don't know when you'll be back for an extended time, right?"

"You're right, Mother. It might be a while before we're in Washington again. Not for another three years once we leave here."

"Stuart wrangled a very good contract for once, and they're treating us much better this time," said Phyl. She took a sip of her martini. "Hmm. It's been ages since I've had a martini. Can't wait to get to Toronto and share a few with Claude Jr. Remember when you treated everyone to our first martinis on Toronto Island?" she asked Stuart. She suddenly felt sad. "With El and Claude?"

Stuart looked at her grimly and nodded. "Seems like a lifetime ago."

"For one person, it was a lifetime."

They looked up to see a waiter arrive with a large platter carrying four dishes of shucked oysters.

"This is one thing I'm pleased about during this war," said Mrs. Redington, "and that is oysters haven't gone up in price at all. Bon appétit."

* * *

Stuart and Phyl sat on the little porch of the clapboard cabin they rented with Claude Jr., her Dad, and K. Phyl bounced little Stuart on her lap as she looked over the white caps of beautiful Georgian Bay. "More," demanded little Stuart. Phyl held the child's hands and yanked him up into the air with a cheer. Little Stuart giggled. "Again," he demanded, grinning, showing his fine, tiny teeth.

Stuart watched and grinned. He flicked his cigarette over the railing into the grassy dune below. "It's chilly for bare feet. Typical Northern Ontario. Hot and flies during the day, and frost at night."

"I hope to see the Northern Lights tonight again. I could swear when I whistled, they came closer," Phyl said, looking up in the sky.

"Just native lore."

"Oh, I don't know, I thought they certainly were about to devour us," said Claude Jr., showing up at the screen doorway and stepping outside. He slapped a mosquito. "The little buggers are out again. Let's go in."

Phyl put the child down and followed little Stuart and his father back into the cabin. Claude Sr. sat in an old wooden armchair reading the local news and smoking his pipe. Jr. walked up to his Dad and rested his bare foot on the edge of his Sr.'s chair. Jr. started to lecture on the changing aspects of Magnetic North. He had read about pilots and the challenges of navigating, but he said the problem was that Magnetic North did not remain static from year to year. Sr. rolled his eyes. Jr. had some outrageous ideas about the earth tipping and rotating according to the weight of the oceans.

Stuart demanded proof that the oceans had an effect, and this kicked off an evening's worth of animated discussion. Claude's arguments were constantly interrupted by his nervous laughter. It was now late, and little Stuart was in bed. K shushed Jr. when she heard little Stuart stir in his cot by the stove in the rustic kitchen.

Stuart changed the subject when he took a closer look at a leather lampshade with a map of Ontario. He decided to trace it with a red pen as to where they had fished over the years, despite Phyl's protestations that he shouldn't mark the lampshade. But Stuart swore he was going to town to buy a new one and would keep the old as a souvenir.

Phyl played with a pair of little socks. "I just love to hear little Stuart talk. He's such a darling. I hope he gets over that timidity, though. We need to take him around more so that he won't mind going into strange homes. If that shyness remains, it may turn into insecurity and self-consciousness in later years. He'll be miserable whenever he has to meet people."

"Maybe we should discourage people from making him the center of attention. He'll only withdraw more," offered K. She sat on a straight-back wooden chair knitting by a tall floor lamp.

"I think shyness is something you inherit," said Phyl, still looking out for the Northern Lights. "He could've from both sides as Eleanor was shy and Dad is shy."

Sr. took out his pipe. "Speak for yourself."

"And so is Claude, Jr." Phyl continued, "but like me, he pretends not to be and brazens it out."

"Oh, is that why you get wild in crowds?" joked Stuart.

Phyl scratched her upper arm. She rolled up her sleeve to check where she had the typhoid and smallpox shots in preparation for their return trip.

"Itchy?"

Phyl nodded. "These shots nearly knocked me for a loop. We have a second of a series of three typhoid shots in Washington on Friday again."

"You're going back to Washington? I thought when you left to come here, you'd be going straight to New York to catch the ship," said K.

"We were wrong. The doctor in Wilkes-Barre suggested we go back to Washington for the shots. Then, one more after that, in New York. We have to have them for the Brazil visa. But, boy, the last typhoid inoculation was bad. I fainted in the elevator, much to my embarrassment, but Stuart was with me and got me into bed. He called the hotel doctor, who said it was a normal reaction, took my pulse, and charged us five dollars."

"Well, another three years without you here," said K quietly. "We certainly miss you when you're gone. And, with censorship and your letters arriving sporadically, sometimes not at all, we don't have the pleasure of reading about your adventures like we used to. We sometimes go for months without hearing from you. Don't we?" asked K, looking at Claude Sr.

Phyl's Dad looked over and nodded. He took his pipe out and poked at the tobacco with the tip of his finger, then searched for matches in his pocket. "Yup, they're pretty sporadic now."

K got up and picked up a book of Hotel Redington matches and handed it to Claude Sr.

"With the war and censorship, there isn't a lot you can write about in detail, is there? Anything can be misconstrued as classified or dangerous and be redacted. It's not worth the effort." Claude Sr. poked at the tobacco with a match before lighting it.

"Surely, not so if we write to *them*." Claude Jr. drank from his beer mug.

"Doesn't matter which way the letters go. Spies are everywhere," said Claude Sr.

"Or they're stolen just for their stamps," said Stuart. "People are getting desperate."

"Are you planning to see anything in New York before you leave?" asked K.

"Yes, I would love to see the Hayden Planetarium and the Metropolitan Museum. And there are two good plays on right now, one with Ethel Barrymore." Phyl wriggled her eyebrows excitedly.

"Speaking of which," said Claude Jr. "When will we ever see those movie pictures you were in?"

Phyl laughed. "Oh, I wouldn't hold your breath. They're for the Latin countries."

Stuart downed his beer and smacked his lips. "You should see your sister, Claude. She looks pretty good even though they painted her in green face and black lips."

"An improvement," quipped Claude Jr.

Phyl jumped up. "Why you!" Phyl raced after Claude Jr. He ran around her and out the front door into the black night. Phyl ran after him and stopped at the top step of the stairs. She gazed upwards.

The Northern Lights were at their best and splendid selves, flowing and moving as if giants shook colorful sheets of light in effervescent greens, yellows, and blues in towering mountains above.

"There you go, Phyl. Like magic." Stuart stood at the screen door, looking up.

"Isn't that just heaven. That's gotta be heaven. What a perfect moment. And it's so quiet, I can almost hear them buzz."

They stood quietly for several moments as if on holy ground.

* * *

"It's cold, Stu."

"Well, it is October, but it's not as cold as the first time we left New York that December when everything was covered in ice," Stuart reminded Phyl. "Even the dock lines were frozen."

"You're right, it's not that cold." They were standing on the stern of the Argentina once again. On board the ship were 120 Norwegian sailors coming down for the British government to take over some other ship from Argentina. They were already having a wild time and had only just left the docks. "Oh, she's so beautiful. New York is such a marvelous sight this time of night. The lights are just going on, and it looks like a fairyland. I think everyone on board feels subdued like I do." There was a round of laughter further back on the ship.

"Except for the 120 sailors back there," said Stuart.

"Indeed," Phyl said. "But, it sure feels strange leaving the docks with no one to see us off."

"Yeah, Mother felt pretty blue. It was best we put her on the train with Marita before we left the hotel. She caught that cold, probably in Washington, and I didn't want her around the damn docks and their filth."

"Did you notice we seem to go up in the world? Every time we go on a ship, our accommodations get better and better. Is it the company this time or compliments of the US government?"

Phyl took Stuart's arm. They sauntered along the deck and looked back at the Statue of Liberty. The light in her wand and spotlights from below just lit up.

"No, I think it's thanks to Schuler, who has been most generous. It cost the company easily $1,800 expenses for us on this trip. And that's without boat fare."

They looked over when they heard screaming and laughter. "Goodness, we're going to have a problem, I think. All these young males on board."

Later, after dinner, they watched as they sped passed the darkened shores of New Jersey.

"Remember when Atlantic City was so bright, the entire sky above it was almost as bright as New York's?" said Phyl. "Now it's just black along the shore. It's another world entirely."

"Subs have been spotted along this coast. In fact, I'm sure there isn't a bit of coastline not having subs pass."

"Oh, what an awful thought!" exclaimed Phyl. She looked around and saw the distant faint glow of their escorts. "I'm so relieved we're not travelling alone. We could still be torpedoed but I guess knowing we're escorted, they kind of hesitate? Do they?" she asked, hopefully.

"The escorts have equipment sensitive enough to hear a sub if there's one nearby. Granted, it's not a guarantee they won't try to torpedo us. But there's three of us against one." Stuart shivered. "Well, nothing to see here. In fact, perhaps it's best to retire, Phyl. There's nothing out here but freezing cold wind and I certainly need my beauty sleep."

"I noticed. In fact, lots of people ask why I'm with such an old man and I look so young."

Stuart pinched her in the ribs and she squealed.

The noise from the raucous sailors' carousing worsened. Phyl and Stuart, still smiling, returned to their cabin when there were more screams and calls from the deck. They rushed back up. Everyone in the dining room scrambled into the cold air to see what the problem was.

A purser scrambled past them toward the pool at the back. Stuart took Phyl's hand and hurried after the purser. When they reached the pool area, where a single light was strung across, Phyl gasped. The edge of the empty pool was lined by young sailors, most swaying and drunk.

"What happened?" Stuart asked a porter.

"One of the sailors took a leap into the tile swimming pool, but he didn't realize there was no water in it. It's pretty dark. We think he killed himself instantly. He must have broken his back or neck."

"Well, that is definitely the second stupidest thing I have ever heard," said Stuart grimly.

"What was the first?" asked Phyl. Stuart looked at her pointedly. "Oh, yes," she said quietly. "How can I forget?"

Stuart frowned at the porter. "What do you do when someone dies on board. Do we turn back?"

"No, we put the body in the icebox for the rest of the trip. At least until we receive authority to dispose of it."

The porter excused himself and wandered toward the edge of the pool. He helped clear away onlookers as two pursers went to the bottom of the pool to retrieve the broken body. They carried it wrapped in a bloody sheet to the shallow end and up the tiled stairs where a third purser stood by.

Phyl tapped a nearby sailor's shoulder. "Do you know that poor boy?"

The young man looked distraught. "Yes, he's from the Falkland Islands. I know his sister in Norway. She will be very upset. But the Nazis have taken over their village, and I'm not sure if we'll be able to get through to tell her."

"Oh, dear. If it isn't the war, it's crazy antics killing the young." Phyl leaned against Stuart. He patted her arm.

"Let's go in. We're sitting at the Chief Officer's table tomorrow night. We'll get more information then. Shall we?"

They left the crowd to go to their luxury cabin. "Let's hope the rest of the trip is uneventful," Phyl said. "No bombings, no submarines. Just plain old-fashioned fun and on-board romances."

Stuart put his arm around Phyl and squeezed her. "You're on. Shall we continue a very famous one, worthy of romance novels."

Phyl looked around comically. "Oh, which one would that be?"

* * *

Three weeks later.

Stuart and Phyl stood in the luxurious lobby of a swank hotel in balmy Rio de Janeiro. Though the height of wealth and class surrounded them, they had been spoiled by their cabin quarters and hated to leave it behind. The day seemed emotionally gloomy, and Phyl was tearful.

"Shhh," Stuart said as he watched their luggage being taken away to an elevator. "We're on the most beautiful beach in the world. Our room has a marvelous view. We have a few weeks before we get to Buenos Aires, so let's have fun. There's lots to do and we can swim and lounge at their massive pool."

"Oh, I don't even want to look at a pool right now," Phyl whispered. "All I'm going to see is that poor broken body wrapped up in that bloody sheet."

Stuart continued to try and distract her. "Well, they also have great tennis courts here. Come, let's go to our room and settle down."

They followed the porter to the elevator and up to the fifth floor. Down the hall, just two doors, they were let into a swank room. Phyl turned on the lights and looked into the bathroom. She turned on the tap but waited a while. The porter was just about to leave after having been given a generous tip by Stuart.

"Excuse me, we don't have any hot water."

"I'm sorry, *Señora*. Power cuts. The war, you see."

"Even in Rio de Janeiro?" she asked, saddened by the realization they couldn't get away from the war anywhere they went. She jumped at a massive bang against the wall from next door. They distinctly heard noisy neighbors hollering in Portuguese. "Oh, Stuart. I already give up. Let's just go to the casino and play roulette."

"The casino is attached to the hotel, *Señora*. I can show you the way."

"Great," said Phyl, checking herself in the mirror quickly. "I'm going to double my money, and I wager Stu, you will lose all yours."

"What do you wager?" asked Stuart, letting her out first to follow the porter.

"A room at the Copacabana Palace Hotel instead."

* * *

The following Monday.

They stepped out of the Copacabana Palace Hotel toward the beach. Phyl carried a rolled blue and white striped towel and wore her bathing suit under a summer dress. They crossed a busy road, and Phyl tripped just as she stepped onto a high cement curb of a gorgeous mosaic boardwalk. Somehow, she remained on her feet and spread out horizontally the width of the sidewalk. At the last moment, she dove to the other side and fell two feet down, head first, into the hot beach sand.

Stuart rushed forward and jumped down into the sand. He helped her back up and saw she had scraped her knee. "I have never seen anyone think so quickly as you do, Phyl, when you fall. I swear you have some cat in you because I've seen you fall so many times and land right side up." He brushed her down as she pushed her sandy hair behind her ears.

She looked around, embarrassed, making sure not too many people stopped to stare. She saw a bulky cement bench. "I guess my number isn't up because this could have been really bad." She looked back at the sidewalk she had just flown over. "I could've split my head quite easily, especially on that cement bench right in front of us. I don't know how I missed that."

"Well, you're going to be sore for a couple of days. Come, let's settle down first before getting saltwater on that raw scrape of yours." He looked at the Gloria Hotel. "We'll go next door for a cocktail."

Phyl limped along with Stuart onto the sidewalk and across the road to the Gloria Hotel. As they settled down into a soft, velvet settee in the lounge, the elevator door opened on the mezzanine with a ding. Phyl saw Jorge and Angelica in the elevator just before the door closed again. "Oh, Stu! I just saw Jorge and Angelica!"

"What? Are you sure?"

"Yes, I'm sure!"

"That would be quite the coincidence, though he comes here often for business." Stuart went to the front desk to see if Jorge and Angelica were registered. He stood at the counter, wrote a note, and handed it to the concierge. He came back and nodded. "Yup, they're registered here. I left a note for them that we're next door in the Copacabana." He bent over and kissed her on the lips. "Did you know that today is our seventh anniversary?"

"What? And we didn't even think about it until just now?"

"Well, at least we both forgot. Let's celebrate tonight with the Piñieros. Come." He held out his hand and helped her up. "We're going back to our room. You're going to freshen up."

"Oh, but the beach," Phyl complained.

"We're here another week. The beach can wait. Right now, we're going back, we'll call Jorge's room, and celebrate tonight."

The Copacabana Palace had five huge luxurious salons for gambling. After much kissing and laughter, when they got together for dinner, Jorge, Angelica, Stuart, and Phyl went gambling and drinking amongst the rich and famous from around the world. Phyl preferred the wheel and usually figured it out pretty well. Stuart dropped ten American dollars in the hole. Jorge won, and Angelica won a little. All around, the anniversary celebration was a resounding success. Late into the night, they sat for nightcaps.

"Did you know that Fred Astaire and Ginger Rogers filmed *Flying Down to Rio* here just eight years ago?" Phyl was drunk and happy. She stood up and swirled, letting the hem of her satin dress furl mid-air. "Look, I'm dancing like Ginger Rogers."

Angelica laughed.

"You could be a Ginger Rogers, being just as good a dancer as she is."

Phyl waved at Jorge, pleased. "Oh, Jorge. That's not true."

"No, it's very true. I can't take my eyes off you when you dance."

Phyl blushed and swayed drunkenly on her feet. "Oh, you."

"Well, I hate to disappoint you, Phyl, but we just missed Walt Disney, Bing Crosby, Douglas Fairbank, Jr., and Ed Sullivan at our hotel. They were here just months ago."

Phyl looked at Stuart, aghast. "No!"

"Yes," Stuart laughed.

Phyl threw up her hands. "Why didn't they wait for me."

"Oh, and your old friend, Errol Flynn, was here."

"You know Errol Flynn?" asked Angelica, surprised.

Stuart laughed. "No, she doesn't. But she was within spitting distance."

Jorge and Angelica laughed. Jorge sat up straight and cracked his neck. He put his drink and cigarette down. "How much longer are you staying?"

"Another six days. Then we go back to our apartment in your building," said Stuart.

"Can you spare a few days?"

"A few days more, you mean?"

Jorge nodded.

Stuart looked at him, a serious expression on his face. He pondered on Jorge for a moment. Stuart nodded silently. He looked at Phyl. Phyl was watching him quietly.

Jorge looked around. "There's a military attaché I want you to meet. He would be a good contact for you. He works here in Brazil."

Stuart, serious now, nodded silently.

"Angelica can return to Buenos Aires with Phyl on the Argentina next Friday. You and I will follow two weeks after on the Brazil."

"Right."

Phyl looked at Angelica, then at Jorge. "So, are you guys going to be okay? No guns involved?"

"Of course not. No, we'll be fine. But there are a few things we need to look into while in Brazil. Too many ears and eyes in Argentina. Here, we have more freedom to move around undetected and talk. But that's all I'll say. Except that things are brewing here in the military as well. Argentina is becoming a problem child claiming neutrality but stubbornly covering for the Nazi Fifth Column." He looked around, then down at his hands.

"But…" Phyl didn't like surprises.

"Listen, you'll have a French Princess, a Russian Duchess, and an Argentine movie star on board," added Jorge. "I heard it from the horse's mouth."

Phyl sat back. "Which horse is that?"

Jorge zippered his lips.

"Oh, well, in *that* case."

* * *

The Duchess and Princess were the worst dressed and rudest passengers Phyl had ever met.

But at least, once they arrived in Buenos Aires, Phyl had terrific things to write about. On the bright side, she and Angelica had met a charming, cultured Brazilian lady who took a liking to them. This woman was very wealthy and took them around in her chauffeured car. She bought Phyl orchids and fed her and Angelica an extravagant lunch in her apartment. They had a cornocopia of French wines and champagne. The woman adored the United States and Canada, having traveled across both countries. Apparently, she had been treated exceptionally well by both, so she wanted to show her appreciation. Phyl was moved when she discovered that the woman had just lost her little girl to infantile paralysis and was chronically broken over it. It was her only child. Life crashed.

When Phyl thought about her new friend and her loss of a child, she cried with a shattered heart. She cried over El leaving her only child. And she cried for herself, for the child who had not yet come and seemed to be taking its time. Perhaps, never.

To add to her meloncholy, letters to Canada and back were fewer and further between as the war progressed. Much mail was lost through torpedoed mail boats, so Phyl wrote airmail, though it was five times more expensive and still not a given. She refused to write long epistles, especially by hand, and send them by sea when there were only two chances in fifty they would survive.

In December, the war took yet another monstrous turn.

While most slept, just before 8:00 a.m. Hawaiian time on December 7th, the Imperial Japanese Navy struck the American Naval Base in Pearl Harbor. Four American Navy battleships were sunk, and four were crippled. Three destroyers, cruisers, minelayers, and an anti-aircraft training ship were also sunk. One hundred eighty aircraft were destroyed, 2,403 Americans killed, and 1,178 wounded. Power stations, shipyards, and a dry dock were blown to shreds.

To Phyl and Stuart's living horror, the United States declared war on Japan.

President Castillo declared an emergency, but his government resisted pressure from the United States to get every Latin American country to join the Allies. The Japanese attack spawned a continent-wide enmity for the Axis. Argentina stoically remained neutral. Naturally, more pressure from the States.

All the more, Argentina resisted, and relations between the United States and Argentina worsened.

As a Canadian and American couple, the situation was much more surreal for Phyl and Stuart.

In 1942, they decided to take up another offer to stay at the *estancia* with Jorge, Angelica and their family. Living in the city was like lingering near a tinderbox about to explode. When Stuart was given nudges to lay low, they decided to leave Mercedes to run the home and take Tony with them indefinitely. Stuart's meetings tended to be out of town now anyway, so he would take the train and go for a week or so when needed. But when he left, at least he knew Phyl would be all right.

One morning, while Stuart was back from one of his trips, he opened the newspaper at breakfast on the terrace. The breeze off the eternal fields lifted the scalloped edges of the awnings, causing them to make startled flapping sounds above his head. It was cool. Winter. But the sun was low, comforting on the skin. Stuart wore a white shirt with a large collar and a heavy cardigan. He no longer had a thin pencil mustache, and had allowed it to grow thicker and broader. His face had filled in, and he had acquired the paunch of a maturing man. He held a hand to his cheek as he read.

Phyl appeared, dressed in her winter riding clothes. She watched Stuart nibble carefully on a piece of freshly baked bread with a plate of eggs, holding the newspaper with one hand.

"Still have a toothache?"

Stuart nodded without looking up.

"More bad news?" asked Phyl. She sat down and nodded to the servant who placed a *café crema* before her.

Stuart looked grim. "If being at war isn't bad enough, things seem to be unraveling here."

"Surprise, surprise," said Phyl, adding sugar to her coffee and mixing it with a silver spoon. "Where's Jorge? I know Angelica's with the baby."

"I don't know."

"I can't believe they have six children now. She just keeps popping them out."

She was tempted to feel sorry for herself. She sighed. It was a strange contradiction. She didn't like children, but she didn't mind Angelica's. She knew of women who died during childbirth and babies being born not quite right, so, fear nibbled at the back of her mind. They were indeed trying their best. She shook her head and grabbed a piece of bread from Stuart's plate. "So, how are things getting worse?"

"It's Ortiz. Even though Roosevelt had sent his best American ophthalmologist to treat him, it hasn't done any good. He's now blind and handed in his resignation yesterday with two years left in office."

Phyl worried about what was coming around the corner. More violence? More threats?

"Remember I mentioned Perón and the group he was involved with?"

"*Accion Argentina* or something like that?"

"Hmm," nodded Stuart. He sipped his coffee. He put the cup down. "They're still trying to push being part of the Allies."

"That's good, right?"

"You'd think so. But Argentina is a problem child, isn't it? It's just as much fascist as it is Nazi, and the rest go with the flotsam. It's a nasty predicament."

Jorge appeared, dressed heavily, ready for what he obviously thought was a cooler morning. "Good morning," he smiled. He bent over Phyl and gave her a kiss on the cheek. She did the same. He pulled a chair out and sat between her and Stuart. "Good sleep?" he asked Stuart.

"Always an excellent sleep. Much quieter than the city."

Jorge laughed. "I feel better here," he said, looking around the terrace. "We're under siege, but when I'm home, here, I can pretend all is well." A servant placed a black coffee before him. He didn't look up. "Though the *estancia* books reflect the uncertain times we live in."

"Stuart's business is suffering, too." Phyl picked up her napkin, wiped her mouth, then swept the napkin across her lap to rid crumbs.

Jorge squinted at Stuart.

"There is no use selling machines here I can't get. I've lost a few thousand in commission already, not being able to fill orders. That's why I go to Uruguay to drum up business, as Uruguay can get machines but not Argentina."

"Can't you just fill the orders here and then get the typewriters in through Uruguay?" asked Phyl.

"The cost of shipping from Uruguay, plus the customs and bribes involved, increases the price exorbitantly. I might as well just do business there." He looked down at his plate and skewered a piece of roasted lamb. "Besides, it's been good to be staying out of the city." He looked at Jorge. "And information is easier to get at and pass along through the contacts in Uruguay now anyhow. We're really watched in the city. I always get the feeling I'm being followed. In fact, I know I am."

"Does that mean I am, too?" asked Phyl. She picked up a spoon and lightly tapped her thumb with it. "I ask because the ladies at the Club have asked me to work at the Red Cross sometime this month. Helping out usually ends up being more social, but a few really go down there to work, like me."

"I don't know. We'll look into that. Things seem to have settled down in the city and it may be time to return in a week or two. So, I guess you can do your Red Cross stint."

Stuart suddenly let his fork drop onto the plate with a clatter. He cradled his face.

"I know a dentist in Rio Negro," said Jorge. "I'll get you an appointment for tomorrow. You've been suffering for a while. This won't go away."

"Cloves have been helping, thanks to Angelica," said Phyl.

Stuart took a deep breath and opened his eyes. They were watery. His face squinted under the pain. "Okay," he whispered.

Jorge snapped his fingers and pointed to the phone by the door. The servant brought the phone over, its long cord unraveling perfectly as he walked to the table. Jorge dialed, spoke briefly, and hung up. "You have a 3:00 appointment."

"Oh, thank goodness," said Phyl. A servant walked over with an envelope and held it out to her. "Oh, *gracias*," she said with surprise. She took Stuart's knife, wiped it on her napkin, and slit open the envelope. "Oh, it's from Berndt."

Stuart's eyebrows shot up. "Berndt? The Swede on the ship?

"Yes, remember how he always said he needed someone who can speak English and Spanish to work in the office? He still can't find anybody suitable. He's sent me another job offer. What perfect timing."

Jorge pushed his chair to lean back. "Berndt August Hjorth? He and his wife are tenants of mine. They live a couple of floors below you."

Phyl looked up. "Yes, that's them. Meeting you in Rio was very lucky for them. They were worried about finding an apartment in Buenos Aires, and there you were, graciously giving them one on the spot."

"Timing is always important," Jorge joked. "I understand his business requires much correspondence all over the world."

"I guess you know, they normally spend their life traveling due to his work."

"Precisely. I suppose you know, Berndt has to get steel from German companies. We have a pretty good idea of what is going on in steel manufacturing in Germany by doing business with them here on neutral territory." Jorge looked at Stuart. "All the steel and shipping businesses are covering up spy activities." He took a sip of his coffee, eyeing him.

Stuart quetly sipped his coffee, acknowledging his look.

"Berndt's tenancy is short-term. He's only staying in Buenos Aires for the duration of the war."

"Which could be a year or more," offered Stuart.

"Or twenty. We don't know," said Jorge.

"Well, he's been looking for some time for a girl with qualifications like that of my father's very talented offspring." Phyl smiled proudly, pointing at herself. She looked at Stuart.

Stuart cradled his face, nodded. He looked sideways at Jorge.

Phyl happily continued. "Last time we were out for dinner, he again said he hadn't been able to find anyone, so I said, very brazenly, if the wages were right, I might have a whack at it, but he'll probably regret it once I start." She laughed.

"Oh, I doubt that," mumbled Stuart.

"Well, I'm very pleased to have something to do," said Phyl. "I don't know if you know, but they both speak beautiful English, French, German, and Swedish. However, neither speaks Spanish. That's why he needs a girl who could take that worry away. It's good practice for me, too. I'll be taking his letters, just like I did for Schuler in Toronto. He draws pictures of gang saws, and I'll have to do some calculations with decimal points and percentages, which will probably be a disastrous exercise."

"Well, I'm pleased." Stuart threw his napkin onto the plate and sat back. "Now I can retire completely from both sales and spying and concentrate on my golf and bowling."

"Well, it's only a five-half-day week job as secretary, translator, and a general office girl for an export manager of a large Swedish company."

"Well, I'm glad that's finally set up." Stuart smiled at Phyl.

"Set up?" Phyl looked at Stuart curiously. "Set up?" She looked at Jorge. She frowned. "So, this is another *movie* role set up by *you*?" she asked Jorge.

Jorge cocked his head. "We've had to scramble to set up a new system of communication, Phyl. We have the radio here, but we're blind if we continue to stay here on the *estancia*." He looked at Stuart. "And Stuart's trips to Uruguay have been fruitful, but we have no eyes on the ground in Argentina anymore." He looked kindly at Phyl. "Phyl, you don't mind, do you? You'll have your finger on the pulse in terms of what's going on behind the scenes. You'll be right in the thick of it."

"Is that why Berndt was so persistent in this job offer?"

"You are the perfect candidate. He can't trust anyone other than someone we can all vet."

Phyl looked away, thoughtful of the paradigm shift she was nudged into. An Alice in Wonderland feel of walking through the Looking Glass. Everything suddenly looked very transfixed. She saw herself typing code into letters, translating obscure numbers, and taking home work to pass on to Stuart to filter and relay to God knew who. She abruptly sobered. She sat up and looked down at her lap.

"Well, we *are* under siege. And what a damn shame I can't write about this to any of my family or friends." She paused, seeing the Looking Glass ahead of her. "It's like the movie I always imagined. Living a high life in Argentina, served by servants." She motioned to a servant puttering around a platter of cakes. "And spying, to boot." She looked up at Stuart.

Stuart admired her silently.

They could hear children chatting and laughing in the house. The Innocents.

"I couldn't do this if I had children, could I?" she said. It wasn't a question. She knew.

Stuart looked down at his hands. "We have no control over that, Phyl. But it does mean you are a very valuable—"

"Asset," quipped Phyl.

Angelica and her bouncing munchkins came through the glass doors with wooden shotguns. One the five-year-olds pretended to shoot Stuart, who mockingly grabbed his chest and pretended to die.

This sobered their Mata Hari.

* * *

Eighteen days later.

Stuart was in the kitchen bent over a toaster. He was still smoking a cigarette and held a spray can of Nafta. Tony at his feet, watched him.

"We'll be in Kingdom Come by morning if you keep spraying Nafta under your cigarette," Phyl yelled from the table, her nostrils spazzing from the smell. She listened to the radio while writing a letter to K. The program was suddenly interrupted by a commercial promoting an upcoming movie. Her ears stood to attention. *Una Novia en Apuros.* "A bride in trouble," she translated to herself, her hold on the language now very functional. Eva Duarte was in it. Phyl grunted.

Mercedes suddenly bolted out of the kitchen, looking frightened, scared. "*¿Oh, Dios. Nosotras vamos a explotar?*"

Phyl shook her head, "*No, no vamos a explotar.*" She raised her voice so that Stuart could hear her. "We're not going to explode, right, Stu? You're smoking while you're doing that, aren't you!"

"Yeah. No. Not at all. So long as it's unplugged, it's okay. Oh, wait."

Mercedes grabbed the top of her uniform. "Ayayay."

"It's okay. It's unplugged now," yelled Stuart.

Phyl gasped and rolled her eyes.

Mercedes did the sign of the cross and hurried into the bedroom. Tony's head poked out from the kitchen. Then he ran after Mercedes, wagging his tail.

Phyl watched him disappear into the bedroom, then returned to her letter.

Speaking of food, it must be the dickens up there looking for ration stuff. You should've seen the shops here for Christmas – packed with every kind of food and liquor and people buying at three times pre-war price.

A couple weekends ago, we went to Mar del Plata with Jorge and Angelica. I sent along to you a couple of pictures. We arrived home without a cent in our pockets, having left it in the casino, so I had to reign in for Christmas. Fortunately, we were invited for lunch on Christmas Day at some good friends, and went to a movie and had dinner with another couple, so I didn't have to buy a turkey. Christmas Eve, we stayed home and had a bottle of champagne and thought of you folks. Stu bought me a lovely compact made in Morocco with a saddle of ivory, rare French perfume, and a box of bonbons. I gave him an ice bucket with Spanish proverbs, two bottles of Chilean wine, suspenders, hankies, etc. Mercedes gave me a nice glass jar for the bathroom, and I gave her two pairs of silk stockings – which are a delicacy these days – and a manicure set. Stu gave her candies. Friends gave me Chanel 22 perfume and Stuart a bottle of Crème de Cacao liquor. I received an enormous bunch of gladioli from a business acquaintance from Sweden. But the things that gave us the most pleasure were a letter from you, a card from Claude - the most beautiful card I've ever seen - and a letter from Stuart's mother.

It was a scorcher for Christmas day, 100°. Before Christmas Eve, it rained, but it was hot for Christmas just so we wouldn't be disappointed, and cool after.

Still haven't heard anything from the Embassy. Tonight, we are having the Military Attaché for dinner. That's all I'll say, and you know why.

This country is overrun with European refugees, mostly Jews. They are an asset to any country. A good healthy pulse in terms of workers, the others? Don't ask.

I started a job. Half days. I love it and was relieved as I hate to leave the apartment so long in the hands of the maid. Mercedes is honest, but she has been with us for 5 years and is beginning to take a few liberties.

The radio program was again interrupted by a news bulletin. Phyl stopped writing and listened.

> *The 18th president of the republic, former president Roberto M. Ortiz, died this morning of bronchial pneumonia, which followed maladies of a chronic nature. He was 55 years old. His death caused deep sorrow in his people, but purely as a human tragedy and not part of the country's political drama since he had resigned from the presidency on June 24. Dr. Ortiz's body was moved to Cassa Rosada, where it will lie in state until tomorrow when burial will take place in the Recoleta Cemetery. He will receive a state funeral. A decree issued today concedes to him all honors that are granted to presidents who die in office.*

"Did you hear that, Stu?"

Stuart moved to the kitchen doorway. "Yes, it was inevitable." He went back to the toaster.

The timer in the kitchen went off to remind her she should start dinner.

"Timer's going," yelled Stuart.

"I can hear it, silly." She got up. "I need my kitchen now, Stu. Mercedes and I have to get supper prepared for tonight." She walked to the kitchen and looked in.

Stuart was sitting on the floor with a screwdriver stuck into the toaster. "Good call," she said.

"What?"

"Unplugging it first."

"Shut up."

Phyl laughed.

"I missed my toast this morning. Damn, if I have another breakfast without it."

"Do we need to ask Mercedes to stay at her sister's tonight? Are you guys going to talk about important things or just chat about normal stuff?" Phyl stepped back into the doorway and looked at the bedroom door. She whispered. "I wonder if she heard the announcement. She may be too upset with the death of her president."

"I don't know. You can ask her." He put the screwdriver aside. "No, tonight it's mostly chat. Though he's bringing over paperwork for me."

"To put in the safe?"

"Yes."

Stuart struggled to get up. He'd gained a few pounds in the last year. He raised his hand for her to grab. She took it with both hands and helped him to his feet. He brushed himself down.

"He's got highly classified information. Both on Japanese spies in Brazil who are purportedly on their way here and information transmitted from the Argentina Under Secretary for Foreign Affairs to the Ambassador's office."

"Ah, our friend the ambassador. How *is* Norman? I miss them."

"He's okay. From what I can gather." Stuart picked up the screwdriver and toaster and tested the lever several times. "There, it's unstuck. Now let's give it a try." He fiddled with the electrical cord. "I also asked him over because I really like him. He's been in Brazil since last year but has been waiting to be transferred to active service. Remember when I had coffee with him in Rio? Nice guy, right?"

Phyl remembered him. He was a good-looking man, a little older than Stuart. They had gone off somewhere to talk or meet someone, but she didn't know exactly. "I do remember him. I liked him. And his name is easy to remember: Camilo Gay. Rhymes with May, haha. A poet, and I didn't know it."

"Yeah, Lieutenant Colonel Camilo Gay. Anyhow, it'll be nice to catch up."

"Why does he want to go back to active service?"

"Well, he's having a hard time." He searched for the power switch on the side of the toaster.

"Hard time?"

"Yeah, like you were. This secret stuff can really frazzle your nerves at times."

"Don't I know it!"

Stuart turned the toaster on and placed it at the highest setting. He picked up a slice of bread near the sink and stuck it in. "Well, here goes." He pushed down the lever. It buzzed and cracked, and the bread popped into flames.

Phyl screamed and she jumped to the sink to run water.

"No, no water! Pull the plug!"

Phyl yanked out the plug. Stuart threw the toaster into the sink and doused it. The toaster sizzled and popped - like what the bread was supposed to do.

Mercedes appeared at the kitchen doorway, wide-eyed. "*¿Qué pasó?*"

"We were talking about frazzled nerves?"

Stuart made a face. "Oops."

Later that evening.

Lieutenant Colonel Gay finished his coffee and dessert. He wiped his mouth and looked around for Mercedes. He was ruddy-complexioned, medium height. A charming enough face. He had spoken of his wife and children, his youth; it was an enjoyable evening. But now, he turned towards the sombre. He took a drag from his cigarette, diverted the smoke to the overhead light, and banked conspiratorially.

Stuart and Phyl closed in to listen to what he was about to share.

About to start confessional, Gay looked gently at Phyl. Then at Stuart. "I won't be upsetting Phyl if I talk shop?"

"No, not at all," Stuart said, nodding at Phyl.

Phyl shook her head and folded her hands on the table.

Gay tapped his cigarette against the ashtray. "Apart from all this ongoing shit," to Phyl, "Sorry."

"I know the word for kaka," Phyl joked.

Gay sighed. "Well, this ongoing shit about exchanging *pesos* and American dollars by people within the ministry. We still don't know who's skimming or charging extra to convert the money. But we think the skimmed money is diverted to the *Accion Argentina* group by the *Grupo de Oficiales Unidos*."

"Oh?"

"We're seeing more evidence that Perón, who has just been promoted to full colonel, is masterminding this. He may have devised this way of bankrolling their activities without it being on the official books."

"Yes. I know the head office is watching him. They think he's a mover and a shaker, but no one mentioned that little tidbit."

"Perón's being groomed for -"

"Hmm. President. *One* day."

"Well, anyhow, I thought I'd mention that. Keep an eye on developments."

Stuart fiddled with his coffee spoon. "Thank you. Anything about Japanese spies in that valise you brought along?"

"Well, it's a moot point, though you have a report. The spies were arrested today in Brazo."

Stuart grunted thoughtfully. "It just gets more interesting by the day."

"Don't we all know it," laughed Gay.

"It's fine, so long as we can all talk about it once it's over," said Phyl grimly.

Gay lowered his gaze and nodded silently, slowly stirring his cigarette through the ashtray.

* * *

Months later, on a Sunday morning.

Phyl saw something in the New York Times sent by her father and K. It had arrived on Friday, but she hadn't had time to give it a good read-through. Tucked into the bottom corner of one of the pages, almost as an afterthought, she read the following, and gasped:

Special Cable to THE NEW YORK TIMES.

RIO DE JANEIRO, Brazil, August 14 — The body of Lieut. Col. Camilo Gay, 44 years old. Argentine Military Attaché in Brazil was found in a cave in a lonesome spot on Gavea Road. He had been shot dead. His automobile was found nearby, and a wallet with $50 in his pocket. Lieut. Col. Gay had been in Brazil since February 1941. Some time ago, he requested a transfer to active Army service.

Whether it was the shock of his death and all that it implied, or the ongoing rain and humidity, Phyl and Stuart ended up quite ill in bed for over a week. Phyl needed sedation, and Stuart had a nasty case of bronchitis, on the verge of pneumonia. All Phyl could think of that whole time was how much fun they had in Rio de Janeiro while, all along, it was just an interlude before Camilo, whom they met there, would be found dead in a cave within minutes' drive from the beach they swam in.

This did not bode well for Phyl. There were days she simply did not want to wake up because she felt in her bones things would only worsen.

And worsen, they did.

Chapter Fifteen

More Coups, Eva, Perón and a Surprise Declaration of a Different War

"Phyl!"

Stuart barged into the flat. Sweating, looking toward the phone on the bar. He saw Mercedes draped over the counter in her maid's outfit, slightly askew. She played with the thick cord while happily chatting in her usual machine-gun Spanish.

"Mercedes!"

She jumped, seeing Stuart in the doorway, with a look of panic, and quickly hung up.

"¿Que?" asked Mercedes, looking as if she had been caught stealing something red-handed.

His voice cracked with duress, having obviously run a great distance in haste. "I've been trying to call through, damn it!" He lunged to the bedroom. "Phyl!"

"Señora en el techo colgando la ropa," croaked Mercedes.

A deep rumble shook the walls. Stuart held the door open and glared at Mercedes. "What the hell is she doing up there hanging wash while you're standing there monopolizing the phone? That's for emergencies, not for your personal entertainment!"

He ran off, Mercedes close to tears.

Stuart hit the stairs to the roof two at a time. His loafers skidded on a dusty marble step near the top. The door to the roof was open, and a cold wind rushed through. He burst onto the roof, wheezing, and coughing, and looked around the wash lines. He saw sheets billowing from the updraft of an icy breeze off the bay.

"Phyl!"

"I'm here, Stu." She sounded terrified.

She leaned over the cement wall facing the parks, the docks, and *Casa Rosada*, the presidential palace. Smoke rose from the city streets leading to the pink structure. Phyl ran to Stuart and held him tightly.

"Stu, what's happening. Are we being invaded?"

Stuart looked down into her pale face. She had lost weight again and had just gotten over a cold, the usual with the damp winters. The last thing she needed was yet another traumatic shock.

"No, it's a coup." He held her tightly. "I've been trying to call through to warn you. I wanted to make sure you were home. Things are getting out of hand."

Stuart shook his head. "Our apartment doesn't face the right direction; otherwise, I'd be watching through the telescope."

"Bring it up here, Stu. Set it up here."

Stuart looked around the pebbled deck of the roof. If it had been any colder, there would've been snowflakes whipped about in the stiff wind. Even the wet sheets looked as if they were stiff in the breeze. He shivered, coughed, and held her closer. "No. Too cold." He looked at her from head to toe. "And why aren't you wearing a coat? It's winter, for crying out loud."

"It was only going to take a few moments."

He took her hand and led her back to the stairs. "We're going to Jorge's. We can see from their flat. I'll give him a call."

Phyl tried her best to keep up with Stuart as he pulled her down the stairs. She almost tripped and fell, so he stopped briefly to let her catch up, and he put an arm around her and led her more sensibly.

"So, a coup? Did you know it was coming?" gasped Phyl.

They reached their floor and hurried along the hallway. Another rumble.

"It's been in the workings for a couple of years," Stuart yelled. "We just didn't know when it would happen. It's the United Officers Group, remember? The *Grupo de Oficiales Unidos*. It's Perón."

They burst into their flat. Mercedes was at the glass balcony doors, craning her neck to see if she could see more in the direction of the booming.

"*Ay, Dios mío. ¿Lo que está sucediendo?*" Mercedes asked, fear etched on her face. She was wringing her worn hands.

"It's a coup, Mercedes," Stuart answered in Spanish. "They're ousting the president."

"*Ayayay*," cried Mercedes, hands to her cheeks. She did the sign of the cross.

Stuart picked up the phone and dialed. He scolded the slow-moving rotary dial. He sighed loudly out of frustration. He banged down on the phone and started to dial again. He glanced at Phyl, shivering at the table, looking lost. "Get your coat on, Phyl." To Mercedes, he ordered, "Mercedes, you stay here and lock the door behind us."

Mercedes and Phyl looked at each other frightfully. Phyl searched the corners of the apartment and clapped her hands. Tony came slinking in from the kitchen, low on the floor. "I'm taking Tony."

Stuart listened to the ringtone at the other end of the phone. He shook his head. "No, leave him here with Mercedes."

Stuart talked to Jorge in clipped tones. Phyl looked at the calendar hanging over the bar. Friday, June 4, 1943. A familiar feeling that it was all too much to bear washed over her. She shook her head and touched her forehead. "The world is already so crazy. Lord, don't these people know when to stop? Enough is enough!"

Stuart hung up. "Phyl, your coat!"

* * *

Jorge and Stuart stood on Jorge's balcony, watching the activities at the palace and the streets through their respective telescopes.

"It looks like about 4,000 soldiers," yelled Stuart.

"Actually, more. Look at the trucks coming down from the north. I'd say maybe another thousand."

Angelica and Phyl stood at the doors, shivering in their coats. Inside the flat, the Piñiero children, one of them holding the youngest in his arms. The servants gathered behind the children. The glass doors rattled from the shock wave of an explosion. The children jumped back, startled. The toddler cried. Angelica swirled around and tapped at the glass, trying to get the toddler's attention.

"Stu, I want to see," said Phyl, stepping forward.

Stuart stood back from the telescope and motioned for her to look. Jorge did the same for Angelica. The women bent over the viewers.

Phyl saw smoke rise from burning cars along the boulevard in front of the pink palace. She swivelled the telescope to the left, further up the boulevard and saw men pushing and rocking a small bus until it toppled over. Then, the men ran to a streetcar and attempted the same. "Oh, my God," Phyl whispered. Suddenly, she saw a flash as the smaller bus burst into flames, the bottom blowing out toward the crowd, forcing men to scatter in all directions. A second later, the concussion and roar of the explosion reached the balcony.

"Geez, I hope no one got killed."

"What do you think they'll do with Castillo? Will they kill him?" asked Angelica.

"I doubt that. They'd lose their heads if they lost their attempt in this uprising. You just don't do that to presidents." Stuart shivered in his coat.

Phyl laughed sarcastically. "They're so good at being gentlemanly when they take over with their guns. That must make it all right!"

Jorge put his arm around Angelica's shoulders. She had gained weight with every child but looked quite content, not at all concerned about the extra handles. In contrast, Phyl looked like a little waif.

"Once it settles down, which it will, I need to get to the palace and join the crowd." Stuart put his hands in the pockets and jiggled coins.

Jorge squinted at Stuart. "I think we should go now."

"No, Jorge. You will not go there! You could get killed." Angelica looked close to tears. She turned to look at the children, who stood terrified.

Stuart simply walked past Angelica, opened the doors, and waited for the children to step to the side. The servants moved away quickly and disappeared. Phyl followed him into the flat. She yanked at the hem of his jacket.

"Stu! Don't!"

Stuart turned and looked briefly, ditching acknowledgement. Jorge entered and walked past them. Stuart stubbed out his cigarette, and followed Jorge to the door.

Jorge, car keys in hand, didn't look back at Angelica. She stood helplessly inside the doors, her arms around her children.

"Jorge, the car! They could burn the car. These people are crazy," she said, frantically.

"We'll drive only so far, and then we do the rest on foot." Jorge opened the door and waited for Stuart.

"Oh, for crying out loud. WHY!?" Phyl turned red in the face as she glared at Stuart.

Stuart turned to her. "You know why, Phyl. We have to. We're eyes for a larger concern here. Remember that." He left with Jorge, and the door closed behind them.

Deep into the night. Angelica and Phyl sat quietly worried at the dining room table, empty coffee cups at their elbows, wringing damp handkerchiefs. The clock ticked loudly on the white marble mantle. The radio was on low as they had been listening to live reporting of the uprising. They could still hear the distant roar of angry voices.

Angelica's head suddenly dropped, but shook immediately awake and settled into a more comfortable position.

Phyl lowered her head and rested it on her arm on the table.

Startled, they sat upright and turned at the sound of the door opening.

Phyl jumped up, almost knocking over her cup. "Oh, Stu! We were so worried!" She raced to the door.

Stuart and Jorge looked tired, their faces haggard and dust-covered, their coats stained and filthy.

Angelica glared at Jorge. She pointed at his coat. "Did they accost you?"

Stuart took off his coat. "No, but we were caught between soldiers throwing tear gas. We couldn't see a thing and were knocked over."

Phyl took the coat from him, looked at it, and draped it over her arm. "We'll get you a new coat," she said glumly. She went back to the table and sat down heavily.

Jorge walked to the table and pulled out a chair. He spied the coffee pot, removed the lid, and peered in. He felt the side of the pot. "Cold," he said.

Angelica picked up a little bell and rang it. A tired-looking servant came in, saw Jorge holding the cold pot of coffee, and nodded. He took the pot and left.

"So, who is *el presidente* today?" asked Angelica wearily.

"General Arturi Rawson," Jorge said.

"General Rawson?" said Angelica, surprised. "Not Perón?"

Jorge shook his head. "Not Perón. I suspect he's happy controlling things in the background."

"Do you think he's biding his time with the war and all? He'd have to show his cards, wouldn't he, and show his Nazi streak? The Americans wouldn't like that one bit." Angelica sat down and crossed her arms.

Phyl looked at Angelica, surprised at how informed she sounded.

"You said that while he was in Italy, he appreciated the notion of authoritarian rule as the only way to impose effective reforms," continued Angelica. "That, in itself, sounds like a very frightening prospect. Like what reforms? Getting rid of us, the landowners? Does he want communist rule?"

"He does have some socialist leanings, and he's Nazi-trained." Stuart coughed.

"I remember you saying he studied at a Nazi military college?" asked Phyl.

"Yes, and we know he, like the rest of the military, is pretty confident the Axis will win." He sighed. "I mean, look at how well Germany's been doing." Stuart counted his fingers as he spoke. "They have superior equipment. They have an army made up of brainwashed youth they started programming years ago —"

Phyl shuddered. "Hitler's Youth. We know the type, don't we."

"The poor kids. They're programmed to fight to their deaths. I mean, look at all the German victories of late?"

"Oh, don't say that, Stu. It sounds like a done deal. Surely, we just have to win!" Phyl's eyes were wide and hollow.

"Well, let's see what this Rawson says and does before we jump to conclusions."

"I've never heard of this General Rawson."

Stuart smiled. "There are a lot of 'em generals, aren't there?"

"They seem to be coming out of the woodwork," said Phyl.

The servant returned with a hot pot of coffee and more *crema*. Phyl touched Angelica's reaching hand. "Please, I'll pour." Phyl took a couple of clean cups and poured coffee. "So, now what?" she asked, handing Jorge his coffee.

"Well," started Jorge. "We pass on what we witnessed today and live another day in another regime."

"Hmm. Same war, same craziness, different faces, with a slightly different mission." Stuart looked at Jorge, who looked worried. "We just have to wait till tomorrow and see what kind of stripes they'll begin to show. Lord knows what changes will be made."

"Do you think they'll stay neutral?" asked Phyl.

"They'd have to stay neutral," said Angelica. She raised her hands and let them drop on the table. "They'd be crazy not to."

"Well, the regime is encouraging Nazi refugees to come at a pretty penny each and harboring thirty U-boats down the shore." Stuart nervously tapped the table with his fingers.

"U-boats down the shore? That's not being neutral." Phyl was aghast. Fearful.

"What are they doing there? Will they attack us?" asked Angelica.

Jorge shook his head. "Some fantastic murmurings of them setting up a base in Antarctica."

Phyl let out a sound of disgust. "Wow."

"If we were to get proof of this sneaky and lucrative sideline of extorting Nazi refugees," continued Stuart, "it would certainly put them at odds with the Allies." He held up his empty cup with a pleading look at Phyl. "Never mind allowing those U-boats a safe refuge. These Nazis come to jobs and homes already waiting for them. That's all part of their deal. And we shouldn't kid ourselves. They're everywhere. Living and working right under our noses."

Phyl slowly poured coffee into Stuart's mug and added a dash of *crema*. She looked as if she was going to be ill. She sat back, put the pot and *crema* on the table, and blinked. She was stunned. "Oh, my God. Crazy."

Stuart held the steaming coffee to his nose and inhaled. Then he lowered the cup slowly, cocked his head, and stared at Phyl.

Phyl covered her mouth and returned the stare, tears welling in her eyes.

* * *

"I just hope if Stuart is called to fight for Uncle Sam, it won't be until the Fall so that it's still Spring here so that we don't freeze up there, as our blood is so thinned out," yelled Phyl.

She carefully sipped on a comforting cup of tea. She waved smoke away from her eyes, sent from a Club member nearby who unknowingly blew in her direction.

"I would imagine the fuel problem is pretty bad back home, Phyl," Vivienne yelled. "So, two consecutive summer seasons would be ideal." She stopped to sip her tea and then took a drag on her cigarette stuck in an elegant holder studded with sapphires. She blew the smoke away from Phyl.

Phyl looked at the tray of cookies at the end of the banquet table. She bit her lip. She looked through a wall of smoke at the women gathered in the American Women's Club main room. "I hope this meeting starts soon. I'm getting nervous about getting home on time."

"Why are you afraid to be out and about?" Vivienne looked around for the Club president and the featured speaker for the day. The topic was what foreigners were to expect in the new regime.

"No. I want to be home in time to listen to Radio Belgrano."

Vivienne tapped her cigarette onto the edge of her saucer. "You're still hooked on that Eva Whatshername?"

"She intrigues me. She's not exceptionally pretty. She's not exceptionally talented. Her voice is getting better, though. She no longer screeches. And lately, she seems to get the odd larger part." Phyl made a face. "I don't understand how she manages to get work. I think I have more talent in my little finger than she'll ever have in her entire being, so what gives?"

Vivienne's eyes sparkled, and she smiled impishly. "I think I have a fairly good idea. You want some juicy gossip?"

Phyl brightened up and moved closer to hear better. "Sure!" She cocked her ear.

"My maid's sister is a maid to Radio Belgrano. She cleans up and helps the women with their make-up and their hair. The actors have a bit of an audience when they perform on air, right?"

"Yeah, I know." She didn't, really.

Vivienne leaned closer to Phyl's ear. "Yeah, so, as you know also, they plunked this General Ramirez in the palace replacing that other general they stuck in during the coup, and he was president for, like, what, a week?"

"General Rawson. The guy who promised the British he'd make Argentina pro-Allies."

"Yeah, poor Rawson. Our moment of hope didn't last long. I guess that didn't sit well with most of the Nazi military," Vivienne said, rolling her eyes.

"Not with Perón, certainly. Did you know he's now in charge of Labor?" Phyl smirked and shook her head. "So, about this Ramirez? What does he have to do with Eva Duarte and Radio Belgrano?"

Vivienne lowered her lids with satisfaction, shimmied her body slightly with pleasure, and smiled. "Apparently…"

"Yes…"

"Apparently, this Eva, who claims she knows everyone, said in the dressing room that she could prove she could have anyone she wanted, even if she desired to go straight to the top of their beloved country, Argentina."

Phyl laughed. "NO."

"Well, wouldn't you know it? Before their show started the other day, she picked up the phone while everyone sat and called the palace. Very loudly she told the palace who she was – as if she was some sort of hoity-toity princess – and asked to speak to President Ramirez. When he actually got on the phone, she announced who she was, told him she was a huge supporter, thought he was the country's savior, and said she was so happy to God he had become president that Argentina would be forever grateful. Then she said she wanted very much to have dinner with him."

"HA. What did he say?"

"He immediately said yes, and she arranged an evening to go in to see him." Vivienne blinked happily.

Phyl almost drooled. "Why that sl—" Phyl covered her mouth with her gloved hand and looked around. "Well, you know what I mean to say!"

"Uh-huh."

"Wow."

"Yup. That's why she doesn't rely on that little tiny bit of talent she barely has."

The knock of a gavel hitting a desk caught their attention, and Phyl looked knowingly at Vivienne as they slowly made their way amongst the chatty ladies to chairs set up in rows in front of the podium.

"I guess it's the old story."

Phyl sat down with Vivienne and balanced her cup of tea as she pulled a cigarette from the bag she had just placed on the floor. A woman beside her held out a cigarette lighter and lit her cigarette. Phyl returned the favor with a smile and leaned back to Vivienne.

"I can't wait to tell Stu. A president so easily swayed and probably so eager to share secrets with pretty new ears. Can you imagine a U.S. president sneaking women in for dalliances and possibly telling them state secrets?"

Vivienne shook her head. "Are you kidding? Absolutely not! That would never happen in a million years!"

* * *

Stuart tossed what little mail they had on the dining room table. Phyl looked up from her knitting. She was struggling with another lopsided sweater for little Stuart.

"Oh, goody." She reached for an airmail envelope. She saw the cost of the postage. "Oh, dear. I hate putting K and Dad through this extra expense."

"Well, it's either that or the mail goes down with another boat sunk by our local neighborhood Nazi sub." Stuart pulled a chair out and sat down.

"You're just in time for dins. It's almost 8:30. Did you have a good day?" Phyl asked. She carefully loosened the edge of the thin, blue envelope.

"I wouldn't call it good necessarily," Stuart coughed hard once, then twice, to clear his airways.

Mercedes came out of the kitchen, holding a T-towel. "*Señor. ¿Quiere un trago?*"

"*Gracias*, Mercedes. A whiskey." Stuart watched Mercedes go to the bar and back to the kitchen with the whiskey bottle. He listened as she chipped away at the ice block in the fridge and then at the pleasing sound of ice clinking an empty glass. He watched Phyl open the letter and squint, reading the letter to herself.

Mercedes returned with the whiskey, the ice in the glass tinkling happily as she walked. Stuart looked up and noticed her stumbling. She put her free hand out as she tried to keep her balance. He looked at Phyl, who now stared at the shaking table.

"Oh, no, Stu. What's THAT?" Phyl cried.

Stuart jumped to his feet as the floor swayed. "Earthquake! Quick. To the bathroom. Mercedes! Tony!" He hustled the two women and dog into the bathroom, put them into the claw foot tub, and stood in the doorway. The bathroom continued to shake. A crack formed in the plaster wall, and a roar bombed the window. Buenos Aires shook. Something crashed in the kitchen.

Mercedes clung to Phyl tightly in the tub. Phyl's eyes were saucers. Mercedes cried loudly, beseeching Mother Mary to help. Slowly, but in what felt like an eternity, the Armegeddon subsided. All three looked around, listening closely, waited for more shaking. Tony finally managed a bark.

Stuart relaxed. "Stay here," he demanded.

He left the bathroom, hurried to the living room, turned the radio on, and tuned it. It was in the middle of playing a rhumba. He stood at the balcony doors and looked out. It was summer, hot and muggy. Looking across the greens to Luna Park and the city streets, other than plumes of dust, nothing seemed amiss. He could see the palace in the distance. A ship's horn expressed surprise and horror. Another ship blew its horn. Finally, the music on the radio was interrupted. Stuart went to the bathroom and looked in on the ladies. "I think you'll be okay coming out."

Stuart help Phyl out of the tub, disentangling her legs from Mercedes' shaking arms. Mercedes shook her head when Stuart reached for her. He left her there with Tony and led Phyl back to the living room. He picked up his drink and killed it. He held his glass up to Phyl with a questioning look.

"Oh, my God, please, yes. Make it a big one." She held her stomach and bent over. "Shoot, what is this country doing to us? I guess this is going to be another juicy news event for K and Dad! Quick, where's my pen?" Phyl joked nervously. "Oh, Stu, they're not gonna be party-poopers again and censor any news of an earthquake, are they?"

* * *

"They say we are 'Nazis'."

Colonel Jaun Perón's voice echoed through the stadium and beyond, into the hot summer night sky. "I declare we are as far from Nazism as from any other foreign ideology."

Clearly, the colonel was emerging as the absolute authority in this new regime. He carried himself stoicly, magnificent in uniform, standing center stage, addressing seated dignitaries, actors, singers, and musicians. They had all gathered to put on a grand show and help raise funds for the earthquake victims of San Juan. The city had been almost entirely destroyed claiming over 10,000 lives. Perón's demeanor was benevolent, and he looked virile in his forties.

"We are Argentines and want, above all, the common good for Argentines. We do not want any more electoral fraud nor more lies. We do not want that those who do not work live from those who do."

In a bleacher seat, Jorge, sweating in a white tux and sitting on the other side of Angelica, leaned over her to speak to his cohort, Stuart, wiping sweat from his brow. "He means us wealthy landowners whose families have been working for centuries, of course," Jorge said grimly.

Stuart nodded slowly and sat back. He looked at Phyl, dressed in a taffeta red evening gown. He took her gloved hand. She smiled at him. He saw she was holding something in her hand. "What ya got there?" he whispered.

Phyl opened her hand. Cradled in her palm was a 1943 Canadian penny. "A new penny. Thinking of home. Look." She held it up in the light and showed one side of the copper coin. "A torch and a large 'V' for Victory," she said thoughtfully. "I hope that happens soon."

Stuart smiled and patted her hand.

Phyl sighed and looked at Eva Duarte, who she had been watching all night. At the moment, Eva sat between a member of the new military regime, Lieutenant Colonel Aníbal Imbert, and the empty seat in which Juan Perón had been sitting before getting up to the podium. Eva looked adoringly at the back of Perón's head with wide eyes. Her face was pale, framed by dark brown ringlets. She was thin-lipped, flat-chested – her lack of cleavage covered by a large bow on her strapless light blue satin dress. Her wrists were crossed over her lap and she wore long white evening gloves. Her posture was terrible, Phyl noted, as she haunched over her lap, leaning forward. Phyl also thought there was a distinct lack of sexuality, something that didn't match the stories she heard.

Earlier, during the various artists' performances, Phyl saw Eva standing near the front of the stage. There, her abundant jewelry shone and sparkled gaily under the spotlights. She was tugging at the emcee's pant leg, seemingly asking to get on the stage to say something. The emcee had shaken his head and continued on with his introduction to the coming musical number. It appeared that Eva Duarte did not have enough clout to influence the proceedings. Yet.

After the musical numbers, Eva was escorted onto the stage, placed in her chair, and invited to speak briefly. Her speech was patriotic, simple, and delivered in a working-class accent. Some in the audience applauded with enthusiasm, evidently fans of her radio appearances and movie roles. Phyl thought of the various radio roles she had heard Eva play — famous women in history: Isadora Duncan, Elizabeth I, Mme Chiang Kai-shek, Sarah Bernhardt among them. Vivienne had told Phyl that since that fateful dinner with Ramirez, Eva's salary had shot up to thousands per week, and she had gotten starring roles one after another. Eva also mysteriously acquired the position of spokeswoman for the Radio Association of Argentina. Both Vivienne and Phyl figured it was one of those 'special favors' bestowed on her by President Ramirez and it got her into the earthquake benefit as a special guest.

"Who are you looking at?" asked Stuart.

"That Eva Duarte. I'm just wondering how she got on that stage to sit with those dignitaries?" She shook her head. "Lordy, what some women wouldn't do to get to where they want."

"You are obsessed with this Eva Duarte."

Phyl shrugged. "Vivienne said she's gone from Ramirez to Perón."

Stuart looked at Perón, still droning on in his political speech. "You don't say?"

"It happened after Perón took over as Minister for Labor."

Stuart blinked at the sight of Eva Duarte looking at Perón adoringly, smiling broadly, legs crossed under her gown and her hands clasped on her lap. "Where'd you hear that?"

"At the Club. They have adjoining apartments. They're keeping it under wraps for now."

"Well, well, aren't you the one up-to-date on secrets."

"We have our own spies at the Club, you know," she said proudly.

"Well, if she's as calculating as you say she is, I'm not surprised." Stuart glanced around the sizeable stadium. "She certainly recognizes in whose hands all the control is being held." He looked back at Perón, still speaking. "Smart cookie."

Phyl slapped Stuart's arm. "Don't say you approve!"

Stuart grinned at her and shrugged. "Greek tragedies are boring without these kinds of women."

* * *

"Well, it's official," said Phyl, throwing her clutch onto the dining room table and loosening up the fingers of her gloves.

Stuart sat in his chair, smoking and reading papers. He had started wearing reading glasses, which made him look like a professor. Phyl smiled at him. She liked the image. He looked up, tearing his eyes away from what he was reading so intently. "What's official?"

"Eva and Perón. They're living together now. And boy, are we ever having a ball gossiping about that! Can you imagine? LIVING together."

"And no marriage announcement in sight," muttered Stuart, somewhat amused.

After checking to see if her gloves would last another day, Phyl turned away, took them off, and put them by the front door. "Nope. Narry an announcement in sight."

Stuart sat back and smoked. "And in a Catholic country. How undignified. What will the Pope think about that?"

Phyl rubbed her hands together and reached up to smooth down her hair. "It is so unbelievably hot. Even the open windows in the taxi couldn't get any breeze in. Vivienne and I melted away into the back seat."

"Now, that's a sight." He looked concerned.

Phyl walked closer and sat on the couch. "You okay?"

Stuart tossed the papers onto the coffee table. He shook his head and covered his eyes.

"Oh, dear," whispered Phyl. "Has this anything to do with what you were up doing with the radio all night?"

Stuart marooned his cigarette on the edge of the over-flowing ashtray. He searched through the papers and retrieved one. He handed it over to Phyl.

Phyl took the paper, and read it. Then she sat back, crossed her legs, straightened her summer skirt, and frowned. "The Argentine army, not happy with President Pedro Ramirez's support of the Allies and his proposed break with the Axis, was forced to relinquish his position and delegate his role to Vice President Edelmiro J. Farrell in what was regarded as another palace coup." Phyl looked up, shocked. "Another palace coup? Already? That's three since June."

"Read on."

"*General Farrell is an intimate friend of Colonel Juan Domingo Perón, Secretary of Labor and Welfare in the Ramirez government, and frequently mentioned as the mainspring of the reactionary 'gou' or 'colonel's group.' Only last week, the 'gou' had been credit with forcing the resignation of Foreign Minister Alberto Gilbert following reports that he favored a declaration of war against Germany.*" She looked at Stuart. "Jeepers."

Stuart shook his head. "They say it's because Ramirez is ill, so his VP had to step up." He shook his head again.

"How'd he get so ill?" asked Phyl, her mind racing to Eva Duarte. She frowned and then shook her head. "Never mind. I just had a silly idea."

Stuart pointed at the paper. "The problem is, even though they think the States and Britain will recognize the Ramirez government through Farrell, the fact is, Farrell is pro-Axis. I don't think the States will be happy with this. Perón's already asked for equipment and ammunition; they've had to remind him he's neutral. They only help countries protect themselves against the *Axis*." He picked up his cigarette and looked at it closely. Before he took a drag, he said, "Perón didn't like that one bit."

* * *

Two days later.

Elegantly dressed, Stuart and Phyl sat at a round banquet table at the Alvear Palace Hotel with their friends, American Ambassador Norman Armour, and his wife, Myra. Two embassy attachées and their wives were included in their party.

Phyl looked around the elegant, smoke-filled, Parisian-style ballroom. "I love coming here, don't you?" she asked Myra.

Myra, her dark hair piled high accentuating her cheekbones, smiled and looked at the gilded ceilings and the crystal chandeliers. "Oh, it's like we're in Paris. I really can't get over it. It's beautiful. And sitting here, it's tough to remember that there's a war going on out there." She touched Phyl's satin-gloved hand. "All the more reason why it's good to come here as often as we can," she laughed. "It's absolutely refreshing to forget about it all."

Myra looked back at the extensive band playing a tango. A tiny dark man sat at the front in the middle, playing guitar, leading the band. His fingers were a blur running up and down the strings. "And I so enjoy listening to Oscar Alemán. What an amazing musician. You know, he used to play with Josephine Baker."

"Oh, goodness. What an experience that must have been for him," said Phyl, looking at Oscar Alemán. "So, he spent a lot of time in Paris."

"Have you heard his latest record? '*Bésame Mucho*'? It's quite titillating, don't you think?" Myra smiled broader, exposing her dimples. "It puts chills up my arms."

"Oh, mine, too." Phyl turned to Stuart and playfully puckered her painted-red lips. She leaned into him. "*Bésame mucho,*" she demanded in a comical, sultry tone.

Stuart humorously eyed her funny expression and pretended to be frightened. He pulled back and coughed, laughing. Everyone at the table laughed along. Pleased with herself, Phyl grinned and sipped her Champagne. She rested her chin in her hand, and looked around, amazed that while she came from practically nothing in Toronto with big dreams, without having to be very wealthy themselves, they seemed to always be living the high life. She watched the other elegantly dressed patrons dance, some of whom were quite serious about the tango.

She turned to Stuart. "Oh, Stu. I do wish you picked up on this tango. I so love it!" Her eyes darted around the table, wondering if any other gentleman would consider taking her to the floor. But, they were all engrossed in conversations, smoking and drinking. She looked at Stuart's cigarette burning between his stained fingers. She eyed his flushed look. He was sweating. She reached out and pushed back a lock of his hair. "Are you alright?"

Stuart coughed briefly but harshly into his hand and nodded. "I'm okay."

"No, you're not. You look like you have a temperature."

"Sweetheart, I'm okay." Stuart took her hand and placed it back on the table. He patted it.

Phyl looked at the other gentlemen, also with nicotined fingers. She looked at the ambassador, who clenched a pipe between his brown teeth. His hands were clean. She sighed deeply and sat back, adjusted the low neckline of her daring new pink evening gown, and straightened out the skirt. She looked at the ambassador again, who sat on the other side of Stuart. Her eyes softened. She liked Norman and Myra very much. They were good people with solid convictions. She was happy to think that perhaps they could somehow keep in touch once they finally settled back at home. Movement at the main doors behind Norman Armour caught her attention. She watched the doorman point over to their table as a military attaché in uniform to the side of him stood looking around the room. The young man then walked straight to their table.

Myra sat up straight as she spotted the young messenger approaching their table. "Uh-oh," she muttered grimly.

Phyl turned to her. "Is this bad news?"

"Well, it's never good news, let me tell you that," said Myra, her eyes glistening.

Phyl watched the uniformed messenger stop at Norman's side, salute, then whisper into his ear. Norman's gaze dropped to his lap. He breathed heavily, and red welts formed on his neck and cheek. He tapped his pipe onto a crystal ashtray, wiped it with his napkin, then put it in his pocket. He threw the stained napkin onto the table, pushed his chair back, and stood. He grimly looked around the table.

"I'm afraid something very urgent has come up. Gentlemen?" He motioned to the other two men at the table. They pushed their chairs back and stood. He looked at Myra and held out his hand. "Myra, you come. You have to start packing."

Myra's eyes widened. "Pack? Oh, my!" She jumped up, accidentally pulling at the tablecloth, and dragged it along with her as she moved away. Phyl grabbed the tablecloth, then stood up. Stuart jumped up and pulled the chair out for her. They looked at Norman, worried.

"Ladies, I will send a car back to take you home. I advise you that you leave now and not be tempted to stay for what is obviously outstanding entertainment. You will hear more shortly," Norman said. As the other ladies stood up, he pulled Stuart to the side. Myra walked ahead with the other young men and stopped to wait for Norman. Norman noticed. He waved her on. "No, you go on. I'm just saying a few words to Stuart here."

Wordlessly, Myra waved at Phyl and turned and left with the others. People around the other tables craned their necks to watch them go. The odd dance couple on the floor slowed their moves and watched. A murmur spread through the room.

"What's going on?" asked Stuart.

Norman's face was set and serious. "Stuart, I would advise you and Phyl to pack up immediately. You're going to have to go back to the States. I just received word that our country is about to declare war on Argentina. All diplomats and American citizens are to leave Argentina. Brazil is standing by as an ally to the United States, ready to invade."

Phyl gasped, "What!?" Her voice carried over the music. More people looked over at them curiously. Phyl covered her mouth and looked around. Stuart held her closer and 'shushed' her.

"Phyl, do not panic. Pretend nothing is happening." Norman quickly glanced around. He shook his suit sleeve straight again. "Argentine diplomats have already been expelled from the U.S. We're ordered to fly out as soon as we can. I advise you to come to the embassy once you're packed. Call your American friends."

Norman was about to turn and leave when he turned again. "And I advise you to get rid of any surveillance equipment you may have. Burn your papers. This is serious." Then, the ambassador abruptly turned and left the ballroom, leaving Stuart and Phyl shocked in his wake.

Stuart coughed. Phyl pounded him on the back, concerned. She looked at the two ladies still standing in shock, and panicked. "The bill. How do we pay the bill?"

Stuart caught his breath, pulled out a handkerchief, and wiped the sweat from his brow. "I think that's the last thing we should worry about. Ladies. Let's go!"

* * *

"Listen, I'm so, so sorry you guys can't go right now," said Vivienne, wringing her hands.

Still in her housecoat and surrounded by clothes and suitcases, Phyl held out a thick envelope. "I know, Vivienne. I hate missing this plane. The ambassador went out of his way to arrange this flight, but Stuart's just too sick. He can't breathe. The doctor says flying is the worst thing for him right now."

Vivienne took the envelope and held it tightly with both hands. "I promise to make sure I get this to your Dad and K as soon as I can when I get to Toronto."

"I know you will. And thank you so much. And please tell them not to worry. As soon as we get on a ship, I'll send a telegram, and I'll write them once we get to New York. But tell them that we don't know when that will be. It could be a couple of months by the time we arrive." Phyl's chin quivered under the emotional strain.

"My, God. I'll be there in a couple of days. Just because you miss this flight, it'll cost you months. I feel sick to my stomach. I hope nothing happens to you guys." Vivienne looked over as Mercedes crossed the room behind Phyl, going from the kitchen to a bedroom, carrying a feather duster. Vivienne motioned to Mercedes as she walked away. "And what's going to happen to your maid? Are you leaving for good?"

Phyl burst into tears, took a handkerchief from her pocket, wiped her eyes and nose. "I have no idea," she said, shaking her head. "For now, we'll keep Mercedes to look over the flat and Tony. I'm sure she won't mind ruling the roost while we're gone." Phyl looked at her friend and tried to smile.

"I'm sure," Vivienne said quickly. She put her arms around Phyl. "Bon voyage, safe trip. I'll see you when you get to Toronto."

Phyl held onto Vivienne tightly, feeling Vivienne's long red hair sticking to her damp cheeks. She pulled back and brushed at her cheeks. "You take care, too. But don't worry. I don't like planes, anyhow. And I'm sure you'll be safe. There'll be a lot of important people on board, including you."

Vivienne silently nodded. "Take care of that ol' mutt. I hope he gets better soon."

"Thank you." She stepped closer to the open doorway and let Vivienne go back into the hall. "I'm glad you're not flying alone. Nice to see you're with some of the other gals and their husbands."

"Yeah, a couple are waiting in the taxi downstairs. Our bags were picked up earlier today." She took a deep breath. "See ya." She kissed Phyl on the cheek.

"See ya, Viv," said Phyl quietly. She watched her go to the elevator held open by the building's doorman. Phyl waved at her again before her friend disappeared into the elevator. She closed the door, pressed her forehead to the cool wood. Her ears perked up at Stuart's muffled cough in the distance. She closed her eyes and felt her body shake rhythmically to the intense pounding of her heart.

Chapter Sixteen
Home for Health, Other Home for Escape

Phyl felt sick to her stomach.

She hadn't eaten for a whole day as she worriedly stood waiting for additional prescriptions to be delivered to the waiting room at the Buenos Aires train station. Stuart's lungs had still not cleared up, but the doctor assured her that Stuart would survive a train and bus trip to Lima, however arduous it would be. She cast her eyes through the large dust-covered windows toward the train's platform and their waiting train. Ghosts of steam pumped around the wheels, track, and around people's legs moving about on the platform. Phyl and Stuart had fifteen minutes before the train left. This was all cutting it a bit too close for her nerves.

She clutched her bag with all the money they had in the world. Though the exchange rate left them years behind in their savings, they had no choice but to withdraw the funds from the bank. The realization of all that hard work and waiting in a godforsaken country and teetering political climates to achieve their dreams seemed to have been for naught. The *peso* had plummeted astoundingly low. This broke her heart.

She wiped her eyes with a sodden handkerchief and tucked it into a heavy bag. She set her eyes on the main doors, looking out for the delivery man. Jorge stood beside her, his hands clasped onto Stuart's wheelchair.

Phyl and Stuart had no choice but to leave everything behind under Mercedes' protection, save the few clothing and precious items they took. Vivienne asked before leaving for her flight, a week before, if Phyl could trust Mercedes. Mercedes had begun to show the same signs as many of the country's other workers who flaunted their newly found courage in the face of expected entitlements. Perón promised them far more than what their share of the wealth and luxuries of life had been. In fact, all workers, laborers, servants, and merchants innocently expected to live as those who held the wealth and had applied their skillful management of lands and stock through hard-won experience. Previously, the economy relied on them. Somehow, that was forgotten. Their traditional roles did not fall within the equation of new changes looming in Argentina. Perónism began to be a popular term. But it all tasted like exploiting the poor to hold office. How would the country survive this new Perón era and the threat of war with the U.S. and Brazil?

No matter. In light of Stuart's condition, Phyl did not care one iota about Argentine politics. It was Mercedes' integrity that Phyl relied on and Jorge's oversight of their home, if only as the building's owner. She had no choice. Secretly, she was adamant she was never coming back and was going to rely on Jorge to wrap up their affairs sometime in the future, foreign affairs and Remington-Rand be damned.

Jorge helped them to the station. Traveling through the streets was treacherous for foreigners, and he promised to ensure they stepped onto that train without incident. Even the plantain merchant at the entrance to the train station looked as if he was going to hurl bunches of the green fruit off his stall as he watched them struggle out of the car. It could've been her imagination. Other than if they spoke English, how would people know they were foreigners?

Jorge stood patiently behind Stuart, slouched in his wheelchair. Jorge had just finished tucking in the corners of the plaid, woolen blanket they had taken to help keep Stuart warm. The last thing Stuart needed along the journey was pneumonia – a certain death sentence.

Phyl felt dismally out of her element. Though she was not a praying person, she reached out with her heart for something grander. Some benign entity, loving, who would look into her soul and say, "I got this. Lean on Me." She took a deep breath and adjusted Stuart's hat. A brisk wind almost knocked it off his feverish head.

"He's here," announced Jorge.

Phyl followed Jorge's gaze to the main doors. A lightening shiver shot down her back. She trembled. She raised a hand to wave at the paunchy gentleman at the threshold looking around the waiting room. The man, unshaven and looking rushed, saw her and hurried over.

Jorge took the paper bag from the man and gave him a tip. The man looked at a generous tip, eyed Phyl and Stuart under hooded eyes, then nodded at Jorge before turning to go.

"Put that somewhere safe," said Jorge gently. He handed Phyl the bag.

Phyl opened the bag, counted the bottles, and crunched it closed again. She crammed it into her bag and put it onto Stuart's lap, tucking it under his gloved hands. She looked at Jorge. Her chin quivered, and she fought back tears. "Thank you so much, Jorge." She lunged forward and collapsed onto his neck.

Jorge, surprised, put his arms around her and rocked her gently. "It's nothing. Nothing at all." He stood back and looked into her face. So pale. So frail. He looked at the train through the window. "You must go. I have a friend on board. You need not speak or worry about him unless you find it's too much,

Phyl. He can help. But in the meantime, he's meant to leave you to yourselves until you get on that bus in Salta. I will ensure someone will also be on the bus to Lima. Once you're in Peru, there will be no threat. I have seen the passenger list on the ship. They're all American and Canadian, and you'll be fine."

Stuart said, "Friend."

He turned from Phyl to Stuart. He held out his hand and smiled.

Stuart, pale and half asleep from heavy medication, raised his hand and smiled wanly. He took Jorge's hand and covered it with his. "Friend," Stuart rasped, "and brother." The effort of speaking brought on a painful cough.

"I will help you get on board and tip the porter generously to ensure he gets you settled comfortably and also to help you disembark," Jorge said, maneuvering the wheelchair toward the platform entrance, dodging people.

Phyl touched Jorge's shoulder. He paused to look at her. She mouthed, "Thank you."

He smiled back gently. He nodded, then turned and focused on getting Stuart to their designated train car. A gentle roar rose amongst the crowd making their way along the dirty, paper-strewn platform. Jorge stopped pushing Stuart and looked around. Phyl, frightened, stopped as well. She was confused when someone in the crowd cheered.

"What's happening?" asked Phyl, too upset to understand the rapid Spanish around them.

Jorge beamed at her. "I can't believe it."

"What?"

"D-Day, I think they're calling it. Allies successfully landed in Normandy. France is liberated!"

Phyl covered her mouth in utter shock and disbelief. She turned to Stuart, grabbed his shoulders, and shook him. "Stu! Did you hear that? France is saved. Oh my God! France is saved!"

Overhead, the warning for "all aboard" was announced.

"We better get you on board. But this is, indeed, a happy omen," laughed Jorge. He put an arm around Phyl's shoulders as he continued to push Stuart and the wheelchair with one hand. "Perhaps this terrible tension between the U.S. and Argentina may pass much quicker than we think. So, hold fast, dear friends. You may end up turning around to come back."

"No," announced Phyl into his ear so as not to disturb Stuart. "And continue this nightmarish Argentine riptide? Never again." She ignored Jorge's shocked look.

"But -"

Phyl quickly kissed Jorge on his cheek and stood back as two porters lifted Stuart and his wheelchair into the train car. "Maybe we'll see you in New York next time you're able to see your American mistress," she yelled over increasing belly rumbles and hisses from the train. She turned and followed the porters, leaving Jorge to stand and wonder whether she meant her comment as sarcasm.

He stepped over to the next train window, frowning and craning to see if he could follow their path through to the car. There were too many people in his way on the platform waving. The train slowly moved away, and he desperately searched the windows. Finally, after a few moments, he recognized Phyl's coat sleeve and gloved hand waving goodbye through an open window.

"We stay in Salta overnight tonight and take the bus very early tomorrow." Phyl read the itinerary to Stuart tucked under a blanket on the long first-class seat, swaying to the train's motion. "I'm not sure how we'll survive this trip. It's going to take three days to get to Lima."

Stuart raised his rheumy eyes. He whispered, "It is what it is, Phyl."

"Yeah, but…" She didn't know how to tell him she was frightened this would be the end of him. She continued reading the itinerary, part of her heart still jubilant from the news of France's liberation. "August 28, we take the ship from Lima, which stops at Panama City." She dropped the itinerary and stared out the window. "God, I wish the Japanese war was finished. What if a kamikaze pilot spots us?"

"That war is too far away," rasped Stuart.

She looked at the itinerary again. "And then we go on to Miami, arriving September 3rd." She looked at Stuart. "Stu, I'd like to take a day or two in Miami. Just to catch our breaths."

Stuart nodded.

"And then we can grab the train up to Washington. I'll send a telegram to let your sister know when we'll arrive."

She leaned back and looked out at the countryside. In the far distance, she saw the setting sun blazing over the hazy tops of the jagged Andes. They had never been in this part of the country before, far from the Pampas, far from tumultuous Buenos Aires, far from craziness. But monsters were waiting in the corners, in her mind. Despite what Stuart said about them being too far, Phyl imagined the Japanese attacking the western shore of the South American continent. She thought of the island of Saipan in Japan. She had read in Time magazine how the Americans finally won over the island and how almost all of the inhabitants of the island intently jumped off the northern cliffs. She looked at Stuart.

"What is it about Americans that the Japanese are so afraid of, Stu?"

Stuart slightly shrugged. "Phyl, don't fret about that." He coughed into his fist and tucked his arm back under the blanket.

"I don't expect you to talk, Stu. Sorry. It's just that, well, how could a civilization be so terrified that they would rather jump off cliffs with their children than to come face to face with Americans?" She held out her hands toward him. "How could they be frightened of someone like you, Stu?"

Stuart tried to talk. "Japanese propaganda." He coughed.

Tears welled in her eyes as she studied her very ill husband. Her heart was overwhelmed with love and tenderness. She switched to his bench to lean her head onto his shoulder and gave him a squeeze. "You are so sweet, kind, gentle, fun, and you wouldn't hurt a fly."

She sat back and looked at him proudly. Though he wasn't physically fighting the war, she realized at that moment that all he had been doing clandestinely was in aid of preventing such a war, however an impossible task it turned out to be.

"Look at you!" she muttered. She kissed his feverish cheek. "I'm so proud of you." Phyl sat back and looked out in time to see the last majestic rays of light shoot up into a vermillion dome above the peaks of the Andes. Stars already sparkled in the heavens. She snuggled against Stuart again, pointing out the window at the beautiful sight. Then she dropped her hand and inhaled. She smelled his sweat, and various ointments lathered onto his chest and neck under all those layers of clothing and blanket.

"Damn that deadly propaganda," she whispered sadly. "It makes the whole world seem so ugly and devious."

* * *

Stuart survived the bus trip — barely.

Much to Phyl's relief, his health dramatically improved once onboard the ship. He quit smoking just before leaving Buenos Aires and was fortunate to find himself in good hands with the ship's doctor, who was most attentive. Phyl was elated to be able to slowly walk with Stuart along the decks of the boat and watch an entirely different body of water pass by. The sun and temperature were in their favor throughout the Panama Canal and the Bahama Islands.

They arrived in Miami in top form, where they stayed beachside and were able to catch a nightclub. Stuart even deigned to attempt a weak tango with Phyl, who happily tried to guide him through the sultry moves. They were well rested when they finally boarded the train to Washington days later, substantially healthier and tanned. Stuart's mother and sister welcomed them at the train station with open arms. His brothers were enlisted men. They found themselves in desk jobs and couldn't get leave, so they sent their happy regards via their mother.

Once in Washington, Stuart was immediately summoned to a briefing on the Hill on activities he witnessed in Argentina. His superiors were particularly interested in Perón and his mounting influence on the Argentine people. Despite what Phyl wished, tensions were still high between the United States and Argentina. Stuart came back from his briefing to tell Phyl that the Brazilian ambassador in Washington was said to have claimed that Buenos Aires could be destroyed entirely by the Brazilian Air Force even without intervention by the United States, who had already committed to supporting Brazil by providing the necessary ships and ammunition. This implied a worsening situation back home in Buenos Aires.

Shortly after, Remington-Rand beckoned Stuart and Phyl to bustling New York, where they had to spend two weeks before returning to Washington once more to pack and finally take the train for Toronto. The company told them they needed to reacquaint Stuart with new products and hash out a new role for him. In New York, Phyl and Stuart were put up at the Hotel Astor, where Stuart hopped on the subway to Head Office each morning while Phyl spent the days sightseeing or reading in the sun on the hotel's famous rooftop garden.

The city's streets teemed with optimistic shoppers and tourists and sailors and soldiers on every street corner. Here and there, Phyl saw the odd soldier or sailor perched on a suitcase or duffel bag, waiting for a bus or taxi, looking simply overwhelmed. First timers. Phyl chuckled, as she knew perfectly well what kind of trouble these young men could get into on leaves of absence in the mighty metropolis.

Near the end of their stay, Phyl called Claude Sr. and K in Toronto long distance from the office and discovered that they were expected earlier, having waited at Union Station a good portion of the Sunday prior. Phyl felt dismayed, and hated thinking they had waited so long for nothing. She couldn't understand how her father and K had gotten their return date wrong, so the following day, she wrote:

September 20, 1944
Hotel Astor, New York

Dear Dad and K,

It was so good to hear you by telephone. We have been in New York nearly 2 weeks and they have bargained hard with Stu until yesterday when the VP made Stu the offer of Morgan's job. It would give us a chance to settle in and for Stuart to get up-to-date on all new equipment and to get the feel again of the North American way of doing business, which is entirely different from the South

American. The disadvantages on the other hand would be a lower standard of living due to lack of apartments and domestic help and the Canadian General might not want to pay what Stuart considers fair. Stu has had a tough break all along what with the exchange, war, etc. and has to get something in return. Taxes are very high in Canada and Stuart has to consider his mother. We are not getting any younger and have to get something put away. Plus, we have our little house to think of. The Canadian General Manager is in New York today talking to the Vice President and things are no doubt to be decided. Poor Stuart, he is always having to make big decisions.

If Stu accepts the proposition, and we come to Canada, it would be best to finish our visit in Washington and then come to Toronto.

The United States is putting more pressure on Argentina. All Argentine companies with ties with the Axis powers are boycotted, and newsprint exports is limited to pro-Allied newspapers. American exports of electronic appliances, chemicals and oil have stopped. Properties of Argentine companies in the U.S. have been taken over. Hull wants to force the present military regime in Argentina to resign. Stu says there's no definite declaration of war against Argentina because they're afraid to affect the supply of food to Britain. Stu says Churchill is nervous about that.

Enough of that. I can't wait to see you both, Claude Jr., little Stuart and meet Dorothy. Love to you all, Phyl.

P.S. Stuart is much better these days. He's gained weight since quitting smoking and he's added years to his life. And that makes me happy to no end.

PPSS Yes, Mrs. Goulding was a pest while we were in her house last time. It's good of her to let us rent again. However, she didn't want the place out of her vision for five minutes. She always asked me about the weeds but I told her gardening was not my forte and she'd have to be satisfied if we kept the grass cut and the place watered so shut up on that subject.

We saw our new little house in Pennsylvania and how far it's come along. It's weather tight, as Stu calls it, but the insides have to be finished. We were hoping to have the money to finish it but the peso is low and we come with far less than planned. Oh well. C'est la vie! We are healthy and alive. So, there you go!

Phyl sat back and looked at the letter, realizing that a good portion would be censored. She shrugged and continued.

Can't wait to see you all. Love, Phyl.

* * *

Stuart walked in through the front door carrying his briefcase. A cold Toronto October day. A gust blew dead leaves past him into the hallway.

"Oh, my gosh! Shut that door, quick!" yelled Phyl.

Stuart slammed the door shut, wiped his shoes, and entered the toasty kitchen. He put his briefcase down and took off his coat and hat and gazed at Phyl sitting at the kitchen table across from six-year-old Little Stuart. Phyl looked flushed.

"Well, hello there, namesake. What are you doing here?" asked Stuart, smiling.

Little Stuart, taller and gangly, held up a bright red paper cut-away.

Stuart peered at the paper. "Ah, a red ghost, I see, with two black eyes."

Little Stuart nodded thoughtfully. "Yes. And I have a witch here." He grabbed a black cutout and held it up. Phyl looked on proudly.

Stuart pretended to be frightened by the paper witch, which made Little Stuart scoff at him.

"How's your baby brother?"

Little Stuart shrugged like an old man. "He smells and keeps falling, so he cries all the time."

"Well, that's what smidgeon human beings do," chuckled Stuart.

"Huh?" Little Stuart looked at him queerly.

"How was your day?" asked Phyl, eyes sparkling, putting scissors and glue into a shoe box.

"Same old, but there's a bit of news of our old buddy, Perón," said Stuart, lifting his briefcase onto the table and opening it. He tossed a newspaper toward Phyl.

She pulled it closer and unfolded it. She looked at the headline. "Goodness! And the drama continues. So, Perón's in jail? But he's the Vice-President and the minister of War."

"He was thrown into the clinker apparently for promoting demonstrations. Read on."

Phyl squinted and read to herself. Her mouth dropped open. "*In a popular uprising, workers organized and marched toward Buenos Aries and petitioned the government to release Perón. Perón was released and is now in complete command of the military government before an election. The popular uprising enabled Perón to personify himself as the hope for the future of workers' rights against the oligarchy of international capitalists and their supporters, the Democratic Union. Perón is known to harass the rich, muzzle the press, and bait the intellectuals."*

"What does muzzle mean?" asked little Stuart.

"You know how a dog can keep barking or biting, and people put something over their nose? That's a muzzle," said Stuart. He pulled out a chair and sat down.

"Do people in 'gentina bite?" Little Stuart flew the black witch through the air.

"Yup," said Stuart loosening his tie. "Keep reading," he said to Phyl.

Phyl bit her lip. "*Perón may decide, now that the Allies have won the war, to eradicate the Nazi presence, giving his complete cooperation to international organizations.*" She looked at Stuart. "Well, kinda late, now, isn't it?"

"Nazis have escaped to Argentina. In a way, the War's still not over."

Phyl put the paper down. "Stu, I've got something to tell you."

"What's for dinner?" Stuart stared at a stove with no steaming pots.

"We're going to Dad and K's for supper. Claude's going to join us there. Dorothy and the baby are at her mother's, so we," Phyl, got up and tickled Little Stuart, who tried not to giggle, wanting to act mature. "have to take care of Little Stuart until then."

"I don't like being called Little Stuart," he protested.

"What do you want to be called, then?" asked Stuart.

"How about Stuart and you be called Old Stuart?" Little Stuart grinned.

"Well, I oughta…" Stuart mimicked the Three Stooges.

"I don't want to go home."

"That's too bad. You're going back."

"No, I'm not. I need a break from my brother."

"That doesn't matter. I'm not having no snot-nosed kid in this house overnight. He might frighten me with his ghost and witch," exclaimed Stuart as he jumped out of his chair and grabbed the boy. Despite himself, Little Stuart squealed as Stuart tucked him sideways under his arm and ran into the living room, hitting the door jamb with Little Stuart's legs.

"Oh, be careful, Stu!" yelled Phyl. She sighed, picked up the paper, and continued reading. "Oh my gosh. Did you know they got married?"

Stuart was in the living room, dipping the boy's body into a kamikazee dive toward the carpet. "Who got married?" he huffed.

"Perón and Eva. And she's a blonde now." Phyl's mouth dropped 8 stories. "Oh my God! Bitch!"

"Oh, dear. Your Aunt Phyl said a very naughty word," Stuart said to his nephew.

"What does it mean?"

"A female dog," yelled Phyl. She scraped her chair back and took the paper with her. She stood in the doorway and held it up. "Look at that."

Stuart glanced at a photo of Eva and Perón, then tickled Little Stuart again. "Yeah. She's blonde."

"No, look at what she's wearing."

Stuart faked slamming the boy onto the floor and stepped over him. Little Stuart clung to his foot, so he had to be dragged along. Stuart took the paper. "What about it?"

"That's a replica of my suit with the brown velvet collar and cuffs. Remember I wore it when I did background for that movie? She kept eyeing me that day." Phyl looked at the photo again. "I can't believe it."

"She looks matronly."

Phyl slapped his arm. "Are you saying I did, too?"

"No. It looked very nice on you. You're slim and beautiful." He shrugged. "I don't know. With her hair slicked back and blonde, she looks double pale. And the outfit just isn't flattering."

"She's shrewd. I bet she changed her appearance just to look less, well, slu…"

"That's a very bad word."

"Another naughty word?" asked Little Stuart, still stuck to Stuart's foot like a barnacle.

Stuart bent down and unglued the boy's hands from his shoe. He lifted him up onto his feet. "Boy, you're getting heavy. Wanna go out and throw a ball?"

"Yeah!"

"No," said Phyl. "We have to go. Time to go to Grandad and Grandma K and eat meatloaf."

"Meatloaf again?" complained Little Stuart.

"Feel lucky we have food to eat," said Phyl. "We're still rationing. Besides, there are children in Europe who don't have enough food."

"And no toys?"

Phyl looked at Stuart, who smiled at her and shrugged. He shook his head. "Too young, Phyl."

"He should learn." She turned back to her nephew.

"But toys are important, too," protested Little Stuart.

"Right. And they have no toys," said Phyl.

Little Stuart looked into the corner of the living room and stepped to a big, battered chest. He lifted the lid and pulled out a small wooden truck. He held it up. "You can give them this. I'm too old for it." He brought it over.

Phyl took the truck and looked at it blankly.

"And you can give them my meatloaf, too."

Little Stuart sat cross-legged in front of the radio, playing with a Tinker Toy set. *Pennsylvania 6-500* played loudly while the adults lingered at the dining room table. Claude Sr. wiped his mouth with a napkin. "Sad loss when that plane went down with that musical genius," he muttered.

"We're always asked to play Glenn Miller when the band gets together," said Claude Jr.

Phyl watched Stuart clean his plate with a piece of bread. "Losses all around," she muttered.

K craned her neck to see how much Little Stuart ate of his dinner. Claude Jr. noticed.

"He doesn't like meatloaf and pork 'n beans," said Claude Jr.

"It doesn't matter," said Claude Sr. "He shouldn't waste his food."

"He wouldn't if someone didn't put so much on his plate," muttered Claude Jr.

K dropped her knife and fork, and turned red.

Phyl raised her arms. "All right! Let's not quarrel for once tonight. Listen. I have very happy news, though I haven't told Stu yet." She grinned at Stuart.

Stuart blinked at her.

Phyl's eyes sparkled as her grin grew wider.

Stuart's face went pale. He looked at her midriff. "It finally took?" he croaked.

Phyl nodded her head proudly. "Finally!"

The other adults erupted with joy, springing out of their chairs to hug Phyl and shake a stunned Stuart's hand.

"So, little Donald is going to have a playmate!" laughed K with tears in her eyes.

At the radio, Little Stuart's eyes widened as the truth dawned on him. "What? Not another stinky baby." He threw down his Tinker Toy and crossed his arms angrily. "I'm running away from home!"

* * *

Bugles squealed. Drums beat. A marching band played Jingle Bells, its happy, jarring notes bounced off the buildings lining snow-covered University Avenue downtown Toronto. Phyl shivered beside Dorothy. Both were bundled up, their frosted cheeks, noses, and foreheads showing from under woolen hats and scarves in an unforgiving wind. Their eyes stung from sparkly flurries as they tried to focus on the uniformed players.

"I have no idea how they manage to play in this cold! Do you see Dad yet?" yelled Phyl at her new sister-in-law.

Dorothy shook her head searching the marching players. "No, and I don't see Claude."

"They already passed," yelled Little Stuart, bundled up and perched on Stuart's shoulders behind Phyl and Dorothy. He bounced, pointed, and waved out of control.

Stuart laughed. "Hold on there, buddy. You'll fall!"

"He's got a better view up there," laughed Dorothy.

"Look, look!" yelled Little Stuart, arms askew.

"Everything all right up there, buddy?" yelled Stuart.

"Clowns are throwing candy canes!"

Phyl looked up to see Little Stuart grinning. She turned to Dorothy. "It's so nice to see him happy for a change."

"Donald takes all the attention away, which is natural. He's still just a baby. It's quite a change for Little Stuart." Dorothy wiped her nose with a handkerchief. "And having a new mother is an adjustment. I sense he isn't quite there yet. He's always so miserable."

"You have to give him more time. He must miss El so," offered Phyl. She touched her own abdomen. "Well, we'll try not to forget Little Stuart and Donald after our own baby's born. We'll give all three as much love and attention as possible." She shivered and looked back, eyeing Stuart and his cigarette. Stuart looked at her, took his cigarette out of his mouth while balancing his nephew, and dropped it onto a snowbank.

Phyl eyed the butt in the trodden snow, then resumed staring at him.

"Phyl, don't give me a hard time, alright?"

Phyl mouthed, *you promised.*

Stuart almost rolled his eyes. Not quite. Almost.

Phyl wondered if it was the same man she had married. He'd been smoking for a month or so, excuse after excuse, saying his lungs were all right again now that they were back. Phyl, disappointed, studied the people huddled around them. Some laughed at something just out of Phyl's sight. She stood on her toes and saw clowns interacting with the happy crowd along the curb. They were tossing candy canes over everyone's heads. Phyl watched a red, green, and white striped cane arc overhead just in time to see Stuart catch it midair, then hand it to Little Stuart. She turned back to Dorothy, wringing her gloved hands together for warmth.

"This is the only thing I don't like about being back," she yelled, the steam of her breath hovering in the midst of a multitude of ghostly breaths. "The winters. But thank God, we'll never have to go back to that godforsaken place again. I've seen enough palm trees and street fights to last a lifetime, paradise or not." She pulled her coat in tighter.

Dorothy looked strangely at Phyl before looking back at the clowns prancing past.

Phyl studied Dorothy's profile.

"Why'd you look at me like that?"

"Pardon?"

Phyl's stomach turned. "You gave me a funny look."

Dorothy looked pained and glanced back at Stuart. Phyl noticed he looked down at her from under heavy lids.

"Is there something I don't know?" she asked him, the wind carrying her words away.

Stuart shook his head, making a face.

Phyl turned fully to face him.

"Is there something you're not telling me, Stu?" asked Phyl angrily.

"I can't hear you, Phyl, speak up," yelled Stuart, his jaw stiff with cold.

Phyl bellowed. "Can you hear me now!?"

Stuart was taken aback by her anger. Dorothy looked concerned.

"Is there something I don't know?" Phyl bellowed again. A few people turned.

Stuart let go of one of Little Stuart's hands and fiddled with his ear lobe. He frowned and glanced at Dorothy.

Phyl snapped her head and looked at Dorothy, who returned the look with wide eyes.

Little Stuart squealed above them, yelling he could see Santa's reindeer coming around the bend.

Phyl's chin quivered with emotion. "Do Dad and K know?"

Dorothy opened her mouth but didn't speak. She looked to Stuart for direction.

"Don't look at my husband. Do Dad and K know, Dorothy? Does my brother know?" Phyl's voice intensified.

Dorothy gulped, "Well, I—"

Phyl pushed Dorothy aside and tried to squeeze past Stuart.

"Where are you going?" yelled Stuart.

"I'm getting as far away from you as possible! You lied to me. You said we'd NEVER have to go back! Why didn't you tell me?"

"Because I knew THIS would happen," he yelled.

Phyl started to cry and couldn't see clearly. She pushed here and there to escape the crowd. All she wanted was to find a restaurant, or a phone booth to hide in, or better, find her way back to the car oh so far away. But she couldn't remember where it was. Stuart tried to grab her with one hand, but she pulled away harshly, stepped back, and fell backward off the curb just as everyone swarmed onto the road to see the Santa Clause float.

* * *

Phyl huddled in bed, sadly listening to Silent Night on the radio downstairs in the living room. The light from the hallway visited her in bed and she stared at the stitching in the quilt stretched over her legs. She imagined K's fingers pushing the needle into the layered materials, then deftly reinserting the needle, creating tiny and precisely spaced stitches. The quilt was a wedding gift from K. It was made with rose bouquets, reds, pinks, and greens on a white background. So much work. So much love. So much love.

She looked at the windows. The shades weren't drawn, and it was pitch black outside. Early winter hours. The room was dark but cozy and warm from the coal fire downstairs. She heard K huff up the creaky stairs. She listened to tinkling cups, pots, and silverware. She slowly inhaled. She turned on her bedside lamp and pushed back into her pillows as K appeared in the doorway with a tray, teapot, cookies, and a cup and saucer. Phyl raised an arm.

"You're so good to me, K," she said so sadly.

"Oh, it's nothing, Phyl," puffed K. "You're a daughter to me. Of course, I would be here to help."

"But Dorothy needs you more."

"Dorothy has a mother with tons of time on her hands. It won't kill her to step in for once."

"Sit down. You're out of breath."

K, gasping for breath, put the tray on the night table, slid the lamp to the side, and plopped onto the edge of the bed. The springs cried out in protest. She picked up the teapot and poured steaming liquid into the cup. She patted her chest. "Phew," she chuckled, embarrassed. She picked up the cup and saucer. It shook as she handed it to Phyl. Phyl took the saucer and held the cup with the other hand.

"You're shaking, K. Are you alright?"

K waved her away. "I just shake sometimes, is all. This asthma..."

"Maybe it's time you stop cleaning houses. It wears you down. Now, with Dad's promotion to supervisor, you could step back. Couldn't you?"

K shook her head. "I've cut two houses out to make time for Dorothy, and we're pretty tight."

"You're cleaning and doing wash there, too."

"Family," was all K said.

Phyl sadly looked down into her black tea. She swallowed. "K, here I am, going to impose on you even more. I need you to do something for me, please."

K pushed a grey hair back behind her ear. Her bun was loosening. "Anything, dear."

"I need to get a message to Stu's Mom and sister. I'm going to Washington and see if our house is okay for me to move in."

"Excuse me?"

Phyl fought back tears. "It pains me to say this, K. But I think our marriage is over."

K reached out to Phyl's cheek and held it lovingly, caringly. She bent her head and looked deeply into Phyl's tearing eyes. "Phyl, you can't mean that."

Phyl's bottom lip quivered, and tears rolled. "I can't face Stuart." She could barely talk. "K, he lied to me." Phyl desperately clung as K rocked her gently, side to side.

"Phyl, you're with baby. The doctor said you had a close call, and you have to rest. Now's not the time for big decisions like this." She pulled back to look at her stepdaughter. "This will all blow over. Besides, Stu won't be going back for another year; there's plenty of time for you to have the baby and get used to the idea again."

"No, not this time. If we go back, K, I know one of us will die, and I will not bring a child back to that place. Not over my own dead body."

Tenderly, K cupped Phyl's hand. "You're worrying about things you don't have to worry about right now, Phyl."

"Well," Phyl said, searching the bedroom. "I'm going to make sure I won't have to worry anymore. I'm going to live in that house we've been saving for all these years. My child will be safe. And if my child has to live without a father in order to stay safe, then that is how it will have to be."

"Oh, my darling Phyllis," gasped K. She covered her mouth, shook her head, and cried.

K lowered her head into Phyl's frail shoulder. Phyl placed her hand on K's head for comfort. But her heart and mind were set. She felt dead inside, grieving the love and the loss of all those years fighting towards a future that continually seemed to drift further asea. She was dead set on stopping that agonizing cycle. She would make that life they fought for possible, one way or another, with Stu or without. His loyalties were to be his downfall. She no longer had room to fear for his safety. He seemed determined to follow a path of self-destruction. The baby was not to have any part of that.

"So be it," whispered Phyl.

* * *

"*The poor like to see me beautiful: they don't want to be protected by a badly dressed old hag.*"

"*She* said that?" asked Phyl. She sat beside her mother-in-law in an old Redington Hotel armchair, snapping peas from their shell.

"Yes, indeed," grinned Mrs. Redington. She folded the newspaper. "That Eva Duarte, or Perón I should say, is quite the character. How interesting that you should know her."

"Well, not really well. It's just she always seemed to be on the fringes of my day-to-day life. And there was no end of gossip about her at the Club." Phyl paused feeling slightly ill.

Mrs. Redington chuckled. "I would say." She laughed aloud and shook her head. "This wouldn't happen in North America. Imagine someone like that being the First Lady. Eleanor Roosevelt, she is not."

Phyl took a deep breath and looked out the window over the Susquehanna River towards Wilkes-Barre. She could make out the top of the Redington's former hotel. She was again aware of the absence of something that had been constant: her breath being kicked away in her abdomen. Out of instinct, she placed a hand on her belly. She felt a chill go up her spine and felt light-headed.

"Kicking again?" Mrs. Redington took off her round reading glasses and peered happily at Phyl.

Phyl shifted her body and squeezed slightly at the side of her belly, hoping to encourage movement. "No, not for a little while."

"Well, he must be resting. They go through spells." Mrs. Redington took a handkerchief from her apron pocket. She wiped her eyes. "Following the doctor's advice to do as little as possible was good, but, dear, coming down here on the train was a gamble, I have to tell you. You were fortunate that Vivienne could accompany you on such short notice. Honestly, when you showed up at my door three months ago, I almost had a heart attack."

Phyl snapped the last of the pea pods. She ignored her mother-in-law's statement. She didn't want to acknowledge that sad and terrible time. She had left Toronto angry and upset, against everyone's wishes. "So, what else did that article say about Perón?" she asked weakly.

Mrs. Redington waved at the air with her handkerchief, tucked it back into the apron, and clasped her hands on her lap. She leaned over slightly, crossed her ankles to the side. Her heavy stockings sagged over Mr. Redington's old slippers she was wearing. They were far too big for her. "That his arrest and the public uprising forcing his release ended up with him winning the election last month."

"Boy, you've really become an expert on South American politics!"

"Well, my son has spent his best years in one of the most unpredictably violent countries. I *need* to understand. His father always scoured the papers for any news on Argentina. I especially panicked when your mail stopped coming for a period of time. We were beside ourselves, let me tell you!" Mrs. Redington looked over the rim of her glasses. "You look pale, Phyllis."

Phyl motioned to the folded newspaper. "Anything positive?"

"Why do you ask specifically about positive?" asked Mrs. Redington. A small, concerned smile lingered on her countenance.

"Well, as you say, the idea of violence or further uprisings…" Phyl was suddenly sad. She brushed non-existent entities from her skirt and put the bowl and pot together on her lap.

Mrs. Redington eyed her for a brief moment. "I know you're worried. He's still in New York."

Phyl blinked at her mother-in-law. She raised her chin with a slightly defiant air. "I don't care either way." She pushed on the armrest with one hand to move her bottom closer to the edge of the chair. "I love him but… I don't need to repeat all what I feel, I guess." Phyl felt a pain in her diaphragm.

Mrs. Redington sighed, stood up and took the pot and bowl from Phyl. She gave her free hand to Phyl to help pull her to her feet. "It seems to me, Phyl, that everything you do shows you care. Right from the fact that it is I with you during your pregnancy, and not K and your Dad."

"Well, you just happen to come with the house we've been working toward having."

"Actually, you tore me away from Washington, D.C." Mrs. Redington led Phyl to the kitchen.

"Yes, but wouldn't you want to be back here? You can keep an eye on your house just up the road." Phyl pointed in the general direction of the Redington home and suddenly stopped. She watched her mother-in-law continue on into the kitchen. She bent over, a spasm in her midriff.

"Well, I don't know if I like seeing how the tenants are neglecting the house, but…" Mrs. Redington sighed as she put the bowl and pot into the sink. She turned on the tap. "I do appreciate being with you, my dear. I didn't think any of my children will ever get to starting their families."

Phyl slowly walked into the kitchen. "To be honest, I think I was too tense, too unwell, to get pregnant. My body wasn't healthy enough and my monthly stopped at one point. That's how sick I was."

"You look very pale; you should sit down."

"And it was as if my body knew we were finally safe at home and we would never have to go back to that place." She looked down at her belly. A tear escaped, and she quickly wiped it away. "This house is what we were fighting for. You'll have to drag me away screaming if you ever try."

"Well, we're not getting too far with the finishing details, I'm afraid." Mrs. Redington looked around at the plywood floors and the doorways missing trim and jambs.

"That will come." Phyl looked at the floor. "I don't know how, but it will."

"Come." Mrs. Redington led Phyl to a highchair, where she continued to watch her mother-in-law rinse the peas.

"So, again, what's happening in Sin City?"

"Oh, yes," said Mrs. Redington. She leaned back against the sink counter. "It seems Perón has delivered a good amount of reforms – for the poor masses, of course."

"Hmm. Yes." Phyl stretched her back.

"Paid and longer holidays." Mrs. Redington wiped her hands dry on her apron. Something caused her to look out the window. She pushed aside the white cotton curtain with a scalloped edge of red and white stripes. "Perón is forcing factories to pay extra bonuses and improve working conditions. He's now calling his followers – let me think." She bit her lip. "*Decami* something or other."

"*Descamisados*," offered Phyl. "It means *shirtless ones*."

"Oh, yes. I keep forgetting you can speak Spanish. It all comes so easily to you."

"At least I gained in one area after all those years," muttered Phyl. She caught the sound of a distant car motor. Only farmland was further up the road, and tractors were more likely to pass.

"He seems to be punishing the elite, that one. The people with the land and money." Mrs. Redington turned and grabbed a tea towel off a hook under the unfinished sink counter. She dried the pot. "Like those friends of yours with that lovely ranch. I would say that would affect an already struggling economy. Am I correct in thinking that?"

"Well, Mother, I'm no expert," said Phyl. "But it seems that's a no-brainer."

Mrs. Redington laughed but stopped. This time, both women heard the engine gear down. It entered the long laneway leading to the house. She took off her apron and kicked off her slippers. She stepped to the wall, slipped her feet into pumps, and exited the kitchen. "Someone's coming up the lane."

Phyl saw a late-model car approach the house. "Who on earth…?"

"Whoever it is must be rich. That's quite the car. I think it's a Lincoln Continental." Mrs. Redington spruced herself up at the old Redington Hotel gilt-framed mirror by the front door closet.

Phyl, held her abdomen, and remained in the kitchen doorway. She fought back a wave of nausea.

Mrs. Redington didn't wait for a knock and threw the door open.

Phyl saw a handsome, swarthy-looking man taking off his hat.

"JORGE!" screamed Phyl.

Then, her water broke.

Chapter Seventeen
The Baby, The Trip, The Shipping Magnate with Secrets

Phyl hovered over a rocky ledge on the rugged coast of Uruguay.

She clearly saw low clouds over Buenos Aires. She strained to see the city, and suddenly, she clearly saw ships at the port and cars along the waterfront. She saw people walking along the streets. She stood wondering how the city could be so clear and close when it should be out of sight. A soothing, cool breeze snaked up her legs from the foaming rollers of the brown, brackish waters, playfully flipping the hem of her long, white gown. She looked down at long, bell sleeves. Her hands glowed.

She gazed toward the setting sun, more intense than ever, yet there was no need to squint. As if the fierce light was an object to behold. Clouds caught on fire, their flames reflected brilliantly off the water between her and the city. A seagull cried like a baby. Her heart lept to her throat and she saw the bird hovering above. She felt dizzy and thought she would surely fall from the sky onto the rocks if she continued to look up. But she couldn't turn her eyes away. She was confused. Before her eyes, the bird morphed into a lovely child, then into a beautiful young girl, smiling lovingly down at Phyl. The girl waved with an alabaster hand, emanating love and peace. Phyl called out.

"Baby?"

"She spoke," said a voice.

Phyl fell into a light grey abyss, stopping just short of an entrance to a black pit. She wasn't afraid. She was filled with joy and an insane intensity of peace though so close to darkness. She realized she has always known that young girl. And that she would see her again.

"Are you sure?"

A ringing intensified in her inner ear until it sounded like a roaring wind. The onslaught of sound was so intense, so painful. She was about to call out in pain. She moaned.

"Phyllis?"

The roar clapped to silence. Immediately, Phyl's senses gathered into a singlular focus, as if all five had legs and arms, and crawled together in a ball as quickly as possible. She was coming home. She knew it. Her eyelids opened to a slit. A wispy, blue light hurt them, and they closed again.

"Phyllis, dear."

It was her mother-in-law. She saw her face in her mind. She saw a doorway around her mother-in-law. Jorge stood behind her on the stoop. Suddenly, Stu stepped into view in a black coat, whipped by the cold March wind. She gasped and opened her eyes.

"Stu," she called out.

"Phyllis, goodness. Hello." Mrs. Redington held Phyl's hand and leaned over her face. She reached out with a warm, moist hand and brushed sticky hair away from Phyl's forehead.

"Mother?" Phyl croaked.

"Yes, I'm here."

Phyl slightly raised her head then dropped it. Jorge stood at the foot of the bed, looking concerned. Sad.

Phyl lifted a hand to her forehead, touched her nose and cheek. She groaned quietly and became aware of a deep abdominal pain. She tried to stir.

Jorge rushed toward her, opposite Mrs. Redington. They put their hands on Phyl's shoulders.

"Stay still, Phyllis," whispered Jorge. "You have gone through a lot. We thought we'd lost you."

"I don't..." Phyl placed a hand on her tummy, but it felt oddly soft. "My baby. I saw her. She called me." She tried to sit up. "Where is my baby?"

Mrs. Redington gasped and burst into tears. She held a handkerchief up to her face and shook her head. Jorge stepped around to Mrs. Redington, helped her up, and led her to the door. He whispered to her. The two stood in the doorway. Phyl, confused and terrified, saw Stu appear behind them. Jorge startled, grasped Stu's hand. Stu didn't look at him. He was staring intently at Phyl.

"Stu," croaked Phyl.

"I came as quickly as I could." Stuart turned to Jorge. "Does she know yet?" He looked beseechingly at Jorge and glanced at his mother as she slipped further into the hallway, crying.

Jorge shook his head.

Stu turned his eyes to Phyl. He was pained, torn, traumatized. He paled even more as he approached Phyl's bed. "Phyl, darling. I hopped in the car and drove down as soon as I heard..."

"Stu? I just saw you."

Stuart looked at Jorge for an explanation.

"She was talking just before she woke. She must have been dreaming."

"What's happening?" whispered Phyl. "Why is everyone acting so strange?" She gazed at Stuart. She suddenly missed him so terribly. She held her hand out to him. "Why are you so sad?"

Stuart took her hand and sat slowly on the bed. He kissed her palm. He leaned his cheek into it.

"Oh, Stu." Her bottom lip quivered, and she fought back tears. "It's the baby, isn't it?"

"Phyl, you miscarried. The baby is gone."

Phyl yanked her hand away and tried to sit up. She wanted to fly off those rocks, to search the skies for her little girl. "I saw her," she whispered, wide-eyed.

Stuart exchanged a look with Jorge.

"I saw her. She's beautiful. Our daughter." A stab in her abdomen knocked her breath away. She fell back. "Couldn't they save my little girl?" she cried. "My God. What was I? Six months? She was a full person, Stu. I know she was tiny, but surely, they could've saved her!"

Stuart swallowed hard. "The baby was stillborn. There was nothing they could do," Stu whispered. Tears escaped, running down and over his lips. He wiped at his face. "I'm so sorry, Phyl. This is all my fault."

Phyl looked queerly at him through her tears. "No, Stuart. She wasn't sad!" She gazed at the wall behind Stuart and remembered their daughter's glowing image. "In fact, we'll see her. Just not yet." She looked at him. "I don't know how to explain this to you. She's as real as you and I. She's there!"

Stuart looked at Jorge. "What kind of medication is she on?"

"Stu, you have to believe me! She's real," Phyl insisted, getting upset.

Jorge came forward. He tried to soothe her by smiling gently and warmly.

Phyl gazed at Jorge. Then at the room's only window. The blinds were drawn, but the bright sun made it glow.

A knock sliced through her frenzied thoughts. She saw at the doorway a doctor standing in his white lab coat, holding a clipboard. He pushed his round-framed glasses higher onto the bridge of his nose. His thick, dark eyebrows were knitted together. He blinked quickly and walked in. "Phyllis. Welcome back."

Stuart stood up. He shook the doctor's hand.

"Stuart. I'm sorry we see each other in such sad and unfortunate circumstances after all these years. But," the doctor said, raising his voice, "The good news is that Phyl will pull through."

Everyone waited for more. The silence begged for answers. Stuart broke the silence.

"What exactly happened?" he asked.

"It's complicated. I know that Phyllis had a fall in Toronto before coming to Pennsylvania. It may not have been a wise move to travel then." He looked directly at Phyl. "Though when she arrived in my office, everything appeared normal."

"Could this have been prevented?" Stuart asked.

The doctor shook his head. "That we will never know." His eyes softened as he looked at Phyl, then back at Stuart. He lowered his voice. "The fetus had been dead a good two weeks, from what I could tell."

Phyl gasped. "Oh, my God," she whispered.

"Well, I won't go into too much detail now. But the little body had been deteriorating. The uterine wall tore, and its arm protruded into Phyl's cavity."

"You mean *her* arm," Phyl said quietly.

The doctor looked confused. "I don't think I told any of you its gender. Yes, it was a little girl."

"I had no idea," said Stuart. He looked at Jorge. "Did you?"

Jorge shook his head.

"Interesting," said the doctor. He took a deep breath. "Phyl," the doctor moved to the foot of the bed. "We had to do an emergency hysterectomy. And I'm concerned about the possibility of sepsis."

Phyl's face drained of color. From the depths of where her beleaguered womb once was rose a primeval cry that echoed the cries of eons of heartbroken women faced with the knowledge that they would never see their little angels born to them. She realized then the finality of knowing her journey would never include holding her own bundles of love in her arms. She saw clearly that her path was different from others. She quite suddenly remembered how she disliked children as a young woman. Did she always know? Or was this a form of punishment for thinking so?

She shrugged off the temptation of blaming herself. It was clear that she had spent so much time blaming the world and Stuart for all her perceived miseries that she had gravely overlooked how incredibly blessed she was. Her tears stopped, and her heart slowed. The image of her daughter had given her love, a sense of fulfillment, and a sense of purpose.

She looked up at the three men looking down at the bed, or the floor, or the clip board. A wave of peace permeated her being. She lowered her head and sadly nodded an acknowledgment of the truth to herself. She realized Stuart was still holding onto her hand. She looked at him gently, then cupped his hands with hers. Stuart leaned his forehead onto hers.

She touched his head and caressed his hair. She closed her eyes. "It's okay, Stu. We're going to be okay." She let out a slow, long, peaceful breath, remembering the love emanating from the image of their daughter. "Everything is going to be fine."

* * *

Almost a year later.

Phyl felt the ship heave under her feet as it entered the Gulf Stream's choppy seas. Many passengers had already resorted to buckets, but it seemed she and Stuart, the officers and crew, were the only ones who went about their business. Seasoned travellers all.

Stuart had just gotten over another attack of bronchitis and had to have a tooth extracted the day before they sailed. Between the fresh air on deck and good shots of whiskey, they both held their own.

Stuart's brother Bob and his mother and sister saw them off in New York. This time, the ship was small - only 8,000 tons. It carried precious and dangerous cargo: The deck was loaded with jeeps, army trucks, and barrels of high explosives and ammunition for Perón. The captain had told them he was worried they might break loose and go overboard in the terrible swells they were enduring. Needless to say, all passengers were quite uneasy about being on board with such cargo.

When Phyl discovered they would be accompanying dangerous cargo for the Perón Administration on their trip back to Argentina, she thought it quite ironic that their personal lives should, again, be intertwined with the ongoing political drama. They didn't even have to wait until they got there. It was in their face from the moment they stepped into their cabin. They were welcomed by a massive portrait of Perón and Eva hanging on the bulkhead.

Phyl tried to brush that aside. She was pleased as this time, she and Stuart had the best cabin and were honored to sit at the captain's table. However, despite his enjoyable company and gracious welcome, the food was horrible. They were fed a supper at 5:30 the night before they left New York and were given nothing more until 8:15 that morning – not even a spot of tea. Regardless, with so many airplane mishaps and crashes in South America, she still preferred the ship from hell to flying.

Phyl saw a school of dolphins through the porthole, diving, racing through the whitecaps and intense spray as if the dangerous ocean swells were nothing for them. Now and then, with each roll of the ship, she heard things clattering and smashing to the floor in the nearby kitchen. She heard concerned voices in the hallway. The crew was Norwegian, and everyone on board spoke English with a thick accent. There were more of them than passengers, as only thirteen paying passengers were on their way to Buenos Aries.

Because of their cargo, they would be on the sea for twenty days without stopping.

No ports welcomed explosives.

Phyl looked at Stuart, resting and rolling in his cot, having a wonderful time reading comics.

She grabbed onto the edge of the sink for balance as the boat suddenly heaved.

"Are you trying to look blasé on purpose?"

"Did you say something?" Stuart joked as he peered at her over the edge of the comic book. Everything in their cabin creaked, groaned, and protested.

She laughed, waited for the ship to drop into a swell and remain somewhat straight, then hurled herself to his cot. She pushed him aside with her hip and snuggled against him. The ship heaved again, its bow slowly arcing to the sky.

"You're not frightened, are you?" he said.

"Not at all. It's strange, but I feel quite calm."

"Norwegians are good sailors, but you could never call them cooks," laughed Stuart. He reached to the bunk above to keep them from rolling off the lower berth entirely.

"Ha!" laughed Phyl. "If they put a plate of raw fish in front of me tomorrow morning again, I'll join everyone else and run for that old bucket pronto!" She twisted to look at him. "How are you feeling?"

"Well, for a guy who was running a temperature of over 101 on Wednesday night and had a complicated extraction Thursday night, I'm not feeling too badly, although everything I ate this morning has been running around my stomach in many directions. If the whole journey's like this, I don't think I'll eat enough to make me fat!"

Phyl poked his shoulder. "You're already fat! Ever since you quit smoking, you've been eating like a pig. Look at that face!" she laughed, squeezing his cheek. "You look strong like bull."

"Whoa!" Stuart called out. He clung to her with his free arm and kept the other clenched over the edge of the upper bunk as the ship practically stood on its bow. Phyl laughed with glee.

"My fearless Phyl," whispered Stuart into her ear.

* * *

The bustling, steaming port of Buenos Aires.

Jorge and Angelica joyfully bore flowers as part of a hearty and warm welcome. The temperatures were balmy, and the humidity thick enough to slice with a knife. Phyl and Stuart stepped off the ramp from the tug boat. Jorge helped by grabbing a bag from Phyl, and led everyone back to his new Lincoln Continental in a filthy parking lot.

"Ooo, I see you have another snazzy car. It looks exactly the same," cooed Phyl.

She let Stuart open her passenger door in the back.

"It *is* the same. I shipped it down from New York." Jorge opened the back door for his wife. The men clambered into the front seat, and Jorge started the engine. He deftly pulled through the throng of dock workers, passengers, and visitors before driving onto the parkway. "Disembarking was quite an ordeal, we saw."

"They were going to unload the jeeps, army trucks, and explosives first!" exclaimed Phyl. "They were going to keep us on the ship as they did. These damn Dupont people and their explosives. They nearly starve us to death for twenty days without a stop or sight of land, jeopardize our lives, and charge us more than the luxury liners used to for the privilege. No one wanted to be there when a spark set the whole thing off! We had a mutiny onboard and insisted on getting off before getting to port. It's as if we were second-rate compared to Perón's special delivery."

"That's precisely what you were," laughed Jorge. "Second rate." He drove them through the city a few blocks until he pulled in front of the beautiful Alvear Hotel. "Does it feel like home yet?"

Phyl laughed as she craned to look at their old apartment building across the road. "Oh, my gosh. Remember having to start your car by pushing it in that godawful storm? How many wonderful nights have we had in that flat and at this hotel?"

"She stalked Errol Flynn here, you know," joked Stuart as he got out.

"I did not stalk Errol Flynn!" argued Phyl. "Vivienne was stalking him. I was just there out of curiosity. I wanted to just get a glimpse of him, which we did." She let Stuart help her out of the car.

"You were stalking him," repeated Stuart, grinning as he let her hand go.

She slapped his shoulder in protest.

A valet took Jorge's keys, and the two couples climbed stone steps and entered the luxurious lobby of the famous hotel. Phyl and Stuart's bags were brought in from the car, and a porter put them on a gold luggage cart before leading them to one of the ornate brass elevators.

Quietly, they rode up to the top floor and stepped out onto the luxurious carpet of the hallway. Everything smelled exquisite to Phyl. She inhaled deeply. She wondered why she hated Buenos Aires so much. She understood she had been frightened, but having survived it all, she now looked back on it as an extraordinary adventure. And she had missed the amenities of servants while back in North America so much. Though the political upheaval and sense of danger were always present in the city, their lives were rich with adventure, beauty, exciting friends, and high living.

They entered their lovely room. Phyl gazed happily at the mahogany furniture, the gold bedspreads and drapes, the luxurious beige broadloom carpeting, green satin upholstered chairs, and the massive crystal chandelier.

"I love it!" she proclaimed.

"You two settle down, and I'll order us Champagne," said Jorge.

Phyl kicked off her shoes and dropped into one of the beautiful armchairs. "So, this is home for the next two months? Thank you, Remington-Rand." She looked at Angelica, grinning. "I guess you know we can't get into that apartment until the embassy's lease ends."

"Hmm," answered Angelica. "The American Embassy is pretty secretive, so as landlords, we left them alone. I don't know what state the apartment will be in, however. Lord knows what they get up to. They didn't allow anyone in to clean or do maintenance. The Embassy took care of it all."

"For security reasons, I'm sure," said Stuart.

Phyl shook her curls and looked around again, grinning. "Did I tell you about the Brazilian fishermen we saw bopping around in little rowboats over a hundred miles from the coast?"

"No," smiled Angelica. She pulled out a cigarette after sitting in a matching chair. She crossed her legs and let Stuart light her with hotel matches. "But you chatted up a storm about the trip in the car."

Jorge ordered Champagne and joined Angelica with a cigarette. He offered one to Stuart and Phyl. Phyl shook her head. Stuart hesitated, looked at the cigarette longingly, and politely waved it away.

"Well, the mother boat was large enough to resist the waves," Phyl continued. "But, gosh, these little boats looked like tiny flies crawling up these massive walls of ocean swells. I mean, I could swear some of those swells were as big as skyscrapers. How don't they drown or capsize?"

She paused and looked at her watch. She absentmindedly rewound the spring, then clicked on the little knob. She shook her arm to let her sleeve drop. "Incidentally," she turned specifically to Angelica, who looked younger than the last time she saw her. In fact, Angelica had become an even more beautiful woman, though she had another child while Phyl and Stuart were in North America. "There's something else I find curious. They say that even though there's a lot of coffee in Brazil, the people there still have to pay two *pesos* and sixty per kilo. I hear it's gone up to three *pesos* and eighty here? What gives?"

"I know. Things have not improved here at all under Perón. On the one hand, the locals and the poorer citizens feel they've hit jackpot, but the economy itself is staggering. The *peso* hasn't leveled out at all," muttered Angelica. She made a face as she blew smoke to the chandelier. She shook her head. Her blonde locks were pinned into an elaborate coiffure. "Not good."

"Tell us more about your trip? I only travel by air now, so I'm curious?" asked Jorge, settling back in a settee. He wore his linens and white shoes, contrasting with the dark suit and black leather shoes he wore back in Pennsylvania.

"Despite storms, unlike the other passengers, we enjoyed the trip. Very much," Stuart said. "We got along quite well with the captain and invited him to drinks. He was very companionable, and we expect to see more of him as he stays in the city for extended periods of time after each trip down."

"Waiting for cargo to take back, I'm sure," Jorge pointed out.

"They were all Norwegian. Good efficient workers."

Jorge jumped to the door when they heard a knock, and took the Champagne from the hotel employee. He tipped him and shut the door. He looked at the label. "Well, I don't think you were served such a fine Champagne on board." He showed the bottle . "Thank the good monk, Dom Pierre Perignon!"

Phyl cheered. "No, we didn't. Oh dear, is it sinful to say it's so nice to see an old friend like that bottle?" She held out her hands and took the bottle from Jorge. "Hello, old friend," she laughed. "We did drink tons of whiskey." She handed back the bottle. "But, oh, my gosh, the food was appalling."

Stuart cleared his throat. "You know, I found it interesting. The captain explained to us that they receive about two dollars per day per passenger as well as $425 for the 20 days to carry the freight."

"Two dollars a day? What was the freight on board?" asked Angelica.

Jorge looked knowingly at Stuart. "It was those military supplies for Perón, remember?"

Angelica frowned. "Goodness. There's no end to it. I hate to think what he is planning. Why on earth would he need more military equipment? To turn them on us?"

Stuart turned to Phyl. "I guess that's why I'm back and what the U.S. wants to keep tabs on."

There was a long pause as they all looked at each other.

"Was the service good?" asked Angelica, deftly changing the subject.

"Well, unfortunately," Stuart began. "We passengers were given the officers' and crew's cabins, so we got the dirty end of the stick as some didn't like us very much. These charter ships are obliged to take passengers to get the cargo trade, otherwise they couldn't do business with the States." Stuart handed a crystal ashtray to Angelica. "However, for some reason, Phyl and I were treated the best of all of them."

"I think because Stuart's American. Since the war ended, people seem to think America is great," Phyl said, watching Jorge loosen the cork to the Champagne. She stood up and went to the sidebar for trumpet glasses. "We were usually seated with the captain and invited for cocktails to his cabin. We were six Jews and six Gentiles, and I don't know what. The Norwegians have no love for the Jews, though, I saw, but they were soft to us. The poor Jews."

"Yes, poor jews. The Perón regime doesn't like to paint Nazis as culprits, so no one is allowed to talk about what they did." Angelica frowned deeply. "Isn't that just criminal?"

"How can something like that possibly be hidden?" asked Phyl.

Despite her youthful look, Phyl noticed that Angelica appeared to have gone through a difficult time. When Jorge popped the cork, Phyl was about to ask if Angelica was all right. The cork shot up into the chandelier, and the grand light erupted into a symphony of chimes. The women giggled with delight.

Jorge quickly poured the frothing nectar into glasses placed on a glass table by Phyl and handed them out. He stood holding up his glass. "To our dearest friends, we missed you terribly." He smiled at Stuart and looked dewily at Phyl as everyone held up their glasses. Phyl smiled back, tears in her eyes.

"Welcome back," he added.

Angelica repeated. "Welcome back, dear, dear friends." She leaned over and hugged Phyl before they all sipped. They stood looking at each other for a moment.

Stuart exhaled slowly. "Well, I guess," he held up his glass again. "To the next adventure."

"To the next adventure," repeated Jorge and Angelica.

"Hear, hear," said Phyl.

* * *

"The heat won't be going on until next month, and then there will be, as usual, mighty little of it."

Sitting in her favorite checked outfit with the brown velvet collar and cuffs, Phyl looked around the American Women's clubhouse at familiar faces, though there were fewer of them.

"Our tenant moves out tonight. And we should receive a few more privileges than most in our building as I understand we now have some high police chief or something living next door. So, the building is protected by no less than four cops permanently stationed on the block."

"Oh, my goodness. A whole security detail at no cost to you!" said Vivienne, a few years older, a few pounds plumper, and wearing a wedding band and an obtrusive diamond engagement ring.

"The cops tipped their collective hat to Stuart the other day as we dropped by to see the flat. One of them asked if we had always rented to Embassy people and mentioned that the *Señor* who had the apartment while we were gone was very good to them. So, we got the hint and can see that our protection will be darn little without a few *pesos* every now and again."

"Well, let's hope for more heat and you making a lot of *pesos*," laughed Vivienne.

"The apartment will need painting and lots of fixing up, but I'm so glad we rented it out and not let it go, as rent seems to have doubled while we were gone. We pay 350 *pesos*, but if we had let it go and taken a new apartment, we'd be paying 500 or 600 a month."

"I know. Of course, we had to take a new apartment altogether. I had let my old one go, thinking I'd never come back," said Vivienne. She and her new husband had arrived the week before from New York and moved straight into a new three-bedroom flat. "There are places to be had, but all up around 600 to 1500 a month. We have to pay 800."

"Oh, my God," exclaimed Phyl. "No! How can you pay that?"

Vivienne shrugged. "Well, in our case, we don't have to worry. Joe's company covers the rent, but he's not working on commission. It's straight salary."

"In *pesos*?" asked Phyl.

"Unfortunately, yes." Vivienne frowned. She had cut her beautiful long red hair into a curled bob. "But at least the cost of a maid is covered, and for a cook, as well."

"Well, I'm just glad I'm fairly well outfitted for clothes. My suits, which are still in good condition, would now cost 600 *pesos* and I paid 240. Everything here is at New York prices, it seems, with the exception of food. Meat is still a quarter of the price and butter, milk and bread are all cheaper than back home, but still higher than when we were here three years ago."

"I know. It's scary." Vivienne glanced around the room at the gathered women. "Is Stuart already working?" She zeroed in on a group of women excitedly chatting in the far corner.

"Stu started right away. He already sold a good contract to the government with many more to come. Everyone here is on the bandwagon selling commodities, it seems. Never saw so many elegant upstarts in my life, either. Fantastic fur coats just in this hall alone. Full-length white mink!"

"Joe says the corruption in the government is really something to behold. If only we weren't so honest. We could gather together enough bribes to take our families down for a glorious vacation!"

Phyl sighed. "Yeah, but that's not our style, is it."

"No, but you can thank the one running the show, who is his ex-mistress, now wife. She's surrounding herself and him with quite a game."

"Eva?"

"Hmm."

"*Señora* Eva *de* Perón."

Vivienne shook her curls. "Here she is, starting from rags, only grade school and now heading a country — she, the daughter of a Madame!"

Phyl made a face. "Do you think that's really true? Would he marry her if she was?"

"Lord knows. Everything goes here. Now she's running half the show like some Madame Du Barry or something. She has her own office, receiving job applications, loans, and favors. So, you can imagine. This is some slap in the face for the Argentine *señoras*, who we know very well are the most straight-laced women in the world. I hear they are fit to be tied over it." Vivienne turned in her seat to look better at the raucous women in the corner. She got up. "What on earth is all that racket about?"

Phyl looked. She stood up and smoothed down her skirt. "Let's go see." The two ladies took their handbags and sauntered over to the corner of the room. Eight women were gathered around two round tables pushed together. They drank martinis.

Vivienne grinned at them. "What are you ladies so excited about?"

"You know who is going to Europe on a Rainbow Tour? She thinks she's going to see the Pope! As if the Pope would lower himself," explained one of the ladies, a brunette with glasses and thick lips.

Phyl held out her hand and introduced herself to the few new members she'd never met. "You're talking about Eva Perón? What's this Rainbow Tour?"

"A goodwill trip. She's going to France, Monaco, Switzerland, Spain, and the Vatican."

Phyl frowned. "Spain? Isn't it still under Franco? The Americans won't like that."

Another lady scoffed. "The whole world wouldn't like that!"

"I think she's going to take most of Argentina's money and deposit it into a Swiss bank account. It's a ruse. She's draining Argentina in plain sight," said another.

Phyl thoughtfully looked at the woman. She had a cigarette holder, was taking a deep drag, and looked very happy with herself. She eyed Phyl and motioned to her outfit. "You trying to start a fad with Eva's line of clothing?"

Phyl looked down at her outfit and touched the front of the top. She laughed. "No. In fact, she copied *me*. She saw me wear this on set during one of the movies I worked in. She was one of the actors. I was only background."

The women squealed with delight.

"You mean she copied *you*?" one asked excitedly.

Phyl smiled again. "Yeah. She kept eyeing me. That was when she was still a brunette."

The women all sat up. A few stood up around Phyl. "Tell us what she was like," asked one.

"Well," Phyl said, looking around. "She was much younger, but, yeah, she was pretty bossy. Kind of a loner, I would say. I wasn't too impressed with her acting skills." She frowned. "And I thought her voice was tiresome. It's improved somewhat now, I noticed."

One scoffed. "Ha! Not quite. Her voice is appalling."

"I bet she's going to act her role as she thinks it should be acted. That's all she knows. Faking it. She has absolutely no class or proper upbringing. Imagine expecting to see the Pope. And she from the streets," said a mousy, older woman sitting with her legs crossed and holding her cocktail glass. She was stirring a toothpick with a maraschino cherry on the end of it.

"Yeah," said Phyl thoughtfully. "Imagine. Quite ambitious, I would say. Amazing."

Vivienne looked at her oddly. "You sound as if you almost feel sorry for her. Surely, that's completely different from how you always spoke about her."

Phyl looked at her pensively. "You're right. But now I can't help but see her as somebody's child. A little girl who, for some reason, felt she needed to fight tooth and nail to get away from where she came from. Something terrible must have happened to her."

One of the ladies piped up. "Phyllis Redington, you are getting soft. That's not how you sounded last time you were here."

"Well, I'm not the same person as I was last time I was here," Phyl said quietly.

* * *

Phyl stood looking at the cracked walls of their living room.

Earlier, she had noticed that someone seemed to have swung off the chrome shower curtain rod in the bathroom, and there was a hole punched into the woodwork next to the tub. In the back of her mind, she imagined someone being tied up, hung and battered. She shook the image from her mind and took out her sodden handkerchief to wipe her nose. She had acquired the obligatory Argentine cold, as had Stuart. And his cough had returned, even though he still wasn't smoking.

She looked further at the state of the apartment. Stuart planned to have everything fixed and painted before they moved back in, but with the housing shortage, getting someone to do the work was like being extorted. There were no regulated or fixed rates, and Stuart had to go around and literally fight for someone to do the work. He told her that Argentines think all North Americans were millionaires and quoted the highest prices he'd ever heard.

Phyl looked at her watch. She was expecting a new maid to arrive. Mercedes had disappeared into thin air while they were in North America after she gave Tony to Jorge. Tony had happily pranced around the *estancia* with the other various animals, waiting for Phyl to come back. He fell ill and died the year before. But he had a very happy doggy life.

This new maid – Maria - was older and had mature daughters who also worked, so she wasn't desperate for money. But Phyl desperately needed *her*, and though Maria wasn't going to do everything Mercedes had done or live with them full time, she agreed to come every afternoon to prepare dinner, do a bit of wash and cleaning, then leave after everything was cleaned up in the evening. Phyl had to pay 175 *pesos* per month, and with the new Perón measures, she would have to give Maria a month's salary as a gift at Christmas; plus, if ever Maria left or was fired, Maria was to receive a month's salary for every month she worked for them. Phyl wryly thought perhaps she should go into the maid business herself.

She walked into the kitchen and looked around. Everything looked abused. She stood on a step stool to look at the higher shelves in the cupboard. She was pleased to see that Mercedes had packed her good things away. Everything was there, a relief. She had moments where she thought Mercedes would steal everything she could. She hated to think that way, but the Argentine masses seemed to disdain the people who hired them. It felt insane.

She carefully got down from the step stool and walked into the dining room. She went behind the bar and searched the shelves. There were used bottles of alcohol, glasses, and a pile of stationery. She took out a sheet. It was the American Embassy stationary. "Well, this will come in handy," she said.

She looked at the ceiling and noticed light bulbs were missing. She shook her head. Lightbulbs were now seventy-five cents apiece. She saw she'd have to get half a dozen or so as some were missing from table lamps.

She planned to recover the lampshades and wanted to reupholster the furniture, but with the prices of upholstery, she opted to have them cleaned instead. The rug was destroyed, so she and Stuart purchased a new one and a small one for the bedroom, a shame since prices were at a premium.

The remainder of their things coming from New York would take months, but at least Stuart had come to the Hotel last night saying their belongings were on the high seas and well on their way. Her vacuum cleaner, sewing machine, hampers, sheets, and towels were coming home. She hoped the moth balls would keep vermin and bugs at bay and that they wouldn't have to bribe or beg someone from high up to quickly maneuver their things through customs.

She walked to the balcony doors and opened them. A cool breeze off the ocean whipped her hair as she stepped out to the railing. She looked to the right. Over the treetops, she could see across the river and the congested port in the foreground, bustling with a backup of freighters offshore waiting to unload. The sky was clear, and the lights were beginning to twinkle. She saw the tops of palm trees, pine trees, and blossoming plantains.

It was a full moon, and she admired its faded presence. Soon, it would shine like a spotlight over the city. She looked again at the packed port, the lights, and the billowing steam from freighters. She shook her head. It seemed there were still periodic shortages of about everything, and the Perón government put a ceiling on flooring, clothing, and other dry goods. She wondered why there could be such a shortage when port trade seemed constant and brisk.

She shivered in the cold. She was about to walk back into the apartment when she spied something behind one of the planters of dead plants. She walked over and picked up an old ball.

"Tony," she whispered. She held it to her nose and missed him so much. She squeezed it and took it into the apartment.

Having a dog again was tempting, but if something were to happen, uprooting and taking it back to North America would be so very unfair to the poor thing. For the first time, she consciously decided not to ever have a dog again. As with children, she would have to be satisfied with seeing the Piñiero kids and pets and consider them almost her own.

She took a deep breath, shivered again, and stepped back into the apartment, closing the glass doors behind her. It was getting dark, and Stuart would return soon from the market. Tomorrow, they were going to the zoo.

And so, their life of intrigue was beginning again.

* * *

The next day.

The weather was hazy and heavy with humidity, and it felt rather cold. She and Stuart were surprised at the changes in the zoo. It appeared that those in charge weren't sure whether to have a simple zoo or a full-fledged amusement park. It wasn't enough to have children riding on llamas and ponies. Now, they laid a miniature train track right down the middle of the main pathways. A sign on a post near the track said the train was not in use due to a pending court order on the city stating that the zoo owed them taxes. Stuart hinted that the owner was being held over a barrel by Eva, who was in the habit of looking for kickbacks. He figured it was to build up a coffer of monies to spend on the *descamisados*.

Phyl eyed her surroundings. She noticed more booths selling sweets and souvenirs, though some stood empty. The animal enclosures were also undergoing changes. She was appalled to see families balancing their children on the edge of a new lower fence around the lion pit. A merry-go-round sat still, looking as if it had been wrecked by hoodlums.

"What a shame," she said to Stuart as she looked around.

Stuart shrugged and shook his head. "The effects of regime changes. It's unsettling, for sure."

Phyl looked to see if the usual benches were in their old positions. "Are we doing the old bench trick, Stu?"

Stuart laughed. "No, we're actually meeting someone for coffee at the new cafeteria. It's quite in the open. We don't have to pretend to be ventriloquists."

"Oh. So, we're actually looking at this person, then?"

"Apparently so."

"A lovely change," she laughed.

They entered an open-air coffee shop with a help-yourself quay similar to a North American cafeteria. They went to the counter, ordered coffee and biscuits on a tray, and walked while Stuart searched the seated crowd.

"Now what?" asked Phyl.

Almost on cue, their noses twitched to a floating sea of nearby perfume. They turned to see a hefty young man with slicked-back hair, a pencil mustache, a fedora and dark suit appear out of nowhere beside Stuart. Stuart jumped and looked to his side.

"*Señor* Redington?"

"*Sí.*"

"Follow me, please," the young man requested.

Stuart and Phyl followed the young man.

"Is this the guy we're supposed to meet?" whispered Phyl.

"I don't know," Stuart whispered. He studied the back of the young man. "I guess we'll find out."

The three meandered between adults and screaming children until they reached a Funny House under construction. "What do I do with this?" asked Stuart, motioning to the tray he was carrying.

The young man took the tray and threw it into a nearby bush.

They slipped through a side door. They stopped as their eyes slowly adjusted to the damp, dark interior. The noise of the crowd bounced against the unfinished walls. Phyl looked back at daylight slipping through the cracks of the door. She heard a little girl giggle. She faced the dark hallway again.

"Please," called the young man from a distance.

He opened a door leading into a hallway. Light from within poured over his form. Another young, muscular man with a hand in one pocket and a cigarette leisurely held in the other stepped through the lit doorway, looked at Stuart and Phyl, and wordlessly stood next to the first. They patiently waited.

As Stuart and Phyl walked to the opening, they heard a voice beckon them. "Come in, *Señor* Redington."

They peeked around the doorframe and saw a slightly balding, swarthy man elegantly dressed, with a thin mustache. He appeared to be in his late fifties. He waved a well-manicured hand and the smoke swirled around him highlighted by a ceiling lightbulb. He looked slightly familiar to Phyl. "Come, sit," he said.

He motioned to two wooden chairs across from him. A small marble-topped table stood precariously perched on uneven legs between the man and chairs. A large glass ashtray bore a smoldering black and gold-tipped cigarette. The man picked up the cigarette, took a drag, and flicked the ash onto the ground. He took another quick, noisy drag, then dropped the half-smoked cigarette. He ground it with the toe of a black leather shoe. He pushed his chair back with a scrape and held out his hand.

"Señor Redington, let me introduce myself properly. I am Alberto Dodero."

Stuart held out his, ready to shake, and froze mid-motion. He knitted his brows. "Dodero?" he choked. He looked at Dodero's hand and slowly, reverently, shook it.

Dodero turned to a curious Phyl. "*Señora de Redington*. I understand you are a talented actress."

"I, uh…"

Phyl, startled, looked to Stuart. She held out her hand. Dodero took it and bent over it, his lips brushing her skin just gently enough to cause her shivers. She pulled her hand away and absentmindedly looked at it.

"Please." He motioned for them to sit.

Phyl slowly sat down, allowing Stuart to adjust her seat slightly to face Dodero. Stuart removed his hat, undid his jacket and vest, and sat down with one hand on his hip to look relaxed, though Phyl could almost hear his heart racing. She could see his neck pulse.

Dodero briskly motioned to the two young men at the doorway. "The Belgian truffles," he said.

He smiled, and a gold tooth twinkled. "As you may know, I am a bit of a – how you say? Go-between between your Embassy and the Peróns. The president and his First Lady are two of my closest friends." He studied his own well-manicured nails. "In fact, I have a tremendous influence on them, having, I believe, greatly helped Juan to his presidency." He turned to Phyl.

"My wife was a professional dancer and tried her hand at acting. She knew Eva from her earlier days, having met her on set. You also met her on a set when she was still a teenager?"

"Yes, I did. I didn't do very much. I was only background, and at the time, I couldn't speak Spanish. But she left an impression on me."

"Yes." He smiled. "I could well imagine. For all her great aspirations, Eva comes from humble beginnings, and, at times, her lack of training has been quite evident. My wife, who is passionate about her clothes, is helping Eva appear more of a – shall we say – First Lady."

"Oh," said Phyl. "I see." She smiled stiffly.

Dodero sat back and glanced at the two young men who appeared in the doorway. One of them entered with a bowl of Belgian chocolate truffles and placed it carefully on the little table. He moved the ashtray.

Dodero waved. "Get me a fresh ashtray," he ordered.

The young man looked back at his own second, who quickly disappeared.

Dodero held out the bowl of chocolate truffles and he took one out. "The most expensive truffle in the world. I had them flown in from Bruges, and they arrived this morning." He offered.

Phyl and Stuart politely took one each. They quietly unwrapped their truffle, every-once-in-a-while looking at Dodero as he smiled, unwrapping his. He popped it into his mouth and chewed, tossing the wrapping back into the bowl and wiping the cocoa off his hands.

Phyl bit into hers and closed her eyes as the chocolate melted and oozed over her tongue like a magical potion baptizing her mouth with the most exquisite taste and texture she had ever experienced. She opened her eyes. She closed her eyes again. She covered her mouth, and slowly sucked at the delicacy with a moan. Then she slowly licked the cocoa off her fingers.

Dodero beamed at her. The second young man hurried in with a clean ashtray. "Heavenly, yes?" he asked, pleased.

Phyl silently nodded. She looked at the beautiful wrapping, smoothed it on her knee, folded it, and carefully slipped it into her purse.

"Please," Dodero motioned. "Take some for later."

Phyl looked at Stuart, then at the bowl. She took two and carefully put them into her purse. She smiled at Dodero, who grinned back, nodding.

Dodero eyed the ashtray as he took out a gold cigarette case, opened it, and held it out to Phyl. Curiosity drove Phyl to accept one and not worry about what Stuart thought. But to her surprise, Stuart also took one. The cigarettes looked more expensive than a bottle of the best whiskey. Dodero leaned forward and lit their cigarettes with a gold lighter. He took a cigarette and lit his.

The smoke curled and snaked around their heads. Stuart coughed, and Phyl automatically patted his back.

Dodero startled Phyl. He pointed at her. "You're the key."

"I'm the key?" She looked at Stuart wide-eyed. Stuart looked confused.

"Stuart, here…" He looked at Stuart. "May I call you Stuart?"

Stuart nodded.

"Stuart, here, is already established in a chain of transfer of information." Dodero looked at Stuart. "Your friend, he keeps in touch with me as well."

"Jorge?"

"Yes. Piñiero. Our mutual friend, Piñiero, no longer has much power. His newer workers have no respect, and he has a problem arranging shipping of his wines and wool."

Stuart shifted. Phyl tried to read his face. If he knew of Jorge's latest problems, he certainly didn't tell her, though, in light of the upsets caused by the shifting of powers from the elite to the poor, she wasn't surprised. But she could kick herself for never asking how Jorge and Angelica were faring.

"Piñiero, as all of us with an interest in the future of our country's economy, feels he helps by gathering and sharing information with you Americans. As you, yourself, have been doing with us, Stuart. I know there are quite a few of you here. Salesmen, attachés, one or two of the journalists still allowed to cover events." He took a deep breath and sat back, slightly scowling. "I, on the other hand, am perhaps the wealthiest Argentine. I have more to lose, so playing both fields is in my best interests." He sat back. "You know how I acquired my wealth?"

Stuart: "In shipping."

"Yes, I bought many defunct ships after the First World War. I built even more. Many more." He shifted forward, leaning on his elbows as he looked down at nothing.

Phyl eyed his array of gold and diamond rings.

"Initially, I could bring out commodities for trade anywhere in the world, but I needed product to bring back." He sat back and held out his palms. "It didn't make economic sense to not secure cargo on the return trips. So, it was crucial for me that countries were prepared to trade with Argentina. I focused on England and the United States. I was able to set up brisk trade with England, but," he shrugged. "The United States was always a challenge. The problem had to be corrected at the base of Argentine politics. We needed a government that the United States would officially recognize. As you know, it's been a challenging journey. And Latin America, after all, is the footstool to North America. Argentina has not been easily influenced by the Americans, and yet, you Americans would rather influence the Argentines into a form of government similar to yourselves. Like England is to the U.S. But…"

Stuart laughed. "Democracy."

"Yes, you laugh. We appear as a problem child when it comes to democracy. No need to explain what a potential storehouse of dynamite we are." He looked at them impishly. "I know things which are helpful to you Americans. Ergo, my vital connection to your Embassy." He flicked his cigarette. "I must say, when diplomatic relations were cut those two years at the war's end, I don't think I slept a full night. You see…" Dodero cracked his back. "I may be one of the wealthiest men in the *entire* world. In fact, I've had the largest private yacht ever built in the Mediterranean. I have multiple homes, mistresses, gold, and diamonds. I shower the Peróns with furs and riches."

He pointed at himself. "I am certainly wealthier and therefore more powerful, in a way, than they are. But if the economy of this country collapses because of their mismanagement, and if a Fascist government takes over and nationalizes everything, well," he made a face and shrugged. "Guess who loses out?" He pointed at himself with his thumb. "Do you see what I mean?"

Stuart studied Dodero thoughtfully. "Absolutely."

Phyl saw that her self-confident husband returned. He seemed comfortable in Dodero's presence.

"Keep your friends close, but your enemies, closer."

"Between you and I, yes." Dodero smiled at Stuart. "You understand me."

"Yes." Stuart briefly glanced at Phyl. "So, why do you think my wife is key?"

Phyl stirred. "Yes," she croaked. "Why did you say that? I'm a nobody."

"Eva leaves on the sixth of June for Spain. Just before she leaves, she will inaugurate the first temporary housing units for single working women in Buenos Aires."

"Well," said Phyl, surprised, "that's impressive. And quick."

"Yes. Perón is practically giving her free reign. So, the question is, why is he doing this? Why is he allowing an uneducated young girl - she's only 28 with no political experience - to take millions of *pesos* and American dollars to do what she sees fit? Oh, I applaud her intentions. It's all about worshipping Perón as the savior to his country, and all she talks about is the *descamisados*."

"The poor shirtless ones," whispered Phyl.

"It's well-intentioned, highly admirable. Yes, the shirtless ones have appeared to be trodden while we," Dodero pointed to himself. "I, your friend Piñiero, our entire class, we're the ones who made Argentina very wealthy into the Depression. And while the rest of the world suffered, we held on fairly well. There is a reason why Buenos Aires is the Paris of the Western World, even throughout the Depression. But trade was affected. So, my country and I were affected. Never mind, I'm going off-topic as usual. Back to you and Eva."

Phyl's heart started to pound.

"You are a member of the American Women's Club, which has over 500 members - wives of diplomats, big business leaders, and mistresses of wealthy men. Powerful men. Men have their women's ears when in bed. Women know more than the collective we," he said, looking at Stuart.

Stuart made a face and chuckled.

Dodero's eyes softened. He also chuckled.

"So?"

Dodero looked at Phyl. "You will be receiving a nomination to become President of the American Women's Club. Piñiero and I need you to accept. Representing the club, you will be invited to all the special openings and gatherings Eva will be organizing. I want you to keep an eye on her. If you can - because I realize she is very off-putting and insular, maybe even arrogant in her lack of self-confidence - you can speak to her. Win her friendship, her trust." He sighed. "My wife is Eva's best and only friend. But she likes to travel and finds these openings a bore. She only wants to attend the special Balls."

"I must decline." Phyl looked at Stuart. "We don't have a car and chauffeur to run to town every day nor the money for all the incidental expenses connected with this position." She looked beseechingly at Dodero. "We would need five servants and a grander flat or house with a swimming pool to put on the necessary show." She looked around the dark room. "There will be many members against me, too, as I am not American, and the Club is the focus of the American colony here."

Dodero waved her away. "All hurdles I can help with, and best not to change flats. You are under the protection of Piñiero at the moment. When you entertain, you can entertain at the hotel."

"Lordy, I don't know how I can be of help to you in any case!" exclaimed a frightened Phyl.

"You will help by watching Eva's mental state. She is unpredictable and can fly off the handle. Perón has given her almost unlimited power, and she is emotionally driven and erratic in her methods."

"Why would Perón give her so much power?" asked Stuart.

"Because the masses adore her and her rhetoric. She claims to be like them. They see her and all her opulence; she claims they should have that, too. This secures Perón's base, and she will deflect attention and criticism away from him while he focuses on things that do not necessarily improve the state of the *descamisados*. He eats, drinks, and dreams military. He plans on becoming a long-standing and almost dictatorial ruler, but he is smart enough to realize where the power lies, not just in the elite and his military. He has learned from the best, you see. You control the emotions and minds of the larger and more manipulative, less educated masses, and you control the foundation of your power."

"Just like Hitler," said Stuart.

Dodero shrugged. "As I said. He learned from the best."

Phyl's mind raced.

"Perón manipulates Eva, who is less educated and easily swayed by his power. She thinks she can be their savior. Their saint. Another role for her to play. Both have, in their own way, Fascist leanings. And that," Alberto Dodero said, as he popped a truffle into his mouth, "is why all this matters to me. They are close friends of Spain's Franco - who, by the way, just declared Spain a monarchy and made himself regent - and those who hold private wealth would become a target. I may lose everything I have. Piñiero, the likes of him, and myself, must have hands on deck to make sure that this particular ship of ours doesn't sink."

"No pun intended," muttered Stuart.

Dodero laughed. "Oh, no. Indeed. Pun intended."

Phyl had a million questions. She still couldn't understand how keeping an eye on Eva and passing on information could be any better than other connections he had. But then again, she thought, she probably was one of many who will bend an ear for the famous and influential Alberto Dodero.

Dodero raised a hand and massaged the back of it. "Eva is insisting on a grand goodwill trip throughout Europe. I suspect it's her way of fingering her nose at the bluebloods of Argentina who regularly spend time in Paris. You aren't cultured until you do, you see. So, she's doing a grand slam, as you say. I will be going along. There is a great deal of opposition. The Peróns have gone through quite a bit of the country's coffers on behalf of Eva's grand social services and so she now promises she'll pay for the trip from her own salary as an actress, but I doubt she makes millions as a radio player."

Dodero cleared his throat. "Whatever. I am covering all costs of the logistics of the trip. We're flying on a Douglas DC-4 and outfitting it as Eva demands. Bedrooms, dining room, vanity table, and curtains. Room for her endless number of trunks. Servants. I'll have it well stocked with Champagne, of course. Then I take her back on one of my ships."

"Other than benefactor, in what capacity are you going on this goodwill mission?" asked Stuart.

"Someone needs to keep an eye on her and what she says. There will be a publicist with us to guide her. And, I am arranging Swiss bank accounts for her and Perón while everyone else is watching her flit about. No one knows it yet, but we're visiting Switzerland, as well."

"Oh, my God," said Phyl. "Are they siphoning money from Argentina?"

Dodero took on a conspiratorial air. "Let me put it this way." He turned to Stuart. "Did you know that the Nazi connections are far from dead despite the agreement between your Truman and Perón?"

Phyl, startled, looked at Stuart to read his expression. Stuart didn't seem surprised. Their recent discovery of the atrocities of Hitler's concentration camps had just fully come to light, and Phyl hadn't slept for nights after seeing some of the images Stuart had brought back to show her.

Stuart quietly looked at his hands for a moment. "Yes, we realize that." He angrily pursed his lips and shook his head. "We also know the Jews are dead set on locating Nazis who had anything to do with the massacre of millions of their people. They know Nazis are flocking here." Stuart smashed his cigarette into the ashtray. He absentmindedly studied his fingers for wayward tobacco. "We also know that Perón welcomes Nazi stragglers with a price on their heads with open arms and offers them new identities. We suspect there are thousands. Maybe tens. And each one of them represents a healthy kickback."

Dodero grinned. "Yes, kickbacks directly into the Perón pockets. In fact, they struck the mother-load of Nazi Jewish gold."

"Excuse me?" asked a surprised Phyl.

Dodero scratched his chin.

"Is she so evil?" hissed Phyl.

"Eva? I don't think she understands where their gold comes from." Dodero shook his head. "I don't think she's that smart. Even if she was, I don't think she cares enough to even wonder. But again, I tell you this: she is being used by Perón." He cocked his head and stopped smiling. "You should know, the most wanted of them, the Nazi leader himself, was secretly brought here," he blinked at Stuart.

Stuart's mouth dropped open.

Phyl looked again at Dodero. "Who?"

Stuart turned to her and the blood drained from his face.

Phyl gasped. "Adolf Hitler?"

"The truth is, he's not well. He hasn't been for a couple of years, though they hid that fact from everyone. It may be, thank God, one of the reasons why they finally lost. He was like Napoleon in the end, refusing to face reality and sick with physical affliction." Dodero noticed Stuart's look of disdain and raised his hand. "I swear to you, I do not know where he might be at this moment, but wherever he is, he may not live long enough to see our Argentine summer."

"How do you know all this?" asked Stuart. His face flushed with anger. Sweat beaded his forehead and shone like stars under the light above.

Dodero put a finger to his lips. "He was smuggled on one of my ships."

"For a kickback to you?" choked Stuart.

"I don't need kickbacks," Dodero announced huffily. He was miffed at the suggestion. "No, the proverbial gun was pointed at my head. If I am to remain a close friend, there are evils I must do, I fear. This was one of the gravest."

Phyl swallowed hard. "But they shot themselves, he and Eva Braun. Their bodies were burned. And they found them in a bunker under what was left of Berlin."

Dodero tapped his temple. "If we are harboring hundreds of war criminals, all capable of escaping, would it not be logical to assume that the chief of all, with an infinite number of resources at his fingertips, could not also escape?" He paused for good effect. "I trust you won't risk your lives by spreading this information." He pointedly looked at his two bodyguards. "People are already disappearing. I don't know if it's the Nazis or the Peróns or both. We live in dangerous times."

Phyl felt sick to her stomach. She was on that fearful roller coaster once again. She took a deep breath to gather her courage. She realized she was at the crux of history. Being in the know of information relating to the truth of one of the worst monsters in history terrified her. And yet, deep down inside, she sensed she had the strength to bear it. She looked at Dodero, wide-eyed but composed.

Dodero silently nodded. He took a deep breath and took another Belgian chocolate truffle. He slowly unwrapped it and held it to the light to admire it. "Exquisite," he whispered. He popped the luxurious morsel into his mouth, closed his eyes, and slowly sucked the cocoa off the tip of each finger.

Chapter Eighteen
Eva's Welcome, Uruguay, Rio and New Year's

"Did you hear the Pope received our First Lady with only a rosary like any other dignitary. For heaven's sake, I would love to have been a fly on that holy wall." Angelica yelled over the din of voices and band music in the port terminal. The floor, walls, and windows trembled with the deep, bone-rattling rumble of ship's engines.

Tucked tightly against Angelica, Phyl pulled her eyes away from the busy wharf to admire Angelica's broad purple hat, elegant white mink, and her mauve and black cinch-waist dress. She glanced back and saw that Angelica's hat blocked the action from those behind them.

Angelica, utterly unaware of how others were affected, squinted from under her thick dark lashes through the streaked window. She looked elegant, refined, deliciously round, and feminine. Jorge stood on the other side of her, his arm around her waist. Angelica raised a petite hand and tapped at the glass. "I hear she had a bit of a screaming session with her brother, who was to have arranged everything precisely," she laughed.

Phyl chuckled. "Poor thing. She must live in a fantasy world if she thought she was going to be treated like a potential saint by the Pope."

Just then, a woman pushed into her, and Phyl grabbed Angelica's arm for balance, almost knocking her and Jorge over. They both laughed.

"I don't know. It boggles my mind because look…" Phyl pointed at the crowd on the wharf and beyond. "Look at these people waiting for her. My God, I see old women crying. Eva Perón really *is* a saint in this fantasy world."

150,000 frenzied Argentines gathered to greet Eva Perón back from her European Rainbow Tour. Women screamed, men hollered, thousands of white and colored handkerchiefs fluttered and waved in the air above the heads of those crammed near Dodero's docked ship, The S.S. Buenos Aires.

Phyl looked past the stern of the ship, at cumbersome but powerful tug boats plowing through the brown harbor's white caps. She glanced around the packed interior of the terminal. People huddled at each tall window. It was bitterly cold outside. But standing amongst the elite inside, they were warmed by the sun cascading through the windows, cozy and warm. She looked at all the conspicuous wealth they rubbed elbows with. It seemed every woman was wearing a fur coat. Elegant men with pocket watches and gold rings, smoked cigars, and sucked cigarette holders. A thick, low-hanging band of ghostly smoke floated above everyone. She worriedly glanced at Stuart, who occasionally coughed in irritation.

Phyl's eyes fell on Jorge again. He stood looking keenly out the window. She studied his handsome profile for a moment, noted how the sun's rays caused the silver at his temple to sparkle. She smiled and sighed. Angelica and Jorge had been such good friends. She felt great adoration for them.

The ship's engines rumbled to a tortured stop. She glanced at the quivering glass window, afraid it might shatter. The crowd in and out erupted in joyous cheers, and she looked beyond to dock workers below, slowly maneuvering a steep and screeching boarding ramp into place.

Jorge had parked a great distance away and they had been swept up by the living current of singing, chanting people flowing through the streets to the port.

Buenos Aires rang with ship and car horns and whistles. Everything was adorned with robin's egg blue and white Argentine flags with the stylized gold sun in the middle. Massive, heavy banners of Eva's image smiled benignly on the packed streets and sidewalks and hung absolutely everywhere. Her frozen, steady gaze was beamed from every rooftop, street light, and tall building. Every once-in-a-while, a stiff, cold wind off the broad River Plate lifted the edges of one or two banners and made them flop and clap like gigantic rugs being flicked. A deafening ring of church bells echoed throughout the city and oceans of tiny Argentina flags waved on balconies and windows by people desperately watching for Eva's ship slowly being piloted into port. There was color and noise and barking everywhere, ringing in everyone's ears. Oh, such passion. Oh, such excitement.

An hour later, Phyl leaned against the window and looked down at the band performing a military number barely audible over the fracas. She saw a series of microphones on a dais being arranged close to the bottom of the ship's ramp finally rested in place. Nearby, groups of reporters, journalists, and cameramen. Behind the press and the surrounding fencing, people jumped over each other to catch a glimpse of movement up on deck. Suddenly, everyone spied the movement of a door, its brass porthole sparkling in the bright sun as it swung open, but just a crew members stepped out from the ship's interior. The false alarm set the crowd off like dynamite. Disappointment engulfed them when they realized it was not their beloved.

Their beloved Eva.

Phyl saw the new American ambassador, James Bruce, at one of the other windows. Phyl knew she and Stuart would meet him at a welcoming reception at the Embassy in a few months. She surmised he came early to catch this historic day.

She looked back at Stuart to see if he had spotted him, but Stuart seemed more interested in the activities onboard ship. He had told her that Eva Perón's grand European trip had been riddled with controversy; parts were highly successful, some bitterly embarrassing, and a great disappointment to the great Eva Perón. Apparently, there were mixed reactions to Argentina's First Lady in one or two of the European countries. Perhaps Ambassador Bruce had heard word and hurried down to keep a finger on the pulse.

The goal of the trip wasn't all as rosy as the Argentine papers depicted. Phyl sensed Machiavellian maneuverings were part of Eva's agenda. Contrary to what they claimed, it was not just for good will and drumming up international trade. The most contentious part of the trip was that she went to fascist Spain first. This greatly concerned the Americans. She had also made a detour through Switzerland. Just as Dodero told them she would. Phyl wondered what monies were squirreled away. So, it was no wonder the ambassador had come long before the official swearing-in of his office.

A flash of reflected sun caught her attention. She looked in time to see a group of men barge through the ship's door, whisking Eva Perón onto the main deck and into the holy light. A deafening explosion of cheers and cries erupted as their Madonna flamboyantly stepped to the head of the ramp. She waved delightedly to another explosive roar of emotion from the crowd.

Phyl eyed Eva with interest. The First Lady was decked out like a movie star. She wore a magnificent dress with a cream-colored fur coat over her shoulders. She wore a broad-rim hat, which she kept in place with a white-gloved hand against an imposing breeze. She allowed herself to be carefully led down the ramp by two sailors. Her smile was broad and impish. She was evidently pleased with the well-orchestrated and majestic welcome.

"She's gone up in the world. She finally has a Christian Dior dress," smirked Angelica.

Phyl squinted at Eva's hem peeking out of the opening of her coat. "How do you know it's Christian Dior? Most of it is covered by the fur coat."

"Oh, believe me. I know."

The band picked up a frenzied Argentine anthem and flocks of pigeons - dyed pink and blue - exploded from hidden cages and swept and darted overhead like cherubs.

Angelica leaned into Phyl. "Talk about topping Madame du Barry," she said, ensuring no one around them could hear. "Fancy rising from the house of prostitution to being decorated with the Order of the Virgin of Guadalupe in Spain, throwing money around and making speeches to women about virtue and a spiritual home life. Does she even know how to cook? What was she before: a nun?"

Angelica dipped under her coat lapel to adjust a bra strap and threw a mischievous smile at Phyl. "I hear the King and Queen of England went to Scotland just to avoid her in London, the poor things. They say she insisted on staying at Buckingham Palace." Angelica gave Phyl a knowing look. "I bet you she was miffed *that* didn't pan out!"

"She was so miffed, she ended up not going to England at all," said Stuart, standing directly behind Phyl.

Phyl wondered what all Stuart knew. She took an extra long look at him and noted how he had gained considerable weight. Since that meeting with Dodero, Stuart had to fight to stay away from cigarettes. He ate everything he could get his hands on. His face had widened and filled out, making his mustache look thinner and broader. They had to cut into their budget and get a new tailor-made suit for him as he couldn't get his trousers buttoned or his vests closed adequately. Oh, but he was still so very pleasant looking. Her heart filled with pride. She smiled at him. He didn't notice.

Slowly, a mounting, bone-rattling rumble shook the overhead rafters and glass. Phyl looked and saw a swarm of planes flying in formation. Her heart lept when she realized they were dumping something over the wharf, buildings, and people. "What are they dropping?"

Stuart studied the strange-looking items as they hit and slid down the windows. "Twigs with ribbons."

Jorge nodded, staring at a couple that landed on the outside windowsill. "Actually, flags on olive branches. Perhaps of countries she visited."

"The olive branches or the flags?" teased Stuart.

Jorge elegantly turned and cast Stuart a long, dry look. Then he smirked and continued looking over the action outside.

"I wonder how much of the planning that went into this was done by her?" muttered Jorge.

Angelica laughed.

"Look, there's Dodero," pointed Stuart.

The sun began to set, and rays poured straight across the upper deck. Once again, the glint of the brass porthole in the deck doorway had caught everyone's attention. Alberto Dodero appeared behind another man who Phyl recognized as Eva's brother, Juan Duarte. Both men moved to the top of the ramp to stop and watch the proceedings below, careful not to take the limelight from the woman of the hour.

Phyl frowned. "Are you sure that's Dodero? He looks different."

"Stress," joked Stuart.

Jorge shook his head. "Shaved off his mustache. And Duarte. I wonder what the story is behind *him* going? Curiously, as Perón's private secretary, he should have stuck close to home."

"Perón insisted on sending him to keep an eye on his sister," Stuart said.

"That's interesting. Trust issues." Phyl studied the two frazzled gentlemen.

"I wonder if Dodero is relieved not to be baby-sitting," chuckled Stuart.

Phyl sighed with contentment. She was pleased Stuart was in a good mood. He had very few lung problems recently and was in excellent spirits. She wasn't sure if Dodero had anything to do with it, but Stuart had sold over a million *pesos*' worth of business since their strange meeting at the zoo. As a result, Remington-Rand, was so impressed they announced they were sending Marcel Rand himself to check Stuart out. At first, Phyl fretted as she would have her hands full entertaining him and whoever else he would bring along while already scheduled to attend Eva Perón's social program receptions, openings of hospitals, women's temporary housing and orphanages.

She also had an opportunity to be in another play, which she seriously considered until she heard Marcel Rand was coming. She was sad to turn the play down. Her life was indeed full. The silver lining to this heavy load was that, true to Dodero's word, he approved the hiring of an extra maid and servant for Phyl for as long as she needed them. Plus, a car and chauffeur for her Eva commitments.

That made it all quite doable and pretty luxurious. She was one of the Argentine elites between the extra servants and being chauffeured like royalty. She whispered a silent blessing for Dodero.

Stuart squeezed her shoulder.

Phyl patted his hand, then frowned as a dull ache raised its ugly head in her abdomen. She took a long, deep breath and fidgeted slightly. She wasn't sure if it was lingering pain from her hysterectomy, phantom monthly pains, or just the usual Buenos Aires nerves. More than likely, it was probably due to the electric lifestyle change in taking on the role of President of the American Women's Club. She decided to be more disciplined with what she ate and drank. She reached over and patted Stuart on his tummy because it had also been affecting him.

Stuart held her hand close to his heart. He jokingly patted his round tummy with his other hand.

Another wave of cheers jarred Phyl's train of thought. Juan Perón, accompanied by generals, soldiers, and a cardinal, marched to the dais. Above their heads, the colorful pigeons settled on every ledge and railing, dropping streaks of white feces on everything, including the posters of Eva smiling down at the massive crowd. This made her chuckle. "Did everyone get a day off from work?"

Jorge whispered in her ear. "Factory workers were threatened with losing their cards and possibly their jobs if they did not come to greet their beloved Eva Perón."

Phyl gasped. "Really? That's outrageous!"

Jorge put a finger to his lips.

"This is all a setup, then?" Phyl looked down at the crammed wharf. "Is that legal?"

"Does it matter?" asked Jorge.

"Yes. It's pure manipulation. All these reporters and photographers recording this for the rest of the world to see, and the world will think everyone loves Eva Perón."

"Precisely the point."

"Well," Stuart cut in. "I think I've seen enough. Shall we drink at the Alvear before the throng attacks it after the usual speeches?"

"Don't you want to hear what she has to say? I wouldn't mind," said Phyl.

"No need," he said sadly. "It's all about how she worships Perón, and she is just a humble servant to him and her people, yada yada. She'll say the poor are without wealth but rich in faith and honor. She'll pour out tears and platitudes to the hardworking, the hungry. She'll boast of coming from nothing, just like them; all the while, she has special cargo on board being unloaded into trucks," he said, pointing out the window at the ship, "Every fur coat you can imagine while her diamonds, rubies, and gems are hauled in bags by her poor, bedraggled and nagged servants. Humble indeed."

Eva smiled tearfully and waved at her adoring crowd. She finally reached Perón at the bottom of the ramp and openly embraced her husband, *El Presidente*, giving him a tearful kiss.

The crowd roared again.

"Stu, I want to stay," whispered Phyl.

Stuart chuckled. "You lucky thing, you'll see her again at that reception at the *Circulo Militar* this weekend. As for me, with this trip to Uruguay next week, I have some work to prepare. But first," Stuart took her arm and smiled down at her. "I need a real stiff one." He gently led her through the crowd.

"Or two stiff ones," joked Jorge, leading Angelica to follow.

Angelica tried to keep up with her husband. "Phyllis, are you coming to the *estancia* in October? The children are so looking forward to it."

Phyl looked back, grinning. "Are you kidding? I'll crawl to your *estancia* if I have to."

Angelica lunged forward and grabbed Phyl's arm, and Phyl let go of Stuart to face her friend inquisitively. Angelica pulled her closer, and the two women allowed the men to push ahead. "Alberto Dodero will be joining us at the *estancia*," said Angelica quietly.

Phyl, after a moment's thought, nodded. She turned and felt her stomach ache again.

Most definitely not rich food, thought Phyl grimly. She was back in the game.

* * *

Phyl didn't make it to the *estancia*.

She advised Angelica she would join her in February instead. Then, quite interestingly, Dodero postponed his visit to coincide with hers. This made Phyl wonder what Dodero was planning. She asked if Dodero wanted to see Stuart, but Angelica didn't know. He seemed only interested in Phyl.

Phyl decided to wait and see. Their schedules were full. In addition to engagements, she and Stuart were to attend leading up to Christmas, Stuart insisted she join him to Montevideo. He didn't explain why, but she knew it meant more than just being there for company. But it pleased her. She would have the freedom of writing home. Sending Christmas gifts and cash safely was virtually non-existent now. She sighed with relief, knowing that all would reach their destination from Uruguay.

Phyl had given up on letter writing in Argentina. When the odd one did get through early in the Perón's reign, they arrived in Canada heavily censored. Now, any mention of Perón, his government, and especially Eva was absolutely forbidden under threat of imprisonment. In fact, spreading any kind of information was severely restricted, especially on Argentine radio broadcasts and newspapers. Eva now controlled all Argentine radio stations and, along with her husband, most of the newspapers. The two remaining independent newspapers were being harassed and severely penalized by Perón. From what Stuart told her, Phyl knew Perón limited the remaining independent newspapers' supply of newsprint to restrict their circulation. The odd voice still spoke truth in print, but these newspapers faced a death knell. Everyone saw the writing on the wall.

Censorship was not limited to Argentine journalists and editors, however. An American Time magazine reporter who tagged along with Eva on her Rainbow Tour wrote about negative responses Eva received. He was sent back to America and banned from Argentina. Many other foreign journalists who had deigned to say anything remotely negative about her and Juan Perón were also barred.

Control didn't stop with the media, however. Most disturbingly, people mysteriously disappeared. Occasionally, a harassed businessman or professor fled to Chile or Brazil. Or just was no more.

Since becoming aware of these unsettling developments, Phyl had been waking in the night with cold sweats, agonized by a tiny worm of fear. She couldn't shake the pain in her stomach. She had her belly and gall bladder checked, but she instinctively knew what really caused physical discomfort.

Stress.

She feared they would be caught. Worse, she feared they would be killed.

She often willed her heart to slow down as she sat in meetings at the American Women's Club or during dinner with the Piñieros. She reminded herself that as foreigners, they were probably somewhat protected from being eradicated. They had, after all, a pseudo-protective umbrella over them.

Did they not?

One night, she thought at length about the bodyguards stationed in and around their building. Yes, they were there because the police chief resided in the other penthouse but perhaps they were also stationed there because the American Embassy had subleased their flat. Then another thought occurred to her: Maybe they were there for Stuart and her. Did Jorge arrange that? Had Dodero?

She considered the important people they entertained at their flat. She remembered Gay, the military attaché, who was found dead in a cave near Montevideo after their dinner. It was then that a seed took hold of her and she became obsessed over the reason for his murder.

Days later, Phyl stood next to Stuart on the ferry crossing the River Plate to Uruguay. She looked back at Buenos Aires in the warm early afternoon and secretly wondered if there was a connection between what Stuart was doing and Gay's death. What did he tell Stuart? Why were Stuart and she entertaining him at all? She dreaded the thought that they may have had some connection to his demise.

Phyl made a brave decision to look into it further.

Settled in their hotel in Montevideo that evening, they enjoyed drinks in the lobby, listening to a piano and violin playing a slow samba. Her face and arms were tanned from sunning on the ferry deck all afternoon. Phyl leaned back in her chair, pondering Gay. Then she looked around her beautiful surroundings. She noticed portraits of Roosevelt and Churchill hanging in the entranceway.

"What a lovely change not to have to look at massive images of Eva everywhere I go," she said to Stuart reading an English newspaper. She took a long, slow sip of her vodka martini and studied him. A wife studying her husband.

They sat in red brocade chairs with gold and white trim. Stuart lounged, his long legs stretched out and crossed at the ankles. He wore his white linen pants, white loose shirt, and a mauve cravat. She loved how mature he looked. She reached out with her rope sandal and nudged his foot. He looked up at her. She smiled at him. He gave her a come-hither side glance and grinned, and went back into the paper.

She leaned in, lightly slapped his knee, and giggled. Aware of movement nearby, she saw a well-dressed, heavy-set man in his early sixties approach them. He looked strangely familiar. He looked directly at her and Stuart. Her smile disappeared and she sat back. She touched Stuart's knee.

"Stu?" she whispered.

"Huh?"

She motioned with her eyes.

Stuart looked up as the gentleman reached them. The man held out his hand to Stuart. "I'm sorry I kept you waiting," he said.

Phyl looked from the strange man to Stuart.

Stuart stood up. "Absolutely no problem. We were enjoying the music." He motioned to Phyl. "Phyl, this is Colonel Atilio Cattáneo. Colonel, my wife, Phyllis."

Phyl stood up. "Oh, yes. Colonel Cattáneo, the aviator." She knew of this man. He had been part of an uprising just before her and Stuart's arrival in Buenos Aires. Cattáneo was a vocal supporter of a fair and democratic system in Argentina. At one point, years earlier, he had been imprisoned. That was before he helped Perón attempt his own coup. Initially, he aligned himself with Perón and the military coup of 1943. However, after Perón came into power, Cattáneo openly criticized his dubious electoral means. Cattáneo was then elected into the Argentine Chamber of Deputies by the official Opposition, and he was a continual pain in Perón's and Eva's side ever since.

"Please, join us." Stuart motioned to a chair and caught a waiter's attention.

"Just a whiskey. Double," said Cattáneo.

"Make that three," demanded Stuart of the waiter. Stuart turned to Phyl. "The colonel is a good friend of Dodero and Jorge. We thought we'd chat and catch up on some things here where it's safer." He turned to Cattáneo. "Where is Dodero?"

"He'll be here shortly."

"Good to be here to talk finally."

"Yes, it's quite refreshing," said Cattáneo. He was cultured, and elegant in speech. Phyl saw his books in stores when they first arrived in Buenos Aires. She had glanced through them, but her Spanish was rudimentary, and the prose a little beyond her. Quite frankly, she wasn't as interested in Argentine politics then as she was now.

The drinks arrived surprisingly quick. Phyl and Stuart slowly sipped theirs while allowing Cattáneo to lead the conversation. He brought Stuart up to date on gossip and rumors but also shared what information he could pass on to the Embassy. At one point, he referred to Dodero's ongoing relationship with Eva and Perón. Cattáneo had a glint in his eye when he carefully searched the lobby for prying eyes. It was a safer territory in Uruguay, but Perón's spy system infiltrated surrounding countries.

"Our friend Dodero is looking to launch his own airline company," he continued in a lowered voice. "He had a problem pushing through the permits and we all know which two people are in charge of permits, trade, business …"

Cattáneo reached into his light summer jacket and took out a cigar with a gold band. He carefully removed the wrapper and shifted the band along the length of the cigar. "The other week, Dodero and his wife were having dinner with Eva and Perón, and he brought up the subject of the permits." Cattáneo slipped the gold band off the end of his cigar and handed it to Phyl.

Phyl looked at it curiously, put it on her forefinger for fun. This made Cattáneo smile.

"Eva didn't say a word, of course. Neither did Perón. Instead, you know what Eva did?"

Phyl's eyes brightened.

"Eva turned to Dodero's beautiful wife – supposedly her best friend - and admired a twelve-carat diamond ring given to her by Dodero for her birthday." Cattáneo shook his head as he pulled out his gold lighter, flicked it, and studied the flame. "Dodero yanked the diamond ring off his lovely wife's finger and put it onto Eva's."

"Oh, my gosh," exclaimed Phyl. "His poor wife. I don't think that marriage will last."

Cattáneo lit his cigar. It had a tight draw, causing very little smoke. He looked at the end and then grinned at them again. "This won't be the straw that broke the camel's back. The man is brilliant but a scoundrel. The fact that he's surrounded by beautiful young women everywhere he goes can't go well for his marriage. My God, he's on the front pages of every social publication wherever he goes. No secrets."

Cattáneo tapped the cigar onto the ashtray at his elbow. "Well, success. Dodero got his permits yesterday," he laughed. "Of course, the Perón duo stand by as he creates this Argentine airline at his own cost because, my dear friends, I guarantee you that at the rate they are breaking every single democratic, ethical, and moral law, confiscating businesses through extortion threats, we will see the day when everything is nationalized under the guise of socialism and for the benefit of the *descamisados*."

"You're saying *guise*?" asked Phyl.

"Forgive me, but I know it is obvious to you and me. The poor *descamisados* don't have the brains to see they're being used."

"Eva seems to honestly care," offered Phyl.

"She is motivated by this dramatic image of herself as a poor little urchin. And this is a role to act. She is an actress, after all. What better role to play than the wealthy controller of an entire country of people who adore her and want to kiss her feet and then *pretend* to be like them? They kill each other in stampedes to see her. She throws money at them. Not hers. Money confiscated from some businessman."

Cattáneo leaned the other way in his chair. It creaked under his weight. "Nationalizing everything would give the Peróns unimaginable power. Dodero's airline will become Eva's personal form of transportation and another source of income. Plus, a more private means of making people disappear."

"Disappear?" asked Phyl.

"Hmm."

Stuart leaned toward Phyl. "By throwing them overboard over a jungle."

Phyl gasped loudly.

Cattáneo looked around and put a finger to his lips. He leaned in as his eyes almost closed, for effect. "Why do so many planes go down over the mountains? And have you ever wondered about those who step onto planes but curiously don't arrive at their destinations?"

Phyl felt ill.

"The White House is quite disturbed by this," said Stuart.

Cattáneo pulled out another cigar and held it toward Stuart, eyebrows raised.

Stuart waved it away. Phyl realized they were sharing information extremely disturbing to him.

"Those closest to the Peróns are upset by developments." Cattáneo said.

"Oh? Who?" asked Stuart.

"For one, the brother."

Stuart pursed his lips. "Juan Duarte."

Phyl blinked at Stuart.

Cattáneo coughed into his fist and sat back. "He has secretly agreed to help."

"He's your contact in the inner circle?" Stuart carefully whispered.

Cattáneo took a deep breath through his nose and slowly let it out.

Phyl was stupefied by what he had just said. She searched for eyes sent to spy on them. No one took any notice of them, it seemed. She sat back, deep in her thoughts, and wondered how she, Phyllis May Redington, from a humble little house in Toronto, should end up sitting on the crest of a mounting political wave in a country where, of all things, Hitler may still be residing and where two power-hungry people were destroying the once magnificently, prosperous nation of Argentina. A country in which people disappeared and were being thrown off planes. It made her head spin and her stomach turn, but her heart pounded not with fear. It was emboldened with pride. A determination took hold of her.

"*Señor* Cattáneo. Do you remember a military attaché, Lieutenant Colonel Camilo Gay?"

"*Si,* I remember. The man was found dead in a cave, shot through the head."

"Is the cave far from here?"

Cattáneo looked at Stuart and then at Phyl. "It's nowhere near here. It's in Brazil."

"Would you show us? You probably have seen the file."

"Phyl, it's near Rio de Janeiro. It's almost thirty-five hours by car."

"We did Rio from here by train once," Phyl insisted, looking intently at Stuart.

"Phyl," Stuart said softly. He leaned forward. "You may have your days free, but I don't. I have meetings set up all this week."

Phyl looked at Cattáneo. "You said Dodero was going to meet us here."

"*Si.*"

"Then you and Dodero take me there."

Stuart's face reddened. "What in hell are you talking about?" he hissed.

Phyl's face hardened.

"Stuart, I've rarely complained about having to be part of whatever you and Jorge do. Yes, I've been frightened to death. In fact, you know I lost weight and my health over it. And perhaps all this upset may even have caused me to lose …"

Her nostrils flared as she stopped short of saying a terrible thing. Referring to her precious daughter in such a terribly accusatory way. Her eyes filled with tears. "Now I'm directly involved again."

Stuart, fumed, refusing to answer.

"I told you that over my dead body was I coming back to that godforsaken place," she said emotionally, pointing toward Buenos Aires. "But," she said, "here I am again. Up to my neck again."

Phyl spied Dodero step off the elevator eyeing a beautiful woman who passed him to get in. "I need to know the truth. I need to know what the possible outcome is for me. I know yours!" she argued. "Your lungs are rotting away. Lord knows how many years you have left because of -"

"Oh, come on, Phyl," Stuart yelled.

Dodero heard Stuart all the way from the elevators. Startled, he looked at them and hurried in their direction, looking anxiously around the lobby. He reached them, and put a hand on Stuart's shoulder. "Shh, my friend."

"Dodero, most don't understand English," Stuart reasoned angrily.

"Unfortunately, most here *do* speak English. Tourists, diplomats, big business, and…," he looked around before acknowledging Cattáneo, who nodded back at him. "And Perón's spies. You may not be concerned, but if you make yourselves more obvious, I would prefer not to be in your presence."

Stuart glared at him. "Oh, come on, Dodero. Everywhere you go, you attract attention. You don't think you do so just by walking over to us?"

"Being caught wooing beautiful women or entertaining movie stars is one thing. Being in the company of loud suspected foreign agents is another." Dodero stood his ground.

Cattáneo stood up. "I agree. I feel like a drink at the bar."

"I'll join you," Dodero barked.

"Wait," whispered Phyl loudly.

The two men stopped, turned, and looked suspiciously at her.

"Dodero, you expect a hell of a lot from me," she muttered. "I want to see what happens to people who sneak around spying like us."

The men fidgeted and looked around.

"I just suggested that you and Cattáneo take me to Rio to see the cave where Lieutenant Colonel Camilo Gay was found dead."

Dodero's face paled. He looked at Cattáneo, who stared back. Then Cattáneo shrugged and nodded almost indiscernibly.

Stuart abruptly stood and threw his newspaper onto a marble table. "I don't know who this woman is anymore." He glared at Phyl. "Go ahead and make it worse." He looked at the gentlemen. "You want to do her bidding? You're free to do so. I want nothing to do with it."

Stuart walked away.

"Stu!" Phyl called out.

Dodero and Cattáneo sat on each side of her. Dodero smiled, pretending to make small talk for the sake of onlookers. "This will be a waste of time, Phyllis."

Phyl simply stared.

"Jorge told me you were a stubborn woman."

"Did he now? Well, Jorge doesn't know the half of it," snapped Phyl.

Cattáneo sighed. "When?"

"Next train out," said Phyl. She turned to Dodero. "And you're paying."

Phyl kicked her white stained running shoes at loose pebbles on a large, cool cave floor off Gavea Road outside Rio de Janeiro. Her eyes darted from shadow to crevice in the rock walls. She trained her flashlight into the darker areas of the cave and pointed it above. She almost choked at the sight of bats hanging directly over her. She fell back and frantically scrambled away like a crab.

Dodero and Cattáneo lunged and helped her back onto her feet. She brushed herself down, eyeing the squirming bats.

"Ignore them. They won't bother us," said Cattáneo.

Phyl pulled her eyes away from the mini-Draculas into the darkness, then back to the light of day at the cave opening behind them. "So, where was he found?" she croaked.

Cattáneo shook his head. "The file said he was under a low-hanging ledge."

"How on earth did they find him?" asked Phyl, looking around for a low-lying ledge.

She was dressed in a man's shirt and pants, her hair slicked back like a young man. She didn't want to be seen alone with two men. Everyone would surmise wrongly what it meant, and she didn't wish tongues to wag in case she was recognized. She trusted Dodero and Cattáneo. She knew they wouldn't take advantage of her, but she was more likely not to be noticed if dressed as a young man.

"And who found him?"

"Young boys exploring the cave for adventure."

Phyl shook her head. "Wow. Poor kids. They sure found their adventure."

She walked to a low-lying ledge and put her hand on the rock and leaned against it to look underneath. She saw something sparkle in the light of her flashlight. She reached underneath and pulled out the back of a pin. "Does this look like the back of a military pin?" She held it up to the two men.

Cattáneo reached out and took it. He studied it closely, shrugged, and sighed deeply. Then he looked around. "This looks like where it was."

"Was it a clean shot through the forehead?" Phyl asked, crouching in the dirt, thinking she might find blood evidence.

"He was shot twice. Once in the chest. Then assassination style, in the back of the head on his stomach." Cattáneo blinked Phyl as she studied him. He looked at the cave opening. "We're losing light."

Phyl ignored him. "Why do you think he was killed? She looked into the deepening shadows. "Perón was already in the scene. Was it him? The Nazis?"

"I wouldn't read too much into this. But why in Brazil?" He shrugged. "We all go to Uruguay. It's just across the river. But Brazil is a location you set out for with a purpose."

Phyl imagined her own body lying under the ledge with a bullet through her head. She imagined Stuart lying there. She checked her gut feeling. She was startled. She couldn't feel anything. She took a deep breath and stood up. She got what she came for. She could face this and still be logical in her commitment to a cause that had become their lot in life. She needed to know she had what it took.

She thought of Gay and was very sad.

"We had him over for dinner, you know. He told us he wanted to quit his Embassy posting and go back to active duty. He was tired – or frightened – of being a military attaché. He didn't say why. Not to me, anyway. But now I think I can understand. He knew things. He disagreed with things."

"Have you seen enough, Phyllis?" asked Dodero. "I am ready to go to Rio. I'll get us a large suite."

Phyl stood and wiped down her pants. She nodded and turned. "Thank you for humoring me, gentlemen. I had to stare death in the face and put what Stuart and I are doing in perspective."

She looked back at the spot under the ledge. "Somehow, I don't envision myself, or Stuart, ending up like this. Whether I'm kidding myself or not, I just don't see it."

"Well, then. I'm glad your gut feelings agree with Cattáneo's and mine," said Dodero impatiently. He turned and climbed up the dusty incline toward the fading light at the cave opening.

Flashlight aimed at the ground, Phyl absorbed the deepening blackness. She shivered at the thought of Gay rotting away in a cave eaten by bugs, undiscovered.

As the three finally emerged from the cave, Phyl wondered if Gay's ghost watched them? Was his spirit in the cave? Or was he where her daughter was, in that safe place, at peace?

She followed the two men down the incline to their car parked about a half mile away. She knew that her gut ache - now subsided - would never return.

She had emerged from that cave a different woman.

* * *

New Year's Eve morning.

Phyl sat at their dining room table staring at their Christmas tree. Her fingers played with American Embassy stationary. She just read a letter from K and pondered how to answer her questions. She took a deep breath. Fabulous aromas wafted around her head. She closed her eyes and could clearly isolate the perfume of various blossoming bushes and plants outside in the park. This was Christmas in the middle of summer in Argentina. This was exotic, special, and beautiful. This smelled like Eden.

Phyl felt far from Canadian wintry days. She tried to capture the joys of snow by scattering cotton over her holiday tree. She clipped candles onto branches and tried to remember the cold tingle in her fingertips when she made snowballs, this while sweat ran down her back from the heat.

She looked past the tree with its fake snow and beautiful baubles and candles, to the bright blue sky over the city. She listened to the sound of traffic, chatter, and music outside. Not exactly Christmas hymns. She heard the bangs of cargo loaded at the port in the distance. She noted the birds calling, chirping, and singing near her balcony. Nests full of beaks to feed, no doubt.

She jumped at a harsh noise behind her. It took her a moment to realize it was Maria in the kitchen banging at phyllo pastry in preparation for their traditional Argentine meal for the night.

Phyl had asked her to make her special beef *empañadas*, and the exquisite smell of simmering and bubbling exotica in a large pot on the stove did its magic. Phyl sniffed garlic, cumin, cinnamon, and paprika wafting from the kitchen. There would be plump currants, olives, and hard-boiled eggs with tomato sauce stuffed into those rolls, then sliced into delicious pinwheels.

She sighed, contented. Life. It was good. After all.

They stayed home for New Year's Eve, for a change. Stuart needed to do something from the house and Phyl was glad for the rest. Constant entertaining had taken its toll. She could tell she was no longer 23. It seemed to her that when they first came to Buenos Aires 12 years earlier, they could party all night and the next without complaint. Now, they had to pace themselves.

But she felt good. The world had shifted. She was at peace. She fully recognized the dangers in their circumstances, but logic now prevailed. As foreigners, they would likely not meet the same strange endings some outspoken Argentines had met. Accidental deaths and disappearances were numerous now. Rumors were the only source of information not reported in the press. Elites, outspoken business owners, and political players criticizing Eva's tactics and demands - they all knew they risked their lives doing so. While in Uruguay and after her trip to the cave, Stuart and Phyl met the odd person who fled for safety, having lost everything directly to the Peróns. These people quietly shared their stories and concerns. Stuart, not writing anything down, listened closely and carefully, nodding occasionally.

It took a while for Stuart to get over his anger with her. In fact, it wasn't until they were on the ferry back from Uruguay, when she reached out for his hand, standing at the railing, watching Montevideo disappear over the horizon, that he didn't yank his away.

The banging in the kitchen abruptly stopped, bringing her back to the moment. She heard Maria bustling noisily, doing things in the kitchen. The sounds were comforting. Phyl grew very used to having servants and hoped she would never have to go without. How that would be possible once they returned to Canada or the U.S., she did not know. For now, she counted her blessings. She picked up the cup of coffee Maria had made for her, took a sip, and raised her cartridge pen to begin writing.

> *December 31, 1947*
>
> *Dear Dad and K,*
>
> *We arrived from Uruguay two days before Christmas. For Christmas Eve, I decided to do lamb on the charcoal burner instead of going out to eat, so I had it ready at eight, but Stuart didn't appear until 10. Just like him, he started to do his Christmas shopping at 7, bought me cologne and red gladiolus, but at 9:30, he was still waiting for a taxi and finally got one at 10.*
>
> *He walked about 30 blocks looking for a store that was still open where he could buy things. The flowers were sad-looking as it was around 95, and the humidity was unbearable. I call him last minute, Luke!*
>
> *Buenos Aires is a madhouse. Everyone has money who never had it before - factory workers, domestics, etc., are paid a month's salary as a Christmas bonus, the elections are this year, and guess who will look like their saviors — so now, inflation is awful. Naturally, these bonuses have to be made up by charging higher prices. The entertainment spots are jammed, no taxis are available in the places they should be so everyone's in a panic. As usual, we don't get in on the big money as Argentina has no dollar exchange and again Stuart has difficulty getting machines. He can't rely on big deals and his salary, so high in Toronto, is just average here.*

Phyl paused. She held off talking about the millions of *pesos* of business Stuart generated as she knew it was all credit to Dodero. She wondered, however, if she could get away with something more precise. She took a deep breath and looked out the window again. Her letter will not arrive with this stuff written in it.

She looked at the letter, and pondered. Life, she thought. She sighed. She must wait until she knows a friend is going to Uruguay. She'll have it mailed from there…

> *I expect the big dict-r will tighten things up once the votes are in.*

She bit her lip. About to cross the sentence out, she left it.

Christmas Day, we had the Piñieros over and sat around. Today, New Year's Eve, we had hoped to play tennis. We had invitations to join parties but don't feel festive, so we'll stay home. Tomorrow, lunch with the Piñieros, and then a reception at the American Embassy from 7 to 9, the new Ambassador Bruce's first official one for the colony, finally. We are required to go, of course.

Stuart has to go to Rio, the hottest time of the year. Not good for his lungs. I'll go down to the estancia. But first, I have a few things to get out of the way.

She stopped, and thought about the opening of a new Children's Village Eva was presiding over the first week in January. There was no way she could mention that.

She looked up when she heard Stuart cough in the next room. He was busy at the radio updating transmissions. She continued writing.

Stu is sleeping at the moment, and is having the usual problem with his lungs. I tell him he's rotting his lungs. I'm such a nag now that he's smoking again.

She wanted to throw the pen across the room.

He didn't like his weight gain, though I thought he looked quite handsome. And I'd rather he was hefty than hacking his lungs out.

She sat back in frustration. There was so much more she wanted to say, such as when they first arrived so long ago, Argentina was potentially one of the wealthiest countries in the world. Bread, butter, and meat were cheap and plentiful. Now, people buy milk by the cup. Or bribe a butcher to give them the best cut of meat for exorbitant prices. Inflation was at almost 100% and rising. And there was a rumor that heads of cattle were down by 10 million and that Perón would introduce a "Meatless Day." In Argentina! The only winners were the occasional American visitor who found everything cheap because he got twenty *pesos* to a U.S. dollar compared to three when Phyl first arrived.

She could not take a chance writing any of these in case the letter was intercepted.

She jumped at a knock on the door. Something clattered into the sink and Maria slapped her slippers to the front door. Phyl twisted in her chair to look.

"Vivienne!" she yelled.

Looking pale but glamorous, Vivienne barged through the door. Maria closed the door behind her and was about to take her hat and purse when

Vivienne waved her away. "Oh, no. I'm not staying." Vivienne sniffed the air. "Oh, my god, my mouth is watering. Can I stay for supper?"

"Sure," laughed Phyl.

"Actually, I just wanted to drop by to wish you and Stuart a Happy New Year, and thought I'd tell you we decided to fly to Rio after I go with you to that Children's Village. We need a break. In fact, we may fly to Miami after that and then to Toronto to see my folks."

"Everything okay at home?"

Vivienne shook her head sadly. "It's Bob. He thinks the Argentines are out to get us."

"Why would he think that?"

Vivienne was about to say something when she caught sight of the Christmas tree. She sashayed to it and touched colorful baubles and cotton batting.

"How quaint. I never thought of using cotton." She smiled and faced Phyl. "Yes, Bob. They're very anti-American at the office and it's wearing him down." Vivienne dipped into her purse for a handkerchief. She dabbed at a tear. "The doctor thinks it's liver cancer," Vivienne said, stopping. She folded the handkerchief in different ways as she searched for words. "But Bob says the symptoms are more like slow poisoning…Oh, he's so paranoid!" She waved the thought away. "He wants to go back to New York."

"You must go as soon as you can if he's that sick!"

"We can't," laughed Vivienne sadly. "Money talks, you know. And the Company rules. He must finish a deal and paperwork before we can leave."

"How long will that take?"

"Probably end of June. Almost a year short of our contract. And I'll still be able to go to this Eva Opening with you. What is she calling them? *Hogar de Transitos?*"

Phyl squeezed her friend's hand. "Er, yes. And I'm glad you're still coming." Phyl took her arm and led her through the open doorway onto the balcony. They stood at the railing and looked over the swaying palm trees. Children's laughter and barking dogs echoed from the park below.

"You have such a lovely view, Phyl."

"Yup, we love it here. After New York, when are you coming back?"

"Never."

"What?"

"Bob's had enough," Vivienne said, shaking her red curls.

"Where is he now?"

"He's in the cab downstairs. We're on our way to a New Year's Eve dinner at one of the girls' places just out of town. But what's with the goons on the floor and down in the lobby?"

Phyl laughed. "We share this floor with the chief of police."

"Of Buenos Aires?"

"Yes," laughed Phyl. She led her back into the house. She walked to the bar, and took a bottle, handing it to her friend. "Here, Happy New Year."

Vivienne read the label. "Wow. Dom Perignon. Who the hell can afford this?"

"Not us," quipped Phyl. "A friend of a friend gave it to us."

"Nice friends." Vivienne looked around. "Where's Stu? I want to wish him a Happy New Year."

"He's in bed, not feeling well," lied Phyl.

"Oh, the poor baby. Let me just say hello for a second." Vivienne headed for the bedroom door. She was so quick Phyl didn't have a second to hold her back. Vivienne opened the door and entered.

Phyl caught up and peered into the bedroom. Stuart sat in his housecoat at the radio with his headphones on, notepad and pen in hand, cigarette clenched in his teeth.

Vivienne looked stunned. "Oh, I didn't know Stuart liked radios." She stepped into the bedroom.

Stuart sat up and twirled. He deftly turned the radio off and tore off his head phones. "Vivienne! Hello, I'm sorry you caught me like this!" He coughed. "I'm a bit under the weather."

"Yes, so Phyl said." She pointed at the radio. "Your hobby?"

"Er, yes." He leaned over to stub his cigarette into a full ashtray. "It keeps me out of trouble."

"Well, hard to get into trouble by staying home on a New Year's Eve." She waved at the smoke in the room and held up the bottle. "Look what I have. We'll drink to your health tonight."

Stuart tightened the belt of his housecoat and nodded, grinning like an idiot. "Say hi to Bob."

"Sure, I will. See you, Stu. Happy New Year." Vivienne gave the room a once over before allowing Phyl to walk her past the dining room table. The embassy letterhead caught her attention.

Phyl opened the door and walked out with Vivienne. She nodded at the goon sitting on a chair at the end of the hallway.

"Vivienne, when you go, to Miami and, later, New York, let us drive you to the airport." She guided her friend to the elevator and pushed the button. The elevator immediately kicked into life. "But do you have to go by plane? It's so dangerous going over the mountains."

Vivienne hugged the bottle of Champagne. She shook her head. "No time for a boat."

Phyl touched Vivienne's shoulder. "Are you okay? You look awfully pale."

Vivienne smiled. "Just stressed out." Vivienne wouldn't look at her.

"That's unusual, Viv." The elevator door dinged open. They stepped in and remained quiet down the nine floors. As they neared the lobby, they heard Eva chatting briskly. Eva's voice echoed louder off the walls as they stepped off the elevator to be greeted by the two goons hovering by the porter's counter listening to the radio. The porter saw them and jumped to open the door.

At the curb, Phyl bent down into the shade of the cab to wave at Bob. He grinned and waved back from the shadows. He looked gaunt and had dark circles under his eyes.

"Gotta go," said Vivienne briskly. She stepped to the passenger door. The taxi driver jumped out and opened the door for her. She faced Phyl. "Have a great Happy New Year." She glanced up at Phyl's balcony at the top of the building. "What are you guys up to, anyhow? Should I be worried?"

Phyl made a face. "Same old, same old. No. My only worry is that Stuart is smoking again."

"Hmm. I'm starting to distrust doctors when they say smoking is good for the nerves. But when I see how many of our friends have lung cancer, I'm not so sure anymore."

Phyl cocked her head. "It makes bloody sense, though, doesn't it?" She smiled.

"It sure does. Me? I haven't stopped smoking. I like it too much."

Phyl poked her friend's shoulder. "You're going to be the exception. You'll live to be a hundred."

"Ha!"

Phyl looked across the road to the park and pointed at the large Eva posters along the boulevard. "I'll never get used to being stared down at by a gigantic sickly, sweetly smiling Eva."

Vivienne rolled her eyes and laughed heartily. She put a finger to her lips and motioned with her eyes to the taxi driver standing nearby. She leaned into Phyl's ear. "Be careful, Phyl. We hear stories, and they're not nice." She kissed Phyl on the cheek and held the bottle of Dom Perignon aloft for Bob to see. "We're living it up tonight, Bobby!" She climbed into the cab.

Phyl watched the cab drive away, then looked up to see Stuart looking down at her, smoking.

She looked up at Eva's face on a massive banner as she let the porter open the door for her.

She listened to Eva's lilting, country voice on the radio over the sound of her own sandals flapping against marble floors. She stepped into the elevator and the brass doors closed on the glare of the sun and the gazes of the porter and goons. As she rose toward the top of the building, Eva's voice faded away. It dawned on Phyl that she had spent almost her entire adult life in Argentina. And that the girl she was when Stuart proposed to her on that hot, dry day on the Guelph campus had somehow morphed into who she was now. She felt glorious. Unique.

Phyl's thoughts drifted to that young teenager, Eva Duarte, the wanna-be she met on that movie set. She shook her head. That young girl, whose face was now plastered all over Argentina, had also grown into quite a woman. Far transcending Phyl in Machiavellian ways.

"Lordy, life is weird," she thought.

Chapter Nineteen

Joining Eva, Back at the Estancia, Spyglass and Wrecked Packard

Phyl nervously eyed a journalist.

He snapped photo after photo, flippantly casting aside spent bulbs with a steady clatter onto the marble floor. It bothered her tremendously that he kept her in the shots along with a few others close to Eva Perón. Eva gaily discussed the virtues of the transitional home for single women, which they were there to explore and praise.

Eva was grand. Proud. Delighted. A burst of sunshine, in an expensive flowered dress and a white, broad-rim hat over, her golden hair swept up in sleek rolls. Phyl read that Eva was described in Italy as another Lana Turner. It was a baseless compliment: The only similarity Phyl saw was the color and sweep of her hair. Nevertheless, Phyl watched intently as Eva waved her hands excitedly to her audience, pointing to needlework displayed on walls and tabletops created by women who purportedly lived in the transitional home. Every once in a while, Eva turned and looked to ensure that Phyl was listening closely, still not believing that Phyl understood her rapid-fire Spanish.

Phyl nodded, indicated that she understood, and smiled benignly. She was painfully aware that she was the only foreigner who followed the First Lady from one display to another, hearing of beautiful plans for more homes. *What would these women do, left alone on the streets?* Eva asked them all. *Isn't it wonderful how they have a place to stay because of me? Perhaps the life of a woman in Argentina will improve through my programs. And she now has the right to vote because of me.*

Because of me. Worship me.

Me. Me. Me. *I am but a humble servant and the wife of El Presidente. I am interested only in social work. And me.*

Basically, that's what Eva was saying and not saying. And, yes, Eva was half right. Because of her, much was being done for the poorer citizens of Argentina. In particular, the women and children.

Earlier that month, at the first opening Phyl attended of a new orphanage, Eva recognized her immediately. "You couldn't understand a single direction on set, I recall." Eva turned to a gentleman beside her. "This lady is American and speaks Spanish fluently. We met on a movie set when we were very young - I was a supporting actress, and she was simply an extra - but she didn't speak Spanish then. Now, she understands absolutely everything we say." Eva had patted her hand like a pet. "If only all Americans would care to do what this woman has done while living in our beautiful country. Learn our language! It's the least they can do. This woman is a foreigner truly worthy of being in Argentina."

Phyl was relieved to be seen in such a positive light by the luminous Eva Perón, so she did not care to correct her about her actual citizenship. After all, she was the American Women's Club president and married to an American. No need to complicate Phyl's already surreal and dangerous mission.

Please don't keep me in that photo, Phyl prayed silently as another flashbulb temporarily blinded anyone unfortunate to be looking in the photographer's direction.

"I expect you to make sure all your American friends are aware of all the terribly good things I am doing here," said Eva. "My wonderful husband, *El Presidente*, and I are anxious to strengthen our relations with the United States of America. We no longer rely on Britain as much as before, you see. They didn't have the time of day for me on my famous tour. But that is beside the point. We have so much to send to the United States. We hope to do so soon in return for loans and the military equipment we so desperately need. This very unfair American embargo against us will soon be lifted when your Congress finally approves what they said they would do at the Rio Conference last year, so we can finally modernize our military for the sake of our people. Americans must know the wonderful things my husband and I are doing for our *Descamisados*."

Eva's voice lowered. "I hear there is much hunger and poverty in your supposed land of milk and honey." She touched Phyl's arm in sympathy and looked around the crowd. "I want everyone to know that I am planning to send foreign aid to Washington, clothing for the poor women and children…"

Phyl's eyes widened at the absurdity, but she smiled broadly. "*Oh, que maravillosa!*" she exclaimed.

When Eva finally looked away and directed the others to another piece of handwork, Phyl quietly slipped off a shoe and wriggled her sore toes. She glanced at her watch and wondered how long the tour would last. They had been there for over two hours, scrutinizing rooms full of elaborate Louis XIV furniture, gifts to Eva while in France. Everything was painted in gold gilt, elegant and luxurious. Eva insisted her plan was to create homes to make women feel like queens. Temporary queens, mind you. They could stay as long as they needed, so long as they eventually find another home or occupation.

Phyl wondered how these women would adjust to reality once they returned to the streets.

She looked around nervously. Something didn't feel right. Were there actual women living in this home? Nothing in the grand, expansive building looked used. Beds and closets, untouched and empty. In fact, earlier, Phyl had touched one of the gold-gilt beds, admiring the satin covering, when all she felt under the comforter was wood instead of a mattress. She quickly withdrew her hand.

It was staged.

She looked closely at two shy women sitting at a smaller table, pushing a needle and yarn through and up linen. Their timid eyes glanced up at the group and Eva, then looked away. They wore dresses that didn't quite fit. Their work-worn hands and fingernails did not match their elegant stockings and new shoes. They looked as if they were put in costumes and told to act. Phyl looked closer and noticed their hands were shaking. One had a runny nose and was too embarrassed to wipe it. Phyl was tempted to give her a handkerchief but did not want to bring attention to herself or the poor girl.

She glanced at the empty shelves along the walls and then up at the high ceilings and elegant crystal chandeliers. She lowered her gaze to the beautiful, rich drapery gracing the tall, stately windows. Through the glass panes, she saw carefully trimmed shrubbery and tall, swaying palm trees, rolling green lawns dotted with tropical birds. Marble, flowing fountains, and statues of Mother Mary of God and other saints were prolific. It was a stunning castle built to suit royalty. Stuart had told her earlier that the property once belonged to an old, longstanding Argentine family of great wealth and political stature whose patriarch had openly criticized Perón. The family ran off to Uruguay, leaving everything behind. Phyl wondered what actually happened to them.

She hoped they did not disappear off a plane over a jungle, instead.

A woman in uniform appeared in a doorway. Thinking she may be a matron running the home, Phyl sidled up to her. "*Hola*," she whispered. "Could you tell me where the women keep their things?"

"Oh," the woman looked at Phyl with angst. "What little they have is stored."

Phyl looked at the women at the table. "But surely there are more women, and also children. They would have toys and a playroom." She glanced out at the expanse of green. "I don't see any playing."

"The children are napping," responded the matron tersely.

"Where?"

The woman refused to answer.

Phyl pushed the point. "And isn't that what the closets and shelves are for? For their clothes and toys?" Phyl argued. "I don't see signs of them anywhere."

The matron's face turned red. Without a word, she turned and disappeared through the doorway.

Fascinating, thought Phyl. She couldn't wait to tell Stuart how strange it all seemed. He was returning from Rio after two weeks with Mr. Lutman from the New York office, and his wife. Lutman, who was to cover for parts of Latin America, accompanied Stuart to Uruguay and Chile to meet clients. Thankfully, the Lutmans weren't returning with Stuart, so Phyl didn't have to entertain them.

She absentmindedly wondered what the Lutmans thought of South America. She remembered the shock she and Stuart felt when they first arrived so many years ago. As a child of a debilitating Depression, she was taken aback by the magnificently Bohemian style of Buenos Aires and its incredible color, music, filth, and strange culture. It was eye-opening. She closed her eyes at the memories. She grieved the loss of that beautiful and poetic Argentine grandeur they once knew and grew to love. The festivities, flowing Champagne, clouds of perfume, even the blatant prostitution on the streets and children defecating and urinating on the sidewalks had almost disappeared. Laughter and debauchery had lessened considerably, and the poorer citizens' suffering, loss, and struggles were continually brought to light. The general attitude of people was much more severe. But then, the entire world had changed since the war. There was a great loss of innocence knowing tens of millions of people had needlessly died, including over 10 million Jews who were brutally eradicated.

Now, with the Cold War and the red threat of communism, there was a strange dampening of wine, women, and song. No one dared speak English in public anymore for fear of physical violence. And absolutely no one could speak freely about Perón, no matter what language. There were ears everywhere. The people no longer feared German bombs, raids, or submarines. They feared the walls around them.

For they had ears.

Phyl shook off a sense of unease and moved closer to Eva. She remembered to carefully memorize details and remind herself she was acting. She had to be careful not to overdo it. She knew that even the smallest and most insignificant detail was to be stored in her brain and shared later with Jorge, Stuart and Dodero at the *estancia*.

She glanced at her watch and thought of the next day's journey. She still had some packing to do and was anxious to get home. They were heading off in their new Packard first thing, picking up Angelica, Jorge, and the younger children on the way out of the city.

She frowned at the thought of leaving Maria alone at the flat. Not that Maria would actually tamper with the locks on their bedroom door and Stuart's office. But what if there was an emergency? What if there was a fire and people had to break into their personal space? What if either one of them had an accident and things came to light that they were, in essence, *spying*?

She nervously took out a cigarette and lighter from her purse. Smoking helped calm her nerves and after taking a few slow, deep breaths, she was able to recognize the irony of the moment: While she was acting for this very special audience of one, Eva was playing the role of a lifetime for an entire world.

"All the world's a stage, and all the men and women merely players," quoted Phyl to herself.

* * *

"So, here we are again — finally,"

Phyl's eyes were closed behind a pair of dark sunglasses shielding her eyes from the bright midday sun. She listened to the Piñiero children splashing, screaming, and laughing nearby in the pool. The temperature was cooler than average. Staying out of the Pampas wind on this side of the main house, the temperature felt quite comfortable. Of course, it wasn't the same as fabulous Rio with its drier heat and beautiful breezes off the ocean. She did wish she hadn't missed the Rio trip with Stuart, but her mission with Eva Perón was her priority. In the grand scheme of things, she knew she had no right to complain as she comfortably lay stretched out in her bathing suit on an elegant lounge chair on the *estancia's* extensive granite patio. The day was still far better than the typical February intense heat and the suffocating humidity they would otherwise suffer in Buenos Aires.

"That was an adventure driving here. Remind me to take the train next time," laughed Angelica, sunbathing in an ornate lounge chair.

"We didn't plan on snapping an axle. It's either the roads or someone purposely did something."

"Oh, come now."

"Well, then, it's the terrible roads. How do people get around in this godforsaken country?"

"I remind you, by train."

Phyl laughed.

Angelica raised an arm and held it over her forehead. She looked at her children, saw they were fine, and lowered her head. "When must you go back to Canada or New York?"

"Our three-year contract is over New Year's 1950, in just under two years. But we already agreed to turn right around for another two-year contract with a possible third year. However, …"

Angelica sat up and leaned toward a small table, picked up her cocktail, swished the liquid in the glass, and swallowed the remains. She held up the empty glass to a servant standing by the patio doors. "However?" she repeated.

Phyl handed her glass to the servant, who took Angelica's and left to refresh the drinks.

"However, one can't bank on anything as things are really grim here? If it gets any more dangerous, the company might decide to send us somewhere else."

"Oh, no," said Angelica, surprised. "We'd miss you terribly."

"This couple in power has really made a mess of this country. No one knows where it's heading." Phyl patted her tummy. She was gaining weight again. All those special dinners and Openings.

"At least we're all in agreement on that." Angelica eyed the servant who stood at the bar mixing the drinks. She lowered her voice. "Prices are unbelievable, Phyl. I'm so concerned. We now pay $1 US for a single electric bulb, the same for a can of sardines and salmon."

"Oh, my gosh. I know. I paid $1.25 US for a can of peaches the other day."

"What do the Peróns expect? They aggressively raise wages at the cost of employers, but the poor still can't afford what they were able to buy a few years ago."

Angelica took a cigarette from a crumpled package on the little table next to her. She reached for a gold lighter. What an irony. There is a great scarcity of rice and soap, kerosene, petroleum. Thank goodness, we had a year's worth of petroleum in barrels here. Perhaps things will change by the time we need to refill them." Angelica held up fingers crossed. "I know, wishful thinking."

Phyl smiled. "Well, I tell you, we're not putting more of our cash into the banks. Not the way the *peso* keeps dropping."

"That's why you bought the Packard?"

Phyl turned onto her stomach and watched the servant come and place her drink on the little table beside her. She smiled, reached over, and played with the straw. "Yes, we figure it will keep its value better than cash. We thought of buying a little house, but the prices are out of this world."

"Jewelry."

"Excuse me?"

"Buy jewelry. Gold."

"Is that what you guys are doing?"

Angelica took a diamond stud out of her earlobe. She handed it to Phyl. Phyl gently took the diamond earring. "Beautiful."

"We just got this." She held up her arm to show a gold tennis bracelet. "Gold never loses value."

Phyl eyed the bracelet, then handed the earring back. "Well, if it works for you. I'm not sure if we actually make enough to buy diamonds and gold."

"You bought a Packard. That could've been a number of beautiful stones and gold."

"Everything seems to be upside down. Even our milkman told me that had he known we would be such a nuisance," she stopped to emphasize the word. "*Nuisance* because we're only taking one liter of milk a day - he would never have accepted us as clients. Our milkman can't read or write, and yet he receives a salary of 1200 *pesos* per month – exactly the amount Stuart got when we first came to Argentina. And Stuart has a degree from Princeton." Phyl felt ill suddenly. "The folks at Stuart's office complain that it costs too much to dress decently because they receive less due to the exchange than our milkman earns driving a horse cart. We were in the Boston bank a couple of days ago when suddenly the wickets closed. One poor man was leaving for Europe the following day and couldn't get a cent of his own money out. They simply refused to listen. How can an economy last this way?"

"I come here and try to forget that hell."

Phyl squirmed. "Yes, sorry to go on about it."

"I joined in. It's hard not to. In the meantime, to the good life." She toasted.

Phyl held her glass aloft. "The good life." She took a swallow of her cocktail and leaned back into her recliner. "Aren't we lucky? We ride, fish, hike and swim in a large beautiful pool with lovely kids, drink martinis served on a beautiful stone terrace in front of a beautiful home looking over a beautiful ranch to the hills beyond – a nice job if one can get it."

Angelica grinned. "Well, we got the job!" she laughed.

Phyl stretched her legs. The sun felt absolutely fantastic. She admired the tan on her legs and smoothed out the skirt of her bathing suit. "Yesterday's barbeque was absolutely luxurious. It was wonderful seeing everyone from *Ventana* again."

"We went through three whole lambs," said Angelica.

"I believe it. There were a lot of folks. And a lot of kids." Phyl laughed. She noticed young Lorenzo walking toward them. "*Hola*, Lorenzo."

"*Hola Tía* Phyllis. Georgie and I are going to hunt for ostriches a little later. Do you want to come?" At what usually would be considered an awkward age, Lorenzo carried himself handsomely with great confidence. He stood, wet, dripping, and grinned at her, tanned and toned.

"Lorenzo, you are such a gentleman." Phyl looked at Angelica. "You know, I think a great deal of the credit for raising the boys so well goes to you, Angelica."

"Oh, I know! Come hell or high water, I bring the boys here every chance I get. But I have to fight with them constantly to wash their necks, comb their hair, and change their filthy underwear."

"*Mama!*" complained Lorenzo.

Angelica motioned at Lorenzo to step closer. She gave him a big smile, played with his wet hair, and turned to Phyl. "You should go along, Phyl. You like hunting for ostriches."

Phyl looked at her watch and Lorenzo. "Okay. But I'd like to be back before your father and Stuart return with Mr. Dodero."

"We'll only take about two hours or so. Musso, our *majordomo*, said he saw fifty of them down by the Sierras early this morning."

"Ha! Well, in that case, you got a deal. I'll get changed."

"We're taking the jalopy. I'm driving," grinned Lorenzo.

Phyl turned to Angelica. "Is Lorenzo old enough to drive?"

"He's going to be twelve in April."

"Twelve?"

Lorenzo turned to his siblings at the pool. "Georgie, *Tía* Phyllis is coming, too!"

Fifteen-year-old Georgie hurried out of the pool. "*Hurra, vámonos.* I'll get the guns!"

Angelica called out as her sons ran off to prepare for the hunt. "Be careful, and don't drive too fast." She grabbed Phyl's arm as she was about to leave. "Phyl, don't let Lorenzo drive too fast. Hit one of those holes with a tire, and you'll crash. Keep an eye out along the fields."

"Not to worry. We'll be fine. I promise."

"And don't shoot our cattle by accident!" added Angelica.

The jalopy raced, rumbled and creaked leaving a trail of dust as Lorenzo headed toward the massive flock of ostriches gathered in a gully by the Sierras. Phyl clutched her rifle with one hand and hung on for dear life to the frame of the passenger door. She squinted at the speedometer and saw they were going 70 miles an hour.

"Oh, my God, Lorenzo. Slow down."

"We can't. We have to catch up." The ostriches exploded in all directions. "I have to keep them together in a group. Otherwise, we'll lose them!"

His voice was sucked away by the wind in Phyl's ears. She saw cattle in the distance, and made a note to be careful shooting. She looked at Georgie, who searched his pockets as he swayed and bounced.

"What are you looking for?" Phyl yelled.

"I forgot shotgun shells."

"Oh, no," yelled Phyl, laughing. She held up her rifle. "Here, use this. I don't really want to kill ostrich. I'm just here for the excitement."

Georgie put the shotgun down and dipped his hand into a duffle bag beside his feet. He pulled out a revolver, braced himself behind Lorenzo, and aimed at ostriches. He shot, missing them.

This was Phyl's cue. She carefully stood up, braced herself with her thighs against the filthy dash, and held her rifle aloft. She aimed as best she could, trying to get into the rhythm of the jalopy. She pulled the trigger and saw an ostrich suddenly jump. Phyl lowered the rifle to see if she had hit the bird. It continued its run with a limp. "I got one in the foot," she yelled.

Lorenzo suddenly lost control of the jalopy, and it almost flipped over. Phyl fell back on the passenger seat and banged against the passenger door. The jalopy righted itself and stopped.

"That's enough! It's my turn to drive," yelled Georgie. He waited for Lorenzo to climb into the back beside him before throwing his legs over the driver's seat. Georgie slipped down and grabbed the gear shift. He stood up, semi-standing, and kept his foot on the accelerator. He put the jalopy into gear and shot forward. They caught up to the flock and continued to shoot: Georgie with his revolver, shooting like mad with one hand, with the other clutched at the wheel. Lorenzo shot with his rifle from one side of the car in the back while Phyl did her best to shoot from the other side from the front.

It took less than an hour for them to realize they weren't going to score any ostrich meat for dinner, but the hunt was thrilling for Phyl. They stopped the jalopy to retrieve stray ostrich feathers as a small private plane flew overhead. Instinctively, Phyl knew it was Dodero. They returned, dusty and happy, to where Angelica was still lounging on the terrace. Phyl had a magnificent ostrich feather.

"Any luck?" asked Angelica, shielding her eyes from the afternoon sun.

"No. But I managed to get this feather and hit a big one in the foot." Phyl twirled the fluffy feather in her hand before letting it float down onto the stone terrace by her feet. She brushed the dust off her slacks and plopped into a lawn chair.

"My Dad and Claude Jr. would be so impressed by your boys. The way they handle themselves in a hunt. And they're such capable shooters." Phyl took off her jacket and shook it. She folded it over the arm of her chair. "They drive like madmen. Just like their father."

"Is the jalopy still in one piece?"

"Barely. We almost flipped and would've totaled it if we had."

"Who was driving at the time? Lorenzo or Georgie?"

"Lorenzo."

Angelica shook her head. "Those boys. That jalopy barely survived the last fiasco."

"That wasn't Georgie's fault. It was that dead cow in the middle of the road at night."

"Look at you standing up for my sons. Phyl, I think my boys bring out the child in you."

"You're right. I don't feel a bit like my thirty-seven years."

"By the way, our labor situation is dire, and Georgie and Lorenzo need help rounding up 400 head of cattle to get them into the corral. You seem to be so keen on doing everything our *gauchos* do."

"I would love that. I'm the mad Canadian here, remember?"

"Wonderful. Thank you." Angelica closed her eyes and settled back to enjoy the sun.

Phyl looked at Angelica's beautiful face. "Your boys have grown into fine young men, and they definitely have your beautiful looks. Though Jorge isn't bad looking either."

"Hmm." Angelica smiled contentedly.

Phyl sat up and took off her sunglasses to see better at a cloud of dust over the hill. "I think the guys are back." Phyl looked at her watch. "Dodero flew over us a while ago, so it must be him."

"Flying in. Quite the playboy," muttered Angelica.

Phyl thought of all the beautiful women Dodero surrounded himself with and felt frumpy. "Oh my God," she exclaimed. "Oh, dear, look at me. I think I better go freshen up."

Angelica raised her head to look in the distance. "Oh, shoot. You're right." She sat up straight. I can't be seen like this!" Angelica swung her bare legs over the side of her chair, spilling a drink she had resting between her knees. "Oh my gosh!" Angelica stood up and looked at the stain over the bottom of her bathing suit and down her legs. "Shoot! I look like I peed myself," she screamed.

Phyl laughed. "Better you than me!" She grabbed Angelica's hand and tugged her. "Come on. Race you," she yelled as she pulled Angelica toward the house.

"If any businessman has the wherewithal to create riches in Argentina, it's me, the great Alberto Dodero."

Dodero patted his chest. "I was the youngest of five sons to Italian immigrants in Uruguay. When my father died, *I* was the one who built his little shipping business into the biggest merchant fleet in South America. Me. *I* did that."

Stuart and Jorge looked at each other. The three men lounged with drinks in Jorge's stately, cool study, surrounded by old leather-bound books and grand portraits of Piñero ancestors in gold-gilt frames. Dark mahogany lined the walls, and hand-carved mahogany and leather furniture reflected local indigenous and old Spanish tastes. They looked up, as Angelica and Phyl shyly looked into the study, opening the heavy, carved mahogany door. Classical music, played somewhere in the sprawling home.

"Knock, knock?" said Phyl, freshly made up. She looked at Dodero. He grinned back at her.

"Two beauties to lift my soul." Dodero politely stood and bowed before the women.

"Are we interrupting?" asked Angelica as she sauntered in, her hand raised toward Dodero.

Dodero took Angelica's hand and kissed it gently. He turned to Phyl, who had closed the door, rendering the music almost undetectable, already standing with her hand out, grinning.

Phyl heard Stuart chuckle at her childishness. Phyl looked at him wide-eyed, warning him not to tease her. Stuart shrugged and smirked as he watched Dodero kiss Phyl's hand. She happily eyed it and pulled out an ostrich feather from behind her back. She held it out to Dodero.

Dodero took the large, beautiful feather. He twirled it in his hand, then pretended to dust the top of a little table nearby. "Just what I needed." Everyone laughed.

Dodero motioned to chairs around them. "Please, join us. I have no secrets from this group."

The two women chose two bull-horn chairs close by.

Stuart leaned forward, leared his throat. "You must be the richest man in Argentina, then."

"I could've been richer if this government knew what they were doing." Dodero sat back in his leather seat and sighed deeply. He gently placed the ostrich feather at his feet on the alpaca wool rug, which covered the extent of the room's dark, oak floors. He turned and looked at the beveled glass of the study's window overlooking distant, rolling hills. He pursed his lips. "Yesterday, this *friend* of mine." He clasped his hands. "This *El Presidente*," he said, hissing. "Gave me a take it or leave it proposition."

Jorge frowned. "Oh?"

Dodero rested his manicured hands over his knees. "Apparently, I made a mistake by giving Perón my humble advice."

"What was that?" asked Jorge.

Dodero ran a hand over his slicked-back hair. "I frankly informed him that he and the *Señora* were running the country down. My shipping business had dropped to one-third of what it was at the war's end. I told him that was unacceptable."

"What was the proposition?" persisted Jorge.

"I sell my shipping interests to Perón and that I had absolutely no choice."

"You had no choice?"

Dodero threw up his hands. "Either I sell, or they nationalize them. He's already taken my ships, airline, and all my business property except for a string of apartment houses, including the one next to Jorge's, where you live." He motioned to Stuart and Phyl. "Would you like to know the terms?" he asked sarcastically. He didn't wait for an answer. "Less than $3 million U.S. It's worth four times that much."

"Oh, my gosh," exclaimed Phyl.

Stuart looked at Phyl, then at Dodero. "Sorry to hear that."

Dodero poked at his chest with a thumb. "Me. I created all this. I told you, at the end of the Great War, I bought 148 unwanted U.S. ships and resold them for a good profit. I kept expanding, buying, selling, and growing my shipping business so that I owned more than 300 ships by this last war. Two years ago, my shipping business alone was worth $6 million U.S."

He picked up his beautiful crystal tumbler and looked closely at the amber-colored scotch. "And I thought by becoming close friends and confidante, I would be able to ensure my interests were safe." Dodero slurped and grimaced. "I showered them with diamonds and Rolls Royces! Here," he said. "Look!" He flipped the lapel of his linen jacket to show two gold pins. "What does this look like to you?"

Phyl squinted at the pins.

"Come closer, look!"

Phyl and Angelica stepped closer. They looked at the finely made pins.

"Oh, they're the Peróns," exclaimed Phyl.

"Precisely."

"Their profiles in gold," said Angelica.

"Unfortunately, after all my generosity, my great respect for them, my obvious admiration - none of it helped. I spoke to your ambassador yesterday morning and briefed him. I told him it was unacceptable. Outrageous. Irresponsible. If Perón does this so easily to me, his closest friend and ally, how trustworthy is he in affairs of the State? How can the U.S. trust him?"

Stuart sighed deeply.

Dodero looked at Phyl. "Understand me: I am still their friend. Not a very happy one, but still their friend. As Alberto Dodero, I am still mighty here and outside Argentina. They still need me."

"Of course," said Jorge.

"Tomorrow, I want to sit down with Phyllis and hear what she says about our *Señora's* mindset. Eva may influence Perón in ways that do not serve his best interests. She acts like a loose cannon."

Phyl nodded. "Of course. Anytime you say."

"Why don't you go riding tomorrow and talk? You might as well enjoy the *estancia* while you are here, Alberto," Angelica offered. She walked to the large desk and lifted a gold and quartz cigarette box lid. She took out a cigarette and absentmindedly tapped it on the surface. She leaned on the edge. "Phyl loves to ride. In fact, we have a beautiful stallion just for her here in our stables."

"Wait a minute, Angelica." Stuart turned to Dodero. "No offense, Dodero, but no playboy's going out with my wife alone."

"Stu!" Phyl was aghast.

"I'm not a playboy. I'm a married man." Dodero grinned, pounding his chest.

"You can't fool us," laughed Stuart.

"Then come along," said Dodero. He turned to Phyl. "Your husband has a right to be concerned. You are a very beautiful woman, and beautiful women are a weakness of mine."

"Oh, dear," muttered Phyl, blushing.

Jorge inhaled loudly. "Are you serious, Stuart, or joking?"

Stuart's smile dropped. "I'm serious. I'm coming along."

"I'll go riding, as well," piped up Angelica.

"So," said Jorge. "I'm now supposed to trust my wife with two men?"

"Oh, come now," said Stuart. "She's safe with me."

"Just making a point."

"This is silly." Phyl stood up. "Eleven o'clock at the stables, then. The four of us." She turned to Angelica as she crossed her arms. "Maybe Lorenzo and Georgie would like to come along." She turned to Jorge. "You don't mind, do you, Jorge?"

Jorge shook his head. "Certainly not. You can all ride together and still talk in peace. I'll tell our *majordomo* you'll be saddling up tomorrow."

"So, eleven it is. Oh, what fun." Phyl turned to Dodero. "You do ride, don't you, Alberto?"

"Not very well or for very long, but our conversation need not be long. I can ride for an hour or so without too much pain afterward." He looked around the room and at the portraits. "This is a beautiful plantation, Jorge. You must be very proud of your ancestral home."

"Thank you. Though, as you, we are quite concerned of how things are developing." Jorge nervously tapped the arm of his chair with his thumb. "I'm afraid it feels as if it's the end of an era."

Dodero nodded sadly. "Indeed. You have much to worry about. We all do."

"What now, Dodero? What are your plans? How is Eva's brother holding out?" Stuart stretched out his legs and held his hands behind his head. Though his body looked relaxed, Phyl saw he was grinding his teeth.

"Juan Duarte is anxious to hear what Phyl has to say. That's why our ride tomorrow. You see, it's the proverbial emperor and his New Clothes. Nobody has the guts to speak the truth to Eva, and all Juan hears from those around her and Eva herself is how wonderful she is. But Juan Duarte is most concerned for her safety as he sees and hears very disturbing things."

Phyl, startled, pushed away from the desk and stood to her feet. "What disturbing things, may I ask?" She imagined herself as an innocent victim during assassination attempts on Eva.

"There are factions within the military who dislike her very much. She's doing admirable things for the *Descamisados*, but the money flows like water, and not all of it to where it *should* be flowing."

"I suppose I can see why that would bother them," said Phyl weakly.

"What are his concerns, exactly?" asked Jorge.

"She blatantly extorts people and businesses. She makes very powerful people quite unhappy. These people like to feel they still have some influence on the outcome of future elections. Quite frankly," Dodero said, as he pulled out a cigar from his inner pocket, "the military is not impressed by how much power is given to unruly and uneducated peasants who wish to live like royalty without the experience and knowledge of how to live responsibly. They are very weary of the hordes. No one has forgotten about the French Revolution. It's still in everyone's minds two hundred years later."

Dodero shrugged and ripped off the cigar cover. "Hordes are hordes. Hungry enough and give them knives and guns, and countries topple. People lose their heads. Literally."

"Like the Spanish revolution. Some of the things done were barbaric," said Jorge.

"I still have nightmares," offered Angelica.

Phyl felt ill at fleeting images of Angelica and Jorge impaled on tree stumps. Her face twisted for a moment and she clapped her hands over her face. "Oh, this is so awful."

Stuart stood up and looked out the glass doors. The light was fading, and the room darkened considerably. Behind him, Angelica stood up and turned on two table lamps. Stuart absentmindedly looked at the two lamps. "You have to admit, Perón is also motivated by a certain amount of fear."

"Fear? Perón is incapable of fear," Dodero said quietly.

"Look at his Five-Year Plan, though. He can't fully depend on foreign or private investment, which would help save what's in the coffers, but he's committed. So, the State has to drain the coffers in order to invest into the Plan's improvement of infrastructure and trade, helping industries expand.

Now, people who once worked the land are pouring into the city for what they think are better prospects."

"That happened here. We've lost quite a few families to the city," muttered Jorge.

"Precisely. These people are looking for hope and a promise of better days. If Perón ensures workers' wages increase again and again, he knows their spending power will increase. They feel happier, more in control, and less likely to be swayed by philosophic pressures from outside the country."

"Like fascism in Spain?" Phyl asked. "And what happened during the French Revolution?"

Jorge's eyes locked onto Phyl's. He smiled sadly. "Add to that, the new threat of Communism," he muttered. "And nuclear warfare."

"Ah," gulped Phyl.

"Well, you are correct, Stuart," continued Dodero. "My friend, Perón, does indeed intend to keep the hordes happy by spending. Absolutely no room for bloody uprisings. But his rhetoric of late, and that of Eva's, *feeds* uprisings, so Perón contradicts himself. He's an idiot." Dodero paused. "Not very bright."

Everyone shifted slightly as the Piñiero children ran yelling past the windows on the terrace.

"When I saw your American Ambassador Bruce, it was precisely what he confided in me. He said he already approached Perón about their imperialistic anti-U.S. rhetoric. Americans aren't idiots, we all know. They hear of his insults and his complaints about the United States in his speeches. Bruce told me he asked Perón why he would want to jeopardize the very relationship he so desperately wants to nurture. Perón said it was innocent prattling. It was how he kept his base together against a concept bigger than their problems. He insisted that when it became necessary, he would stand by the U.S. no matter what."

Jorge chuckled.

"What did Bruce say then?" asked Stuart.

"Bruce believes him."

"Is your ambassador an idiot?" yelled Dodero.

Stuart looked at his hand and started biting a nail. "Perón's also afraid of another Great Depression. Depression and another war happened after the First Great War. Why wouldn't the same happen again after this last war, right? Communism, the Cold War, the Iron Curtain, nuclear war…"

"Oh, Stuart. That sounds so awful. Like there's no hope," whined Phyl.

"Perón is taking extreme measures to prevent any of these outcomes. You see," Stuart sat on a cushioned windowsill. "Perón needs to continue agricultural exports on a level that would maintain favorable foreign exchange. He also needs imported materials for Argentina's growing industrialization."

Phyl shook her head. "Stu, are you saying he's forcing the creation of a larger industrial base to get the economy going and be less *dependent* on imports."

"No, but yes, that's part of it."

"I'm confused because, at the same time, he needs to *increase* imports to ensure good, strong trade relations and allies." Phyl took a deep breath. "There's no way around that, right? That's quite a balancing act."

Jorge fidgeted in his armchair, causing the leather to squeak comically and suggestively.

Phyl looked around, and smirked, but the moment was too severe to break for frivolity.

Jorge took a deep breath, smiled at her, and shook his head.

Stuart frowned.

Jorge: "Perón may claim he wants to maintain agricultural exports, but everything he is doing to *us*, the agricultural *base*, which provides the meat, wool, wine, and fruit, emasculates us. His focus is *away* from us."

"Could he nationalize agriculture?" asked Phyl innocently.

"That would end up being communism. That wouldn't go over well," said Stuart. "Not with us, the Americans, anyway."

"On our home front, as you know, we've lost workers. Though quite capable, my children have had to step in and carry a larger load while here. But we can't always be here." Jorge stood up and stretched. "We simply don't have enough staff."

"And we've had long periods of droughts here in the Pampas," said Angelica. "So, it looks like our harvests may be dismal this coming year."

"Yes, droughts. Damn droughts," muttered Jorge.

"As well, Argentina lost Britain as a major trading partner. That affects our business," offered Angelica.

Dodero took a deep breath. He looked at his empty glass and held it up questioningly. Jorge tried to get up, but Dodero put up his hand. "Friend, allow me to help myself." Dodero pushed himself out of his chair and walked to the bar. He perused the bottles quickly and chose a single malt. He poured a hefty amount into his glass and took a swig. He pursed his lips. "I know for a fact, that Perón is deep in discussion with Britain to renew trade in exports of meats. But Britain is driving a hard bargain, Perón told me. He needs sterling area petroleum. But they insist on exporting materials Perón is already trying to manufacture in this country in exchange for imports."

"What does he want instead?" asked Stuart.

"Luxury goods, automobiles, machinery. The stuff he can't do here. He hopes to also import them from the United States as part of forming a strong partnership. In spite of his rhetoric, he does not want to jeopardize U.S.-Argentina relations, especially since the U.S. will see it as competition if Perón bends to Britain's terms. But we have to somehow stop the trade deficits. It's depleting the coffers."

"Fair enough." Jorge crossed his legs and looked at Angelica, who sadly looked back. "To get back to you, *Querida*, and what you said about Britain. As you just heard, it's not that Britain will not be a partner, just the conditions have changed, and not in Argentina's favor."

"There's another thing: The U.S. is overstretched, helping European countries and Japan get back on their feet. Even Germany. Perón's furious that the U.S. is giving non-repayable financial support to them while, at best, they offer only temporary loans to him," said Stuart. "Loans with interest."

"What does he expect?" laughed Phyl. "After all that running around with Nazis and refusing to side with the Allies during the war?" Phyl shook her head. "What a silly thing for him to assume."

Jorge: "Silly or not, politics doesn't have to make sense, Phyllis. Each day brings in new variables. Nothing is black and white."

"Well, it's sometimes beyond me. Why can't it be black and white, good or bad?" Phyl impatiently crossed her legs.

"We live in a very imperfect world," offered Stuart.

A gentle knock on the door precipitated a servant quietly entering the room, wondering if the *Señora* would like supper to be served. Jazz, the new rage in Paris, wafted into the room.

Jorge stood up suddenly. "Well, look at the time. Light's fading. Shall we retire to the dining room? Angelica?" He motioned to his wife. She looked at her gold wristwatch.

"Yes, of course." She stood up and turned to the servant, and gave him instructions. She ran her hands down the front of her summer dress and rearranged loose, sunbleached hair. She forced a smile and motioned to the door. "Shall we? I hope you don't mind. We are having cold roast lamb and fresh salads."

"Pampas leftovers?" said Jorge. He motioned to Dodero. "We have a special guest here tonight!"

"I have a love for cold mutton," said Dodero. "But I do insist on sampling your best wine. My shipping interests may be going out the window, but that doesn't stop me from continuing my import and export business. Perhaps I can find a broader market for your vineyard."

"Well," Jorge said, surprised. "That would brighten our day. So long as we are able to meet the demand. Let's talk. Come. We'll all drink till we drop."

"I won't say no to that," grinned Dodero. He inhaled his scotch and slammed the empty tumbler on the desk on his way out of the study. He was about to reach Phyl and had his hand ready to put on her back to lead her through the door when Stuart jumped in and took Phyl's hand, stemming the tide.

"Come, Phyl. Let your husband take you to the dining room," Stuart said, eyeing Dodero.

"Oh, Stu," grumbled Phyl.

"Sorry, Dodero," said Jorge, as he held the door.

Dodero grimaced and shook his head. "That's my plight, Jorge, my friend. Another man sees my looks and great wealth and is threatened by me."

"Well, it doesn't help when you blatantly run around with hordes of beautiful women. Do any of them resist you?"

"Well, perhaps one or two," grinned Dodero. "But I still try."

"I'm surprised no man has killed you in a jealous rage yet," joked Jorge.

"No man has the spine to stand up to Alberto Dodero."

Jorge stepped closer to Dodero with a twinkle in his eye. "Stuart Redington just did."

"That didn't count."

The late morning sun offered warmth and comfort.

Phyl swayed gently straddled on her proud, glistening-black Arabian horse. She gazed at the long, beautiful mane before her. She crossed her hands at the wrists and let them rest, holding the reins. She looked over at a vineyard dotted with workers pruning vines. She heard Dodero cough, looked to her right, and squinted at him. He seemed pretty comfortable on his white Arabian mare. He waved away flies, a cigarette holder balanced between stained teeth.

"I think I am happiest when I go riding," she told him.

"Is that so?"

"Yes," said she, almost shyly. "Well, next to dancing. Dancing has always been my passion and easier to do than ride."

"Dancing? Does Stuart like to dance?"

"He used to hate it, but when he realized I loved to dance, and strange men always swept me away from him, he decided to put his best foot forward, so to speak," she laughed, "and now he always keeps me happy. No strange men dancing with me anymore."

Dodero squinted. "I am not surprised at all. He is easily jealous. But I am not strange."

Phyl grinned and shrugged apologetically.

"But, of course, I can understand completely. You are a very beautiful woman."

Phyl, surprised, sat up straighter, blushed, and looked back quickly. They were a reasonable distance ahead of the rest of the riding party, who were just leaving the stable yard. But she saw Stuart staring at them while leading Angelica, Lorenzo, and Georgie at a quick pace.

"You are uncomfortable with compliments, I see," Dodero announced boldly.

"Well, I find it odd to be so complimented by you since you are married to one of the most beautiful women in the world, and you always surround yourself with more beautiful women," Phyl laughed, throwing up a hand for emphasis. She averted her eyes. She returned to gazing at the beautiful horse's mane before her. "I don't feel so beautiful that I could be compared to these women."

They were headed along a path of conversation she desperately didn't want to follow. She tried to change the subject. "Do you like to ride?" she abruptly asked.

"*Si*, absolutely, but..." He shifted his body slightly "Excuse me," he said. I have never ridden without a saddle. I keep feeling I will slip off this sheepskin."

Phyl laughed. "Well, I prefer the sheepskin. I must admit, it's a bit difficult adjusting to an English saddle back at the Women's Club after spending time here."

"Hmm," grumbled Dodero.

Two workers rode past on mules and tipped their *gaucho* hats at them. Whips, revolvers, and large gloves slapped and bounced to the mules' gaits.

Phyl nodded at them.

At the sound of a whistle, she and Dodero twisted to look back.

Stuart, his eyes glued on them, put two fingers to his eyes, then pointed them at Dodero.

Dodero laughed heartily and turned away.

Phyl, embarrassed, looked back at the path and continued.

"Jorge's *estancia* is interesting, don't you think? He and his brother, Diego, their business is mainly wine and champagne, so there are miles and miles of vineyards." Phyl laughed, motioning to the vineyard. "We are such champagne snobs now, having it whenever we please. Of course, you certainly spoil us with your Dom Perignon."

Phyl absentmindedly brushed down stray hair on the horse's mane, ruffled in the hot breeze. "Their second most important product is wool," she continued, "and they have hundreds of Merinos and other kinds of lambs whose names I've forgotten."

She turned to the rolling hills past large tracts of bushes and momentarily listened to the horses' hooves clopping. She pointed. "Over there, beyond those bushes, they have fruit orchards, and past those are barns with cows just for the milk supply of this place. They have over a hundred horses, including twenty-five saddle horses and lots of mules. All the *peons*, the *majordomo*, and their families live nearby. It is quite a little *pueblo* on this *estancia*."

"If I wasn't such a globetrotter, I wouldn't mind settling for a time here in the *Pampas*." Dodero tucked the reigns under his sheepskin and frowned at his cigarette holder. He took out a cigarette stub, squeezed the end with his fingers, and flicked the butt onto the dirt.

Phyl glanced back at the butt to ensure it wasn't smoking. Fire was always a concern.

Dodero tucked the cigarette holder into the inner breast pocket of his sports coat and picked up the reigns. He whistled and kicked the horse in the sides to quicken the pace. "Beautiful horse," he said.

Phyl quickened her gait. "Yes, did you know you can buy a pure-blood Arab horse bred from an Argentine champion, unbroken, for only 80 pesos? That's about $30 at the present rate of exchange. If we still actually had exchange, that is." She chuckled. "We once discussed buying a raft of them, having them broken here, and then taking them to North America to sell."

"They're beautiful, but I see these Arabians aren't suitable for cattle rustling."

"No, you're right. They're only suitable for *Señoras* to ride since they are small and nervous and have such dainty feet."

"Who? The *señoras* or the horses?" he laughed.

Just then, Lorenzo and Diego, hands firmly on their *gaucho* hats, howled and pounded past Phyl and Dodero, causing their Arabs to nervously pull at their reigns. Phyl settled her horse down and, a little perturbed, watched the boys' backs pull ahead. The horses' hooves violently scattered dirt, and swirls of dust rose into the air.

Something caught her attention in the hills ahead of them. A flash of light. A reflection. Reminiscent of the afternoon she and Stuart were at the dam.

"Someone's spying on us," she said out of the corner of her mouth.

"What?"

She turned to Dodero, dumbfounded. She glanced back at Stuart. He frowned, curious. She pointed to the hills. She saw Stuart look up. But when she turned back to look, there was no flash.

"Maybe it's my imagination, but I could swear I saw the flash of a spyglass."

Dodero pulled at the reigns, stopped his horse in its tracks. "Let's head back. I'm not too happy about Perón knowing where I am."

"Well, they may not be spying on you. We seem to be the subject of snoopers ourselves."

"Either way, it's not good. Talk to me about Eva, and then I should get back to the airfield." Dodero turned his horse to face where they came from. Stuart and Angelica slowed down when they saw.

"Stu, we're heading back," yelled Phyl. She led Dodero to Stuart and Angelica.

"I saw. We're being spied on again." Stuart looked grim.

"Indeed." Dodero surveyed the surroundings. "And I thought I could be discreet by coming here. Stuart, I will need to be driven back to the airfield as soon as possible. Phyl and I will talk some more on our own back to the stables and house, but then I must go." Dodero slipped his horse past everyone, then stopped to wait for Phyl.

Stuart looked at Phyl. "Well, that's unfortunate."

"Yes. Very. I don't like being spied on."

"No one does," roared Dodero. He continued on ahead.

Stuart squinted off at the hills. "There. I saw it again. We're definitely being watched."

Phyl saw the reflection. "Shoot. Well, I'll go back with Dodero. I'm sorry. I've been wasting our time talking about the *estancia*. I better catch up." She kicked the horse's side, clucked her tongue, and hurried to catch up with Dodero.

"Sorry, Alberto. I better give you my update about Eva," she yelled at Dodero.

"Please, do."

"Okay, so this is what I've observed, but this is only my observation."

"Yes, yes. I know." Dodero was not in a good mood.

"My Spanish is excellent, so I understand everything Eva says except for the odd country slang, which she falls into at times. I get the impression she truly cares about the poor, women and children. But whenever we go to an Opening, I don't see evidence of these places being used. Sometimes, I get the feeling that people are bussed there, given instructions, sit at tables to embroider or sew something, and stand in a row to meet us all. But they look oddly dressed and out of place. Their shoes look new and don't always seem to fit. I can't say that these people will stay after the presentation. I asked one woman at one of the transitional houses about something, but she didn't know anything."

Dodero was hastening even more, and she had to quicken her horse's gait. The extra bounces and rocking caused her voice to skip. "Also, I'm not exactly on top of all the news and of what goes on politically. I only know what I read in the papers, and of course, nothing is written truthfully, except for in *La Prensa*, but their circulation has been cut back, and we can't always get a copy. Perón is holding back—"

"Yes, I know. The idiot is holding back newsprint supplies from them specifically."

"Yes. And they're the only ones who stick to facts. But when I hear Eva talk, she never speaks about facts or details or makes promises based on careful aforethought. It's as if she only cares about her connection to the voting poor and doesn't bother with the more educated voters who are more discerning. She goes on about how the *Descamisados* are wronged and they should stand for their rights. She tells them they are wealthier than the filthy elites because they are wealthy in spirit, if not in earthly riches. That they deserve everything the elite have. She sounds quite angry at times. As if she wants to stir up all their frustrations and get them more upset than they are. It's as if it's a power trip for her."

Dodero pulled the reigns and stopped his horse. He looked at her, trying hard to keep his horse still. "That's precisely what her brother, Juan Duarte, is concerned about. The military and those around Perón know of this. They don't want an uprising by uneducated, emotionally driven, and frustrated people. She may be maintaining a strong hold on the very people who put Perón in office, but to continue with unsettling rhetoric distracts from allowing them to govern peacefully. It is not Perón's inention to alienate the rest of Argentina, or to start a rebellion."

"Yes, I can see that. Well, she does it well enough on her own, is my opinion." Her Arab settled down, and she was able to sit and ponder. She frowned. "I don't think Eva is very educated and is capable of speaking of anything else. She also seems limited in her vocabulary."

"She has very little education."

"Well, all I can say is I think, amazingly, she found her calling. This is her best acting role yet."

"But her acting this time may lead her and Perón to trouble. And the country. Phyllis. It's time to go. However short this was, I have heard enough." He roughly dug his heel into the horse's ribs and galloped toward the stables.

Phyl winced, hoping Dodero's horse didn't feel too much pain.

Stuart and Angelica caught up to her.

"What happened?" asked Stuart.

"He heard enough, he said." Phyl took one last look at the distant hills. "He needs you to take him to the airfield now."

Angelica spoke up. "May I come along? I need to pick something up in town, and I'd rather go with you in the Packard than with Lorenzo in the jalopy." She was breathless as they hurried along.

Stuart went ahead of the women, trying to catch up to Dodero. The dust bothered the women's eyes, and Phyl squinted as she watched Stuart's back. She turned to Angelica.

"There's lots of room. Unless Dodero wants to be alone."

"What happened that he suddenly has to go?" asked Angelica.

Phyl motioned back at the hills with her head. "We're being spied on."

Angelica looked back. "Jorge and Diego are very outspoken, so Perón's goons keep an eye on them whenever they're here. It's never there when I'm here alone with the children."

Phyl silently looked at Angelica. Her friend didn't appear to be disturbed, just slightly miffed. But Phyl was *very* concerned. If other elites, property, and business owners have fled or mysteriously disappeared, could that not happen to the Piñieros? Phyl felt ill but feigned disregard. "Well, let them look, then." She waved in the direction of the spyglass. Angelica laughed. Phyl turned to Angelica, grinning. "You know, if I were a different woman, I would be tempted to give them a show."

"Oh, Phyl," laughed Angelica. "You mean like this?" Angelica lifted her blouse to expose her brassiere and hefty cleavage. She pulled the blouse back down and looked around quickly to ensure no one saw. One vineyard worker stood straight up in surprise. He readjusted his *gaucho* hat and shook his head before bending over the vines to continue pruning.

Phyl screamed with shock and delight, her voice echoing off the distant hills. They looked back to where the spyglass was. There was a flash of reflection.

They howled with glee and galloped back to the stables.

The Redington's Packard kept a steady 45 miles an hour on a clear, narrow highway on their way to the airfield near the train station. Lorenzo and Georgie were squeezed into the back with Angelica and Phyl while Stuart drove and Dodero sat brooding beside him. The adults had let the two boys chat and entertain them while they were deep into their own thoughts.

Phyl absentmindedly watched an oncoming car stir the dust on the broken pavement and straddle the center of the road. It swerved, and then straddle the center again. Suddenly, it swerved into their path and made a 180-degree turn in their lane, cutting right across the Packard's nose. The two cars' bumpers hooked together – the other car's back bumper into their front – and both cars slid off the road over a steep embankment. Everyone in the car flew off their seats and the Packard crashed nose-down on top of the other vehicle.

As if in slow motion, Phyl reached out for Stuart's shoulder with one hand. Her other hand grabbed Lorenzo's before impact.

"Oh, my god, my children!" screamed Angelica as they crashed into the other car.

"Stuart!" screamed Phyl.

Dodero fell against the windshield while the two boys were thrown against the back of Stuart's side of the front seat. Phyl was pulled away from Stuart and thrown over the boys against Angelica, who smashed sideways into the door.

The car settled at a precarious angle. After a dazed moment, people groaned and attempted to move and untangle themselves.

Angelica crawled over the boys and grabbed them. *"Dios mío, ¿Estás bien?"*

"Si, Mama!" yelled Lorenzo.

Georgie groaned, held a hand to his head, but nodded at his mother.

Phyl grunted as she scrambled to right herself. She braced her knees against the back of the front seat and tried to reach over to touch Stuart's back again. "Stu! Are you okay?"

Stuart winced and groaned and pushed away from the steering wheel. He turned his head and nodded. He tried to reach back and touch her hand. "Are you hurt?"

"I think I hurt my knees, but I don't think I have any broken bones. How about your chest?"

Stuart touched his chest. "I'm not sure. But I'm not bleeding anywhere, I don't think."

"Alberto! Alberto!" Phyl yelled as she realized Dodero was slumped against the dash. She reached over and gently nudged him. He stirred. He slowly pushed up from the dash and righted himself. "Are you okay?"

Dodero shook his head. *"No. Si."*

Phyl noticed through the shattered window the driver in the smashed car beneath them trying to open his door. He managed about an inch. Finally, the man kicked the door open. It came off its hinges with a squeak and fell to the bottom of the ditch. He crawled out, his face covered in blood.

"That idiot!" muttered Stuart. He slowly twisted against the steering wheel and reached to open his door. At first, it wouldn't budge, but then it fell wide open with a groan as gravity prevailed.

Georgie put a shoulder to his door. Dodero struggled to take off a shoe to clear the shattered glass out of the window of his door. He awkwardly maneuvered himself so that he pushed and pulled himself out of the window backward. Stuart and Dodero dropped down into a dry, parched ditch to the side of the wrecked car. Stuart dropped almost on top of the other driver.

Dodero leaned one foot on the hill's incline and yanked at Angelica's door, moving out of the way as it swung open.

Georgie jumped out and helped Lorenzo down.

On the other side, Stuart reached up to help Phyl crawl out. She had to shimmy along the back of the front seat. She took a step back, lost her balance against Stuart, and fell onto the incline of the hill, knocking the wind out of herself. She remained there, stunned and wide-eyed, and saw the devastating scene. She watched the other driver try to keep his balance, looking unsteady.

It was then that the women in their car cried out. Dodero leaned down and tried their door handle, but the door had buckled and was impossible to open.

"You, get these women out. This door is stuck," yelled Dodero at the other man.

The man was bleary-eyed and had difficulty focusing on Dodero.

Stuart angrily knocked him down into the parched ditch. He reached into the car, and helped two women crawl out. They cried and bled from their foreheads, their clothing askew.

Phyl turned her head at the sound of engines. Two old trucks came from both directions on the highway and slowed to a stop. Men jumped out and scrambled down the steep embankment to help. Slowly, each victim was supported, pushed, and pulled as they crawled back up to the road. When they finally reached the pavement, Phyl and Angelica checked the boys, Stuart and Dodero.

"It's a miracle no one died," said Stuart angrily. He watched the other driver being helped up the embankment. Phyl held Stuart back as she anticipated he wanted to lunge at the man. Stuart fumed. Phyl held back tears. His chest was his Achilles Heel, and she felt deathly afraid for his wellbeing.

The man and women appeared to be too drunk or drugged to answer any of Stuart's terse questions, or even converse. Finally, Stuart allowed Dodero to pull him away to the side.

"Come, I need to keep going. I'll pay one of these truck drivers to take me to the airfield. I'm sorry, friend, I'm afraid I am leaving you in this, which is my doing." He put his hand on Stuart's shoulder but quickly pulled it away when Stuart winced. Dodero looked around at the dry plains and distant hills. He then looked at the two wrecked cars. He shook his head. "I will pay for the damages."

Stuart shook his head. "No. I have insurance. And if anyone is paying for anything, it would be that guy." He pointed at the other driver.

Phyl carefully made her way to Dodero's side. "I know what you are thinking," whispered Phyl.

Dodero glared at her. "Absolutely. The guy might've been put up to this." He waved his hands. "Either way, look at him. He's not fit to drive." He shook his head. "It could be a coincidence, but I'll have my plane checked with a fine-tooth comb before I fly back to the city; I could tell you that much!" He saw Angelica huddled with her sons. "Apologies. Are you and your sons hurt?"

Angelica licked her dry lips and pushed back disheveled hair. She looked at her sons, stunned, and stared down at the wrecked cars. "All I can say is that this one time, the drought saved our lives. These ditches are usually underwater. We could all have drowned." She visibly shook.

Dodero nodded and marched to a third truck, which he saw slowing down to perhaps help.

Phyl watched Stuart glare at the other driver, now talking to one of the truck drivers, motioning this way and that. She put her hand on Stuart's back. "You're shaking."

"I'm always such a careful driver." He covered his eyes. "God, I don't know why we're not dead." He turned to Phyl and held her gently against his sore chest. "This could've been so much worse."

"I know. It's a miracle. But it wasn't your fault, Stu. I know you're always so careful."

A cool breeze swirled dust and dead grass around their feet. Phyl looked at the sky and saw large, grey clouds racing over the hills. Thick, grey shafts of distant rain slanted toward them. "Oh my God, look, we're getting rain."

"That's all we need," said Stuart, cutting into her thoughts. "These cars will be stuck if we don't hurry and get them out."

"Rain! Let's get these cars out of the ditch!" yelled one of the truck drivers.

"I will send back a team of horses," yelled the other driver who agreed to take Dodero.

Stuart lunged toward Dodero about to climb into the truck. "Will you be able to take off in rain?"

Dodero grimly eyed the distant rainclouds. "If I get the hell out of here now, I can beat it." He nodded curtly. "Take care." He turned and climbed up into the truck with a grunt.

Stuart slammed the door shut for him and waved as the truck pulled away. Dodero cranked open his window and held out his arm as a farewell.

It took an hour before a team of four horses rode back to the waiting crowd, all gathered inside two remaining trucks pounded by rain. To their relief, as they hooked up the horses to the Packard, they saw the *estancia's majordomo* arrive in the jalopy. He stopped, jumped out into the rain, and ran to the truck where Phyl and Angelica hid from the elements.

"*Ay, Dios mío. ¿Qué pasó?*" he yelled, leaning into the truck, aghast. "*Señor* was worried!" He eyed the horses, men, and the wrecks in the watery ditch. He waved at Lorenzo and Georgie, who were in the ditch and excited to help Stuart with a hook and rope. "What can I do to help?"

"Oh, thank God, Musso." Angelica turned to Phyl. "I hope you don't mind. I'd like Musso to take the boys and myself back. Jorge must be beside himself right now."

"Of course, you and the boys should go back to Jorge. I'll stay here with Stuart and the car." Phyl opened the truck door and carefully lowered herself onto the wet pavement. She bent to brush herself off but winced and stopped as her joints pulsed with pain.

Angelica allowed herself to be helped down by Musso. She wrapped her arms around herself and went to the embankment's edge, and called her sons. They saw Musso, and waved. Angelica yelled. "We're going back with Musso."

The boys shook their heads.

"They're having too much fun helping," yelled Phyl, shielding her eyes from the rain.

They watched Stuart turn to the boys. They had a friendly argument, which Stuart won. Lorenzo and Georgie dropped the rope, scrambled, slipped, and crawled back up the embankment past the horses to their mother. Angelica put her arms around them, led them to Phyl's side, and paused.

Stuart hollered at her from the ditch. "Phyl, go back with them."

Phyl shook her head. "No," she yelled. She turned to Angelica and gave her a long, tight hug. The women momentarily stood in the rain, swaying together. "Oh my God, I hurt so much," whined Phyl.

"I do, too. All my muscles ache," agreed Angelica.

Phyl wiped her eyes. "We may not make it back tonight, so don't worry about us."

Angelica smiled as best she could, then herded the boys into the jalopy and clambered in herself. The *majordomo* jumped behind the wheel and put the jalopy forward, but just as quickly, he stopped and went into reverse. Musso jumped out, holding a bottle. He rushed over and handed it to Phyl. She squinted through the rain at the label.

"*Aguardiente de Caña!*" her eyes brightened. "Oh, my gosh. Where did you get this? This will do quite nicely for us. Thank you." She turned and held the bottle aloft. "Stu. Look!"

Standing back while the horses pulled the ropes taut, Stuart saw what the bottle was. A grin broke out across his bedraggled face, and he nodded, holding up his thumb. "Just what the doctor ordered."

Musso jumped into the jalopy, and tore away toward the *estancia*. Phyl waved goodbye at everyone, then climbed into the truck to watch horses being coaxed to nudge the Packard free.

It was almost midnight when the rain stopped.

The horses pulled both cars out of thick mud formed in the ditch. All work done now was by the light of flashlights. After the soaked and exhausted horses were finally driven away, a weary Stuart climbed into the filthy, muddy Packard and tried to start the car. A truck driver held a flashlight for him to see. The engine came to life after a couple of tense tries. Despite missing a front bumper, smashed headlights, cracked windshield, smashed passenger window and a rumpled hood, Stuart figured they could drive carefully to the next town. There, he would contact the insurance company the next day. They had no choice but to stay the night.

"Thank God Jorge wasn't here. He would've had us in an asylum with nerves," announced Phyl.

They carefully made their way through the black night, following one truck while the other trailed. After half an hour, they arrived at the closest *pueblo*. They woke a family for accommodation and thanked and paid the two truckers for their time. Stuart and Phyl, though exhausted, could not sleep. Huddled on a narrow cot behind a torn curtain in the corner of the little ramshackle house, Stuart decided to crack open the bottle of *Aguardiente de Caña*. They looked at it longingly as if it were a sacred relic.

"You know, two sips of this, and we would step into the ring with Joe Lewis," whispered a wounded Stuart, his voice hoarse, his nose runny. He wiped his nose with a mud-splattered sleeve.

She wiped the tip of Stuart's nose with a moist handkerchief. Phyl looked like a drowned rat. Bleary-eyed, she licked her lips. "I know," she whispered. "But after today, we deserve it."

"You know, you don't just feel it down in your toes," Stuart warned her. "Hell, it will hit your brain, then your toes in thirty seconds, bounce back to your innards, do a double flip, and run down your arms to your fingertips, where it will evaporate in tiny blue flames. And that's just the first sip. If you're still sentient."

Stuart took Phyl's hand and looked at her fingers. "Your fingernails will go pink, your ears will throb, you'll smell the hairs in your nose singeing, your biceps will begin to bulge, and you'll yell, *where is that goddamn polar bear!*" Stuart pursed his lips into a tight smile.

Phyl grinned impishly, pulled the curtain to the side to see if everyone else was asleep, and put a finger to her lips. "Sounds perfect!" she whispered. She grabbed the bottle and took a swig and was immediately knocked back against the wall, wide-eyed. Her free hand grasped at her throat.

"That good, huh?" whispered Stuart. "Give that to me." He freed Phyl's fingers off the bottle. Phyl fell off the bed when he let her go. "Oh, shoot." Stuart grabbed her by the arm and lifted her to the bed as best he could. He squinted at her. "I have a feeling we should go outside."

Phyl tried to focus on Stuart's face and nodded, red-faced.

Stuart dragged Phyl out of the humble little house. They scrambled into the dark bush nearby, where he took off his mud-crusted shirt and spread it on flattened branches. He let Phyl drop onto her behind on one end of his shirt and then dropped down beside her with a grunt and muffled cry. The moon had come out, and he could see Phyl's stunned face. She started to sway and then make a retching sound. He patted her back as he held up the bottle in the moonlight, took a deep breath, and bent over his sore ribs. He shook his head and winced. Momentarily, the pain subsided, and he straightened out.

"Okay, here goes. Here's to you, you bastard, Dodero!" He took a swig.

Try as they might, they would never remember the events of the rest of those early morning hours, but they did recall waking up halfway into the next day to grunting pigs snuggling at their faces in the *pueblo's* clearing and feeling as if a train had ridden over them and then in reverse for good measure.

In the meantime, the farmer who so kindly accommodated them the night before found the almost full bottle on the discarded shirt in his bushes and placed it in his little house on the stucco shelf above his almost barren mattress. Unable to read the label as he was illiterate, he knew enough to see that this elegant bottle with the beautiful label was probably more expensive than everything combined in their whole *pueblo*. So, he decided to keep it as a symbol of his brush with unbelievable wealth, thus affording him a higher station amongst his poor peers.

His wife was not impressed. So, unknown to him, would put it to practical use and throw a dash of the potent liquid onto her cooking fire whenever it stubbornly refused to burn. This she continued to do until, one day, she had finished the bottle and then filled it with water.

The following year, her poor husband lost his head to his neighbor's machete in a dispute after selling him the bottle for two cows, and their neighbor angrily declared he had been duped with a bottle of water.

Later, the wife married the neighbor, bringing along the two cows.

She still kept the pretty bottle.

Chapter Twenty

November 1949, Dodero, Eva's Brother, Trouble Brewing

"We've been summoned again."

"What?" Phyl looked up from brooding over a letter to K, when Stuart walked into the bedroom. She was fully dressed under her housecoat, sitting in the sun by the window.

"Cold?"

Phyl wrapped the housecoat tighter, nodded and sniffed. "I know it's summer, but it's damn cold, and there's absolutely no heat, and we've run out of propane. Maria can't even make me a hot cocoa."

"Oh, okay." Stuart thought for a moment and motioned to the window. "It's probably warmer outside in the sun. You should go to the park."

Phyl looked out the window and frowned. "I still can't get used to being outside alone."

Stuart chuckled. "Well, I think since Evita made sure women had the vote and a say in how things are run, men aren't on the prowl as they used to. And, in case you haven't noticed, you are no longer considered bait age."

Phyl glared at him. "Let me inform you that thirty-seven is NOT not being bait age. I am told I am quite attractive."

Stuart didn't answer. Instead, he threw her a kiss and wiggled his eyebrows.

Phyl put her pen down. "Fresh!" She tried to slap him, but he moved out of the way. "You were saying? We are summoned?"

"Dodero. Zoo." He shot his cuff and looked at his gold Bulova watch. "In an hour."

"What? It's been six months and suddenly," she snapped her fingers, "he summons us?"

"Hmm." Stuart took a folded paper from the breast pocket of his linen jacket and unfolded it with a severe expression.

"What's that?"

Stuart looked at her and sighed deeply. "Nazi trouble again."

"Nooooo." Phyl reached for the paper. Stuart held it back.

"Kind of for my eyes only, but the gist of it is that one of the Peróns' bodyguards is an escaped Nazi war criminal, Otto Skorzeny."

Phyl pursed her lips and shook her head.

Stuart blinked at her. "Israel is about to consolidate their Intelligence agencies with a major T-bone in their mighty jaws. They're going after Nazi war criminals here in Argentina. And according to this," he said, slapping at the paper. "Perón is still accepting and harboring them."

"Wow." Phyl looked at her letter to K. "Such juicy news, and I can't write any of it."

Stuart's face paled.

Phyl laughed. "Don't be silly. I would never write what you tell me. In any case, you're going to send it for me from Rio next week. It won't go through censors."

Stuart coughed, plopped down on the edge of the bed, and pulled out a handkerchief. He folded it twice before spitting into it, then wrapped it gently and put it back in his pocket. "Too bad you're acting in that play and can't come along."

"Bad timing," Phyl said. "And I see you're not upset about missing my play. Although…"

"Although?"

Phyl shrugged. "Most of the Club members have left the country, so the audiences aren't going to be as big as they used to be. We almost cancelled. I would be surprised if we sell enough tickets for all five performances." Phyl stood up and looked at her watch. She took off her housecoat and lay it over the small rose-colored armchair she sat in.

Stuart pulled her onto the bed beside him. He retrieved an envelope from his hip pocket and held it out to her.

"No, Stu. I must get ready if we have to see Dodero in an hour."

"You gotta look at the envelope. Notice it doesn't have postage. It doesn't have to."

Phyl took the envelope and looked at it. It had the emblem of the *Partido Perónista Femenino* on the front. "A letter from Eva's feminist organization?" she said.

"Let me remind you, she goes by *Evita* now."

Phyl chuckled as she ripped open the envelope. "Evita, then." She unfolded a two-page letter, the second page of which slipped out and floated onto the bed. Stuart picked it up as Phyl read the first page. "It's from Eva herself!" Phyl's heart skipped a beat as she placed a hand firmly on her heaving chest. "Goodness. Now what? I haven't been invited to anything since our stay at the *estancia*, so this must be a hate letter."

"Hmm. Eva found out we were with Dodero, you can be sure of that."

"I'm afraid I blew my cover, didn't I? I'm still walking, though."

"What does she say?"

Phyl read for a moment. "She says she expects me to share with the Club all she accomplished since Perón took office." She looked at Eva's signature at the bottom of the typed letter. It started with an elegant "E," then the rest of the name became chaotic. Phyl figured Eva was either in a hurry or gave in to disgust with her. "She ends the letter saying a country which forgets its children renounces its future and that she demands more rights for women because she knows what they have to put up with."

"Sounds as if she had a tough life if you read between those lines." Stuart handed over the second page, which they saw was a list of information. "And she pontificates, as usual. Does she give an explanation as to why you didn't get invited to any more openings or dinners?"

"Nope," she said, shaking her head. "I'm really surprised I'm not dead in a ditch somewhere."

"Don't be silly. As I said, it was only because we were caught with Dodero. Who knows. Maybe she's just jealous." Stuart took the letter and started to read it.

"Of me? Ha! They're destroying their friendship with poor best friend, Dodero, by practically stealing everything from him," Phyl announced loudly.

Stuart grabbed her arm and motioned to the door. Phyl looked back. The door was shut but Maria would hear her voice if raised. She gave Stuart an apologetic look, then reviewed the second page. "It's a list of all she has accomplished." She read to herself for a bit. "In 1947, she created the Eva Perón Foundation, and it seems…" She looked closer. "Wow. Quite a list. She's built hospitals, homes for the elderly, single mothers, two polyclinics, schools, the Children's City."

"You already knew most of that."

"Yeah, but when written down like this, it's impressive." She continued reading. "She says she distributes cider and sweet bread to the poor on holidays. She organized children's and youth sports tournaments. She published *The Rights of the Elderly*. Created Senior Citizen Day. This year, she formed this Perónist Women's Party to help militarize women." She looked again at the envelope and the Party's emblem.

"Militarize? Interesting."

"That's what she wrote here in Spanish."

"No matter what people say about her, she's a force, and, it pains me to say, admirable."

"You mean things like Whore? Sneaky? Overbearing? Unreasonable? Pushy?"

"I'd say some of that is quite unfair, don't you?"

Phyl shrugged.

"Well, one makes enemies when moving mountains."

"Oh, Stu. You're right. You make me almost like her now. That's no fun." She pointed at her letter to K on the windowsill. "I can't send this now. What I wrote is so wrong after what you just said."

"What do you mean?"

She picked up the letter. "This is what I wrote, '*As I see it, this little white mother is definitely from the other side of the railway tracks. She has it in for everyone who isn't. Between her and her husband, they are going to do away with the landowners, make them rent out their lands to a lot of Diego small farmers who will work it ragged only to leave the soil, when they are finished, in a frightful state of erosion, which will take years to be rich again. I have seen some of the lands treated this way, and it is a disgrace. I've never had a lot of money and suppose I never shall, but by observance of this country, I'm all for the oligarchy. You certainly know who are making a wreck of this country. There are certain things I don't approve of and am not allowed to say, but generally speaking, the landowners are educated, decent, and simple people who treat those who work for them warmly and fairly. There are always exceptions, but I am speaking from my own experience.*"

Stuart's mouth dropped. "Phyl! Dem's killing words, you know that? Are you *crazy*?"

"Well, you were going to send this letter from Rio, not from here. No one was going to see this at the censorship board."

"You don't know that. I could lose it. It could be misplaced. Burn it! Immediately. Here."

Stuart snatched the letter and took out his lighter. He stood up, pulled a metal wastepaper bin, and held the letter over it. Stuart lit the lower corner. They watched the flame climb up the paper, then he dropped it before the fire reached his fingers. Very quickly, the paper burned, nothing but curling ash left at the bottom of the bin. "You can't go around writing things like that about the Peróns. *Especially* Eva."

"Evita."

"Evita. You'll get us killed."

"I'm so sorry, Stu. But she can be so infuriating. What I wrote was also true."

Stuart kicked the bin back into place and pulled Phyl closer. "Don't ever do that again."

Phyl looked at him closely. He had grown broader, larger than life. More handsome than ever. If only he didn't have tobacco stains on his dark blond mustache. Phyl stared at the stain.

Stuart shook her gently to get her attention. He peered into her eyes. "Phyl, come on. You made a mistake. Have Maria make a quick sandwich. I'm starving. And then we'll hurry over to the zoo."

"That creepy half-finished Tunnel of Love ride again?"

"Yup."

"It's still not finished? Aren't people going to get suspicious after all this time?"

Stuart laughed. "It works now. You get to ride the Tunnel of Love with an extremely handsome and intelligent man."

Phyl looked around the room with a glint in her eye. "Which extremely handsome and intelligent man are you talking about?"

Stuart picked Phyl up and threw her onto the bed. She squealed and didn't give a fig if Maria heard her.

Phyl stood perspiring in the sun.

She stood in line with Stuart impatiently eyeing the young man at the controls of the little rusty boats stopping and crawling through the creepy-looking Tunnel of Love. He looked strangely familiar. Her nostrils twitched at the smell of the tunnel's foul-smelling, streaming water. She saw him seemingly recognize her and Stuart further up the waiting line behind three young couples. She sensed Stuart nodding at him from behind her.

The young man got up, walked toward them and strolled past. He hung a chain across the entrance behind their backs and put up a sign saying the Tunnel of Love was closed, and returned to his controls. Phyl and Stuart watched the young man maneuver the little boats into place with his lever. He released each couple and boat and watched as they floated into the darkness, always carefully stopping the next little boat with his lever to allow returning couples to scramble out.

Stuart and Phyl were next. The young man held his hand out for Phyl to grab as she stepped into the little boat and made sure she sat on the red metal bench welded into the middle before he let Stuart step in. The bench was slightly wet and very cold. Phyl was afraid to move to wipe the bench underneath her, but reached out and wiped the moisture off the remainder of the seat with her handkerchief for Stuart.

She looked up at the young man again, and recognized him. He was one of the two bodyguards they had met the first time they were taken to Dodero so long before. This time, he looked more rugged, dressed in a cap, a heavy shirt, and dungarees. Stuart climbed into the boat, making it almost tip on its side. The young man bent over them to say something. Phyl leaned forward and tried to hear over the sound of the rushing water and the laughter coming out of the tunnel.

"I will stop your boat, and you will get out to the side. You'll see a doorway." He stood up, pulled the lever, and let them float with the cigarette-butt littered current.

Children's laughter, adult's voices, music, and the call of zoo animals echoed off the condensation-covered metal walls. They floated into the dank darkness, and all they could hear were the giggling couples ahead of them and the sound of water lapping about. They were almost in complete darkness when their little boat stopped and locked into position. Phyl saw a ledge next to Stuart.

"Here we are," Stuart said.

He carefully climbed out of the boat and reached for Phyl to take his hand. They slipped into an opening and saw light stream from under a door at the end of a small cubicle. Stuart opened the door. They were met by the other young bodyguard from the last meeting. He motioned for them to go to the same back room as before. This time, Dodero was not alone under the ugly glare of a lightbulb.

Juan Duarte, Evita's brother, sat smoking beside Dodero and Colonel Atilio Cattáneo.

Phyl's eyes widened, and then she grinned, surprised to see Cattáneo.

Dodero stood up in deference to Phyl, as did a smiling Cattáneo. Duarte did the same. Dodero looked older and worn. He and Stuart shook hands, smiling and Phyl held out her hand with a gentle smile. Then Stuart and Phyl shook hands with Cattáneo and Duarte.

Phyl eyed Cattáneo. "Old friend."

He nodded with smiling eyes.

She turned to Dodero. "Alberto," she whispered. "How are you? We missed you. I was most concerned."

Dodero smirked and shrugged.

"It is a surprise to meet you, *Señor* Duarte," Stuart said politely before looking pointedly at Dodero and Cattáneo. "I suppose we have been summoned for a reason other than catching up with you globetrotters."

Phyl noticed Duarte look away sadly as the others chuckled. He took a deep breath and nodded slightly. He was short, round-faced with a black mustache and balding. He wore a summer suit and tie, gold cuff links, and a large diamond ring, which he nervously fingered with his other hand. He had deep, dark circles under his eyes.

Dodero sat down, adjusting his vest and tie. "First, in answer to our lovely Phyl, as you may know, my wife and I have separated. She wants a divorce. Though being Catholic and in Argentina, we technically can't be divorced."

Phyl sat down and cocked her head. "But you were divorced already once before marrying? How'd that work?"

Dodero made a face. "Though a divorce would be recognized in the rest of the world, Argentina would always consider my wife my, er, wife."

"Which wife would that be?" asked Stuart, smirking and making himself comfortable beside Phyl. He briefly watched the other men sit before looking back at Dodero.

Dodero slapped the table. "All right. That is enough about me."

Cattáneo cleared his throat and adjusted his body in a creaky chair. "Dodero and I thought we needed this one last catch-up. And *Señor* Duarte…" He paused and looked at Stuart. "I'm sorry, do we need to make clear who…?"

Stuart shook his head. "No. We know you are Evita's brother." He looked kindly at Duarte.

"Well, *Señor* Duarte is most concerned that the United States does not misunderstand his sister's mandate." He blinked at Duarte. "As I said earlier, Duarte, you can rely on them both to help share information. I understand there are issues related to your sister's safety."

Stuart leaned forward. "I feel we will have an earnest discussion here."

"Indeed," said Duarte. He looked at Dodero and Cattáneo. Duarte cleared his throat and continued. "Both Dodero and the Colonel said I could feel confident that what I am about to share with you today will be passed on through your contacts." He looked at Dodero. "You see, your ambassadors come and go. Your Bruce has gone, and Stanton Griffis will be leaving soon, but each ambassador is mostly concerned about policy and your country's influence on our country. And each has his own mandate. I need to know if I can rely on American intervention in case we need it. So," he motioned to Stuart and Phyl. "I understand that Eva wrote to you, *Señora* Redington, hoping you would continue to share all she has done for the *Descamisados* with your American Women's Club members."

"I just received the letter this morning. But I don't know how I can be of help."

"Your American women have influence. They tend to be open with their opinions. They know American journalists back home; some are married to men of note and power. They travel to where they are free to express their views and speak of their thoughts on Eva, on our country."

It suddenly felt hot and stuffy in the room. Duarte took out a handkerchief, wiped his beaded forehead, and put it back. He did so with his little finger raised in the air, something Phyl thought was unusual for a man. "With Alberto now having less influence on my sister and brother-in-law, and with his wife spending less time at my sister's side, I fear that Eva is falling back into her old habits. It may not be obvious, but she has a serious lack of self-confidence."

Phyl and Stuart looked at each other. "But she seems so sure of herself," said Phyl. "She does a wonderful job of making her people love her."

"There is a certain amount of bravado in what she does and says. It's why she is so driven. Acceptance. Love. Adoration. Yes, all things she's always craved for. We all did growing up. We were considered bastards and were treated like dirt, though our father cared enough to give us his name. His real family refused to acknowledge us when our poor father died. They are quite wealthy, but we were left impoverished. I'm sure with this deep in her psyche, Eva has been very generous with my mother and us, her siblings, making sure we live as royalty." He motioned to no one in particular. "I am doing quite well, myself. I have land and investments. Of course, I must be careful not to appear to gain from my position as personal secretary to *El Presidente*."

"And brother to the first lady," added Stuart.

"Precisely," Duarte said. He made a slight motion with his head that appeared effeminate. Phyl realized he was of another ilk.

"Your sister must care very much about you and your family," offered Phyl. She looked at Stuart, and he looked back. He raised his eyebrows.

"Oh, yes. I owe her much."

"You have children?"

"I am not married."

Dodero cleared his throat. "Duarte, here, is a bit of a playboy." He grinned, showing tobacco-stained teeth.

"Yes, I like the ladies," Duarte said emphatically and not too convincingly. "In any case, all attention must go to what my sister does out of love for others. Not *how* she does it or any personal gain through her efforts."

"Oh," said Phyl. She frowned, searching for a diplomatic way of saying she disagreed as she believed Eva's tactics were harsh and suspicious.

"She is not, particularly, a well-educated and well-read individual," Duarte continued. "Our family was quite startled when she and Perón became an item." Duarte lowered his chin and gazed at one of the pearl buttons on his vest. "But I fear for her as she is so quick to fight anything and anyone who might imply she is not good enough."

"Well then, how can I help?" asked Phyl.

Duarte motioned toward her. "As club president, please read that letter to your members, or better yet, make copies and ensure your members have one and are well aware of her accomplishments."

"Then, I will do that."

Duarte raised his bloodshot eyes and smiled sadly. "And she is not well, I fear."

"Oh? Perhaps she is overworked and needs rest." Phyl wanted to sound empathetic. She looked at Cattáneo, who scratched his eyebrow. He looked discouraged and occupied with his own thoughts. She saw Duarte glance sideways at the men beside him before clearing his throat. He leaned closer.

"She has, er, female problems."

Phyl glanced at Dodero and Cattáneo. "Are they serious problems?"

Duarte made a face. "I am led to believe so. You see, I located the doctor who treated my brother-in-law's first wife." He cocked his head. Phyl saw his eyes tear up. "I learned she died because of something he may have passed on to her." He held up tiny, pudgy, soft-looking hands, then frustratingly scratched at his receding hairline. "I'm not saying he did so intentionally, but, perhaps, a sexually-transmitted disease." His face collapsed into tears. He covered his face and shook his head.

Everyone paled and looked at each other but waited patiently. Stuart coughed nervously.

After a moment, Duarte stopped crying, took out the handkerchief again, and wiped his eyes and nose. "I apologize. My reaction may seem a bit extreme, but I must tell you that I see all correspondence that comes into the office, and we receive constant death threats. I read them before *El Presidente* does. For the most part, I pass them on to him. But I dread Eva knowing about them. Her death or threat of death is always on my mind." He covered his eyes and shook his head. He sat up straighter.

"Where do these threats come from? Can't Perón stop them or at least catch and jail these people?" asked Phyl innocently.

Duarte's nostrils flared. "No. Because these threats come from the Church and the military. It isn't a matter of simply eradicating a single source of threat. These do not always come from individuals. These threats come from higher up."

Phyl gasped softly, frowned at Duarte. "The Church?" She looked at Stuart. "Correct me if I'm wrong, but I thought a church represents love, forgiveness, and peace. Thou shalt not kill, and all that."

Dodero laughed heartily. "Dear pretty woman. You are such a sweet, innocent child. Where do you come from again?"

"Canada."

"Precisely. You Canadians are such nice people. You have no idea what the real world is like outside your borders."

"What do you mean?"

"Let me explain, Duarte" Cattáneo interrupted. He turned to Phyl, holding up a hand to underline a point he was about to make. "In this country, the Catholic Church is number one," he held up one finger. "All-powerful. Immovable. Ultimately, in control. As they are with most of the military. And they used to be in control of the people."

"Oh," said Phyl, understanding where Cattáneo was heading.

"Suddenly, *Perónisma* and *Evita* have all the power."

"I see."

"Two," Cattáneo held up another finger. "Evita is doing the Catholic Church's work. She is doing a better job than the Catholic Church ever did in helping the *Descamisados*. That does not bode well."

Phyl nodded.

Cattáneo held up a third finger. "Three: Consequently, Evita is now considered a Virgin Mary in her own right, which, you can imagine, causes the Church to be apoplectic."

"Ah." Phyl stifled a laugh.

Cattáneo held up a fourth finger. "Four: *Perónisma* is taking over the dogma of the Church in its own schools. Perón has made his political philosophy, which is neither fascist nor communist and is a separate entity all on its own, as compulsory education elbowing out religious studies in the classroom."

"Oh, my God," said Phyl, covering her mouth.

"And they, of course, can't easily threaten Perón, *el presidente*. So, they target Eva," said Stuart.

"Yes, which brings number five." Cattáneo held up all five fingers. "Evita has now given women the right to vote and the right to social programs the Church would never have thought of or cared about. You see, the Catholic Church is patriarchal. They do not *want* women to have power or have a voice. To them, women are evil creatures, having to live in shame ever since Eve and the Garden of Eden fiasco. They are servants, having to succumb to the men. They have no rights. Other than bearing children for the Church and caring for their husbands, they are not much more valuable than dogs."

Phyl felt nauseous.

"*Evita* is not safe anywhere, anytime. But she won't listen to me." Duarte looked pale, worried, sick. "You understand what I am saying? What would help is if your United States could recognize her good deeds for this country and, yes, the world. Then the less likely something will happen to her."

"But she doesn't care less what the United States thinks of *her*," said Stuart.

"Oh, that's not true, Stu," Phyl piped up. "She's always saying Argentina depends on what the United States can do for them. I've heard her say this often. She desperately wants Argentina to get loans, military equipment, and materials for their own industries."

Stuart silently studied Phyl.

Duarte: "Your country must understand what motivates her. And people must stop spreading terrible rumors about her. They can be most hateful and ugly."

Phyl cleared her throat and shifted in her seat. She looked at Stuart. She swallowed hard, knowing she had been one of the perpetrators. She thought of all the times she stood with wine and cigarette in hand, listening to and sharing the latest gossip, all invariably very cutting and almost entirely baseless.

She thought of the letter she had almost sent K. Her voice croaked. "I will try my dandiest to set things straight every time I hear something that is not truthful."

Duarte sat back, somewhat satisfied.

Stuart cleared his throat and looked at Cattáneo. "Um, I don't mean to change the subject, but why are we blessed with your presence here today, Colonel?"

Cattáneo good-naturedly shot up his eyebrows and smiled. He leaned to the side and pulled an envelope out of a briefcase next to his chair. He handed it to Stuart.

Stuart looked at the plain envelope and flipped it over. It had been taped shut.

"Put it somewhere safe until you can either pass it on or decipher it and transfer the information to the powers that be. I will no longer be able to do so myself. I'm stepping out."

Stuart frowned. "What do you mean?"

"I can read the writing on the wall. I, too, get continuous threats. A few of my peers have disappeared and I am not interested in becoming a martyr. Perón didn't like a speech of mine recently and he is introducing a new law that doesn't allow disrespect for him and his office through public speeches."

"Wow. No free speech allowed in Argentina," muttered Stuart.

"Hmm. To do so would mean prison. I represent the Opposition and what do they expect? How can I *not* point out his shortcomings? I have a family to think of. So, I'm leaving the country with my wife and children until things settle down *after* Perón. If that day will come within my lifetime."

"Who will lead the Opposition then?" Stuart asked.

"You American. You're still assuming we are a democracy. To oppose Perón now means to be a sitting duck in that carnival shooting gallery outside these walls." Cattáneo stood up and stubbed out his cigarette. He held out his hand to Dodero, who stood.

Dodero shook his hand.

"Perhaps I will see you in Rio, Dodero."

Dodero shook his head. "Don't stay in Rio. That's not far enough. Remember that man with bullets in his back and head in that cave Phyl dragged us to? Whether it's Perón, the Church, or the military, there's secret police everywhere."

Cattáneo inhaled deeply. "Well, I don't have the resources you have, Dodero. I can't just up and go to Cannes or the Riviera."

Dodero slapped Cattáneo's arm. "Contact me when you are ready. I can help."

Cattáneo no longer smiled. Phyl saw tears gather in his eyes. He nodded. He quickly kissed Phyl's hand, shook Duarte's hand, and looked at Stuart. "Thank you for passing on my last correspondence. I'm sorry, I no longer can work with your country." He smiled sorrowfully.

Cattáneo bowed abruptly, stepped to the door, and knocked. The bodyguard opened the door to allow him through and then closed it behind him.

"Wow," said Stuart as he and everyone sat back down.

"Speaking of Cannes," jumped in Dodero. He picked up a beautifully wrapped box, and put it in the middle of the table directly under the light.

Phyl eyed the object of beauty. The wrapping paper looked as fine as gold leaf, and there was a large, elegant gold bow on top. Her eyes glistened as she wondered what it was and who it was for.

Dodero turned to Duarte. "As you know, I was at Rita Hayworth and Prince Aly Kahn's wedding in Cannes recently."

"Yes, I heard it was magnificent and ever so elegant. Over five hundred people were invited." Duarte smiled. "They filled the pool with eau de cologne, I hear."

"They did, indeed."

"You met Rita Hayworth?" gasped Phyl.

"Who is Prince Aly Kahn?" asked Stuart, frowning.

Dodero ignored Stuart. He pushed the gift toward Phyl. "For you."

"Oh, my!"

"This is from their circus of a wedding," grinned Dodero.

"My wife does not receive gifts from other men," announced Stuart tersely.

"My friend, do not fear. If I were to woo your wife, it would be in secret and with diamonds and furs." Dodero looked amiably at Phyl. "I did not buy this for Phyl. All guests received this. But I thought of Phyl." He looked at Stuart. "I don't think that is a sin, is it? A friend thinking of a friend?"

"Oh, Stuart!" whined Phyl. "Please."

Stuart angrily waved at her, crossed his arms and legs, and sat back in his chair.

Phyl looked at Dodero and held out her hands. "May I open it?"

Dodero grinned. "Be my beautiful guest."

Phyl carefully loosened up a side flap. She unwrapped the gift slowly, leaving the bow attached to the paper. It was a shiny black box with a gold square logo on the front and the word *Shalimar* in the middle. She opened the box and pulled out an elegantly shaped perfume bottle. She gasped. Carefully, she unscrewed the top and passed it under her nose. The aroma, like delicate long fingers, reached up into her nostrils, and titilated a garden of joy in her very soul. She sat back, feeling heady, her heart skipping. "Oh, my God. This is so amazingly beautiful. Smell this!" Phyl said, holding the bottle out to Stuart.

Stuart waved it away.

Phyl ignored him and sniffed at the aroma again. She screwed the beautiful top back on. "Oh, thank you, Dodero. It's the most elegant perfume I have ever smelled."

"It's Rita Hayworth's favorite." He grinned at her, pulling out his cigarettes and offering them to Stuart.

Stuart shook his head and motioned to the perfume bottle, eyeing Dodero with distrust. "Man, how am I supposed to top that?"

"Wait till I tell Vivienne!" Phyl turned to Stuart. "I'm going to write to her about Rita Hayworth getting married on the Riviera with this Prince..."

"Prince Kaka." Stuart was not happy.

Dodero shrugged amiably. "Don't worry. We all kind of know the marriage won't last."

"How can you say that?" asked Phyl, astounded.

"I don't care if he *is* the richest prince in the world, he's no Prince Charming. And you think I'm a lady's man?" He laughed. "I wouldn't be surprised if he, er, did the servants the morning of."

"Oh, that's awful."

"What do you expect from the filthy rich and Hollywood?" asked Stuart.

"I'd like to think Rita Hayworth is smarter than that," retorted Phyl.

"Well, guess again. Why do you think the smartest man in film divorced her?" asked Stuart.

"You mean Orson Welles?"

"Hmm."

"Oh. She's not smart? But she must be the most beautiful woman alive today."

Dodero grinned. "They can't all be beautiful and smart at the same time like you."

Phyl bit her lip and grinned, pleased.

"You stole my line, you bastard!" protested Stuart.

* * *

When Phyl left the apartment a couple of days later for her meeting at the Club, the goon who always sat at the end of the hall was gone. No chair. Nothing.

As too often happened of late, the power had gone out, so she had to take the stairs to go down. In the lobby, only the porter sat at his console. The vestibule lights were out, and the radio was dead. Usually, the two goons and Dodero's assigned chauffeur normally waited for her chatting, laughing and smoking with the porter.

"*Hola*," said Phyl, looking around. Then she noticed he sat looking at her dolefully. "*Que pasa?*"

He wordlessly pointed out the door, and she looked. No car. No chauffeur.

"Oh," she said. "What happened? Is he late?"

The porter shrugged. Phyl looked at her watch. "I'll wait outside." The porter jumped up, opened the door, and stood with her on the sidewalk, looking up and down the street. Phyl took a deep breath and looked around. They stood together for a minute more.

"Taxi?" he asked decades later, seemingly.

Phyl looked at her watch again. "*Si*. All right. Otherwise, I will be late for my meeting."

Minutes later, Phyl sat in the back of a taxi and was deep in thought when she realized they had stopped. She saw traffic wasn't moving. Slowly, she became aware of the roar of a crowd approaching. Eventually, a tsunami of bedraggeled-looking country folk, flew between the cars, banging at doors and windows, yelling angrily, like the dead had arisen for the dawn of the Apocalypse.

The taxi driver leaned out and asked a passerby what the problem was.

Phyl sat closer to listen. "What did he say?"

The taxi driver threw his hands up when he was finished with the man. "He says there was an attempted assassination on Evita and Perón."

"What?" Phyl's heart beat hard against her chest. "Do you think it's the same people who tried to kill her when she pushed through the woman's vote last year?"

Suddenly someone was thrown against the hood of the taxi. His face smashed against the windshield before he slipped off the car and disappeared onto the road somewhere. They waited *nervoso* as the taxi rocked, blindsided by several fist fights. Finally, the fighting men were torn off and away from the car and cast aside. The mob moved on and traffic started to crawl forward again. Phyl kept a hand on over her pounding heart.

An eternity passed. Still shaken, Phyl entered the nearly empty meeting room at the American Women's Club. The Club had backup power, so the main building functioned. The noise of generators vibrated the walls slightly as she put her purse down at the head table and sat. She moved the gavel to the side and picked up a copy of the Agenda left for her. Club members trickled in, clucking over the apparent uprising and rumor of the attempted assassinations.

"This dictatorship is as bad as Hitler and his henchmen ever were," said one of the women.

Phyl opened her mouth to caution against rumors, as was asked of her by Duarte, but hesitated.

"Did you know women were jailed just for talking about the high cost of food at the market?" asked another.

"It's not safe for us downtown today. When I saw people walking around with hangman's ropes, I had to ask the taxi driver to take a detour around the park."

One member rushed in, breathless. "Did you hear? They think it's an American living in Montevideo who is the ringleader for this attempted assassination."

More women poured into the room, and soon the walls echoed with calls, cries, and concerns as they shared stories and gossip, both true and maybe not.

Phyl stood and slammed the gavel on the table. Women looked at her, surprised. It wasn't yet time to start the meeting. But Phyl wanted to kill the frenzy of speculation. "Ladies, calm down. Grab some coffee and have a seat. We'll share once we get more information, but don't speculate. We don't have all the facts."

"Sure, we do. The fact is, we're sitting in a hellhole!"

Many agreed. Some sat in shock, fearful.

"That's not the point. We'll wait to hear—"

The phone in the main lobby rang shrilly, and one of the ladies standing in the doorway stepped toward it. There was a lull in the room as everyone eavesdropped. The woman at the phone listened to the caller at length, said two or three words, and slowly hung up. She looked into the room and locked eyes with Phyl. Phyl motioned for her to come closer.

"A bunch of antigovernment people were rounded up this morning and almost tortured to death. They were discarded and are beyond recognition. It's recommended we all go home immediately and stay until this ugly dust settles."

"Who called?" asked Phyl.

"The American ambassador himself."

The room exploded with a frantic exit of thirty women. Phyl quickly gathered her things and rushed out along with the others. Her blood ran cold. She prayed that all would be well with her Stuart.

* * *

"For the last few weeks, they have been busy bringing hundreds of thousands of people down from the north, practically all Indigenous Peoples, to stage a massive demonstration next Sunday," said Stuart.

He sat at the dining room table scraping his burnt toast with a butter knife. He held the toast up in disgust for Phyl to see.

"No power, so Maria toasts it over the gas flame," explained Phyl.

"During the war, we knew the Nazis were behind some of the uprisings, but now, at the office, they're saying perhaps it's communists," Stuart brushed burnt breadcrumbs off the embroidered tablecloth. "Or even Evita herself though I can't prove that." He pointed the knife in Phyl's direction. "Don't you dare quote that."

Phyl made a surprised face.

"We're closing the office; no one knows for how long."

"So, what do we do? Just wait in our flat?"

Stuart tossed the toast onto his plate. "Nope. We're going to Rio. My contacts there will fill me in, and I can piece it all together before my next report."

"Oh, thank God. I'm ready for a luxurious beach break, though those tanned and beautiful Nubian bodies sure make me feel old."

"Don't let them get you down; at almost 40, you look exceptional. Mind you, you're no Rita Hayworth."

Phyl slapped Stuart's arm, jokingly picked up his knife, and held it up menacingly, trying to look tough. "I'm 37 and going on 20, if you don't mind."

"Well, when you put it that way, you can be 18 for all I care!" He leaned over and whispered in her ear. "It's a good thing you're smart."

Phyl picked up the toast and threw it at Stuart.

* * *

Hotel Regente
Rio de Janeiro, Brazil

Wednesday, January 11, 1950

Dear Dad and K,

Argentine Riptide

It's seven years since I last saw Rio, and it hasn't lost any of its beauty. We arrived on Monday, and the view from the air was really something – you think you've seen all the beauty the world has to offer until you see this place.

I also wish I could be there with you to be of some comfort, K. Stuart is worried that Dad isn't feeling too well. We received his letter and were thrilled about it. Tell him we can't seem to find out anything more about the monster snake here. I think they call it an Anaconda. But he should see some of the funny things they pull in the fish nets. There is a Ling Bass, about four feet long. It has a top fin but no lower fin. They take the boat out, leave the huge nets, and start hauling both ends and this way, they scoop up fish by the ton. All the suntanned boys and girls make a nuisance of themselves kibitzing. The fishermen yell at them in Portuguese to get out of the way, but they keep on crowding around. The thing that keeps them back is the slime splashing around from all the fish flipping.

Phyl sat back against the aqua-blue and white striped cushions of the lounge chair. She looked at the lights and billowing smoke stacks of two cruise ships maneuvering into place in the darkening harbor. The sight of them made her feel mellow. She looked around the colorful surroundings, and caught the city lights coming on. Above her, in the vermillion blue sky, two planes with their navigation lights on - one coming in to land and another on its way north. She looked across the effervescent turquoise rollers crashing into the beach below. People had, for the most part, left the beach to nap or dress for dinner. Workers from the hotels were stacking chairs and closing umbrellas, moving around the wicker domed love seats, and picking up used hotel towels and debris.

She looked at the letter she was writing. She moved to allow light from the balcony sconce to brighten the paper. She wiped a tanned knee, squinted at the paper and continued writing.

Two ocean liners are just now coming through the channel. Planes constantly take off and arrive from the Santos Dumont Airport. Their silver wings shine and reflect the city's lights and the moon's as they bank over the ocean – oh boy! I wish you and Dad could come and see. The glamor is still here even though the roulette casinos no longer exist due to the religious convictions of the President's wife, who died last year, but not before she spoiled one of the biggest attractions of this place. Anyway, the game was a weakness of mine, and it is just as well as I would have to leave a lot sooner, as to me, the croupiers' call is just like a moose calling me in the Canadian wilds!

She looked back into their darkening hotel room as she heard the door open and glasses clink. "Stu?"

"Yup. Martinis as ordered from the bar. It was packed so it took a while," he yelled from inside. A shaft of light cut across the balcony. Stuart turned on a lamp. His shadow blocked the light as he showed up in the glass doorway. "Wow, it gets dark fast." He stepped closer. "What ya doing?"

"I'm writing home. It's great writing anything I want from here." She saw Stuart hold out her martini. "Oh, thank you." She held the beaded glass aloft and Stuart pulled a chair closer to her. Above them, the scalloped edging of the aqua and white awning flapped in the evening's salted breeze.

"You have to be careful what you write, Phyl. We're still followed here in Rio."

"I think I'll take the chance, though I promise," she lowered her voice to a whisper, "I will not say anything about the Peróns."

They clinked glasses and sipped cool drinks.

Phyl licked her lips. "Yum."

Stuart wore khaki shorts, a white cotton shirt, and leather sandals. "So, what are you writing?"

"How beautiful it is here. And I'm going to talk about when I thought your plane crashed coming back from here a few weeks ago."

"We didn't almost crash. The pilot knew exactly what to do."

"Well, you *could've* crashed. That storm was awful."

"Right, the storm held us up, and we turned back."

"One plane went down."

"It doesn't take brains to know flying over the mountains is a challenge in good weather, never mind flying blind and being knocked around by wind and rain." He shook his head and looked down at his martini. "It was a private plane. Dumb."

"Believe me, I got some gray hairs waiting and worrying. You were a whole day late. The next morning, I devoured the newspaper and when I saw a plane went down, I almost died. But then I read it wasn't yours. Thank God, you eventually buzzed up and said you were downstairs in the lobby. I was still trying to make mince tarts in the gas stove, while hallucinating airplane crashes and lightning flashes."

"Some homecoming. I had to walk up the nine flights of stairs. Good time to have a power outage, on Christmas Eve."

Phyl grinned. "You poor thing. Your tongue was hanging out for a drink, and I felt so bad having to tell you that the ice in the icebox had melted." She threw up her hands. "No ice! You should've seen your face. At least you didn't miss Christmas!" Phyl noticed Stuart staring at his martini. "You okay?"

"I got some news from my contact, some of it unexpected."

"Is it all bad?"

"Well, first," he leaned back. "This will have something to do with you."

"Oh?"

"Evita fainted two days ago and was rushed to hospital. Apparently, they operated on her. They *say* an appendectomy."

Phyl sighed. "Her brother said she was sick," she whispered, looking at the surrounding balconies. She held a finger to her lips.

"Hmm." Stuart sighed, looked around as well. He lowered his voice. "Also, extreme changes are being made for those entering Argentina, though us old-timers remain as we are."

She frowned. "What do you mean? Us as in old-time foreigners?"

"Yup. But newcomers, if they are lucky to be approved to enter, must take out papers and keep them on their persons."

"Like criminals?"

Stuart nodded.

Phyl fidgeted. "It's getting worse by the day, Stu."

"I know. Things are getting impossible and dangerous. And you won't like this, Phyl, but there's something else."

"More bad news? What won't I like?"

"It is now prohibited to take anything out of the country when leaving." He patted his breast pocket for cigarettes. "Darn, I must have left my cigarettes at the bar."

Phyl's face went pale. "You're saying we can't take our private *things* with us back home?"

"Right."

"But our entire marriage here was spent carefully picking and choosing what we wanted to invest our money in. We have nice rugs and oil paintings. I don't want to give them up. Lord, we have some decent mahogany furniture and silverware." Phyl started to panic. "How can they do that to us?"

"They're doing it."

"You mean we have to sell everything when we leave, even the car?" she cried.

Stuart coughed into his fist. He searched between the cushions around Phyl.

Phyl reached behind her between the cushions and pulled out cigarettes and a gold lighter. She frowned when Stuart coughed again. It didn't sound good. "Are you sure you want a cigarette?"

Stuart held out his hand, and she gave him the package and lighter. He lit two cigarettes and handed one to her.

"All right. For the sake of argument, if we sell everything and manage to get all our money out of all our wonderful stuff, won't this also leave us holding a raft of useless *pesos* to convert to dollars? Isn't it about ten to the dollar, now?"

"Yup."

Phyl threw up her hands. "We're poor again!"

"We have very little choice. It's a moot point, anyhow. What you don't know is that the banks won't do the exchange. We can only buy dollars on the black market at an exorbitant high rate of exchange. The only other angle is to put our money into a small property, but that wouldn't make sense if things are going the way they are and we have to leave."

"We can follow Jorge's advice," she said. She held out her arm and pointed at her fingers and wrist with the hand that was holding her burning cigarette. "I could start looking like Eva Perón."

"Jewelry," Stuart snorted. He cleared his throat. "I'm not too happy about that, but it's probably the best approach. My contract is until December of this year, but I'm thinking I'll ask to leave early."

"Would they allow that?"

"It's getting pretty iffy here for us, Phyl. I'm hearing rumors…"

She covered her face. "No. No more bad news. What a way to ruin a perfectly beautiful day."

Stuart allowed the calming sound of the waves rolling onto the beach below to stifle the moment's tension. Laughter rose from the boulevard below, and music wafted up from the open lobby nearby. People gathered for the usual late supper in the neighboring cafés and dining establishments. Stuart inhaled the aroma of exquisite spices mixed with the ocean air. He coughed.

Phyl sniffed, wiped at moist eyes. "Okay. What kind of rumors? To do with us?"

"Well, it has to do with all of us moonlighting on the government's dime. The G-Man program. Things are getting very tense and surreal because those who spy on us no longer hide the fact that they're following us and our contacts. They don't seem to care if we spot them. They've become quite brazen."

Phyl felt nauseous, and her heart raced.

"I've sent a cable to head office inquiring about working and living in Brazil instead for this coming year," he said, looking around for the ashtray.

She picked up the ashtray behind her on the balcony floor, and placed it between them. "Stu," she whispered. "If what you say is true, then Brazil is still too close for comfort. They have their spies out here, too."

"It's not in the books, anyhow, Phyl. It was only my suggestion and they didn't take it. They came back with Harrisburg, Pennsylvania instead."

Phyl stepped to the railing. She violently shook her head. "Uh-uh. No way am I going back to Pennsylvania." She hung halfway over the top of the railing and blindly searched the hotel entranceway below her and thought of her terrible miscarriage. She watched but her eyes didn't see the tops of heads milling about. She heard laughter and wondered how people could be so unaware of the dangers lurking about in a country going crazy.

Stuart looked at her with hooded eyes. He stood up and touched her back. She buried her face into his shoulder. "Harrisburg is nothing at all like Wilkes Barre. This would be in a small suburb."

"Anywhere in Pennsylvania is not living," she mumbled into his shirt.

The phone rang. Stuart and Phyl looked back and stared at the almond and gold phone on the white and gold-trimmed credenza by the fancy bronze table lamp. Stuart let go of Phyl and walked through. He noted that the bottle of Shalimar perfume sat next to the phone. He turned and looked at Phyl, still on the balcony, watching him forlornly, too stunned to move. Stuart answered the phone, listened momentarily, and held the receiver against his chest. "It's for *Señora de Redington*."

Phyl raised her eyebrows. She sadly shook her head. "It's probably the Club with an update. Please ask the desk to take a message."

Stuart quietly studied her and looked at the receiver. "Perhaps you should take it. You never know what it might be."

"Oh." Phyl took a deep breath, shook her head, and hurried to Stuart. She meekly took the phone and listened. As she did, she eyed the Shalimar perfume next to the phone, picked up the bottle, and sniffed it with her eyes closed, hoping to have her spirits lifted by the exquisite mixture of scents and oils. Suddenly, her breath was knocked out of her; she dropped the bottle in shock.

Having walked back to the balcony railing to look at the beautiful ocean, Stuart turned in surprise. He rushed back in, saw the bottle on its side on the white carpet, and picked it up and sidled closer to Phyl. She stood shaking and holding the receiver. She slammed it down and broke into tears.

Stuart held her close. "Shh. It's okay, Phyl. Shh."

"No, it's not okay, Stu!" Phyl pushed him away. She pointed at the phone, distraught. "That was Selina from Membership. She said they just got word that Vivienne died in Toronto yesterday." She covered her face and shook her head. "Oh, my God, Stu. Her husband died last year, and now it appears Vivienne died of the same thing, but no one really seems to know what it is."

Stuart reached out for her again and rocked her gently from side to side. After a moment, Phyl opened her eyes and saw the bottle of Shalimar in Stuart's hand. She took the bottle and looked at it. "I'll never wear this again," she whispered.

"Now, why would you say that?"

"It'll always remind me of Vivienne dying. Poor Vivienne. Beautiful, smart Vivienne." She put the bottle on the credenza. "Stuart," she announced. "This place is killing everyone. And if we're not careful, it'll kill us."

Chapter Twenty-One

Harrisburg Twice, Death on Her Mind, Jorge Update and Toronto

The spectre of death held a constant grip on Phyl's mind.

She could not shake it even a year later, living in Harrisburg.

It nibbled at her psyche as she hung up from her call with the Remington-Rand New York head office. She told them Stuart was too ill to take the train to Manhattan to attend his weekly meeting.

She shook her head from pinpricks of chronic anxiety. She compulsively scratched at the nail polish on her index finger. She hadn't expected to feel so uprooted since leaving Buenos Aires, and perhaps that didn't help. She had developed a syndrome, almost a need for living on the edge. Life was shockingly different on American soil. She expected to feel relieved and safe away from Argentina, but her fears remained unchanged.

The fear did not reside in Argentina. It lived in her. It didn't help that they could only afford a cleaning lady for half a day once a week, leaving Phyl burdened with everything else. She knew she'd been spoiled, but she was always physically spent.

She shifted in her kitchen chair, hunched over the table and continued with her to-do list. In the distance from their bedroom upstairs, she heard Stuart cough. She shook her head. That was another thing: She had hoped Stuart's lungs would clear up once back, but he was still struggling. It had been a terrible winter, and early February 1951 was a far cry from the beautiful, hot weather they were undoubtedly having back in Argentina. She covered her eyes. She thought of Stuart's father dead after years of constant lung problems and feared Stuart inherited his weak lungs. She fought back depression, though she wouldn't have known the word. Ennui, perhaps.

Melancholy. The spectre of death. The blues. The incessant doldrums.

Phyl wearily checked her watch. It was just past 8:00 o'clock. She would typically have taken Stuart to the station to catch the 6:30 a.m. train so he could arrive in Manhattan for a full day of work. These Head Office meeting days were long and arduous for Stuart. He would hurry to catch the 5:00 o'clock train back and arrive weary to be picked up at 8:00 o'clock. Phyl cupped her face into her hand and leaned on an elbow. She felt her body sway slightly to her heartbeat.

A clump of snow plopped onto the kitchen windowsill outside, and Phyl looked up past the sheer curtains in the frosted window. She looked past the bottom edge of the outside metal awning, and could make out a thin blanket of freshly fallen snow on the Packard parked by the back door. The day was starting to lighten. No doubt an overcast day. A heavy snowfall in the last few days left behind a winter wonderland, though slush on the roads was pitch black.

The summer before, after years of living in colorful and vibrant Buenos Aires, Phyl and Stuart thought their two-bedroom house and surrounding neighborhood looked plain and colorless. Everything was covered with an ever-present layer of soot. Even the grass lacked the luscious emerald luster of Buenos Aries' parks. Determined to create a bright and cozy home by adding color, they installed expensive turquoise and white metal awnings over all the windows. These did a bang-up job of reminding them of brightly-colored hotel awnings flapping in the ocean breeze in Rio de Janeiro, or of those on the *estancia*, or the awnings flapping in the salty air at Jorge and Angelica's Buenos Aires flat. All happy memories. The sight of them made Phyl think warmly of Jorge and Angelica. She was so grateful they could store their belongings in one of the *estancia* stables, even though their return to Argentina was a toss-up. Jorge was able to smuggle the Packard out of the country to New York. The previous October, he also smuggled in a Goucho statue, which presently perched on the fireplace mantle in the living room. She couldn't wait for Jorge's subsequent visit the next month to see what of their other precious items he would bring. She did, at least, have his visits to look forward to.

Phyl pushed back from the white enamel table, folded the to-do list, and stuck it into her black leather handbag on the other red and white faux leather chair. She straightened out her woolen skirt and hurried to the front hall to climb the hallway stairs, each wooden tread creaking under her fuzzy, pink slippers as she grasped the railing. Halfway up the staircase, she paused to look out the small side window. She frowned at the street.

"Yup," she muttered. "There you are again." She eyed a black car sitting along the curb. She hurriedly continued up the stairs. "Stu?" she yelled.

Stuart muttered back unintelligibly.

Phyl opened the bedroom door. Warm, moist air caressed her face. "I'm going. 'You going to be okay for a few hours?"

Stuart in pajamas under the covers, coughed, shifted and moaned. "Yes. I'll be fine."

Phyl walked in and eyed the humidifier. She shook it, heard water gurgle, and saw it still spewed soft steam. "Do you need anything?"

Stuart coughed again. "Nope," he rattled. "Just you." He smiled sweetly. He had dark rings under his eyes and looked flushed.

"Ah," said Phyl. She smiled before taking long strides to his side to kiss him on his hot sweaty cheek. "Okay, then. I have to do some groceries, get a few things for the kitchen at Kresge's, and maybe grab a grilled cheese. Is that okay?"

Stuart nodded slightly.

"Stu, that car's up the street again."

Stuart stirred and looked at her with one eye. He twisted with a groan to lie on his back and he put an arm over his eyes. "Phyl. We spoke about this before. You're reading into things. You thought we were being watched on the train to Washington and were being followed in Toronto."

Phyl wordlessly played with Stuart's thinning hair.

"I know you're not happy, Phyl."

Phyl sat on the edge of the bed. She let her eyes be drawn to the bedroom window, covered in condensation, and a rolled-up towel tucked along the bottom edge to hold in the moisture. She looked at the soft snowflakes gently floating down, sticking to the window, and slowly rolling down, leaving a snake-like melt trail on the glass. There was no wind. She felt a clammy hand cover hers.

"I know you're disappointed about not seeing the boys as often as you'd like. You have to remember, they're not babies anymore. You miss them more than they miss you."

"I know, but I thought after being gone for so long, they'd be happy to see us come more often. Or want to come down to spend time with us. Especially little Stuart."

"Well, Stuart's not so little anymore," he said, slightly shifting against the pillows. He patted her hand and turned onto his side toward her. He tucked both his hands under his head. "And it's not just the boys who are important. K, your Dad and my mother are as well. Who knows how long they'll live."

Phyl sadly looked down at him. "That's kind of part of it. Death. I'm always thinking about death. I can't shake it." She felt tears welling in her eyes.

"I'm not dying," Stuart muttered.

She pushed his shoulder. "Who says I'm worried about you, silly oaf!" She sniffed.

"It's obvious," Stuart snorted. He changed the subject. "How was the rehearsal yesterday with Theatre Harrisburg, by the way?" Stuart softened his tone. He coughed into his palm, and then put his hand back under his flushed cheek.

Phyl took a deep breath and made a face. She looked back out the window.

"That good, huh?" Stuart chuckled.

She peered down at her nails. "The play's good. Very funny."

"What's it called? Good Housecleaning?"

"No, silly," she laughed. "Good House*keeping*."

"Whatever," he smiled. His eyes looked dewy. "I'm proud of you. You got the female lead."

"I know. Maybe that's the problem. The others seem to shun me. They try not to look at me."

"They're intimidated by you. Aren't you the only one who can claim to actually be in movies?"

"That's not it. I should just keep my trap shut. I made the mistake of sharing a few things we've done in South America. I spoke too much at Bridge, as well."

"Well, that's your problem. No one wants to talk while playing Bridge," laughed Stuart. He reached out and grabbed the upper part of her sleeve. He pulled her closer. She lay beside him with her back to him. She could smell his heavy breath. Smoke, jungle mouth, but familiar. His sweat. Home.

"You're too beautiful and talented for little Harrisburg," Stuart added. "You have to remember: A lot of the locals have never even left the state. In fact, I don't think some were really aware of Europe until their kids shipped off to fight in the war. Pennsylvania is full of farmers and people who hunt wild turkey on weekends. Or miners and deer hunters. They're as American as can be. They're good folk."

"I know. You're right. It's me. I'm a square peg trying to fit into a round hole."

Stuart brushed Phyl's hair away from his face and kissed the back of her head. "You go and enjoy today. Be good to yourself."

Phyl groaned and pushed herself back up. She smiled down at him, gave him a kiss on his feverish lips, and stood. "So, nothing you need?"

Stuart reached to the nightstand and checked his pack of cigarettes. He shook it. "Cigarettes."

"Oh, Stuart."

"Cigarettes. That's all."

Phyl made a face. "See you a little later, then."

"Okay."

Phyl walked into the bathroom, filled a plastic cup with water, and walked to the humidifier and opened the top. She poured in the water, checked the level, peered at the melted glob of Vic's Vaporub in the receptacle, then went back to the bathroom and replaced the cup on the edge of the sink.

"That should do."

"Thank you," muttered Stuart.

"You're welcome," whispered Phyl.

She left the room, gently closed the door, and hurried back down. She stopped, opened the front closet for her heavy winter coat and overshoes, and scampered to the back door. She quickly donned her jacket, kicked off her slippers, and put her feet into loafers. Then she stepped into the overshoes, strapped them shut, and walked through the mud room out onto the little back cement porch. She stopped and thought for a second, her breath hanging as ponderously as her thoughts.

She imagined someone getting into the house and hurting Stuart. She blinked back her angst and paranoia for the hundredth time. She turned, locked the door behind her. She pulled on her gloves, and carefully made her way down the cement steps to the snow-covered driveway.

She unlocked the Packard and looked around. She was not in view of the suspicious car. She opened the car door and settled into the driver's seat. Her breath hung heavy in the car's interior. She turned the car on and let it warm up a moment before putting it in reverse. She carefully backed it up over the sidewalk, onto the quiet, plowed street. She looked into the mirror, her eye on the black car, and slowly drove down the long street toward town in the opposite direction. She was strangely satisfied when the car pulled away from the curb and followed her. She hoped it meant they didn't know Stuart was home. It was evident to her, no matter what Stuart said about her paranoia, that the car was following her. It was *not* a coincidence. She tightly grasped the wheel, feeling ill.

"No time to die," she whispered.

At the stop sign, Phyl waited for cars to crawl by before pulling out into traffic. After a few blocks, she noticed the black car had dropped so far back that she couldn't see it anymore. She kept her eyes equally on the road and the rear-view mirror. After a moment, she forgot about it and focused on the piled snow lining the road on both sides. Children waddled in thick coats, snow pants, hats, scarves, and mitts and followed each other along the tops of the snowbanks on their way to school. She was worried one of them would slip and slide into the traffic under chained tires. She kept glancing at the children as she passed. She saw them laugh and chat, and every once in a while, one would inadvertently kick a chunk of snow down the embankment onto the street or throw a snowball at a passing car. One little girl with dark brown braids hanging from under her snow cap waved at her, showing a missing tooth.

Phyl thought of her daughter. She felt her heart swell and subside as she continued driving.

Two hours later, with three paper bags of groceries in the car, she sat at the counter in the diner section of Kresge's. She had bought a new colander and hair pins after browsing the bins and shelves. Most merchandise was imported from Japan, part of America's attempt to help boost the struggling Japanese economy. Everyone still felt the effects of the war, and cheap imports from war-torn countries paid tribute to hope for a recovering world economy.

Phyl listened to a radio high on a shelf over the kitchen serving window. Nat King Cole sang his latest, *Unforgettable*. Soothing, gentle, perfect for a wintry day, she enjoyed Cole's sultry voice over the chatter of women along the counter having coffee and pie.

Phyl looked past the customers, at the winter cityscape outside the plate glass window. She saw the sun peek out from between the clouds. She remembered the time she and Stuart sat together having a grilled cheese in Toronto, that first time he officially introduced himself to her after starting at Remington-Rand. It felt like another world, another universe, sixteen years before. She smiled at the lovely memory. Her eyes fell on someone she knew from Bridge. She smiled and raised a hand to wave, but the woman pretended not to see her.

Saddened, she faced the counter. A waitress placed a perfectly browned and melting grilled cheese and pickle in front of her with a brimming cup of coffee. She sighed, feeling a twinge of bitter-sweet delight as she wiped her fingers on her lap before reaching for the sandwich. Nat King Cole finished singing, and a determined-sounding announcer reminded listeners that train and car traffic was being diverted to accommodate work being done on the new New Jersey Turnpike. This set off some women to chat about the new Turnpike and how traveling would be so much faster, but darn, those tolls.

Phyl couldn't imagine driving the Turnpike would be faster than riding the train, especially the one named The Broker, which Stuart took every week. It was called so because most of the passengers were Wall Street workers who commuted to Manhattan daily. She closed her eyes, and took a bite of her grilled cheese. She quietly moaned with delight and chewed. She opened her eyes to look as she dipped a corner of the bread into a dollop of ketchup on her plate. She was suddenly in such a good mood she decided she would treat Stuart by digging up her 1937 American Womens Club Commemorative Pan American cookbook later and choose a lovely Argentine recipe to warm the cockles of his heart. It might mean another trip into town late afternoon for the odd ingredient she may not have at home, but that was okay. The roads were quickly drying up.

She would do something very special for her poor, sick darling.

Absolutely nothing turned out the way she had planned.

Having left all the cooking to Mercedes and Maria all those years, Argentine cooking wasn't readily coming back to her. She stood in the kitchen, frustrated, scraping burnt rice from the bottom of a pot. She would have to go out for more to finish the *Cacedrola de Choclo y Arroz*, or Baked Corn and Rice. She wasn't happy about that as it had started to snow again, and it was already dark. Dirty slush and lousy driving conditions after sunset vexed her. She frowned at the sink as the radio on the kitchen window sill played the Boston classical music station. She thought she heard Stuart bang on the floor above her, so she turned the tap off and listened.

"Stu?" she called out, one hand in the soapy water, the other on the volume knob.

No answer.

She shrugged, put up the volume, and turned on the tap again to continue cleaning the pot. Abruptly, the beautiful symphony was interrupted by a news bulletin. She dropped the scrub brush and turned up the volume.

> *This evening, a crowded steam locomotive locally called The Broker and carrying over a thousand passengers along the Pennsylvania Railroad Jersey Central rail line to Bayhead in South Jersey, derailed and plummeted down the embankment, killing scores of people and injuring hundreds more. The horrific sound was reportedly heard from miles away, and the crash shook many homes and shattered the windows of other residences in downtown Woodbridge...*

Phyl stood, pale and stunned. She forgot to breathe. She was stunned at the incredible timing of Stuart staying home. In her mind, she saw him flung, mangled, into the snow next to burning railway cars.

She stepped back from the sink and clutched her stomach. Her mind raced, and for a moment, she was tempted to believe it was part of a conspiracy against Stuart alone. Fantastically stupid, but it was too easy to read danger into everything, and this was fertile food for the imagination. She ran, dripping soapy water, into the living room and looked out the window. She peered into the dark, up and down the street. No strange car. Just their empty, snow-covered street and a neighbor shoveling his walkway.

She turned, fled upstairs, and bolted into the bedroom. Stuart was sitting up, wearing his reading glasses, and looking at the day's newspaper. He looked up, unshaven, his hair comically poking upwards like a clown's wig. She just stood there, her chest heaving.

"Is supper ready? I'm starved," said Stuart.

Phyl slowly climbed into the bed, burrowed into the blankets, and tightly held onto him.

* * *

"He's dead," said Stuart.

Phyl looked up from her knitting. She listened to a tango playing on their phonograph. She was determined to complete sweaters for little Stuart and Donald before her next visit to Toronto.

"Who is dead?" *No time to die.*

"Dodero." Stuart sat in the livingroom next to the fireplace. He folded the New York Times and dropped it on the carpet

Confused, Phyl slowly put her knitting needles and wool to the side and got up. She bent down and picked up the paper. She looked through the pages and found what she was looking for. She slowly sunk down onto the carpet to read.

> *Alberto Dodero Dead in Uruguay*
> *Shipping Leader, an Intimate of Perón,*
> *Was Used by the U.S. for Intermediary Roles*

"Oh my gosh, can they say that?" asked Phyl, surprised.

"They said it." He covered his eyes.

Phyl read aloud.

> *Montevideo, Uruguay, March 2 – Alberto Dodero, shipping leader and one of South America's best-known personalities, died here tonight after having suffered a heart attack. He was 65 years old. Señor Dodero was identified with the major shipping enterprise linking the Rio de la Plata countries with one another and with Europe. He was one of the closest intimates of president Juan D. Perón of Argentina and an unofficial liaison between General Perón and United States diplomats.*

"Shoot," whispered Phyl.

"Hmm," muttered Stuart.

> *The Argentine government purchased Señor Dodero's Argentine lines and seaplane service in May 1949, but Dodero's name continued to be used in shipping advertising. His sons, Pedro, and Alberto Jr., by his divorced, first wife, still were identified with the lines' management.*
>
> *The industrialist built a great fortune in shipping and related financial operations between the world wars and greatly increased his holdings as a result of World War II. He acquired such influence with President Perón that at least two United States Ambassadors – James*

Bruce and Stanton Griffis — used him constantly as their primary intermediary with the Argentine chief.

Señor Dodero was a frequent guest at the United States Embassy in Buenos Aires. In one instance, a severe anti-United States outbreak in the Argentine capital in September 1948 was calmed largely because the United States Ambassador, then in New York, got Señor Dodero, who also was there, to phone President Perón.

Recently, Señor Dodero was known to have had less contact and cooler relations with the Peróns.

"No kidding," snapped Stuart.

Phyl reached up and comfortingly touched Stuart's knee. "Oh, my God, Stuart. How could he die? He looked so good!"

Stuart shook his head. "Stress, maybe. He lost almost everything to Perón. And his wife left him. Lord knows how much she took as part of the divorce."

"But would that be enough to kill him?" She blinked back tears. Speechless.

They sat silently, not hearing the cheerful tango secretly tugging at the Argentine part of their hearts and souls. The fireplace cracked with the fluctuating temperature of the room.

"The last of the tycoons," whispered Stuart.

Phyl leaned her head on his lap. He placed a hand gently on her face.

It rested for a very long time.

* * *

"She's dying, you know that?" asked Jorge.

Phyl and Stuart sat opposite Jorge on love seats in his Waldorf Astoria suite in New York.

"Oh, Lord, that word again," thought Phyl.

"We heard she started chemotherapy," said Stuart.

"Yes, the first person in the country to receive it." Jorge's eyes wandered to the fireplace. It was late spring 1952.

Phyl looked at him, concerned. "There's more?"

Jorge flicked his cigarette distractedly, ash floating gently onto the carpet. Phyl leaned forward.

Jorge gazed at the ash on the carpet. "Oh dear. I didn't realize I did that."

"Your mind is so far away, Jorge. What is it?" Phyl asked.

She glanced at Stuart, then at Jorge, and waited for an answer. They had discussed the possibility of returning to Argentina at the end of their Pennsylvania contract, but it didn't sound promising. It was still too dangerous. Stuart had been briefed of the continual upheaval in Argentina and wasn't very optimistic. And after what Jorge said next, she understood the depth of the craziness in Buenos Aires.

"Eva's brother told me something alarming, and I wish you to pass this on," Jorge said, motioning to Stuart, returning his search for something in the fireplace. Jorge paused. "Eva had a hysterectomy a while back. Part of an attempt to remove the tumors."

"Yes?" said Stuart.

Jorge pulled his eyes away from that unknown something in the fireplace, then at Stuart and Phyl. "Duarte told me it was done by an American surgeon. The same surgeon who tried to help Perón's first wife. In the meantime," Jorge fiddled with an impeccable crease on his pant leg, "Eva had become more of a handful for her enemies. And Peron."

Phyl laughed. "More?"

"Yes, she was caught promising arms for the poor from her bedside."

Phyl pulled at her diamond earring. "You mean, like in guns? For hunting?"

"No, as in guns for an uprising."

Stuart sat back in surprise. "Well, isn't that what tops it all!"

Phyl felt a chill go up her arm. "That doesn't sound sane."

"No, indeed." Jorge reached for a half-full glass of whiskey and downed it. He smacked his lips and stared at the crystal tumbler, then gently put it down on the table.

Phyl frowned. "Goodness, she's already in so much danger."

"We're at a point of no return." Jorge tipped his head. "Duarte discovered that while she had the hysterectomy, they did a lobotomy at the same time. Without telling her. Without telling anyone. It's not for public knowledge."

Phyl gasped and covered her mouth. Her mind raced. She shakily touched her forehead. "I think I'm going to be sick."

Jorge held up a hand. "Oh, Duarte was told it was to control her pain as she was suffering quite badly. They told him they targetted that part of the brain which controlled pain." He looked around the grand suite, at the brocade armchairs and sofa in the next open area, the fancy wall sconces, the fine dining table and chairs, and the rich oriental rugs on the carpet. As if wondering what it was all for?

Phyl looked around, then back at Jorge. "So, that kind of makes sense."

"Lousy excuse. It's to control her."

"Precisely," agreed Stuart.

"But she's still so popular with the *Descamisados*, yes? With a lobotomy, is she still able to do speeches? I mean, what exactly happens after a lobotomy? Can she talk?" Phyl asked.

Jorge picked up his glass, and walked to the bar to pour more whiskey. He pointed the empty tumbler questioningly toward them. "She can't talk coherently anymore, though she goes out canvasing with Perón for a second term."

He turned and faced them and made a funny motion with his free hand. "She's so weak she can't sit or stand on her own for any length of time. She even needs support for her arm so she can wave. So, they made this contraption for her to be strapped into when she stands or sits in the touring car while campaigning."

"Oh, the poor thing," said Phyl.

"So, Perón forces her to canvass despite being made a vegetable," said Stuart.

"Oh, Stu!" exclaimed Phyl.

"He can't win without her by his side. You know the people demanded that she run for vice president?"

Stuart laughed, then checked himself. "I'm sorry, but I could just imagine what the military thought of that."

"I think if it wasn't for her being so ill - and now, of course, incapacitated - she certainly would have hoped Perón would let her run." Jorge returned to his loveseat with his drink, crossed his legs, and primly straightened his crease.

"That would've been potentially very dangerous. Perhaps even civil war, right?" asked Stuart.

Jorge nodded. "Certainly, if the peasants were armed to the teeth as she intended. They have this hatred for the rich and the military."

"She was forgetting the big picture, the wellbeing of Argentina. I think her power is going to her head." Phyl bit her lip.

"Well, it *did*. There no longer is a functioning head," said Jorge. "And, she refuses to eat. Duarte thinks they inadvertently erased the need to eat. She's starving herself to death and she's completely oblivious to it."

Phyl took a deep breath. "Oh, my God." She played with her rings.

Stuart placed his hand over hers.

"Phyl, darling. I don't think we'll be doing a new contract back home at the end of this one. Or even at the end of the next. Things are too dangerous."

"Oh, but Stu, I can't stand Harrisburg. I'll go mad if we stay any longer."

Jorge's eyes twinkled. "So, you miss Argentina! Lovely to hear."

"I know. I couldn't wait to run away. What was wrong with me? But if it *was* safe this time around, yes, I would've wanted to go back. Our life is there. Our things, we miss the food, the music, our friends."

"The help," joked Stuart.

Phyl slapped him. "Stop it. That's not all." She suddenly looked sad. "My Lord, here we're joking while Eva's starving, dying…"

Stuart cleared his throat. "It's true. You're always complaining about not having people to boss around."

"Oh, you," Phyl said. "Okay. Stu's right. I do complain about not having help. I've been spoiled. Look, Jorge. Look at my dish-worn hands."

Jorge reached over the coffee table and took one of her hands. He looked at it and kissed it. "It feels fine to me." He grinned.

"You leave my wife alone," joked Stuart.

"Yeah, keep that stuff for your New York mistress," quipped Phyl, snatching back her property.

"I don't have a New York mistress anymore."

"You don't?" asked Phyl.

"No. No mistress. No mistresses at all." He made an innocent face. "Just to make you like me for a change."

"Oh, I like you, Jorge. And it's none of our business, anyhow."

"I know, but it bothered you to no end."

"Yes, it did. It didn't sit right with me. For Angelica. Why, if Stuart ever even considered…"

"And Stuart never did," said Stuart, cutting in. He took her hand. "And Stuart never will."

"Oh, look at this." Jorge raised his hands in blessing. "How am I supposed to compete with your Prince Charming husband? I was hoping Phyl would tire of you, Stuart, and eventually would…"

Stuart cut him off. "Would what?"

Jorge blushed.

"Don't even think about it," joked Stuart, holding up an exaggerated fist.

Everyone laughed. Needed medicine for a general malaise.

Phyl turned to Stuart. "Well, if we're not staying in Harrisburg, this next three-year contract…"

"Er, that's not what I said. I'm sorry, Phyl. It will be another three years in good ol' Harrisburg."

"Noooo."

"But, if we still can't go back to Argentina after that, we'll go as far away from North America as possible."

Jorge cocked his head. "Why must you go as far away from North America as possible?"

"Phyl thinks we're in danger here and in Canada," said Stuart.

Phyl squirmed with embarrassment. "We're always being followed."

"Well, of course you are. But not necessarily by those with evil intentions," explained Jorge. "You may be followed for your protection."

Phyl sat back, surprised. She looked around the suite. "Protection? My God. Protection from what? From whom?"

"I don't think that helped, Jorge," muttered Stuart.

Jorge took a deep breath. "Well. I guess there's no way around it," he said. "I don't have business in Australia…so I will miss you two terribly."

Phyl looked at Stuart. "Australia?"

"I discussed this with Jorge. We have another option after these next three years."

"Australia?"

"Would that do to make you feel safe?" asked Jorge with melancholy.

"In three years? But I will go mad if we have to stay in Harrisburg again."

Stuart exchanged a look with Jorge.

"Well, I guess we'll have to get an apartment in Toronto, then, so that you have a place to stay for extended periods. Get you away from Harrisburg as much as you want. The boys will soon be teenagers so now is a good time to take advantage of being around. Once they have girlfriends, you'll rarely hear from them. By that time, distance won't be such an issue."

"Can we afford an apartment?"

Stuart shrugged. "I've sold a couple of Univacs. Great commission. And I could always request work periods out of the Toronto office."

"What are Univacs?" asked Jorge.

"Oh, my gosh, Jorge. You would be so impressed. They call it a computer. It has how many vacuum tubes?" Phyl turned to Stuart.

"Five thousand, and it weighs sixteen thousand pounds and can perform a thousand calculations in a second. We sold the first one last year—the Univac 1—to the U.S. Census Bureau."

"I saw one. It looks like a huge desk with a massive console," said Phyl.

"At a pretty price tag, I am sure," offered Jorge.

"Yup. A million clams," said Stuart. "So, we can afford a studio apartment in Toronto if my wife wishes."

Tears of relief filled her eyes. Phyl nodded. "Your wife wishes."

* * *

Phyl stood outside in the healing light of an Ontario sun at the entrance to the Riverdale Zoo.

Her two nephews, Little Stuart and Donald, had gone to the men's room to drink out of the tap. She sniffed a strange cocktail of animal smells. Mercifully, the smell of fresh popcorn overrode the scent of dung, and it brought to mind the many movies she had seen with El so many years before. If El only knew that her son, little Stuart, had a sweet, gentler half-brother. The pain she felt in her heart as she thought of her friend drew her back into lingering grief. She felt a door open in her mind to the memories of a dear one gone. One of many doors of people passed from her life. This one was named "Dearest Best Friend, El."

She looked around at vendors. Her mouth watered at the sight of gleaming, red toffee apples hanging upside down at one of the carts. She adjusted her summer hat to stay put in the breeze, and began to whistle. As thoughtful as ever, Stuart arranged for one of the Toronto office secretaries to purchase a new record for her as a gift. She played it constantly at the apartment, an earworm by Jo Stafford, You Belong to Me.

See the pyramids along the Nile,
Watch the sunrise on a tropic isle.
Just remember, darling, all the while.
You belong to me.
See the marketplace in old Algiers.
Send me photographs and souvenirs.
Just remember, when a dream appears,
You belong to me.
I'll be so alone without you.
Maybe you'll be lonesome too, and blue.
Fly the ocean in a silver plane,
See the jungle when it's wet with rain.
Just remember till you're home again,
You belong to me.

Well, they never went to see the pyramids or Algiers, but they certainly flew breathlessly over jungles. And, yes, she was lonesome for Stuart, too. Thank goodness, he was scheduled to come to the Toronto office for meetings, and he was to take a two-week break. A full three weeks together. She promised to return to Pennsylvania with him for a couple of months afterward, and hoped she would survive them before feeling the ache of missing the boys again.

She heard a squeal and turned to see thirteen-year-old Stuart drag a cringing and struggling seven-year-old Donald by the ear. She rushed forward and slapped Stuart, causing him to release Donald.

"Stop that now!" she ordered. "Why are you always picking on him, Stuart?"

"I can't help it. He's such a squirt."

Donald glared at him. "I'm not a squirt!"

Stuart offered a toothy grin.

Phyl touched Donald's head. "Are you okay?"

He pouted, looking down at his scuffed Keds runners, still glaring his headlights at Stuart.

Phyl tutted and sighed, she directed Donald to the gate, ensuring Stuart followed.

"Do we have to go in?" young Stuart asked.

"Yes, Stuart. We're going in. What else would you do on a Sunday in Toronto the Good? Besides, we're going home with Grandad for Sunday supper later after he's finished for the day."

"He's only mucking out the crap of cages. Big *schlemiel*."

Phyl went ballistic. "What kind of language is that? Do you even know what that means?"

Stuart shrugged.

"Your Grandad's superintendent of the zoo now. He doesn't muck out dung, anymore."

Stuart kicked a pebble. "He smells like it."

"Geez. Where is the respect?"

Stuart shrugged again, staring at the ground.

Phyl took a deep breath and looked at her watch. She looked at the sun to verify the time of day. She had a flashback of her trips to the zoo in Buenos Aires. That old troubled feeling nibbled at the back of her head. Tensions at the zoo. Though this zoo was so very different from Buenos Aires. Everything about the Riverdale Zoo was somehow gentler. There were more trees, kinder breezes off the nearby Don River, and certainly not as hot and overcrowded. And no spies.

No Dodero.

Phyl glanced at Stuart again, concerned for his lack of empathy. She shook her head, sighed and looked at Donald. She never had to drag an argumentative teenager into a zoo before. It may have been easier just to take Donald on his own.

"Why do you want to spend time with us anyhow?" asked Stuart.

"Excuse me?"

"Why drag us around? I thought you didn't like kids."

"Where did you hear that from?"

"Dad told me."

"My own brother said such a terrible thing?"

Stuart shrugged.

Phyl wondered how to respond. She wondered why she hadn't polished her shoes for Sunday. She wondered what that had to do with a belligerent child. "Okay. I'll open my heart to you right now and you better not trample all over it." She stared pointedly at Stuart. Then lovingly roughed up Donald's hair to comfort him in light of her stern sidebar.

Stuart looked at his aunt sideways. He stuck his hands into his dress pants pockets.

Phyl motioned for them to follow her to a bench. She didn't bother to wipe away the dust and small debris before dropping onto its wooden slats. Obediently, they sat on both sides of their aunt.

"My brother, your Dad, doesn't know everything. When I was very, very young, I was sick. At that time, many people died from the same sickness. I brought this sickness back home. I survived. My mother didn't. So."

"So, you think it was your fault that your Mom died?" Light appeared to shine from the depths of Donald's eyes.

"Yes. I was a little snotty kid and I killed my mother. At least, that's how I saw it. Whenever I saw snotty-nosed kids, I thought of me. I was frightened of having children."

"Were you relieved when your baby didn't live?" asked innocent Donald.

"Oh, my God." She felt as if she had been punched in the diaphragm.

"Donald, that was a stupid thing to say," said young Stuart.

Phyl took Donald's small hand and squeezed it. "Darling. It almost killed me to lose my precious baby. And I will never be able to have children. Ever. That's why you both are so precious to me."

"If we're so precious to you, why do you always disappear for years on end?" asked Stuart.

"Now, how am I supposed to answer that? What do you think I'm doing here in Toronto while my husband is alone in Pennsylvania?"

An elephant bellowed ferociously not far off, reflecting the anger welling up in Phyl. She looked at her watch and knew at that moment that Donald's mother, Dorothy, was helping K with the Sunday dinner. Later that night, her Stuart was to call her Dad's place long distance from Harrisburg. It was a weekly event and costly, but well worth the money. She wondered if she would be able to fight back the tears when she shared with her own Stuart the conversation she just endured. She inhaled a ragged breath.

"Let's have some fun, okay? Let's see if that baby monkey is still alive."

"Can I have some popcorn first, Auntie Phyl?" asked Donald, holding her back as she stood.

"Yes. Of course."

They headed to the popcorn stand. They passed a newspaper vendor and she looked down at the New York Times. A photo of Eva caught her attention. She picked up the paper, and absentmindedly searched her purse for coins as she read the headlines. She gasped.

Eva Perón Dies in Argentina; A Power as President's Wife

Phyl found coins to give the paperboy. She didn't wait for change; instead, she shook out the paper and moved further into the shade. She continued reading, her heart beating hard.

BUENOS AIRES, July 26—Señora Dona Maria Eva Duarte de Perón, wife of President Juan Perón, one of the most powerful women in the history of Argentina and of the New World, died at 8:25 o'clock p.m. She had long been ill.

According to the Argentine Who's Who, she was 30 years old…

The people of Argentina, who had been celebrating masses for the recovery of the First Lady who was called "The spiritual chief of the nation" were prepared for the event. During the course of the day, the Sub-Secretariat of Information issued three bulletins in rapid succession that clearly indicated the end was near.

President Perón, at her bedside when she died, had been staying all week close to his wife in the Presidential Residence. Members of the cabinet were there.

Señora Perón was operated upon last November for cancer. Her last public appearance was June 4, when, looking pale and worn, she attended the ceremony at which Perón was inaugurated to succeed himself as president—largely through her help. As news of the death was received throughout the country, each Province decided to send here special delegations, presided over…

Continued on Page 58, Column 4

Phyl frantically searched for page 58, dropping her purse in the process. A disgruntled Stuart walked over and picked up her purse.

"So, when are we going in?" he asked impatiently.

Phyl took her purse from him, placed it at her feet, and continued flipping the pages of the newspaper. She continued reading.

…by the Provincial Governors, as a mark of honor to the First Lady, who, although she had not held an official position in the government, will receive the honors usually accorded a President.

"Wow," she whispered.

"Auntie Phyl," whined Donald.

"Wait. Just one minute. This is important." She rushed toward the bench and sat down.

> *It was expected that, temporarily, burial will be at the Basilica of St. Francis, an order in which Señora Perón held the rank of first degree lay sister.*

"Shoot, the church won't like this," she muttered. "This is going to come back at Perón." Stuart and Donald sat at both ends of the bench, staring at her with disappointment. She lowered the paper and let the last bit of information sink in before continuing. "They're making her into a saint. Almost a martyr."

"Who?" asked Stuart.

Phyl saw that Stuart appeared sincerely interested.

"Eva Perón." She squinted at him, then at Donald. "Do you know about Eva Perón and her husband, Juan Perón, the president of Argentina?"

Stuart nodded. "Yeah. You always keep on about them to Grandad and K."

"Do I?"

Stuart nodded, rolling his eyes.

"Well, she died yesterday. She was, well, a very interesting woman. I just can't figure out if she was good or bad for Argentina. She was so unusual." She frowned and paused for a moment. "Do you mind if I just finish reading this?"

Stuart cocked his head and snorted impatiently.

Phyl dipped into her bag and took out her change purse. "Here, you go on in. I'll catch up."

Stuart took the change purse and opened it. He looked inside and then over at the popcorn vendor. "So, we can we *finally* get our popcorn?"

"Go." She waved them away. "Get your popcorn and candy apples. I'll catch up."

The two boys scrambled to the popcorn vendor.

> *Shortly before midnight, a resolution adopted at a conference of Cabinet Ministers announced national mourning. It decreed that all official activity in the country would be suspended for two days with thirty days of official mourning…*

She felt the pressure to hurry, and frantically glanced ahead into the article.

> *At her bedside when she died were, besides President Perón; a dozen of relatives and close political friends. They were her mother, Señora Juana Ibarguren de Duarte; three sisters, Elisa Duarte de Arrieta,*

Bianca Duarte de Alvarez Pereya and Ermida Duarte de Bertoloni; her brother, Juan Duarte...

"Poor Juan," she whispered. She decided to read the remainder of the article later. She folded the paper and stuffed it in her bag and hurried to the popcorn vendor.

"One popcorn, please," she asked the man at the cart. She dug into her bag for her change purse and threw up her hands. She had forgotten the boys went into the zoo with it. She sighed, weakly smiled at the man. He stared at her blankly.

"Well, I know this sounds silly, but a funny thing just happened."

"Funny?" the man asked in a very thick accent, eyeing her with suspicion.

"Yes, or rather, silly" Phyl said, waving toward the gate. She looked at the man. A refugee. An immigrant. From where? Italy? "I gave my change purse to my nephews..."

"Nephews?" the man looked blankly toward the gate. He shrugged and shook his head. There was a deep sadness about him. An intense sense of loss.

Phyl could feel it. She studied his haunted eyes. "Well, yes, they have my money. You see, I was distracted by something very sad." She had to stop to fight back tears.

The man frowned and slowly nodded.

A strong wave of emotion, solid as an iron hammer, rose from the depths of her being. "I mean, well, you see," she continued weakly, her chin trembling. She pointed to the gate and stared at it. *Time to die.* "My father..."

"Sorry. No, understand."

Phyl looked at the pain etched across his unshaven face. Time stood still. Birds fell silent. The leaves ceased to rustle in the breeze she no longer felt. No elephants called. No lions and tigers roared. Hot tears gathered in her eyes, and she shook her head to stem a wave of grief. Deep in her soul, she realized that to live and live long enough meant to know loss. *Time to die.* And each loss left a vacuum. And grief abhorred a vacuum. A cavernous space formed in her heart. Unsettling, curious, unnatural. She understood that was life. Even this poor man standing in front of her oozed a deep sense of loss and understanding of such. The war?

She never got over El. El hung over her day and night, now that she spent so much time in Toronto. She found herself constantly in their old stomping grounds. The streetcars, the houses, the sights, the sounds, the smells – all memories. All real. The tiny shop where they bought penny candy. Black balls, which took years, it seemed, to melt in their mouths, exposing layers of colors and staining their teeth. Perhaps it was this mindset, this walking around with an exposed heart, that allowed grief and fears of further loss to take root and grow. And now this amazingly cruel conversation with the boys.

Stuart's fragile health didn't help. It hung over her like a black storm cloud offering endless commiserations over those who left this world unnaturally, prematurely: the military attaché, Reiner, Vivienne, her husband, Stuart's father, mother, Dodero, Eva… above all, her sweet unborn daughter. All the aunts, uncles, and cousins on both sides of the family having passed while she lived in Argentina. So many family funerals she had missed.

Embracing all this inner turmoil, the cruel losses still felt by all from the war – almost a dozen years ago - tormented her. Every family seemed to have lost a son, uncle, father, brother. And there was constant news coverage about the Holocaust. Like the rest of the world, she was mortified to learn more and more of what human beings were capable of doing to each other. The papers spoke of the Jewish people's search for surviving Nazi war criminals.

Nazi criminals who were probably still hiding back in Argentina. Back *home*. Vengeance raised its ugly back.

"Missus?"

Phyl blinked and was suddenly aware of the man looking at her with concern. She looked down and saw tatooed numbers on the inside of his wrist. Suddenly, sounds returned amplified, rich smells accosted her, and the sunlight – was it always so brilliant? Phyl searched for her handkerchief in her purse and wiped her eyes and nose.

"I'm so sorry," she whispered to the man.

He looked at her puzzled. Then down at his wrist.

She heard a shuffle and chatter behind her and was surprised to see pods of distracted people all in their own worlds. She felt as if she was an observer, no longer a member of the human race. She saw so clearly. They, however, walked around with blinders to their eyes.

"*It's always time to die.*"

Did Phyl hear this right? Phyl stared at the man. "What did you say?"

"I say'a, this time no'a pay." The man handed her a paper bag of buttered popcorn. He nodded and smiled with two teeth missing.

Phyl swallowed hard and nodded. "Thank you."

She stepped away from the cart and walked toward the gate she had known since she was very young. She looked back at the vendor, but he was already taking change from the next person. In his own world. One of an infinite number. She turned, tucked the newspaper further under her arm, balanced her purse over her forearm, and munched dumbly from her popcorn. She followed the dirt path toward the animal enclosures.

She felt ancient, walking towards an uncertain future.

Chapter Twenty-Two

Beautiful Australia, the General and Back to Friends

"I can't imagine why we haven't heard from K for so long. Something is wrong."

Phyl sat in the breakfast room by windows overlooking Sydney Harbour in back of their high-end bungalow. The sun shone brightly onto the white tablecloth and the PIX magazine she absentmindedly perused. She shook her head. "I just feel like something really bad is going to happen. I can't shake it."

Stuart paused from the morning paper, opposite her. He took a sip of his coffee cup and gently placed it back on its saucer. "You worry too much at times."

"Hmm."

"Our storage in Toronto should be renewed," he offered, changing the subject.

Phyl shivered though she sat in the sun. She rubbed her slim arms. "My goodness, it's freezing indoors. Can't we buy a kerosene lamp?"

"It's too bad we left the one we bought in Argentina in that storage unit."

"What were we thinking, leaving it in Toronto?"

"Well, for one thing, I don't think we were told how cold it is in Australia." He looked around and out into the cream-colored living room. "Ask Mavis to put a fire on in the fireplace."

"It takes too much time, hauling filthy coal. And I'm always afraid Mavis will drop the coal onto the carpet." Phyl looked up into the sky. Bright billowy clouds and birds everywhere. She reached over and touched the cold glass of the large window. "We should hang curtains. Help keep the cold out."

"No. It would ruin the new modern look. No curtains."

Phyl pouted. "Well, I sure wish we had a stove like Dad has in his living room."

Stuart made a face. "That sells for about $100 here."

"I wish I brought my flannel nightgowns and pajamas. And your long underwear."

"It wouldn't fit you. The long underwear."

She laughed.

"Did you write to your Dad about the zoo here? He'd find it very interesting."

"Oh, I did. I told Dad the koalas were cute and so defenseless that the government had to stop people from shooting them before they became extinct. I can't imagine subsisting on nothing but the leaves of a gum tree, can you?" Phyl placed her bare feet on the edge of her chair and hugged her leg as she flipped the magazine page. She clasped her cold toes. Her hand felt nice and warm.

"If you're so cold, wear socks and slippers."

"True."

Something in the magazine caught Phyl's eye, and she brightened up. Then she looked sad again. "Oh, darn, they say Auntie Mame won't be shown in the theatres here in Australia until two years from now. How unfair! Everyone back in New York has seen it already!"

"Well, I have a surprise for you, then. The Club is having a private screening."

"Of Auntie Mame?" She sat up. "Oh, how wonderful! When!"

"This, my dear wife, is part of our welcome to our new vice president, retired General Leslie Groves. Friday night."

"Can't wait." Phyl's smile waned. "Hmm. The VP. I have so much to do before tonight. Aren't we the lucky ones who are always entertaining everyone."

Stuart nodded to himself. "What do you expect? I'm the executive here. So, it falls on us just as it did in Argentina." He stepped around the table, and kissed her. "Do not fear. After all these years of entertaining, you should know, by now, how so perfect you are at it."

She smiled. "You're so nice, Stu. But it's just that food is different here, the customs, the help…"

"Be happy we have help. All paid for by the company. This remarkable house has breathtaking views of Sydney Harbor and the Pacific from the front. What more can you ask for?"

"I know. The extra $600 a month put into our Harrisburg bank account doesn't hurt, either."

"Precisely. Count your blessings. The average Joe would be happy if he made $200 a month, so it's all icing on the cake for us."

"You're right. I shouldn't complain."

"No. You shouldn't. You're a spoiled brat." Stuart turned away, but Phyl grabbed his sleeve.

"Just curious." Phyl cocked her head. "How come a retired general becomes an executive with Sperry Rand? I mean, wouldn't you think he's a tad overqualified?"

Stuart raised his eyebrows. In her life with him, there has always been some hint of mystery. The true Stuart.

"Well, you said he organized and oversaw the Manhattan Project. He had a hand in ending the war. Why would he want to be a vice president in the business world?"

Stuart took a deep breath. He looked down at her, his blue eyes shining. "Mysterious machinations working in the background, maybe?"

Phyl frowned. A thought dawned on her. "Stu. Are we still…? Are you still…?"

"I'm not as active, but I am asked to keep my eyes and ears open."

"So…"

"Okay, I'm off."

Deep in thought, Phyl followed Stuart to the front hallway. She let him give her a kiss on the cheek. She lifted some lint off his back as he bent over to retrieve his briefcase.

"Don't forget. I'll be home early to change, and then we're off to the Club. After drinks, we come home for dinner this time, and then we take the VP back to his hotel, probably for nightcaps. Very late."

He reached for his fedora off a brass hook and placed it on his head. "But not as late as it will be Friday at the Club's special dinner in his honor. We're also supping with the Ambassador and his wife."

"I know, I know," she said quietly. She brightened and held up a finger. "Ah, but we also see Auntie Mame!" she said triumphantly.

Stuart waved and walked down the stone path to his new white cream Buick Electra convertible. She watched him drive down the hill towards the city and allowed her gaze to swivel over the harbor where a yellow haze stretched out toward the ocean. To the left, she spied the milk delivery truck across the street. She looked up and down her road to see if the milkman was nearby so that she could add an extra cream to her morning order. The road was strangely quiet. She looked at the truck again and frowned. Had it been there long? She sniffed and looked past the houses on the other side of the street to spy bits of the blue Pacific. She tried to quell the sour panic beginning to rise in her throat. Was she supposed to be on guard again? Would that terrible monster she fought in Pennsylvania return? She rushed back into the house and hurried to the kitchen.

She heard Mavis talking to someone. She was relieved to see the milkman chatting with Mavis at the back door. She tutted at herself. "You stupydoo, it really is the milkman," she grumbled. She relaxed, pushed the slatted saloon doors open, and sauntered into the kitchen. The rose-red countertops and the contrasting white tiled floors returned her to a joyful disposition. Especially when she saw the coffee pot still on the gas stove, its chrome gleaming. Phyl grabbed a mug, poured hot coffee, and searched the cupboards for her cookbook from Argentina. She found it behind the big mixing bowls. She looked for a recipe for dinner and absentmindedly listened to what Mavis was saying to the milkman.

"White lady a bloody lizard, can't make a bloody johnny cake, whole lot of 'em - nothing! Yes, all the native lady bin cookin" n showin' 'em. You know why? Well, them White men bin learn 'em them native, and they start cookin' bread and everything. White lady bin come, can't cook nothin'! Got to have a look in a cookbook first to cook 'em meals. Hahaha! The Black woman bin learnin' fast how to cook bread, cakes, everything they want ... Oh, they White women gave us Black women clothes ... learn 'em how to sew. That's all White lady bin come up and mendin' them clothes, but can't cook a bloody tucker without a book, nothing ..."

Surprised, Phyl snapped the book shut.

Mavis, holding a cigarette aloft, her black bobcut hair flipping around her face, poked her head through the back door. Her eyes widened at the sight of Phyl leaning against the countertop not far from the door. They widened even more at the sight of the cookbook in Phyl's hands.

Mavis disappeared. "You bist git goin'. White lady lookin' lizard red," Phyl could hear.

Phyl heard the rattle of empty milk bottles as the delivery man left. Then Mavis, sans cigarette but cradling two bottles of milk, hurried into the kitchen. She inadvertently slammed the door shut behind her, making herself jump, and frantically motioned at the door with her chin.

"Oh, so sorry, Miss." Mavis, a young half-cast aboriginal in a black maid's outfit, quickly opened the refrigerator, placed the milk on the top shelf, and slammed the door shut. Then she blindly took a damp cloth from the sink and briskly wiped surfaces within reach, pretending to busy herself.

Phyl pursed her lips and silently watched. Her eyes fell back down on the cookbook in her hands. She stretched, cracking her elbows. She threw the cookbook into the trash bin and gave Mavis a pointed look. Then she smoothed down her house dress and cleared her throat.

"Okay, Mavis. We have much work before this afternoon's special guest arrives."

"Yes, 'M!" Mavis' eyes darted to the trash bin as she held the cloth aloft.

Phyl looked at the bin. She retrieved the cookbook, and returned to the recipe in question. In defeat, she pointed at it. "Mavis, this white lady bloody lizard would like you to fix this cookin' meal from this white lizard cookbook." She slammed the cookbook onto the counter and pointed at it. "N' you git white lizard money for doing so."

Mavis, no more than eighteen, covered the yawning cave of her open mouth. She dropped her hand and nodded in total defeat. "Yes, 'M!" Slowly, she took the heavy cookbook, and her dark eyes rested on the page Phyl pointed at.

Phyl nodded in spiked victory. She pointed over her shoulder with her thumb. "Okay. Well, then. This white bloody lizard lady will go see what lizard should wear for big white man later today." She appeared satisfied to hear Mavis almost choke. She turned and sauntered out, pushing the saloon doors as far forward and back as possible like Calamity Jane, but they bounced back and slapped her face more like the Three Stooges. Phyl raised her hands to stop the saloon doors from hitting her again.

She could swear she heard Mavis snicker. Score tied. She looked back, chin up, and glared at Mavis until she wiped that smile off her face. Phyl heard the milk delivery truck start outside while she genteelly stepped back into the living room. As she hurried along the white carpeted hallway toward the master bedroom, she slapped her forehead and shook her head.

"Dumb, dumb, dumb." She laughed despite herself.

* * *

"I could stretch my work forever in Australia and New Zealand. My main problem is sorting out the important from the unimportant as all the company men from here to Tasmania want me to run around to see their prize prospects."

Stuart paused to sip his scotch. He glanced around the American Club's dining room. Everyone gathered after the screening of the new movie, Auntie Mame. People stood and sat in groups, chatting and laughing, all in a jubilant mood after Rosalind Russel's performance.

"I think they feel flattered to have a New York executive give them some of his attention," cut in Phyl, standing next to Stuart, looking glamorous and smiling at General Leslie Grove's handsome face. Next to her, their guests, American ambassador to Australia, William Sebald, and his petite wife, Edith.

Groves, holding an empty glass, looked around the candle-lit banquet room for a passing waiter.

"Would you like another soda?" asked Stuart, feeling slight guilt about drinking while his VP abstained.

General Groves shook his head. "One can only drink so much soda."

William Sebald laughed heartily, attached to a healthy tumbler of scotch. He sipped and shook his head, still smiling. "I can't get used to this British scotch. Japanese scotch is so much more elegant in taste."

Edith, ten years Phyl's senior and very exotic-looking, tugged at her husband's cuff. Ambassador Sebald looked at her curiously but in good humor.

"Ah, yes, my lovely wife always reminds me to be discreet when discussing anything Japanese."

Edith looked at Phyl, Stuart, and General Groves shyly. She was half Japanese and half American.

"Even though I was American-educated from twelve years of age, with the war and marrying my husband, I lost my Japanese citizenship. Our famiily went through terrible things during the war. I'm still cautious about my status."

"Darling, you were given your American citizenship years ago. All is well." Sebald turned to the others. "For years, Edith wouldn't follow me to my postings outside of the U.S. for fear she would never be allowed back in. It was quite an ordeal for her, I'm afraid."

"Well, for *all* us Japanese and one gets quite sensitive," added Edith.

Everyone stood quietly for a moment.

Stuart cleared his throat. "Yes, that was quite unfortunate. War is complicated, I'm afraid."

"You have such a fascinating background, Edith," said Phyl, lightening the mood.

"Yes, well," smiled Edith. "My father had a very successful legal firm back home in Kobe, Japan." She looked up at her taller husband. "That's where Bill and I met." She smiled broadly. She turned to Phyl. "Enough about me. I truly enjoyed that movie. I'd like to think Bill and I live just like that. After all, we have seen some wonderful places during our marriage, especially since the war."

Phyl laughed. "Yes, wasn't the movie wonderful? I loved how Auntie Mame kept redecorating according to the land she just visited. And I love her saying, 'Live, live, live! Life is a banquet and most poor suckers are starving to death.' I'd like to think I live like that, too."

"You do," laughed Stuart. He coughed, then stretched his back, looking around for a place to sit.

Phyl motioned to a nearby table. "Shall we sit and take some weight off our feet?" She led everyone to a table, cleared from their earlier dinner, reset with flowers and opened bottles of Champagne on ice. "Oh, Champagne." She held out a beaded bottle from the silver ice bucket. "Anyone?"

Edith waved it away politely as she allowed her husband to hold her chair so she could sit.

"I'll have a wee drop," said Ambassador Sebald. He watched Phyl take a Champagne flute and fill it halfway, bubbles rising to the edge. She handed it to the ambassador, her bracelets over long, satin gloves, flashing in the candlelight. She looked at Edith again, nodded happily. Phyl served her bubbly.

"We are leaving for New Zealand on Sunday morning at eight, weather permitting." General Groves said. "The flight takes about six hours, and we will arrive in Christchurch first. Then we leave the next day for Wellington, do we not?"

"Indeed," said Stuart. He lit a cigarette and offered one to the General, who waved it away politely.

"Of course, the New Zealand manager has dates all over New Zealand, Oakland, Dunedin. We are supposed to cover the whole place in three weeks, but I have no intention of doing so." Stuart coughed, then raised his hand apologetically. "Sorry. This damp weather doesn't help my chronic bronchitis." Stuart took out a handkerchief, wiped at his lips, and tucked it back into his breast pocket. "I've been trying to get it into their thick heads at head office - sorry, the present company is excluded," added Stuart, motioning to the General next to him. "That New Zealand has Yankee dollars, which Australia doesn't. These two countries with equally small populations are always jealous of one another. Just like Argentina and Brazil."

"Ah, Argentina and its habit of coup d'etats!" chuckled the General. "I believe they have, yet again, a new president?"

"Yes, Arturo Frondizi Ércoli," offered Stuart. "Though that is on the heels of the last coup," he laughed. "The last was Eduardo Lonardi, who ousted Perón."

"Ah, Perón." The General pursed his lips as he leaned back in his chair, creaking under his weight. "He did an idiotic move by taking an anti-American stand after he was elected to a third term."

"Indeed, we didn't like that up at the White House, did we?"

"No. Then the idiot goes and arrests five leaders of the opposition, the Radical Civic Union, including its vice-presidential candidate."

"Growing discontent over inflation, oppression, and corruption finally got him ousted. He no longer had Evita to hide behind. She at least was able to reach the base and kept patriotism alive."

"You mean, Perónism," interrupted Phyl.

Stuart nodded at Phyl. "More precisely, yes. Now he's exiled but snug as a bug in Spain."

"He made a deal with Frondizi, you know. Perón said he would instruct his supporters to vote for Frondizi if he promised they would give back all his possessions, which were taken when he was ousted."

"Ha! All that wealth he and Evita accumulated? From dubious sources? Goodness, the wheeling and dealing we don't know about behind the scenes," exclaimed Phyl.

"I heard that Evita cried '*Mi vida por Perón!*' a thousand times before the roaring crowds and then died." Edith placed her empty glass on the table. She looked at the glass and put her gloved fingers on her lips. "Oh, dear. Did I finish that already?"

"Well, it wasn't that cut and dry. These fairy tales make her all the more a saint. But, you know, there are parallels that could be drawn between her life and the lives of other obsessively ambitious women who force themselves out of poverty through skillful manipulation. Except in her case," Phyl paused as she weighed her words, "I believe she truly did care for the people."

"Certainly not for the church or military." Stuart coughed into his hand.

"Hmm. Which was Eva's downfall."

Edith frowned and leaned toward Phyl. "What do you mean, 'downfall'? She died from cancer at the height of her popularity, did she not?"

Phyl thought perhaps she had said far too much. "Well, there was a …" Phyl looked to Stuart.

Stuart glanced around and nodded.

Phyl leaned closer to the middle of the table. "Perón had her secretly lobotomized. She was getting out of hand." Phyl looked at General Groves with big eyes. "We believe Perón was forced into doing it by the military. She was dying anyway, and he needed her to win his campaign, but I don't think he expected it to quicken her death in the manner in which it happened."

"How would a lobotomy quicken anyone's death? I thought it was to settle a person down somewhat," frowned Edith, quite appalled.

"Well, it completely took away her urge to eat."

"She starved to death before cancer got to her," muttered Ambassador Sebald.

"Hmm," nodded Phyl.

"You knew?" asked Edith, looking at her husband.

"I heard the rumors."

"Another indication of a failed system," said the General. "Someone's always being knocked off."

"Chronically," said Stuart. "Do you remember when Evita's brother was found dead? Juan Duarte?"

The ambassador sat back, crossed his legs, and rested his clasped hands on his knee. He nodded.

"I remember Juan Duarte," said the General. "Eva appointed him as private secretary to her husband. He committed suicide a couple of years after his sister's death, I believe."

"Well, it was made to *look* like a suicide," said Stuart.

"*Made* to look?" repeated the General.

"Hmm. The bullet lodged in his brain was a different caliber from the handgun found near his body." He pursed his lips, half smiling as he looked from the ambassador, to the General and to Edith.

"Oh, my," said Edith.

"There was a multi-page letter left as a suicide note," the ambassador pointed out.

Stuart made a questioning face. "Yes, but it went on and on about how wonderful Perón was."

"Why'd they have him killed and make it look like a suicide?" asked Edith.

Stuart took a deep breath. "Perhaps he knew too much. And he was made the brunt of negative publicity. Alleged corruption in every aspect of Perón's government was blamed on him."

"A scapegoat." The General sniffed.

"Yes! That crafty Perón."

"But the letter…" Edith was deep in thought.

"He could've written that letter under force," offered her husband.

Everyone sat silently for a moment. The band played Bobby Darin's newest hit, Mack the Knife. The singer sounded just like Bobby Darin with a slight Australian accent:

> *Oh, the shark, babe, has such teeth, dear*
> *And it shows them pearly white*
> *Just a jack knife has old MacHeath, babe*
> *And he keeps it, ah, out of sight.*
> *You know when that shark bites with his teeth, babe*
> *Scarlet billows start to spread…*

The General pushed his chair back. "Would you care to dance, Edith? You don't mind, do you, Bill?"

The ambassador grinned and motioned to his wife. "Be my guest."

Edith beamed. "That would be very nice, General. Thank you."

"Well, then. I must ask Phyl to dance. Sorry, Stuart." Ambassador Sebald pushed his chair back and held his hand out for Phyl. Phyl beamed and quickly got up and let him lead her to the floor.

"Quite the lyrics," yelled the ambassador over the music.

Phyl laughed gaily and deftly followed his lead. She was light on her feet, and her skirts twirled around her with energy and grace.

"You are quite the dancer, Phyllis."

"I love to dance. Always have. I take it quite seriously."

"Well, Stuart's a lucky man."

"Well, I'm the lucky one. I'm very proud of Stu. He works so very hard." She turned her head to see Stuart watching them from the table. He waved at her, and she twiddled her fingers back. "I must point out, Ambassador Sebald —"

"Call me Bill."

"I believe, Bill, giving lectures and showing movies on the Univac computer has become quite effective for Stu. Sometimes, he has up to 125 people attending."

"Who all attends these lectures?"

"Engineers, executives of other companies, government top brass. He ends the lectures with ample time for questions, which is no easy task as they're all quite inquisitive and technical, and the paperwork afterward is endless. On top of that, Stu has to keep up with the ever-changing electronics at the other end of the business. I must admit, sometimes it takes a toll on him."

"Well, I heard from the General that his sales are impressive."

"These new Univacs go for a minimum of half a million dollars. Though the old dinosaurs used to go for much more. But those were huge and cumbersome."

"Yes, I understand they've managed to whittle them down in size. Remington Rand computers used to be as big as a truck and cost a million U.S. I saw the one purchased for the Census Bureau back in 1950. Things have developed quite a bit since Sperry took over Rand."

Phyl looked at him inquisitively. "How do you know so much about the company?"

"Phyl. It's not just a company now, is it?"

Phyl was about to ask what he meant when the music suddenly came to an end, and before a new number would start, he gently maneuvered Phyl back to the table.

The General also arrived with Edith. They sat back down and motioned shyly for more Champagne.

Stuart did the honors, filling Phyl's glass as well. The bottle emptied. Stuart held it up high. A waiter immediately rushed over, took the bottle, and left to get another.

The General, still standing, looked over the ladies' heads at Sydney Harbour. "Beautiful view, even at night."

Phyl looked out at the darkened harbor, lights shimmering in the waves. There were many smaller craft anchored in the harbor, their mast lights shining brightly and swaying with the rolls. "There's a bit of a chop out there."

"The anchorage is full of vessels tonight due to the oncoming cyclone," said Stuart.

"It's bound to hold up your flight," said Phyl.

Stuart shook his head. "No, it should blow over before then."

"It's such a violent climate here," said Phyl, turning to everyone else. "No wonder all the poor animals in Australia have pouches for their babies. They'd all be blown away!"

Stuart pushed back his chair. "Well, that being said." He grabbed the bottle of Champagne from the waiter who returned. "Shall we take you all back to the Redington's on John Dyke's Avenue for a nightcap? You can see the harbor from an entirely different angle and also see over the darkened Pacific. You just might see the lit buoys out in the ocean." He pointed into the distance. "Perhaps a slight glow on the horizon. Maybe even catch one of those new fan-dangled U.F.O.s everyone's talking about these days."

Everyone laughed.

"Oh, don't be silly, Stu," yelled Phyl, gathering her things.

Stuart looked at Phyl gleefully. "I mean it!" Then he feigned surprise and held a finger to his lips in secrecy. "Or, is it one of those new secret military aircraft?"

Phyl made a face. "Well, that's more like it."

Stuart waved at everyone to follow him.

"Can we all fit in one car?" asked Edith. She looked back at a young military attaché in uniform, watching wide-eyed, waiting at a pillar a short distance away. She motioned at him with a gloved hand to follow. "Don't forget, we have our entourage!"

"No problem," announced Stuart. "We have a limousine waiting." He hurried to the front lobby. "The last one to the limousine gets no Champagne!"

Phyl carefully dropped the needle onto the record on their new stereo player.

The General stepped to the stereo and opened the side cupboard to view the LPs. An orchestra picked up the sound of a tango, and Phyl swayed to the beat. Thank goodness, the house was nice and warm. She had instructed Mavis to be doubly careful putting on the coal stove.

"I see you have a lovely collection of records here," the General muttered. He sifted through the albums, flipping one over the other. He pulled one out and read the jacket. "You got the new Frank Sinatra album, I see. Come Dance with Me." He shook his head, looking at Frank Sinatra's image appreciatively. "No one like this crooner."

"Oh, I love that one," cooed Phyl. She danced and shimmied to the music. She noticed the General didn't have a drink. She looked around and saw that Mavis hadn't yet come in with the tray of drinks. Something didn't feel right. She saw Stuart chatting with Edith and the ambassador by the sliding doors. He was pointing out landmarks in the distance along the dark but shimmering cityscape. "Stu? Have you seen Mavis?"

Stuart, a forelock hanging over his eyes, shook his head.

Phyl waved at him. "Geez. Just like a teenager. He sure is in a good mood tonight." She looked up at the General. He looked as fresh and crisp as five hours before. Of course, he didn't have a single drop of alcohol all evening. "Would you excuse me? I just need to find my maid."

The General smiled politely, reassuringly. "I'm not going anywhere. I will listen to this blue-eyed wonder after this tango is finished, if you don't mind." He leaned over the record and studied the needle following the ridges in the vinyl record. Phyl scurried to the kitchen.

"Mavis?" Phyl called. She pushed the saloon doors apart. She heard the loud 'tap tap' of winged bugs hitting the lamp overhead. She looked down at the floor where more appeared to be in death throes. Phyl saw the back door ajar. Upset, she stepped toward it. As she approached the door, she realized that Mavis was standing outside. Phyl hesitated with her hand raised to push the door wider.

"No can do. Bloody lizard lady got me here all night," argued Mavis, standing out under the back oriental-motif light, bugs slapping and skirting its glass sides.

"Sure, you can do. I sneak in, and no one be wiser," cooed a young man just out of sight.

Phyl cleared her throat loudly and threw the door wide open. "Mavis, the bugs are coming in, and bloody lizard lady needs you!"

Mavis fell back and crashed into the white brick of the house. The young man, whoever he was, turned tail and raced along the path, and evaporated into the bushes. Then she heard his feet stomping on the pavement on the other side. "Stop!" she yelled. Suddenly, Phyl saw the young military attaché who was stationed outside by the front door, pursuing the young man into the dark.

Phyl ran back into the house. "Bill! Bill!" She ran into the living room. Everyone expectantly turned to the sound of her voice. Edith put a hand to her chest.

"What happened?" Edith cried.

"Your attaché is in pursuit of a young man who really shouldn't be here," cried Phyl.

Stuart frowned and ran past her to the front door. "What young man?"

"I don't know. But he must have been up to no good; otherwise, why would he run? He ran off like a scared rabbit." She jumped when she heard a gunshot. She screamed, as did Edith.

The General and the ambassador raced out the door after Stuart. Phyl took Edith, and they scrambled into the front hallway and peered out, but they couldn't see anything. However, they heard voices and someone yelling.

"Oh my," said Phyl. She and Edith watched the attaché and the General drag the young man back to the house into the pool of the front light. The women stood back as the men marched in with the captive. Stuart slammed the door shut.

"Was that a gun I heard go off?" asked Phyl, her eyes like spotlights searching his expression.

"It was." Stuart held up a pistol. "He shot at us with this." Stuart grimly looked at her expression before following the others into the living room. The two men threw the young man down onto the couch. Stuart checking for bullets first, then held the pistol at the young man's face. Stuart looked back at Phyl.

"Where's Mavis?"

Phyl saw Mavis standing, shocked, in the kitchen doorway, partially hidden by the saloon doors. Phyl angrily motioned at her to come into the living room.

Mavis, one hand at her neck, slowly pushed the saloon doors open and stepped onto the white carpet. She seemed not to know where to look.

"Who is this young man?" demanded Stuart.

"He bins comin' up wid the milk. He new." She fussed with the skirt of her maid's uniform. "He white man and done bin good t' me. He's my friend."

"Why was he here this night?" demanded Stuart.

"He bin wantin' spend dis night wid me," Mavis said, lowering her eyes.

"Specifically, this night?" asked Stuart.

Mavis shrugged sadly.

Stuart turned back to the young man. "Why did you shoot at us? Why are you here?"

The young man's face was red with excitement. He eyed the pistol in Stuart's hand. He glanced at the ambassador. He jumped when the General suddenly dipped his paw into the young man's jacket breast pocket and pulled out a wallet. The man slowly sank back into the couch and Stuart stepped closer and held the gun at his head.

The General took out an ID card. "Vladimir." He took a deep breath and held the ID out to the ambassador. Bill took it and glared. He looked at the young man.

"Is this your real name?"

The young man stared back.

"Answer him," sneered Stuart. He kicked the man in the shin.

"Ow!" He nodded. "Yes, Vladimir Olgavich."

"Russian."

"Well, this doesn't bode well, Stu," yelled Phyl. "A Communist spy?"

"Who said anything about a spy?" asked Stuart. "Or communism? He could be just a punk."

"Or maybe white man *do* like me," offered Mavis, offended, and completely out of line.

Phyl turned to Mavis. "How dare you take such liberties! In my home. With my guests!"

Mavis, stubbornly held her ground. "I no care. Dis is my lizard life. I need da love, too!"

"Well, not on my clock; you don't." Phyl was spitting mad and felt humiliated. All her past paranoias quickly took root in the center of her being.

Mavis lunged forward to grab Vladimir's hand. Stuart pushed her back.

"Mavis, get back," Stuart said menacingly.

"He no white lizard spy!" she retorted.

Feeling the alcohol and andrenaline in her veins boil, Phyl maniacally shook Mavis, making an absurd face. "What else could he be?" She pointed to the Ambassador and the General. "Do you have any idea as to who we have here at the house? As if it's normal to have the American ambassador here and the very man," she pointed at the General, "The very man who created the Manhattan Project. The H Bomb, for crying out loud. And who designed the Pentagon. He practically stopped the war. You don't think he'd be of any interest to enemy countries?"

Phyl turned to the General. "And excuse me for being so rude, but…" She turned to Edith and placed a trembling hand on her chest. "I'm sorry, Edith. But you have no idea what kind of life we've had since we set sail for Buenos Aires so, so long ago. What…?" She looked around drunkenly. "Twenty-two years ago?" She looked myopically at Stuart.

"Sir?"

Everyone turned to see the military attaché standing by the stereo and holding the phone receiver.

"They're sending help, sir."

Everyone looked at him blankly as Frank Sinatra kicked in with a new song:

> *When an irresistible force*
> *Such as you*
> *Meets an old immovable object like me*
> *You can bet as sure as you live,*
> *Something gotta give*
> *Something gotta give*
> *Something gotta give*

Phyl stepped toward the stereo to turn off the music and yelled, "Something absolutely gotta give! Either that or my heart's gonna give out!"

* * *

Phyl stood at the railing. She looked down, mesmerized by the white caps assaulting the sides of the hull before being swept aft and swallowed into the wide 'V' formation of the ship's wake. Phyl looked into the far distance from where they came and sighed. She held the railing tighter and leaned back, tipping her head to look at the dome of endless sky and clouds above. She tried to focus on an Albatross floating at a great height. Suddenly, the bird – a wingspan of almost twelve feet – shot down as if to dip into the swells, then careened back into the heights. Phyl was amazed once again, having witnessed this scores of times over the years. It didn't flap its wings once. Just hovered, and waltzed on the current of the wind.

Over the sound of the wind, waves, and rumbling of the ship's engines, she heard that familiar cough. She turned to see Stuart, wrapped in an overcoat and wearing his fedora, carefully make his way over the salt-sprayed deck toward her. She reached out for his coat sleeve and pulled him closer. She smiled. Then she patted him on the back before rubbing the front of his coat.

"How are you?" she yelled over the wind and surf.

Stuart gazed at the uninterrupted horizon. He took a deep breath and coughed into his palm. He waved at Phyl to not worry. She poised to pound him on the back. He took out a handkerchief, blew his nose, and then coughed into it. He looked at it. His face went white, and quickly bunched the handkerchief and tucked it deep into his pocket.

The good wife noticed his expression. "Wait a minute. What are you hiding?" she asked, concerned. She went to take out his handkerchief, but he quickly put his hand over hers in prevention.

"Just a lot of phlegm," Stuart said. He took her hand and kissed it. She playfully pulled it back.

"Ewe, you just coughed into that hand," she laughed.

He made a face. "If we don't have the same germ colonies by now, I don't know what would kick them in. Besides," he added, turning to face Phyl. "You can't catch what I have."

She blinked against the wind. Phyl had a strange vibe, but let it go. She focused on his well-shaven and now lined face. She smiled. "Now, aren't you a handsome catch? How did I get so lucky?"

"It was your long legs," he said, pulling her closer.

"Now that's silly, I don't recall showing them off. My hems were halfway down to my ankles." She laughed.

"Oh, I had my ways. Sometimes, you did the naughty and crossed your legs while typing. I saw those knees of yours." Stuart grinned.

"Well, I'm delighted you did," she said. She suddenly saddened, and touched Stuart's lapel. She stared at it momentarily, studying the tiny water droplets on the heavy wool. She swallowed. "I'm sorry about our fight. After that night with the General and …"

"I know. You flipped into the depths of a melancholy I had never witnessed before."

"Yeah, I'm sorry."

He looked deep into her eyes. "I assumed you always knew it would never go away," he said, close to her ear.

She nodded. "I know." She sniffed. Cold, wind, or emotion. She wasn't sure. "I was trying to ignore it. I thought if we didn't talk about it anymore, it wasn't happening."

"And if you ever cared to look at my passport, it is now official. It's stamped Foreign Service."

Phyl's lips trembled. "I hadn't known that. I don't know where my head was."

Stuart took another deep breath, fought back a cough, then let Phyl go. He looked around. "I can't wait until we're in warmer climates. I'm glad we did it this way. A long flight back to the States, a quick turnaround, and then packing off to Argentina again with everything in the world we own."

"I'm glad we took every single item from Toronto and Australia on this ship this time. It's like carrying our nest along with us."

"And, of course, Jorge has that flat ready for us. Good of him to arrange our things to come out of storage."

"I don't know what we would've done without Jorge's help over the years."

"Hmm. I remember the first time I met him. I did not like him one bit!"

Phyl laughed. "Oh, I know. I remember leaving you two on that deck as we approached Buenos Aires. I thought you were going to throw him overboard. You were so upset with him."

Stuart took out a gold cigarette case from his breast pocket.

"Good luck getting that lit out here," laughed Phyl.

Stuart grabbed Phyl's upper arm. "I'm not lighting it out here. We're going back in. It's time we got dressed for dinner. Sitting at the captain's table is still a big deal, you know. I have to show off my beautiful wife."

"Oh, please dance with me tonight, Stuart. All these other men who politely ask me to dance, well, they're worse than you. At least you don't step over my toes, and you let me feel free enough to twirl and do my fancy footwork."

They carefully hurried toward the closest entranceway into the ship. Stuart kissed Phyl's head. He roughed it up more than the wind.

"What are you doing? You're messing up my hair."

Stuart opened the gangway door for her and smiled as she stepped up over the threshold. "I like that salt and pepper look," he said.

"Well, enjoy it while you can. I'm having it dyed pitch black as soon as I get to Buenos Aires. Angelica's already made an appointment with her hairdresser for me."

"I don't know if I could handle the young version of Phyllis May Redington," joked Stuart. He unbuttoned his coat and led Phyl to the lounge.

"Oh, I'm sure you'll remember how," teased Phyl.

"How about this? This look okay?" asked Phyl, holding up a black taffeta dress with full skirt and straps.

Stuart adjusted his grey silk tie, his chin jutting out. He stiffly glanced sideways to look at the dress Phyl was holding. "Isn't it a bit too cool to wear nothing over your shoulders?"

"It has a matching bolero jacket." Phyl looked at her hand. "Darn. My nails." She placed the dress onto the bed, hurried to the little bathroom, and opened the metal medicine cabinet over the sink. She retrieved a small bottle of red nail polish and closed the cabinet shut. As she turned, she spied another red object. Thinking perhaps she had inadvertently spilled nail polish earlier, she bent down with a frown.

Red peeked out from under a used pair of nylons she didn't remember throwing away recently. She bent down and lifted the nylons and stared at a tissue soaked in blood. With her other hand, she slowly lifted the tissue from the waste. With both nylons and tissue raised in the air, she walked back into the stateroom. She stared at Stuart.

Stuart felt her gaze. He didn't quite look back. "What? You okay?"

"The question is," Phyl's quivering voice whispered, barely audible over the stateroom's low rumble. "Are you okay?"

Stuart stopped fussing with his tie. He slowly lowered his hands and looked down at his shoes. "I'm okay," he muttered.

Phyl jumped between Stuart and the mirror. "Stop it!" she yelled, pushing at his shoulder.

He feigned surprise. "Stop what?"

"Stop LYING to me!" She pushed him hard.

Stuart stared at Phyl, his mouth agape. He swallowed hard. He looked at the bloody tissue.

"Ah, yes, that."

The ship's doctor carefully listened to Stuart's chest.

He was good enough to leave the ship's clinic and head to their stateroom. Phyl and Stuart's standing amongst the passengers was special. Phyl took this for granted. Spoiled perhaps. Expect the best service, the most attention, and ongoing and beautiful compliments. All this didn't matter anymore beyond her appreciation for immediate and personal service.

Phyl sat on the bed, wringing her hands. She straightened up when the doctor finally stood and took off his stethoscope. She watched his expression closely.

"Well," started the doctor. He cleared his throat and thought for a moment. "Spotting of blood is quite typical with your history of lesions on your lungs. You say this has been a chronic problem?"

"For years, doctor." Phyl made a face. "Ever since I've known him. Twenty-five years."

The doctor removed his glasses and wiped them with a handkerchief eased out of his pants pocket. He studied Stuart, Phyl noticed. She saw his look settle on Stuart's nicotine-stained fingers. "You are a heavy smoker, I see."

Stuart buttoned up his dress shirt, stood, and tucked in his shirt tails. "I like to smoke," he muttered. He glanced at Phyl's stare. "I quit off and on. But with business, both drinking and smoking are very hard to shake when everyone you meet offers you both."

"He entertains clients a lot," added Phyl.

The doctor rolled up his stethoscope and tucked it into his medical bag. "I don't like the sound of your lungs, though it could be just a flare-up. I would advise you to see a doctor for tests immediately after disembarking in Buenos Aires." He put a hand on Stuart's shoulders. "Get all the tests they can throw at you. You're still young, so you should be able to pull through whatever this is."

"And what *is* this?" asked Phyl quietly.

"I don't know. A conservative guess is you will need some heavy-duty antibiotics." He looked at his watch. "As a matter of fact, I think I will start you on penicillin immediately. I have time to get you a few days' worth before the dinner bell rings." The doctor picked up his bag and stepped toward the door. He opened it and looked back at Stuart. "I would definitely advise you to immediately stop smoking."

"Ah, doc. One more day. We're having dinner with the captain, and he's a chain smoker."

The doctor snorted softly. "And yes, that there is another stubborn patient of mine. I've given him orders to quit, too." He made a grim face, adjusted the glasses on his nose, and turned. "A purser will come with your medication shortly. See you at dinner." He smiled at Phyl before closing the door.

Phyl looked sadly at Stuart.

"I know. You've warned me over and over again." He grabbed his tie from the bed and threw it over his neck. Silently, Phyl took it and started to adjust the lengths. As she tied the knot, Stuart studied her with the solace of a man longtime married to his soulmate.

"It'll be fine. A good dose of penicillin is all that is needed. Lesions. Aggravated from coughing."

Phyl took a deep breath and nodded. Right.

Stuart looked down at the knot. "Well done."

Phyl turned to retrieve her bolero jacket. Stuart turned to look at himself in the mirror. "I should brief you," he said.

Phyl adjusted the jacket over her shoulders.

Stuart took his dinner jacket off a nearby hook. "You should know the underlying purpose of returning to Buenos Aires."

Phyl sat on the bed and picked up her high heels. She carefully slipped one on.

"With Perón gone and with enough time having gone by, some of the more dangerous factors have also fallen by the wayside."

"You mean they've all been killed off?" Phyl quietly slipped the other shoe on.

Stuart adjusted his lapels. He cocked his head. "I look pretty good for an old guy."

Phyl didn't respond.

"Something quite big is about to happen in Argentina."

"I don't want to know."

"The Mossad is about to finally abduct a major Nazi player in the Holocaust."

"Mossad?" asked Phyl, without emotion.

"Israeli secret service."

Phyl sadly looked at Stuart. "And this is supposedly happening *after* we get there?"

"Yes, I have to be there. But the CIA is trying to prevent it from happening."

Tears rose in Phyl's eyes. She looked away and pretended nothing bothered her.

"Are you listening to me? We want to help Israel, but the CIA has some sort of agreement with ex-Nazi criminals who have Russian connections. They're using them as spies in our fight against communism. If Eichmann gets caught, he may let the bag out as he's associated with these individuals. Phyl?"

Phyl grabbed her long black evening gloves and headed for the door.

"Phyl, listen to me."

"Why are you telling me all this?"

Stuart lunged forward and stood between her and the door. Phyl refused to look at him.

"It's Eichmann."

"Eichmann."

"Yes, Adolf Eichmann. One of the chief masterminds of the Holocaust. Because of him, millions have died. It's a bit of a dance, as we're not supposed to give the impression we're helping. In fact, the CIA knew of his whereabouts since '58 but refused to let the Israelis know."

"And now they know," muttered Phyl.

"Yes, a little leak here and a little whisper there…"

"From you?"

"No. I'm not that big a player."

Phyl looked down at her gloves.

Stuart grabbed her upper arms. "Phyl."

Phyl put up her hands and pressed them against Stuart's chest. She looked up into his face, studied it solemnly, then lowered a hand to find his smoking hand. She drew it up to her face to look at the yellow stains. "The day I don't see any stain on these fingers would be wonderful. Until then, I don't think I have it in me to understand the depth of anything you do. Or even care anymore."

She kissed his knuckles and gently pushed him aside. She opened the door and listened to Stuart follow her out into the hallway. That was the point. He was always there. At least in spirit when he was gone. They were a team.

She always had an acute sense of being on the dangerous side of watching history in the making. But now she prayed she would never find herself standing on the side alone. Without him, it all added up to nothing.

* * *

"Angelica! Jorge!"

Phyl frantically waved at the dear friends who waited behind a glass partition. She and Stuart collected their trunks and baggage. He, a cigarette clenched between his teeth, was instructing a porter.

"Look, there they are!" she screamed.

Stuart turned and smiled as best he could and did a quick wave. He handed the porter a piece of paper with instructions on where to deliver the bulk of the trunks. He took Phyl's arm and led her and the porter to the exit doors.

Phyl flew into Angelica's arms and they hugged joyously. The women rocked and danced for a moment while the men watched.

Stuart shook Jorge's hand, and accepted a massive hug from Angelica. He turned back to the matter of the luggage. "What car are you driving? I hope you have room."

Angelica waved off Stuart's concerns. "Not to worry. We know what you both are like. We hired a truck." Angelica, an arm around Phyl, led her and the men away from the throng of humanity. "Wait till you see the children. You won't recognize any of them. They're adults now."

"The boys are doing okay?" asked Stuart. He flicked his cigarette butt to the side. It rolled and joined its all too many brethren. Stuart took out his handkerchief and wiped his mouth. He gently coughed into it.

Jorge felt concern, but smiled. "The three older boys are engaged to be married."

"Wow, that's fabulous!"

Phyl turned to Jorge. "We have to call our doctor. Do we have a phone in the flat yet? Otherwise, we'll have to call from yours. Stuart's on penicillin for a lung infection, but the ship's doctor suggested getting tested as soon as possible."

"Still fighting that bronchitis?" Jorge asked. He slapped Stuart's back like an old chum.

"Same old, same old."

Phyl stopped to take sunglasses out of her leather bag. She held them up in the light for smudges and put them on. "My goodness. Here we are finally," she laughed. "Back in the heat and sun. I can't tell you how good it feels to be back."

"I told you it was more like home than you may have thought," quipped Jorge.

Phyl grinned. She looped arms with Angelica into the parking lot. "I must admit, as soon as I saw the city on the horizon, my heart quickened. However much we went through, the angst I felt had nothing to do with the beauty of this country and its people. And, of course..." She faced Angelica as they sauntered. "Our dear friends."

"Well, let's get you settled in that apartment. We had it arranged for you, your stored furniture and all. You can always rearrange things later."

"Thank you. Did you hire the maid and cook?"

"Yes, all arranged."

Phyl let go of Angelica. "Stu, I'm a happy woman once again." She threw up her arms. "Not only a maid but a cook to boot!" She raised her face and heart to the sky. "Oh, it feels good to be alive."

"Are you going back to the American Women's Club?" asked Angelica.

"Eventually. But one of the first things I'd like to do is visit your *estancia*. I can't wait to see everyone again."

"Well, there have been changes," said Jorge.

"Oh?"

"We've lost many of our workers and farmers to the city. Our *majordomo* left after all these decades. But the children have picked up a good part of the slack." Jorge stopped and turned to face Stuart. "We also lost our vote."

Stuart did a double take. "What do you mean, you lost your vote?"

"A glitch in the new government. The provincial constitutions were abolished by the military in '56. Only provinces with a constitution in force as of December 1, 1957, can participate in the election. In Las Palmas, as in most provinces, we still don't have one. So, we didn't vote in the presidential election of '58. And won't in any elections until we sort this out."

"You've lost your voice?" exclaimed Phyl, astounded.

"Indeed." Jorge took keys from his pant pocket and jiggled them in the air. "We're here." He stopped at an old delivery van.

The porter rolled a heavily stacked dolly to the back of the van and waited for Jorge to open the back doors.

Jorge unlocked the car and walked to the back. "Careful. It's hot in there. Let it air out a bit."

Angelica went to the other side and opened the door wide. She fanned the heat that rolled out of the interior.

"No chauffeur?" Stuart joked.

"We don't use chauffeurs anymore," said Angelica. "They expect to be paid so much. We're supposed to be well off, but we find that more and more things we used to do simply aren't as affordable." She rolled down the passenger side window and leaned against the open door. "Besides, we want to make sure our children have a good start. We're giving them each land and building a home for them. With all their hands-on experience, they should do better than most."

"Priorities," said Phyl.

"Indeed."

Stuart pulled his tie off and ran a finger along his collar. "It's awfully hot and sticky."

"Take your jacket off, Stu. I don't know why you wore one. We're back in the tropics." Phyl took a close look at his flushed face. She frowned. "Are you okay? Shall I get some water for you from somewhere?"

Stuart struggled with his jacket and inadvertently pulled the sleeves inside out. He folded it as best he could and placed it on the trunks and closed the rear doors. He dipped into his pocket for the porter's tip.

Jorge interceded his billfold already open. He thanked the porter, handed him *pesos* and nodded him away. The porter tipped his hat and dragged the large dolly back to the terminal.

"Thanks." Stuart took out his handkerchief again and wiped at his forehead. He wavered on his feet. Jorge took hold of his upper arm.

"Come. As we drive, you'll feel better with a breeze flowing through the van."

Stuart went to take a step but suddenly leaned back against the side of the van.

Phyl, seated in the back, felt the van jolt. She quickly rolled down the window and poked her head out. "Stu? Are you okay?"

Stuart coughed and hacked. He grimaced and spat blood into his handkerchief. This time, the blood did not stop. Eyes wide, he looked at Jorge, surprised. "Ah, geez," he gurgled.

Jorge quickly dug out his handkerchief and put it against his friend's mouth. Stuart bent forward and spit more blood. And more.

"Time for the hospital!" yelled Jorge. He pushed Stuart into the front seat and rushed to the steering wheel. "Hold on, everyone. This is going to be a rough ride."

* * *

Stuart was heavily sedated.

He slept on his side with a medical vomit basin at his face. There was evidence of mucous and blood from an earlier cough. Phyl stared at the basin. She was poor at the hands-on part of helping a sick husband. She made a distressed face and stood. She swallowed hard and reached for the basin. She did not look in and carried it to the washroom to rinse. She fought back sudden nausea. She shivered by the sink. The doctor, in his light greens over a white shirt and black bowtie, entered the room, a clipboard in hand and a stethoscope around his neck.

"*Buenos dias, Señora de Redington*," he greeted quietly. "How is your husband today?"

Phyl tapped the basin against the edge of the sink and walked back into the room. She held the basin aloft. "A little spit and blood, but he's been able to sleep this past hour."

"Good." The doctor nodded and looked at his clipboard.

"You have the results?"

"*Sí.*"

"Are the lesions causing all this bleeding?"

"Have a seat, *Señora*, please."

She held her eyes on the doctor and she felt her way over to one of two chairs near the bed. The doctor sat in the other. He placed a hand on Stuart's hip. Stuart's eyes flickered. Then, slowly, he opened them.

"*Buenos Dias, Señor Redington*. How are you? I see you are able to catch some sleep."

"I could be better," whispered Stuart. He stirred and slowly turned onto his back. He put a hand on his chest and winced. "I'm afraid to cough."

"Try not to, Stu. Please," beseeched Phyl. She turned to the doctor. "Please, tell us what's going on. I've never seen him this bad. All this blood worries me."

The doctor took off his glasses and looped them over his bowtie. "Our tests show tumors. There are many lesions, and I really had to take a good long look at the X-rays, but what is clear is that there are many obstructions. Anomalies. I recommend we see what they are."

"You mean, as in opening him up?" asked Phyl, her voice feeble with emotion.

"Medicine has gone a long way, but sometimes it's still a guessing game until we look for ourselves."

She clenched her teeth.

Stuart tried to sit up. No go. He looked drained. He tried to talk, but his throat was dry.

Phyl jumped and grabbed a glass of water by a roller table. She held the glass to Stuart's lips but he took it from her and sipped on his own. He gave the glass back to Phyl.

"I have work to do," rasped Stuart. "So, I need to know when you suggest you open me up. Also, how long will it take me to get back to work after you do?"

Phyl felt faint. "Can't we keep Stuart for a few days until he heals and rests? Can't we do that? Maybe it's really nothing."

"Phyl, I can feel it. I don't feel right."

"Have you been losing weight recently?" asked the doctor.

"A little."

The doctor nodded.

"Stu, we should talk to Head Office. See what they say." She struggled to make sense of this unexpected turn of events.

"Right." Stuart slid into a lying position. He held up his hand and shook his head. He pointed to his chest and throat, turned, and spit blood and mucous into the basin.

Phyl jumped up.

Stuart held a hand up to stop her. He motioned for tissue.

Phyl scrambled to the trolley table and grabbed a tissue. She slapped it into his palm and looked away as Stuart wiped his bloody lips. She turned to the doctor. "Doctor, I'll go with our friends to our apartment here and contact the head office in New York to see what they advise."

"Fine. It would be good to know by tonight so we can strategize," said the doctor.

"Strategize. Like it's a battle," whispered Phyl. Stuart appeared to have fallen asleep, sweat on his grey skin. "It's just another battle. We'll win. We always do."

"I will wait for your decision," said the doctor. He shook Phyl's hand. "Stay strong."

"I know nothing else than to be strong, doctor."

"She's the Rock of Gibraltar," croaked Stuart.

The doctor looked at the basin and back at Phyl.

She grimaced and motioned to the basin. "Er, except for when it comes to this kind of stuff."

The doctor nodded and left.

Phyl cried like a baby in Angelica's arms.

Jorge stood by the phone. He dialed a number from a piece of paper Phyl handed him. She heard him speak but she was too distraught to make out the words. After a moment, she felt a hand on her head. It wasn't Angelica's. She stopped sobbing, wiped her nose and eyes, and looked up, wearily.

Jorge, tears in his eyes, witnessed her beautiful frailty. He held the receiver out to her. "It's the office. I explained the situation, but they need to speak with you."

Phyl took the receiver. Her hand shook. She sadly confirmed all the details while the secretary reiterated everything Jorge said to her. She instructed Phyl to stay on the line as she tried to connect her with either the president or vice president.

"Oh, let me talk to the vice president, General Groves," said Phyl with renewed hope. "He's a good friend of ours." She waited to be connected, and told Angelica and Jorge how they had such a lovely time with the general in Australia. Suddenly, she heard the familiar voice cut in on the phone. She held up a finger to Jorge and Angelica.

"General, oh, General. I have such sad news," she cried. "It's Stuart. He's not well. Please. I wonder if you could advise me."

*   *   *

A few weeks later.

Phyl sat in a daze. She held Stuart's hand in his hospital bed at the Memorial Sloan Kettering Cancer Center on Manhattan's Upper West Side. He was rolled back in after a lengthy operation, hooked into bottles of fluids.

The operation took longer than they had forewarned, and she wasn't sure if that was a good or bad sign. She took a deep and shaky breath. The squeaks of shoes continually passed their door. Announcements made over the intercom. She scanned the room. Cards and flowers everywhere, from family, friends, and the office. The general personally delivered a huge bouquet. There was a beautiful arrangement from Jorge and Angelica, and some smaller ones from her Dad and K, Claude Jr. and Dorothy, and Stuart's sister and brothers.

We are so blessed, she thought. The love shown to them moved her to tears. She dwelt on what a charmed life they had always led. She smiled at some memories and frowned at others.

She smoothed her skirt. She wore the same skirt and jacket for days, and they looked awfully wrinkled. She packed so few things when they were rushed on a flight back to New York with a nurse. Stuart was hardly aware of what they were doing. Once they arrived in New York, everyone meant business. Sperry Rand put her in the best hotel, as close to the hospital as possible. They had the best surgeon the country could offer, and the attention to every need for her Stuart was exemplary.

Phyl heard determined footsteps approach and a familiar voice greet nurses. She turned to see the general fill their door. He raised his hand and knocked on the door. His eyes locked on hers. She shot out of the chair and ran to him. He cradled her and patted her head gently.

"I'm so frightened, General," she cried.

"Hush. No need to be frightened. Lobectomies are no longer life-threatening, Phyl. They've found out so much in the field of medicine since the war. He just needs to change his lifestyle, that is all."

Phyl wiped her face with a sleeve. "I'm sorry. I'm a real mess. I just hope it's not too late to change things."

"Well, take heart. Look at him. He'll pull through," he said, looking keenly at Stuart. "Has he woken up from surgery yet?"

Phyl shook her head. "Not yet. He's on heavy painkillers and massive amounts of streptomycin to fight possible infection. Oh!" She was surprised to see Stuart's eyelids flutter. She hurried to his side, grabbed his hand, and held it to her chest. "Stu? Can you hear me?"

Stuart turned his face toward her voice. He tried to smile.

Phyl turned hopefully to the general.

He stepped to the other side of the bed, carefully pushed the IV tower to the back wall, and looked down. He placed a hand on the railing of the bed. "Stuart. It's the General. Can you hear me?"

Stuart slightly nodded and groaned.

"No need to talk. Just wanted to give you my best, buddy. And give you an update." He leaned down and whispered into Stuart's ear. "They got him. The Mossad got Eichmann."

Stuart half-opened his eyes and grunted.

"He's in Jerusalem awaiting trial. It's probably the hangman's noose for him."

Phyl watched Stuart fall asleep. She looked up at the general, and he glanced at her before stepping away from Stuart's side. He walked to her and took her hands. She stood.

"He could live another twenty years, Phyl. Don't fret."

"But his other lung still has so many lesions. I mean, his odds, they don't look good."

"With today's medical advances, he'll be fine. He's in superior hands. I understand you can fly back in less than three months. You'll be home again soon."

"Home," she whispered.

"I understand he'll convalesce at his sister's in Washington?"

Phyl nodded. "Yes."

He patted her shoulder. "Before you know it, you'll be on that plane going south. At least you're missing the worst of the winter weather there. You'll be back, what?" He looked up at the ceiling in thought. "It's the end of May now." He made a face. "Yes, you may be home in Buenos Aires in July or August before the blossoms return." He looked at his watch. "Say, I have time yet. How about a coffee down in the cafeteria? We can reminisce about that strange young Russian man spying on us in Australia."

Phyl rolled her eyes. "Ha! Well, that was surreal. But I sure would like to tell you other stories that don't sit well with me. Especially a young Hitler Youth leader called Reiner."

He held his arm out to her. "Shall we then? Off to the best cafeteria coffee you can find in Manhattan?"

Phyl bent over Stuart and kissed his forehead. She touched it. "He feels cold to the touch," she whispered.

"No fever," the general said, approvingly.

"I love you, Stu. I'll be right back." Phyl didn't wait for an answer. Stuart floated somewhere far away. She stepped to the General to take his arm, looked back at Stuart again, then allowed herself to be walked out of the room. "Are you sure he'll be all right? You're not just saying that, General?"

"Phyl, if he had to be sick, now in history is the bestest of times."

* * *

But the bestest of times was not good enough. Six months later, two months after they returned to their new home in Buenos Aires, Phyl woke up to find that Stuart had died peacefully in his sleep.

Chapter Twenty-Three

But that was one big fat lie.

Phyl didn't wake up to find a Stuart peacefully deceased next to her. It's what she preferred to tell the world. The truth is Stuart died a horrible death. It was her mother's death all over again. Stuart awoke one morning ragged and unable to breathe and was rushed to hospital. After two days, it was evident that Stuart would not pull through no matter what they did. He was clear-headed enough to know that he didn't want to die in an antiseptic, cold and noisy environment. He requested that Jorge take him and Phyl to the *estancia* where he wanted to live out his last remaining days.

He also needed to see that his papers were destroyed.

So, in the middle of the beautiful Pampas, Stuart lay in a darkened room lit only by candlelight in the Piñiero's home. Jorge hovered near a metal barrel at the stables burning Stuart's files, papers and maps. Once done, Jorge joined Phyl and the rest of his family at Stuart's side with a local priest, rushed in to solemnly give Stuart the last rites.

Then it was an excruciatingly difficult and grief-stricken waiting game. Angelica and the eldest of her children held vigil as Jorge and Phyl rested or slept before it was their turn to try and lessen Stuart's suffering and keep him as comfortable as possible. But Phyl could not rest and more often than not slumped in a leather armchair, looking on, exhausted, while Angelica gently cooled Stuart's face and arms with a damp cloth or moistened his parched lips with honey and warm water.

Phyl was astounded at the inhumane lengths the body would go to to fight to stay alive. Stuart's desperate gasps for air heaved his chest as he fought for oxygen. He fell in and out of consciousness. She was desperate to help but there was absolutely nothing she or Jorge could do but stand by and watch poor Stuart suffer. When he finally fell silent and she and Jorge thought Stuart had come to the end, he startled them by suddenly opening his eyes wide to fight further, to take another agonizing and body-wracking breath. It had been a while since she had any form of communication with Stuart, and when his eyes were open, they simply gazed through her. She believed she lost him in spirit and mind, that before her was but the carcass kicking in an extended death rattle.

Unexpectedly, as if by magic, Stuart came to and looked around. His breathing calmed and he reached out for Phyl, and smiled. She clung to him, around his neck and shoulders, and bawled like a baby. He soothed her with words of love and comfort. But this lasted less than a minute for, once again, he sank into the abyss of delirium.

Phyl clung to Stuart's neck and screamed, "Don't leave me! Stu! Don't leave me!"

He started to drown in his own lung fluids. Jorge quickly put him into a half sitting position against a mound of pillows. Stuart fell into a rhythm of deep gasping and gurgling breathes. Slowly, the pauses between each breath lasted longer and longer until there was a moment or two when it appeared he finally died. Phyl squealed the first time this happened. She grieved when, suddenly, he inhaled noisily before grinding back into the pillows.

Phyl buried her head into Jorge's chest. "Oh, Jorge. I can't take this anymore. How do we stop this? He's drowning! He's literally drowning to death in his bed. I can't take this anymore. I just can't!"

Jorge held her closely. His bloodshot eyes quietly and sadly rested on his struggling friend. "I wouldn't want to wish that on my worst enemy."

Phyl jumped onto the bed. "Oh, Stuart, don't go," she cried. Don't you dare leave me!" She clutched at his shoulders and shook him. "Stuart! We have so many plans. I can't do this without you."

Angelica cried, more because of Phyl's broken heart. She turned away, as did Jorge and their children, to give Phyl her privacy in these final moments. Surely a body could take only so much suffering before it succumbed. Suddenly, Phyl jolted back when Stuart noisily gulped for air, suffocating. She pounded Stuart's chest. She willed him to breathe, to no avail. Now she willed him to die quickly so as not to go through such torture.

She bent over him and whispered into his ear. "Stu, my love. My darling," she cried tearfully. "I'm sorry. You can go. Let go. I can't stand you suffering like this anymore. It's all right. I love you."

Stuart took one last long rasping breath and Phyl's giant of a man - her Adonis, idol, lover and soulmate – slumped, and his eyes dulled and stared unseeing down at the bed covers under his chin.

Jorge reached over and gently closed Stuart's eyes. Phyl stood, wide-eyed, with her hands over her mouth. Then Jorge held out his arms to Phyl and Angelica. The women moved into the reach of his arms and clutched each other in grief. Their adult children looked on, startled and appalled at seeing their first human death throes. They watched Phyl pull away from their parents and crawl up on the bed to cling to Stuart's lifeless body.

Jorge opened the door. A servant and the waiting priest sat in chairs in the hallway, He nodded at their servant and she immediately left to ring their bell to inform the rest of the family and working crew of Stuart's passing. The priest entered the dark room to pray.

Phyl didn't listen to the prayer as the bells rang and echoed over the *estancia* grounds. She wasn't as devoted to a God as Stuart was and, at the moment, she did not think that God was at all on their side. Why take Stuart away at such an early age? He was barely into middle age. But she had to remind herself that Stuart had a choice. He knew his lungs were compromised, as were his father's, and he also knew that it was smoking that hastened his own father's death. Phyl shook her head at their stupidity. If only she had argued till she was blue in the face. If only she didn't care if he ever got angry.

If only.

Early the next morning, a searing hot wind from the dry Pampas plains whipped Phyl's hem across her nyloned calves. She impatiently yanked away a moist and clinging tendril of hair from behind her dark glasses and defiantly cocked her head into the wind. She grimly focused on a herd of ostrich playing freely on a distant hill. She half-heartedly listened to the priest's words and, instead, willed herself to believe that Stuart stood next to her enjoying the iconic view along with her. "See, Stu?" she thought to herself. "Look at those crazy ostriches. Do you remember how we used to chase them?" She smiled.

She was startled when she felt a warm and gentle touch on her shoulder. Half expecting to see Stuart standing behind her, she saw Jorge. She blinked back unwelcome tears and turned to finally face the priest and noticed he was perspiring heavily in his black robe and white collar, still praying over the simple casket resting before the Piñiero's family mausoleum.

Phyl fearfully glanced into the dark abyss of the mausoleum, then at Stuart's casket. She felt ill at the thought of leaving his body in that stiflingly hot space and wavered on her feet. Jorge steadied her. She leaned on Jorge's shoulders, her eyes drawn to a flash of light in the distant hills. A reflection. She snorted. Jorge looked at her curiously. She motioned with her chin into the distance and Jorge looked over the rolling hills. The reflection flashed again.

Angrily, Phyl stepped away from the group and held up her hand sporting her middle finger. "See that? Are you happy now" she yelled. "Go to hell!"

Jorge lunged at her and held her by the shoulders, leading her back to the group. She finally looked into his eyes, the intense grievous loss in her own reaching out and squeezing his heart. He shook his head almost imperceptibly before directing her attention to the ongoing ceremony.

Prayers and benedictions finished, Jorge and Angelica's older children and two servants bent down and lifted the casket, their necks and arm muscles betraying the fact that a large and once strong man was cocooned within that wooden box.

Phyl fell into a folding chair and doubled over. She barely heard the noises of a coffin being hauled into the mausoleum and the large iron doors being pulled shut and locked. For the longest time, she refused to move. Eventually, as the others started to walk back toward the house, Angelica and Jorge stood by as she slowly lifted her face to look at the closed iron gate. She allowed herself to be lifted out of the chair and guided back to the house. In her grief, her hearing was amplified and her eardrums were assailed by a concert of singing and chirping birds, the cawing and calling of the rooster and hens, and the neighing and roar of horses, cows, alpacas and pigs. Suddenly, a piercing screech above her head made her look upwards into the breathtaking sky. There, hovering as if frozen in place, glided a majestic condor. She stopped in her tracks and squinted to get a better look at its massive contours. She could see its head looking this way and that as if focused on her. Or so she believed.

"Fly free, my darling. Fly free."

The condor screeched once more, dipped and then glided off to the rolling Pampas hills to where she saw another flash of light. She burst out laughing. "Go get 'em, Stu!"

* * *

The soft and fluid skat of Duke Ellington and John Coltrane swirled throughout the New York apartment.

Elegant people of all shapes, sizes and ages, carried martinis and Champagne while they mingled in every room. Vases of multicolored dahlias adorned every nook and surface of the eclectic flat. Creamy whites, palest of pinks, sunny yellows, crimson reds beautifully complimented the large Argentine landscapes which adorned the walls. White furniture stood in striking contrast to the dark brown and maroon alpaca wool rugs. Germanic themed plates adorned the kitchen walls. Gold-painted, carved Indigenous faces lined the grand hallway. Argentine ceramic vases and pottery, painted in the colors of hills, stood alongside *Siwani* Argentine woven baskets on glass shelves, lit individually by small lights above.

Elsewhere, framed photos of Phyl and Stuart over the years plus photos of the Piñieros on their *estancia*. Next to these, she had more recent professional photos taken of her in dancing costume.

Nancy, a blond woman with her hair brushed high into a clip stood in a tight-fitting lime green mini-dress. She admired Phyl's dance photos. Phyl wore a black and white small hounds-tooth mini-dress and slowly glided amongst her noble guests. She stopped and savoured her photos.

"Phyl, these are lovely," Nancy announced. "Were these taken while you were working at that Fred Astaire School of Dance?"

Phyl cocked her head. Her hair was now kept short and softly curled, offset by long dangling earrings dipping from her ear lobes. "I wasn't just working there, as you put it. I *own* the Fred Astaire Dance Studio."

"Oh, I'm sorry, Phyl. I didn't mean to imply…"

Phyl shook her head. "Not to worry. I'm fine, but after Stuart died, I was faced with the fact that one of his pensions were in *pesos*. Fine if I stayed in Argentina, but here the *peso* is worthless. Oh, don't get me wrong. Stuart left me in a very secure position. We always invested wisely."

Phyl motioned to her flat and looked from wall to wall. "I was able to purchase this from one of our investments. But it's the day to day." She waved her hand toward a servant in a maid's outfit serving from a tray of hors d'oeuvres. "I am so used to the finer things in life that I thought, why not combine what I so love to do with something that augments an already nice cash flow."

"Oh, Phyl, you are such an inspiration!"

"Oh, maybe I'm just a ham." Phyl laughed softly. "I love to perform, that's all."

Nancy pointed to a print of Phyl dancing with a male partner. "And who is he?"

"He was my partner for a little while. We danced in ballrooms all over New York."

"What happened to him?" Nancy looked at Phyl suggestively.

Phyl shook her head. "He got married and his wife didn't like us being so close." She laughed. "She had no idea how harmless I really am. I would never hurt another marriage. Besides, Stuart's a hard act to follow. I would never, ever, in my life, find a man like Stu, again. When I married him, heaven blessed me to no end."

The front doorbell rang over the chatter and light jazz. She turned to make sure that a servant answered. She and Nancy watched the door open, and a handsome young man walked in, wearing a paisley Neru jacket and slacks.

"Who's that?" asked Phyl. She frowned. "I don't think I invited him."

"Oh, sorry, Phyl. I knew how much you love to chat with other dancers. That's a friend of Steven and mine. His name is Barry Del Rae. He's an actor from California." Nancy whispered, "He knows Frank Sinatra and Marlon Brando."

Phyl blinked. Another dancer and actor. But he was at least twenty years younger than her. "Well, it *would* be interesting to talk to him. Especially about Hollywood." Phyl turned to Nancy. "I used to act, you know."

"Oh?"

"Oh, yes. Movies and theatre."

"Oh, my. You are full of surprises," offered Nancy. She followed Phyl's curious gaze at the door.

A delivery man appeared in the open doorway behind Del Rae and handed a package to the servant. Phyl turned to Nancy. "Excuse me. I see I have a delivery." Phyl walked to the hallway but stopped briefly to extend her hand. "Welcome, it's Barry Del Rae, is it?"

Barry, surprised at the vision of brunette elegance and charm, held out his hand. "Yes, Barry Del Rae." He shook her hand pleasantly enough. "And you are?" He smiled politely, sweetly.

"I'm Phyllis Redington. You can call me Phyl. This is my party."

"Oh, I'm sorry. This is your home?"

"Hmm."

"Yes, well I'm…"

Phyl smiled. "Yes, you're crashing the party."

Barry spied Nancy, and waved, then turned shyly back to Phyl. He ran a finger around the collar of his jacket. "Um, yes. I'm sorry."

"Listen, that's absolutely fine. I understand you're an actor and dancer?"

Del Rae, slicked back his hair and grinned charmingly. "Yes, I am."

"So am I." Phyl, almost sadly, looked up at him, he was taller, so young. Blue eyes. "I have some business to attend to. Please make yourself at home. We'll have lots to talk about later, I'm sure."

Phyl took the package from the servant. She thanked her and took it to the privacy of her bedroom. Cut off from the ongoing sound of chatter, laughter and jazz, she took a deep breath, kicked off her black leather heels and sank into a pink brocade and gold trimmed armchair. She ripped open the package and took out a letter and a small box. Frowning, she read the letter.

My Dearest Phyllis,

If you would do me the honor of seeing me next week while I am in New York, I would like to make a proposition. Your presence is sorely missed and I realize you may not want to consider this, but your company would be greatly appreciated. Would you consider accompanying me on my business trips? We can elegantly put it as you are my personal secretary and business manager. I will do my routine trips to Paris and Rome, and have to return to New Zealand and Australia.

You are organized, efficient, charming and elegant. You are wonderful with people. It would greatly enhance my business by simply having you at my side. And it would enhance my happiness. I know you so well, Phyllis. I guarantee you will be happy with the outcome.

Love and adoringly,
J.

Phyl shook her head. "You never give up, do you, Jorge?" she said to herself. She opened the little box. When she saw what it was, she gasped. A solid gold armband with a feather formation of diamonds. She covered her mouth and blinked at the beautiful piece of jewelry. She sat back, dumbfounded. In spite of herself, she reverently put the band on her wrist. It felt heavy and absolutely rich. She stared at it for an eternity.

"Well, Jorge, if you knew me that well, you know I would never accept your proposition." She whispered. "How on earth am I going to talk to Angelica now?"

She took a deep breath, folded the letter and put it back into the envelope. She took another look at the bracelet and decided to keep it on for the time-being. She stood up, slipped into her heels once again, then opened the door. She looked back at her bed, the bed she and Stuart shared all those years in Argentina. She swallowed back grief and walked back to the sea of people, drinks, food and music.

"I was looking for you," said Nancy. "Come. I really want you to get to know Barry. He can't stay for very long."

Phyl followed Nancy down the hall toward the living room. "Why? Where is he going?"

"He has to catch a cruise ship. That's why he's here in New York. He dances on cruise ships when he's between acting jobs in California."

Dancing on ships?

Nancy spotted Barry at the windows looking down onto the street of beautiful brownstones and motioned him to come over.

Barry came from where he stood. He waved at smoke hanging in the air, coughed slightly, and reached them smiling sweetly. He nodded at Phyl, with moist eyes.

"Are you alright?" asked Phyl.

Barry frowned, questioningly. "What do you mean?"

"You coughed," said Phyl in a small voice.

"Oh, yes. I'm trying to quit so I find it hard to be in a room with others who smoke." He shrugged. "It's almost impossible not to be surrounded by it everywhere you go." He looked around. "Don't get me wrong, I love to smoke."

He pointed at his chest. "But it's the lungs, you know. They're so important. Especially, as a dancer."

Phyl didn't know what to say. She stifled the beast who nudged her insides.

"Please. Let me get you ladies a drink." He looked around for a servant and didn't see one. He held up a finger. "One moment. What would you like, by the way? Martini, Champagne?" He laughed and motioned to Phyl. "Here I'm offering you your own alcohol."

Phyl smiled slightly. "Champagne."

"Me, too," said Nancy.

Barry walked away on drink safari. Phyl watched him go into the kitchen.

"Isn't he nice?" asked Nancy.

Phyl nodded.

"He's mafia, though."

"Oh?"

"Just thought you should know."

Phyl shrugged nonchalantly. "Nancy, if you're trying to match make me, sensationalism won't do it, however much you know me. But you have to understand, I'm not interested." She poked at Nancy with a glint in her eye. "And he is just a baby."

Nancy grinned, also a glint in her eye. "So? Look at you. You look twenty years younger than you actually are."

Pleased, Phyl snorted. That made them both laugh.

Barry returned with two Champagne flutes, the bubbles popping above the rims and pleased to see such glee. "Two Champagnes for two beautiful, happy ladies."

Phyl noticed how slim he was. A dancer's body.

"Barry, Phyl owns a dance studio here in Manhattan. She also performs in ballrooms across New York."

Phyl looked at Nancy, not sure if she wanted to talk about herself at all with this perfect stranger.

"Oh, really? Oh, my gosh. I can't believe it. I'm actually looking for a new partner. My present one just got pregnant and won't be dancing for much longer."

Phyl's eyebrows raised, slowly.

He looked intently at her and blushed. "Oh, no no. It's not mine," he said shyly. "She's very happily married." He cleared his throat. "Seriously, there's nothing like performing on cruise ships, which is what I do between acting gigs. It only takes a few days to a week or two, several times a year."

Phyl hesitated.

Nancy perked up. "Oh, I gotta go. Steven's motioning at me." She gave Phyl a quick kiss on the cheek. "We're going to his parents' in the Hamptons. We have to be there for supper. Thank you so much for everything, Phyl." Nancy waved at Barry and rushed to the door to where her husband held a fur coat.

Phyl was taken aback. "Um…"

"Phyl," Barry began.

"Yes?" Phyl answered politely, thinking of ways of hurrying Barry out the door.

"When I come back from this cruise, I have a few days before I go back to Hollywood for a bit part in a Western. But I have an uncle with the best little Italian restaurant in Little Italy. Would you join me for dinner while we talk about dance and these contracts I have this coming year? I guarantee you, it's the best spaghetti sauce this side of Italy."

"Listen, Barry. I'm guessing I'm old enough to be your mother. And I am not at all interested …"

"I think you must exaggerate."

Phyl opened her mouth to retort. He held up a finger.

"Before you say anything, let me remind you of what the character, Auntie Mame, always said."

Phyl's heart skipped a beat. "Auntie Mame?" Her eyes glazed over.

"Yes, in that movie, Auntie Mame. Live, live, live!" Barry dramatically threw out his arms. "'Life is a banquet and most poor suckers are starving to death.'"

Phyl was stunned. She felt a loving hand rest on her shoulder. She turned to see no one there. "Stuart?" she whispered.

The record player dropped another LP and a light and happy French bossa nova stirred.

"I would like one dance before I go. Phyl, would you care to join me?" Barry held out his arm.

Phyl looked around at the eyes gazing at them. They looked as if they appreciated the sight of the two of them together. Despite her caution, the music took hold of her body and she couldn't help but go with it. She knew she could absolutely blow away her friends with her expertise and elegance. And this young man. The challenge quickened her heart. She cocked her head at Barry.

"Sure, let's see how good you really are." She straightened her shoulders and firmed her legs and sauntered into a clearing with him. People moved away to give them room, as if they were ionized.

"You ready?" he whispered. He held her firmly, authoritatively and respectfully. His blue eyes sparkled and danced as he looked deep into hers.

Over Barry's shoulder, Phyl thought she saw Stuart. She was dumbfounded. She imagined him smiling at her encouragingly. She felt a kick in the behind. She took a deep breath.

"Life's always been a glorious banquet for me," she said to Barry. "And I have never, ever been a starving sucker. In fact, I was a glutton." She laughed.

Barry's smile widened. "A very beautiful one, I'm sure." He bent into her and swept her around and around the room. The elegance. The smooth and agile movements. The surrender. She tilted her head back joyfully. Barry smiled broadly and he twirled her, dipped her, and made her fly and feel beautiful.

"So," he said, as he held her close again, "What do you say? Little Italy next week?"

Phyl warmed up to him a little more but it wasn't enough. She shook her head. "No, I'm afraid I'm terribly busy."

"*Phyl,*" Stuart whispered.

Phyl twisted her head around, searching the gathering as she continued to dance.

"*If you let this fish go, it would be the third stupidest thing I ever saw.*"

Phyl almost fainted and missed a step.

"Are you alright?" asked Barry, continuing to twirl her around.

Phyl kept dancing, stunned. "*You are still in the land of the living, Phyl. Live.*"

Phyl gulped back a shout of surprise as her body jolted under the sudden release of grief, fear and loss and showered, instead, by hope and joy. She grinned. She flung her arm up above her head and looked to the ceiling. She sent her love to her daughter, her family, friends and acquaintances, passed on to the next world.

"*This is another adventure, Phyl.*"

"It wouldn't be the same without you, Stu," Phyl whispered to him, all around her.

"*Go. Beautiful ships going to exotic places? You've always loved that. You can dance to your heart's content. And Hollywood? What's not to like?*"

"More ships, huh?

"*More goddamned ships!*"

In her heart, she heard Stuart laugh.

"Just promise me, no more zoos in this next life," she joked.

"*Well, Little Italy's a zoo, Phyl. The Mafia is a completely different animal. And Hollywood? Don't get me started. You think you can handle all that?*"

The music stopped and Barry dipped her into an elegant frieze. The guests applauded heartily. She straightened out and let go, and gave this intriguing young man a long and appreciative look.

She sighed and whispered to Stuart, "After all that *we* went through...? Piece of cake!"

About the Author

Liesje Wagner was born in The Hague, The Netherlands, and immigrated with her family to Canada in the late '50s. She studied at York and Guelph universities and is a certified Deeper Path Speaker. After several careers, Liesje has wholeheartedly embraced her love of writing.

She is also author of *Corrie and the Rose Accordion: Dutch Girl, Hitler's War, Symbol of Hope*, and a children's book, *Bully Swan Gone*.

She lives in Brighton and has two wonderful sons.

dollivertwist2014@gmail.com

Coming soon from Tina Assanti Books:

Italian Bones Scattered East
Italian Bones of Contentions Pride Series Part Three

Italian Bones: Andy's Ghostly Revenge
Italian Bones of Contentions Pride Series Part Four

Corrie and the Rose Accordion
Audio Book

www.tinaassantibooks.com
tinaassantibooks@gmail.com

www.ingramcontent.com/pod-product-compliance
Lightning Source LLC
Chambersburg PA
CBHW072142070526
44585CB00015B/985